FUNDAMENTALS OF
HUMAN NEUROPSYCHOLOGY

A SERIES OF BOOKS IN PSYCHOLOGY

EDITORS:
RICHARD C. ATKINSON
JONATHAN FREEDMAN
GARDNER LINDZEY
RICHARD F. THOMPSON

FUNDAMENTALS OF
HUMAN
NEUROPSYCHOLOGY

BRYAN KOLB AND IAN Q. WHISHAW

UNIVERSITY OF LETHBRIDGE

W. H. FREEMAN AND COMPANY SAN FRANCISCO

TO OUR PARENTS, WHO PROVIDED THE BEGINNING,
AND TO GAY, SUSAN, GAVIAN, AND PAUL,
WHO HAD BETTER THINGS FOR US TO DO,
BUT WAITED PATIENTLY

SPONSORING EDITOR: W. HAYWARD ROGERS
PROJECT EDITOR: PEARL C. VAPNEK
MANUSCRIPT EDITOR: KEVIN GLEASON
DESIGNER: PERRY SMITH
PRODUCTION COORDINATOR: WILLIAM MURDOCK
ILLUSTRATION COORDINATOR: AUDRE W. LOVERDE
ARTISTS: JUDY MORLEY AND GEORGE KLATT
COMPOSITOR: BI-COMP, INC.
PRINTER AND BINDER: ARCATA BOOK GROUP

LIBRARY OF CONGRESS CATALOGING IN PUBLICATION DATA

KOLB, BRYAN, 1947–
FUNDAMENTALS OF HUMAN NEUROPSYCHOLOGY.

(A SERIES OF BOOKS IN PSYCHOLOGY)
INCLUDES BIBLIOGRAPHIES AND INDEX.
1. NEUROPSYCHOLOGY. 2. HUMAN BEHAVIOR.
I. WHISHAW, IAN Q., 1939–   JOINT AUTHOR.
II. TITLE. [DNLM: 1. NERVOUS SYSTEM DISEASES.
2. NERVOUS SYSTEM—ANATOMY AND HISTOLOGY.
3. PSYCHOPHYSIOLOGY. 4. NERVOUS SYSTEM—PHYSIOLOGY.
WL102 K814f]
QP360.K64   612'.8   80-17987
ISBN 0-7167-1219-9

3 4 5 6 7 8 9 HL 0 8 9 8 7 6 5 4 3 2

CONTENTS

20

DISCONNECTION SYNDROMES   432

PART NINE

APPLIED HUMAN
NEUROPSYCHOLOGY

21

NEUROPSYCHOLOGICAL
ASSESSMENT   449

22

APPLICATIONS OF
NEUROPSYCHOLOGY   463

PREFACE

In recent years psychologists have given increasing attention to study of the human brain. As a result of their newfound interest, a rich, established literature on human brain function has been rediscovered, many old problems have received fresh attention and reanalysis, and many new lines of inquiry have been developed. Indeed, a new scientific discipline has arisen: human neuropsychology, the study of the relationship between human brain function and behavior. The excitement in this new field has attracted the attention of undergraduate university students, and has created the need for an introductory textbook, one that summarizes the contributions of traditional approaches to the study of brain function and combines them with the new approach of human neuropsychology. *Fundamentals of Human Neuropsychology* was written to satisfy this need.

Comparative and physiological psychologists will find much that is familiar in this book, as befits our backgrounds in comparative and physiological psychology. The book is comparative in that it applies principles derived from the study of the nonhuman brain to the study of the human brain. It is physiological in that physiological principles are treated as important in understanding the function of the human brain. But psychologists in other areas will also find much that is familiar in the book, because its central aim is to arrive at an understanding of behavior by knowledge of brain function. Accordingly, many problems that have been explored in the areas of perception, cognitive psychology, developmental psychology, psycholinguistics, and clinical psychology are discussed in the context of human brain function.

Since this book is written for students who may have little knowledge of basic neuroscience and only a limited knowledge of psychology, we have taken a number of liberties in our presentation that would be unacceptable in a more advanced text. We have omitted the dates of many recent works from the chapter text, instead presenting appropriate references at the end of each chapter. We have not cited all of the studies that might be relevant to particular problems, expecting that interested students will find more detailed accounts of the relevant literature in the many reviews and texts that we do cite. We occasionally present tables summarizing the studies that are relevant to particular issues but that include details beyond the scope of our objectives. We have often simplified complex issues. Where facts were absent or unclear in their implications, we have speculated and theorized. These liberties should make the book more readable for students who are not yet comfortable with the style and format of more advanced texts.

The book is organized into nine parts of two or three chapters each. Parts One and Two (Chapters 1–4) provide background material for those unfamiliar with basic terminology and knowledge of neuroscience. Part Three (Chapters 5 and 6) provides a technical framework by which material in the remainder of the book can be interpreted. Parts Four–Seven (Chapters 7–17) present at once the core of human neuropsychology and the core of a course in the discipline. Part Eight (Chapters 18–20) addresses issues that are relevant to understanding the current directions of thought presented in the earlier chapters. Finally, Part Nine (Chapters 21 and 22) describes applications of the new technology of neuropsychology to the everyday clinical problems facing psychologists.

It is our pleasure to thank our colleagues and students who have read the book and helped us to improve it. We owe much to the students at the University of Lethbridge and the University of Michigan who read and criticized the entire manuscript in the spring term of 1979. They helped us to remember who the book was written for. We are grateful to Roger Barnsley, Charles Beck, Gus Buchtel, Delee Fromm-Auch, Graham Goddard, Robert Hicks, Robert Sainsbury, Laughlin Taylor, and William Webster for their encouragement and helpful comments on given chapters. We are especially indebted to Paul Cornwell, Doreen Kimura, Terry Robinson, Case Vanderwolf, and Mike Warren for their extensive and thoughtful comments on the entire manuscript. We must also acknowledge the enthusiasm and effort of Kevin Gleason, Buck Rogers, Pearl Vapnek, and the staff of W. H. Freeman and Company, who have demanded and attained a level of excellence that we could not have managed on our own. Finally, we express our gratitude to Adria Allen, who typed the manuscript and put up with our whims and numerous revisions.

June 1980   Bryan Kolb and Ian Q. Whishaw

PART ONE

BACKGROUND

Chapters 1 and 2 present background information about the anatomy and physiology of the brain for the beginning student who has not previously had a course in neuroscience, neuroanatomy, or physiological psychology. Students who have had such courses and feel comfortable in their knowledge of these areas can either review the material or proceed directly to Part Two.

1

THE ORGANIZATION
OF THE NERVOUS SYSTEM

As Oedipus approached the city of Thebes his way was blocked by a Sphinx, who posed him a riddle: "What walks on four legs in the morning, two legs at noon, and three legs in the evening?" The answer given by Oedipus, "A man," was correct, for a person crawls as an infant, walks as an adult, and uses a cane when old. The riddle posed by the Sphinx is a riddle of the nature of man, and the reply by Oedipus indicates not only that he knew an answer but that he understood the underlying significance of the question. The riddle of man's nature is still unanswered, and the object of this book is to pursue the answer in the place where it should most logically be found—the brain.

The simplest and most obvious questions to ask about the brain concern its size. Does size mean anything? Some information suggests that it does. The human brain is 400 grams at birth, 850 grams at 11 months, 1100 grams at three years, and 1450 grams at maturity. This suggests that the development of adult behav-

ior is related to brain size. Furthermore, beginning at about 30 years of age the brain begins to grow smaller, until by 75 years has lost on the average about 100 grams. This suggests the suspected decline in human abilities during aging may be related to decreased brain size. The brain has also grown bigger during evolution; for example, the brain of the great apes weighed about 400 grams, that of Java man about 850 grams, and that of Peking man about 1100 grams. This growth suggests that the evolution of modern man's abilities may have been dependent upon the evolution of a greater brain size.

But despite these relations, there are facts about brain size that suggest that these conclusions are not unassailable. It is curious that modern man's direct hominoid ancestors, Neanderthal man and Cro-Magnon man, may have had slightly larger brains than modern man. It is also curious that the human brain may have gotten somewhat smaller in the last few thousand years. It is curious that although adult brain size is related to body size (larger people have larger brains than smaller people, and females, who are generally smaller than males, have proportionately smaller brains), the brain size of people of extraordinary ability is no different from the brain size of people of ordinary ability. It is curious that the brains of both gifted and ordinary people can vary in weight between 1100 and 2000 grams. Finally, it is curious that although man is apparently unique in his cultural achievements, dolphins may have larger brains, relative to body size, than man has. Together, this information suggests that although brain size may be important, size alone does little toward answering the riddle of man's nature.

The next most obvious questions to ask about the brain concern the relations between the brain's structure and behavior, and this is the focus of modern neuropsychology. Unfortunately, the complexity of the brain's structure makes it incredibly difficult to relate its components to individual capacities. The brain is composed of 140 billion cells, and of these, the 20 billion directly engaged in information processing each receive up to 15,000 physical connections from other cells. If there were no order in this complexity it would be incomprehensible. Fortunately, some tentative answers about how this machinery works can be obtained because the cells of the brain are not organized haphazardly. They are arranged in assemblies, many of which are large and obvious enough to be identifiable on superficial examination. Although the brains of individuals vary in their features just as the faces of individuals vary, the different structures of the brain are common to all men. In fact, these structures seem common to all mammals. The anatomist Lorente de Nó, after examining the mouse brain through a microscope, remarked that its fine structure was little different from that of the human brain. Since many features of the brain are common to most animals as well as to man, and since many of the behav-

iors of man and animals are similar, it is possible to learn about the function of the human brain by studying the brains of other animals, and to learn about the function of other animals' brains by studying the human brain. In the science of **neuropsychology** both kinds of study are pursued. Perhaps this procedure more than any other has influenced the organization of this book. Consequently, although we are specifically interested in discussing the functions of the human brain, we will, throughout the book, frequently do so indirectly, through examination of the brains of other animals. It is our view that the answer to the riddle of the nature of man lies as much in the study of those other animals as it does in the study of man.

COMPOSITION OF THE NERVOUS SYSTEM

As we have stated, the nervous system is composed of cells, and these cells and their processes are grouped in an organized fashion. Since brain anatomy is the study of this organization, it is helpful to know how cells give the different parts of the brain their characteristic appearance.

Neurons and Glia

The germinal cells of a developing embryo give rise to two primitive types of nervous system cells: **neuroblasts** and **spongioblasts** (a blast is an immature cell). The neuroblasts develop into **neurons** (from the Greek for nerve), or *nerve cells,* which form the functional units of the nervous system. The spongioblasts develop into the **glial cells** (from glia, the Greek for glue), which provide various types of support functions to neurons. These two types of cells, neurons and glia, make up the composition of the adult brain. Figure 1-1 shows the relative size, shape, and location of

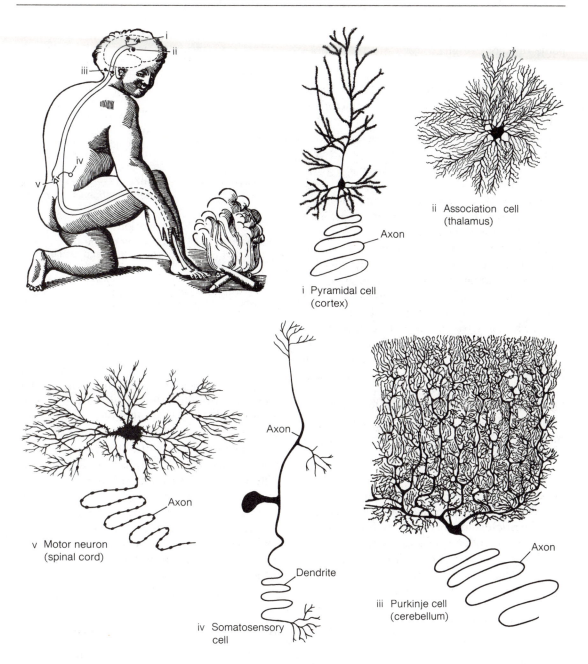

i Pyramidal cell
(cortex)

ii Association cell
(thalamus)

v Motor neuron
(spinal cord)

iv Somatosensory
cell

iii Purkinje cell
(cerebellum)

FIGURE 1-1. The nervous system is composed of neurons, or nerve cells, each of which is specialized for its function. The schematic drawings show the location, size, shape, and configuration of some neurons.

some neurons, and Table 1-1 summarizes some functions of glia.

Grey, White, and Reticular Matter. Different parts of the nervous system characteristically appear either grey or white or mottled and are called grey, white, and reticular matter respectively. Mixtures of capillary blood vessels and cell bodies of neurons have a grey-brown color and so areas composed predominantly of cell bodies constitute the **grey matter.** From the cell bodies of neurons, long processes, called axons, extend to form connections with other neurons in other brain areas. These processes are generally covered with an insulation of glial cells. The glial cells are composed of a fatty (lipid) substance with a high refractive index that gives them a white appearance, much as fat droplets in milk give it a white appearance. As a result, an area of the nervous system rich in axons covered with glial cells looks white and is called **white matter.** An area of the nervous system where cell bodies and axons are mixed together is called a **reticular formation** (from the Latin rete, meaning net), because of its mottled grey and white, or netlike, appearance.

Nuclei and Tracts. A large number of cell bodies grouped together are collectively called a **nucleus** (from the Latin nux, meaning nut); a large collection of axons from neuron cell bodies is called a **tract** (from Old French, meaning path), or sometimes a fiber pathway. Since cell bodies are grey, nuclei are a distinctive grey; since glial cells make axons appear white, tracts are a distinctive white.

Staining

Because of their color, the larger nuclei and tracts of the brain can be seen in fresh brain tissue or brain tissue cut into thin sections, but

TABLE 1-1

Glial cells and their function

Type	Function
Astroglia	Give structural support to and repair neurons
Oligodendroglia	Insulate and speed transmission of central nervous system neurons[a]
Schwann cells	Insulate and speed transmission of peripheral nervous system neurons
Microglia	Perform phagocytosis
Ependymal cells	Produce central nervous system fluid and insulate the brain's ventricles

[a] Central nervous system neurons are those found within the brain and spinal cord; peripheral nervous system neurons are those in the rest of the body.

the appearance of smaller nuclei and tracts must be enhanced to make them visible. The technique of enhancing differences in appearance is called staining and consists of placing brain tissue into different color dyes. Because there are variations in the chemical composition of cells, their various parts selectively take different dyes. Staining techniques aid immensely in differentiating brain tissue, and they are continually being refined. For example, if a nucleus of the brain is destroyed in some way, the axons leaving the cells die. Stains have been found that are selectively taken up by this dying tissue, making it easy to trace axons to their destinations.

A Wonderland of Nomenclature

To the beginning student, the terminology used to label nuclei and tracts of the nervous system might at first seem chaotic. Many structures have a number of names, often used interchangeably. For example, one structure, the

precentral gyrus, is variously referred to as primary motor cortex, area 4, the motor strip, the motor homunculus, Jackson's strip, area pyramidalis, the somatomotor strip, and gyrus precentralis. Clearly such proliferation of terminology is an obstacle to learning; but it is some consolation to know that it reflects the culture and history of the neurosciences. There are many other examples of brain structures that have a number of names, some of which seem quite peculiar. Greek terminology is interchanged with English (e.g., mesencephalon for midbrain), Latin with English (fasciculus opticus for optic tract), and French for English (bouton termineau for synaptic knob). The neuroanatomist's imagination has sometimes strayed to body anatomy (e.g., mammillary bodies), to flora (amygdala, or almond), to fauna (hippocampus, or sea horse), and to mythology (Ammon's horn). Some terminology is a tribute to early pioneers: Fields of Forel, the fissure of Rolando, and Deiter's nucleus. Other terms are colorful: substantia nigra (black substance), locus coeruleus (blue area), and red nucleus. Some names seem excessively long: nucleus reticularis tegmenti pontis Bechterewi. Other labels are based on the consistency of the tissue, for example, substantia gelatinosa (gelatinous substance); some seem somewhat mystifying: substantia innominata (nameless substance), zone incerta (uncertain area), nucleus ambiguus (ambiguous nucleus); and finally, some reflect a modern and more technical outlook, as with the nuclei A-1 to A-10.

In the present text, we have attempted to use consistent and simple terms, but in many cases alternate terms are widely used and so we have included them where necessary.

Approaches to the Study of Anatomy

Neuroanatomists study the structure of the brain by any of four main approaches: (1) comparative, (2) developmental, (3) cytoarchitectonic, and (4) biochemical.

The *comparative* approach consists of describing the brain's evolution from a primitive cord in simple wormlike animals to a large, complex "ravelled knot" in the head of man. Since new types of behavior have developed as each new layer or protuberance has evolved, clues about the function of new areas can be gained by correlating structure and behavior. However, such analysis is not necessarily simple. The limbic system, a middle layer in the mammalian brain, evolved in amphibians and reptiles. Is its function to control new modes of locomotion, the orientation of the animals in a terrestrial world, new types of social behavior, or more advanced learning abilities? The answer is still uncertain. The comparative approach, however, has yielded a key piece of information in neuropsychology: mammals can be distinguished from other animals by their large neocortex (outer covering of brain tissue). Furthermore, this structure is particularly large in man. It is understandable, then, that this structure is thought to have an important function in conferring abilities unique to mammals, and thus receives proportionately more attention in neuropsychology—particularly human neuropsychology—than other structures.

In the *developmental,* or ontogenetic, approach the changes in brain structure and size are described during the development of an individual. This approach allows for two useful perspectives. First, the development of new structures can be correlated with emerging behaviors, much as is done in comparative studies. Second, the immature brain can frequently provide the anatomist with a simplified model of the adult brain. The Spanish anatomist Ramón y Cajal pioneered this type of analysis to good effect. With the crude equipment and techniques available at the end of the nineteenth century he was unable to determine whether the adult brain was composed of a net of connected tissue or of individual units. But using embryonic tissue he was able to show that it was composed of units. Furthermore, by examining successively more mature animals he discovered how these units developed their adult form. Neuropsychologists widely assume that in newborn infants the neocortex is particularly immature in comparison to the rest of the nervous system. As a result, correlating the development of the neocortex with emerging behavior is viewed as a powerful method of uncovering its structural and functional relations.

Cytoarchitectonic analysis consists of describing the architecture of cells: their differences in structure, size, shape, connections, and their distribution in different parts of the brain. This type of analysis is possible because different parts of the nerve cell have affinity for different types of dyes, so that when the brain is cut into thin sections and stained the cells can be examined under a microscope. The cytoarchitectonic approach has been used to particular advantage by neuroanatomists, such as Brodmann, who have described regional differences in cell structure and have constructed maps illustrating the topography of these regional differences. These maps have particular value, for they correlate rather well with maps that illustrate functional differences in brain areas. Cytoarchitectonic techniques are being continually refined as new and better microscopes, such as the electron microscope, are developed and new and more ingenious staining procedures are employed. Recently, for example, it was found that all of the processes of a single cell can be stained by injecting a protein, called horseradish peroxidase, into the cell through a very small glass pipette. With this technique not only can one cell's place in the brain be located but its connections with other cells can be traced.

The most recent analytical technique of studying brain structure is to describe its *biochemical* organization. It is now clear that discrete clusters of cells that send projections to other cell areas contain unique biochemical substances that play a special role in intercell communication. This finding illustrates a new dimension of brain organization, and is of immense practical importance. First, the activity of these systems can be related to different aspects of behavior. Second, abnormalities in the functioning of these systems can be related to some types of abnormal behavior. For example, the chemical dopamine occurs in reduced levels in victims of Parkinson's disease and occurs in heightened levels in victims of certain types of schizophrenia. Third, as these biochemical systems become better understood, the means by which psychoactive drugs work will likewise be better understood. Various techniques for studying biochemical organization of the nervous system include: performing assays on different regions of the brain to determine their chemical composition; labelling a chemical of interest with a radioactive substance so that its course and destination in the brain can be found; and staining the tissue with dyes that produce distinctive colors in areas rich in particular biochemicals. The chemical organization of the brains of a number of animals has been mapped, and studies of the human brain show that its biochemical organization is similar to that of these animals' brains.

THE ORIGIN AND DEVELOPMENT OF THE BRAIN

The anatomical and functional organization of the adult human brain is difficult to grasp because of the complicated clustering of nuclei and the intricate pathways of their axons. It is easier to understand the nervous system's organization by examining the way it developed phylogenetically. The nervous system developed in four somewhat general steps, as is shown diagrammatically in Figure 1-2.

1. The nervous system was first a simple tube, or *spinal cord,* receiving sensory fibers from the different segments of the body and sending motor fibers to them.

2. One end of the cord then became specialized to respond to special features of the sensory world and so made up the primitive brain, or *brainstem.*

3. The front and the hind end of the brainstem then sprouted two new, large structures. In front, the cerebral hemispheres developed to become the initiators of movement; at the rear, the cerebellum developed to become the coordinator of movement. These final additions completed the *mammalian brain.*

4. With continued growth, the mammalian brain developed into the *human brain.*

The Spinal Cord

In primitive animals (and in the first weeks of mammalian embryonic development), some of the outer, or ectodermal, cells of the dorsal surface of the body formed a trough running the length of the body; the upper edges of the trough folded to form a tube (the precursor of the adult mammalian spinal cord). At this stage of development the body and the cord were arranged in segments, with sensory receptors on the body sending input to the dorsal part of the cord, while the cord sent axons from its ventral portion to control muscles in each of the segments. This primitive system, shown diagrammatically in Figure 1-2 A, provides the basis for the development of two important mammalian functions: the dorsal portion provides the neural basis of the somatosensory system (skin and muscle senses), while the ventral portion provides the

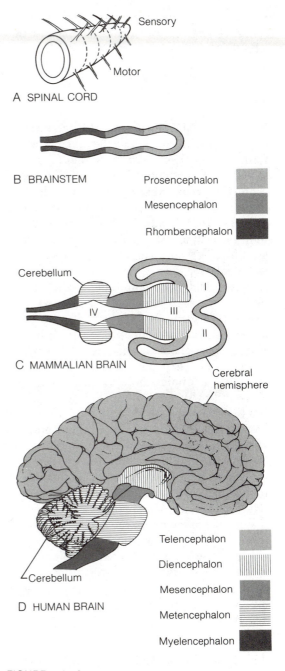

FIGURE 1-2. Steps in the development of the brain. A. Spinal cord. B. Brainstem. C. Mammalian brain. D. Side view of the center of a human brain.

neural basis for the execution of movement. In ancestral vertebrates, such as amphioxus, this was the extent of nervous system development.

The Brainstem

Further neural and functional specialization began at the front end of the spinal cord to form an *encephalon* (from the Greek, meaning in the head), or brain. This was probably because the first vertebrates were mobile, and found it easier to travel predominantly in one direction; thus, it was adaptive to have special sensory analysis take place at "the-end-that-goes-first." At any rate, the front end formed three enlargements or vesicles (bladders). The cells surrounding each multiplied to form centers specialized for receiving and responding to special features of the world. The front enlargement, the **prosencephalon** (frontbrain), became specialized mainly for olfaction and possibly also taste. The second enlargement, the **mesencephalon** (midbrain), became specialized for vision and audition. These parts of the brain allowed for reception of the distant environment. The posterior enlargement, the **rhombencephalon** (hindbrain), became specialized for equilibrium and balance, and gave the animal better perception of its place in its immediate environment. The same organization found in the spinal cord continued to be maintained in the brain: the dorsal portion was sensory, the ventral portion motor. This relatively simple brain, similar to the brain of present fishes and amphibians, forms the basis of the brainstem of mammals. The general organization of the brainstem is shown in Figure 1-2 B.

The Mammalian Brain

The brain next developed primarily at its first and third segments. The prosencephalon de-veloped to form two major new divisions: the **telencephalon** (endbrain) and **diencephalon** (between brain). The most important addition in the telencephalon was the cerebral hemispheres, which functionally became the level of highest control for behavior. The rhombencephalon also divided to form two major new divisions: the *metencephalon* (across brain) and the *myelencephalon* (spinal brain). The distinguishing feature was the growth of the cerebellum in the metencephalon, which became the coordinating center for all movement. The mammalian brain is diagrammed in Figure 1-2 C.

The Human Brain

The human brain evolved from the mammalian brain with no change to the basic design plan (see the saggital, or side, view of the human brain in Figure 1-2 D). The only real difference between the two types of brains is that the cerebral hemispheres and the cerebellum of humans have become tremendously larger than those found in other mammals.

The Ventricles

The primitive spinal cord, remember, had the form of a tube with a hollow center. Further, Figure 1-2 shows that the central core of the brainstem and of the mammalian brain remains hollow. This cavity is not empty but is filled with fluid called **cerebrospinal fluid,** which is produced by **ependymal cells,** or glial cells, that line the inner surface of the cavity. The cavity is larger in some portions of its length than in others; these enlargements are called **ventricles** (from the Latin, meaning belly). There are four ventricles, numbered I to IV. It is conventional to call the lateral ventricles the first and second ventricles, the ventricle in the diencephalon the third ventricle, and the ventricle in the metencephalon

TABLE 1-2

The divisions of the nervous system

Primitive brainstem divisions	Mammalian brain divisions	Portion of fully developed brain	Behavioral division
Prosencephalon (frontbrain)	Telencephalon (endbrain)	Neocortex Basal ganglia Limbic system Olfactory bulb Lateral ventricles	Forebrain
	Diencephalon (between brain)	Thalamus Epithalamus Hypothalamus Third ventricle	Brainstem
Mesencephalon (midbrain)	Mesencephalon (midbrain)	Tectum Tegmentum Cerebral aqueduct	
Rhombencephalon (hindbrain)	Metencephalon (across brain)	Cerebellum Pons Fourth ventricle	
	Myelencephalon (spinal brain)	Medulla oblongata Fourth ventricle	
			Spinal cord

and myelencephalon the fourth ventricle. The ventricle that was in the mesencephalon of the brainstem has become constricted and is called the cerebral aqueduct. The ventricles are distributed in the human brain exactly as in the mammalian brain.

ANATOMY OF THE HUMAN BRAIN

Table 1-2 summarizes the development of the brain from having three primary embryonic divisions to having five. In addition, the table shows some of the major brain structures found in each division of the fully developed brain. Whereas embryological neuroanatomists have divided the nervous system into five major divisions, behaviorists are often content to divide it into three divisions, to simplify discussion of its function. The lowest

division is the **spinal cord,** which includes its connections with organs and muscles in the body. The middle division is the **brainstem,** which is equivalent to the embryologic or primitive pre-mammalian brainstem and includes the diencephalon, the midbrain, and the hindbrain. The highest functional division is the **forebrain,** which includes all of the structures in the telencephalon plus the thalamus of the diencephalon.

Many structures of the brain are labeled according to their location with respect to each other. The conventional terms used to indicate anatomical direction number six: *superior* (top), *lateral* (side), *medial* (middle), *ventral* (bottom), *anterior* (front), and *posterior* (back). Thus, one structure can be said to lie superior, lateral, medial, ventral, anterior, or posterior to another. The nervous system is also symmetrically arranged and so consists of left and right sides. If two structures lie on the same side they are said to be **ipsilateral**; if they lie on opposite sides they are said to be **contralateral**; if they lie on both sides they are said to be **bilateral**. Structures that are close to each other are said to be **proximal**; those far from each other are said to be **distal**. Finally, a process that is approaching the center is said to be **afferent**; one leaving it is said to be **efferent**.

THE SPINAL CORD

The spinal cord, the musculature, and the internal organs of the body have a segmental organization (see Figure 1-3). Each segment of the cord is linked with the organs and musculature of a given body segment. As Figure 1-3 B shows, there are 30 spinal cord segments: 8 cervical (C), 12 thoracic (T), 5 lumbar (L), and 5 sacral (S). Figure 1-3 A shows the segments of the skin and musculature of the body, each labelled to match its corresponding cord segment. Each of the body segments, called a **dermatome** (meaning skin cut), encircles the body in a ring formation. Of course, because man has an upright posture the ring formation seen in a quadrupedal animal is distorted into the pattern shown in Figure 1-3 A. It is worth noting that because the cord and body have this segmental structure, rather good inferences can be made about the location of spinal cord damage or disease from changes in sensation or movement in body parts.

Figure 1-3 C shows a cross-section of the spinal cord. Its outer portion consists of white matter or tracts, arranged so that with a few exceptions the superior tracts are sensory and the inferior tracts are motor in function. The inner portion of the cord, which has a butterfly shape, is grey matter, that is, composed largely of cell bodies. These are arranged so that the cells in the superior portion act as relays for sensory projections from the body, while the cells in the inferior portion send axons to connect with muscles or glands of the body. As can be seen in Figure 1-3 C, two larger fiber tracts (or roots) of the **peripheral nerves** enter each section of the spinal cord, one on each side. The superior tracts contain projections from the receptors in the body, and the inferior tracts consist of axons from cells in the inferior grey matter that project to muscles or organs in the body. Because of this arrangement, damage to the cord's superior regions will produce changes that are selectively sensory in nature, whereas damage to the inferior portion of the cord will produce changes that are selectively motor in nature.

THE BRAINSTEM

The Diencephalon

The **diencephalon** consists of the three thalamic structures (thalamus meaning inner room or chamber, though sometimes translated as couch upon which the forebrain rests): the epithalamus (or upper room), the thalamus (described below with the forebrain), and the hypothalamus (or lower room) (see Figure 1-4). The diencephalon has often been called the interbrain, and appropriately so, for in addition to having its own nuclei it is also a relay or thoroughfare for fibers connecting the forebrain and lower brainstem areas.

The **epithalamus** is of primitive origin, and its function in humans is not known. One of its structures is the **pineal body**, the only nonbilateral structure in the brain. This body has an interesting history, for Descartes, impressed by its solitary nature, suggested that it was the rendezvous between mind and matter and the source of the cerebral spinal fluid that powered movements. Although its function in man is still not known, the pineal body of

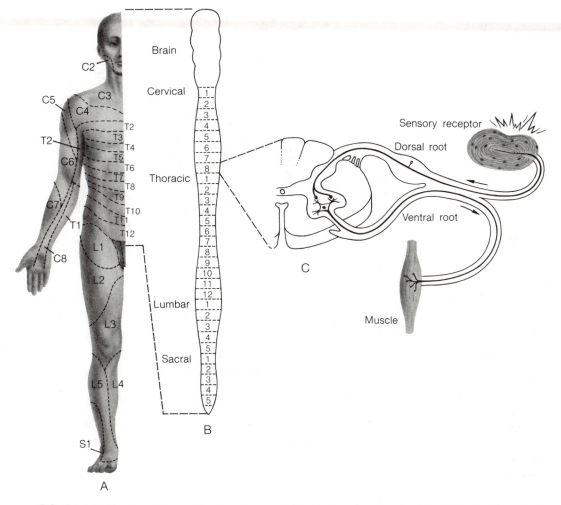

FIGURE 1-3. Relation between the dermatomes of the body and segments of the spinal cord. A. Body dermatomes. B. Spinal cord segments. C. Cross-section through one segment of spinal cord showing that sensory input from a dermatome arrives through the dorsal root, whereas motor output to the same dermatome goes through the ventral root. (After Truex and Carpenter, 1969.)

some animals plays a role in organizing biological rhythms.

The **hypothalamus** is composed of about 22 small nuclei, fiber systems that pass through it, and the pituitary gland. Although composing only about 0.3% of brain weight, its small size is deceiving because it is involved in nearly all aspects of behavior, including feeding, sexual behavior, sleeping, temperature regulation, emotional behavior, endocrine function, and movement. It has been a favorite area of study in animal neurobiology, but unfortunately less is known about the role of the hypothalamus in human behavior.

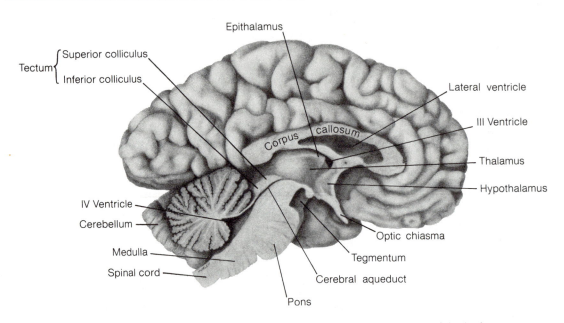

FIGURE 1-4. Medial view through the center of the brain showing structures of the brainstem.

The Midbrain

The **midbrain,** shown in Figure 1-4, consists of two main subdivisions: the **tectum,** or roof, which is the area lying above the aqueduct, and the **tegmentum,** or floor, which lies below the aqueduct. The tectum consists primarily of two sets of bilaterally symmetrical nuclei: the **superior colliculi** (upper hills) are the anterior pair, and the **inferior colliculi** (lower hills) are the posterior pair. In birds and phylogenetically lower animals these sets of nuclei are their visual and auditory brains respectively. In mammals, which have neocortical visual and auditory systems, these structures mediate whole body movements to visual and auditory stimuli respectively. The tegmentum contains four types of structures:

1. Next to the aqueduct are nuclei for some of the cranial nerves.

2. Beneath these are sensory fibers coming from the body senses.

3. Below these are motor fibers coming down from the forebrain.

4. Intermingled among these three structures are a number of motor nuclei such as the red nucleus and substantia nigra and some of the nuclei of the reticular system.

The Hindbrain

The **hindbrain** is organized in much the same way as the midbrain. Sensory nuclei of the vestibular system overlie the fourth ventricle; beneath the ventricle are more motor nuclei of the cranial nerves, ascending sensory tracts from the spinal cord, descending fiber tracts to the cord, and more nuclei composing the reticular activating system. Overlying the brainstem is the cerebellum.

The **cerebellum** (see Figure 1-4) is very old and was probably first specialized for sensory–motor coordination. The precise function of the cerebellum varies from one part of the structure to another, depending on connections with the rest of the nervous system. Parts that receive most of their impulses from the vestibular system help to maintain the body's equilibrium, whereas parts receiving impulses mainly from body senses are involved with postural reflexes and coordinating functionally related muscles. The major part of the cerebellum receives impulses from the neocortex and functions primarily to promote the efficiency of skilled movements.

The surface of the cerebellum is marked by narrow folds, or folia, beneath which lies a thick cortex of grey matter covering a larger central mass of white matter. Within the white matter are several nuclei. The cerebellum is attached to the brainstem by three major fiber pathways in which all afferent fibers pass to its cortex and all efferent fibers originate in the underlying cerebellar nuclei and then pass on to other brain structures.

Damage to the cerebellum results in impairments of equilibrium, postural defects, and impairments of skilled motor activity. Smooth movements may be broken down into sequential components, thus making movements jerky; ability to perform rapidly alternating movements may be impaired; and directed movements may overshoot their mark. In addition, muscle tone may be abnormal so that movements are difficult to initiate.

The *reticular formation* consists of a complex mixture of nuclei and fiber tracts that stretch from the diencephalon through the hindbrain. These nuclei and fiber tracts have two distinguishing features: first, they do not have clearly defined sensory or motor functions; second, each sends fibers to a number of areas of the forebrain, brainstem, and spinal cord. The reticular formation is now well known as the *reticular activating system;* it obtained this distinction in the following way. Up to the 1940s it was thought that sleep could be attributed to a lack of sensory stimulation, whereas

waking could be attributed to reception of an adequate amount of sensory stimulation. In 1949, Moruzzi and Magoun stimulated the brainstem of anesthetized cats while brain electrical activity was being recorded from them on an electroencephalogram, or EEG. The EEG of the cats consisted of large-amplitude slow waves, similar to those typically recorded from a sleeping animal, but when electrical brain stimulation was administered, a low-amplitude EEG pattern, similar to that commonly recorded from a waking cat, was recorded. As a result of their experiment, Moruzzi and Magoun proposed that the function of the reticular formation was to control sleeping and waking. Through the influence of these findings the reticular formation gradually came to be known as the reticular activating system, the function of which was to maintain "general arousal" or "consciousness." More recently, research has focused on the details of individual nuclear groups within the formation, and the results from these studies suggest a number of functions for different cell groups in this area.

There are 12 sets of **cranial nerves** (summarized in Table 3-1), which convey sensory information from the specialized sensory systems of the head and control the special movements of muscle systems in the head, i.e., movements of the eyes and tongue. A knowledge of their organization and function is important for neurological diagnosis; their functions and dysfunctions are discussed in Chapter 3.

THE FOREBRAIN

The forebrain is conventionally divided into five anatomical areas: (1) the neocortex, (2) the basal ganglia, (3) the limbic system, (4) the thalamus, and (5) the olfactory bulbs and tract. The following section will describe the first of these four structures. Since the content of this book is related substantially to the neocortex, it will be described in greatest detail.

The Neocortex

The **neocortex** comprises most of the forebrain by volume. It consists of four to six layers of cells (or grey matter) beneath which their axons form pathways (white matter). The term cortex (from the Latin, meaning bark) is used to refer to any outer layer of cells. Frequently the terms cortex and neocortex are used interchangeably, and so conventionally cortex refers to neocortex unless otherwise indicated. The neocortex has expanded most during evolution, and comprises 80 percent of the human brain. Whereas the brainstems of a man and a sheep are so similar in size that a novice may confuse them, their neocortexes can easily be distinguished. The human neocortex has an area of up to 2500 sq. cm but a thickness of only 1.5 to 3.0 mm. The cortex is wrinkled; this wrinkling is nature's solution to the problem of confining the huge neocortical surface area within a shell that is still small enough to pass through the birth canal. Just as a crumpled sheet of paper can fit into a smaller box than a flat sheet, folding of the neocortex permits the relatively fixed volume of the skull to contain more neocortex.

Fissures, Sulci, and Gyri. The wrinkled surface of the neocortex consists of clefts and ridges. A cleft is called a **fissure** if it extends deeply enough into the brain to indent the ventricles, and a **sulcus** if it is shallower. A ridge is called a **gyrus**. Figure 1-5 shows the location of some of the more important fissures, sulci, and gyri of the brain. There is *some* variation between the location of features of two sides of one individual's brain, and *substantial* variation in both the location and features of the brains of different individuals.

Two of the external features of the brain are relatively easy to locate. The lateral fissure is relatively easy to locate because it begins in a cleft on the anterior-inferior surface of the cortex. The central sulcus can be found because it curves toward the posterior part of the brain as it moves medially across the superior surface of the cortex.

The Hemispheres and Lobes. As Figure 1-6 shows, the neocortex consists of two nearly symmetrical hemispheres, the left and the right, separated by the medial longitudinal fissure. Each hemisphere is subdivided into four lobes: frontal, parietal, temporal, and occipital. The **frontal lobes** have fixed boundaries: they are bounded posteriorly by the central sulcus, inferiorly by the lateral fissure, and medially by the cingulate sulcus just above a large interhemispheric band of fibers called the corpus callosum. The anterior boundary of the **parietal lobes** is the central sulcus and their inferior boundary is the lateral fissure. The **temporal lobes** are bounded dorsally by the lateral fissure. The **occipital lobes** are separated from the parietal cortex medially by the parieto-occipital sulcus. On the lateral surface of the brain there are no definite boundaries between the occipital lobes and the parietal and temporal lobes. The areas between the lobes are sometimes referred to as the parietal-occipital area and the temporal-occipital area. It should be noted that the lobes are not functional regions but convenient anatomical regions. Nevertheless, because there are functional differences between them they are used in a rather loose and descriptive way to indicate different functional regions.

As shown in Figure 1-5, in a lateral view there are four major gyri in the frontal lobe: the superior, middle, and inferior; and the precentral (which lies in front of the central sulcus). There are five in the parietal lobe: the

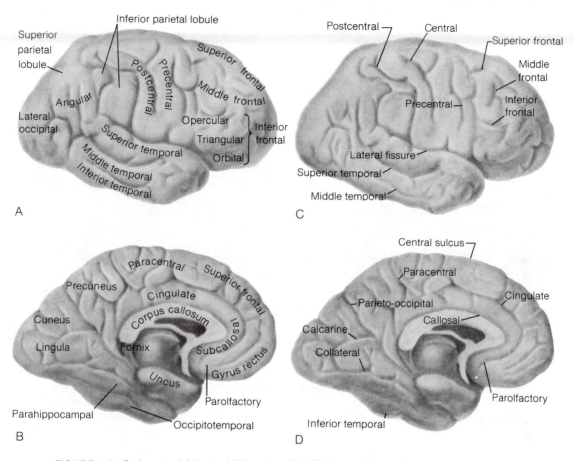

FIGURE 1-5. Gyri and sulci. Lateral (A) and medial (B) views of the gyri. Lateral (C) and medial (D) views of the sulci.

superior and inferior; the postcentral (lying behind the central sulcus); and the supermarginal and angular (on either side of the lateral fissure). There are three in the temporal lobe: the superior, middle, and inferior gyri. Only the lateral gyrus is obvious in the occipital cortex.

Topography of the Neocortex. The several different kinds of maps that have been made of the neocortex are called **topographic maps.** These maps are constructed from in-

formation obtained by the application of specific research techniques:

1. **Projection maps** are constructed by tracing axons from the sensory systems into the brain, and tracing axons from the neocortex to the motor systems of the brainstem and spinal cord.

2. **Functional maps** are constructed by stimulating areas of the brain electrically and noting the elicited behavior, or by recording the electrical activity of the cortex during cer-

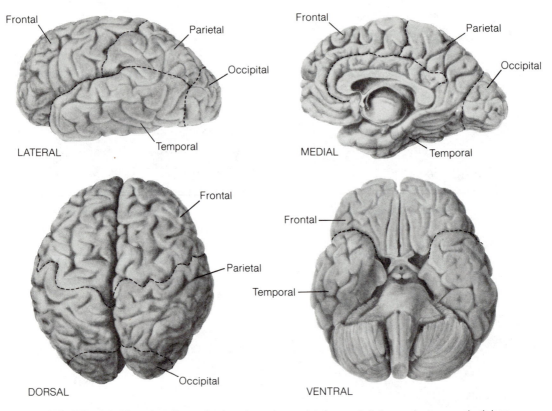

FIGURE 1-6. The location of the frontal, parietal, occipital, and temporal lobes of the human brain.

tain behaviors. Functional maps can also be constructed by relating specific types of brain damage to changes in behavior.

3. **Cytoarchitectonic maps** are constructed from study of the distribution of different types of cells in the neocortex.

Projection Maps. Figure 1-7 shows an example of a projection map constructed by tracing the axons from the sensory systems to the neocortex, and by tracing the motor axons from the neocortex to subcortical motor systems. As the figure shows, the projections from the eye, the ear, and the body's soma-

tosensory system can each be traced to a specific region of the neocortex: the visual system projects to the posterior occipital lobe; the auditory system projects to the superior temporal gyrus of the temporal lobe; and the somatosensory system projects to the area of the postcentral gyrus in the parietal lobe. The major motor projection appears to originate in the precentral gyrus of the frontal lobe. These areas are called **primary projection areas,** but it should be noted that the lateral view does not represent their entire extent, because they also project down into the gyri and fissures. The auditory zone, for example, is much larger within the lateral fissure.

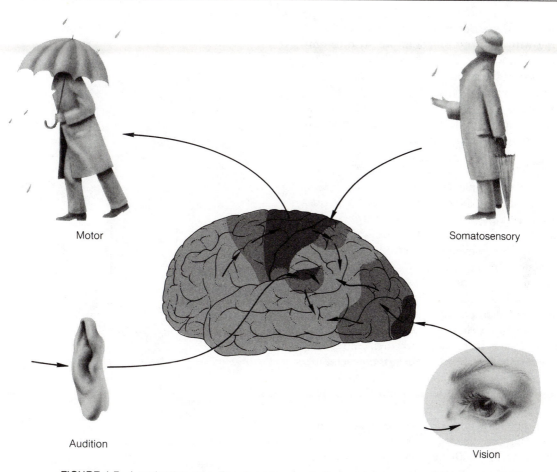

Motor

Somatosensory

Audition

Vision

FIGURE 1-7. A projection map. The darkest areas indicate primary zones, which receive input from the sensory system or project to spinal motor systems. The intermediate shaded areas are secondary zones. The unshaded areas are tertiary, or association, zones.

Once the primary projection areas are described, the relation they have to the rest of the neocortex can be understood. The sensory systems send projections into areas that are adjacent to them, whereas the motor area receives fibers from an area adjacent to it. These areas, also indicated on Figure 1-7, are called **secondary projection areas.** The secondary areas receive fibers from (in the case of the motor projection) or send fibers to (in the case of sensory projections) **tertiary areas,** also frequently called association cortex.

It is clear from this topography that the neocortex is highly organized. It is also clear why the posterior neocortex is considered to be largely sensory, and why the anterior neocortex is considered to be largely motor. Finally, it is apparent why each of the lobes is thought to be associated with a particular general function: frontal with motor, parietal with somatosensory, occipital with visual, and temporal with auditory function. We wish to emphasize, however, that this is a simplified description of the neocortex. Motor fibers can be found coming from every part of the neocortex, and sensory fibers project to other areas. The map simply reflects the most concentrated projections of both kinds of fibers.

Functional Maps. Of the many functional maps of the somatosensory and motor areas, the best-known is by Penfield and his coworkers. During the course of brain surgery, they stimulated the brains of conscious people through thin wires, or electrodes, with low voltages of electric current. The protocol of such an experiment was to stimulate the cortical tissue briefly, observe whether the person made a movement or reported some sort of body sensation (itch, tickle, etc.), record the location and response, and then move the stimulating electrode to repeat the procedure. The results of several such experiments are shown diagrammatically in Figure 1-8. Areas that produced movement lie in the precentral gyrus in the primary motor projection area. Areas that produced sensations lie in the postcentral gyrus in the primary somatosensory area. For both the motor and sensory areas there is a point-to-point relation between parts of the body and parts of the neocortex. Note that in the figure these distributions of the body on the cortex are distorted, the face and hands being far larger proportionately than are other parts of the body. This topography is shown schematically by the cartoon men (or *homunculi*) drawn over the motor and sensory areas to indicate the parts of the body represented in different cortical areas.

The face and hands of the homunculi are larger because they are capable of finer perceptions and movements than are other body areas and so require proportionately more neocortex to represent them. The foot area lies

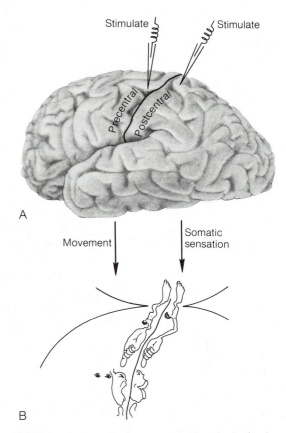

FIGURE 1-8. A projection map. A. Electrical stimulation to precentral or postcentral gyrus through small electrodes. B. Movement or sensation is produced at the locations shown by the homunculi, or "little men." (After Penfield and Jasper, 1954.)

in the longitudinal fissure (flexed up in Figure 1-8). The cortical representation of the eyes is actually not in the head region of the motor homunculus; they have their own area just anterior to the head area.

The visual and auditory systems have a neocortical distribution as precise as that for the motor and somatosensory systems. The visual field (the area of the world the eyes see) is represented across the visual projection area in the occipital lobe, while the sensory area for sound, the basilar membrane, is represented in the primary auditory area of the temporal lobe. The taste area of the brain lies across a tongue-shaped area in the postcentral gyrus in Figure 1-8. Whether or not the olfactory system has any representation in the neocortex is at present uncertain.

Cytoarchitectonic Maps. Cytoarchitectonic maps are constructed by examining the neurons of the neocortex and grouping areas with similar cell structure together. The many cytoarchitectonic maps of the neocortex differ chiefly in their degree of simplicity or complexity. The one presented in Figure 1-10 is by no means the simplest, but it is the most widely used, and it will be used throughout this book.

The neurons of the neocortex are arranged in about six layers, as is shown in Figure 1-9. The number of layers distinguishes the neocortex from other brain areas, such as the limbic system, which has only three layers. The cell layers of the neocortex can be separated into two groups by function: the outer four layers receive axons from other brain areas; the inner two layers send axons to other brain areas. The cell layers are not distributed uniformly in the neocortex (in fact, it is debatable whether there are really six layers in all neocortical areas). For example, a primary sensory area such as the visual area has a large number of layer 4 cells receiving axons from the eyes but fewer layer 5 cells, whereas the primary motor area has a large number of layer 5 cells sending axons to subcortical motor systems but fewer layer 4 cells. Areas that are neither primary motor nor primary sensory have fewer cells in layers 4 and 5 and a greater density of cells in layers 2 and 3. It is on such differences in cell distribution, as well as differences in cell sizes and shapes, that cytoarchitectonic maps are based.

In **Brodmann's map,** a cytoarchitectonic map, shown in Figure 1-10, each of the areas is

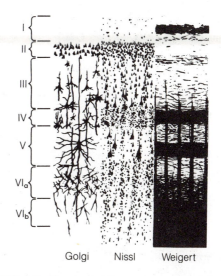

FIGURE 1-9. Structure of the cortex revealed through the use of three different stains. Golgi stain stains only a few neurons but reveals all of their processes; a Nissl stain highlights only cell bodies; and a Weigert myelin stain reveals the location of axons. Note that these staining procedures highlight the different cell types of the cortex and reveal that it is composed of a number of layers, each of which contains typical cell types. (After Brodmann, 1909.)

numbered, but the numbers themselves have no intrinsic meaning. To do his analysis Brodmann divided the brain at the central sulcus, and then worked through each half in random order, numbering new conformations of cells as he found them. Thus, he found areas 1 and 2 in the posterior section, then switched to the anterior section and found 3 and 4, and thereupon switched again, etc.

Table 1-3 summarizes some of the known relationships between each of Brodmann's areas and its functions. As it turns out, the relation between structure and function is stunning. For example, area 17 corresponds to the primary visual projection area, and area 18 and 19 to the secondary visual projection areas. Similar relations exist for other areas and functions. The boundaries of Brodmann's

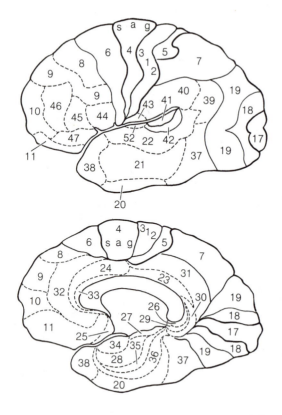

FIGURE 1-10. Brodmann's areas of the cortex. A few numbers are missing from the original sources, including areas 13–16 and 48–51. Some areas have histologically distinctive boundaries and are outlined with heavy solid lines; others, such as 6 and 18–19, for example, have less distinct boundaries and are outlined with light solid lines; the remainder have no distinct boundaries but gradually merge into each other and are outlined with dotted lines. (From H. Elliott, *Textbook of Anatomy*. Philadelphia: Lippincott. Copyright © 1969. Reprinted by permission.)

TABLE 1-3

Functional areas and Brodmann cytoarchitectonic areas

Function	Brodmann area
Vision	
primary	17
secondary	18,19
Auditory	
primary	41
secondary	22,42
Body senses	
primary	1,2,3
secondary	5,7
Sensory, tertiary	7,21,22,37,39,40
Motor	
primary	4
secondary	6
eye movement	8
speech	44
Motor, tertiary	9,10,11,45,46,47

point the best advice we can give a student with respect to Brodmann's system and its relation to function is to commit the numbers and the location of the primary and secondary areas to memory and then keep in mind that the remaining areas (composing the greater area of the neocortex) are tertiary cortex.

Cortical Connections

The various regions of the neocortex are interrelated by three types of axon projections: (1) relatively short connections between one gyrus and another, (2) longer connections between one lobe and another, and (3) interhemispheric connections, or **commissures**, between one hemisphere and another. Most of the interhemispheric connections link homotopic areas, or the same points, of the two hemispheres. Figure 1-11 shows the locations and names of some of these connections. The cortex also makes other types of connections with itself; cells in any area may, for ex-

areas also appear to be related to function because the primary sensory and motor areas have fairly distinct boundaries and functions. The secondary areas have less distinct and the tertiary areas still less distinct boundaries. This has been taken to mean that they have less specified sensory or motor function and more associative or integrative function. At this

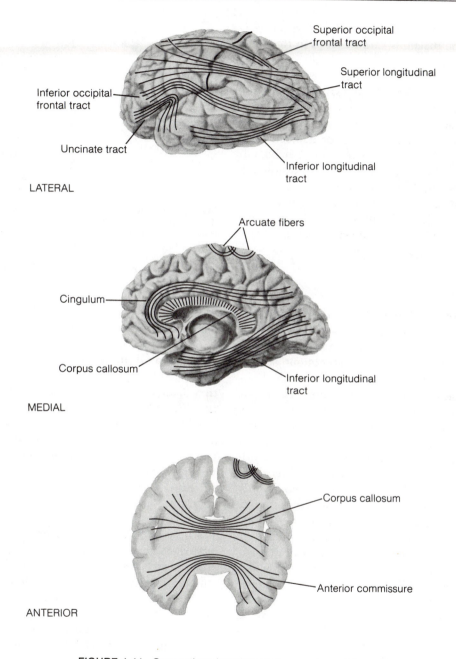

Superior occipital
frontal tract

Superior longitudinal
tract

Inferior occipital
frontal tract

Uncinate tract

Inferior longitudinal
tract

LATERAL

Arcuate fibers

Cingulum

Corpus callosum

Inferior longitudinal
tract

MEDIAL

Corpus callosum

Anterior commissure

ANTERIOR

FIGURE 1-11. Connections between various regions of the cortex.

ample, send axons to cells in a subcortical area such as the thalamus, and the cells in the area of the thalamus may then send their axons to some other cortical area. These types of relations are more difficult to establish anatomically than those that are based on direct connections. Yet the connections are of considerable functional interest, for damage to a pathway is often reflected in behavioral deficits as severe as those suffered following damage to the functional areas they connect. A glance at Figure 1-11 will show that it would indeed be difficult to damage any area of the cortex without damaging one or more of its interconnecting pathways.

Limbic Lobe

During the evolution of the amphibians and reptiles a number of three-layered cortical structures developed, sheathing the periphery of the brainstem. With the subsequent growth of the neocortex they became sandwiched between the new and the old brain. Because of the evolutionary origin of these structures some anatomists have referred to them as the reptilian brain, but the term limbic lobe (from the Latin *limbus,* meaning border or hem), coined by Broca in 1878, is more widely recognized today. The limbic lobe is commonly referred to as the **limbic system** (which may very well be a misnomer). The limbic lobe consists of a number of structures, including the **hippocampus** (sea horse), **septum** (partition), and **cingulate** (girdle) **gyrus,** which may all have different functions (see Figure 1-12). Nevertheless, the history of how the limbic "lobe" became the limbic "system" is one of the most interesting chapters of the neurosciences.

Initially, anatomists were impressed with the connections between the olfactory system and the limbic lobe. On this evidence it was suggested that the limbic structures were

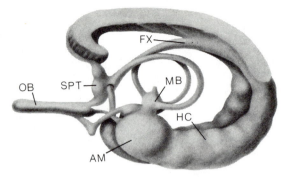

FIGURE 1-12. Model of the human limbic system. Major structures include the hippocampus (HC), amygdala (AM), septum (SPT), mammillary bodies (MB), olfactory bulbs (OB), and fornix (FX). (From L. W. Hamilton, *Basic Limbic System Anatomy of the Rat.* New York: Plenum. Copyright © 1976. Reprinted by permission.)

elaborated to deal with olfactory information, and so together they were called the **rhinencephalon,** or smell brain. Because a number of experiments demonstrated that they had little olfactory function, for a time their putative olfactory function lay in a scientific limbo. Then in 1937, Papez, in a scientific *tour de force,* asked, "Is emotion a magic product, or is it a physiologic process which depends on an anatomic mechanism?" He suggested that emotion, which had no known anatomic substrate, was a product of the limbic lobe, which had no recognized function. It is a historical irony that the structures he emphasized as primary, e.g., the hippocampus, have been subsequently found to have little emotional function, whereas those he ignored, such as the septum, may indeed have such a function. It would be inappropriate, however, to suggest that the function of limbic structures is in any way settled. Recently a variety of different functions have been proposed for different limbic structures. The hippocampus, for example, has been successively postulated to play a role in inhibition, learning, memory, organization of movement, and spatial orientation. Certainly to suggest that the limbic system is the emotional brain now seems as much an oversimplification as it is to say that the limbic system has only one function.

Basal Ganglia

The **basal ganglia** are a collection of nuclei lying mainly beneath the anterior regions of the neocortex (Figure 1-13). They include the **putamen** (shell), **globus pallidus** (pale globe), the **caudate nucleus** (tailed nucleus), and **amygdala** (almond). These nuclei have intimate connections with the neocortex and thalamus, and are connected by ascending and descending fibers to midbrain structures such as the red nucleus and substantia nigra. Figure 1-13 shows suggested relations to the neocortex.

The principal function of the basal ganglia has historically been described as motor. Damage to different portions of the basal ganglia can produce changes in posture, increases or decreases in muscle tone, and abnormal movements such as twitches, jerks, and tremors. The basal ganglia may have other functions, such as sequencing a number of complex movements into a smoothly executed response, as occurs during talking.

Thalamus

The **thalamus** can be divided into two areas, the ventral and dorsal thalami. The ventral thalamus provides a general, nonspecific input into the neocortex that may modulate the activity of the neocortex. The dorsal thalamus, or thalamus proper, is composed of a number of nuclei, each of which projects to a specific area of the neocortex as shown in Figure 1-14. These nuclei receive input from the different body sensory systems or from other brain areas. The lateral geniculate body receives vi-

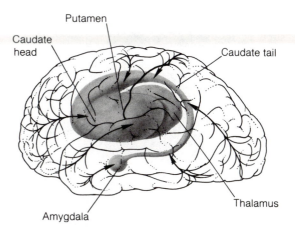

FIGURE 1-13. Relation between the basal ganglia and cortex. Arrows indicate proposed projections of various cortical areas into basal ganglia structures.

sual system projections; the medial geniculate body receives auditory system projections; and the ventral lateral posterior nuclei receive touch, pressure, pain, and temperature projections from the body. In turn the lateral geniculate body projects to area 17, the medial geniculate body projects to area 41, and the ventral lateral posterior nuclei project to areas 1, 2, and 3. Note that the olfactory system does not project through the thalamus to the neocortex. A large area of the posterior secondary and tertiary cortex sends projections to and receives projections back from the pulvinar. Some of the subcortical motor nuclei, such as the globus pallidus, substantia nigra, and dentate nucleus, project to the anterior and lateral ventral nuclei, and these areas project to primary motor area 4 and secondary motor area 6. The dorsomedial nucleus receives projections from the amygdaloid complex, temporal neocortex, and caudate nucleus and projects to the remainder of the frontal lobe. The significance of some of these connections will be discussed in subsequent sections of the book.

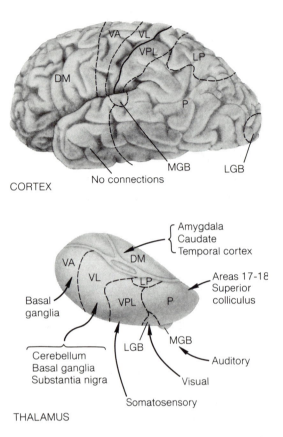

CORTEX

THALAMUS

FIGURE 1-14. Relation between thalamic nuclei and various areas of the cortex to which they project. The arrows indicate the sources of input into the thalamus. DM, dorsal medial nucleus; VA, anterior ventral nucleus; VL, lateral ventral nucleus; LP, lateral posterior nucleus; VPL, lateral posterior ventral nucleus; P, pulvinar; LGB, lateral geniculate body; MGB, medial geniculate body.

THE CROSSED BRAIN

One of the most peculiar features of the organization of the brain is that each of its symmetrical halves responds to sensory stimulation from the contralateral side of the body or sensory world, and controls the musculature on the contralateral side of the body. (See Figure 1-15.) The visual system achieves this effect by crossing half the fibers of the optic tract as well as by reversing the image through the lens of the eye. Nearly all of the fibers of the motor and somatosensory system cross. Projections from each ear go to each hemisphere, but there is substantial evidence that auditory excitation from one ear has a preferential route to the opposite hemisphere. As a result of this arrangement, along the center of the nervous system there are numerous crossings, or **decussations,** of sensory and motor fibers. Throughout the book details of this anatomy will be described where they are relevant to discussions of the function of each of these systems. It is sufficient to say here that because of this arrangement, damage to one side of the brain generally causes sensory and motor impairments, not to the same side of the body but to the opposite side.

Anyone reflecting on this crossed arrangement must ask why it occurs and how. There have been a number of imaginative answers to each of these questions.

The Spanish anatomist Ramón y Cajal was obsessed, as he says, with the following thought: "Everything will have a simple explanation if it is admitted that the correct perception of an object implies the congruence of the cerebral surfaces of projection, that is, those representing each point in space." He suggested that crossing in the visual system is necessary so that a continuous representation of an object is retained in the visual cortex. His explanation of what might happen in an uncrossed section is shown in Figure 1-16. He argued that since the lens reverses the image, and since each eye sees only part of the visual field, an uncrossed system would produce a representation in the cortex in which each half of the image was in one hemisphere but with the peripheries of the image juxtaposed in the center. He suggested that a prey taking the path of the external arrow would be difficult to

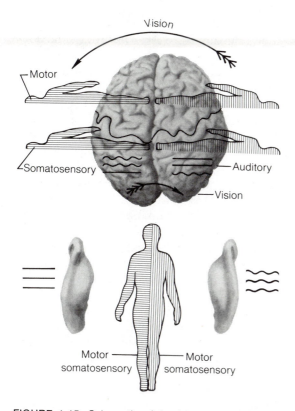

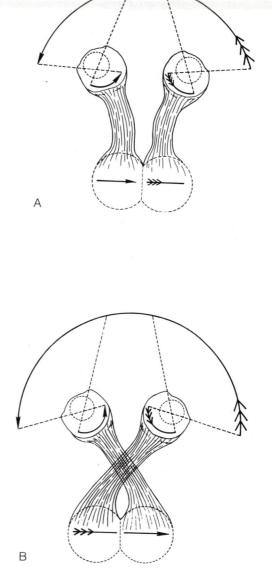

FIGURE 1-15. Schematic of the human brain from a dorsal view showing the projection of visual, auditory, and somatosensory input to contralateral areas of the cortex, and the crossed projection of the motor cortex to the contralateral body.

catch, since its path in the visual cortex would be discontinuous. Crossing the pathway introduces a continuous image. Cajal thought that reversal of the image's direction was not a problem, because it was compensated for by crossing the motor outflow from the brain.

A second theory advanced to explain crossing is the coil reflex theory shown in Figure 1-17. Coghill studied the development of movement in the primitive vertebrate *Amblystoma* and found that its first movement was a coil, which when repeated a number of times formed its basic swimming movement. In this

FIGURE 1-16. A. Illustration of the incongruous central projection of the images from the two eyes if there were no intercrossing of the optic nerves. B. Continuity of the visual image obtained by crossing the optic nerves. (From S. Ramón y Cajal, *Recollections of My Life*. Copyright © 1937. Reprinted with permission of the American Philosophical Society.)

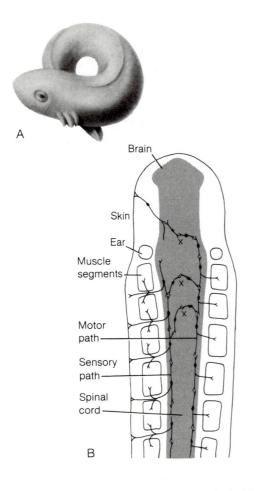

FIGURE 1-17. A. Coil reflex in the embryonic *Ambly-stoma*. B. A diagram of the mechanism which accounts for the coil reaction. Sensory neurons are shown on one side of the body, motor neurons on the other. Excitation of a sensory neuron leads to excitation of an inter-neuron (X) and then to sequential contraction of the contralateral muscles in a head-to-tail direction. (After Coghill, 1929.)

that by their action produce the coil. The coil allows the animal to flex away from a noxious stimulus, and as swimming develops, ensures that stimulation will elicit swimming at the animal's front end. Sarnat and Netsky suggest that this anatomical arrangement forms the basis for the crossed systems in all vertebrates. William Webster has suggested to us that this model explains why the olfactory system is the only sensory system that is uncrossed. The assumption is that the primitive function of the olfactory bulb was to bring an animal to food and so a primitive animal would coil toward an olfactory stimulus that signaled food. Therefore, it would have to contract muscles on the same side of the body and would use an uncrossed projection to the muscles.

An imaginative explanation of how the nervous system became crossed has been proposed by Kinsbourne. He notes that invertebrates have an uncrossed and ventrally located nervous system, a dorsally located heart, and a posterior flow of blood in central blood vessels. Vertebrates have a crossed and dorsally located nervous system, a ventrally located heart, and an anterior flow of blood in ventral blood vessels. He proposes that in the transition from invertebrates to vertebrates the body rotated 180° with respect to the head. As a result, blood circulation reversed direction, the heart became located ventrally, the nervous system adopted a dorsal position, and decussations were formed by the rotation.

One weakness of Kinsbourne's theory is that it predicts that the sensory and motor pathways of the brainstem should be reversed in a dorso-ventral direction with respect to the spinal cord. This is not the case, for the dorsal portion of the midbrain is sensory, as is the dorsal portion of the spinal cord. A second weakness of the theory is that it does not explain why a 180° rotation would prove adaptive. It may have been a chance occurrence, or it may have occurred to effect the coil reflex.

animal, input from sensory receptors goes only to motor cells on the opposite side of the body through an interneuron at the rostral end. The sensory input is passed to successive motor cells in a rostral-to-caudal sequence, causing contraction of successive myotomes

(Alternatively, we could suggest, tongue in cheek, that had the nervous system remained below the esophagus the brain could not have evolved lest it choke off respiration and the route of food to the stomach.)

PROTECTION

The brain and spinal cord are supported and protected from injury and infective invasion in three ways: (1) The brain is enclosed in a thick bone, the *skull,* and the spinal cord is encased in a series of interlocking bony *vertebrae.* (2) Within these bony cases are three membranes: the outer **dura mater** (from the Latin, meaning hard mother), a tough double layer of collagenous fiber enclosing the brain in a kind of loose sack; the middle **arachnoid** (from the Greek, meaning resembling a spider's web), a very thin sheet of delicate collagenous connec-

tive tissue that follows the contours of the brain; and the inner **pia mater** (from the Latin, meaning soft mother), which is a moderately tough membrane of connective-tissue fibers made from reticular, elastic, and collagenous fibers, and clings to the surface of the nervous tissue. (3) The brain is cushioned from shock and sudden changes of pressure by a fluid called the *cerebrospinal fluid* (CSF), which fills the ventricles inside the brain and which circulates around the brain beneath the arachnoid layer, in the subarachnoid space. This fluid is a clear, colorless solution of sodium chloride and other salts and is made by a plexus of cells that evaginates into each ventricle. The CSF is made continually, and flows from the ventricles, circulating around the brain, to be absorbed by the venous sinuses of the dura mater. Although it is unlikely that the CSF nourishes the brain, it may instead play a role in excreting metabolic wastes from the brain.

REFERENCES

Brodmann, K. *Vergleichended Lokalisations lehre der Grosshirnrinde in Prinzipien dargestellt auf Grund des Zellenbaues.* Leipzig: J. A. Barth, 1909.

Coghill, G. E. *Anatomy and the Problem of Behavior.* Cambridge: Cambridge University Press, 1929. (Reprinted by Hafner, New York, 1963.)

Curtis, B. A., S. Jacobson, and E. M. Marcus. *An Introduction to the Neurosciences.* Philadelphia: W. B. Saunders Co., 1972.

Elliott, H. *Textbook of Neuroanatomy.* Philadelphia and Toronto: J. P. Lippincott Co., 1969.

Everett, N. B. *Functional Neuroanatomy.* Philadelphia: Lea and Febiger, 1965.

Hamilton, L. W. *Basic Limbic System Anatomy of the Rat.* New York and London: Plenum Press, 1976.

Kinsbourne, M., ed. *Asymmetrical Function of the Brain.* Cambridge: Cambridge University Press, 1978.

MacLean, P. D. Psychosomatic disease and the "visceral brain": Recent developments bearing on the Papez theory of emotion. *Psychosomatic Medicine, 11* (1949), 338–353.

Papez, J. W. A proposed mechanism of emotion. *Archives of Neurology and Psychiatry, 38,* (1937), 724–744.

Passingham, R. E. Brain size and intelligence in man. *Brain Behavior and Evolution, 16* (1979), 253–270.

Penfield, W., and E. Boldrey. Somatic motor and sensory representation in the cerebral cortex as studied by electrical stimulation. *Brain, 60* (1958), 389–443.

Penfield, W., and H. H. Jasper. *Epilepsy and the Functional Anatomy of the Human Brain.* Boston: Little, Brown, 1954.

Ramón y Cajal, S. *Recollections of My Life,* Memoirs of the American Philosophical Society, 8 (1937).

Ranson, S. W., and S. L. Clark. *The Anatomy of the Nervous System.* Philadelphia: W. B. Saunders Co., 1959.

Sarnat, H. B., and M. G. Netsky. *Evolution of the Nervous System.* New York: Oxford University Press, 1974.

Truex, R. C., and M. B. Carpenter. *Human Neuroanatomy.* Baltimore: The Williams and Wilkins Co., 1969.

Van Valen, L. Brain size and intelligence in man. *American Journal of Physiology and Anthropology, 40* (1974), 417–424.

2

PHYSIOLOGICAL ORGANIZATION
OF THE NERVOUS SYSTEM

When male Grayling butterflies are ready to copulate they fly upward toward females passing overhead. The male's response to females is not unerringly accurate, because sometimes they fly toward other passing objects. This fact suggested to the ethologist Tinbergen that the stimulus that is most effective in releasing the male's approach response could be discovered by controlled experiments. Tinbergen made model butterflies, attached them to the line of a fishing rod, and "flew" them to determine which were most effective in attracting males. Although females are brightly colored, and males can see color, color was not an important feature of the stimulus. Males were attracted by dark, large, and irregularly moving stimuli. Furthermore, these characteristics were mutually reinforcing, which suggested to Tinbergen that the nervous system of male butterflies has a "pooling station" that integrates the different features of the stimulating object.

Tinbergen's experiments are an example of excellent behavioral research that, although done with no knowledge or study of the physiology of the butterfly's nervous system, still gives clues about how that system must work. But knowledge of how the process of integration takes place, that is, of how the pooling station works, involves physiology. This is also true of neuropsychology. Much can be learned about people's behavior through careful observations and controlled experiments, but detailed knowledge of how the nervous system controls behavior requires the study of its physiological organization. This requires knowing the structure of cells and how they work. Although an extensive knowledge of electrophysiology (study of neuron activity) and neuropharmacology (study of biochemical activity of neurons) is not essential for understanding neuropsychology, a general understanding of them is helpful. The following sections give a brief description of: (1) the physical features of neurons, (2) the electrical activity of neurons and the techniques used to record their activity, and (3) chemical communication between cells and the pharmacological techniques used to manipulate their communication.

NEURON STRUCTURE

Neurons are cells that are the integrating units of the nervous system, and although they share many of the characteristics of other cells in the body, they have special characteristics that make them particularly adaptable to their function.

A broad analogy can be drawn between a neuron and a person. Neurons, once formed, do not regenerate, and unless they suffer lethal damage, they live as long as the person in which they are found. Each neuron is separated from physical contact with every other neuron, but it bridges this separation by communicating with a language that is part electrical and part chemical. Neurons vary enormously in bodily proportions, the differences making each neuron particularly adaptable to its specialized function. Neurons are aggregated into communities, or nuclei, each of which makes a special contribution to behavior. Neurons are modifiable: they change their behavior with experience; they learn; they remember; and they forget. At times neurons can malfunction, causing disruptions in normal behavior. There are similarities in the behavior of neurons, but the full significance of their behavior can only be understood within the context of the community in which they function. In summary, this anthropomorphic analogy serves to caution us that the function of a neuron within the context of a working brain is not as simple as the neuron is small.

Figure 2-1 shows a neuron schematically. The neuron is enclosed in a specialized membrane, and consists of a **cell body,** processes called **dendrites** (from the Greek, meaning tree), a process called an **axon** (from the Greek, meaning axle), and little **end feet** on the terminal branches of the axon. Associated

with each of these parts are other specialized structures that are described where appropriate in the following sections. The **dendrites** collect information, which is then integrated at the **axon hillock** close to the cell body; a summary of the input received by the cell is then passed along the axon, through the end feet to other cells. ("Information" is used here loosely to mean any event or events that the cell actively codifies.)

Although neurons have these basic structures, their configurations differ among neurons. For example, a *sensory* cell of the somatosensory system has one very long dendrite coursing from the skin to a point adjacent to its cell body, located near the spinal cord. Here the dendrite connects directly to its axon, which may then travel to the hindbrain. This sensory cell has developed a system of direct information transmission that requires no modification of the signal between receptor and brain. On the other hand, a *motor* cell in the inferior spinal cord has a number of dendrites collecting input and a long axon extending from the cord to muscles. This cell appears specialized to integrate a variety of inputs for a specific action.

Between these sensory and motor cells are many interneurons of various shapes. Some have a densely arborized dendritic system that suggests that their primary function is to collect a great deal of diversified information for integration (for examples of different neuron types see Figure 1-1). Also, although many neurons communicate chemically—and we stress this feature of their function—some probably do communicate electrically.

The Cell Membrane

The cell membrane surrounds the entire cell and consists of a double layer of lipid (fat) molecules. These molecules are polar in structure, each having a head and two tails; the heads face outward, the tails face inward. The

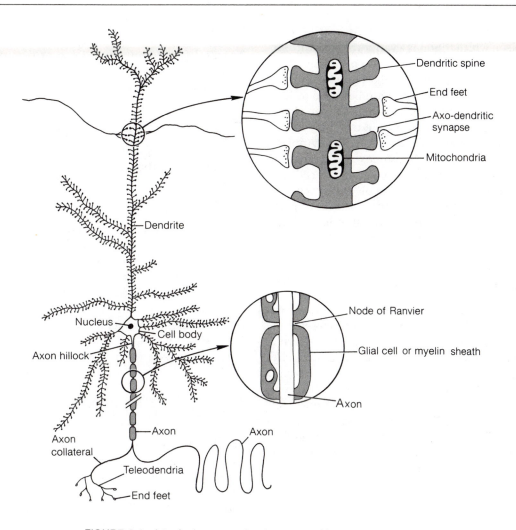

FIGURE 2-1. A typical neuron, showing some of its major physical features.

inner portion made up by the tails is believed to be largely impermeable, thus providing a barrier to free movement of ions through the membrane. Channels exist in the membrane, however, that allow it to be selectively permeable to ions under appropriate conditions. Proteins lie at or near the surface of each layer or penetrate it completely. The proteins provide a structural framework, are involved in the transport of chemicals across the membrane, and act as receptors for various substances that affect the transport mechanism.

The Cell Body

The cell body has a nucleus containing chromosomes that code the cell's genetic information in deoxyribonucleic acid (DNA). Within the nucleus there is also a nucleolus, which is packed with ribonucleic acid (RNA).

Surrounding the nucleus is the cell's cytoplasm, which contains a variety of structures including mitochondria, an endoplasmic reticulum, ribosomes, Golgi complexes, and lysosomes. Mitochondria are believed to have an energy-producing function. The endoplasmic reticulum may provide a transport system between cytoplasm and nucleus and cytoplasm and the cell wall. Ribosomes are believed to be the site of protein synthesis in the cell. The Golgi apparatus may be involved in packaging material to be extruded from the cell, or packaging lysosomes that presumably have digestive functions within the cell.

The Dendrites

The **dendrites** are actually extensions of the cell body that allow the neuron to increase the area of surface upon which it receives information from other cells. The number of dendrites varies from neuron to neuron, some having a few, others over 20; and each dendrite may branch profusely. Dendrites vary from a few microns to millimeters in length and taper as they branch; some have rough projections called dendritic spines upon which they receive end feet from other cells.

The Axon

The **axon** originates in the cell body at a transition point called the axon hillock. Its function is to transmit to other cells information that it receives from the axon hillock. Each cell has only one axon, which varies in length from a few microns to more than a meter in different cells. Most axons have branches called collaterals. At the end of the axon and its collaterals are fine terminations called teleodendria. The teleodendria are covered with little knobs, called end feet, which make junctions with other cells.

The End Feet

The **end feet** terminate in close proximity to other cells. Sherrington coined the term **synapsis** (from the Greek, meaning union) for the "almost" connection between an end foot and another neuron; consequently the end feet became technically known as **synaptic knobs,** abbreviated to *synapses* when speaking functionally or in more general terms. They contain packages of chemical substances that when released will influence the activity of other cells. End feet may synapse with any part of a neuron; they are called axo-dendritic, axo-somatic, axo-axonic, and axo-synaptic, depending upon whether they synapse with, respectively, dendrites, the cell body, axons, or synapses of other cells. Neurons may make other types of contact with each other (for example, somas may touch, or axons may touch), but we will limit our description to the most common, axo-dendritic connections.

NEURON ELECTRICAL ACTIVITY

Much of the pioneering research on the neuron's electrical activity, such as that done by Hodgkin and Huxley, used the giant axon of the squid, on the recommendation of the biologist Young. This axon measures up to a millimeter in diameter and is a hundred times larger than the axons of human nerve cells. The squid's axon is used to contract muscles that squirt water out the end of the squid's body to propel it through the water. Because effective propulsion requires all of the muscles of the body to contract at the same time, the largest axons, which conduct the fastest, connect to the most distant muscles. Because of its size, the giant axon is easily removed from the squid by dissection, and is easy to use for experiments on how electrical conduction takes place in axons.

Probably everyone knows that if a salt is put into a liquid medium it will dissolve into positive (+) and negative (−) ions that will eventually become distributed equally through the solution. In distributing themselves the ions respond to two forces, concentration and charge, and the equilibrium they obtain represents an equal distribution of both concentration and charge. The membrane of a nerve axon separates two fluid compartments, the intracellular and extracellular fluid, each of which contains many ions. Of these, negatively charged organic ions (An⁻) and chlorine ions (Cl⁻), and positively charged potassium ions (K⁺) and sodium ions (Na⁺) are particularly important in electrical conduction. These ions would be equally distributed on both sides of the membrane if it did not act as a barrier to their easy passage. It does this in three ways. First, it provides passive resistance to An⁻ ions because they are simply too large to pass through it; consequently they are retained in the intracellular fluid. Second, it is semipermeable to the other ions, allowing some of them to pass through more freely than others. Normally, K⁺ passes more freely than Na⁺ (Na⁺, although smaller than K⁺, is bound more strongly to water molecules, which add to its bulk). The permeability of the membrane also changes in certain situations, allowing these ions to pass more freely through the membrane at some times than they can at other times. In particular, the membrane contains Na⁺ channels and K⁺ channels, which close or open to control the flow of these ions. Third, the membrane contains a pumping system, or Na⁺–K⁺ pump, which exchanges intracellular Na⁺ for extracellular K⁺. Since the membrane is less permeable to Na⁺ than to K⁺, Na⁺ accumulates on the outside of the membrane. Some K⁺ flows back out of the cell when pumped, to equalize the K⁺ concentration across the membrane. The unlimited outward flow of K⁺ is checked, however, by

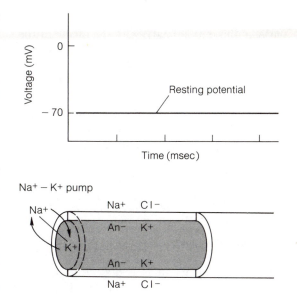

FIGURE 2-2. The nerve membrane, because of its semipermeability and through the action of the Na⁺–K⁺ pump, accumulates anions (An⁻) and potassium (K⁺) in its intracellular fluid and sodium (Na⁺) and chlorine (Cl⁻) in its extracellular fluid. As a result of the charge differences of these ions, the inside of the membrane has a charge of −70 mV compared with the outside. This charge difference is called the *resting potential*.

the accumulating extracellular charge carried by the Na⁺ (like charges repel each other). As a result of the action of these three processes there are 350 times as many An⁻ and 20 times as many K⁺ on the inside as are on the outside of the cell membrane, and 9 times as many Cl⁻ and 20 times as many Na⁺ on the outside as are on the inside of the cell membrane.

Figure 2-2 shows the distribution of the various ions on the two sides of the axon. Because the ions are distributed unequally, and because they are charged, there is a voltage across the membrane, produced largely by the high extracellular concentration of Na⁺. If this voltage is measured with a voltmeter, with one of its poles placed inside and one placed outside the cell, the voltage is found to be −70 mV (millivolts) in the squid axon (and −70 to −90 mV in different animals) with the inside of the axon negative with respect to the outside. If this voltage is plotted for a period of time it is found to be relatively stable signifying, presumably, the constant action of the Na⁺–K⁺ pump. In Figure 2-2 the voltage is plotted on a graph. The voltage across the membrane of the cell is called the **resting potential** of the membrane.

Stimulation

There are, of course, normal influences on the cell that change the voltage of the membrane in systematic ways. In addition, a wide variety of external agents such as electrical currents and chemicals and irritation from manual displacement, foreign tissue, etc., can also produce changes in the membrane voltage. The normal processes provide the mechanisms for the normal functioning of the cell; the other processes more generally lead to various types of pathology. Despite these differences, both the normal and abnormal influences act in very much the same way; thus, any influence or irritation which leads to a change in the voltage can be called a **stimulus,** and the process, whether normal or abnormal, can be called **stimulation.** In experimental situations stimulation is usually provided by giving brief pulses of electric shock to the axon through small wires called stimulating electrodes. The response of the axon is then recorded by measuring its voltage change with a voltmeter or oscilloscope attached to the axon by small wires called recording electrodes.

Depolarization, Threshold, and Action Potential

When an axon is stimulated with a very small electric current, its membrane becomes more permeable to Na⁺ and K⁺, and they move more freely across the membrane. Consequently, Na⁺ enters and K⁺ leaves the cell, causing the voltage across the membrane to decrease toward 0 mV. (Because K⁺ already moves more freely across the membrane than Na⁺ the main change is caused by increased inward flow of Na⁺.) When this small voltage change occurs the axon is said to undergo **depolarization.** This change in voltage is local—restricted to the area stimulated—and brief, so the resting potential of the membrane is rapidly restored.

Although the neuron membrane responds to weak stimulation by decreasing its permeability to ions in a relatively orderly way, it undergoes a peculiar change of behavior if stimulation is sufficiently intense to cause the transmembrane voltage to depolarize to about −50 mV. At about this voltage the membrane becomes completely permeable to Na⁺ and K⁺; that is, Na⁺ rushes into the cell and K⁺ rushes out of it, until the voltage across the membrane falls through 0 mV and reverses to about +50 mV. The depolarizaton of the membrane is largely attributable to Na⁺ influx; its repolarization is due to K⁺ efflux. The sudden permeability of the membrane occurs independently of any further stimulation once the membrane has depolarized to about −50 mV. The loss of permeability is quite brief, about ½ millisecond, after which normal permeability is regained, the Na⁺–K⁺ pump resumes its action, and the resting potential of the membrane is restored. The voltage at which the membrane undergoes this autonomous change is called its **threshold.** The sudden reversal of polarity and the restoration of the resting potential are called an **action potential.** These are displayed graphically in Figure 2-3. One can say, therefore, that the threshold for eliciting an action potential is −50 mV.

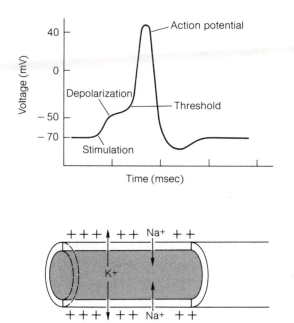

FIGURE 2-3. Stimulation of the membrane causes it to become more permeable to K⁺ and Na⁺. As a result the transmembrane potential declines or depolarizes. At about −50 mV, its threshold, the membrane becomes completely permeable to Na⁺ and K⁺ and its charge momentarily reverses. This reversal is called an *action potential.*

Conduction of the Nerve Impulse

When an action potential occurs in a region of the membrane it acts as a stimulus, causing adjacent portions of the membrane to lose their permeability and undergo a similar voltage change. Consequently, an action potential triggered at one end of an axon will be conducted along its length. (Action potentials can travel in either direction, but they normally begin at the cell body and travel away from it.) This movement of the action potential along the length of the axon, shown in Figure 2-4, is called a **nerve impulse** (or, more colorfully and descriptively, *firing* or *discharging*). The rate at which the impulse travels along the axon, varying from 1 to 100 meters per second, is quite slow, but neurons can sustain a wide range of firing rates. Usually they fire fewer than 100 times a second, but they can fire as frequently as 1000 times per second.

The All-or-None Law

A peculiar property of a neuron's behavior is that its threshold is stable, and every action potential, and hence nerve impulse, once it is triggered, has an identical threshold and height. These properties of the neuron's behavior are formulated in the *all-or-none law:* action potentials either occur or they do not; there is no in-between condition.

The Origin of the Nerve Impulse

Graded Potentials. So far we have described the events that occur on an axon when it is stimulated. What happens on dendrites, which are normally the origin of the cell's electrical activity? Dendrites have a membrane similar to the axons', and a similar resting potential, and they also undergo changes in potential when they are stimulated. But unlike the axon, the dendrites do not produce action potentials. If a dendrite is stimulated the voltage changes from resting potential in proportion to the intensity of the stimulation; the change then spreads along the dendrite away from the point of stimulation, getting smaller with distance (as the size of a wave in water decreases with distance from its source). These voltage changes undergone by dendrites are called **graded potentials,** which can occur as a decrease in transmembrane voltage (depolarization) or an increase (hyperpolarization), depending upon the nature of the stimulation. How each of these occurs will be discussed after we have described how graded potentials trigger the nerve impulse on the axon.

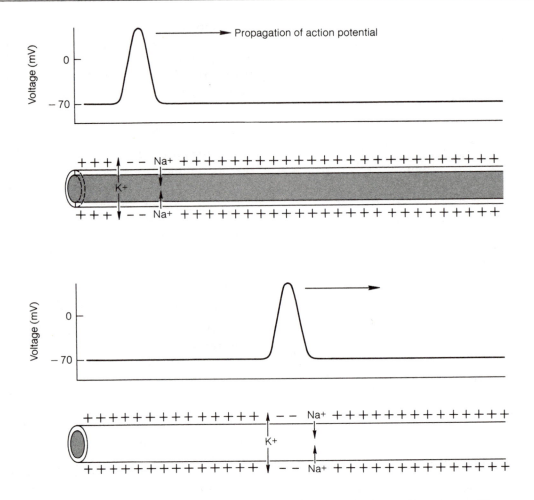

FIGURE 2-4. Because an action potential on one part of the axon stimulates adjacent areas of the axon to produce one, the action potential is propagated along the axon. (After Katz, 1967.)

Spatial and Temporal Summation. Because dendrites respond to stimulation with graded potentials they have some interesting properties. If a dendrite is stimulated at two points in close proximity the graded potentials produced at each point will add. If the two stimuli are identical the graded potential will be twice as large as would occur with only one stimulus. If the two stimuli are given at widely different points on the dendrite the graded potentials will dissipate before they reach each other and will not add. Stimuli given at intermediate distances will produce additive graded potentials, but only at the points that receive the potentials from both sources. Also, the potentials will be smaller because they decay with distance. Similar rules apply when one stimulus hyperpolarizes the membrane and one depolarizes the membrane, with the difference that the graded potentials subtract. This property of adjacent graded potentials to add and subtract is called **spatial summation.**

Another type of change that can occur on dendrites is called **temporal summation.** The graded potential of a stimulated dendrite will decay with time after the stimulus has terminated. A second stimulus given some time later at the same site will produce a similar response. If the second stimulus is given soon after the first, the potentials will add, becoming larger than either is alone. The strength of the graded potential will be determined by the strength of the two stimuli and the interval between them. If one stimulus hyperpolarizes the membrane and the other depolarizes the membrane, then the two will subtract, and the graded potential will accordingly be decreased in size.

If the features of spatial and temporal summation of graded potentials are considered, it is possible to see how the nerve impulse is generated. It will be recalled that the threshold for an action potential is −50 mV. If the entire dendritic system is influenced so that it is depolarized to −50 mV, and if this graded potential spreads over the cell body to a point adjacent to the axon, then the necessary conditions for eliciting an action potential will be met. In fact, the point of transition between the cell body and axon, called the **axon hillock** (Figure 2-1), is the site where the nerve impulse originates. As long as this area is depolarized below −50 mV by spread of graded potentials, the cell will fire. However, if graded potentials are not sufficiently strong to depolarize the axon hillock to threshold, the cell will not fire. In summary, therefore, the origin of axonal firing can be traced to the influence of graded potentials from the dendrites of the cell.

The Origin of Graded Potentials: The Synapse, EPSPs, and IPSPs

The idea that chemicals play a role in the transmission of information from one neuron to another, from a neuron to a muscle, or from a neuron to a body organ originated with the experiments of Otto Loewi in 1921. He stimulated the nerves going to a frog heart, collected a fluid perfused through the ventricles of the heart, and transferred it to the heart of another frog. The activity of the second heart was changed by introduction of the fluid in the same way that the activity of the first heart was changed by electrical stimulation. The stimulated nerve had been releasing a chemical, and it was the chemical, not some direct action of the nerve, that was causing the heart's activity to change. It is now widely accepted that neurons communicate chiefly through the agency of the chemicals they release when they fire. These chemicals, each known as a **neurotransmitter,** are released by the end feet of the neuron.

Figure 2-5 shows a diagram of an end foot. The end foot is separated from other neurons by a very small space called the *synaptic space.* The membrane of the end foot is called the **presynaptic membrane,** and the membrane it synapses with is called the **postsynaptic membrane.** Penetrating the end foot from the axon are neurofibrils, which may transport precursor chemicals for the manufacture of neurotransmitters into the end foot. There are *mitochondria* that provide energy for metabolic processes. There are also two types of vesicles in the end foot: **storage granules,** which are presumed to be long-term storage sites for neurotransmitters; and **synaptic vesicles,** which hold neurotransmitters for immediate use. On the postsynaptic membrane there are specialized proteins that act as *receptors* for the neurotransmitter. The synapse functions in the

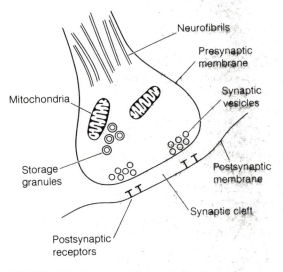

FIGURE 2-5. Diagram of the major features of a synapse.

following way. When a neuron fires, some synaptic vesicles release their neurotransmitter content into the synaptic space. The neurotransmitter binds weakly to the receptors on the postsynaptic membrane, after which it is quickly washed away by extracellular fluid and is destroyed or taken back into the presynaptic membrane for reuse.

How neurotransmitters, released by the firing of a presynaptic neuron, produce graded potentials in a postsynaptic neuron has been clarified in part by Eccles and his coworkers, who stimulated the axons of presynaptic neurons while recording from a postsynaptic cell body. Postsynaptic graded potentials followed each volley of presynaptic stimulation. These postsynaptic potentials, or PSPs, had a very small amplitude, 1 to 3 mV; but depending upon which presynaptic axons were stimulated, they consisted either of depolarization or hyperpolarization of the postsynaptic membrane. Because depolarizing PSPs of course increase the probability of the neuron firing, they are called *excitatory postsynaptic potentials,*

or *EPSPs;* and because hyperpolarizing potentials decrease the probability of the neuron firing, they are called *inhibitory postsynaptic potentials,* or *IPSPs.* It is now accepted that the EPSPs and IPSPs are produced by the action of neurotransmitters on the postsynaptic receptors of the cell. Neurotransmitters from certain synapses, called *excitatory neurotransmitters,* are responsible for EPSPs, while other neurotransmitters, called *inhibitory neurotransmitters,* are responsible for IPSPs. Eccles suggests that excitatory neurotransmitters produce EPSPs by making the membrane slightly more permeable to Na^+, which enters the cell, lowering the transmembrane voltage. Inhibitory neurotransmitters, on the other hand, make the membrane more permeable to K^+ and Cl^+ ions; K^+ flows out and Cl^- flows into the cell, raising the transmembrane voltage.

It can now be seen that the origin of the graded potentials of dendrites can be traced to the release and action of neurotransmitters from the end feet of other neurons. It will be remembered that there are thousands of end feet synapsing with the dendrites and cell body of any one neuron; thus, the summed graded potential of the cell is produced by the action of all of these inputs. The integration of these inputs by spatial and temporal summation determines whether the neuron will fire or not. If EPSPs predominate, and if there are enough of them to produce depolarization to threshold at the axon hillock, the neuron will fire. If IPSPs predominate the neuron will not fire.

Factors Determining Nerve Impulse Speed

The nerve impulse does not travel at exactly the same speed in all neurons. At least two factors affect speed. One factor is resistance to current along the axon. Impulse speed is increased as resistance is decreased; and resistance is most

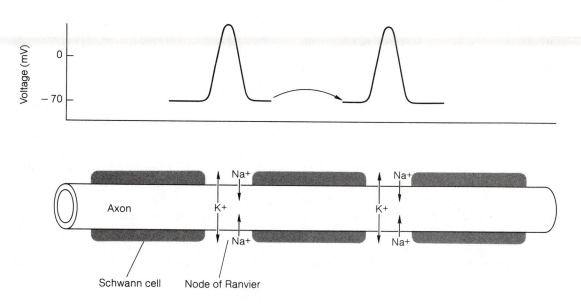

FIGURE 2-6. The nerve impulse jumps from one inter-Schwann cell space, called a *node of Ranvier*, to the next. This process, *saltatory conduction*, greatly speeds impulse transmission.

effectively decreased by increase of the axon size. Thus, large axons conduct at a faster rate than small axons. Were the nervous system to rely only on this procedure, axons would have to be cumbersomely large. An alternative procedure has evolved that uses the glial cells to aid in speeding propagation. Schwann cells in the peripheral nervous system and oligodendroglia in the central nervous system wrap around some axons, forming a compact sheath of **myelin** (from the Greek, meaning marrow) against the cell membrane, as shown in Figure 2-6. Between each glial cell the membrane of the axon is exposed by a gap called a **node of Ranvier.** In these myelinated axons the nerve impulse jumps along the axon from node to node, a type of conduction called **saltatory conduction** (from the Latin, meaning skip). Saltatory conduction is an extremely effective way of speeding the impulse because a small myelinated axon can conduct as rapidly as an unmyelinated axon 30 times as large.

The Integration of Neural Activity and Information Processing

It can be seen from the preceding sections that the dendritic system of the neuron sums the activity from many other neurons by producing graded potentials that will determine whether or not the neuron fires. The firing of the neuron is an all-or-none response, which will continue for as long as the firing threshold of the axon hillock is maintained. But how do these series of activities code information?

It is now thought that the nervous system works by a combination of analogue (how much) and digital, or binary (yes–no), principles. Analogue functions are the property of the dendritic system, and digital functions are the property of the axons. We can see how these principles determine behavior if we return to the opening description of the male Grayling butterfly's behavior. Recall Tinbergen's suggestion that in the male butterfly's nervous system there is a pooling station that integrates the different features (dark, large, and irregular) of a stimulus object to determine whether or not the male will approach the stimulus. Theoretically, all of the male butterfly's behavior could be accounted for by the activity of one central neuron. The dendrites of that neuron would serve as the pooling station and the axon would be the system that initiates an approach response. If three channels of input converged upon the dendrites (one signalling darkness, one size, and one movement), simultaneous activity in the separate channels signalling dark, large, and irregular would produce EPSPs that when summed would trigger axonal firing and thus approach by the butterfly. Activity in only one channel might not be sufficient to fire the neuron; activity in two channels might be sufficient to produce a response, if input in each were particularly intense. At any rate, it can be seen that the analogue function of the dendrites will integrate the various sources of input, while the digital activity of the axon will determine whether or not approach is to occur. Of course, the analogue feature of dendritic integration can be put to many types of use, and the digital properties of the axon can be expressed in many codes (frequency, pattern of firing, etc.).

Many other factors contribute to information processing. Synapses proximal to the axon hillock may have special access to influence cell firing. Inhibition or excitation by more distal axosynaptic connections may allow for more subtle control of intercell communication. Some synapses may also change structurally with use or disuse, thus becoming increasingly or decreasingly effective in communicating. These factors, and many others, are beyond the scope of the present discussion, but they do contribute to the brain's incredible synthesizing and storage abilities.

ANALYZING THE BRAIN THROUGH ITS ELECTRICAL ACTIVITY

Because the activity of nerve cells has an electrochemical basis the activity can be recorded with instruments sensitive to small changes in electrical activity. The several techniques for recording the brain's electrical activity include: (1) intracellular unit and extracellular unit recording, (2) electroencephalographic (EEG) recording, and (3) evoked potential (EP) recording. Relating each of these types of activity to behavior can be used as a way of determining the function of particular brain areas, and as a way of determining the normality of function in a given brain area. Because of its electrochemical mode of activity, the brain can also be artificially stimulated with electrical current. This technique has been used as a method of analyzing the function of different areas, as a possible source of therapy, and as a method of producing experimental models of diseases such as epilepsy.

Unit Recording

If small wires or pipettes containing an ionized conducting solution are inserted into the brain so that their tips are placed in or near a nerve cell, the changes in a single cell's electrical potentials, i.e., **unit activity,** can be recorded in relation to some indifferent electrode or ground. *Intracellular* recordings are made from electrodes with very tiny tips, less than $1/1000$ of a millimeter in diameter, which are placed in the cell, whereas *extracellular* recordings are made when an electrode tip is placed adjacent to one or a number of cells. Both techniques require amplification of the signal and some type of display. The cell's activity is either displayed on an oscilloscope for photographing or recorded on a tape recorder for computer analysis. In many experiments the signal is played through a loudspeaker so cell firing is heard as a beep or pop. Both recording techniques require considerable skill to perform because it is difficult to place the electrode in or sufficiently close to the cell without killing it, and when a cell is "captured," it is often difficult to hold it for more than a few minutes or hours before the signal is lost.

Unit recording techniques provide a particularly interesting insight into the brain's function. For example, cell records obtained from the visual cortex of cats and monkeys reveal that each cell has a preferred stimulus and a preferred response pattern. Some cells fire to horizontal lines, others to diagonal lines, and still others fire only to lines that are oriented in a special way and that also move in a particular direction. Unit recording techniques have also been used to analyze such abnormal cell activity as occurs in epilepsy. In epilepsy, the activity of cells becomes synchronized in an abnormal pattern, and an understanding of epilepsy depends in part upon analyzing and controlling this feature of the cell's behavior. Much of the information obtained with unit recordings has of necessity come from experiments performed on anesthetized animals. Future research is likely to repeat these tests in freely moving animals to confirm and elaborate upon the findings.

EEG Recording

A simple technique for recording electrical activity of the brain was developed in the early 1930s by Hans Berger. He found that it was possible to record "brain waves" from the scalp. These waves, called **electroencephalograms,** or **EEGs,** have proved to be a valuable tool for studying problems such as sleep-waking, for monitoring depth of anesthesia, and for diagnosing epilepsy and brain damage.

To record a person's EEG a small metal disc is attached to the scalp, and the change in electrical activity in the area of this electrode is compared to some electrically neutral zone such as the ear lobe. The electrical changes recorded on the scalp are rather small, usually much less than a millivolt, so they must be amplified for display on an oscilloscope or on a paper chart recorder called an electroencephalograph, or EEG machine.

The electrical activity recorded from the scalp is the sum of all neural activity, action potentials, graded potentials etc., but it is mostly the measure of the graded potentials of dendrites. As a result, it represents the summed dendritic activity of thousands of nerve cells and can only be considered a rather general measure of the brain's activity. Although it can be used as a crude index of the brain's level of excitation it tells very little about the activity of single cells as such. During a given EEG pattern any particular single cell may be active or inactive.

It was originally thought that each cytoarchitectonic area of the brain had its own pattern of EEG activity, but it is now recognized that variations in patterns do not correlate closely with cytoarchitectonic areas. Figure 2-7 shows the characteristic *resting* rhythms obtained from different parts of the cortex. The patterns are obtained only under optimal conditions, when the person is awake, resting quietly, with eyes closed. The dominant rhythm of the posterior cortex is an 8-to-12 cycles/second waveform called the **alpha rhythm.** The dominant rhythm of the precentral and postcentral sensorimotor area is a 20-to-25 cycles/second **beta rhythm.** The secondary frontal areas have a 17-to-20 cycles/second beta rhythm. And the tertiary frontal area has 8-to-12 cycles/second waves.

The resting EEG patterns desynchronize or flatten into a low-voltage asynchronous activ-

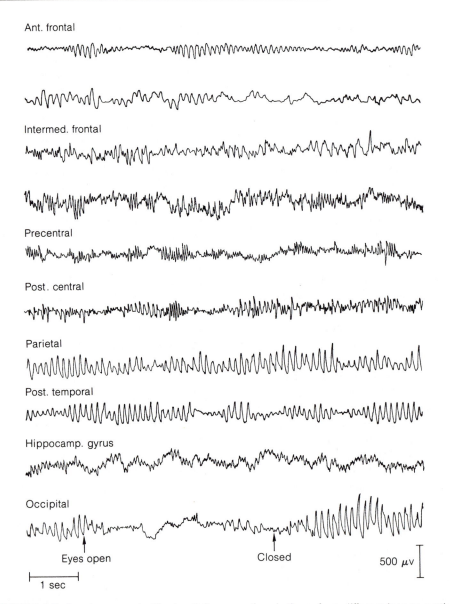

FIGURE 2-7. Spontaneous electrical activity, or resting rhythms, from different human cortical areas. Sample tracings were taken directly from the exposed cortex with bipolar silver-chloride cotton wick electrodes. (From W. Penfield and H. H. Jasper, *Epilepsy and the Functional Anatomy of the Human Brain*. Boston: Little, Brown and Co. Copyright © 1954. Reprinted by permission.)

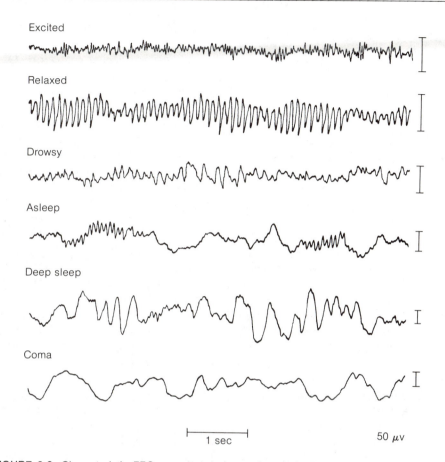

FIGURE 2-8. Characteristic EEG recorded during various behavioral states in man. (From W. Penfield and H. H. Jasper, *Epilepsy and the Functional Anatomy of the Human Brain.* Boston: Little, Brown and Co. Copyright © 1954. Reprinted by permission.)

ity when the person opens the eyes or becomes active (see Figure 2-8). They also disappear during sleep, coma, after epileptic seizures (postictal stupor), and anesthesia, at which time they are replaced by slower, larger-amplitude waveforms. Jasper and Penfield have recorded from the motor cortex (area 4) while it was exposed during a surgical procedure. They found that the beta rhythm was blocked during voluntary movement, i.e., arm movement. Imagining the movement did not cause the same blocking. In some cases

blocking of the beta rhythm was restricted to the cortical area representing the part of the body that was moved, i.e., moving the hand blocked only the beta rhythm in the hand area.

Electroencephalography is used clinically to detect malfunctioning brain areas, and so is useful for diagnosing epilepsy, or for locating brain lesions or tumors. Large-amplitude spike-and-wave activity may indicate the presence of epilepsy, and slow waves in a behaviorally alert individual may indicate brain damage. Figure 4-6 shows some abnormal EEG waves recorded from epileptics. Although the EEG is only a general measure of the brain's activity, rather sophisticated averaging procedures have been developed to localize areas that generate abnormal EEG activity.

Evoked Potentials

Evoked potentials, or EPs, consist of a short train of large slow waves, and are like the EEG in that they are recorded from the scalp and largely reflect the activity of dendrites. But they occur only under special conditions. If a bright light or noise is presented very briefly, say for 250 milliseconds, electrodes placed on the cortex will record a large slow wave that is clearest and largest over the area of cortex processing the sensory event. For example, in the case of a bright light, the EP will be largest over the visual cortex. Since these potentials vary somewhat in their actual size and shape it is customary to average several together to obtain an accurate estimate of the "typical" EP. This average is often called an AEP, or **average evoked potential.** The evoked potential technique is very tricky because the size of the EP can be influenced by many variables. In animals, the most important variable seems to be movement, for the magnitude of the evoked potential may vary according to what the animal is doing. Movements that affect EP size may be as small and subtle as eye movements or changes in respiration. Nevertheless, the EP is considered by some people to be a useful indicator of the brain's activity in processing information.

Electrical Stimulation

The object of electrical stimulation of the brain is to activate neurons. Usually a fine insulated wire with an uninsulated tip is placed in the brain so that the tip lies in a predetermined location. Low-voltage pulses of current,

usually 60 to 100 pulses per second, are then passed through the electrode to stimulate neural tissue adjacent to its tip. Use of this technique on freely moving animals was pioneered by Hess, who developed the procedure of permanently attaching electrodes to the skulls of cats. The electrodes produced little discomfort to the animals and so they could receive brain stimulation while their reaction was observed. Hess found that virtually every behavior that a cat spontaneously performed could be induced by brain stimulation. The elicited behaviors were usually "stimulus bound"; that is, they lasted only as long as the stimulation was applied. Every part of the brain of many animals has since been mapped for the effects of electrical stimulation.

Electrical stimulation has also been used in surgery and as a treatment of some neurological disorders. In certain situations requiring brain surgery it is considered important not to damage areas of the brain involved in controlling speech. Under local anesthesia the patient's cortex is exposed and stimulated electrically to identify speech areas. During a stimulation test the patient is asked to speak, electrical stimulation is applied, and if it is found to disrupt speech in particular ways the stimulated area is defined as a speech area.

Therapeutic brain stimulation, although not widespread, has been used. A few seconds of electrical stimulation of the midbrain may arrest otherwise unmanageable pain for periods lasting many hours. Brief periods of stimulation given in the cerebellum have sometimes been found effective in arresting epileptic attacks.

Recently Goddard has found that if certain portions of the limbic system are given from one to two seconds of stimulation each day, the stimulation, which initially has no observable effect on behavior, will begin to produce epileptic attacks. That is, the animals will show convulsions after stimulation. If the treatments are continued for a long enough period of time the seizures may begin to occur spontaneously. This procedure has been given the name **kindling,** and is providing a much-needed model for studying human epilepsy.

ANALYZING THE BRAIN THROUGH ITS BIOCHEMICAL ACTIVITY

As we have pointed out, neurons communicate with each other and with glands, muscles, and other body organs by releasing small quantities of substances, neurotransmitters, onto receptors of the neurons or organs they synapse with. At the present time many different neurotransmitters are suspected to be active in the nervous system, but it is known that any given neuron will have only one type of transmitter in all of its synapses. Substances that are postulated to be neurotransmitters include: acetylcholine, adrenaline, dopamine, noradrenaline, serotonin, enkephlins, some amino acids, histamine, prostaglandins, ergothioneine, substance P, and GABA. There are many others, and as biochemical technology develops the list continually grows. These substances can be called suspected neurotransmitters only advisedly, because only acetylcholine has been conclusively shown to be a transmitter in the central nervous system. Proof of neurotransmitter function requires that a number of rigorous criteria be met; these include:

1. The chemical is shown to be present in the end feet.

2. It is shown to be released when the neuron fires.

3. Placing the chemical on the innervated organ mimics the effect of nerve stimulation.

4. There is a chemical or uptake mechanism present in the area of the synaptic space to inactivate the neurotransmitter.

5. Placing in the synaptic space a substance that will destroy or inactivate the neurotransmitter must block the effects of nerve stimulation.

At the present time, technology is simply unable to meet the rigor of all of these demands; and so, chemicals that are strongly suspected of having neurotransmitter function are labeled **putative** (or supposed) **transmitters.**

Distribution of Putative Transmitters

The distribution of putative neurotransmitters in the brain can be determined in a number of ways. Samples of tissue can be taken from different brain areas and the concentrations of chemicals in the samples compared. This type of analysis gives only a relative measure of neurotransmitter distribution, and most neurotransmitters have been found in all regions of the brain, though in considerably varied concentrations. Generally it is not wise to conclude much about function from concentration differences; for example, a small quantity of neurotransmitter in one region may be just as important for a particular function as a large quantity in some other region. Another technique of determining distribution is to stain the brain tissue with stains that interact with neurotransmitters or with some chemical closely related to the neurotransmitter's function. For example, noradrenaline and dopamine can be stained by exposing sections of tissue to formaldehyde vapor and then illuminating the tissue with ultraviolet light. Both substances fluoresce with a green color, but to slightly different shades that can be distinguished. The presence of acetylcholine can be identified by staining tissue with a substance called butylthiocholine, which turns acetylcholinesterase, a chemical that breaks down acetylcholine, black. In most, but not all, brain sites acetylcholinesterase indicates the presence of acetylcholine.

Neurochemical mapping procedures have been revealing some extremely interesting insights into the organization of the brain. Some neurochemicals, although widely distributed in all regions of the brain, are located in neurons whose cell bodies are found in a number of restricted nuclei. The origin and distribution of some fibers of these systems in the rat is shown diagrammatically in Figure 2-9. These systems resemble hormone systems, except that hormones are carried from their origin throughout the body by the blood rather than by axons.

Brain Dysfunctions, Mental Illness, and Neurotransmitters

Since neurons containing specific neurotransmitters appear to be organized in systems, it seems pertinent to ask whether these different neurochemical systems can be associated with specific functions. Indeed they seem to be. The problem, however, is not to find a function but to find the *appropriate* function.

Since before the turn of the century it has been often suggested that **psychosis**—e.g., an illness such as schizophrenia or manic-depressive psychosis—was the result of brain malfunction. It was variously proposed that psychoses were due to actual brain damage, ingestion of toxins that poisoned the brain, or synthesis by the brain itself of a toxin that caused it to malfunction. These ideas were reinforced by the observation that various chemical agents, e.g., atropine, when ingested, produced behavior resembling that of psychotics. Then, in 1952, French physicians observed that a preanesthetic agent, chlorpromazine, had a tranquilizing effect on surgical patients. When tried on psychotic patients, it was found to have striking therapeutic action. By 1955 it was in use in North America and was probably instrumental in drastically reducing the patient population of mental hospitals (Figure 2-10).

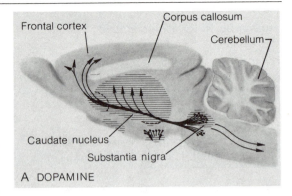

A DOPAMINE

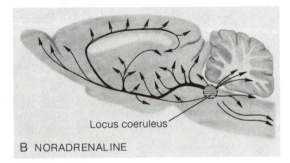

B NORADRENALINE

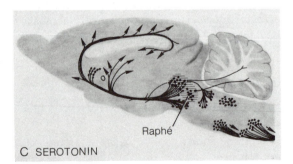

C SEROTONIN

FIGURE 2-9. Location of cell bodies, shown as black dots, and the projections of dopamine, noradrenaline, and serotonin pathways in the rat. (From J. R. Cooper, F. E. Bloom, and R. H. Roth, *The Biochemical Basis of Neuropharmacology*. New York: Oxford University Press. Copyright © 1978 by Oxford University Press, Inc. Reprinted by permission.)

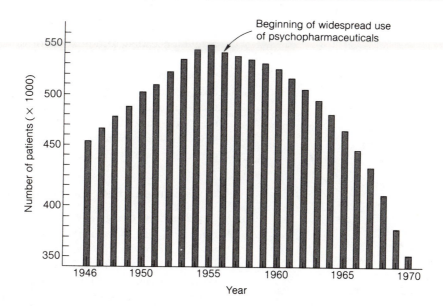

FIGURE 2-10. Numbers of resident patients in state and local government mental hospitals in the United States from 1946 through 1970. Note the dramatic change in the total population of patients in mental hospitals that began in 1956, when therapeutic use of psychoactive drugs began. (From V. C. Longo, *Neuropharmacology and Behavior*. San Francisco: W. H. Freeman and Company. Copyright © 1972. Modified from D. H. Efron, ed., *Psychopharmacology: A Review of Progress*. Washington, D.C.: U.S. Department of Health, Education, and Welfare, 1968.)

Since then many other antipsychotic drugs have been introduced, and an intense search for the mechanisms of their action has been under way. Since many psychoactive drugs are now thought to produce their effects by modifying synaptic activity, the following sections will describe the synaptic organization and pharmacological influences of some of the better-known neurotransmitter systems.

Sites of Drug Action on Synapses

Figure 2-11 is a diagram of a generalized synapse showing many of the features typical of most synapses. The following is the sequence of biochemical events outlined in the diagram.

1. *Synthesis.* Precursor chemicals obtained from food or manufactured in the cell are transported down the axon into the synapse, where they are synthesized into the neurotransmitter.

2. *Storage.* The transmitter is stored in the synapse in one or more of several ways, at least one of which is in vesicles available for release.

3. *Release.* When the nerve discharges, some of the vesicles release their content into the subsynaptic space.

4. *Receptor Interaction.* The released neurotransmitter crosses the synaptic space and binds weakly to specialized receptors on the postsynaptic membrane, where it initiates depolarization or hyperpolarization of the postsynaptic membrane. In many systems more than one type of postsynaptic receptor may be sensitive to the neurotransmitter.

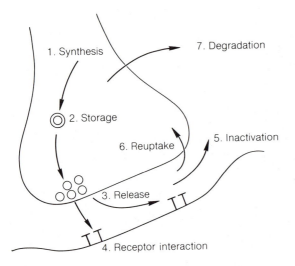

FIGURE 2-11. Steps in synaptic transmission in an idealized synapse.

5. *Inactivation* or

6. *Reuptake.* In some synapses the neurotransmitter is inactivated in the area of the synaptic space, in others it is taken back up into the synapse, and in some both mechanisms may be active.

7. *Degradation.* The free neurotransmitter within the synapse may be degraded to control internal neurotransmitter concentrations.

Many of the chemicals that people ingest by accident or as recreational drugs or medicine may influence one or more of these steps in one or more neurochemical systems. This realization has revolutionized modern pharmacology and neuropharmacology, and has led to an intense investigation directed toward disclosing the specific action of different drugs and toward synthesizing new drugs with specific actions. This investigation also involves a search for a neural substrate for such mental disorders as schizophrenia and depression, on the logic that if a particular drug can ameliorate one of these disorders, and if the transmitter substance upon which the drug

acts can be identified, then that might be taken as evidence that some excess or deficiency of that neurotransmitter may be causally related to the disorder. Although this line of reasoning has disclosed some intriguing possibilities, there are many pitfalls in the logic, and as yet there is no unequivocal evidence proving that any neurotransmitter is causally linked with a particular mental disease.

Classification of Psychoactive Drugs

Psychoactive drugs, drugs that affect cognitive functions, can be classified in a number of ways, among the most useful of which is by their behavioral effects. Table 2-1 summarizes such a classification. The table also shows the neurotransmitter systems upon which various drugs in each category are thought to act and the effect the drug has on the respective neurotransmitter function. As pointed out above, a drug may intervene in the process of intercell communication at any of a number of stages, but irrespective of its site of action it will have one of two effects: it will either increase or decrease the effectiveness of transmission at the synaptic junction. Thus, the arrows in Table 2-1 indicate by their direction whether the drugs listed have the effect of increasing (upward arrows) or decreasing (downward) activity at that synaptic junction.

Sedative-hypnotics are drugs that at low doses reduce anxiety, at medium doses produce sedation, and at high doses produce anesthesia or coma. They are a diverse group of drugs and include barbiturates, benzodiazepines (known as minor tranquilizers, of which Valium is an example), and alcohol. They are widely used for their antianxiety actions. It is thought that these drugs depress the activity of the systems that produce arousal or initiation of behavior. At low doses the sedative-hypnotics may depress the activity of noradrenaline synapses, but their precise mechanism of action is unknown. At higher doses

TABLE 2-1

Relation between psychoactive agents
and neurotransmitter systems

Drug classification and drug	Neuro-transmitter	Action
Sedative-hypnotics		
Barbiturates	Noradrenaline	↓
Benzodiazepines	Noradrenaline	↓
Alcohol	Noradrenaline	↓
Stimulants, antidepressants		
Amphetamine	Noradrenaline	↑
Cocaine	Noradrenaline	↑
Desipramine	Noradrenaline	↑
Imipramine	Serotonin	↑
Antipsychotic agents		
Chlorpromazine	Dopamine	↓
Reserpine	Dopamine, noradrenaline	↓
Opiates		
Heroin, morphine	Endorphins	↑
Psychedelics		
Atropine	Acetylcholine	↓
Muscarine	Acetylcholine	↑
Mescaline, cannabis	Noradrenaline	↑
LSD, psilocybin	Serotonin	↑ or ↓
	Noradrenaline	↑

they may block neurotransmission in many systems and thus produce anesthesia or even coma.

Stimulants are drugs that increase behavioral activity either by producing increases in motor activity or by counteracting fatigue. One group of stimulants, the amphetamines, is thought to potentiate release of noradrenaline from the presynaptic membrane and to also block the reuptake mechanism that reabsorbs noradrenaline back into the synapse after it has acted on the receptor. Both actions would increase the amount of noradrenaline available and the duration of its availability for action on the receptors. The amphetamines have antidepressant properties, but their major clinical use is to counteract narcolepsy, an uncontrollable tendency to fall asleep. Amphetamine is also given to hyperactive chil-

dren, whom it may help by prolonging their attention span. Another group of stimulants includes cocaine and the tricyclic antidepressants, including desipramine and imipramine. There is good evidence that these drugs block the reuptake of noradrenaline and serotonin, and thus facilitate transmission by prolonging the time during which the neurotransmitter can act on the receptor. Some tricyclics, such as desipramine, have a more potent action on noradrenaline reuptake, whereas others, such as imipramine, more selectively block serotonin reuptake. The ability of cocaine to counteract depression was first documented by Sigmund Freud, but today the tricyclics, which are in some ways structurally similar to cocaine, are the treatment of choice for depression. Because different tricyclics are more effective than others in treating quite different depressive populations, van Praag has suggested that there may be at least two types of depression: one referable to reduced noradrenaline transmission, the other referable to reduced serotonin transmission.

The *antipsychotic agents* (often referred to as major tranquilizers) are drugs that have been effective in treating schizophrenia; the most widely used of these drugs are chlorpromazine and reserpine. Although both drugs act on noradrenaline and dopamine systems, their antipsychotic action appears attributable to their action on dopamine. Chlorpromazine is thought to reduce dopaminergic transmission by blocking dopamine receptors, whereas reserpine reduces dopamine levels by destroying storage granules within the synapse. Although the effectiveness of these drugs in treating schizophrenia has led to the "dopamine hypothesis of schizoprenia," which states that schizophrenia may be related to excessive levels of dopamine, this hypothesis should be viewed with caution. Neurotransmitter systems have complex interactions with each other, and it is quite possible that schizophrenia is caused by imbalances in any of a number of known or unknown systems that normally check the level of dopamine transmission.

The *opiates*, such as heroin and morphine, although widely abused because of their addictive properties, are nevertheless among the most effective pain-relieving agents available. Their mechanism of action has been clarified recently by the discovery of endogenous, natural opiatelike substances in the brain. It has been suggested that these natural opiates such as endorphins (a class name meaning that the chemicals act like opiates) are neurotransmitters in the brain, and that the opiates produce their effects by mimicking the postsynaptic stimulation from these neurotransmitters. The discovery that there are endogenous opiates has of course provoked tremendous excitement, particularly with respect to the possible new avenues they open up for controlling pain.

The *psychedelic drugs* are a mixed group of agents that alter sensory perception and cognitive processes. There are at least three major groups of psychedelics: (1) Acetylcholine psychedelics block or facilitate transmission in acetylcholine synapses. Drugs such as atropine block acetylcholine postsynaptic receptors, thus reducing acetylcholine action; those such as muscarine, on the other hand, stimulate these receptors much as acetylcholine does, thus mimicking acetylcholine activity. (2) Noradrenaline psychedelics include mescaline and possibly cannabis, and they may act by stimulating noradrenaline postsynaptic re-

ceptors. (3) Serotonin psychedelics include LSD (lysergic acid diethylamide) and psilocybin, which may mimic serotonin by stimulating postsynaptic receptors of serotonin synapses or which may block the activity of serotonin neurons. In addition they may stimulate noradrenaline receptors.

In summary, it can be seen that many commonly used drugs interact with neurotransmitter systems in the brain. The object of this section was to point out the usefulness of considering drug action and behavior within the context of neurotransmitter function. Consequently, this should not be considered a comprehensive discussion of either neurotransmission or drugs. There are, of course, many more drugs that act on neurotransmission (curare, for example, blocks acetylcholine nerve-muscle junctions), and many other drugs have effects other than at neuron junctions (such as caffeine, which may stimulate metabolic activity in neurons). In addition, the seeming simplicity of neurotransmission is deceptive, because many neurotransmitter systems have a number of types of postsynaptic receptors that are sensitive to the effects of different drugs. For example, the nerve–muscle acetylcholine receptors are blocked by curare, whereas the brain acetylcholine receptors are for the most part blocked by atropine. For a lucid and more detailed review of neuropharmacology we recommend the reader to Cooper, Bloom, and Roth; and for a comprehensive source book on drug and drug action we recommend Goodman and Gilman.

REFERENCES

Cooper, J. R., F. E. Bloom, and R. H. Roth. *The Biochemical Basis of Neuropharmacology.* New York: Oxford University Press, 1978.

Eccles, J. The synapse. *Scientific American, 212* (January 1965), 56–66.

Goddard, G. V., and D. McIntyre, Some properties of a lasting epileptogenic trace kindled by repeated electrical stimulation of the amygdala in mammals. In L. V. Laitinen and K. E. Livingston, eds. *Surgical Approaches in Psychiatry.* Baltimore: University Park Press, 1973.

Goodman, L. S., and A. Gilman, eds. *The Pharmacological Basis of Therapeutics.* 4th ed. New York: Macmillan, 1970.

Hodgkin, A. L., and A. F. Huxley. Action potentials recorded from inside nerve fiber. *Nature, 144* (1939), 710–711.

Katz, B. How cells communicate. In J. L. McGaugh, N. M. Weinberger, and R. E. Whalen, eds. *Psychobiology.* Readings from *Scientific American.* San Francisco: W. H. Freeman and Company, 1967.

Longo, V. C. *Neuropharmacology and Behavior.* San Francisco: W. H. Freeman and Company, 1972.

Penfield, W., and H. H. Jasper. *Epilepsy and the Functional Anatomy of the Human Brain.* Boston: Little, Brown, 1954.

Tinbergen, N. *The Animal in Its World.* London: Allen & Unwin, Ltd., 1972.

Van Praag, H. M. Significance of biochemical parameters in the diagnosis, treatment, and prevention of depressive disorders. *Biological Psychiatry, 12* (1977), 101–130.

PART TWO

BASIC NEUROLOGY

There are a number of reasons why it is very important to the student of neuro-psychology to have a basic grasp of clinical neurology. First, one method by which neuropsychologists study the normal function of the central nervous system is by studying it when it is behaving abnormally. It is therefore of fundamental impor-tance to understand the ways in which the nervous system can become disordered, as well as the methods for identifying and studying these disorders. This need is particularly acute because different disorders affect the nervous system in dis-tinctly different ways, and the inferences that can be drawn about normal function thus differ somewhat according to the exact disorder being studied.

Second, the principles of neuropsychology can be applied in a variety of ways to the treatment of people suffering from neurological disorders. This application, however, requires that the clinical neuropsychologist understand the nature of the disorders well enough to apply the theory most efficiently and appropriately. For example, it is pointless to consider occupational therapy in a person with certain disorders, since the disturbance of cognitive function will be profound and ir-reversible. In other cases, people are able to function fairly normally, working around their sometimes considerable cognitive limitations. The neuropsy-chologist who fails to fully understand the nature of the disorders afflicting a given patient not only does the patient a disservice but also harms the credibility of the entire field of neuropsychology itself.

Thus, the two chapters of Part Two consider the clinical examination and spe-cialized tests used to assess the disorders (Chapter 3) as well as providing a basic survey of disorders of the nervous system (Chapter 4). These chapters introduce an array of specialized terms that are likely to overwhelm the beginning student, but with repeated exposure throughout the book they will become relatively simple and straightforward. One ought not be frightened of them.

3

THE NEUROLOGICAL EXAM
AND CLINICAL TESTS

People suspected of having some disorder of the nervous system are usually examined by a **neurologist,** a physician specializing in the treatment of such disorders. Although a comprehensive understanding of the neurological exam is not essential to an understanding of the basic principles of neuropsychology, a sense of what this exam entails is useful nevertheless, for a number of reasons. First, since a diagnosis is only as reliable as the procedure used to make it, the neuropsychologist should be aware of the limitations of diagnostic procedures. Second, since neuropsychologists often see clients who should be referred for a neurological exam, they should be aware of the procedures involved and the questions that are asked in this type of examination such that they can recognize when to make referrals and what information can be gained by the referral. Finally, since neuropsychological tests are extremely effective in spotting certain brain dysfunctions, the psychologist should be able to understand a neurological report in

order to compare diagnoses and make recommendations.

The neurological examination is guided by the principle that every function is abnormal until it is examined and found to be normal. The neurologist first takes a history from the patient and makes a general assessment of the patient's appearance; i.e., what impression does the person's personality, facial appearance, and body structure make? The neurologist then examines every square centimeter of skin and mucous membrane, every orifice, every sensory system and motor function; listens to every sound over the chest, abdomen, head, and blood vessels; and examines every organ system. If what appears to be a deviation is found, it is evaluated with respect to the way and degree it is different from the body part on the opposite side, the body part of family members, and the theoretical norm for a person of like age and sex. In addition, the neurologist may recommend additional tests (EEG, brain scans, etc.) as indicated by the person's history or the initial neurological exam. At the end of an examination the neurologist writes a case summary. This usually consists of a summary of positive and negative historical and physical findings, a provisional diagnosis, a plan for further diagnostic tests to discriminate between diagnostic possibilities, and suggestions for therapy, therapeutic goals, etc. The following section summarizes the types of tests administered by the neurologist and some aspects of the rationale underlying their use.

THE NEUROLOGICAL EXAM

The History

The art of diagnosis has been described as coming to a correct answer with too little information. The neurologist's first step is to ask the patient about the problem, and it is a useful rule of thumb that the patient's first descriptive statement about his illness is the most important. Information is collected about the person's own background with emphasis placed on previous disease, accidents, and the occurrence of symptoms such as headache and attacks of loss of consciousness and sleep disturbances. Often, incidents that do not seem important to the person can be relevant to the diagnosis of the disorder. Family background is also significant because many diseases, such as epilepsy, have a high familial incidence. While the history is being taken some aspects of the neurological exam are completed. For example, mental status is assessed (i.e., Is the person aware of where he is, the date, etc.?); facial features are examined for abnormalities or asymmetries; speech is assessed for abnormalities; and posture is observed. State of awareness is described by adjectives such as alert, drowsy, stuporous, confused, etc. Facial features and behavior reveal whether the per-

son is agitated, anxious, depressed, apathetic, restless, etc. Some of the simpler aspects of memory may be tested by presenting digits and asking for their recall. Delusions and hallucinations are noted when present. The neurologist may also determine whether the person is left- or right-handed and the history of handedness in the family, since this may provide clues about which hemisphere controls speech. A number of simple tests for speech may be given: asking the meaning of words, having rhymes or words repeated (e.g., "la-la," "ta-ta"), having objects named, having the patient read and write.

Although the information obtained in a history gives clues about where emphasis should be placed in the subsequent neurological examination, the neuropsychologist should not accept uncritically the neurologist's evaluation of mental state. Many people who appear lucid to cursory examination are found to have severe impairments when thoroughly tested with appropriate neuropsychological tests.

The Physical Examination

To make a physical examination the neurologist puts out a number of instruments that then guide the course of the examination. These include: (1) a measuring tape for measuring head and body size, the size of skin lesions, etc.; (2) a stethoscope for listening to the sounds of the heart, blood vessels, etc., and an otoscope for examining the auditory canal and drum; (3) a flashlight for eliciting pupillary reflexes; (4) tongue blades for depressing the tongue, for eliciting the gag reflex, and for eliciting abdominal and plantar reflexes; (5) a vial of coffee for assessing smell, and vials of salt and sugar for taste; (6) a 256 cycle per second tuning fork for testing vibratory sensation and hearing; (7) a cotton wisp for eliciting the corneal reflex and for testing sensitivity to light touch, plastic tubes for testing temperature sensations, and pins for testing pain sensation; (8) a hammer for eliciting muscle stretch reflexes, such as knee jerk; (9) some coins and keys for testing **stereognosis,** the knowledge of objects through touch; and (10) a blood pressure cuff for taking blood pressure.

Examination of the Head

One of the most important parts of the neurological exam is the study of the head. Its general features such as size are assessed and a detailed examination is made of sensory and motor functions. The head is innervated by 12 sets of cranial nerves, many of which have both sensory and motor functions. These nerves have different origins within the brainstem, and their pathways occupy different portions of the brain. The study of their function may reveal malfunctions providing important clues about the location and nature of nervous system damage. Table 3-1 summarizes the cranial nerves, their function, and some of the more common symptoms that occur after damage to them. Rather than discuss the function of each nerve in detail we will give some examples from the visual system to illustrate the type of information the neurologist can obtain in the examination.

In examining the eye the neurologist first looks at its external covering, the eyelid. If it droops, a condition called **ptosis,** there is an indication of damage to some portion of the third nerve, which normally elevates it. The visual field can be examined for blind spots or reductions of sensitivity in the area that a person should normally be able to see. The occurrence of visual field defects can reveal quite precisely the existence of damage at nearly any location between the retina and visual cortex (see Chapter 10). The pupil is controlled by two interocular smooth muscles: the pupilloconstrictor and pupillodilator muscles of the

iris, which act in opposition to each other. When the retina of one eye is illuminated with a light the pupil constricts to block out most of the light, and at the same time the pupil of the unilluminated eye is constricted through a relay of the third nerve in the midbrain. Thus, the pupillary constriction and the lack of the consensual response of the opposite eye can be used as indicators of possible damage in the retina, optic tract, or midbrain. The pupils also constrict or accommodate when a person looks at a near object. Constriction to accommodation but not to light, the so-called **Argyll-Robertson pupil,** has been used to diagnose syphilitic or other damage to midbrain relays of the third nerve. Examination of the optic fundus, or central area of the retina, is done with an ophthalmoscope, which is a light source with a viewing aperture. This allows for the condition of blood vessels (which are visible on the retina) to be examined, and for determining whether there is blurring or swelling in the central retina. The swelling, called **papilledema,** can indicate the presence of such abnormalities as brain tumors; because cerebrospinal fluid extends along the optic nerve, increased pressure in the brain will be reflected as retinal swelling. Finally, symmetrical movements of the eyes are controlled by the third, fourth, and sixth nerves, and asymmetries may indicate malfunctions of these nerves or of their central relays.

The Motor System

The motor system is examined to assess muscle bulk, tone, power, to test for the occurrence of involuntary muscle movements such as shaking and tremors, and to assess the status of reflexes. In addition, coordination is examined by having a patient do such tasks as walking heel to toe in a straight line, touching the neurologist's finger and his own nose repeatedly, making rapid alternating movements

TABLE 3-1

The cranial nerves

Number	Name		Functions	Method of examination	Typical symptoms of dysfunction
I	Olfactory	(s)[a]	Smell	Various odors applied to each nostril	Loss of sense of smell (anosmia)
II	Optic	(s)	Vision	Visual acuity, map field of vision	Loss of vision (anopia)
III	Oculomotor	(m)[a]	Eye movement	Reaction to light, lateral movements of eyes, eyelid movement	Double vision (diplopia), large pupil, uneven dilation of pupils, drooping eyelid (ptosis), deviation of eye outward
IV	Trochlear	(m)	Eye movement	Upward and downward eye movements	Double vision, defect of downward gaze
V	Trigeminal	(s,m)	Masticatory movements	Light touch by cotton baton; pain by pinprick; thermal by hot and cold tubes; corneal reflex by touching cornea; jaw reflex by tapping chin, jaw movements	Decreased sensitivity or numbness of face, brief attacks of severe pain (trigeminal neuralgia); weakness and wasting of facial muscles, asymmetrical chewing
VI	Abducens	(m)	Eye movement	Lateral movements	Double vision, inward deviation of the eye
VII	Facial	(m)	Facial movement	Facial movements, facial expression	Facial paralysis
VIII	Auditory vestibular	(s)	Hearing	Audiogram tests hearing; stimulate by rotating patient or by irrigating the ear with hot or cold water (caloric test)	Deafness, sensation of noise in ear (tinnitus); disequilibrium, feeling of disorientation in space
IX	Glossopharyngeal	(s,m)	Tongue and pharynx	Test for sweet, salt, bitter, and sour tastes on tongue; pharyngeal or gag reflex by touching walls of pharynx	Partial dry mouth, loss of taste (ageusia) over posterior third of tongue, anesthesia and paralysis of upper pharynx
X	Vagus	(s,m)	Heart, blood vessels, viscera, movement of larynx and pharynx	Observe palate in phonation, palatal reflex by touching palate	Hoarseness, lower pharyngeal anesthesia and paralysis, indefinite visceral disturbance
XI	Spinal accessory	(m)	Neck muscles and viscera	Movement, strength, and bulk of neck and shoulder muscles	Wasting of neck with weakened rotation, inability to shrug
XII	Hypoglossal	(m)	Tongue muscles	Tongue movements, tremor, wasting or wrinkling of tongue	Wasting of tongue with deviation to side of lesion on protrusion

[a] s and m refer to sensory of motor functions (or both) of nerve.

of the fingers, tapping the foot as rapidly as possible, and so on. Generally, all the muscles of the body are tested in head-to-foot order, and the status of each can be recorded on a standard chart.

A knowledge both of reflex and muscle function and of the central motor pathways can allow a fairly accurate estimate of the location and nature of possible central motor damage. Various types of motor dysfunction are also characteristic of certain motor diseases. For example, people with Parkinson's disease may show limb tremors when they are resting that are reduced or absent when they move. The analysis of reflexes can give important clues about the nature and function of nervous system damage, for some, such as the knee jerk, involve only spinal circuits, whereas others, such as abdominal reflexes, involve circuits that course through the brainstem, midbrain, or cortex. In addition, as we have indicated previously, different motor pathways cross from one side of the body to another at different levels of the nervous system. This arrangement allows the locations of lesions to be deduced, for when motor deficits occur in the same person, a lesion must be located at a point where motor pathways lie adjacent.

The Sensory Systems

A complete sensory examination includes investigation of sensitivity to painful stimulation, touch, temperature, vibration sense, joint position sense, two-point discrimination, tactile localization, stereognosis (recognition of objects by touch alone), and **graphesthesia** (the ability to identify numbers or letters traced on the skin with a blunt object). These sensory tests allow the functions of individual sensory systems to be assessed, and also give information about the location of possible dysfunctions. For example, if a person has no tactile sensation in a hand there could be a prob-

lem with the spinal cord or with peripheral nerves. If the person can feel a stimulus but not recognize what it is, the problem is likely at a cortical level. Comparing functions of different sensory systems and comparing sensory functions with motor functions also give information about the location of possible dysfunctions. For example, pain and pressure information from a given part of the body have separate routes through the spinal cord; pain fibers cross to the opposite side of the cord on entering, but the pathways are adjacent through the brainstem, where pressure fibers also cross. Thus, weakness in one modality and not the other may indicate a spinal problem, whereas weakness in both may indicate a problem in the brainstem or higher. Similarly, because sensory fibers lie adjacent to particular motor fibers at some levels of the nervous system but are separate at others, sensory and motor deficits that occur together provide diagnostic clues.

CLINICAL TESTS

A variety of clinical tests have been designed to quantify and augment the neurological exam and assist in diagnosis. It would be unusual for all of the tests to be done on a single patient, but because all the tests are widely used we describe what they are intended to do.

Electroencephalography

Electroencephalography, more commonly called EEG analysis, consists of sampling the electrical activity of the cortex through electrodes posted in specific areas of the skull. The electrical fluctuations are usually amplified and displayed on an inkwriting polygraph. EEG analysis is only a very crude measure of underlying brain activity, because it gives a measure of only the summed activity of millions of dendrites. Nevertheless, abnormalities in dendritic activity can be diagnostic of conditions of epilepsy, brain tumors, or other disorders. In cases of suspected epilepsy abnormal discharges may be present in the absence of overt epileptic signs such as convulsions; or the discharges may be elicited by various drugs or by such photic stimuli as a flashing strobe light. Differential recordings made with different combinations of electrodes can be used to quite accurately localize the source of abnormal brain activity.

Electromyography

Electromyography, or EMG, is the analysis of the electrical activity of muscles. The record is made by inserting a needle electrode into the muscle to be tested. When a normal muscle is completely relaxed no electrical activity can be recorded, but as contraction occurs a characteristic recording, somewhat similar in appearance to an EEG recording, is produced. EMG recordings are useful for diagnosing the presence of damage or abnormalities in nerves innervating the muscles from which recordings are being obtained. For example, in disease of the motor neurons of the spinal cord there is a marked reduction in the number of spikes present in the record, because there are fewer normal motor neurons to contract the muscles. By using the EMG the neurologist is able to diagnose the disorder and evaluate its extent in the spinal cord.

Cerebrospinal Fluid Studies

Analysis of cerebrospinal fluid (CSF) provides the only method of looking at the subarachnoid space without opening the skull. CSF is most easily obtained by a puncture made in the lumbar, or lower, portion of the spinal column. CSF is removed for a variety of

purposes: (1) to relieve intracranial pressure and to remove toxic, inflammatory, or other substances in the CSF, as would be found in disorders such as encephalitis, meningitis, etc.; (2) to allow an analysis of the CSF for the presence of blood (indicating a vascular accident) or a variety of other substances that might indicate the presence of a variety of central nervous system dysfunctions; (3) to introduce therapeutic substances into the subarachnoid space; and (4) to introduce air or opaque media for radiographic studies (see below).

Roentgenography

Roentgenography, or photography using x-rays, has been modified in a number of ways to serve in nervous system diagnosis. *Routine* x-rays are used to scrutinize the skull for evidence of fractures, calcification, or erosion of bone. **Contrast x-rays** can be obtained after special radio-opaque dye or air is injected into the ventricles or dye is injected into the arteries. Having a different density from surrounding areas, these introduced substances can be visualized, along with the outline of the arteries or ventricles, on the x-ray negatives. These procedures also make it possible to delineate the presence of occlusions or of swellings in the vessels, displacements of vessels or ventricles (indicative of the presence of a tumor), and sometimes actual visualization of a tumor.

The use of the x-ray technique after dye is injected into the vertebral or carotid artery is called **angiography;** Figure 3-1 shows an example of an angiogram. Angiography is particularly valuable in diagnosing and locating vascular abnormalities and some tumors, since they can be visualized in the x-ray. For example, if an artery appears displaced from its usual position it can be inferred that something, such as a tumor, has developed, pushing the artery out of place. In **pneumoencephalog-**

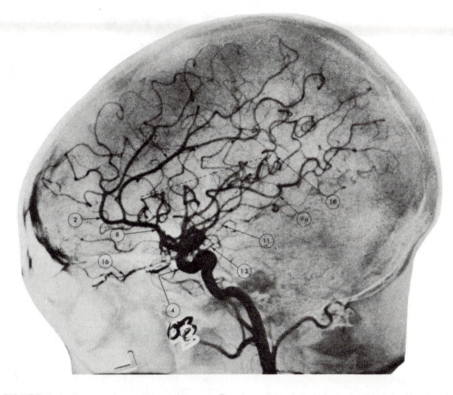

FIGURE 3-1. A normal carotid angiogram. The face is pointed down to the left. Number key: 2, callosomarginal artery; 4, internal carotid artery; 8, anterior cerebral artery; 9a, middle cerebral artery; 11, anterior chloroidal artery; 13, posterior communicating artery; 16, ophthalmic artery; 18, approximate end of the Sylvian fissure. (From S. J. DeArmond, M. M. Fusco, and M. Dewey, *Structure of the Human Brain: A Photographic Atlas,* 2nd ed. New York: Oxford University Press. Copyright © 1976 by Oxford University Press, Inc. Reprinted by permission.)

raphy, x-rays are taken after the cerebro-spinal fluid is replaced by air introduced by a lumbar puncture. By manipulating the posture of the patient the radiologist is able to force the air to travel through the ventricular system. Since the air can be seen on an x-ray, it is possible to locate blockages in the ventricles, displacements in the position of the ventricles (as might occur with a tumor), or enlargements of the ventricles as in hydrocephalus. **Ventriculography** is a similar technique, except that the air or opaque medium is introduced into the ventricle through a cannula inserted through the skull. It is chiefly used when there

is an increase in intracranial pressure and when other procedures have not proven enlightening.

Computerized transaxial tomography, or the **CT-scan,** is a new and exciting x-ray procedure that has revolutionized diagnosis. With conventional roentgenography the two-dimensional projections of a three-dimensional body appear on the x-ray films as overlapping structures that are difficult to distinguish from one another; the CT-scan, on the other hand, provides a three-dimensional representation of the brain. The CT-scan works on the mathematical principle that a three-dimensional object can be reconstructed from the infinite set of all of its projections. In actual fact a finite set is used to produce a rough approximation. Briefly, the technique is as follows: A narrow beam of x-ray is passed through the brain from one side of the head and the amount of radiation not absorbed by the intervening tissue is absorbed by radiation detectors. The x-ray tube is moved laterally across the patient's head and the amount of radiation detected is recorded at 160 equally spaced positions. These data are stored in a computer. The x-ray beam is then rotated one degree and the procedure is repeated. In all, the beam is rotated through 180 degrees. When all the projections are completed, the resulting x-ray sums (160 × 180) are processed by the computer. A reconstruction of the patient's head in cross-section is then printed out by the computer (see Figure 3-2). Ordinarily, eight or so cross-sections are printed out, allowing a simple noninvasive examination of the patient's brain in about 25 minutes.

The CT-scanner is an expensive apparatus, but is fast becoming an indispensable tool in neurology because of its greater safety, speed, and accuracy when compared to other x-ray techniques. Its greatest potential lies in locating tumors, assessing vascular accidents and head injuries, and locating a variety of intracranial lesions or brain atrophy. It is not perfect, however, as it is unable to identify many neurological abnormalities, such as epilepsy, and does not replace a careful neurological and neuropsychological examination in an overall assessment of the patient's condition.

Radioisotope Scanning

In the **radioisotope scan** (or **brain scan**) an intravenous injection of a radioisotope is given, and the cranial surface is then scanned

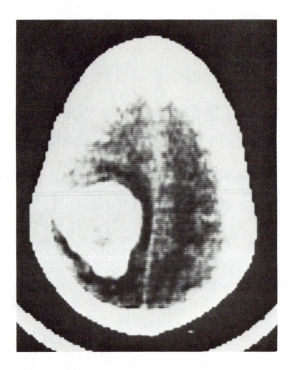

FIGURE 3-2. Image of a brain obtained by a CT-scanner, showing a section through the top of the cerebral hemispheres. The large white zone in the left hemisphere outlines an intracerebral hematoma. The white ring surrounding the shaded brain tissue is a portion of the skull.

with a Geiger counter. Any alteration in blood supply can be detected, including alterations associated with the growth of a tumor (see Figure 3-3).

THE NEUROPSYCHOLOGICAL EXAM

The neurologist carefully examines primarily the sensory and motor functions but leaves other nervous system functions, especially those involved in cognition (i.e., thought) to the neuropsychologist. Indeed, it is not uncommon for patients to exhibit no neurological impairment at all in the neurological exam,

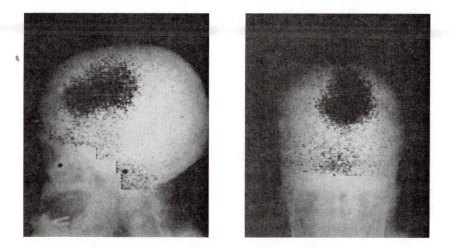

FIGURE 3-3. Radioisotope scan (brain scan) showing a tumor as a darkened area. (From R. Bannister, *Brain's Clinical Neurology*, 5th ed. Oxford: Oxford University Press. Copyright © 1978 by Oxford University Press, Inc. Reprinted by permission.)

only to be found to have clear neuropsychological deficits. This is because many neuropsychological deficits are not obvious without careful assessment of cognitive functions by tests of memory, intelligence, problem solving, and spatial relations, among others. These tests may take 6 to 8 hours to administer, so it is hardly surprising that a neurologist is unable to assess them in a cursory mental status exam. Neuropsychology is a relatively new field but it has become a useful, and in many cases necessary, tool in the diagnosis and treatment of neurological disorders. We will discuss the procedures of neuropsychological assessment in detail at the end of the book because they are best discussed in the context of neuropsychological theory. However, in order to demonstrate the usefulness of neuropsychological assessment we will provide an example here.

Mr. R. was a 21-year-old left-handed man who struck his head on the dashboard in an auto accident two years prior to our seeing him. He was unconscious for a few minutes, but other than a cut on the right side of his forehead and amnesia for the period just before and after the accident, Mr. R. appeared none the worse for his mishap. Prior to his accident Mr. R. was an honor student at a university, with plans to attend professional or graduate school. However, a year after the accident he had become a mediocre student who had particular trouble completing his term papers on time, and although he claimed to be studying harder than before the accident, his marks had fallen drastically in courses requiring memorization. He was referred for a neurological exam by his family physician but it proved negative and the EEG and CT-scan failed to demonstrate any abnormality. He was referred to us for neuropsychological assessment, which revealed several interesting factors. First, Mr. R. was one of about one-third of left-handers whose language functions are represented in the right rather than left hemisphere. This discovery was significant not only in interpreting his difficulties but also in the event that Mr. R. should ever require neurosurgery, since the surgeon would want to respect the speech zones of the neocortex. In addition, although Mr. R. had a superior IQ his verbal memory and reading speed were low average, which is highly unusual for a person of his intelligence and education. These deficits indicated that his right temporal lobe may have been slightly damaged in the car accident, resulting in an impairment of his language skills. (Two years later Mr. R had an epileptic seizure, confirming our diagnosis of brain damage.) On the basis of our neuropsychological investigation we were able to recommend vocations to Mr. R. that did not require superior verbal memory skills, and he is currently studying architecture. This example illustrates that many effects of brain damage are subtle and difficult to detect without careful neuropsychological assessment. Even the most astute neurologist would have been unable to detect Mr. R.'s deficits without using extensive neuropsychological testing. Indeed, we anticipate that as neuropsychology continues to develop, neurology will place increasing demands on neuropsychological assessment as a tool in the diagnosis of cortical dysfunction.

REFERENCES

Bannister, R. *Brain's Clinical Neurology,* 5th ed. New York: Oxford University Press, 1978.

Curtis, B. A., S. Jacobson, and E. M. Marcus. *An Introduction to the Neurosciences.* Philadelphia: W. B. Saunders Co., 1972.

DeArmond, S. J., M. M. Fusco, and M. Dewey. *Structure of the Human Brain: A Photographic Atlas,* 2nd ed. New York: Oxford University Press, 1976.

DeMyer, W. *Technique of the Neurologic Examination.* New York: McGraw-Hill Book Co., 1974.

Gordon, R., G. T. Herman, and S. A. Johnson. Image reconstruction from projections. *Scientific American, 233* (October 1975), 56–68.

4

NEUROLOGICAL DISORDERS

The normal functioning of the central nervous system can be affected by a number of disorders, the most common of which are headache, tumors, vascular disorders, infections, epilepsy, trauma from head injury, demyelinating diseases, and metabolic and nutritional diseases. The following is a brief overview of those disorders that a neuropsychologist is most likely to encounter either clinically or in the literature.

HEADACHES

Headache is so common among the general population that rare indeed is the person who has never suffered one. Headache may constitute a neurological disorder in itself, as in migraine; it may be secondary to neurological disease such as tumor or infection; or it may result from psychological factors, especially stress, as in tension headaches. The pain-sensitive structures within the skull that can be responsible for a headache include the dura; the large arteries of the brain; the venous sinuses; and the branches of the fifth, ninth, and tenth cranial nerves and the first to third cervical nerves. Pain can be elicited from these structures by pressure, traction, displacement, or inflammation.

Types of Headaches

Migraine. **Migraine** is perhaps the most common neurological disorder, afflicting some 5 percent of the population at some time in their lives. It is experienced as an aching, throbbing pain, frequently unilateral and often coincident with pulse beat. A migraine attack is often preceded by a visual disturbance (aura) that occurs within a restricted region of the visual field. This is experienced as a zone of flashing, whirling, or shimmering light that slowly increases in size, lasting 15 to 30 minutes. This aura is presumed to occur because vasoconstriction of one or more cerebral arteries has produced ischemia of the occipital cortex. The actual headache begins as the vasoconstriction reverses, thus ending the visual disturbance, and vasodilation occurs. The headache is manifested as an intense pain localized in one side of the head, although it frequently spreads on the affected side and sometimes to the opposite side as well. A severe headache can be accompanied by nausea and vomiting, and may last for hours or even days. The frequency of migraine attacks varies from as often as one per week to as seldom as once in a lifetime. In cases where migraine is frequent the occurrence generally drops with aging and usually ceases in middle age. Migraine was generally believed to be rare prior to adolescence, but in recent years it has been recognized as afflicting children as well, although the actual incidence in this population is uncertain.

A large number of environmental factors appear to trigger migraine attacks, including anxiety, the termination of anxiety (relaxation), fatigue, bright light, and in many persons specific allergies, particularly to food and wines.

Headache Associated with Neurological Disease. Headache, a common symptom of many nervous-system disorders, usually results from distortion of the pain-sensitive structures. Common disorders producing headache include tumor, head trauma, infection, vascular malformations, and severe hypertension (high blood pressure). The characteristics and location of these headaches vary according to the actual disorder. For example, headache from brain tumor is almost always located on the same side of the head as the tumor, particularly in the early stages of the tumor. However, headaches related to brain tumor have no characteristic severity, for they vary from mild to excruciating. Likewise, hypertension headache, although it is nearly always located in the occipital region, is also highly variable in severity.

Tension Headache. These headaches, sometimes known as psychogenic or anxiety headaches, are characterized by sensations of tightness and persistent band-like pain in the forehead, temples, or occipital region. They result from sustained contraction of the muscles of the scalp and neck caused by constant stress or tension, especially if poor posture is maintained for any period of time.

Treatment of Headache

Migraine is treated by specific drugs at the time of attacks and preventive measures between attacks. In an acute attack **ergotamine** compounds, often given in conjunction with caffeine, are useful in alleviating the headache, probably because they produce constriction of the cerebral arteries, thus reducing tension in this pain-sensitive structure. In addition, most migraine sufferers find the headache is reduced in a totally dark room. In view of the unpleasantness of migraine, the sufferer should try to avoid those circumstances that experience shows precipitate the attacks.

The most obvious treatment of headache arising from neurological disease is to treat the disease itself. Tension headache can be relieved by muscle-relaxant drugs, minor tranquilizers, application of heat to the affected muscles, and improvement of posture. They can also be prevented by avoiding the life situations that give rise to them.

TUMORS

A **tumor** (or **neoplasm**) is a mass of new tissue that persists and grows independently of its surrounding structures and that has no physiologic use. Brain tumors do not grow from neurons but rather from either glia or other support cells. The rate at which tumors grow varies widely, depending on the type of

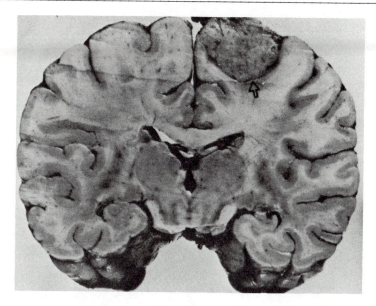

FIGURE 4-1. Frontal section showing a meningioma (see arrow) arising in the dura and compressing the right cerebral hemisphere. Notice that the tumor has not infiltrated the brain. (From S. I. Zacks, *Atlas of Neuropathology*. New York: Harper & Row. Copyright © 1971 by Harper & Row. Reprinted by permission.)

cell that gives rise to the tumor. Tumors account for a relatively high proportion of neurological disease, and next to the uterus, the brain is the most common site for tumors. It is possible to distinguish between benign tumors, those not likely to recur after removal, and malignant tumors, those likely to recur after removal and that frequently progress, becoming a threat to life. Although the distinction between benign and malignant is well founded, the benign tumor may be as serious as the malignant one, since many benign tumors in the brain are inaccessible to the surgeon without risk to life. The brain is affected by many types of tumors, and no region of the brain is immune to tumor formation.

Tumors can significantly affect behavior in a number of ways. A tumor may develop as a distinct entity in the brain, a so-called encapsulated tumor, and produce effects by placing pressure on the rest of the brain (Figure 4-1). Encapsulated tumors are also sometimes cystic, which means they produce a fluid-filled cavity in the brain, usually lined with the tumor cells. Since the skull is of fixed size, any increase in its contents will functionally compress the brain, resulting in dysfunctions. Other tumors, so-called infiltrating tumors, are not clearly marked off from the surrounding tissue; they may either destroy normal cells and occupy their place, or surround existing cells (both neurons and glia) and interfere with their normal functioning (Figure 4-2).

Symptoms and Diagnosis of Brain Tumors

The recognition of a brain tumor may be divided into three phases: (1) the suspicion that a tumor may be present; (2) the diagnostic confirmation of tumor; and (3) the precise lo-

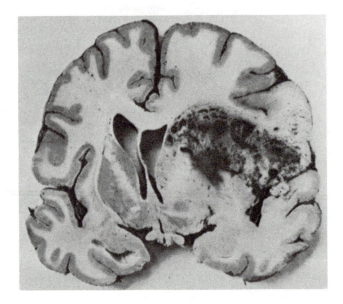

FIGURE 4-2. Frontal section showing a glioblastoma in the right cerebral hemisphere. Note the displacement of the ventricular system and the invasion of brain tissue. (From R. Bannister, *Brain's Clinical Neurology*, 5th ed. Oxford: Oxford University Press. Copyright © 1978 by Oxford University Press, Inc. Reprinted by permission.)

cation of the tumor within the nervous system. The generalized symptoms of brain tumors, which result from increased intracranial pressure, include: headache, vomiting, swelling of the optic disc (papilledema), slowing of the heart rate (bradycardia), mental dullness, double vision **(diplopia),** and, finally, convulsions. It would be rare indeed for a patient to exhibit all these symptoms, most of which result from a marked increase in intracranial pressure. Other signs and symptoms of tumors depend on the exact location of the tumor. Thus, a tumor in the speech zones would be more likely to disrupt speech than would a tumor in the visual cortex.

Types of Brain Tumors

There are three major types of brain tumors, distinguished on the basis of where they origi-nate: gliomas, meningiomas, and metatastic tumors. Each is discussed in turn.

Gliomas. **Glioma** is a general term for those brain tumors that arise from glial cells and infiltrate the brain substance. Roughly 45 percent of all brain tumors are gliomas. Gliomas, ranging from relatively benign to highly malignant, vary considerably in their response to treatment. Because the detailed description of types of gliomas is more important to the neurologist and neurosurgeon than to the neuropsychologist, we briefly describe only the most frequently occurring types of gliomas: astrocytomas, glioblastomas, and medulloblastomas.

Astrocytomas result from the growth of **astrocytes** and are usually slow growing. They account for about 40 percent of gliomas, being most common in adults over 30 years of age.

Because they are not very malignant, and because of their slow growth rate, they are relatively safe once treated. Thus, the prognosis is relatively good, with postoperative survivals occasionally being over 20 years.

The **glioblastoma** is a highly malignant, rapidly growing tumor most common in adults, especially males, over 35 years of age. Glioblastomas account for roughly 30 percent of gliomas. This tumor results from the sudden growth of spongioblasts, cells that are ordinarily formed only during development of the brain. The tumor may be made up of a variety of cell types (glioblastoma multiforme) or of a single cell type (glioblastoma unipolare). Because these tumors are so rapidly growing the life expectancy is usually short, seldom extending beyond one year after surgery.

Medulloblastomas are highly malignant tumors that are found almost exclusively in the cerebellum of children. Medulloblastomas account for about 11 percent of all gliomas. The tumor results from the growth of germinal cells that infiltrate the cerebellum or underlying brainstem. The prognosis for children with these tumors is poor; the postoperative survival period ranges from 1½ to 2 years.

Meningiomas. Meningiomas are growths attached to the meninges and grow entirely outside the brain. These tumors are well encapsulated and are the most benign of all brain tumors. Although these tumors do not invade the brain, they are often multiple and disturb brain function by producing pressure on the brain, often producing seizures as a symptom. Although most meningiomas lie over the hemispheres, some occur between the hemispheres. The latter location makes removal more complicated. It is not uncommon for meningiomas to erode the overlying bone. If meningiomas are removed completely they tend not to recur.

Metatastic Tumors. *Metastasis* is the transfer of disease from one organ or part to another not directly connected with it. Thus, a **metatastic tumor** in the brain is one that has become established by a transfer of tumor cells from some other region of the body, most commonly lung and breast. Indeed, it is not uncommon for the first indication of lung cancer to be evidence of brain tumor. In the event of metastasis to the brain, usually multiple metatastic tumors occur there, making treatment complicated and prognosis poor.

Treatment of Brain Tumors

The most obvious treatment is surgery, which is the only way to make a certain histological diagnosis. If feasible, tumors are removed, but, as with tumors elsewhere in the body, success depends on early diagnosis. Radiotherapy is useful for treating certain types of tumors, such as glioblastomas and medulloblastomas, as well as for some metatastic tumors. Chemotherapy has not yet been very successful in the treatment of brain tumors owing in part to the difficulty in getting drugs to pass the blood–brain barrier and distribute in the brain.

VASCULAR DISORDERS

A neuron or glial cell can be damaged by any process that interferes with its energy metabolism, whether it be a reduction in oxygen or glucose; an introduction of some poison or toxic substance; or, more important, an interruption in blood supply. Vascular disease can produce serious—even total—reduction of both oxygen and glucose resulting in a critical interference of cellular energy metabolism. If such interference is longer than 10 minutes, all cells in the affected region die. Cerebral vascu-

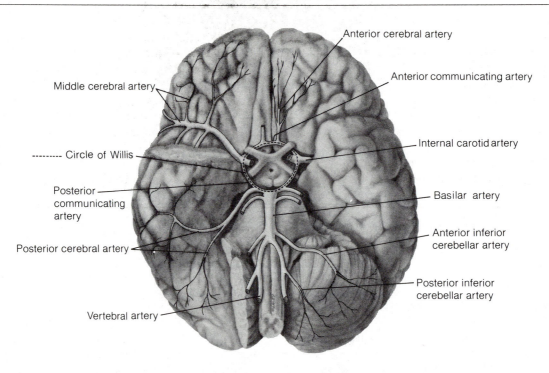

FIGURE 4-3. Major arteries of the brain viewed from below. The cerebellum and temporal lobe on the right hemisphere (left side of the figure) have been cut away to reveal the pattern of irrigation normally hidden from view. The connections formed by the anterior and posterior communicating arteries form the circle of Willis.

lar diseases are among the most frequent causes of death and chronic disability in the Western world. They are of particular concern to the neuropsychologist, because neuropsychology plays an important role in assessing the effects of vascular disorders on cognitive functioning.

The brain receives its blood supply from two *internal carotid* and two *vertebral* arteries, one of each in either side of the body, as shown in Figure 4-3. The internal carotid arteries enter the skull at the base of the brain and give off a number of smaller arteries and two major arteries, the *anterior cerebral artery* and the *middle cerebral artery,* which irrigate the anterior and middle portions of the cortex. The

vertebral arteries enter at the base of the brain, and then join together to form the *basilar artery.* After giving off several smaller arteries that irrigate the cerebellum, the basilar artery then divides into the *posterior cerebral artery,* which irrigates the medial temporal lobe and the posterior occipital lobe (Figure 4-4).

The middle cerebral and posterior cerebral arteries are actually joined together on each side by the *posterior communicating artery,* and the two cerebral arteries are joined by the anterior communicating artery. These interconnections of arteries form the *circle of Willis,* which may compensate a half of the brain that has lost one of its carotid or vertebral arteries. In swimming mammals the circle of Willis may

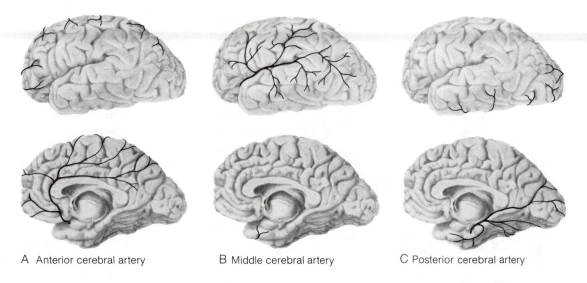

A Anterior cerebral artery   B Middle cerebral artery   C Posterior cerebral artery

FIGURE 4-4. Distribution of the major cerebral arteries in the hemispheres: top, lateral view; bottom, medial view.

also rapidly equalize arterial pressure in the two hemispheres during diving.

The distribution zones of the anterior, middle, and posterior cerebral arteries are shown in Figure 4-4. Notice, however, that these arteries irrigate not only the cortex but also subcortical structures, as shown in Figure 4-5. Thus, a disruption of blood flow to one of these arteries has serious consequences for subcortical as well as cortical structures. As we shall see in ensuing chapters, the occurrence of both cortical and subcortical damage following vascular accident is a major reason why studying the victims of vascular accidents is such a difficult way to study brain function.

The veins of the brain are classified as external and internal cerebral veins and cerebellar veins. The venous flow does not follow the course of corresponding arteries, but follows a pattern of its own, eventually flowing into a system of venous sinuses that drain the dura. Because adequate illustration of the venous-sinal drainage system requires more technical

detail than is appropriate to this book, the interested reader is referred to more advanced discussions for more detail.

Symptoms and Diagnosis of Vascular Disorders

A common term used in discussion of cerebral vascular disorder is stroke, or **cerebral vascular accident.** By **stroke** is meant a sudden appearance of neurological symptoms as a result of severe interruption of blood flow. Stroke can result from a wide variety of different vascular diseases; but not all vascular disorders produce stroke, for the onset of dysfunction can be insidious, spanning months or even years. Stroke often produces an **infarct,** an area of dead or dying tissue resulting from an obstruction of the blood vessels normally supplying the part.

Most disease of the cerebral vascular system affects the arterial system, disease of venous drainage being uncommon in the central ner-

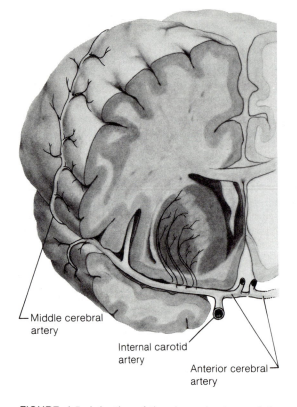

Middle cerebral
artery

Internal carotid
artery

Anterior cerebral
artery

FIGURE 4-5. Irrigation of the deep structures of the brain by the same arteries as irrigate the surface structures. Interruption of the blood supply can thus produce both cortical and subcortical damage. (After Raichle, de Vivo, and Hanaway, 1978.)

vous system. The type of damage, or **lesion,** its extent, and its symptoms depend on a number of factors, including especially: the size of the blood vessel involved, the health of the remaining vessels, the presence of preexisting vascular lesions, the location of tissue involved, the type of disorder, and the presence of anastomoses. These are now discussed in turn.

Size of Blood Vessel. If small blood vessels, such as capillaries, are interrupted, the effects are more limited than the often devastating

consequences of damage to large vessels, such as the major arteries diagrammed in Figure 4-4. Disturbance of these arteries can result in lesions that include large portions of the brain and produce serious deficits in behavior.

Health of Remaining Vessels. If a stroke or other cerebral vascular disorder occurs in one restricted portion of unusual weakness, prognosis may be rather good, because vessels in surrounding zones are often able to supply blood to at least some of the deprived area. On the other hand, if a stroke affects a region that is surrounded by weak or diseased vessels, the effects may be much more serious, because there is no possibility of compensation; in addition, the surrounding weak zones may be at an increased risk of stroke themselves.

Presence of Preexisting Vascular Lesions. A small vascular lesion in a healthy brain will, in the long run, have a good prognosis for substantial recovery of function. However, in the event of preexisting vascular lesions, the effects of the second lesions may be extremely variable. The lesions can sum to obliterate a functional zone of brain tissue, producing serious consequences. Or, less commonly, the lesions can produce what is known as a serial lesion effect, in which case there is remarkably little chronic effect of the second lesion. Although the mechanism of the serial lesion effect is unknown (see Chapter 19), the phenomenon is assumed to result from the process of recovery from the first lesion.

Location of Tissue Involved. The behavioral symptoms following vascular lesions depend, as with other lesions, upon the exact location of damage. For example, a lesion in the primary visual cortex can produce an area of blindness; a lesion in the hippocampus can produce an impairment in memory; and a lesion in the medulla can produce arrest of breathing, resulting in death. Thus, the behavioral symptoms resulting from vascular disorder are important clues to the neurologist in locating the area of brain damage and assessing the extent.

Type of Disorder. Exact symptoms of vascular disorder depend upon the precise nature of the disorder. Slowly developing disorders can be expected to produce symptoms that differ from those of disorders of sudden onset. Warning symptoms of many disorders may be similar, however; these include headache, if there is compression of the brain, as well as dizziness and vomiting.

Presence of Anastomoses. An **anastomosis** is a connection between parallel blood vessels that allows them to intercommunicate their blood flows. The presence of an anastomosis in the brain thus allows cerebral blood supply to take more than one route to a given region. If one vessel is blocked, a given region might therefore be spared an infarct because the blood has an alternate route to the affected zone. The presence of anastomoses is highly idiosyncratic among individuals, making it very difficult to predict the extent of damage resulting from a stroke to a given vessel. The difficulty is exacerbated by substantial variation in the exact route of even major blood vessels in the brain.

Types of Vascular Disorders

Of numerous vascular disorders that affect the central nervous system, the most common are encephalomalacias, cerebral hemorrhage, angiomas, and arteriovenous aneurysms, each of which is now described.

Encephalomalacias. Encephalomalacias (**encephalomalacia** means literally "softening of the brain") are vascular disorders that produce a softening of the brain resulting from inadequate blood flow. Decreases in blood flow can have any of three causes: (1) a thrombosis: a plug or clot, in a blood vessel, of blood that has coagulated and remains at the point of its formation; (2) an **embolism:** a clot or other plug brought through the blood from another vessel and forced into a smaller one, where it obstructs circulation. An embolism can be a blood clot, a bubble of air, a deposit of oil or fat, or a small mass of cells detached from a tumor. Curiously, embolisms most frequently affect the middle cerebral artery of the left side of the brain; (3) reduction in blood flow such that not enough oxygen and glucose are supplied. This reduction in blood flow can result from a variety of factors that produce a narrowing of the vessels. The most common example of such narrowing is **cerebral arteriosclerosis,** a condition marked by thickening and hardening of the arteries. Other causes of narrowing include inflammation of vessels (vasculitis) or spasm of the vessels.

Aside from embolism, which produces sudden onset, encephalomalacias usually develop gradually, taking hours or sometimes days. The disease may also be episodic, in which case it may be termed cerebral vascular insufficiency or **transient ischemic** attacks to indicate the variable nature of the disorder. Onset of transient attacks is often abrupt, frequently occurring as fleeting sensations of giddiness or impaired consciousness.

Cerebral Hemorrhage. Cerebral hemorrhage is a massive bleeding into the substance of the brain. The most frequent cause is high blood pressure (hypertension). Other causes are congenital defects in cerebral arteries, blood disorders such as leukemia, or toxic chemicals. Onset of cerebral hemorrhage is abrupt and may quickly prove fatal. It usually occurs during waking hours, presumably because the person is more active and thus has higher blood pressure. Prognosis is poor in cerebral hemorrhage, especially if the patient is unconscious for more than 48 hours.

Angiomas and Aneurysms. Angiomas are congenital collections of abnormal vessels, including capillary, venous, or arteriovenous (A-V) malformations, that result in abnormal blood flow. Angiomas are composed of a mass of enlarged and tortuous cortical vessels that are supplied by one or more large arteries and are drained by one or more large veins, most frequently in the field of the middle cerebral artery. By causing abnormal blood flow, angiomas may lead to stroke, because they are inherently weak, or to inadequate distribution of blood in the regions surrounding the vessels. In some cases arterial blood may actually flow directly into veins after only briefly, or sometimes not at all, servicing the surrounding brain tissue.

Aneurysms are vascular dilations resulting from localized defects in the elasticity of the vessel. These can be visualized as balloonlike expansions of vessels which are usually weak and prone to rupture. Although aneurysms are usually due to congenital defects, they may also develop from hypertension, arteriosclerosis, embolisms, or infections. Symptoms of aneurysm especially include severe headache, which may be present for years because of pressure on the dura from the aneurysm.

Treatment of Vascular Disorders

Most vascular disorders have no specific treatment, although the most common remedies include support and surgery. Supportive measures include anticoagulants to dissolve clots or prevent clotting, agents to produce vasodilation, drugs to reduce blood pressure, and hypertonic solutions or steroids to reduce cerebral edema (swelling). Surgical techniques have been greatly improved in recent years but are practical only for some disorders. For example, the only certain cure for aneurysm is total removal, which is usually not feasible. Aneurysms are sometimes painted with various plastic substances, but the efficacy of this treatment is disputed. In the case of cerebral hemorrhage it may be necessary to operate to relieve the pressure of the blood from the ruptured vessel upon the rest of the brain.

INFECTIONS

Infection is the invasion of the body by disease-producing (pathogenic) microorganisms and the reaction of the tissues to their presence and to the toxins generated by them. The central nervous system can be invaded by a wide variety of infectious agents, including viruses, bacteria, fungi, and metazoan parasites. Thus, the diagnosis and treatment of infection are an important component of clinical neurology. Although infections of the nervous system usually spread from infection elsewhere in the body—especially the ears, nose, and throat—they also may be introduced directly into the brain as a result of head trauma, skull fractures, or surgery. Infections of the nervous system are particularly serious because usually neurons and glia die, resulting in lesions.

There are a number of processes by which infections kill neural cells. First, infections may interfere with blood supply to neurons, thus producing thrombosis, hemorrhage of capillaries, or even the complete choking off of blood vessels. Second, there may be a disturbance of glucose or oxygen metabolism in the brain cells that is serious enough to kill the cells. Third, the infection may alter the characteristics of the neural cell membranes, thus altering the electrical properties of neurons; or alternatively, it may interfere with the basic enzymatic processes of the cell, producing any number of abnormal conditions. Fourth, a by-product of the body's defense against infection is pus, a fluid composed basically of white blood cells, their by-products and those of the infectious microorganisms, and a thin fluid called liquor puris. Pus impairs neuronal functioning in at least two ways: (1) it significantly alters the extracellular fluids surrounding a neuron, thus altering neuronal function; (2) because pus occupies space, its production increases pressure on the brain, disturbing normal functioning. Fifth, and finally, infection often causes swelling (known as edema), which compresses the brain, again resulting in brain dysfunction.

Symptoms and Diagnosis of Infection

Many infections of the nervous system are secondary to infections elsewhere in the body and are accompanied by symptoms associated with those other infections, including: lowered blood pressure and other changes in blood circulation, fever, general malaise, headache, and delirium. In addition, symptoms of cerebral infections include both generalized symptoms of increased intracranial pressure, such as headache, vertigo, nausea, convulsions, and mental confusion, as well as focalized symptoms of disturbance of specific brain functions.

Diagnostic studies of infection include CSF studies in addition to conventional methods of infection identification, such as smear and/or culture studies. CT-scans and brain scans may also be used to diagnose and/or locate some infectious disorders.

Types of Infections

Unfortunately, there is a good deal of semantic disagreement about terminology of infections. We will use the term **encephalitis** for inflam- mation of the central nervous system caused by infection, and the term **encephalopathy** for chemical, physical, allergic, or toxic inflammations. Note that, strictly speaking, encephalitis and encephalopathy do not refer to specific diseases, but rather to the effects of disease processes.

Four types of infections can affect the central nervous system: viral infections, bacterial infections, mycotic (fungi) infections, and parasitic infestations. We now discuss each of these types.

Viral Infections. A **virus** is an encapsulated aggregate of nucleic acid that may be made up of either DNA (deoxyribonucleic acid) or RNA (ribonucleic acid). Some viruses, such as those causing poliomyelitis and rabies, are called **neurotropic viruses,** because they have a special affinity for cells of the central nervous system. These are differentiated from **pantropic viruses** (such as those causing mumps and herpes simplex), which attack other body tissue in addition to the central nervous system. Most viral infections of the nervous system produce nonspecific lesions affecting widespread regions of the brain, as occur in diseases such as St. Louis encephalitis, rabies, and poliomyelitis.

Bacterial Infections. Bacterium is a loose generic name for any microorganism (typically one-celled) that has no chlorophyll and multiplies by simple division. Bacterial infections of the central nervous system result from an infestation of these organisms, usually via the blood stream. The most common disorders resulting from bacterial infection are meningitis and brain abcess. In **meningitis,** the meninges are infected, by any of a variety of bacteria. **Brain abcesses** are also produced by a variety of bacteria, and are secondary to infection elsewhere in the body. They begin as a small focus of purulent bacteria that cause necrosis (death) of cells in the affected region. As the organisms multiply and destroy more brain cells, the abcess behaves as an expanding mass, frequently hollow in the center; as it expands it produces increasing intracranial pressure.

Mycotic Infections. Invasion of the nervous system by a fungus is known as a **mycotic infection.** A fungus is any member of a large group of lower plants that lack chlorophyll and subsist on living or dead organic matter; the fungi include yeasts, molds, and mushrooms. Ordinarily the central nervous system is highly resistant to mycotic infections, but fungi may invade the brain whose resistance has been reduced by various diseases such as tuberculosis or malignant tumors.

Parasitic Infestations. A **parasite** is an organism that lives upon or within another living organism (the host) at its expense. Several kinds of parasites invade the central nervous system and produce significant disease, the most important diseases being amebiasis and malaria. Amebiasis (also known as amebic dysentery), caused by an infestation of the protozoan ameba (*Entamoeba histolytica*), results in encephalitis and brain abcesses. Malaria is caused by protozoa of the genus *Plasmodium,* which are transmitted by the bites of infected mosquitoes. Cerebral malaria occurs when the plasmodia infect the capillaries of the brain, producing local hemorrhages and subsequent degeneration of neurons.

Treatment of Infections

Treatment varies with the type of infection. Viral infections are extremely difficult to treat, for there are no specific antidotes, the only treatment being to let the diseases run their course. Sedatives are sometimes administered to make the patient more comfortable. The important exception to this is the treatment of

rabies. Once it is ascertained that a person has had contact with a rabid organism, antirabies vaccine is administered over a period of two to four weeks in order to produce an immunity before the disease actually develops. Once the disease does develop, rabies is fatal.

Bacterial cerebral infections have become less common with the introduction of antibiotic drugs, the usual treatment for these infections. In some cases it may be necessary to drain abcesses to relieve intracranial pressure, or to do spinal taps to remove CSF and reduce pressure where there is edema or a buildup of pus.

Neither mycotic nor parasitic infections can be satisfactorily treated, although antibiotics are often used to treat associated disorders.

EPILEPSIES

Epilepsy is a condition characterized by recurrent electrographic seizures of various types that are associated with a disturbance of consciousness. Although epileptic episodes have been termed convulsions, seizures, fits, and attacks, none of these terms is entirely satisfactory, since attacks vary greatly in nature. Epileptic seizures are very common; one person in 20 will experience at least one seizure during his or her lifetime. Most of these people are not truly epileptic, however, for the seizures do not recur. The prevalence of multiple seizures is much lower, about one in 200.

The cause of epileptic seizures was unknown until the development of the EEG, by Berger in 1929. This technique made it possible to demonstrate that different varieties of epilepsy are associated with different abnormal electrical rhythms in the brain (see Figure 4-6). Sometimes epileptic seizures are classifiable as symptomatic seizures; that is, they can sometimes be identified with a specific cause, such as infection, trauma, tumor, vascular malformation, toxic chemicals, very high fever, and other neurological disorders. But other seizure disorders, called **idiopathic seizures,** appear to arise spontaneously and in the absence of other diseases of the central nervous system. The cause of the abnormal electrical discharge within the cell is poorly understood, although it is likely that it causes some type of abnormality in the neuronal membranes.

Although it has long been known that epilepsy runs in families, it is unlikely that there is a single gene responsible for the seizures, because the incidence is lower than would be predicted from genetic models. It is more likely that certain genotypes have a predisposition to seizure problems given certain environmental circumstances.

Symptoms and Diagnosis

The most remarkable clinical feature of epileptic disorders is the discontinuity of symptoms with widely varying intervals between attacks—minutes, hours, weeks, or even years. Thus it is almost impossible to describe a basic set of symptoms to be expected in all, or even most, people with the disease. Three symptoms, however, are found in many types of epilepsy: (1) An aura, or warning, of impending seizure. This may take the form of sensations such as odors, noises, and the like, or may simply be a "feeling" that the seizure is going to occur. (2) Loss of consciousness. This may take the form of complete collapse or simply staring off into space. There is often amnesia, the victim forgetting the seizure itself and the period of lost consciousness. (3) Movements. It is common for seizures to have a motor component, although the characteristics vary considerably. In some cases there are shaking movements; in others, automatic movements such as rubbing the hands or chewing.

The diagnosis of epilepsy is usually con-firmed by EEG. However, in some epileptics, seizures are difficult to demonstrate except under special circumstances (e.g., EEG recorded during sleep); and not all persons with abnormal EEG actually have seizures. In fact, some estimates suggest that 4 in 20 people actually have abnormal EEG patterns!

Types of Epilepsies

Several classification schemes are published for epilepsy. Table 4-1 summarizes the one in use at the Montreal Neurological Institute.

Focal seizures are those that begin locally and then spread. For example, in Jacksonian seizures the attack begins with jerks of single parts of the body, such as a finger, a toe, or the mouth, and then spreads. If it were the finger, the jerks might spread to other fingers, then the hand, arm, and so on, producing a so-called Jacksonian march. Jackson made the prediction in 1870 that such seizures probably originated from the point (focus) in the neocortex representing that region. He was later proven correct.

Complex partial seizures most commonly originate in the temporal lobe, and somewhat less frequently in the frontal lobe. Complex partial seizures are characterized by three common manifestations: (1) subjective feelings, such as forced, repetitive thoughts, alterations in mood, feelings of déjà vu, or hallucinations; (2) automatisms, repetitive stereotyped movements such as lip smacking or chewing, or the repetition of acts such as undoing buttons and the like; (3) postural changes, patients sometimes assuming catatonic, or frozen, postures.

Generalized seizures are bilaterally symmetrical without local onset. The **grand mal** attack is characterized by loss of consciousness and stereotyped motor activity. Typically, patients go through three stages: (1) a tonic stage, in which the body stiffens and breathing

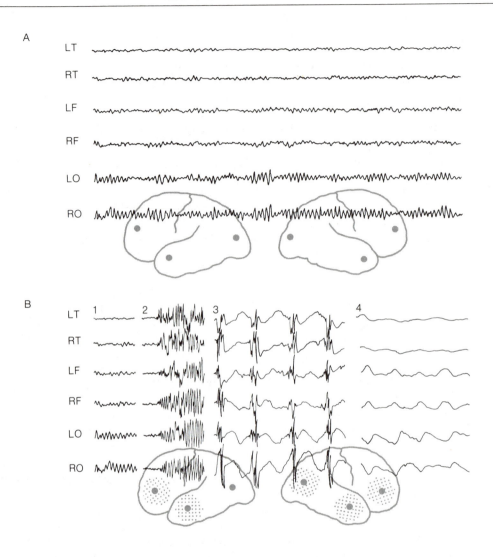

FIGURE 4-6. Examples of EEG records from different forms of epilepsy. LT: left temporal. RT: right temporal. LF: left frontal. RF: right frontal. LO: left occipital. RO: right occipital. Black dots on the hemispheres indicate the approximate recording sites. A. Normal adult EEG. B. Brief excerpts from an EEG during a grand mal seizure: (1) Normal record preceding the attack. (2) Onset of attack. (3) Clonic phase of the attack. (4) Postictal period of coma. Shaded areas represent regions picked up by scalp electrodes. C. An episode of 3/second spike-and-wave EEG characteristic of petit mal discharge. D. Hypsarrhythmia in the EEG of a child. Notice diffuse slow waves with occasional spikes. (From W. B. Hardin, Pathophysiology of clinical epilepsy. In S. G. Eliasson, A. L. Prensky, and W. B. Hardin, eds., *Neurological Pathophysiology,* 2nd ed. New York: Oxford University Press. Copyright © 1978 by Oxford University Press, Inc. Reprinted by permission.)

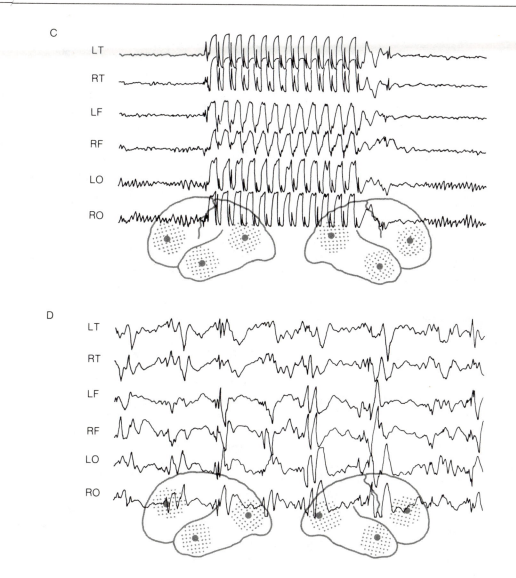

stops; (2) a clonic stage, in which there is rhythmic shaking; and (3) a post-seizure (also known as postictal) depression, in which the patient is confused. About 50 percent of these seizures are preceded by an aura.

In the **petit mal,** or **absence attack,** there is loss of awareness during which there is no motor activity except blinking and/or turning the head, rolling the eyes, etc. These attacks are of brief duration, seldom exceeding about 10 seconds. The EEG record has a typical pattern known as 3/sec spike and wave.

Akinetic seizures are usually only seen in children. Usually the child collapses suddenly

TABLE 4-1

Classification of the epilepsies

1. *Partial seizures* (*focal*)
   a. Simple partial seizures
      i. Motor (Jacksonian)
      ii. Sensory (Jacksonian)
      iii. Autonomic
   b. Complex partial seizures (temporal lobe, psychomotor)
      i. Absences
      ii. Complex hallucinations
      iii. Affective symptoms
      iv. Automatism
   c. Partial seizures secondarily generalized
2. *Generalized seizures*
   Bilaterally symmetrical without local onset
   a. Absence attacks (petit mal)
   b. Tonic-clonic (grand mal)
   c. Bilateral myoclonic
   d. Drop attacks (akinetic)
3. *Unclassified seizures*
   Because of incomplete data, includes many patients with apparently generalized seizures.

and without warning. These seizures are often of very short duration, and the child may get up after only a few seconds with no postictal depression. The falls that these children have can be quite dangerous in themselves, and it is not uncommon for them to wear football helmets until the fits can be controlled by medication.

Myoclonic spasms are massive seizures that basically consist of a sudden flexion or extension of the body and often begin with a cry.

As mentioned earlier, seizures are not continual in any epileptic patients, even though the EEG may be chronically abnormal. Table 4-2 summarizes the great variety of circumstances that appear able to precipitate seizures. Although one is struck by the wide range of factors that may precipitate seizures, one consistent feature is that the brain is most epileptogenic when it is relatively inactive and the patient is sitting still.

Treatment of Epilepsy

The treatment of choice is use of an anticonvulsant drug, such as diphenylhydantoin (DPH, Dilantin), phenobarbital, and several others. Although the mechanism by which these drugs act is uncertain, they presumably inhibit the discharge of abnormal neurons by stabilizing the neuronal membrane. If medication fails to alleviate the seizure problem satisfactorily, surgery can be performed to remove the focus of abnormal functioning in patients with focalized seizures.

The surgical treatment of epilepsy dates back to the late 1800s, when Horsley and others removed the cortex in an attempt to alleviate seizures. The modern technique of surgery for epilepsy was pioneered by Otfrid Foerster in the 1920s in Germany. Wilder Penfield, stimulated by his studies with Foerster, began a prolonged scientific study of the surgical treatment of epilepsy in 1928, when he founded the Montreal Neurological Institute for that purpose. Penfield was soon joined by Herbert Jasper, who introduced EEG to the operating room, and by D. O. Hebb and Brenda Milner, who introduced the neuropsychological assessment of Penfield's surgical patients. Together these four and their colleagues developed a technique of cortical removal of the epileptogenic tissue from victims of focal epilepsy. The technique has been remarkably successful for this form of epilepsy. This team approach to the treatment of a neurological disease provides a model of the marriage of basic and applied disciplines in developing an effective treatment for a neurological disorder.

Today, epilepsy is a particularly important disease for the neuropsychologist, because patients treated surgically for the relief of epilepsy form one of the best patient populations for neuropsychological study. Because the extent of surgical removal can be carefully

TABLE 4-2

Factors that may precipitate seizures in susceptible individuals

Hyperventilation	
Sleep	
Sleep deprivation	
Sensory stimuli:	Flashing lights
	Reading-speaking, coughing
	Laughing
	Sounds—music, bells, etc.
	Reading
Trauma	
Hormonal changes:	Menses
	Puberty
	Adrenal steroids
	Adrenocorticotrophic hormone (ACTH)
Fever	
Emotional stress	
Drugs:	Phenothiazines
	Analeptics
	Tricyclic mood elevators
	Alcohol
	Excessive anticonvulsants

After Pincus and Tucker, 1974.

charted at surgery and correlated with both preoperative and postoperative behavior, neuropsychologists have an excellent source of information on brain–behavior relationships in humans.

TRAUMATIC HEAD INJURIES

Brain injury is an all too common result of automobile and industrial accidents. The brain can be seriously injured from blows to the head whether or not the skull is fractured. (Conversely skull fracture is not necessarily accompanied by brain damage.)

Cerebral trauma may have significant effects on brain function in a number of ways: (1) The trauma may result in direct damage to the brain, such as in a gunshot wound, in which neurons and support cells are damaged directly. (2) Trauma may disrupt blood supply, resulting in ischemia and, if the interruption is prolonged, infarction. (3) Compound fracture of the skull opens the brain to infection. (4) Head trauma can produce scarring of brain tissue; the scarred tissue becomes a focus for later epileptic seizures. Indeed, the sudden appearance of epileptic seizures in adulthood can frequently be traced to head injury (particularly from automobile accidents) in the preceding months or years.

Types of Head Traumas

Concussion. **Concussion** is defined by Bannister as "a condition of widespread paralysis of the functions of the brain which comes on as an immediate consequence of a blow on the head, has a strong tendency to spontaneous recovery, and is not necessarily associated with any gross organic damage in the brain substance." It is, however, believed to produce permanent microscopic morphological changes in brain cells. Concussion produces loss of consciousness and loss of memory of events just preceding it. Severe or repeated concussion also may produce diffuse cerebral atrophy, which may be seen as an increase in ventricle size. The appearance of the so-called punch-drunk syndrome in professional boxers is believed to result from the cumulative effects of cerebral concussion and subsequent cortical atrophy.

Cerebral Contusion. **Cerebral contusion** is primarily a vascular injury, resulting in bruising, edema (swelling), and hemorrhage of

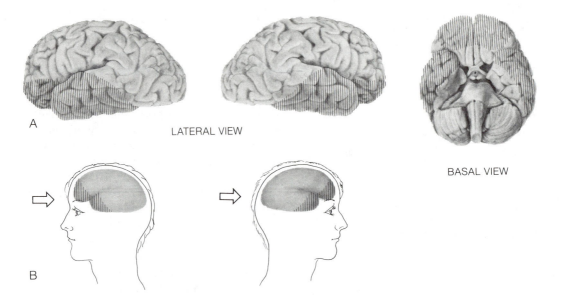

A

LATERAL VIEW

BASAL VIEW

B

FIGURE 4-7. A. Shading represents regions of the cerebral hemispheres most frequently damaged in cerebral contusion. B. Demonstration of how a blow to the forehead or occipit can produce a cerebral contusion on the frontal and temporal poles. Left, the blow (arrow) directly damages the brain; right, the blow causes the brain to be compressed forward. (Both after Courville, 1945.)

capillaries, most often at the poles of the frontal and temporal lobes (see Figure 4-7). Such contusions are a particular problem for both the neurologist and neuropsychologist because they often produce puzzling behavioral changes suggestive of damage to areas distant from the point of impact. For example, it is common for blows to the back of the head to produce symptoms of frontal-lobe damage. This paradoxical effect occurs because the brain is thrust forward by the blow, being bruised on the frontal pole as it compacts against the interior of the forehead (see Figure 4-7). Note, however, that direct blows to the forehead also can produce frontal contusions and pursuant symptoms of frontal-lobe damage.

Cerebral Laceration. Cerebral laceration is a contusion severe enough to physically breach the brain substance. Laceration is most often produced by missiles or fragments of bone penetrating the brain substance.

Cerebral Compression. If head injury is followed by hemorrhage (either extradural, subdural, or intracerebral), a **hematoma** (a local swelling or tumor filled with effused blood) occurs. The hematoma compresses brain substance, thereby producing behavioral changes much as a tumor would. A hematoma may take days to slowly develop after a relatively minor head injury, especially in elderly patients, making diagnosis more difficult, particularly if the patient has forgotten about the head injury.

Treatment of Head Injury

As in most disorders, the duration and mode of treatment depend upon the severity of the disorder. Concussion often requires only bed rest, but many cases of hemorrhage, hematoma, and cerebral laceration require surgery. If the patient is unconscious, special nursing procedures are necessary to maintain clear respiration and adequate nutrition until the patient revives. In cases of severe head injury neuropsychological assessment is often mandatory to assess the extent of cognitive impairment so that special rehabilitation programs can be designed.

PSYCHOSES

The Diagnostic and Statistical Manual of Mental Disorders (DSM-II) of the American Psychiatric Association defines psychosis as occurring when mental functioning is sufficiently impaired to interfere grossly with the capacity to meet the ordinary demands of life. This impairment may result from a serious diminution in the capacity to distinguish reality from nonreality. Psychoses are not generally discussed in neurology texts, but it can be assumed that all psychological processes, normal and abnormal, depend upon brain function. Current limitations in our knowledge about brain function make it impossible to ascertain whether a given behavioral disturbance results directly from abnormal brain functioning or, at the other end of the spectrum, from a response to psychological or social factors. However, because recent research has demonstrated that psychotic behavior has a neurological basis, the study of such behavior has become a legitimate concern of all neuroscience and of neuropsychology in particular.[1]

According to most current neurological theories of psychotic behavior, psychotic disorders result from disturbances in the synthesis and/or degradation of synaptic neurotransmitters, especially acetylcholine, dopamine, noradrenaline, and serotonin. Thus, psychotic behavior is theorized to result from excessive or insufficient neurotransmitter quantities or imbalances among them. Furthermore, it is assumed that treatment of psychotic behavior is effective only insofar as it restores the proper balance among neurotransmitters. Additional evidence comes from studies of patients treated for various disorders of movement by drug therapy. Such therapy, which alters neurotransmitter levels, often produces psychotic behavior as a side effect.

Symptoms and Diagnosis

It is generally easier to identify symptoms of psychosis than to precisely describe them. Nonetheless, it is possible to describe several symptoms characteristic of psychotic behavior, although the precise nature of the symptoms varies considerably from disorder to disorder. These include: cognitive distortion, emotional distortion, distorted reality contact, and hallucinations and delusions.

Cognitive Distortion. The most characteristic symptom of psychosis is profound change in basic cognitive functions, particularly those tested in intelligence and memory tests. These changes are not specific deficits but are global, resulting in an overall decrease in cognitive ability. This decrease is often manifested as a distortion of thought processes. Thus, a psychotic patient is apt to make statements that appear completely unrelated to previous conversation. For example, one psychotic patient suddenly said to us, in the midst of a discussion concerning his medication, "I'm sorry to bother you, I didn't know you were playing baseball"!

Emotional Distortion. Many psychotic patients display altered emotion, as either

---

[1] Current neurological and neuropsychological theories of psychotic behavior are discussed in Chapter 17, in the broader context of the neurological control of affective behavior.

blunted affect or emotional lability as the individual swings from one mood to another, often within just a few minutes.

Distorted Reality Contact. Many psychotic patients are unable to separate events or things that are actually happening from those that they imagine are happening. (An analogy would be the inability to be certain whether events in one's dreams really took place or were merely dreams.)

Hallucinations and Delusions. Hallucinations are perceptions for which there is no appropriate external stimulus, such as hearing voices that are not really there. **Delusions** are beliefs that are opposed to reality but that are held firmly in spite of evidence to the contrary. Hallucinations and delusions are characteristic only of some types of psychotic disorders, especially schizophrenia.

The diagnosis of psychotic disorder is usually made by a psychiatrist on the basis of clinical experience. There are no diagnostic neurological tests of psychoses in current use, but research suggests that CSF studies and neuropsychological tests may one day be used as diagnostic tools.

Types of Psychoses

Psychoses can be divided into those resulting from known neurological disorder, that is, **organic brain syndromes,** and those that cannot be directly attributed to physical conditions. We shall discuss each separately.

Organic Brain Syndromes. Defined as mental disorders associated with brain pathology, organic brain syndromes include psychosis related to alcoholism (Wernicke's disease); psychosis associated with intracranial infection, neoplasm, and vascular disturbance; and psychosis associated with other physical condi-

tions, including endocrine (i.e., hormone) disorders, metabolic or nutritional disorders, and drug or poison intoxication, as well as psychosis resulting from diseases producing senility (senile and presenile dementias).

Psychoses Not Attributed to Organic Brain Syndrome. Nonorganic psychoses make up a broad category of psychotic disorders; the most common are **schizophrenia** and such affective disorders as depression, mania, and manic-depression. Schizophrenia is extremely difficult to define, the most salient characteristics being: (1) disordered cognitive functioning usually associated with delusions and hallucinations, and (2) poor social adjustment. The major symptom of affective disorders is mood disturbance, usually accompanied by an alteration of the individual's perception of both the environment and the self. Depression is characterized by profound sadness; mania is characterized by periods of excitement and hyperactivity that are often impulsive; and manic-depression is characterized by alternation of periods of mania and depression.

Treatment of Psychoses

The treatment of psychotic behavior varies with the type of disorder. Psychosis resulting from organic brain syndrome is usually treated indirectly by treating the neurological disease producing it, whereas psychosis resulting from other causes is most effectively treated by antipsychotic drugs. Different disorders require different drug treatments presumably because different neurotransmitters are involved. For example, it is proposed that depression is associated with an insufficiency of either noradrenaline or serotonin—or even both. Thus, the effective drug treatment is one that corrects the insufficiency. Because different drugs may be necessary to treat the same behavioral symptoms in two different people, it is possible that each psychotic disorder may actually represent a collection of disorders. Thus, it may be more accurate to describe types of psychosis as "depressions and schizophrenias."

Various other treatments of both schizophrenia and affective disorders have been used in the past that are seldom used today. These include **electroconvulsive shock therapy (ECT or ECS)**, which is essentially a massive electric shock applied across the brain, and psychotherapy, which is a treatment designed to produce a response by talking to the patient and offering reassurance, support, and insight. Electroconvulsive shock therapy may be beneficial in depression if drug therapy fails, although there is little theoretical basis for expecting it to work. Psychotherapy may be useful after the psychosis is successfully treated by drug therapy, when the patient must negotiate the particularly stressful period of resuming normal life in society.

REFERENCES

Alpers, B. J., and E. L. Mancall. *Clinical Neurology,* 6th ed. Philadelphia: F. A. Davis Co., 1971.

Bakal, D. A. Headache: A biopsychological perspective. *Psychological Bulletin, 82* (1975), 369–382.

Bannister, R. *Brain's Clinical Neurology,* 5th ed. New York: Oxford University Press, 1978.

Coleman, J. C. *Abnormal Psychology and Modern Life,* 5th ed. Glenview, Ill.: Scott, Foresman & Co., 1976.

Courville, C. B. *Pathology of the Nervous System,* 2nd ed. Mountain View, Calif.: Pacific Press, 1945.

Eliasson, S. G., Prensky, A. L., and W. B. Hardin. *Neurological Pathophysiology,* 2nd ed. New York: Oxford University Press, 1978.

Forster, F. M. *Clinical Neurology,* 3rd ed. St. Louis, Mo.: C. V. Mosby Co., 1973.

Gloor, P. Contributions of electroencephalography and electrocorticography to the neurosurgical treatment of the epilepsies. *Advances in Neurology, 8* (1975), 59–105.

Hardin, W. B. Pathophysiology of clinical epilepsy. In S. G. Eliasson, A. L. Prensky, and W. B. Hardin, eds. *Neurological Pathophysiology,* 2nd ed. New York: Oxford University Press, 1978.

McNeil, E. B. *The Psychoses.* Englewood Cliffs, N.J.: Prentice-Hall, 1970.

Pincus, J. H., and G. J. Tucker. *Behavioral Neurology.* New York: Oxford University Press, 1974.

Raichle, M. E., D. C. de Vivo, and J. Hanaway. Disorders of cerebral circulation. In S. G. Eliasson, A. L. Prensky, and W. B. Hardin, eds. *Neurological Pathophysiology,* 2nd ed. New York: Oxford University Press, 1978.

Rasmussen, T. Cortical resection in the treatment of focal epilepsy. *Advances in Neurology, 8* (1975), 139–154.

Slager, U. T. *Basic Neuropathology.* Baltimore: The Williams and Wilkins Co., 1970.

Spitzer, R. L. *Diagnostic and Statistical Manual of Mental Disorders,* 3rd ed. Draft manuscript prepared by the American Psychological Association, 1978.

Vinken, P. J., and G. W. Bruyn. *Handbook of Clinical Neurology.* New York: John Wiley and Sons, 1969.

Zacks, S. I. *Atlas of Neuropathology.* New York: Harper & Row, 1971.

PART THREE

APPROACHES AND LIMITATIONS

In principle, it would seem simple to study human brain function: one need only remove or stimulate a piece of brain, note the behavioral changes, and from them infer the function of the region involved. Experiments clearly not feasible in humans could be done on nonhuman animals and the results generalized to humans. Unfortunately, there are problems with these techniques that must be considered if the conclusions inferred from the results are not to be seriously confounded.

In this part, consisting of Chapters 5 and 6, we address two of the major difficulties of drawing inferences about brain function in neuropsychology. First, as discussed in Chapter 5, there is the problem of making inferences from patients with brain damage. It is not universally accepted that the functions of missing tissue can be inferred from the behavioral changes observed to follow damage to the region. Second, as discussed in Chapter 6, although nonhumans have been valuable models in understanding general body physiology, their neuroanatomy and behavior may differ from that of humans, thus limiting the generality of information obtained from the use of nonhumans as models of human brain function.

5

TECHNIQUES AND PROBLEMS

The oldest and still most widely used approach to the problem of human brain function is to analyze the effects of **lesion,** or damage, of circumscribed regions of the central nervous system. In this approach the behavior of humans with restricted lesions resulting from head injury, vascular accidents, tumor, or brain surgery is compared to the behavior of normal control subjects on a variety of standardized behavioral tests. Similar research is done on nonhumans, with the difference that brain lesions can be more precisely located surgically in these species by gently sucking out small portions of tissue with a vacuum pump; by electrolytic lesion, passing strong electric current through a localized area of brain tissue; by heating or cooling tissue; or by placing toxic chemicals in restricted portions of tissue.

The rapid expansion of neuroscience in the last two decades has led to important advances in research methodology that antiquate the lesion technique. For example, with microtechniques, minute quantities of chemicals

can be injected into a single neuron of a conscious animal; the effects of this chemical on the behavior of this neuron and others can be recorded; and, if special labeling materials are injected into these neurons, the cells and their connections can be located histologically after the death of the animal. Thus, because the macrotechniques of neuroscience research have become disused in favor of the microtechnology of the 1970s and 1980s, in recent years the study of the effects of brain lesions on behavior has come under widespread criticism.

There is a problem in neuropsychology, however: it is not feasible to use most of the modern microtechnology when studying human subjects. Furthermore, because the technology of human neuropsychology is limited, the most direct technique for studying the effects of brain lesions in humans is still to study the effects of analogous lesions in nonhuman animals. Thus, the lesion technique continues to be an important tool in all of neuropsychology. But its use is fraught with considerable problems. Although brain lesions are relatively simple to produce, the correct interpretation of their effects requires a thorough understanding of the problems involved. In this chapter we consider the effects of brain lesions on brain function, the difficulties associated with the interpretation of lesion studies, the difficulties in equating lesions in patients with varying neurological disturbances, and finally the problems in drawing inferences from studies of a single subject, so-called $n = 1$ studies.

EFFECTS OF BRAIN LESIONS ON BEHAVIOR

Brain lesions can have three quite different effects on behavior: (1) loss of function, (2) release of function, and (3) disorganization of function.

The most obvious and direct effect of brain lesions is a loss of function. For example, if the visual cortex is completely destroyed, pattern vision is permanently lost. Loss of function can also be partial, as when only a portion of the visual cortex is destroyed. It is a general rule that the larger the lesion, the greater the loss of function to be expected.

A release of function is said to occur if, after brain lesion, a new behavior appears or the frequency of a particular behavior is drastically increased. An example of new behavior occurs in victims of Parkinson's disease (the shaking palsy), who develop a tremor in the fingers and hands. Since the loss of some brain area or system could not produce the tremor directly, it is assumed that the lost area normally functioned to prevent tremor, and in its absence tremor is released. An example of increased frequency of a behavior occurs in victims of frontal-lobe damage, who often perseverate on particular behaviors. For instance, say such a person were asked to sort playing

cards according to color, and after sorting several cards were then asked to sort by suit; it would be typical of persons with frontal-lobe damage to continue sorting by color, even if asked a second or third time to sort by suit. Perseverative behaviors imply that one function of the frontal lobe is to inhibit behavior, and in its absence behavior is released from inhibitory control.

Disorganization can also follow brain lesion such that bits or pieces of behavior still occur but now do so in the incorrect order or at the wrong time and place. Thus, people with lesions in certain regions of the left hemisphere may be unable to make a cup of tea because they are unable to place the necessary behavioral components (heating water, pouring it over the teabag in a teapot, pouring the tea into a cup, and adding sugar and/or milk) in the correct order. Instead, they might place the teabag in the milk, add sugar to the teakettle, and pour the heated water onto the saucer. It is clear that these people are capable of all of the pieces of the behavioral sequence; they are simply unable to organize them into the correct order.

It can be seen that the inferences drawn from the study of lesion effects depend upon whether there is loss, release, or disorganization of function, or in some cases a combination of these effects. Behavior must be carefully described, and each of the three principal effects considered, before solid conclusions can be made from the study of brain lesions.

LIMITATIONS TO INTERPRETING LESION EFFECTS

A number of factors restrict the inferences one can make about brain function from the study of either humans or nonhumans with brain lesions. These include (1) locus of damage, (2) recovery from damage, (3) sparing of function,

(4) side effects of damage, (5) disturbances in regions not directly damaged, and (6) source of damage.

Locus of Damage

It has been recognized for hundreds of years that damage in the brainstem can have more devastating effects on behavior in general than a similar extent of damage in the neocortex. For example, in the winter of 1977 a young skier had a catastrophic spill in a downhill race and landed on his head at a speed in excess of 60 miles per hour. The resulting compression and twisting of the brainstem from the impact of the fall produced a lesion in the brainstem resulting in permanent coma. Autopsy studies of people with similar traumatic accidents indicate that the lesion in the brainstem responsible for the coma may be very small indeed. This observation stands in stark contrast to the famous case of Phineas Gage. Gage suffered an accidental removal of his frontal lobes when an iron bar was blown through his head, but, remarkably, Gage was merely stunned for a few seconds, and managed to walk to medical assistance. The comparison of the skier and Gage is particularly surprising when one considers that Gage's lesion was 20 to 30 times larger than the skier's.

Recovery from Damage

Following brain injury there are often a number of behavioral changes that are transient and gradually disappear. A middle-aged man, Mr. B, suffered a small stroke in the left hemisphere and was subsequently unable to talk, read, or write. We followed his recovery over a period of six weeks, and he gradually began to regain his language skills, although even three months after the stroke he was still seriously impaired. When we next saw him, a year later, he was much improved and was capable of carrying on a conversation, although his speech was somewhat slower than normal because he had difficulty finding words. Mr. B illustrates clearly the phenomenon of recovery of function. Although recovery processes such as those observed in Mr. B are as yet poorly understood, their study is an important part of lesion studies because they are a source of inferences regarding function. Had Mr. B been examined two weeks after the stroke, the conclusions about the effect of his lesion would be rather different from those made a year later. This issue is further complicated by the variability of recovery in humans: the recovery period may take days, weeks, or, in some cases, even years; or recovery may not even occur. Many people with lesions similar to Mr. B's never regain the ability to talk, read, and write, even with years of therapy.

Sparing of Function

It has long been known that brain injury sustained in infancy has far less severe effects on behavior than similar damage inflicted in adulthood; if the injury occurs early enough, it may have no effect at all on behaviors that have not yet developed at the time of injury. Thus, just as some functions recover with time, some functions are spared from disruption if the brain lesion occurs early in life. The best example of this phenomenon can be seen in the effects of left-hemisphere lesion on speech. Children who suffer cortical damage between about 5 and 10 years of age may initially experience a period in which they are unable to talk; but they usually recover this ability, and are likely to do so more completely than did Mr. B. On the other hand, children who suffer left-hemisphere damage before they begin to speak will not experience a period of language disturbance; they begin to speak at the usual time, or may be retarded by only a few months. These children are said to have sparing of function, rather than recovery, since the function was never lost. Thus, the conclusions one may draw from brain–behavior relations obviously differ according to whether the brain damage was sustained early in life or in adulthood.

Side Effects of Damage

Brain damage may affect behavior not only directly but also indirectly. A common cause of epilepsy is brain damage in which cells in the region of the lesion are not destroyed but remain to act in an abnormal way, thus producing the seizure disorder. The appearance of a seizure disorder complicates the study of brain lesions, since changes in behavior may be secondary to the seizures. Furthermore, certain lesions may produce significant changes in personality that in turn obscure or distort the effects of the lesions on other behaviors. For example, Ms. P was a 22-year-old undergraduate psychology major who suffered the rupture of a large aneurysm of the middle cerebral artery, resulting in extensive damage to the right temporal and parietal lobes. Prior to the accident she was an excellent student, but subsequent to it she was experiencing difficulties, especially in writing term papers—not because she was unable to read or write, but rather because she had become obsessed with writing the perfect paper, an obsession that resulted in no paper at all. Thus her lesion indirectly prevented her from writing by producing a change in personality.

Disturbances in Regions Not Directly Damaged

Changes in behavior following brain damage can sometimes be attributed to disturbances in regions not directly affected by the lesion. It is naive to assume that brain lesions affect only the region actually damaged, because any lesion initiates changes in those regions that are connected to the damaged area. For example, if lesions occur in the neocortex, cells die in the thalamus, because the axons of thalamic cells, which project to the neocortex, are damaged by the cortical lesion. Further, lesions in some regions of the brain have been shown to produce morphological, biochemical, and physiological changes in areas far removed from the damaged area. To illustrate, lesions of the hypothalamus destroy not only the cells in that region but also fibers of passage coursing through it en route from lower centers of the brainstem to the forebrain. Thus, fibers projecting from the substantia nigra to the basal ganglia can be damaged by hypothalamic lesions, resulting in a reduction in the levels of dopamine in the caudate nucleus. It is therefore reasonable to assume that some effects of hypothalamic lesions are actually caused by imbalances in the basal ganglia, thus making it difficult to make inferences about hypothalamic function.

Source of Damage

Although both naturally occurring and surgical lesions result in the death of neurons, not all brain lesions in a given zone of tissue produce exactly the same behavioral effects. Tumor patients frequently do not behave like patients with lesions from other causes, because tumors may produce pressure on widespread parts of the brain, resulting in symptoms unrelated to the region where the tumor actually resides. Furthermore, whereas the primary effects of tumors such as meningiomas result from pressure, the primary effects of infiltrating tumors such as glioblastomas may result from interference with the normal functioning of neurons in the affected area. An additional problem in equating lesions of different sources is that the extent of naturally occurring lesions is usually documented poorly, if at all. CT-scans can provide an estimate of the extent of the damaged region, but visual inspection provides the only certain measure. Since surgically induced lesions of the neocortex can be photographed at the time of surgery, these lesions provide a more precise relation between brain and behavior. However, even here there are other difficulties, since surgical lesions are not performed on normal brains. The patient would not be receiving surgery had there not been some prior neurological disorder; thus, there is a potential interaction between disease and surgery. For example, although epileptics are often nearly seizure-free after surgery, it is the usual practice to require continued medication, to ensure the absence of seizures. There is the added problem that years of poorly controlled seizures may have produced significant abnormalities in regions of the brain far removed from the lesion. Considering these problems, it is hardly surprising that there is controversy in the literature.

PROBLEMS WITH CASE STUDIES

Many neuropsychological and neurological journals publish articles based on the study of a single patient. Although these studies are often detailed and competent examinations of the behavior of a patient with a circumscribed lesion, they are of limited value in constructing a general theory of human neuropsychology because there are serious difficulties in generalizing from the behavior of one person to the behavior of all people. It is commonly recognized that the behavior of individuals varies enormously, but it is also necessary to recognize that brain structure also varies considerably from person to person. A mass of grey matter known as the **massa intermedia,** which connects the left and right thalami across the midline, is missing in nearly one-quarter of the population; at present there is no known relationship between the presence or absence of this structure and behavior. Karl

Lashley once remarked that the thalamus of each rat was so distinctive that individual animals could easily be distinguished by their thalamic anatomy. Indeed, even though the convolutions of the human brain are drawn and photographed in every textbook of neurology and neuroanatomy, the pattern of convolutions is not precisely the same in any two brains.

To complicate matters, even when there is no gross variation in the structure of two brains, two people can vary on neuropsychological tests even to the point that one person appears brain-damaged! It is because of such normal variation that most scientific studies of behavior require the use of at least simple statistics to clearly demonstrate the results. Studies of individual cases therefore run the risk of making serious errors of inference because of peculiarities in the subject's neuroanatomy or behavior, or an interaction of the two. Although in this book we emphasize studies of more than one patient, we still consider single case studies, keeping in mind their weaknesses.

CONCLUSIONS

The clear weaknesses of lesion studies are not an argument against doing such studies. Inferences based on lesion studies can be strengthened by results from other techniques, including electrical stimulation, electrical recording, and chemical or drug work. Much of such work will of course necessarily be done on nonhuman species. Although it would seem conceptually simple to integrate the results of lesion studies and other work into a unified neuropsychological theory, this is unfortunately not the case. A simple example will illustrate the problem.

Imagine that four neuroscientists, α, β, δ, and γ, are studying an imaginary brain area called area 101. Area 101 consists of two local

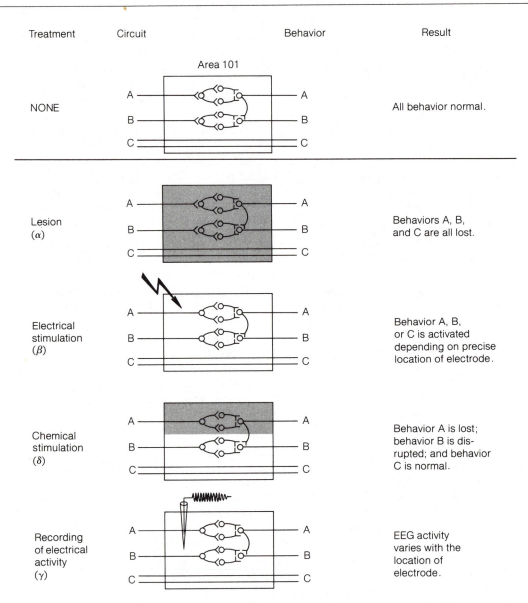

FIGURE 5-1. The different techniques of studying the brain used by scientists α, β, δ, and γ. Each uses a different procedure to study brain–behavior relationships, and each arrives at a different conclusion regarding the function of area 101.

circuits, A and B, which generate, respectively, behaviors A and B. Circuit A, however, sends synapses onto circuit B so that behavior B occurs smoothly and not in jerks. Also in area 101 are fibers of passage that course through the neighborhood of circuits A and B but have nothing to do with either circuit. These fibers are responsible for the control of behavior C (see Figure 5-1).

Scientist α lesions area 101 and destroys circuits A and B and fibers of passage C. He concludes that area 101 produces a syndrome in which deficits in behaviors A, B, and C always go together; this becomes known as α's syndrome in neurology texts. When scientist β stimulates area 101 electrically he obtains either behavior A, behavior B, or behavior C depending upon where his electrode is placed, but concludes that they are all independent and do not go together. In addition, he stimulates other areas of the brain and obtains behaviors A, B, and C (he is in fact stimulating fibers going to and coming from these areas) and concludes that area 101 really is not all that important for controlling behaviors A, B, and C. Scientist δ chemically stimulates area 101 with a drug that blocks the synaptic activity in circuit A. He concludes that the area might control behavior A, that the drug also disrupts behavior B because it makes it so jerky, but that area 101 has nothing at all to do with behavior C. Finally, scientist γ records the electrical activity of circuits A and B and the fibers of passage. He finds two forms of electrical activity: one is related to the details of movement, and the other to the amount of sleep the animal had in the previous 24 hours. Scientist γ concludes that circuits A, B, and C all form some sort of functional system involved in sleep and movement.

Clearly, all four scientists are correct, but it is obvious that if they pooled their information they would not be able to construct the circuitry of area 101 without a unifying theory and considerably more experimentation to test the theory.

Something like the problem outlined for area 101 currently exists in the neurosciences, but on an absolutely massive scale. Many clinical disorders like schizophrenia appear to occur because the brain is behaving abnormally, yet no lesions of the brain produce anything quite like schizophrenia. Many children with no apparent damage to the brain have incapacitating learning disorders, yet others with extensive brain damage are bright and intelligent and show little impairment in learning. These paradoxical effects have led one neuropsychologist we know to make the cryptic comment: "No brain is better than a bad brain." The beginning student will be mystified by these phenomena unless it is recognized that the brain is a large-scale, and considerably more complex, area 101, and that present neuropsychological theory is limited by the experimental techniques available.

6

GENERALIZING IN NEUROPSYCHOLOGY

Although this book is primarily about the functions of the human brain, it is not possible to study human neuropsychology without serious consideration of the neuropsychology of other mammals, particularly nonhuman primates. In this chapter we will consider how and why interspecies comparisons are made, whether the human brain is different from those of other primates, and, finally, whether there is consistency in brain–behavior relationships in mammals.

WHY STUDY NONHUMAN ANIMALS?

To many people, including many psychologists, human neuropsychology is seen as being wholly independent of the study of animals. It is the study of the *human* brain and *human* behavior. This view largely assumes that both human neuroanatomy and human cognitive processes (i.e., thinking) fundamentally differ from those of other animals. After all, humans talk, read, write, and do all sorts of things that

no monkey or rat has ever done. It is our view that this line of reasoning is shortsighted and wrong. There is no compelling evidence of a qualitative difference in the structure of the human and chimpanzee brains (see below). One would surely expect there to be such a difference if neuropsychological processes in chimpanzees and humans were fundamentally different. Few psychologists who work with rats or chimps (or any other species) affect a strong interest in rats or chimps for the sake of these animals; their primary interest is in the human brain and in human brain–behavior relationships.

Many psychologists agree that comparisons between humans and nonhuman primates such as monkeys and chimpanzees are reasonable, but many argue that comparisons with other species such as rats or cats are not. The evolutionary distance between humans and rats is viewed as too great to allow valid generalizations. Indeed, Lockhart and several other authors have argued that the laboratory rat in particular is an indefensible choice for behavioral research. They argue that it has been bred for laboratory work and so for many purposes is a freak, an unnatural animal, and a degenerate compared to its wild cousins. Although domesticated strains of Norway rats no doubt differ in some ways from their wild cousins, we are in complete agreement with Dewsbury's conclusion that there is little or no evidence that they are "inferior, freaks, unnatural animals or degenerates." Indeed, many aspects of neocortical function in laboratory rats are remarkably similar to those of other mammals, including primates. For example, the effects of frontal-lobe lesions in rats are strikingly similar to those of monkeys and, strangely enough, humans.

We are not proposing that rats are merely little men in white fur suits. They obviously are not. We are proposing that monkeys, rats, and other animals have an important role in understanding human brain–behavior relationships, and that to dismiss research on them when discussing human neuropsychology is myopic, unreasonable, and enormously wasteful of valuable information. Furthermore, to insist that nonhuman research be done on primates is morally indefensible at this stage in our knowledge. Many species of nonhuman primates are becoming endangered, and many currently relevant questions can best be studied today through the use of animals that are in no danger of extinction.

What questions can best be addressed through study of nonhuman species? There are three such primary lines of neuropsychological research:

1. Studies directed toward an understanding of the basic mechanisms of brain function.

2. Studies designed to produce models of human neurological disorders.

3. Studies whose aim is to provide a description of the phylogenetic development of the brain.

We consider each of these separately.

The chief purpose of cross-species comparisons in neuropsychology has been to arrive at an understanding of basic mechanisms of brain function.

> An early example of this method is Harvey's investigation of the function of the heart. In establishing that the blood is transferred by the heart from veins to arteries, Harvey used the fish as a model. In the absence of a secondary circulation to the lungs, the passageway from veins to arteries is apparent. Harvey argued that the pulmonary circulation in mammals had obscured our realization that the function of the heart is the same in all vertebrates. (Diamond and Chow, 1962, p. 174)

In this type of comparative work the species chosen for study depends upon the nature of the question under study. For example, neurophysiologists may choose to study the neural activity of giant nerve fibers in the squid because the nerve is so large and accessible. It is assumed that fundamental properties of these nerves are generalizable to mammals and presumably to humans. In addition, sometimes species are merely chosen for convenience; Schneider chose to study hamsters in his work on subcortical visual mechanisms, not because of an intrinsic interest in hamsters, but because the superior colliculus is more accessible in them than in other mammals.

The second goal of comparative work is to produce models of human neurological disorders. The aim is to produce the disorder, then to manipulate numerous variables in order to try to understand the cause of the disorder and its course, and ultimately to formulate a treatment. For example, a model of Parkinson's disease has been developed in the rat—not out of interest in parkinsonian rats per se, but rather to find the causes of their abnormal behaviors and to find treatments to eliminate them. In this type of comparative work animals are really substitutes for humans, and it is

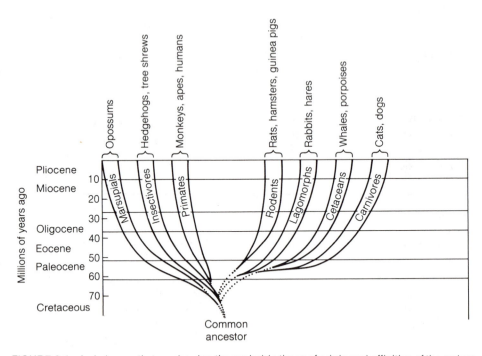

FIGURE 6-1. A phylogenetic tree showing the probable times of origin and affinities of the orders of mammals most commonly studied in comparative psychology and neuropsychology. (After Young, 1962.)

assumed that similar principles underlie the cause and treatment of these disorders in humans and nonhumans alike. Indeed, there are strong grounds for supposing that this assumption is valid for the parkinsonian rat. We and our colleagues have found that these animals show most of the symptoms of parkinsonian humans and respond to various pharmacological manipulations in a manner analogous to that observed in humans.

The final rationale for using nonhuman species is to provide a neurology of mammalian behavior that emphasizes the phylogenetic development of the human brain. It is assumed that an understanding of the evolutionary development of the human brain is important both for human neuropsychology and, in a broader perspective, for anthropol-

ogy and related fields. In addressing this question, the choice of species is critical. Experiments with rats, cats, dogs, and rhesus monkeys do not permit inferences regarding evolutionary development because these animals do not form an evolutionary sequence: rats were never ancestral to cats, nor cats to monkeys. All of these species evolved independently from some primitive mammalian ancestor, as shown in Figure 6-1. To do comparative work from a phylogenetic perspective, it is necessary to choose closely related species that constitute what Hodos and Campbell have termed a quasi-evolutionary sequence. Thus, a series of animals should be used that includes the available living descendants of groups that are believed to be ancestors of more advanced forms (see Figure 6-2). For ex-

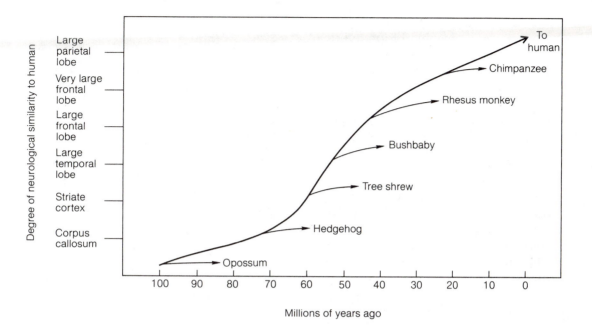

FIGURE 6-2. Phylogenetic relationships among the experimental subjects forming a quasi-evolutionary lineage. Notice that hedgehogs, tree shrews, bushbabies, monkeys, and apes are living animals taken to be close approximations of the ancestors of humans. (After Masterton and Skeen, 1972.)

ample, Masterton and his colleagues have studied the phylogenetic development of auditory processing by using opossums, hedgehogs, tree shrews, bushbabies, macaques, chimpanzees, and humans. Each succeeding species is believed to have evolved from a species something like the one listed before it.

NEUROANATOMICAL COMPARISONS

The most obvious question to ask is one of the easiest to answer: Is there a significant structural difference between the brains of humans and those of other animals—in particular, other primates? It is not necessary to review the evolution of the brain in detail (see Jerison; Sarnat and Netsky) to answer the question. The answer, quite simply, is that there are no qualitative differences, although there are clear quantitative differences. Consider the following points.

Brain Size

The most obvious characteristic of the human brain is that it is larger than the brains of most other animals. But what does this imply? After all, one might expect this difference simply because the human body is larger. Likewise, the elephant would be expected to have a larger brain than humans, and indeed it is roughly three times larger. Neuroanatomists long ago realized it was necessary to factor out brain size, and beginning with Snell in 1891 and Dubois in 1897, they compared the relative sizes of brains by taking body weight into account. From this earlier work of Snell, Dubois, and others, Jerison has recently developed what he terms the **encephalization quotient,** or **EQ:** the ratio of actual brain size to expected brain size. The expected brain size is a kind of average for living mammals that takes body size into account. Thus, the average, or typical, mammal (which incidentally is the cat) has an EQ of 1.0. Animals that deviate from 1.0 have brains larger or smaller than would be expected for a mammal of that particular body size. Table 6-1 summarizes the EQs for common laboratory animals and for humans. Notice that the rat's EQ is only .4, whereas the human's is 6.30. The rat's brain, then, is only .4 times as large as expected for the typical mammal of that body size, and the brain of a human is 6.3 times as large as expected for the typical mammal of that body size. Notice that the chimpanzee brain is much larger than predicted for a typical mammal of that body size (EQ = 2.48), but the EQ is only about one-third as large as the human brain. The EQ makes it clear that the human brain is really larger than those of other primates. (This high EQ is not unique to humans, however; the EQ of the dolphin is comparable, having a value of about 6.0.)

Brain Structure

What is the significance of the fact that the human brain is much larger than the brains of other primates? Is the human brain qualitatively different from those other brains, or is it just a larger version of the same basic brain? Stephan and Andy compared the brains of over 60 species of mammals and found that although nearly all structures of the brain increase in size as the EQ increases, it is the neocortex that shows the most dramatic increase in size. It would seem reasonable to suppose that if the human brain is different in some way, this difference would most likely be found in the neocortex. This possibility can be

TABLE 6-1

Comparison of brain sizes of species most commonly studied in neuropsychology[a]

Species	Brain volume (ml)	Encephalization quotient
Rat	2.3	0.40
Cat	25.3	1.01
Rhesus monkey	106.4	2.09
Chimpanzee	440.0	2.48
Human	1350.0	6.30

[a] Values estimated by using Jerison's formula (EQ = Ei/(.12 × Pi ⅔)) and body and brain values from Blinkov and Glesner, 1968.

considered by comparing the human brain to the brain of other primates on a variety of measures of neocortical structure, including: (1) volume and distribution of neocortex, and (2) cell density.

Total Neocortex. Stephan and Andy calculated what they called a progression index: the ratio of actual neocortex to the expected neocortex of a typical mammal. (This index is an analogue of the encephalization quotient, except that it measures only the neocortex.) The progression index shows that the volume of human neocortex is 3.2 times greater than the predicted volume for nonhuman primates in general and nearly three times greater than that predicted for a chimpanzee of the same body weight. These figures mean that the increase in neocortex from the apes to humans is greater than would have been expected from the trends within the other primates. Where in the neocortex is this increase?

Passingham found that the increase in human neocortex does not appear to occur in the visual, somatosensory, or motor cortex. In fact, there is actually a decrease in the relative extent of area 17. But because there is a trend in primate phylogeny for visual (striate) cortex to decrease relative to total neocortex, this reduction in striate cortex is predictable.

Within primate phylogeny the association cortex increases progressively as a proportion of the total neocortex. Thus, although the association cortex makes up a greater proportion of the human neocortex than would be expected from looking at the chimpanzee brain, Passingham concludes that, given the phylogenetic trend, humans do not have more association cortex than would be predicted for a primate with so much neocortex.

There has been some controversy over whether or not nonhuman primates have any association cortex analogous to the human speech zones. Passingham reviews the evidence and concludes that they do. We will return to this question in Chapter 16.

Cell Density. Although the human brain does not differ from other primate brains in gross anatomy, it is reasonable to suppose that it might differ in fine structure. And it does appear to do so in cell size and density: cell size increases and cell density decreases with increasing volume of neocortex. Thus, as the volume of neocortex increases, neurons increase in size but are spaced further apart, perhaps reflecting an increase in the number of synaptic connections. Although there is a marked change in cell size and density in humans as compared to other primates, Passingham calculates that these changes are predictable given the increase in volume of neocortex.

Conclusion

The overall conclusion that is forced upon us for all of the differences between human and other primate brains is the most parsimonious one: the main selection pressure was for a larger brain with more association neocortex. In other words, although the human brain is larger than would be expected for a primate of the same body weight, this increase in brain size is attributable to a general increase in association cortex. There is no compelling evidence that there is qualitative difference between the brains of humans and those of other mammals.

FUNCTIONAL COMPARISONS

Each mammalian species has a unique behavioral repertoire. There has been a tendency to assume that the brain structures necessary to produce different behaviors must also be unique. This view ignores the fact that mammals share many similar behavioral traits and capacities, although the details of behavior may differ somewhat. For example, all mammalian mothers provide milk and maternal care for their young, although details of care differ from species to species. Warren and Kolb have thus suggested that there are behaviors and behavioral capacities that could be designated **class-common behaviors**: behaviors common to all members of the phylogenetic class Mammalia. Thus, it is recognized that many behaviors are not species-specific; it is in these behaviors that generalizations in neuropsychology should be most meaningful.

If class-common behaviors are considered to be a basis for generalizing in neuropsychology, it is then possible to argue that there is no qualitative difference in the neural control of sensory, associative, and motor functions in mammals. This position is in direct contradiction of the widely held idea that function in mammals has undergone **encephalization**[1] and **encorticalization**. According to the former concept, during evolution

---

[1] There is some disagreement in the literature as to the use of the term encephalization. For example, Ruch, Patten, Woodbury, and Towe use the term to describe the idea that in the course of evolution the forebrain has in-

there was a shift of function from lower centers, such as the brainstem, to higher centers, such as the neocortex and limbic system. According to the latter concept, as the neocortex developed, it assumed functions that were previously controlled by lower structures. If this view were correct, it would imply that the functions of the neocortex would be different in highly corticalized species, such as humans and chimpanzees, from the neocortical functions in species with less neocortex, such as rats or cats. As appealing and widespread as this idea is, it is based on inadequate evidence and can be discredited—as it previously has been by others such as Weiskrantz, Jerison, and Warren. The best evidence that lesions produce class-common behavioral effects actually comes from the very experiments that disconfirm the encephalization concept. So widely held is this concept of encephalization that it is incumbent upon us to at least briefly review the evidence against it. This is most easily done by reviewing the evidence demonstrating functional similarities of the sensory, motor, and association cortex among all mammals.

The Visual System

Until recently there was believed to be a steady phyletic progression from rats to monkeys in the severity of the syndrome resulting from destruction of the visual cortex. Rats were considered to be less impaired than cats, cats less impaired than monkeys, and monkeys less affected than humans. Work done in the

last 5 to 10 years has shown that this conclusion was in error, the error resulting from differences in experimental procedure with different species. For example, monkeys are not nearly as impaired as had been believed; earlier studies employed larger lesions that, going beyond the primary visual cortex, included surrounding cortex involved in the visual guidance of behavior. Also, the behavioral assessment techniques used in these studies were crude and misleading, and for one reason or another did not accurately assess visual capacities after the removal of visual cortex. Recently, Humphrey studied a single monkey, with almost no striate cortex, over a period of years. He observed that the monkey could avoid obstacles and find even small objects such as currants with great efficiency. Humphrey was thus able to demonstrate that the effect of removing the visual cortex was really no more severe in the monkey than in the rat. There is no compelling evidence that the effects of visual cortex lesions differ in humans from those observed in monkeys or rats.

The Auditory System

In a recent review Ravizza and Belmore have shown that the effects of removing the auditory cortex are strikingly similar in many different species of mammals. Monkeys so treated are severely impaired in their ability to approach the site of a brief sound. They can, however, respond differentially to sounds presented at different spatial locations, if the required response is pressing a lever rather than walking through space. This result is apparently also true of other species such as opossums, hedgehogs, bushbabies, and cats. If the functions of the auditory cortex are similar in mammals they should be affected in the same way by the same variations in experimental parameters, as is true in this illustration.

---

creased its domination over lower midbrain and spinal centers. Other authors use the term to describe the course of ontogenetic development of the brain. We are referring here, however, to the idea of a phylogenetic shift of function from lower to higher structures, especially within the neocortex, and we do not take issue with the other uses of the term.

The Somatosensory System

The sense of touch is organized in a remarkably similar way in mammals, although the fine details vary somewhat. Figure 6-3 illustrates the organization of the somatosensory cortex of rats, cats, and monkeys, and compares favorably with the similar organization of the human somatosensory cortex illustrated in Figure 1-8. Although the snout of the rat occupies relatively more cortex than that of the monkey, the class-common basic organization is clearly similar.

The Motor System

As for the visual system, it was widely held a decade ago that the effects of motor cortex removal became progressively more serious as one went from rats to cats to primates. For example, Lassek contrasted the effects of motor cortex removal in monkeys and carnivores, such as cats and dogs, by stating that removal of Brodmann's area 4 in primates causes "an enduring paralysis of isolated movements especially in the digits. A flaccid type of paralysis occurs in the proximal joints whereas the wrists and fingers pass through a period of moderate spasticity" (Lassek, 1954, pp. 65–66). On the other hand, "the motor cortex appears to be largely dispensable in mammals ranking below primates. Ablation of area 4 in the cat or dog is attended by only negligible and transitory deficits" (Lassek, 1954, p. 67).

Lassek's comparison between primates and carnivores is invalid, because it is based on different behaviors. The most profound deficits in monkeys were in manual activities, whereas only posture and locomotion were observed in cats and dogs. It is well known that, in monkeys, posture and locomotion are less severely disturbed by motor cortex lesions than are

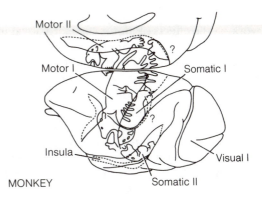

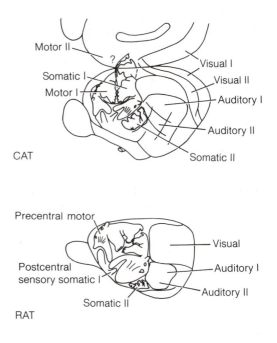

FIGURE 6-3. Functional divisions of the neocortex of three species of mammals as defined by electrical stimulation and recording. The regions not so defined are called association areas. (From C. N. Woolsey, "Organization of somatic sensory and motor areas of the cerebral cortex." In H. F. Harlow and C. N. Woolsey, eds., *Biological and Biochemical Bases of Behavior.* Madison: University of Wisconsin Press, pp. 63–81. Copyright © 1958. Reprinted by permission.)

manual activities. Furthermore, more recent work on the effects of motor cortex removal in cats has shown a permanent impairment in the ability to manipulate objects and to make controlled extension responses with the forepaw. Rats are not capable of very refined movements of the digits of the forepaws, but even they have deficits in manipulation of food and objects following motor cortex removal. This deficit would easily be overlooked, however, if one simply observed rats making gross movements such as walking or swimming—activities that require little fine control of the digits.

To sum, careful observation shows no difference among mammals in the effects of motor cortex damage. The apparent differences described a decade ago do not reflect a functional difference within the motor cortex of various species, but rather a difference in their most obvious behaviors.

Association Areas

Since the association areas undergo such marked expansion in primates, and in humans in particular, it is reasonable to expect that there might be a qualitative difference in the functions of these regions. But the evidence to date does not support this proposition. Although the higher primates are doubtless capable of more complex associations (i.e., learning) than the lower mammals, lesions of the association cortex have remarkably similar general effects on mammals. This conclusion is in contradiction to much of the prevailing literature. For example, in 1969 Diamond and Hall made a convincing case that the cat had no association cortex in the temporal lobe that could be considered analogous to that found in the primate, suggesting a major difference between carnivores and primates. Recent anatomical and behavioral work indicates that this

conclusion was unwarranted. The temporal region had simply not been properly identified in the cat. And Campbell has recently shown that lesions of the temporal association cortex produce deficits in visual learning by cats that are strikingly similar to those observed in primates.

CONCLUSIONS

Cross-species comparisons in neuropsychology are made primarily for three reasons:

1. To arrive at an understanding of the basic mechanisms of brain function.

2. To produce models of human neurological disorders.

3. To provide a neurology of mammalian behavior, with a particular emphasis on the phylogenetic development of the human brain.

We note that the use of nonhumans is not impugned by qualitative differences in the central nervous system of humans and nonhumans, for there are no such differences. The brains of human and nonhuman primates differ chiefly in overall size and in the volume of neocortex.

We have argued that mammals have to deal with the same basic problems imposed by the environment, and the behavioral capacities to cope with these problems are class-common. The evidence indicates that class-common behaviors are mediated by class-common neural mechanisms sufficiently similar among mammals to permit valid generalizations across species. There is no strong evidence for unique brain–behavior relationships in any species within the class Mammalia.

The possibility of considerable generalization across mammalian species does not imply that neuropsychologists should expend their major energies studying rats or monkeys. It does imply, however, that the results of studies on rats, monkeys, and animals of other species are valuable in understanding brain–behavior relationships in humans, and should not be ignored or dismissed simply because nonhumans do not talk.

REFERENCES

Blinkov, S. M., and J. I. Glesner. *The Human Brain in Figures and Tables.* New York: Basic Books, 1968.

Campbell, A. Deficits in visual learning produced by posterior temporal lesions in cats. *Journal of Comparative and Physiological Psychology, 92* (1978), 45–57.

Campbell, C. B. G., and W. Hodos. The concept of homology and the evolution of the nervous system. *Brain, Behavior and Evolution, 3* (1970), 353–367.

Dewsbury, D. A. Comparative psychologists and their quest for uniformity. *Annals of the New York Academy of Sciences, 223* (1973), 147–167.

Diamond, I. T., and K. L. Chow. Biological psychology. In S. Koch, ed. *Psychology: A Study of a Science,* Vol. 4. New York: McGraw-Hill Book Co., 1962.

Diamond, I. T., and W. C. Hall. Evolution of neocortex. *Science, 164* (1969), 251–262.

Hodos, W., and C. B. G. Campbell. Scala naturae: why there is no theory in comparative psychology. *Psychological Review, 76* (1969), 337–350.

Humphrey, N. K. Vision in a monkey without striate cortex: a case study. *Perception, 3* (1974), 241–255.

Jerison, H. J. *Evolution of the Brain and Intelligence.* New York: Academic Press, 1973.

Lassek, A. M. *The Pyramidal Tract.* Springfield, Ill.: Charles C Thomas, 1954.

Lockhart, R. B. The albino rat: a defensible choice or bad habit. *American Psychologist, 23* (1968), 734–742.

Masterton, B., and L. C. Skeen. Origins of anthropoid intelligence: prefrontal system and delayed alternation in hedgehog, tree shrew and bushbaby. *Journal of Comparative and Physiological Psychology, 81* (1972), 423–433.

Passingham, R. E. Anatomical differences between the neocortex of man and other primates. *Brain, Behavior and Evolution, 7* (1973), 337–359.

Passingham, R. E., and G. Ettlinger. A comparison of cortical functions in man and the other primates. *International Review of Neurobiology, 16* (1974), 233–299.

Ravizza, R. J., and S. Belmore. Auditory forebrain: evidence from anatomical and behavioral experiments involving human and animal subjects. In R. B. Masterson, ed. *Handbook of Behavioral Neurobiology.* New York: Plenum Press, 1978.

Ruch, T. C., H. D. Patten, J. W. Woodbury, and A. L. Towe. *Neurophysiology.* London: W. B. Saunders Co., 1965.

Sarnat, H. B., and M. G. Netsky. *Evolution of the Nervous System.* New York: Oxford University Press, 1974.

Schallert, T., I. Q. Whishaw, V. D. Ramirez, and P. Teitelbaum. Compulsive, abnormal walking caused by anticholinergics in akinetic, 6-hydroxydopamine-treated rats. *Science, 199* (1978), 1461–1463.

Young, J. Z. *The Life of Vertebrates.* New York: Oxford University Press, 1962.

Warren, J. M. Evolution, behavior and the prefrontal cortex. *Acta Neurobiologiae Experimentalis, 32* (1972), 581–593.

Warren, J. M., and B. Kolb. Generalization in neuropsychology. In S. Finger, ed. *Recovery from Brain Damage.* New York: Plenum Press, 1978.

Weiskrantz, L. The interaction between occipital and temporal cortex in vision. In F. O. Schmitt and F. G. Worden, eds. *The Neurosciences: Third Study Program.* Cambridge, Mass.: MIT Press, 1974.

Woolsey, C. N. Organization of somatic sensory and motor areas of the cerebral cortex. In H. F. Harlow and C. N. Woolsey, eds. *Biological and Biochemical Bases of Behavior.* Madison: University of Wisconsin Press, 1958.

PART FOUR

GENERAL PRINCIPLES OF HUMAN BRAIN FUNCTION

In the three chapters of this part the principles underlying human brain function are described. The remainder of the book builds and elaborates upon these principles.

Chapter 7 describes the historical beginnings of neuropsychology, showing how and why neuropsychology has become a study of the function of the cerebral hemispheres. Chapter 8 describes the functional organization of the hemispheres in relation to the organization of the other major divisions of the nervous system. It also describes some of the problems more commonly encountered in the analysis of cortical function. Chapter 9 describes a dominant feature of cerebral organization in the human brain: functional asymmetry. This chapter considers the anatomical, electrophysiological, and behavioral evidence of lateralization of verbal function to one hemisphere and the complementary specialization of visuospatial function to the opposite hemisphere.

7

THE DEVELOPMENT OF NEUROPSYCHOLOGY

The term neuropsychology was apparently first alluded to by D. O. Hebb, in a subtitle to his 1949 book *The Organization of Behavior: A Neuropsychological Theory.* Although neither defined nor used in the text itself, the term was probably intended to represent a study that combined the neurologist's and physiological psychologist's common interests in brain function. By 1957 the term had become a recognized designation for a subfield of the neurosciences, since Heinrich Klüver, in the preface to *Behavior Mechanisms in Monkeys,* suggested that the book would be of interest to neuropsychologists and others. (Klüver had not used the term in the 1933 preface to the same book.) The term was given wide publicity when it appeared in 1960, in the title of a collection of K. S. Lashley's writings—*The Neuropsychology of Lashley*—most of which were rat and monkey studies. But again neuropsychology was not used or defined in the text.

The term, then, is of relatively recent origin. We define neuropsychology as the study of the relation between brain function and behavior. Although the study draws information from many disciplines—e.g., anatomy, biology, biophysics, ethology, pharmacology, physiology, physiological psychology, and philosophy—its central focus is the development of a science of human behavior based on the function of the human brain.

Although neuropsychology was developed only recently (as was much of science itself), its contemporary definition is strongly influenced by two traditional foci for experimental and theoretical investigations in brain research: the *brain hypothesis,* the idea that the brain is the source of behavior; and the *neuron hypothesis,* the idea that the unit of brain structure and function is the neuron. In this chapter the development of these two ideas is traced, after which the more recent advances leading to the modern science of neuropsychology are described. It will be seen that although the science is new its major ideas are not. A consensus that these were important ideas was not easily arrived at, however. For much of our past we humans were groping in the dark for concepts that would help to describe the brain's function. From time to time an idea was serendipitously formulated, was sometimes grasped, sometimes examined, and then was discarded only to be later rediscovered. Today we are still finding, examining, and reexamining ideas. Through this history we hope to encourage the reader to become a participant and to see the science not as a dogma but as a dialogue about some of the ideas that have emerged.

THE BRAIN HYPOTHESIS

The Brain Versus the Heart

Since earliest times humans have believed that their behavior is controlled by a soul, spirit, or rational system. We have also held a variety of views about its nature and location; among the earliest that survive in record were those of Alcmaeon of Croton (ca. 500 B.C.) and Empedocles (ca. 490–430 B.C.). Alcmaeon located mental processes in the brain, and so subscribed to what is now called the brain hypothesis; Empedocles located mental processes in the heart, and so subscribed to what could be called the cardiac hypothesis.

The relative merits of those two hypotheses were debated for the next 2000 years, evidence and logic being presented in support of each. For example, Plato (420–347 B.C.) developed the concept of a tripartite soul, and placed its rational part in the brain because that was the part of the body closest to the heavens. Aristotle (384–322 B.C.) had a good knowledge of brain structure and realized that, of all animals, humans had the largest brain relative to body size. Nevertheless, he decided that because the heart was warm and active it was the source of mental processes; the brain, because it was cool and inert, served as a radiator to cool the blood. He explained away the large size of the brain as evidence of

a relationship to intelligence by stating that humans' blood was richer and hotter than other animals' and so required a larger cooling system. Physicians such as Hippocrates (430–379 B.C.) and Galen (A.D. 129–199) described some aspects of brain anatomy and argued strongly for the brain hypothesis. They were no doubt influenced by their clinical experience. For example, before becoming the leading physician in Rome, Galen had spent five years as a surgeon to gladiators and was well aware of the behavioral consequences of brain damage. He went to great pains to refute Aristotle on logical grounds, e.g., by pointing out that the nerves from the sense organs went to the brain, not to the heart. He also did experiments to compare the effects of pressure on the heart and brain. He noted that light pressure on the brain caused cessation of movement and even death, whereas pressure on the heart caused pain but did not arrest voluntary behavior.

Although the cardiac hypothesis is no longer a serious scientific position, it left its mark on our language. In literature as in everyday speech, matters of emotion are frequently referred to the heart: love is symbolized by an arrow piercing the heart; a person distressed by unrequited love is said to be heartbroken; an unenthusiastic person is said to be not putting his heart into it; an angry person is said to have boiling blood. Thus, it was not initially obvious what organ controlled behavior, and elegant arguments for the brain hypothesis developed only gradually and then only as a result of logical argument, careful observation, and experimentation.

Localization of Function: Early Developments

Of course, simply knowing that the brain controls behavior is not enough: formulation of a complete hypothesis required knowledge of *how* it controlled behavior. Much of the research directed to this end has addressed the issue of **localization of function**: the notion that given behaviors are controlled by given areas of the brain. Theories of localization of function are as old as theories about nervous-system involvement in mental processes. Today, localization of function is usually used to mean that functions are distributed among different segments of the neocortex: visual perception in the occipital lobe, auditory perception in the temporal lobe, etc. This idea took some time to develop: the first problem to be solved was whether mental processes were the product of the brain, or mind; the second problem was locating the control of different aspects of behavior within the brain.

Modern thinking about the mind begins with René Descartes (1596–1650). Descartes replaced the Platonic concept of the tripartite soul with that of a unitary mind that is the reasoning or rational soul. Being nonmaterial and having no spatial extent, the mind is fundamentally different from the body. The body is a machine that is material and thus clearly has spatial extent; it responds reflexively to sensory changes by action of the brain. Nonhuman animals have only bodies and no rational minds; thus, their behavior can be explained, according to Descartes, as purely mechanical action. However, any account of human behavior requires that the functions of both mind and body be considered. In proposing that the mind and body are separate but can interact, Descartes originated the *mind-body problem,* namely: What is the relation between the mind and body; or, more simply, how do they interact? Some dualists (as those holding body and mind to be separate are called) have argued that the two causally interact; but they have never convincingly explained how. Other dualists have avoided this problem by reasoning either that the two function in parallel without interacting, or that the body can affect the mind but that mind cannot affect the body. Thus, both latter positions

allow for theorizing about behavior without considering mind. Those philosophers called monists avoid the mind-body problem by postulating that the mind and body are both the same and either are both material or both nonmaterial. Clearly, the latter monist position might be an embarrassing one for a neuroscientist.

The belief, widely held through Descartes' influence, that the mind was an indivisible substance forced two conclusions, also widely held. First, since the mind was indivisible, theories that subdivided brain function could not be correct. (Some of the history of this debate will be traced in subsequent pages.) Second, since mind existed apart from the body, the functions of mind would require separate consideration; complete understanding of the body and how it worked would not bring complete understanding of human behavior. During the nineteenth century physiologists would often describe the physiology of some newly discovered reflex system and then speculate as to how mind worked through it. (Even today some physiologists devote a portion of their writing to the problem of mind—for example, Eccles, *The Neurophysiological Basis of Mind: The Principles of Neurophysiology,* 1956.) Many modern neuroscientists assert that the body portion of the mind-body polarity is their proper domain of study, and ignore the mind or dismiss it by saying that, although it may very well exist, it cannot be studied by using recording or stimulating electrodes. Others, more skeptical, refer to the mind as the bogey in the brain, the ghost in the machine, or, as some psychologists have referred to it, the little green man in the head. They argue, as does the philosopher Gilbert Ryle, that mind is simply a term for the brain and its activities and not a separate entity, just as city is a term for a collection of buildings and people and not a separate thing. Still others, equating mind with the soul, keep their views on the mind private and make no pretense that once everything about neural systems is known the mind–body problem will be solved.

Prior to Descartes there had been a persistent belief, held by Galen and many subsequent writers, that mind was located in the fluid of the ventricles rather than in the matter of the brain. This belief was reinforced, in the tenth century, when it came to be thought that the muscles were moved by being filled with a fluid that traversed the nerve centers. Ventricular fluid was the prime candidate for being that fluid. In fact, some of the theories of how fluid in different ventricular cavities controlled different aspects of behavior were quite elegant. The cogent arguments of Andreas Vesalius (1514–1564) finally discredited the ventricular theories. Vesalius dissected brains and noted that the relative size of the ventricles in animals and humans was the same. He concluded that since rational man distinguished himself by having the largest brain, it was the brain and not the ventricles that mediated mental processes. Descartes, however, was the first to locate mental processes precisely within brain tissue. He located the mind in the pineal body, on the logic, first, that this body was the only structure in the nervous system not composed of two bilaterally symmetrical halves, and, second, that it was located in proximity to the ventricles. (The rest of the brain was seen not as functioning neural tissue but as the cortex, or bark, that protected the important internal mechanisms.) Thus, by thinking of the mind as unified and located precisely in a single structure, Descartes simultaneously initiated the debate on localization of function and enunciated the negative position.

Localization of Function: The Phrenologists

The argument *for* localization of function began with the phrenological theory of Franz Josef Gall (1758–1828) and Johann Casper Spurzheim (1776–1832). Their theory, in the broad lines of its arguments, was of such scope and brilliance that it could not be ignored, but its details were so improbable that it was immediately rejected by most of their contemporaries. Their theory of localization of function stunningly resembles modern theories; had their methodology been a little different they could have anticipated much of modern neuropsychology.

Gall and Spurzheim, both anatomists, made a number of important discoveries in neuroanatomy that alone would have given them a place in history. They realized that the cortex was composed of functioning cells that were connected with the subcortical structures. They described the crossing of the pyramids and recognized that the spinal cord was divided into white and grey matter. They also recognized that the two symmetrical halves of the brain were connected by commissures. But as soon as they went beyond anatomy and attempted to ascribe functions to different parts of the brain, everything they did was conceptually brilliant but hopelessly in error.

From observations made in early youth Gall believed that students with good memories had large, protruding eyes. He thought it possible that a well-developed memory area of the brain located behind the eyes could cause them to protrude. From this beginning, Gall and Spurzheim undertook to examine the external features of the skull and to correlate its bumps and depressions with what they thought to be important aspects of behavior. A bump on the skull indicated a well-developed underlying cortical gyrus and therefore a greater faculty for a particular behavior; a depression in the same area indicated an underdeveloped gyrus and a concomitantly reduced capacity. Thus, a person who had a high degree of what they called **amativeness** had a large bump in the area shown in Figure 7-1, whereas a person who had a low score on this trait had a depression in this same area. Their behavioral traits consisted of a long list of faculties such as wit, inquiry, and faith. Each of these faculties, which they had devised or had borrowed from English or Scottish psychology, they assigned to a particular portion of the skull or by inference to the underlying portion of the brain. Figure 7-2 shows the resulting map. Spurzheim called the study of the relation between the skull's surface features and the person's faculties **phrenology.**

Despite the ingenuity behind Gall and Spurzheim's research it failed, for four reasons. First, the psychology of faculties bore little relation to real behavior: faculties such as faith, self-love, and veneration were hopelessly impossible to define and to quantify objectively. The first breakthroughs in localization came only when people chose an objective behavior, such as speech, to correlate with an area of the brain. The second cause of failure was their belief that the superficial features of the skull, the analysis of which they called cranioscopy, could be used to estimate brain size and shape. Incredibly, they failed to realize that the outer skull did not mirror the inner skull or the surface features of the neocortex. Had they instead investigated gyral size, history might have been kinder to them. They might have discovered the asymmetries, such as the larger planum temporale of the left posterior cortex, which is now thought to reflect lateralization of language to the left hemisphere. The third cause of failure was that phrenology invited quackery and thus, indirectly, ridicule by association. Because its followers devoted themselves to extremely superficial personality analysis, the entire endeavor was quickly brought into disrepute. In the eyes of their contemporaries, however, there was a more damning criticism—the fourth cause of their failure.

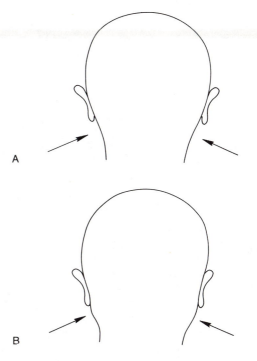

FIGURE 7-1. According to phrenologists, depressions (A) and bumps (B) on the skull indicate the size of the underlying area of brain, and when correlated with personality traits indicate the part of the brain controlling the trait. Gall, examining a patient (who because of her behavior became known as "Gall's Passionate Widow"), found a bump at the back of her neck that he thought located the center for amativeness in the cerebellum. Flourens refuted this hypothesis by removing the cerebellum from a dog to show that the cerebellum was involved in coordinating movement. As phrenology was popularized, bumps and depressions were indicated on the head in places that were no longer adjacent to the brain—as occurred with amativeness, as shown in this figure. Figure 7-2 shows the correct location. (From C. H. Olin, *Phrenology.* Philadelphia: Penn Publishing Co., 1910.)

Gall and Spurzheim had postulated that the brain was the organ of the mind, that personality characteristics were innate, and that the brain (or mind) was composed of independent functioning units. The prevailing opinion still reflected Descartes: the mind was nonmaterial and functioned as a whole. Since these views

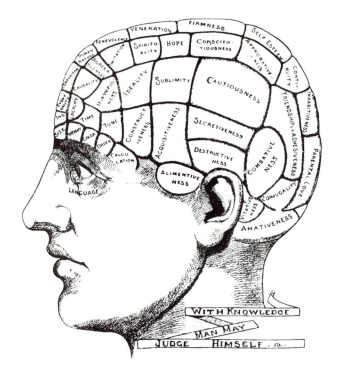

FIGURE 7-2. Originally Gall's system had 27 faculties. As phrenology (Spurzheim's name for the theory) expanded, the number of faculties increased. The figure shows the location of faculties according to Spurzheim. Language, indicated in the front of the brain, actually derived from a case study of Gall's: a soldier had received a knife wound that penetrated the frontal lobe of his left hemisphere through the eye. The soldier became aphasic; he was thus the first reported case of aphasia following left frontal damage.

are still held by many people today, it is possible to understand the hostility they evoked nearly 200 years ago.

Localization of Function: The First Experiments

Because of its weaknesses and the hostility it provoked, Gall and Spurzheim's phrenology had little chance of success. Nevertheless, Pierre Flourens (1794–1867) is generally credited with the definitive demolition of their science. Flourens, who accepted the concept of a unified mind, buttressed philosophical arguments against Gall and Spurzheim with experimentation. Nor was he above using ridicule to discount them, as the following story from Flourens' book *Comparative Psychology,* excerpted by Krech, shows:

> The famous physiologist, Magendie, preserved with veneration the brain of Laplace. Spurzheim had the very natural wish to see the brain of a great man.
>
> To test the science of the phrenologist, Mr. Magendie showed him, instead of the brain of Laplace, that of an imbecile.
>
> Spurzheim, who had already worked up his enthusiasm, admired the brain of the imbecile as

he would have admired that of Laplace. (Krech, 1962)

In his experimental work, Flourens developed the technique of lesioning the brains of animals to study the changes produced in their behavior. He concluded that the cerebrum was the seat of intelligence; that the cerebellum coordinated locomotion; and that the medulla oblongata, since damage to it arrested respiration and resulted in death, was the seat of the principle of life. He concluded that there was no localization of function in the cerebrum, that all intellectual faculties resided there coextensively. He argued that loss of function was correlated with the extent of ablation of cortical tissue; that if all tissue was gone all intellectual functions were gone; and that if sufficient tissue remained intact there was recovery of all function.

The conclusion that Flourens' experiments devastated Gall and Spurzheim was persuasive at the time, but is difficult to support in retrospect. Most of Flourens' experiments were performed with pigeons and chickens—animals with virtually no neocortex. His behavioral tests were assessments of activities like eating and wing flapping, and bore no relation to the faculties proposed for the cortex by Gall and Spurzheim. Finally, many of the deficits from which his animals appeared to suffer may have been the result of postsurgical shock, brain swelling, or removal of far more tissue than the forebrain. Certainly subsequent workers who removed only the cerebrum did not find that pigeons lost all intellectual faculties as Flourens had defined them.

Localization of Language

Gall and Spurzheim's theory of localization of function was in disrepute for about 50 years while Flourens' concept of holistic function was dominant. Jean Baptiste Bouillaud (1796–1881), however, by supporting Gall's idea that language function was localized in the frontal lobe, provided the impetus for localization theory to take a new direction. On 21 February 1825 he read before the Royal Academy of Medicine, in France, a paper in which he argued from clinical studies that function was localized in the neocortex, and specifically that speech was localized in the frontal lobes just as Gall had suggested. (Gall had correlated the frontal cortex with language after studying a penetrating brain injury.) Observing that acts such as writing, drawing, painting, and fencing were carried out with the right hand, Bouillaud also suggested that the part of the brain that controlled them might possibly be the left hemisphere. Why, he asked, should people not be left-brained for the movements of speech as well? A few years later, in 1836, Marc Dax read a paper in Montpellier about a series of clinical cases demonstrating that disorders of speech were constantly associated with lesions of the left hemisphere. Dax's manuscript was published by his son in 1865.

Though neither Bouillaud's nor Dax's work had much impact when it was first presented, Ernest Auburtin, Bouillaud's son-in-law, took up Bouillaud's cause. At a meeting of the Anthropological Society of Paris in 1861 he reported the case of a patient who ceased to speak when pressure was applied to his exposed anterior lobes. He also gave the following description of another patient, with a challenge:

> For a long time during my service with M. Bouillaud I studied a patient, named Bache, who had lost his speech but understood everything said to him and replied with signs in a very intelligent manner to all questions put to him. This man, who spent several years at the Bicetre, is now at the Hospital for Incurables. I saw him again recently and his disease has progressed; slight paralysis has appeared but his intelligence is still unimpaired, and speech is wholly abolished.

Without a doubt this man will soon die. Based on the symptoms that he presents, we have diagnosed softening of the anterior lobes. If, at autopsy, these lobes are found to be intact, I shall renounce the ideas that I have just expounded to you. (Stookey, 1954)

Paul Broca (1824–1880), founder of the society, attended the meeting and heard Auburtin's challenge. Five days later he received a patient, Leborgne, who had lost his speech and was able to say only "tan" and utter an oath. He had paralysis on the right side of his body but in other respects he seemed intelligent and normal. Broca invited Auburtin to examine Tan, as he came to be called, and together they agreed that if Auburtin was right, Tan should have a frontal lesion. Tan died on 17 April 1861, and the next day Broca submitted his findings to the Anthropological Society. The left anterior lobe was the focus of Tan's lesion. By 1863, Broca had collected eight more cases similar to Tan's and stated:

Here are eight instances in which the lesion was in the posterior third of the third frontal convolution. This number seems to me to be sufficient to give strong presumptions. And the most remarkable thing is that in all the patients the lesion was on the left side. I do not dare draw conclusions from this. I await new facts. (Joynt, 1964)

It is usual to credit Broca with four contributions to the study of cortical function: describing a behavioral syndrome that consisted of an inability to speak despite the presence of intact vocal mechanisms and normal comprehension; coining the word aphemia to describe this syndrome; correlating aphemia with an anatomical site now known as Broca's area; and elaborating the concept of *cerebral dominance* of language in the left hemisphere, or, as he phrased it, "nous parlons avec l'hemisphere gauche."

Largely because these contributions marked a change in the approach to analysis of brain function they have been carefully scrutinized by historians, some of whom have judged them as either not original, not enduring, or not accurate. First, the clinical symptoms that he described were already known, as is demonstrated by Auburtin's account of the aphasic Bache—and this Broca acknowledged. Second, the term aphemia was criticized by Trousseau, who argued that it meant infamy and was thus inappropriate as a clinical designation. Trousseau suggested the word aphasia, which Broca criticized as also inappropriate, since it meant "the state of a man who has run out of arguments"; but it nevertheless became universally accepted whereas aphemia was discarded. Third, language and the frontal lobes had previously been correlated by Gall, Bouillaud, and Auburtin, whose priority Broca recognized. Fourth, Broca's anatomical analysis was criticized by Pierre Marie, who reexamined the brains of Broca's first two patients, Tan and Lelong, 25 years after Broca's death. Marie pointed out in his article, "The third left frontal convolution plays no particular role in the function of language," that Lelong was probably a victim of a senile dementia, with general nonspecific atrophy of the brain common in senility, and was not aphasic, and that Tan had additional extensive damage in his posterior cortex that may have accounted for his aphasia. In fairness, Broca had been aware of Tan's posterior damage but had concluded that, whereas the posterior damage contributed to his death, the anterior damage had occurred earlier, producing his aphasia. A fifth criticism is that Dax was the first to suggest the doctrine of cerebral dominance. This Broca also acknowledged, although, according to Joynt, he was never able to establish to his own satisfaction that Dax had read a paper in Montpellier in 1836 in which he stated that speech was lateralized on the left.

There is substance to the details of all of

these criticisms, but in a way they miss the mark, for Broca's more enduring contribution was to synthesize the theory of localization of function, the clinical descriptions of brain-damage effects, and neuroanatomy with such clarity that it excited neuroscientists and the lay public alike and so altered the direction neurobehavioral analysis was to take.

Wernicke-Sequential Programing and Disconnection

From Broca's description of aphasia resulting from left frontal lesions (as confirmed by findings from a number of other sources), Broca could be interpreted as having made two rather simple, but fundamental, points for localization:

1. A behavior is controlled by a specific brain area.
2. Destroying the area selectively destroys the behavior.

People who interpreted Broca in this way have been called strict localizationists. There were, however, those who disagreed with these points on both logical and clinical grounds. Among the most notable to dissent were Hughlings-Jackson, Bastian, and Wernicke. The position of Carl Wernicke (1848–1904) initially gained widest recognition (and it was he who, like Broca, had an area of the brain named after him). He also made two findings devastating to strict localization: first, there is more than one language area; second, damage that spared an area could produce deficits indistinguishable from those that followed damage to the area per se. The first finding suggested that behaviors such as language were *sequentially programed;* the second advanced the concept of **disconnection.**

Theodore Meynert (1833–1892) had first suggested that the cortex behind the central

fissure was sensory in function, and in addition had described the projection of the auditory nerve to the cortex of the Sylvian fissure of the temporal cortex. He suspected a relation between hearing and speech, and had even described two cases of aphasic patients with lesions in this auditory projection area. It was his associate Wernicke, however, who subsequently described the details of this temporal-lobe aphasia—or, as it has come to be called, **paraphasia,** or **fluent aphasia**—and placed it within a theoretical framework.

Wernicke described four major features of the aphasia that made it different from what Broca described:

1. There was damage in the first temporal gyrus, in what is now known as Wernicke's area.
2. There was no contralateral hemiplegia or paralysis.
3. The patients could speak fluently, but what they said was confused and made little sense—hence the term paraphasia.
4. Although the patients were able to hear, they could not understand or repeat what was said to them.

In addition to describing a new kind of aphasia, Wernicke provided a model for how language is organized in the left hemisphere; it involved sequential programing of activity in two language areas (see Figure 7-3). Wernicke theorized that the sound images of objects were stored in the first temporal gyrus (**Wernicke's area**), whence they were sent over a pathway (later identified as the arcuate fasciculus) to **Broca's area,** where the representations of speech movements were retained. If the temporal lobe was damaged, speech movements could occur but the speech would make no sense, because the person was unable to monitor what he said. Because damage to Broca's area produced loss of speech move-

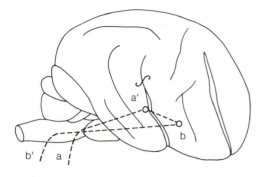

FIGURE 7-3. Wernicke's (1874) model showing how language was organized in the brain. Sounds entered the brain on the auditory pathway (a); sound images were stored in Wernicke's area (a'), and were sent to Broca's word area (b) for articulation over the motor pathway (b'). Lesions on the pathway a-a'-b-b' could produce different types of aphasia, depending upon lesion location. It is curious that Wernicke drew all of his language models on the right hemisphere and not the left, which is the dominant hemisphere for language, as Wernicke believed. (After C. Wernicke, *Der Aphasische Symptomencomplex.* Breslau, Poland: M. Cohn and Weigert, 1874.)

ments without the loss of sound images, aphasia was not accompanied by a loss of comprehension.

Wernicke suggested that if the fibers connecting the two speech areas were damaged (disconnected), then, without damage to Broca's or Wernicke's area, a speech deficit would occur. Wernicke called such a disconnection **conduction aphasia:** both speech sounds and movements would be retained, as would comprehension, but speech would still be paraphasic because the person would not be able to judge the congruity of what he said.

The analysis of brain-lesion effects by subsequent neurologists was much influenced by Wernicke's concept of disconnection, because it provided a methodology linking anatomy and behavior in such a way that it permitted prediction of new brain syndromes and the testing of hypotheses. Using this methodology, Dejerine, in 1892, was able to describe a case in which dyslexia—loss of the ability to

read—resulted from disconnecting the visual area from Wernicke's area. And Wernicke's student Liepmann (1863–1925) was able to show that **apraxia,** an inability to make movements in response to commands, followed disconnection of motor areas from sensory areas. The importance of the idea of disconnection cannot be overemphasized, for the behavioral deficit that follows a disconnection without a lesion in a given locus can be identical to a deficit that follows damage to that locus. As a result, any concept of strict localization of function becomes unworkable.

Electrophysiological Confirmation of Localization

The work of clinical neurologists such as Broca, Wernicke, and others seemed to indicate that behavior was somehow localized in the neocortex. Although many were excited by the idea, others maintained strong objections: what was needed was a different research approach that would support one or the other position. Almost on cue, this was provided by development of the technique for electrically stimulating the brain.

In 1870, Gustav Theodor Fritsch (1838–1929) and Eduard Hitzig (1838–1907) published their extraordinary paper "On the electrical excitability of the cerebrum." Working in Hitzig's bedroom they had examined the effects of stimulating the exposed neocortex of a dog. At the time nearly everyone was of the opinion that the neocortex was inexcitable by electrical stimulation. They demonstrated that not only was the neocortex excitable, it was selectively excitable. Direct application of galvanic current to portions of the anterior neocortex caused movements on the opposite side of the body, whereas stimulation of the posterior neocortex produced no movement. They also found that stimulation of restricted portions of the anterior neocortex elicited movement of particular body parts, which suggested that on the neocortex there were *centers* or topographic representations of the different parts of the motor system. Over the next few years David Ferrier (1843–1928) refined the stimulation technique, and confirmed Hitzig and Fritsch's results in monkeys, dogs, cats, rabbits, guinea pigs, pigeons, fish, and frogs. Hitzig and Fritsch summarized the interpretation of their findings in the conclusion to their 1870 paper:

> Furthermore, it may be concluded from the sum of all our experiments that, contrary to the opinions of Flourens and most investigators who followed him, the soul in no case represents a sort of total function of the whole cerebrum, the expression of which might be destroyed by mechanical means in toto, but not in its individual parts. Individual psychological functions, and probably all of them, depend for their entrance into matter or for their formation from it, upon circumscribed centers of the cerebral cortex. (Fritsch and Hitzig, 1960)

Although Fritsch and Hitzig may have stimulated the cortex of wounded soldiers, the first experiment in which electrical stimulation on the cortex of a human was formally reported was performed by R. Bartholow (1831–1904) in Cincinnati, in 1874. Mary Rafferty, a patient in his care, had a cranial defect that exposed the posterior part of each cerebral hemisphere. The following is an extract from his report of that experiment:

> Observation 3. *To test faradic reaction of the posterior lobes.* Passed an insulated needle into the left posterior lobe so that the non-insulated portion rested entirely in the substance of the brain. The other insulated needle was placed in contact with the dura mater, within one-fourth of an inch of the first. When the circuit was closed, muscular contraction in the right upper and lower extremities ensued, as in the preceding observations. Faint but visible contraction of the left orbicularis palpebrarum, and dilation of the pupils, also ensued. Mary complained of a very strong and unpleasant feeling of tingling in both right extremities, especially in the right arm, which she seized with the opposite hand and rubbed vigorously. Notwithstanding the very evident pain from which she suffered, she smiled as if much amused. (Bartholow, 1874)

Bartholow's work was not met with acclaim. In fact its publication caused such an outcry that he was forced to leave Cincinnati. Also, it is unlikely that he had stimulated the cortex, because in his account his electrodes were inserted about an inch into the brain tissue. Nevertheless, he had demonstrated that the electrical stimulation technique could be used on people; that is, the technique could be used with a conscious person, who could report the subjective sensations produced by stimulation. (The pain that Mary was reported to have suffered was not caused by stimulation of pain receptors in the brain—since there are none—but was probably a genuinely evoked sensation from brain stimulation.) It was not long before electrical stimulation was being used on humans in other experimental situations. And, of course, from there it has evolved into a standard part of many brain surgery procedures.

The Antilocalization Position of Goltz

In his extremely vigorous history (1926) of this period, Henry Head labeled Wernicke and others of his school the "diagram makers." This somewhat derogatory term was a reference to their oversimplification of the deficits that followed brain damage, as well as to their selection ("lop and twist," as he phrased it) of symptoms to fit their models. In fact, Head's criticisms were not unreasonable, because in the period preceding and following 1900 there was a proliferation of maps and diagrams showing the supposed location of all types of functions. Furthermore, Head argued, they persisted in concluding that because we had words for behaviors such as speech, eating, walking, etc., there must be one place in the brain that controlled each behavior. Head preferred to argue that there were many forms of speech, eating, walking, etc., each of which was probably controlled by many different parts of the brain. Rather than review the complexities of the work through this period, it is perhaps more instructive to look at the type of evidence brought forward in opposition to localization of function. The most instructive opposition came from Goltz's experiments with dogs.

When Hitzig and Fritsch made their historic discovery that stimulation of a restricted portion of the neocortex resulted in specific movements, they concluded that the cortex was "the place of entry of psychic functions into matter." The electrophysiological localization of Hitzig and Fritsch, Ferrier, and others led quite logically to the view that the cortex produced and controlled specific movements as well as other behaviors. The experiments performed by Friedrich L. Goltz (1834–1902) in 1892 were intended specifically to question this position. Goltz's methodology resembled Flourens' in that he was addressing the question of what would happen if the entire neocortex was removed from an animal. But unlike Flourens he chose dogs with a well-developed neocortex and a repertoire of easily observable mammalian behaviors. He took his animals throughout Europe and displayed them everywhere, and even made sure that when they were sacrificed to confirm brain-lesion extent, many of the important neurologists and physiologists of the day had a chance to examine the brains to ensure that the lesions were complete.

Goltz reasoned that if a portion of the neocortex had a function, then removal of the cortex should lead to a loss of that function. Goltz removed the neocortex, most of the basal ganglia, and parts of the midbrain from three dogs, which he then studied for 57 days, 92 days, and 18 months respectively. The dog that survived for 18 months was studied in

greatest detail. It was more active than a normal dog, alternated sleep–waking periods (though these were shorter than normal), and panted when warm and shivered when cold. It walked well on uneven ground and was able to catch its balance when it slipped. If placed in an abnormal posture it corrected its position. After hurting a hind limb on one occasion it trotted on three legs, holding up the injured limb. It was able to orient to touches or pinches on its body and snap at the object that touched it, although its orientations were not very accurate. If offered two portions of food—the first a piece of meat soaked in milk, the second a piece of meat soaked in bitter quinine—it accepted the first and rejected the latter. It responded to light and sounds, although its response thresholds were elevated.

Goltz interpreted his findings as indicating a general lowering of the will and intellect that was proportional to the size of the lesion. He argued that his findings did not support the localization-of-function hypothesis. With reference to experiments of his time, he stated that if stimulation of a particular portion of the brain were found to produce movement, and if the stimulated area were concluded to be a motor center, it followed that removal of this area should abolish movement. Goltz's experiments had elegantly demonstrated that cortical removal did not abolish movement. In fact, decortication did not appear to completely abolish any function, though it seemed to reduce all functions to some extent. This demonstration appeared to be a strong argument against localization of function.

Hughlings-Jackson and Hierarchical Organization

Goltz's experiments should not be ignored, because they reiterated what had been said previously by Flourens, and because arguments very much like them were to be made again through the first half of the twentieth century, particularly by Lashley. The fundamental difference between Goltz and those whom his experiments were intended to criticize was to be resolved by the hierarchical concept of brain function proposed by the English neurologist John Hughlings-Jackson (1835–1911). Hughlings-Jackson was extremely prolific, writing over 300 papers; but his work was often not given the attention it deserved, perhaps because he was more reflective and philosophical than is usually popular.

Hughlings-Jackson thought of the nervous system as being organized in a number of layers arranged in a functional hierarchy. Each successively higher level was thought to control more complex aspects of behavior but to do so through the lower levels. Often Hughlings-Jackson described the nervous system as having three levels: the spinal cord, the basal ganglia and motor cortex, and the frontal cortex. But equally often he designated no particular anatomical area for a nervous-system level. He had adopted the theory of hierarchy from Herbert Spencer's argument that the brain evolved in a series of steps, each of which brought animals the capacity to engage in a constellation of new behaviors. But what Hughlings-Jackson did with the theory was particularly novel. He suggested that diseases or damage that affected the highest levels would produce **dissolution**—the reverse of evolution: the animal would still have a repertoire of behaviors, but they would be simpler, more typical of an animal that had not yet evolved the missing brain structure.

If the logic of this argument is followed, it becomes apparent how the results from Goltz's experiments can be reconciled with those of his opponents. Goltz's dogs were "low-level dogs": they were able to walk and to eat, but if food had not been presented to them—had they been required to walk in order to find food—they would have failed and starved. For them walking would not have served a useful biological function. Similarly, all of the other behaviors of the dogs were low-level behaviors. For example, they could thermoregulate by shivering and panting, but had they been placed in a situation requiring them to perform a complex series of acts to leave a cold or warm area for a neutral thermal zone, they would have failed and so would not have been able to behaviorally thermoregulate as do normal dogs. It can be seen, therefore, that Hughlings-Jackson's concepts allowed the special role of the cortex in organizing purposeful behavior to be distinguished from the role of subcortical areas in supporting the more elementary components of behavior.

Hughlings-Jackson applied his concepts of hierarchical organization to many other areas of behavior, including language and aphasia. It was his view that every part of the brain was involved in language, with each part making some special contribution. The relevant question was not where language was localized, but what unique contribution was made by each part of the cortex. Thus, if, for example, the nondominant hemisphere is not involved in language but in spatial organization, then damage to that hemisphere would be revealed not just in spatial disabilities but also in language impoverishment because spatial concepts cannot be employed. With respect to this logic Hughlings-Jackson was particularly modern—so much so, in fact, that his ideas are receiving more serious consideration today than they did in his own time.

THE NEURON HYPOTHESIS

The second major influence on modern neuropsychology was the development of what has become known as the *neuron hypothesis:* the hypothesis that the nervous system is composed of discrete, autonomous cells, or units, that can interact but are not physically connected. The opposite position, known as the *nerve net hypothesis,* that the nervous system is composed of a continuous network of interconnected fibers, was held at one time. At the cellular level, support for the neuron theory depended upon the solutions to three problems:

1. How the nervous system conducts information.
2. How it is constructed.
3. How it is itself interconnected and how it is interconnected with muscles.

The first problem was solved by advances in physiology and physiological recording techniques; the second by advances in anatomy; the third by advances in biochemistry and pharmacology.

Information Conduction

Early views of how the nervous system moved muscles involved some type of hydraulic theory requiring gas or liquid to flow through nerves into muscles. Such theories have been called balloonist theories, since movement was thought to be caused by filling and emptying muscles. Certainly Descartes espoused the balloonist hypothesis, for he argued that a fluid from the ventricles flowed through nerves into muscles to make them move (Figure 7-4). Francis Glisson, in 1677, made a direct test of the balloon theory by immersing a man's arm in water and measuring the change in the water level when the muscles of the arm were contracted. Since the water level did not rise, Glisson concluded that no fluid entered the muscle. Swammerdam, in Holland, reached the same conclusion from similar experiments on frogs.

Isaac Newton may have been the first person to advance a theory of nerve function that approximates a modern view. In 1717 he suggested that nerves were not hollow tubes but were solid. He then postulated that they

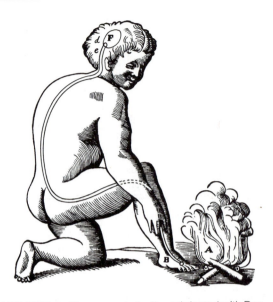

FIGURE 7-4. The concept of reflex originated with Descartes. In this example heat from the flame causes a thread in the nerve to be pulled, releasing ventricular fluid through an opened pore. The fluid flows through the nerve, causing not only the foot to withdraw but also the eyes and head to turn to look at it, the hands to advance, and the whole body to bend to protect it. His concept was stimulated by the mechanical principles of displays used in water gardens fashionable in France in his day. A visitor in the gardens would step on a plate that mechanically caused statues to hide, appear, or squirt water. In actual fact, his use of the reflex concept was for behaviors that would today be considered more than reflexive, while what is held as reflexive today was not so conceived by Descartes. (From R. Descartes, *Traité de l'Homme.* Paris: Angot, 1664.)

worked by the vibration of an "elastic aether" that was propagated along their length. Albrech von Haller (1708–1777) seems to have developed the concept of nerve irritability; that is, when irritated by touch or chemicals the nerves would make muscles move. Haller was aware that electricity was a candidate for medium of nerve conduction, but he and others of his time, thinking of electrical conduction in a wire, believed that nerves lacked the insulation prerequisite for conduction.

The impetus to adopt a theory of electrical conduction came from Stephen Gray, who in 1731 attracted considerable attention by demonstrating that the human body could be electrified. In an ingenious demonstration he showed that static electricity from a rod could pass through the body: when a charged glass tube was brought close to the feet of a boy suspended by a rope, a grass-leaf electroscope was attracted to the boy's nose. It was only much later, however, that Luigi Galvani (1737–1798) demonstrated that electrical stimulation of a frog's nerve could cause muscle contraction, and Friedrich Humboldt (1769–1859) confirmed that nerves contained intrinsic "animal" electricity. In 1859, F. Pflüger suggested that electricity did not flow along the nerve but set up a wave motion within it. Finally, J. Bernstein, in 1886, developed the theory that the membrane of a nerve was polarized, and that the action potential was a propagated depolarization of this membrane. Many of the details of ionic conduction were worked out during the last 30 years, and A. L. Hodgkin and A. F. Huxley received the Nobel Prize in physiology in 1963 for their pioneering efforts in this field.

As successive findings brought hydraulic models of conduction into disfavor and more dynamic electrical models into favor, hydraulic theories of *behavior* were also critically reassessed. For example, Freud's theory of behavior, involving the different levels id, ego, and superego, was very much a hydraulic model. Although conceptually useful for a time, it had no impact on concepts of brain function, because almost as soon as the theory was proposed it became clear that the brain did not function as a hydraulic system.

Nervous-System Structure

Early views of the nervous system showed little concern for its structure, probably because to superficial examination it resembled little more than a bowl of jelly. There was a general awareness that nerves led to muscles, and it was widely believed that the nerves were hollow, fluid-containing tubes. One of the first cellular anatomists, Anton van Leeuwenhoek (1632–1723), examined nerves with a primitive microscope, but was unable to find hollow tubes. By 1717, he had described what may have been a nerve fiber surrounded by myelin. Van Leeuwenhoek also described what he called globules, but it is doubtful that these were cell bodies. They may have been either blobs of fat or optical aberrations produced by the crude microscopes of the day. From van Leeuwenhoek's time until the 1830s, when the achromatic microscope was developed, the frequency of artifacts aroused a general distrust of microscope results. However, in 1781, Felice Fontana did succeed in describing the nerve fiber. Then, in 1833, using the achromatic microscope, Christian G. Ehrenberg described nerve cells in the brain; in 1836, Gabriel G. Valentin described the cell body, nucleus, and nucleolus; and, in 1838, Robert Remak distinguished myelinated and nonmyelinated fibers and suggested that fibers connect to cell bodies. From these findings and others Theodor Schwann, in 1839, enunciated the cell theory; that is, that cells are the basic structural unit of the nervous system. It was not until 1849, however, that Rudolf A. van Koelliker had definitely established that nerve fibers were linked to the cell body.

Understanding of cell structure was advanced chiefly by improvements in technology. The earliest anatomists who tried to examine the substructure of the nervous system were faced with a gelatinous white substance. In 1809, Johann C. Reil developed the technique of fixing and hardening tissue by placing it in alcohol to remove fluid from the plasma. A more effective fixer, chromic acid, was found by Adolph Hannover in 1840. The formaldehyde technique, the preferred modern fixative procedure, was discovered in 1893 by Ferdinand Blum. In the 1830s Luigi Rolando had devised techniques for cutting thin sections of tissue, and in 1842 Benedikt Stilling discovered that the tissue could be cut into extremely thin sections if it was first frozen. The technique of freezing permitted serial reconstruction of fibers and of cellular tissue components, and also permitted a more effective use of stains.

The most exciting development in neuroanatomy was the technique of staining, which allows different portions of the nervous system to be visualized. In 1858, Joseph von Gerlach devised the carmine stain, which turns cells and their processes red; in 1882, Carl Weigert developed a technique for staining myelin; and, in 1894, Franz Nissl developed the methylene blue technique (Nissl stain), which stains cell bodies but not fibers, and reveals many of their internal structures. The most amazing cell stain was developed by Camillo Golgi in 1875. Impregnating tissue with silver nitrate, Golgi found that a few cells would take up the stain, and that each of these cells in its entirety—cell body, dendrites, and axons—became encrusted with reduced silver. Thus, finally the entire neuron and all of its processes could be visualized at one time.

As cells were visualized with microscopes it became clear that, far from resembling a bowl of jelly, the brain had an enormously intricate substructure with components arranged in complex clusters, each of which was interconnected with many others. Psychologists who were fractionating behavior into parts and faculties could only have been encouraged by the details of the brain revealed by the anatomists. There was a genuine theoreticians' banquet on hand, and for every conceivable behavioral trait there was a newly discovered nucleus or pathway begging to be attached. The feast may have been too rich, for the clear message from anatomists to psychologists was that things were probably more complex than they appeared to be. This may have been why for the first half of this century many psychologists turned away from the brain and not toward it, for enlightenment.

Nervous-System Connections

Was the brain a net of physically interconnected fibers, or a collection of discrete units? If it was an interconnected net, then it would follow that changes in one part would, by diffusion, produce changes in every other part. Since it would be difficult for a structure thus organized to localize function, a netlike structure would favor a holistic or gestalt type of brain function and psychology. Alternatively, a structure of discrete units would favor psychology based on localization of function, since—at least theoretically—each unit could function autonomously.

The concept of a nerve net was originated in 1855 by Franz von Leydig, who observed and described numerous interlacing fibrils in the nervous system of a spider. Later, J. von Gerlach (1820–1896), while studying dendrites in vertebrates, found what he considered a similar network. In 1883, Golgi dismissed Gerlach's hypothesis of an interlinking network of dendrites, suggesting instead that axons were interconnected, forming an axonic net. A number of anatomists opposed Golgi's idea; the most definitive work in opposition was done by Santiago Ramón y Cajal (1852–1934), using Golgi's own silver staining technique. In 1891, summarizing Cajal's work on nerve cells, Wilhelm Waldeyer coined the term neuron (from the Greek for nerve) and popularized the *neuron hypothesis,* which stated that neurons are not physically connected through their axons. Golgi and Cajal jointly received the Nobel Prize in 1906; each in his acceptance speech argued his position on the neuron hypothesis, Golgi supporting the nerve net and Cajal supporting the position now considered to be correct, the neuron hypothesis.

Largely because of the development of the electron microscope, more recent work in the early part of the twentieth century fully supported the neuron hypothesis. It is accepted that axons have terminal knobs on their ends, and that cells are separated by gaps, which are bridged by chemical messengers. (It is a nice historical irony that something like the idea that a fluid passes from the end of a nerve to activate a muscle turns out to be true.) It has been repeatedly demonstrated that neurons have a certain autonomy of function; thus, localization of function could be argued at the level of the cell. On this principle Hebb, in 1949, brilliantly advanced association learning theory by proposing that individual cells could, by being activated at the same time, come to form cell assemblies that formed the structure in which memory was housed.

In conclusion, many of the constituent concepts of the neuron hypothesis were formulated at roughly the same time as the developments in behavior we reviewed earlier, and they did so almost in parallel, seemingly without influencing how people thought behavior was produced. But the influence was there: knowing that the nervous system was composed of a uniform substance allowed it to be viewed as a single organ; knowing that it was electrically active led to experiments in which it was stimulated; knowing that some parts of the nervous system were composed of cell bodies and other parts of fibers permitted speculation about the relative effects of cell damage versus fiber damage; and being able to see subtle differences in cell structure in a microscope permitted the development of cytoarchitectonic maps that were strikingly similar and that gave support to functional maps constructed from lesion studies. Thus, although it may seem that behavior was effectively studied in ignorance of the brain's fine structure, in fact it was not—and it is unlikely that it will be in the future. In fact, the discovery that cells are organized in neurochemical systems may now be the predominant influence on how we think about behavior. In our view, although the influence of cell study on psychological theory has perhaps lagged somewhat, it is likely that the neuron hypothesis is catching up and may soon begin to shape psychological theory.

THE DEVELOPMENT OF MODERN NEUROPSYCHOLOGY

Given the nineteenth-century developments in knowledge about brain structure and function—the brain and neuron hypotheses, the concept of the special nature of cortical function, the concepts of localization of function and of disconnection—it seems surprising that psychologists did not become more interested in the brain earlier. Why was a science of neuropsychology not developed by 1900 rather than by 1949, when we first dated the use of the term? There are several possible reasons for the latency. One factor was that in the 1920s neurologists, such as Henry Head, rejected the classical approach of Broca, Wernicke, and others, arguing that their attempt to correlate behavior and anatomical site was little advanced over the approach of the phrenologists. This criticism was partly reasonable at the time, since some people, such as K. Kleist, had attempted to correlate every aspect of behavior and language with a particular anatomical location. A second reason was the intervention of two world wars, which disrupted the development of science in many countries. A third reason may have been that psychologists, who traced their origins to philosophy rather than to biology, were not interested, directing their attention instead to behaviorism, psychophysics, and the psychoanalytical movement.

A number of modern developments have contributed to a renewed interest in neuropsychology as a discipline. Improved anatomical techniques allow nervous-system damage to be specified with greater certainty. The development of neurosurgery as a practical method of dealing with certain brain dysfunctions (such as focal epilepsy) has occasioned demand for more careful appraisal of how neural tissue removal affects behavior. Because psychosurgery has been advocated by some as a way of coping with certain unwanted behaviors, there is now a strong demand that the effects of this procedure be assessed more carefully than they have been. Advances in animal neuropsychology have made it possible to develop and test models of human neuropsychological function with some effect. Developments in **psychometrics,** the science of measuring human abilities, permit objective and standardized measures of normal abilities and disabilities. It was only in 1940 that IQ tests were first given to brain-damaged people, by D. O. Hebb, with the resultant surprising discovery that lesions in the frontal lobes—until then considered the center of highest intelligence—did not decrease IQ score. It has also been realized that the neurological causes of mental illness and learning disorders may be found in abnormalities of neural connections; and that these abnormalities may be revealed by comparing the behavioral changes following brain damage with those that occur as a result of more subtle neurological dysfunctions. Furthermore, it is thought that if brain function is understood, it may be possible to develop alternate modes of coping for those who are disabled by brain lesions: for example, it may be possible to develop symbolic visual languages for those who become aphasic following brain damage. But perhaps most important has been the realization by psychologists that understanding the function of the brain is a prerequisite for understanding behavior.

REFERENCES

Bartholow, R. Experimental investigation into the functions of the human brain. *American Journal of Medical Sciences,* 67 (1874), 305–313.

Beach, F. A., D. O. Hebb, C. T. Morgan, and H. W. Nissen. *The Neuropsychology of Lashley.* New York, Toronto, and London: McGraw-Hill Book Co., 1960.

Benton, A. L. Contributions to aphasia before Broca. *Cortex, 1* (1964), 314–327.

Brazier, M. A. B. The historical development of neurophysiology. In J. Field, H. W. Magoun, and V. E. Hall, eds. *Handbook of Physiology,* Vol. 1. Washington, D.C.: American Physiological Society, 1959.

Broca, P. Remarks on the seat of the faculty of articulate language, followed by an observation of aphemia. In G. von Bonin, ed. *The Cerebral Cortex.* Springfield, Ill.: Charles C Thomas, 1960.

Broca, P. Sur le siège de la faculté du langage articulé. *Bulletin of the Society of Anthropology,* 6 (1865), 377–396.

Clark, E., and C. D. O'Malley. *The Human Brain and Spinal Cord.* Berkeley and Los Angeles: The University of California Press, 1968.

Descartes, R. *Traité de l'Homme.* Paris: Angot, 1664.

Eccles, J. C. *The Neurophysiological Basis of Mind: The Principles of Neurophysiology,* Oxford: Clarendon Press, 1956.

Flourens, P. Investigations of the properties and the functions of the various parts which compose the cerebral mass. In G. von Bonin, ed. *The Cerebral Cortex.* Springfield, Ill.: Charles C Thomas, 1960.

Fritsch, G., and E. Hitzig. On the electrical excitability of the cerebrum. In G. von Bonin, ed. *The Cerebral Cortex.* Springfield, Ill.: Charles C Thomas, 1960.

Geschwind, N. *Selected Papers on Language and Brain.* Dordrecht, Holland, and Boston: D. Reidel Publishing Co., 1974.

Goltz, F. On the functions of the hemispheres. In G. von Bonin, ed. *The Cerebral Cortex.* Springfield, Ill.: Charles C Thomas, 1960.

Head, H. *Aphasia and Kindred Disorders of Speech.* London: Cambridge University Press, 1926.

Hebb, D. O. *The Organization of Behavior: A Neuropsychological Theory.* New York: John Wiley and Sons, 1949.

Hebb, D. O., and W. Penfield. Human behavior after extensive bilateral removals from the frontal lobes. *Archives of Neurology and Psychiatry, 44* (1940), 421–438.

Joynt, R. Paul Pierre Broca: his contribution to the knowledge of aphasia. *Cortex, 1* (1964), 206–213.

Klüver, H. *Behavior Mechanisms in Monkeys.* Chicago: The University of Chicago Press, 1933 and 1957.

Krech, D. Cortical localization of function. In L. Postman, ed. *Psychology in the Making.* New York: Alfred A. Knopf, 1962.

Lenneberg, E. H. *Biological Foundations of Language.* New York: John Wiley and Sons, 1967.

Luciani, L. *Human Physiology.* London: Macmillan and Co., Ltd., 1915.

Luria, A. R. *The Working Brain.* New York: Penguin Books, 1973.

Olin, C. H. *Phrenology.* Philadelphia: The Penn Publishing Co., 1910.

Pribram, K. H. *Languages of the Brain.* Englewood Cliffs, N.J.: Prentice-Hall, 1971.

Rothschuk, K. E. *History of Physiology.* Huntington, N.Y.: Robert E. Krieger, 1973.

Stookey, B. A note on the early history of cerebral localization. *Bulletin of the New York Academy of Medicine, 30* (1954), 559–578.

Taylor, J., ed. *Selected Writings of John Hughlings-Jackson,* Vols. 1 and 2. London: Hodder and Stoughton, Ltd., 1931.

Wernicke, C. *Der Aphasische Symptomenkomplex.* Breslau, Poland: M. Cohn and Weigert, 1874.

8

A GENERAL THEORY OF
BRAIN ORGANIZATION AND FUNCTION

Once upon a time six blind men from Hindustan examined an elephant to satisfy their curiosity about what it was. Alpha, touching its body, thought it a wall; Beta, touching its tusk, thought it a spear; Delta, touching its trunk, thought it a snake; Gamma, touching its leg, thought it a tree; Terry, touching its ear, thought it a fan; and Tim, examining its tail, thought it a rope. The story illustrates a well-known problem in the neurosciences: How can a concept of brain functions be developed from the disparate descriptions given by the different branches of the neurosciences? This problem is compounded: How can anyone assimilate the staggering amount of data about the brain being collected each year by these different branches of neuroscience?

Fortunately, the answers to both of these questions, although not completely adequate, are at least practical and helpful. First, it is possible to sketch a silhouette of the elephant (i.e., a theoretical framework describing the brain's organization and function) that is agreed upon by people in most neuroscience areas. Second, because much of the new information published each year is simply a more refined description of the composition of the "elephant's tusk," it adds little to knowledge about the elephant and so it can be temporarily ignored.

In this chapter, which gives a general overview of the brain's function, we emphasize the brain's hierarchical organization. That is, the brain is organized in a *functional* hierarchy, the higher levels providing the animal with more precision in its behavior. The concept of hierarchy is important because it prevents the attribution of behaviors to one anatomical area that are in fact controlled by another. Other important aspects of brain organization receive less emphasis in this chapter because they are discussed in some depth elsewhere. For example, the lateralization of the brain with respect to function, particularly in humans, is described in detail in Chapter 9. Also, within the hierarchically organized brain are a number of parallel systems. On the input side are the projections and relay stations of the five major senses, each with a similar yet partly independent organization; these are discussed in Chapter 10. On the output side are three relatively independent motor systems: one for whole body movements, one for relatively independent limb movements, and one for relatively independent finger movements; these are discussed in Chapter 11.

LEVELS OF FUNCTION FROM SPINAL CORD TO CORTEX

The idea that the brain is organized in functional levels is not new. It can be dated at least to the mid-nineteenth century, to Herbert Spencer's speculations that each "step" in evolution added a new level of brain and accordingly a new level of behavioral complexity. Certainly it was the basic principle that underlay all of Hughlings-Jackson's writings on brain function. Because of the nature of the questions addressed, the evidence in this section comes primarily from animal studies. Nevertheless, the general principles are applicable to humans, as attested by evidence from clinical studies.

The typical question to which an experiment is addressed is something like: What can an animal do without a neocortex? The question is answered by surgically removing the animal's neocortex and studying changes in behavior. The question is then rephrased: What can an animal do if the neocortex and the basal ganglia in addition are removed? By removal of successively more brain tissue in different preparations, eventually the functions of the spinal cord can be studied in isolation from the rest of the brain. Thus, a brain area can be studied in isolation from some area to which it is normally connected, yielding information about what the removed structure did as well as what the remaining structures do.

Of course, the success of such research depends upon the ability of a damaged nervous system to continue functioning after the surgical procedure is complete. As it turns out, the brain has a remarkable ability to survive after parts are destroyed. This resiliency to insult was given popular exposure in 1700 by DuVerney; in a public demonstration he showed that when a nerve and muscle were dissected away from a frog, the nerve continued to function, for when touched it produced muscle contractions. In 1853 Pflüger demonstrated that a frog with only an intact spinal cord could survive and display quite complex responses. If acid was placed on the frog's right side the right leg would reach up and remove the acid. If the right leg was restrained, then after a number of ineffective efforts, the left leg would be used to remove the acid. Other workers, among them Ridi in 1810, demonstrated that if parts of the brainstem were intact, amphibians could walk. In 1884 Fano studied the locomotor patterns of a tortoise with only a lower brainstem; attached to its tail was a brush dipped in aniline, which traced the animal's pathway as it walked. These early experiments were followed by more systematic research into the capacities of different portions of the nervous system as well as the details of their structure.

The following section presents the case for levels of function by describing the capacities of spinal animals and animals with successively more intact nervous systems. Figure 8-1 lists each experimental preparation and the brain tissue that remains intact, and summarizes the types of behavior the animal can perform. Parallel conditions that may occur in humans will be noted in the discussions following.

The Spinal Animal: Reflexes

The spinal animal has a very simple nervous system. Nerve fibers from sensory receptors in or on the body enter the spinal cord through

ANATOMY	PREPARATION	BEHAVIORS
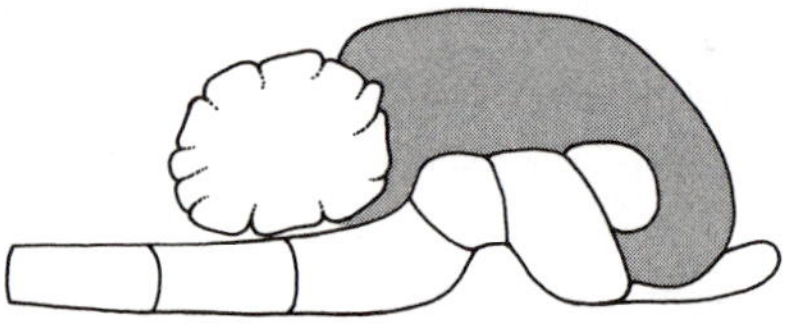	Normal (cortex)	Performs sequences of voluntary movements in organized patterns; responds to patterns of sensory stimulation.
	Decorticate (basal ganglia)	Links voluntary movements and automatic movements sufficiently well for self-maintenance (eating, drinking) in a simple environment.
	Diencephalic (hypothalamus thalamus)	Voluntary movements occur spontaneously and excessively but are aimless; shows well-integrated but poorly directed affective behavior; thermoregulates effectively.
	High decerebrate (midbrain)	Responds to simple features of visual and auditory stimulation; performs automatic behaviors such as grooming; performs subsets of voluntary movements (standing, walking, turning, jumping, climbing, etc.) when stimulated.
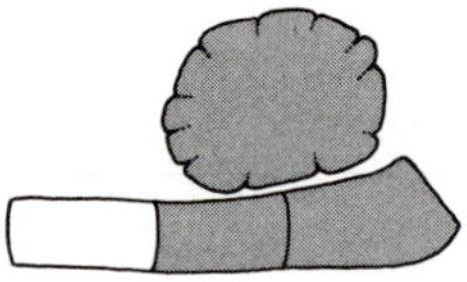	Low decerebrate (hindbrain)	Performs units of movement (hissing, biting, growling, chewing, lapping, licking, etc.) when stimulated; shows exaggerated standing, postural reflexes, and elements of sleep-waking behavior.
	Spinal (spinal cord)	Shows reflexes (stretching, withdrawal, support, scratching, paw shaking, etc.) to appropriate sensory stimulation.

FIGURE 8-1. Behavior that can be supported by different levels of the nervous system. Shading indicates the highest remaining functional area.

its superior or dorsal roots. They then project to interneurons or to motor neurons in the same or other segments of the cord. (**Interneurons** are neurons located between sensory neurons entering the cord and motor neurons leaving the cord.) The motor neurons send projections to the muscles of the body through the cord's inferior or ventral roots. Behaviorally, a spinal animal is also simple: it cannot stand or move spontaneously; however, if a sensory receptor is stimulated, one or more limbs move. Such movements are called *reflexes*. The **spinal reflex** was first described in detail by Sherrington in 1906 and Liddell and Sherrington in 1924. The following is a brief summary of an extensive literature.

The simplest of the spinal reflexes is the **stretch reflex**: the contraction of a muscle to stretch a limb. The stretch activates a receptor in the muscle, and its sensory neuron, on stimulation, activates the motor neuron in the cord, which then contracts the stretched muscle. The function of the stretch reflex is to allow the muscle to maintain a limb in position. Stretching a muscle can also influence muscles that work in opposition to it. In this more complex reflex, called **reciprocal inhibition,** the opposing muscle relaxes in response to the stretch. This reflex is clearly intended to permit a joint to move, for if a muscle is to move a limb, the muscles that work in opposition must relax.

Other sensory stimulation can also elicit reflexes. Pressure on the pads of a foot causes the foot to extend, a reflex that is the basis of the supporting reaction, a prerequisite for standing. Pinching the paw produces a withdrawal reaction, a response necessary for escaping painful or potentially injurious events. Spinal reflexes can be quite well directed: tickling the sides of a spinal dog elicits a scratch response sufficiently accurate to remove the stimulus. Reflexes can also appear to be very complex: penile stimulation in male cats can produce erection and pelvic thrusting, and vaginal stimulation in female cats can produce treading responses. As described by Grillner, a spinal cat suspended in a sling on a treadmill will display coordinated walking, and after some recovery from midspinal section it can use the isolated rear limbs for spontaneous walking.

Kuhn has given a detailed description of the effects of complete spinal-cord transection in humans. He notes considerable variability in the extent to which spinal reflexes recover after cord section. Some people show virtually no recovery, and their muscles atrophy; others recover sufficiently that their legs will support their weight, and they show no muscle atrophy. For those who show pronounced recovery of spinal reflexes, Kuhn describes four major stages or steps in the process of recovery:

1. *Spinal shock.* Spinal shock is a state of profound depression of all reflexes below the level of section. Shock varies in severity from person to person and in duration, lasting from one to six weeks. Some reflexes, such as penile erection in males, may not be depressed at all. As stated above, for some few individuals there is no evidence of recovery beyond this stage.

2. *Minimal reflex activity.* In this stage slight flexion or extension of the foot, some toe twitches, and extension of the large toe occur. Anal and bladder reflexes for waste secretion may also be present.

3. *Flexor activity.* The first major reflexes to return are flexor reflexes, consisting of such movements as dorsiflexion of the big toe and fanning of the toe, dorsiflexion of the foot, and flexion of the leg and thigh. Stimuli found most effective in eliciting limb flexion were tactile; particularly effective were unpleasant stimuli, and the zones with the lowest thresholds were the foot area and the genital area.

4. *Extensor activity.* Extensor movements generally become apparent as early as six months after injury, and continue to develop for years. They consist of extension and stiffening of one or both legs; in some patients there is only a slight tightening of limbs, whereas in others the limbs assume pillarlike rigidity. In some people in the latter group this activity is sufficient to permit prolonged standing in warm water without support.

The most effective stimuli for eliciting extension were proprioceptive, such as stretching the flexors of the thigh muscles at the hip (as occurs during shifting from a sitting to a lying position) or squeezing the thigh muscles. Tactile stimulation became effective in eliciting extensor responses somewhat later, and the lowest thresholds were on the thigh or back of the knee and spread distally to include the foot surface. It can be seen from this description that recovery from spinal-cord section can be quite extensive. However, patients can make no voluntary movements, and receive no sensation from below the area of the lesion.

In summary, the apparent function of the spinal cord is to produce a number of simple responses to stimulation of the somatosensory system. Such reflexes characteristically are produced by stimulation acting directly on the body. The movements are brief adjustments to the stimulation, are stereotyped, and usually last only for the length of the stimulation.

The Low Decerebrate Animal: Support

In the low decerebrate animal both the hindbrain and the spinal cord remain intact. The sensory input into the hindbrain comes predominantly from the head and is carried over cranial nerves IV and XII. Most of these nerves also have motor nuclei in the hindbrain whose efferent fibers control muscles in the head and neck. Whereas interneurons in the spinal cord are sometimes located between sensory projections and motor projections, interneurons in the hindbrain have multiplied to form nuclei as well as more complex coordinating centers such as the cerebellum. Sensory input to the hindbrain is not limited to the cranial nerves, for, as we shall see, the spinal somatosensory system has access to hindbrain motor systems, just as the hindbrain has access to spinal motor systems. Before the function of the hindbrain is discussed, a description of the behavior of low decerebrate animals might be helpful.

Low decerebrate cats are described by Bazett and Penfield and by Bard and Macht in experiments in which the animals are kept alive for periods of weeks or months. The animals are generally inactive when undisturbed and show virtually no effective thermoregulatory ability, but otherwise are relatively easy to maintain because they swallow food placed on their tongues and so can be fed. If the animals are stimulated lightly in any of a variety of sensory modalities—e.g., touch, pain, sounds—they right themselves from their normal lateral position into a crouched position. If stimulation is stronger they walk, somewhat unsteadily. These stimuli can also elicit some of the movements of the affective behavior of normal cats, because the cats are observed to bite, hiss, growl, and lash their tails.

One of the most characteristic additions to behavior accorded by an intact hindbrain is a peculiar kind of stiffness called **decerebrate rigidity**: excessive muscle tone, particularly in the antigravity muscles of the body, which are the strongest muscles. Because of this rigidity, when an animal is placed in an upright position its limbs extend and its head flexes upward. Sherrington referred to this rigidity as exaggerated standing. Against this background of support, a number of *postural reflexes* can be elicited by changes in head position. If the head of a standing animal is pushed down toward the floor the front limbs flex and the hind limbs extend; if the head is pushed up the hind legs flex and the front legs extend. The first type of posture would be used by a normal cat looking under a couch, the second by a normal cat looking up onto a shelf. Turning the head to the side elicits extension of the limbs on the same side and flexion of the limbs on the opposite side of the body; this type of response occurs in a normal cat that has turned its head to look at some object and is prepared to pursue it. When the animals are placed on their sides they extend their lower limbs, which are in contact with the floor surface, and semiflex their upper limbs, a static reaction that represents the first stage of the **righting reflex.**

There are two types of sleep in normal animals: *quiet sleep,* characterized by muscle tone; and *active sleep,* characterized by an absence of muscle tone. Low decerebrate animals are described as showing characteristics of both types of sleep at different times. Animals left undisturbed gradually lose their rigidity and subside or droop into a prone posture. Any mild stimulus such as a noise or touch reinstates rigidity. This type of behavioral change seems analogous to quiet sleep. The animals also show a sudden collapse, accompanied by the loss of all body tone, which lasts from 15 seconds to 12 minutes. This type of behavioral change seems analogous to active sleep, particularly since some people with an illness called **narcolepsy** similarly collapse into active sleep.

The low decerebrate animal's behavior, then, differs from the spinal animal's in a number of ways. First, responses such as tail lashing and biting are elicited by several modes of stimulation, which often summate. Such responses can be explained in the following way. In its simplest form tail lashing is a withdrawal reflex of the tail produced by noxious tail stimulation; it is a spinal reflex. Biting is a jaw reflex elicited by facial stimulation; it is mediated through the hindbrain by the sensory and motor components of the trigeminal (V) nerve. If the sensory component of the spinal reflexes taps into the motor components of hindbrain reflex circuits, and if the sensory components of the hindbrain reflexes tap into the motor component of spinal-cord reflex circuits, then pinching the cat's lip can produce tail withdrawal (tail lashing) as well as biting, and pinching the cat's tail can produce biting plus tail withdrawal. Spontaneous occurrence of these behaviors may either be elicited by spontaneous activity in the spinal-hindbrain circuits, or be triggered by less obvious stimulation carried into the spinal-hindbrain circuits by other nerves such as the vagus (X) nerve. This principle of interlinking sensory and motor components of different levels is an organizational feature of all levels of brain function.

The **vestibular system,** by means of nerve VIII, makes an obvious contribution to the behavior of low decerebrate animals. There are two vestibular receptors in the middle ear: the **saccule** signals when the head is oriented in the normal position; the utricle signals changes in orientation. It is probable that the upright posture of the head and body is maintained by the saccule or its motor nuclei in the hindbrain. The decerebrate rigidity of the low decerebrate animal is no doubt the exaggerated product of unchecked activity in this system. When the head is moved the posture of the animal changes in characteristic ways. These postural changes are probably mediated by the macula and its motor nuclei.

Since part of the function of the vestibular system is to maintain and adjust posture it seems logical that a mechanism be built into the hindbrain to check its activity when an upright posture is not needed. Otherwise an animal might remain in a rigid position until its musculature were exhausted. Decerebrate animals do relax, which suggests that there is an inhibitory system in the hindbrain. The inhibition provided by this system is most likely the neurological basis of sleep. The observation that any type of stimulation can restore rigidity after relaxation occurs suggests that spinal and hindbrain sensory systems have input into the nuclei that maintain support, and are capable of activating them. Stimulation from these systems probably provides part of the neurological basis for awakening.

The behavioral changes seen in low decerebrate animals are paralleled in people who have brainstem damage of the type that essentially separates the lower brainstem from the rest of the brain. Barrett, Merritt, and Wolf have documented a number of such cases. These people may alternate between states of consciousness resembling sleeping and waking, make eye movements to follow moving stimuli, cough, smile, swallow food, display decerebrate rigidity, and display postural adjustments when moved. When cared for, people with such brain damage may live for months or years with little change in their condition.

The High Decerebrate Animal: Voluntary and Automatic Behavior

The high decerebrate animal has an intact midbrain containing, in the tectum, the coordinating centers for vision (superior colliculus) and audition (inferior colliculus), and, in the tegmentum, a number of motor nuclei. Visual and auditory inputs are different from any sensory input received at lower levels because they allow the animal to perceive events located at a distance. Correspondingly, it is not surprising to find that the high decerebrate animal is able to respond to distant objects by locomoting toward them. However, the assessment of how active high decerebrate animals are varies from study to study.

Bard and Macht report that high decerebrate cats can walk, stand, resume upright posture when turned on their backs, and even run and climb when stimulated. Bignall and Schramm found that kittens decerebrated in infancy could orient to visual and auditory stimuli. The animals could even execute an attack response and pounce on objects at the source of a sound. In fact, Bignall and Schramm fed the cats by exploiting this behavior, for they placed food near the source of the sound; attacking the sound source the cats would then consume the food. Although the cats attacked moving objects they gave no evidence of "seeing," for they bumped into things when they walked around. Woods has reported that high decerebrate rats are active and make all the movements of normal rats; Grill and Norgren report that they are generally inactive and show normal locomotor abilities only when disturbed. Bignall and Schramm and Woods may have left some hypothalamic tissue intact, which would account for why their animals were more active than animals observed in other studies.

These experiments demonstrate that all the components (or subsets) of **voluntary movements**—movements that take an animal from one place to another, such as turning, walking, climbing, swimming—are present at the level of the midbrain. Intact animals use voluntary movements in a variety of motivational conditions, e.g., to find food, water, or a new home territory, or to escape a predator. These movements have also been variously called appetitive, instrumental, purposive, or operant. Voluntary movements, being executed through lower-level postural support and reflex systems, can also be elicited by lower-level sensory input; that is, a pinch or postural displacement can elicit turning, walking, or climbing. Thus, this new functional level is integrated with lower levels by both ascending and descending connections, exactly as the hindbrain and spinal levels are interconnected.

High decerebrate animals are also able to effectively perform **automatic behaviors:** units of stereotyped behavior linked in a sequence. Grooming, chewing food, lapping water, and rejecting food are representative automatic behaviors of the rat. Generally, automatic behaviors (also variously called reflexive, consummatory, or respondent behaviors) are directed toward completing some sort of consummatory act, and are not specifically directed toward moving an animal from one place to another. Grooming is an excellent example of an automatic behavior since it consists of a large number of movements executed sequentially in an organized and quite stereotyped fashion. If the rat's fur is wet it first shakes its back, then sits on its haunches and shakes its front paws, then licks water from them, wipes its snout rapidly with bilateral symmetrical movements, wipes its face with slight asymmetrical movements, and then turns to lick the fur on its body. Food rejection is similarly complex. If decerebrate rats are satiated and given food they perform a series of movements consisting of tongue flicks, chin rubbing, and paw shaking to reject the food. These behaviors are similar to the rejection behaviors made by normal rats in response to food they find noxious. If the animals are not sated they will lap water and chew food brought to their mouths.

There are a number of accounts of infants born with large portions of the forebrain missing. One child studied by Gamper (Figure 8-2) had no brain present above the diencephalon and only a few traces of the diencephalon intact, and was thus anatomically equivalent to a high decerebrate animal. This child showed many behaviors of newborn infants. It could sit up; it showed periodic sleep and wakefulness; it could suck, yawn, stretch, cry, and follow visual stimuli with its eyes. How-

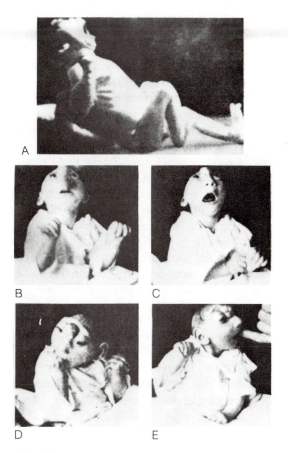

FIGURE 8-2. Instinctive behavior and oral automatisms in Gamper's mesencephalic human. A. Yawning with spreading of arms. B. Oral adversive movements, after the lips are touched, with deviation of the eyes. C. Coordinated gaze and snapping movements after finger was removed. D. Spontaneous sucking of own hand. E. Oral adversion to the left side with deviation of head and eyes and tonic neck reflexes in the arms. (From E. Gamper, *Ztschr. ges. Neurol. Psychiat.* 104: 49, 1926.)

ever, the child showed little spontaneous activity and if left alone remained mostly in a drowsy state. Brackbill studied a similar child and found that in responses to stimuli such as 60–90 decibel sounds it oriented in much the same way normal children did. Unlike normal children, however, the responses did not change in size and did not habituate to repeated presentation. She concluded that the forebrain is not important for eliciting responding, but is important for attenuating and inhibiting responding. Generally, children born with such extensive brain abnormalities do not live long, and among those that live for a number of months there is no development of complex behaviors seen in normal children. They appear to have the same behavioral capacities of high decerebrate animals.

In summary, the midbrain adds at least three new components to behavior. First, the presence of the auditory and optic systems allows the animals to receive sensory input that originates at some distance. Most evidence suggests that these sensory systems respond to only the simpler features of stimuli such as intensity and place. Second, these sensory systems appear to be linked with voluntary motor systems that allow the animal to respond to distant stimuli by moving toward or away from them. Third, the midbrain appears to contain programs that allow the animals to chain together a number of movements to form complex behaviors of the consummatory type, called automatic behaviors.

The Diencephalon: Affect and Motivation

Probably the diencephalon has been studied more than any other brain structure, yet its contribution to the organization of behavior is not well understood. The diencephalic animal has an intact olfactory system, enabling it to smell odorous objects located at a distance. The hypothalamus and pituitary are also intact, and their control over body hormonal systems no doubt integrates the body's physiology with the brain's activity. In physiological literature the hypothalamus is thought to be involved in homeostasis; that is, maintaining body temperature, water balance, energy reserves, etc. Diencephalic animals do maintain

normal body temperature, but they do not eat or drink well enough to maintain themselves. In the traditional literature of physiological psychology, diencephalic functions are often discussed under headings of affect and motivation. Although these terms have never been defined to everyone's satisfaction, the diencephalon does seem to add a dimension of affect and motivation to behavior if the terms are used in the sense that behavior becomes "energized." Some examples of the diencephalic animal's behavior will illustrate this point.

As we have mentioned, high decerebrate animals show many of the component behaviors of rage, but the behaviors are not energetic, well integrated, or sustained. Cannon and Britton studied forebrain-lesioned cats and described what they called "quasi-emotional phenomena" (or sham rage, described below) such as are usually seen in an infuriated animal; the behavior consists of lashing the tail, arching the trunk, making limb movements, displaying claws, snarling, and biting. Sympathetic signs of rage are present, including erection of the tail hair, sweating of the toe pads, dilation of the pupils, micturation, high blood pressure, high heart rate, and increases in adrenalin and blood sugar. These emotional attacks sometimes last for hours. Bard removed various amounts of forebrain and brainstem and found that for this effect to occur it was necessary to leave at least the posterior portion of the hypothalamus intact. Clinical reports indicate that similar sham emotional attacks can occur in people who have suffered hypothalamic lesions; thus, there are reports of people who show unchecked rage behavior, or who literally laugh until they die.

One of the most pronounced features of the diencephalic animal's behavior is its constant activity; this has been observed by Sorenson and Ellison and by Grill and Norgren in rats and by Goltz in dogs. We have watched diencephalic rats and found that although they attempt to eat they are unable to remain still long enough to ingest more than a few grams of food over periods lasting for hours. Since normal animals deprived of food and water become active, it is possible to argue that the diencephalic animal's hyperactivity is driven by a deficiency condition; that is, the animal is searching for food or water. Grill and Norgren, however, have found that feeding the animals as much as control rats does not arrest hyperactivity.

These two examples of diencephalic behavior suggest to us that the diencephalon adds an "energizing" dimension to behavior that may justify labeling the behavior affective or motivated. Britton and Cannon, however, were aware of the inappropriateness of the rage behavior of the diencephalic cat (it is overdone and not directed) and so they called it sham rage, to distinguish it from the directed rage of the normal cat. Perhaps the hyperactivity of the diencephalic animal should be called sham motivation to distinguish it from the goal-oriented behavior of the normal animal. In this sense the sham affect and sham motivation of the diencephalic animal are something like the exaggerated standing observed in low decerebrate animals. Under appropriate forebrain control it can be manipulated for functional purposes, but in the absence of that control the behavior of the animal is excessive and seems inappropriate. (These are classic examples of Jacksonian release phenomena.) At present it is unknown whether the energizing aspect of the diencephalic animal's behavior can be attributed to the hormonal or neural connections of the diencephalon.

The Basal Ganglia: Self-Maintenance

Decortication is removal of the neocortex (either alone or with the limbic system as well), leaving the basal ganglia and brainstem intact.

Decorticate animals have been studied more closely than any others because they are able to maintain themselves without special care in laboratory conditions.

The results obtained by Goltz with decorticate dogs have already been described (Chapter 7), but the most thorough studies have used rats as subjects. Experiments by ourselves and our colleagues show that within a day after surgery they eat and maintain body weight on a wet mash diet, and eat dry food and drink water brought in contact with the mouth. With a little training at drinking (holding the water spout to the mouth) they find water and become able to maintain themselves on water and laboratory chow within 10 days. They have normal sleep-waking cycles, run, climb, and swim, and even negotiate simple mazes (which admittedly they learn with great difficulty). The hyperactivity characteristic of diencephalic animals is greatly reduced.

What is observed in the decorticate rat, and what is presumably conferred by the basal ganglia, is the ability to link automatic movements to voluntary movements so that the behaviors are biologically adaptive. A major portion of this linking probably involves inhibition or facilitation of voluntary movements. For example, the animal walks until it finds food or water and then the basal ganglia inhibit walking to allow the consummatory act to occur. As well as inhibiting voluntary movements at specific times, the basal ganglia probably also help them occur. For example, we have observed that during training in a straight alley decorticate rats increase their running speed to obtain food. Our proposal that the basal ganglia control voluntary movements in order to allow the more automatic components of consummatory acts to occur at the right time and place is supported by the observations of Villablanca, Olmstead, and others. They observe that if the basal ganglia are removed, cats show a "compulsive approach syndrome" in which they follow or approach any moving object indefinitely. They are apparently no longer able to inhibit approach behavior.

The Cortex: Sequencing Voluntary Movement and Pattern Perception

What the neocortex *does* can also be ascertained by studying what the decorticate animal (with neocortex alone removed or with limbic system also removed) *cannot* do. Generalizing from the following deficits, it appears that the function of the cortex is to construct sequences or patterns of voluntary movements in response to external and internal cues, and to discriminate pattern in sensory input.

Sequencing Voluntary Movements. Studies by our group and others on decorticate rats show them unable to hoard food, construct nests, care for young, or avoid or bury a stimulus object that emits shock (as do normal rats described by Pinel and Treit). Their motor responses are awkward; they are unable to negotiate narrow ledges, swim with their forepaws immobile in the normal way, or use their forepaws to lift and manipulate food. They keep their fur clean, but they interrupt the normal sequencing of grooming movements with irrelevant locomotion. They tend to neglect the caudal part of their body when grooming, and they grow long nails on their hind feet (either because they fail to clip their nails or to use them to scratch their fur with sufficient frequency). They have difficulty responding appropriately when placed in some situations: when held in the air they clasp their feet together or clasp their bodies rather than reach for an edge in the normal way; when placed in a narrow alley blocked at one end they are unable to rear and turn around or back out; and when placed on a platform elevated a few inches they are unable to climb

down. Beach reports that decorticate male rats do not mate and decorticate females do not show normal soliciting behavior. (Brooks, however, reports that decorticate male rabbits do mate. This species difference may be due to the greater learning prerequisite for sexual behavior in the male rat as compared with the male rabbit.) All of the behavior described above involves appropriate sequencing of a series of voluntary movements. The deficits shown by the animals are less an inability to perform the components of the movements than an inability to put the components into sequences. For example, a decorticate rat can walk forward and can rear, but in a narrow alley it does not walk forward far enough to rear against the end and turn around, and so it traps itself. Also, the animals may pick up and handle nesting material, but they do not position it to form a nest. Any similar deficit shown by humans with forebrain damage is called an **apraxia** (impairment of the ability to use objects correctly).

Pattern Perception. It is well known that the function of the cortical sensory areas is to discriminate pattern. Klüver, using monkeys, found that the animals with visual cortex lesions were unable to discriminate between two objects that differed in their pattern (i.e., horizontal versus vertical stripes), but they were able to respond to lights in different locations or of different brightness. Bauer and Cooper, and Goodale have made a similar point with respect to visual cortex function in rats. Their research suggests that whereas the superior colliculus and other midbrain visual centers are adequate for discriminating place and intensity, the neocortex is required for pattern discrimination. Other studies on other sensory systems agree that the function of the cortical sensory areas is to discriminate patterns.

In summary, as early as 1906 Sherrington had suggested that the function of higher centers was to break up, by inhibition or facilitation, the simpler movements coded at lower levels, and so produce new movements appropriate for new situations. Sherrington's view can be restated thus: the cortex organizes subsets of voluntary movements into patterns of movements that are appropriate to the patterns of internal or external cues. In other words, the cortex extracts pattern from the sensory world and imposes pattern on the movements animals make through that world. As described earlier, Descartes argued that the body was a machine operated by brain reflexes but that in man the machine was controlled by the mind. It seems appropriate here to restate this view: all components of normal behavior are produced by subcortical systems, but the cortex exerts control.

The Generality of Levels of Function

After summarizing some of the available information on levels of function, it seems appropriate to ask: Are the results from these lesion studies consistent with those obtained from research using other approaches? The answer is that there is a good relation. For example, Flynn and his coworkers have studied the organization of predatory behavior in the cat by stimulating the brainstem electrically. Stimulation in the midbrain gives responses that are not associated with the autonomic signs of arousal that typically accompanied attack behavior elicited by hypothalamic stimulation. Similarly, many other stimulation studies on rats and other animals confirm that the simpler components of motor behavior are organized in the lower brainstem (e.g., Bernston and Micco, Buchholz, and Robinson).

Another source of confirmatory evidence for levels of function is studies on the electrical activity (EEG) of the forebrain. Vanderwolf and his colleagues find that the electrical activity of the neocortex and hippocampus changes with behavior in such a way that "activated" patterns of EEG always occur during voluntary movements but not always with automatic behaviors. The hippocampal EEG of the rat shows this relation most clearly (see Figure 8-3): a rhythmical wave pattern called **theta activity** (having a frequency of 4–7 Hz) is found to be correlated with voluntary movements (Type 1), but is generally absent during automatic movements (Type 2). According to the argument that the forebrain's function is to produce patterns of movements by putting together subsets of voluntary movement, it is understandable that the forebrain is in an "active mode" during these behaviors. It is controlling voluntary movements to ensure that they are appropriate in sequence, time, and place. The forebrain need not be active in the same way during automatic movements, since, once the animal is in a position to perform them, they are executed wholly at lower functional levels. It is instructive that Bland and Vanderwolf have reported that interference with the theta activity of the hippocampus will disrupt voluntary but not more automatic behaviors, whereas facilitating the theta activity facilitates voluntary but not more automatic behaviors.

Why Levels?

Why is the brain organized into functional levels integrated in such a way that each level controls a large number of behaviors? Satinoff suggests the answer has three parts. First, the selective pressure for the development of new brain was to refine the animal's ability to respond to specific features of the world. A good example is thermoregulation: any physiological or behavioral response intended to maintain normal body temperature. Response to temperature change in spinal animals begins at temperature extremes of 36 to 41°C; in decerebrates the range narrows to 37 to 39°C; in

Hippocampus	Behavior
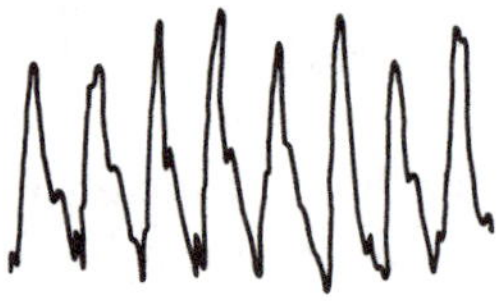	Type 1. walking, running, swimming, rearing, jumping, digging, manipulation of objects with the forelimbs, isolated movements of the head or one limb, shifts of posture. Related terms: voluntary, appetitive, instrumental, purposive, operant, or "theta" behavior.
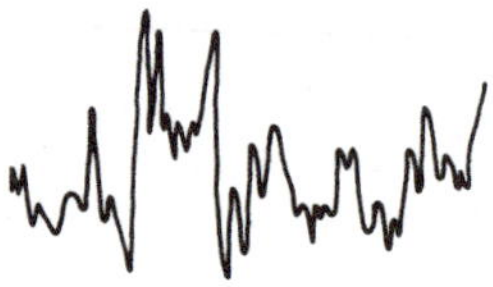	Type 2 (a) alert immobility in any posture (b) licking, chewing, chattering the teeth, sneezing, startle response, vocalization, shivering, tremor, face-washing, scratching the fur, pelvic thrusting, ejaculation, defecation, urination, piloerection. Related terms: automatic, reflexive, consummatory, respondent, or "non-theta" behavior.

FIGURE 8-3. Hippocampal activity in relation to spontaneous behavior in the rat. (After Vanderwolf et al., 1975.)

it is around 38°C; whereas in normal animals thermoregulatory responses are ongoing to maintain a precise body temperature that seldom deviates more than a fraction of a degree. The second part of the answer is that the brain took a great deal of time to evolve, and the development of any new structure conferring a new behavior had to integrate its activity through the systems already present. The third part is that once a new ability was developed it was frequently co-opted to be used for other purposes in addition to those for which it was initially evolved. For example, upright walking on four legs was evolved to move an animal rapidly from one place to another, but the upright posture, once developed, could then be used as the support for shivering. As Schallert et al. point out, it is therefore not surprising to find some aspects of walking and thermoregulation related. In fact, Satinoff has

used this logic to explain why many components of thermoregulation are found at different levels. Another example might be that once an animal was able to balance on its hind legs to rear or jump, its front paws were free for manipulating objects. As a consequence of these three developments, we find behaviors integrated at each level in such a way that the entire organization of the brain can be viewed as a hierarchy of functional levels.

FUNCTIONAL LEVELS AND LATERALIZATION OF THE CORTEX

Since the mid-nineteenth century the anterior cortex has been recognized as being more involved than the posterior cortex in motor functions, and the posterior cortex as being more involved than the anterior cortex in sensory functions. It has also been recognized that the cortex can be divided into three types of areas:

1. Primary sensory and motor areas.
2. Secondary sensory and motor areas.
3. Tertiary, or association, areas.

From this knowledge Luria and others have proposed a general theory of cortical function.

The Organization of the Cortex

Luria divides the cortex into two functional units (Figure 8-4). The first, the posterior portion of the neocortex (parietal, temporal, and occipital lobes), is the *sensory* unit. It receives sensory impressions, processes them, and stores them as information. The second, the anterior cortex (frontal lobe), is the *motor* unit. It formulates intentions, organizes them into programs of action, and executes the programs. In both cortical units there is a hierarchical structure with three cortical zones arranged functionally one above the other. These zones are distinguished by the cytoarchitecture, and can therefore be described with Brodmann's numbering system.

The Sensory Unit. In the sensory unit the *primary zones* consist of the projection areas of vision (area 17), audition (area 41), and body senses (areas 1–3). In these zones the general features of sensory stimulation are organized in an array representing the topography, intensity, and pattern of stimulation. The *secondary zones* comprise the projection areas of these primary zones; in the case of vision, for example, areas 18 and 19. The secondary zones retain the modality (e.g., visual) of sensation, but have a less fixed topographic organization (e.g., for vision its re-representation of the retina). The *tertiary zones* lie on the boundary of the occipital, temporal, and parietal cortex and include Brodmann's areas 5, 7, 21, 22,

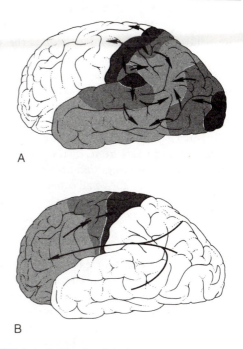

FIGURE 8-4. A. The first functional unit of the cortex: the sensory unit. (Dark shading = primary zones; medium shading = secondary zones; light shading = tertiary zones.) Sensory input travels from primary to secondary to tertiary, and concomitantly is elaborated from sensation into symbolic processes. B. The second functional unit of the cortex: the motor unit. Symbolic processes from the first functional unit are translated into intentions in the tertiary and then into patterns of action in the secondary and primary zones. (After A. R. Luria, *The Working Brain*. The Copyright Agency of the USSR. Reprinted by permission.)

37, 39, and 40—an area of about one-quarter of the posterior unit's total mass. The function of the tertiary zones is to integrate the excitation arriving from the different sensory systems. It is in these tertiary zones, Luria believes, that sensory input is translated into symbolic processes, and that concrete perception is translated into abstract thinking.

The Motor Unit. The motor unit, or frontal lobes, also consists of three hierarchically organized zones. The *primary zone* is the motor strip, area 4, which is the final cortical motor command area. The *secondary zone* is the premotor area, area 6, where motor programs are prepared for execution by the primary area. The most important part of this functional unit is the *tertiary zone,* comprising the prefrontal, or granular frontal, cortex: areas 9, 10, 45, 46, 47. It is here that intentions are formed. Luria describes the tertiary zone of the frontal unit as the most highly integrated area of function: "the superstructure above all other parts of the cerebral cortex."

An Example of Cortical Function

Luria conceives of the cortex as working in the following way: sensory input enters the primary sensory zones, is elaborated in the secondary zones, and is integrated in the tertiary zones of the posterior unit. For an action to be executed, activity from the posterior tertiary sensory zones is sent to the tertiary zone of the frontal unit, then to its secondary zone, and then to the primary zone, where execution is initiated.

To give a very simplified example of how Luria's model of the cortex might function, say one were walking along and came upon a soccer game. In the primary visual area the actual perception of the movements of people and the ball would occur. In the secondary zone, recognition that those activities constituted a soccer game would occur. In the tertiary zone the sounds and movements of the game would be synthesized into the realization that one team had scored and was ahead and that the game had a certain significance for league standings, etc. These cortical events could lead, in the tertiary zone of the frontal cortex, to formation of the intent to play soccer. The programs to execute this intent would be formulated in the secondary frontal zones. The actual movements to execute the programs would be initiated in the primary zone of the frontal cortex and the lower structures it controls.

Using the same example of a soccer game we can describe the effects of brain lesions. A lesion in the primary visual area would produce a blind spot in some part of the visual field, requiring the person to move his head backward and forward to see the entire game. A lesion in the secondary area might produce a perceptual deficit making the person unable to recognize the activity as a soccer game. A lesion in the tertiary area might make it impossible for an individual to recognize the significance of a soccer game in its abstract form; e.g., that one team wins, that league standings change, etc. A lesion in the prefrontal area might prevent the formation of the intention to become a soccer player and join a club, buy a uniform, get to practice on time, etc. A lesion in the secondary frontal zone might make it difficult for the individual to execute the sequences of movements required in plays. Finally, a lesion in the primary zone might make it difficult for the individual to execute the discrete movements, e.g., kicking the ball, required in the game. Again, this example is a grossly oversimplified version of Luria's model and the possible effects of brain lesions according to the model.

Properties of the Cortical Zones

Diminishing Specificity. A cortical area is said to show *specificity* if it analyzes only one mode of sensory input, e.g., visual or auditory. According to Luria, the lowest cortical zones are very specific in function (e.g., the primary visual zone analyzes only visual input), whereas the highest zones are very nonspecific (e.g., the tertiary zone analyzes all sensory information—visual, auditory, tactile, etc.). In other words, the primary zones process a specific sensory modality, recording chiefly its primary features of intensity and spatial distribution, whereas the higher zones process the more abstract features, with the highest zone synthesizing the abstract features of a number of modalities.

Progressive Lateralization. A cortical area is said to show *lateralization* if it has a function that is not shared by the homotopic area of the contralateral hemisphere. Speech, for example, is lateralized in the left hemisphere of most right-handed people. Luria postulates that there is progressive lateralization at higher levels of the cortical hierarchy. In other words, lateralization should be expected to be absent in primary visual area 17, but should be expected to be most pronounced in the tertiary areas. These expectations appear to be correct, because the most lateralized functions (speech in the left, spatial perception in the right) are functions of the tertiary zones. Lateralization does not appear to be as pronounced in the tertiary zone of the frontal cortex, if available evidence is accepted; but Luria predicts that this area, which he describes as the superstructure above all other cortical structures, should show the most pronounced lateralization.

Assessment of Luria's Model

Although Luria's model is a useful way to begin thinking about how the cortex works, it contains some pitfalls, at least two of them worthy of mention. First, whereas it is extremely difficult to make distinctions between sensory and motor functions at any level of nervous-system function, it is more so at the level of the cortex. Consider the following points. (1) Any movement we make produces changes in sensation, just as changes in sensation provoke movement. It could be argued, then, that movement is partly a sensory function, since it produces changes in sensation,

and that sensation is partly a motor function, since it provokes movement. (2) The perception of the same object in different instances can produce different responses. For example, a dog perceiving a man begins to bark and run away; then, "recognizing" the man as its master, it runs forward wagging its tail. (We can all recall similar experiences of our own in which changes in perception have produced changes in behavior.) Since, in Luria's model, perception occurs in the posterior unit, changes in perception could arguably produce changes in movement; thus, posterior cortex is partly motor and not entirely sensory. In fact, many neuropsychologists argue just that point. (3) It might be thought that the corticospinal tract from area 4 of the motor cortex is "very motor"; Sherrington in fact called cells of this tract upper motor neurons. The sensory tracts in the dorsal cord carrying fine touch and pressure directly from body sensory receptors might be thought to be "very sensory." Yet Adkins, Morse, and Towe have shown that the two are intertwined functionally: the corticospinal fibers give off collaterals to the ascending sensory fibers presumably to amplify the input on the sensory channel. When a motor tract is found to perform such functions it is difficult to argue that it is purely motor in its function. We could give many other similar examples of sensory-motor integration, but suffice it to say that the terms sensory and motor are used relatively: the former means more sensory than motor; the latter, more motor than sensory.

A second difficulty with Luria's model is that it is not clear just how much behavior is elaborated through a circuit that involves sequential processing from primary to tertiary sensory cortex and then from tertiary to primary motor cortex. As we shall see in subsequent chapters, there are ways in which information can bypass frontal cortex completely, and other ways in which it can bypass primary motor cortex. We must therefore accept that the model is simply that: a model, from which it should be accepted that there will be deviations. Should it be found in future that the deviations are excessive, the model will no doubt be dropped in favor of one more closely corresponding to the true situation.

APPLICATIONS FOR HIERARCHICAL PRINCIPLES

As we stated earlier, it was John Hughlings-Jackson who adopted (from the psychology of Herbert Spencer) the idea of a hierarchically organized nervous system and applied its principles to the analysis of the brain's function. Some 50 years later the usefulness of Hughlings-Jackson's approach was reaffirmed by Henry Head, and again by Luria still another 50 years later. The following sections describe some of the ways in which hierarchical principles have been used in the analysis of behavior. It should be noted that when levels of function, or centers, are used in these theoretical approaches to problems the structures are *theoretical constructs;* that is, a known structure is not necessarily being described.

Brain Damage

Using the concept of functional levels for clinical diagnosis, Hughlings-Jackson reasoned that two types of symptoms should follow brain damage: loss of function, or negative symptoms; and release of function, or positive symptoms. The *negative symptoms* were those behaviors that, being absent after brain damage, were presumably generated by the damaged area. The *positive symptoms* were those that emerged or became more common after brain damage, and were thus presumed to reveal the function of remaining structures. We can illustrate these types with a hypothetical

example: say a person stops eating, becomes excessively active, is unable to sleep, and is given to outbursts of rage at the slightest provocation. The negative symptoms are the absence of normal quiet behavior, sleep, and eating; the positive symptoms are hyperactivity and excessive emotional response. These symptoms, reminiscent of the behavior of diencephalic animals, suggest that the diencephalon is released from normal forebrain control—which could occur because of a tumor or an infection in the forebrain. (Symptoms not unlike these have been associated with encephalitis or infections of the forebrain.) Quite often positive symptoms take bizarre forms; yet if they are thought of as reflecting lower levels of function, situations in which they are, or once were, appropriate can be found. For example, Denny-Brown has described the reappearance of rooting and sucking reflexes in adults who have suffered some forms of frontal-lobe damage. With such damage and loss of normal frontal-lobe function, the normal smooth flow of behavior disappears, and the disappearance is labeled the negative symptom. The frontal lobe also inhibits lower levels that produce reflexive behavior so in its absence reflexive behaviors reemerge, and are labeled as positive symptoms. Although the positive symptoms appear peculiar in the adult, by the logic of this example they were once appropriate, for they supported feeding in infancy. The disappearance of both the positive and negative symptoms can be used as diagnostic indicators to gauge the rate and extent of recovery from brain damage.

Insanity

Hughlings-Jackson's concept of insanity was entirely hypothetical. When he discussed brain damage he generally had particular anatomical structures in mind—e.g., frontal cortex, basal ganglia, spinal cord—but with reference to insanity he reasoned that at the highest level, the cortex, there must be sublevels that are also arranged hierarchically. Disorders of these levels, he reasoned, would produce insanity with positive symptoms manifest as aberrant behaviors. In fact, he reasoned that the highest levels of the hierarchy would be the most complex in structure and therefore the most susceptible to dysfunction. In his own words:

> Cases of insanity should, I think, be classified and investigated on the basis supplied by the doctrine of evolution of nervous centers. We shall have enormous help in the work Spencer has done in his *Psychology*. We have already explained that we use the term dissolution as the opposite of evolution. Insanity is dissolution, beginning in the highest nervous system processes. Moreover, of course, what we call the scientific investigation of insanity is really an experimental investigation of mind; and in this regard the slightest departures from a person's standard of mental health are to be studied, and not only the cases of patients who require to be kept in asylums. (Hughlings-Jackson, 1932, p. 4)

Although Hughlings-Jackson's reasoning has been little applied to the study of mental disorders, it may become increasingly relevant since those disorders are increasingly studied as neuropsychological problems. His conceptualizations suggest that at the very least the problem in some types of mental disorders lies in the highest zones of the cortex. For example, the inappropriate chatter of hebephrenic schizophrenia resembles in some respects fluent aphasia; thus, it could be taken as a positive symptom of a dysfunction of the highest language zones.

Dreams and Illusions

Hughlings-Jackson considered both dreams and illusions to be positive symptoms revealing the activity of particular brain structures released from inhibition. Dreams, he thought, were released by the inhibition through sleep of higher levels of the brain that were normally inhibitory. Illusions, hallucinations, and similar phenomena had an analogous cause, with the difference that higher centers were inactivated by mental disease, drugs, or brain damage. His intriguing suggestion has never been put to the test. It is interesting to contrast Hughlings-Jackson's theory with Freud's wish-fulfillment theory of dreams, which was predicated on the absence of the ego (or rational part of the personality) during sleep. There are similarities in the two theories.

Development

Perhaps no area of psychology makes more use of hierarchical concepts than developmental psychology (for example, see Bronson): many aspects of the development of behavior are believed to reflect the maturation of successively higher levels of the nervous system. From a developmental perspective negative symptoms (the absence of certain behaviors) can be attributed to the immaturity of higher centers, whereas positive symptoms (e.g., play behavior, hyperactivity) can be considered as reflecting the activity of lower centers. Developmental approaches to brain function analysis have an advantage over brain transection studies insofar as they can reveal brain organization in intact individuals.

SPECIAL PROBLEMS OF CORTICAL FUNCTION

Two problems of cortical function have been repeatedly debated: mass action and equipotentiality. According to the **mass action hypothesis,** the entire brain participates in every behavior, and therefore the removal of any cortical tissue produces, with respect to any task, a deficit that is proportional to the amount of tissue removed. According to the **equipotentiality hypothesis,** each portion of a given area is able to encode or produce the behavior normally controlled by the entire area. Since these two ideas are either explicit or implicit focal points in many discussions of cortical function their status warrants brief review. As can be seen from their definition they are more sophisticated reformulations of the old problem of localization of function.

Mass Action

The idea of mass action was most recently and most clearly formulated by Karl Lashley, between 1920 and 1950. Lashley developed his work largely in reaction to strict localizationists, who adopted the view that each restricted portion of the cortex had a function, and that damage to that area produced a loss of only that function. He envisioned that mass action applied largely to complex behaviors, for he argued in 1939:

> It has been assumed that properties of experience are represented at the level of some simple nervous activity or in a single locus: sensations in the sensory areas, volitional patterns in the motor regions or particular forms of intelligent behavior in restricted coordinating centers. Such conceptions of localization are oversimplified and must be abandoned. Nothing is known of the physiological basis of conscious states, but there is some reason to believe that these states can be correlated only with the summated activity of all centers simultaneously excited. (Lashley, 1939, p. 341)

Of numerous experiments undertaken to examine the problem of mass action, none can be called conclusive. It is generally agreed, however, that Lashley's arguments are not a refutation of the idea that function is localized. It is clear that functions are localized to some extent, although to what extent and how are under debate. It is also clear that damage to many brain areas can produce deficits on a given task. The more relevant question asked today is: How is performance disrupted by a specific lesion? Language, for example, can be disrupted by damage to Wernicke's area, to Broca's area, and to the arcuate fasciculus connecting the two. But language can also be disrupted by deafness at an early age, by damage to areas of the thalamus, and by damage to the nerves controlling the face muscles. In each case careful experimentation can delineate the contribution of each of these factors.

Equipotentiality

If it is accepted that function is localized, at least in a general sense, within an area of the brain, how is that organization achieved? Many people have been impressed by the demonstration that destruction of a portion of a particular "functional" area produces a general behavioral deficit followed by either substantial recovery or only a slight general impairment of function. Usually only complete destruction of an area produces sustained impairment. From such findings it has been concluded that each portion of the tissue within a given area must have the capacity to encode or produce the behavior normally controlled by the entire area. According to Lashley's formulation, equipotentiality meant that every point within an area was able to encode a particular habit. To demonstrate this point it is worthwhile considering two of the most convincing types of supporting evidence.

If a portion of area 17 of the visual cortex is destroyed the cells in the lateral geniculate nucleus that project to that area die. The extent of remaining visual cortex can be estimated by counting the remaining lateral geniculate cells. Lashley trained rats on a visual discrimination task and then removed various portions of area 17. The rats were able to retain the habit with as few as one-fiftieth of the total number of cells in their visual system (682 of about 34,100). Humphrey also reported that a monkey with a small remnant of visual cortex restricted to the left hemisphere was able to localize objects in space, reach out and touch objects in a precise fashion, and avoid bumping into obstacles placed in natural and artificial settings. Similarly, we have examined a person with extensive bilateral damage to the visual cortex who was still able to process visual information with a visual field a couple of centimeters in diameter. This is not to argue that large visual area lesions do not produce visual distortions: they do. But the point is that a small portion of visual cortex can process a substantial amount of visual information. This suggests that there is some degree of equipotentiality within the primary visual area.

In experiments designed to examine recovery in the motor cortex, Glees and Cole defined the thumb area of the motor cortex in monkeys by electrical stimulation. They then removed this area and followed the course of recovery of thumb movements from the flaccid paralysis caused by the lesion. After complete recovery the brain was reexposed, and they found that the borders of the lesion now produced thumb movements whereas they had not during the first stimulation session. This area was then removed, flaccid paralysis occurred, followed again by recovery. These findings are consistent with an enormous amount of clinical evidence that the cortex does have the capacity to reorganize and compensate for damage.

What accounts for this capacity? Lashley suggested that a pattern of excitation is reduplicated throughout an entire functional area, enabling any portion of the area to sustain the response. Recently, Pribram has reformulated Lashley's idea with an imaginative hypothesis.

He suggests that the brain might operate on holographic principles, producing interference patterns similar to those formed in holographic photography. A hologram, which is formed by the interference patterns of light reflected from an object, has two properties that make it a relevant equipotentiality model. First, the image is distributed across the negative in such a way that the negative can be divided into two or many pieces, each of which contains the entire image. Second, each negative can contain many different superimposed pictures that can be recalled when illuminated with varying wavelengths of light. Holograms can be stored in solids, and each bit of information can be stored throughout the solid and still be individually retrievable. In experimental work, some 10 billion bits of information have been stored holographically in a cubic centimeter, and it has been estimated that it is feasible for holographic processes to handle the phenomenal amount of information stored by a human brain in a lifetime.

Another explanation of equipotentiality is that there are large overlapping fields of neurons engaged in each function. Under normal conditions those with the most direct control of a behavior are functional and hold the others under inhibition. If the more prepotent areas are damaged, neurons with lower thresholds are released from inhibition and become functional, thus restoring the behavior. One of several other ideas is that neurons sprout when their terminals are damaged and innervate surrounding intact areas to produce a measure of recovery. At the present time a combination of these two processes is viewed as being adequate to explain both recovery and the latency required for recovery. Thus, it would be appropriate to say that a more restricted concept of overlapping field of control is considered more adequate today than the general equipotentiality theory of Lashley.

REFERENCES

Adkins, R. J., R. W. Morse, and A. L. Towe. Control of somatosensory input by cerebral cortex. *Science, 153* (1966), 1020–1022.

Bandler, R. J., C. C. Chi, and J. P. Flynn. Biting attack elicited by stimulation of the ventral midbrain tegmentum of cats. *Science, 177* (1972), 361–366.

Bard, P. A diencephalic mechanism for the expression of rage, with special reference to the sympathetic nervous system. *American Journal of Physiology, 84* (1928), 490–515.

Bard, P., and M. B. Macht. The behavior of chronically decerebrate cats. In G. E. W. Wolstenholm and C. M. O'Connor, eds. *Ciba Foundation Symposium on Neurological Basis of Behavior.* London: J. and A. Churchill, 1958.

Barrett, R., H. H. Merritt, and A. Wolf. Depression of consciousness as a result of cerebral lesions. *Research Publications of the Association for Research in Nervous and Mental Disease, 45* (1967), 241–276.

Bauer, J. H., and R. M. Cooper. Effects of posterior cortical lesions on performance on a brightness discrimination task. *Journal of Comparative and Physiological Psychology, 58* (1964), 84–92.

Bazett, H. C., and W. G. Penfield. A study of the Sherrington decerebrate animal in the chronic as well as the acute condition. *Brain, 45* (1922), 185–265.

Beach, F. A. Effects of cortical lesions upon the copulatory behavior of male rats. *Journal of Comparative Psychology, 29* (1940), 193–245.

Bernston, G. G., and D. J. Micco. Organization of brainstem behavioral systems. *Brain Research Bulletin, 1* (1976), 471–483.

Bignall, K. E., and L. Schramm. Behavior of chronically decerebrate kittens. *Experimental Neurology, 42* (1974), 519–531.

Bland, B. H., and C. H. Vanderwolf. Diencephalic and hippocampal mechanisms of motor activity in the rat: effects of posterior hypothalamic stimulation on behavior and hippocampal slow wave activity. *Brain Research, 43* (1972), 67–88.

Bland, B. H., and C. H. Vanderwolf. Electrical stimulation of the hippocampal formation: behavioral and bioelectrical effects. *Brain Research, 43* (1972), 89–106.

Brackbill, Y. The role of the cortex in orienting: orienting reflex in an encephalic human infant. *Developmental Psychology, 5* (1971), 195–201.

Brazier, M. B. A. The historical development of neurophysiology. In J. Field, H. W. Magoun, and V. E. Hall, eds. *Handbook of Physiology,* Vol. 1. Washington, D.C.: American Physiological Society, 1959.

Bronson, G. The hierarchical organization of the central nervous system: implications for learning processes and critical periods in early development. *Behavioral Science, 10* (1965), 7–25.

Brooks, D. M. The role of the cerebral cortex and of various sense organs in the excitation and execution of mating activity in the rabbit. *American Journal of Physiology, 120* (1973), 544–553.

Buchholz, D. Spontaneous and centrally induced behaviors in normal and thalamic opossums. *Journal of Comparative and Physiological Psychology, 90* (1976), 898–908.

Cannon, W. B., and S. W. Britton. Pseudoaffective medulliadrenal secretion. *American Journal of Physiology, 72* (1924), 283–294.

Denny-Brown, D. The nature of apraxia. *Journal of Nervous and Mental Diseases, 126* (1958), 9–32.

Flynn, J., H. Venegas, W. Foote, and S. Edwards. Neural mechanisms involved in a cat's attack on a rat. In R. E. Whalen, R. F. Thompson, M. Verzeano, and N. M. Weinberger, eds. *The Neural Control of Behavior.* New York: Academic Press, 1970.

Freud, S. *The Standard Edition of the Complete Psychological Works of Sigmund Freud.* J. Stachey and A. Freud, eds. London: Hogarth Press, 1950.

Gamper, E. In J. Field, H. W. Magoun, and V. E. Hall, eds. *Handbook of Physiology,* Vol. 2. Washington, D.C.: American Physiological Society, 1959.

Glees, P., and J. Cole. Recovery of skilled motor functions after small repeated lesions of motor cortex in macaque. *Journal of Neurophysiology, 13* (1950), 137–148.

Goltz, F. On the functions of the hemispheres. In G. von Bonin, ed. *The Cerebral Cortex,* Springfield, Ill.: Charles C Thomas, 1960.

Goodale, M., and R. M. Cooper. Cues utilized by normal and posterior neodecorticate rats in the Yerkes brightness discrimination task. *Psychonomic Science, 3* (1965), 513–514.

Grill, H. J., and R. Norgren. Chronically decerebrate rats demonstrate satiation but not baitshyness. *Science, 201* (1978), 267–269.

Grill, H. J., and R. Norgren. Neurological tests and behavioral deficits in chronic thalamic and chronic decerebrate rats. *Brain Research, 143* (1978), 299–312.

Grillner, S. Locomotion in the spinal cat. In R. B. Stein, ed. *Control of Posture and Locomotion.* New York: Plenum Press, 1973.

Hughlings-Jackson, J. Remarks on dissolution of the nervous system as exemplified by certain post-epileptic conditions. In J. Taylor, ed. *Selected Writings of John Hughlings-Jackson,* Vol. 2. London: Hodder and Stoughton, Ltd., 1932.

Humphrey, N. K. Vision in a monkey without striate cortex: a case study. *Perception, 3* (1974), 241–255.

Jung, R., and R. Hassler. The extrapyramidal motor system. In J. Field, H. W. Magoun, and V. E. Hall, eds. *Handbook of Physiology,* Vol. 2. Washington, D.C.: American Physiological Society, 1959.

Klüver, H. Functional significance of the geniculo-striate system. In H. Klüver, ed. *Visual Mechanisms.* Lancaster, Pa.: Cattrell, 1942.

Kolb, B., and I. Q. Whishaw. The behavior of the neonatally decorticated rat. In preparation.

Kuhn, R. A. Functional capacity of the isolated human spinal cord. *Brain, 73* (1950), 1–51.

Lashley, K. S. The mechanisms of vision. XVI. The functioning of small remnants of the visual cortex. *Journal of Comparative Neurology, 70* (1939), 45–67.

Lashley, K. S. Functional determinants of cerebral localization. In F. A. Beach, D. O. Hebb, C. T. Morgan, and H. W. Nissen, eds. *The Neuropsychology of Lashley.* New York: McGraw-Hill Book Co., 1960.

Liddell, E. G. T., and C. S. Sherrington. Reflexes in response to stress (mystatic reflexes). *Proceedings of the Royal Society of London, 96* (1924), 212–249.

Luciani, L. *Human Physiology,* London: Macmillan and Co., Ltd., 1915.

Luria, A. R. *The Working Brain.* Harmondsworth: Penguin, 1973.

Pinel, J. P. J., and D. Treit. Burying as a defensive response in rats. *Journal of Comparative and Physiological Psychology, 92* (1978), 708–712.

Pribram, K. H. *Languages of the Brain.* Englewood Cliffs, N.J.: Prentice-Hall, 1971.

Robinson, T. E. Electrical stimulation of the brain stem in freely moving rats: I. Effects on behavior. *Physiology and Behavior, 21* (1978), 223–231.

Satinoff, E. Neural organization and evolution of thermal regulation in mammals. *Science, 201* (1978), 16–22.

Schallert, T., I. Q. Whishaw, M. DeRyck, and P. Teitelbaum. The postures of catecholamine-depletion catalepsy: their possible adaptive value in thermoregulation. *Physiology and Behavior, 21* (1978), 817–820.

Sherrington, C. S. *The Integrative Action of the Nervous System.* New Haven: Yale University Press, 1906.

Sorenson, C. A., and G. D. Ellison. Striatal organization of feeding behavior in the decorticate rat. *Experimental Neurology, 29* (1970), 162–174.

Vanderwolf, C. H. Hippocampal electrical activity and voluntary movement in the rat. *Electroencephalography and Clinical Neurophysiology, 26* (1969), 407–418.

Vanderwolf, C. H., B. Kolb, and R. K. Cooley. Behavior of the rat after removal of the neocortex and hippocampal formation. *Journal of Comparative and Physiological Psychology, 92* (1978), 156–175.

Vanderwolf, C. H., R. Kramis, L. A. Gillespie, and B. H. Bland. Hippocampal rhythmical slow activity and neocortical low voltage fast activity: relations to behavior. In K. H. Pribram and R. L. Isaacson, eds. *The Hippocampus: A Comprehensive Treatise.* New York: Plenum Press, 1975.

Villablanca, J. R., C. E. Olmstead, and I. de Andrés. Effects of caudate nuclei or frontal cortical ablations in kittens: responsiveness to auditory stimuli and comparisons with adult-operated littermates. *Experimental Neurology, 61* (1978), 635–649.

Whishaw, I. Q., T. Schallert, and B. Kolb. Feeding, sensorimotor, and motor behavior in the deneocorticate rat. Unpublished manuscript.

Woods, J. W. Behavior of chronic decerebrate rats. *Journal of Neurophysiology, 27* (1964), 634–644.

9

CEREBRAL ASYMMETRY

It is over 100 years since Dax and Broca discovered that damage to the left hemisphere produced an inability to talk whereas damage to the right hemisphere did not affect speech production. Since then it has been generally accepted that the left hemisphere plays a special role in language that is not shared by the right hemisphere. But language is not the only special function of the left hemisphere; at the beginning of this century Leipmann compared the movements of patients with lesions of either the left or the right hemisphere, and demonstrated that the left hemisphere has a role in controlling movement that is not shared by the right. The special functions of the right hemisphere remained a mystery until comparatively recently, when the work of Zangwill, Hécaen, Milner, and others showed that it was more involved than the left in the analysis of the visuospatial dimensions of the world.

Although these findings superficially appear to simplify the problem of understanding lateralization, the problem is complicated by the following three variables:

1. Laterality of function can be affected by environmental factors as well as genetically determined factors such as gender and handedness; the cerebral organization of some left-handers and females appears to have less functional asymmetry than males.

2. Laterality is relative and not absolute, for both hemispheres play a role in nearly every behavior; thus, although the left hemisphere is especially important for the production of language, the right hemisphere also has some language capabilities.

3. Whereas a functionally asymmetrical brain was once believed to be a uniquely human characteristic—one that suggested a straightforward relationship between asymmetry and language—this idea has proven to be naive and incorrect. There is evidence that certain songbirds, rats, cats, monkeys, and apes have a functionally, and possibly anatomically, asymmetrical brain.

This chapter addresses some of the more general questions of cerebral asymmetry. The answers to most such questions are as yet incomplete, but our tentative answers take into account information about the brain's anatomical and functional asymmetry, the relation of hand preference and gender to asymmetry, the nature of lateralized functions, and finally the incidence of asymmetry in nonhumans.

ANATOMICAL ASYMMETRY IN THE HUMAN BRAIN

According to Hughlings-Jackson, Gratiolet first observed in the 1860s that the convolutions on the left hemisphere matured more rapidly than those on the right. Anatomical asymmetry was described again in 1878 by Heschl, around 1890 by Eberstaller, and later by Cunningham, but these observations were largely ignored until 1968, when Geschwind and Levitsky described significant anatomical asymmetry in a large series of human brains. They reported that the **planum temporale,** which is the cortical area just posterior to the auditory cortex (Heschl's gyrus) within the **Sylvian fissure,** was larger on the left in 65 percent of the brains. On the average, the planum temporale on the left was nearly 1 cm longer than on the right. (See Figure 9-1.) This report has generated renewed interest in anatomical asymmetries in humans and other animals, and has put to rest the notion that the two hemispheres are structurally identical.

Several anatomical differences between the two hemispheres of the brain have now been reported.

1. A number of studies have replicated the Geschwind and Levitsky finding, although the percentage of cases having a larger planum temporale on the left varies from 65 to 90 percent in different samples. Wada has even reported this difference to be significant at about 20 weeks gestational age.

2. There are usually two Heschl's gyri on the right and only one on the left, an asymmetry complementary to the larger planum temporale on the left (see Figure 9-1). We shall see that the anatomical asymmetry of the planum temporale and Heschl's gyrus may provide an anatomical basis for the functional dissociation of the temporal lobes in language and musical functions respectively.

3. The slope of the Sylvian fissure is different in the two sides of the brain, being gentler on the left than on the right (see Figure 9-1). This difference can be seen by gross inspection of the brain or by angiograms, since the middle cerebral artery follows the course of the Sylvian fissure. The region of the temporal-parietal cortex lying ventral to the Sylvian fissure thus appears larger on the right. We shall see that this enlarged region has a specialized role in integrating the spatial characteristics of sensory stimuli.

4. The **frontal operculum** (Broca's area) is significantly larger (by about one-third) on the right than on the left. The larger size on the right is puzzling, since to date no specific function has been ascribed to the larger frontal operculum on the right, whereas the importance of Broca's area on the left for language has been known for over 100 years.

5. Anatomical asymmetry is significantly greater in males than in females, as is functional asymmetry, as we see later in the chapter.

6. The distribution of noradrenergic neurons is strongly lateralized in the thalamus, being more heavily concentrated in the pulvinar of the left hemisphere and the ventrallateral thalamus of the right hemisphere. Since the pulvinar on the left has a significant role in language, this neurochemical asymmetry may prove significant. The discovery of this neurochemical asymmetry may be especially consequential because it is likely to lead to

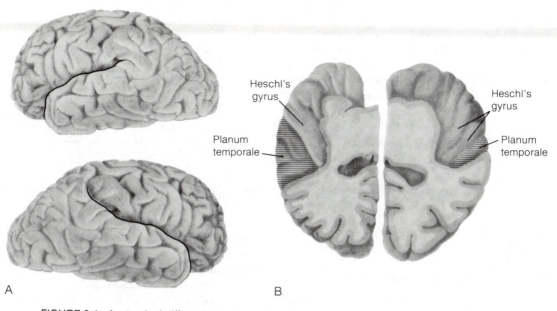

FIGURE 9-1. Anatomical differences between the two hemispheres are visible in temporal lobes. A. The Sylvian fissure on the left (top) has a gentler slope than the fissure on the right. B. A knife has been moved along the Sylvian fissure of each hemisphere and through the brain, cutting away the top portion. The planum temporale (darkened area) is larger on the left than on the right. (B after Geschwind, 1972.)

increased study of asymmetry in the microstructure of the hemispheres, particularly with respect to the distribution of neurochemicals.

7. The right hemisphere extends further anteriorly than the left, and the left hemisphere extends further posteriorly than the right, and the occipital horns of the lateral ventricles are five times more likely to be longer on the right than on the left. The implications of these observations are uncertain since the mass of the two hemispheres is virtually identical.

Because these anatomical asymmetries of the left hemisphere center primarily on the language areas, it is tempting to speculate that they evolved to subserve the production of language. Moreover, the presence of these asymmetries in preterm infants might be taken as support for the proposition that hu-

mans have an innate predisposition for language. It should be noted, however, that because the two hemispheres of the brain have equivalent weight, enlarged areas on one side must be balanced by smaller areas elsewhere on the same side or larger areas in other lobes on the contralateral hemisphere. The possibilities of anatomical asymmetries elsewhere have been neglected to date, largely because language and language areas have been of focal interest in neuropsychology.

DEMONSTRATIONS OF FUNCTIONAL ASYMMETRY

In the past two decades considerable attention has been focused on how the two hemispheres are specialized; accordingly information from traditional sources as well as from newly devised techniques has been used in the analysis in this chapter. Information about asymmetry has been collected from neurological patients and from normal subjects. Neurological patients included (1) those with lesions; (2) those who were subjected to brain stimulation during surgery; (3) and those who received unilateral hemisphere anesthetization with intracarotid injections of sodium Amytal. Another source of information was regional blood flow analysis. Normal subjects were studied by (1) selective presentation of information to the two hemispheres, and by (2) electrical recording from the two hemispheres.

Studies of Neurological Patients

Lesions. The oldest method of studying hemispheric specialization has been to study the effects of circumscribed unilateral lesions that occur as a result of strokes, surgery, etc., and to infer the function of the area from behavioral deficits. However, for it to be concluded that the area has a special or lateralized function it is also necessary to show that lesions in other areas of the brain do not produce a similar deficit. The method that has proved strongest for demonstrating lateralization of function is one that Teuber calls **double dissociation,** an inferential technique premised on the following observations. It has been consistently demonstrated that lesions in the left hemisphere of right-handed patients can produce deficits in language functions (speech, writing, and reading) that do not follow lesions of the right hemisphere. Thus, the functions of the two hemispheres can be said to be dissociated. On the other hand, anecdotal and experimental evidence suggests that performance of spatial tasks, singing, playing musical instruments, and discriminating tonal patterns, is more disrupted by right-hemisphere than by left-hemisphere lesions. Since right-

TABLE 9-1

Hypothetical example of
double dissociation behavioral test

		Reading	Writing
Neocortical lesion site	102	Impaired	Normal
	107	Normal	Impaired

hemisphere lesions disturb tasks not disrupted by left-hemisphere lesions, *and vice versa,* the two hemispheres can be said to be doubly dissociated. A similar logic is used for localizing functions within a hemisphere. That is, behavioral tests that are especially sensitive to damage to a specific locus and not to others can be used to localize functions within a hemisphere, as illustrated in Table 9-1. Two hypothetical neocortical regions, 102 and 107, are doubly dissociated on tests of reading and writing: Damage to area 102 disturbs reading, whereas damage to area 107 impairs writing. In principle, this logic can be extended to functionally dissociate additional areas concurrently, by triple dissociation, quadruple dissociation, and so on.

A second type of lesion, called **commissurotomy,** has provided a way of examining the functions of the two hemispheres when they are not mutually interacting. In some epileptic seizures the abnormal discharges begin in one hemisphere and spread to the other across the connecting fibers of the corpus callosum. To prevent the spread of the seizure when medication has failed to impose control, the corpus callosum has been cut, using a procedure called commissurotomy. Figure 9-2 shows the effect of this section on the normal function of the brain. After sectioning, the two hemispheres are independent; each receives sensory input from all sensory systems, and each can control the muscles of

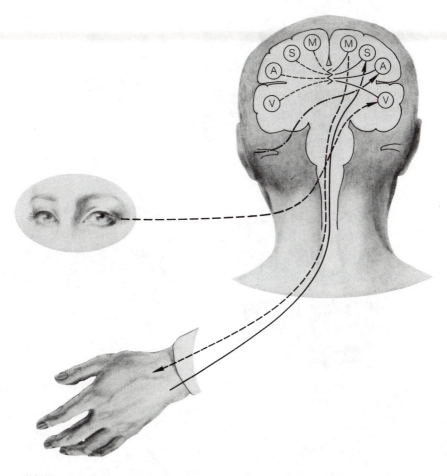

FIGURE 9-2. The effect of commissurotomy on connections between the hemispheres and to the sensory and motor systems. Note that although the connections
between the visual (V), auditory (A), somatosensory (S), and motor (M) cortical
regions and the receptors and effectors are unaffected, the connections between
homotopic points in the two hemispheres are severed. Each hemisphere therefore
functions independently of the other and without access to its sensations,
thoughts, or actions.

the body, but the two hemispheres can no
longer communicate with each other. Because
the functions in these separate cortices or
"split brains" are thus isolated, sensory information can be presented to one hemisphere,
and the hemisphere's function studied, without the other hemisphere having access to the
information.

From the numerous studies performed on
split-brain patients it is now widely recognized
that when the left hemisphere has access to
information it can initiate speech and thus
communicate about the information. The right
hemisphere apparently has reasonably good
recognition abilities, but is unable to initiate
speech because it lacks access to speech mech-

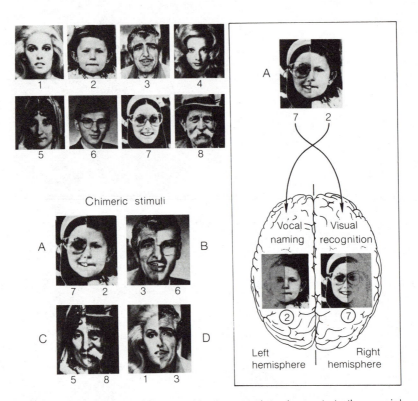

FIGURE 9-3. Composite faces used by Levy et al. to demonstrate the special role of the right hemisphere in facial recognition. Commissurotomy patients were shown the chimeric stimuli (composite pictures) A–D. When asked to choose the face they had seen from among the array of original pictures, 1–8, the patients chose the face that was in the left visual field, as the right-hand side of the figure illustrates. (From J. Levy, C. Trevarthen, and R. W. Sperry. Perception of bilateral chimeric figures following hemispheric deconnection. *Brain, 95* [1972], 61–78. Reprinted by permission of Oxford University Press, Oxford.)

anisms of the left hemisphere. On the other hand, the right hemisphere has a special role in other functions such as facial recognition, which is not shared by the left hemisphere. Levy made a rather good demonstration of this by using the *chimeric figures test,* which consists of faces and other patterns that have been split down the center and recombined (see Figure 9-3). When the recombined faces were presented selectively to each hemisphere the patients appeared unaware of the gross discor-

dance between the two sides of the pictures. When asked to pick out the picture they had seen they chose the face seen in the left visual field and thus by their right hemisphere, demonstrating that the right hemisphere has a special role in the recognition of faces. We return to the split-brain patient in Chapter 20.

Brain Stimulation. A practical treatment of intractable focal epileptic seizures has been found to be removal of the region of the cortex where the abnormal discharge originates. Since this is an elective therapeutic surgery it can be planned for, and considerable care can be taken to ensure that areas of the cortex that are critical for the control of speech and movement are not damaged. To identify these areas the surgeon stimulates the exposed cortex and records the responses of the conscious patient. Cerebral asymmetry has been demonstrated with this technique, because stimulation of the left hemisphere can block the ability to speak whereas seldom does stimulation of the right hemisphere do so. The exception occurs when the motor or somatosensory representation of the face in the right hemisphere is stimulated, for then facial movements necessary to talk are blocked. Stimulation results have revealed other asymmetries: stimulation of the right temporal lobe produces illusions and hallucinations more frequently than stimulation of the left temporal lobe, which suggests that the right hemisphere has perceptual functions not shared by the left hemisphere.

Carotid Sodium Amytal. Although language is usually located in the left hemisphere, a small percentage of people, most of them left-handed, have language represented in the right hemisphere. In the event of elective surgery for the treatment of disorders such as epilepsy, avoiding inadvertent damage to the speech zones requires that the surgeon be certain of their location. To achieve certainty in doubtful cases Wada pioneered a technique of injecting sodium Amytal into the carotid artery to produce a brief period of anesthesia of the ipsilateral hemisphere. This procedure results in an unequivocal localization of speech, for injection into the speech hemisphere results in arrest of speech lasting up to several minutes, and as speech returns it is characterized by aphasic errors. Injection into the nonspeaking hemisphere may produce no, or only brief, speech arrest. Further injection

into the right hemisphere is reported to affect singing, which becomes monotone, devoid of correct pitch rendering. The carotid Amytal procedure has the advantage that each hemisphere can be studied separately in the functional absence of the other, anesthetized one. Since the period of anesthesia lasts several minutes it is possible to study a variety of functions including memory, movement, etc., to determine the capabilities of one hemisphere in the absence of the anesthetized one.

Regional Blood Flow. It has been assumed that the blood flow in the neocortex increases in areas where neurons increase their activity, presumably because neurons in the area have a more active metabolism. For example, during speech there should be more blood flow in speech zones because these areas are more active than other areas. A novel technique has been developed to detect such variations in blood flow. A solution containing a substance called xenon$_{133}$, which accumulates in areas of increased blood flow, is injected into an artery while special detectors on the skull monitor its concentration. If a subject is asked to engage in a task such as speaking, an increase in xenon$_{133}$ concentration is found over the central zones of the left hemisphere, suggesting their involvement in speech. The technique can similarly be used to look for areas of the brain active in controlling other behaviors (see Figure 9-4).

Studies of Normal Subjects

The study of neurological patients, then, often demonstrates an absolute functional difference between the hemispheres on some behaviors, particularly those related to language. Although subjects with an intact nervous system do not show this absolute difference, they do show a relative functional difference if studied

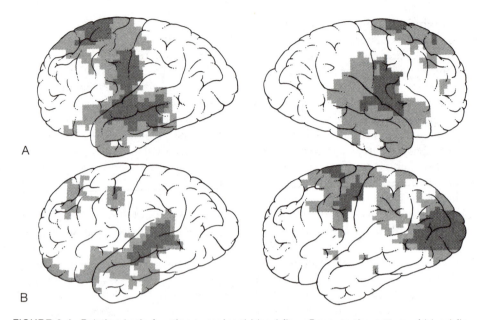

FIGURE 9-4. Relating brain function to regional blood flow. Because the pattern of blood flow varies with the behavioral task the relative importance of different areas in different functions can be inferred: light shading indicates the average level of blood flow; dark shading indicates higher-than-average blood flow; the absence of shading indicates lower-than-average blood flow. A. Speaking activates the mouth-tongue-larynx of the motor and somatosensory cortex, the supplementary motor area, and the auditory cortex. These images, averaged from nine different subjects, show differences in the activity of the left and right hemispheres: in the left hemisphere the mouth area is more active and the auditory cortex, including part of area 22, is considerably more active. B. Sensory perception changes the pattern of blood flow in the cortex, revealing the localization of areas that mediate the processing of sensory information. During the study at the right the subject followed a moving object with his eyes, resulting in high activity in the visual cortex and frontal eye fields. During the study at the left the same subject listened to spoken words, resulting in increased activity localized to the auditory cortex. Note that the position of the Sylvian and central fissures is approximate; the actual position could be determined only by opening the skull. The squared shapes are an artifact of the recording and averaging procedure, and thus do not accurately indicate the shapes of areas in the brain. (Simplified from Lassen, Ingvar, and Skinhøj, 1978.)

by carefully—often ingeniously—designed experiments.

Tachistoscopic Presentation. Figure 9-5 shows the relation between the visual field and its field of projection in the visual cortex. It can be seen that sensory events in the left visual field are projected to the right visual cortex. This anatomical organization can be used to present information to each visual field in-

dependently by using a special instrument, the **tachistoscope.** In tachistoscopic experiments subjects are asked to fixate on a center point marked by a dot or cross. An image is then flashed in one visual field for about 50 milliseconds—a short enough time to allow the image to be processed before the eyes can shift from the fixation point. Another variation of this test is to present images simultaneously in each visual field and then compare the accuracy with which information from the two visual fields is processed. Tachistoscopic experiments have shown that verbal material is processed more accurately when presented to the right visual field than when presented to the left, presumably because right-field images have more direct access to the left language hemisphere. On the other hand, nonlanguage images are processed more accurately when presented in the left visual field than when presented to the right field, presumably because the right hemisphere processes nonverbal material.

Dichotic Listening. The auditory system is not completely crossed as the visual system is: both hemispheres receive projections from each ear. However, the connections from the contralateral ear do appear to have preferred access to the hemisphere; thus, sounds projected to the right ear are primarily processed by the left hemisphere, as shown in Figure 9-6. Kimura has demonstrated that when words or musical notes are simultaneously presented to the two ears through stereophonic earphones, verbal material is more easily analyzed if presented through the right ear, so that it gets to the left hemisphere, whereas musical material is more easily analyzed if presented to the left ear, so that it gets to the right hemisphere. From this difference it has been inferred that the left hemisphere specializes in language analysis and the right hemisphere in music analysis.

Sensory-Motor Tests. The somatosensory system of fine touch and pressure, deep muscle and joint senses, and pain and temperature, as well as the motor system, are so arranged that sensations and movements of the right half of the body are controlled by the left half of the brain (see Figure 9-7). These systems can be studied by blindfolding subjects and requiring them to perform various tasks,

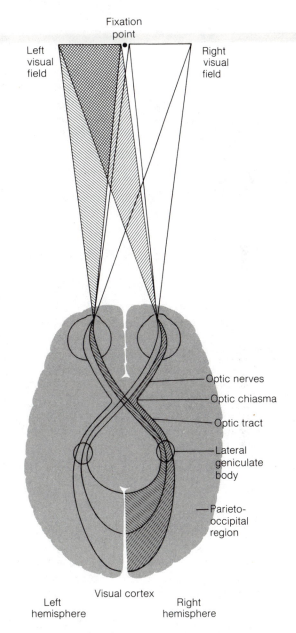

FIGURE 9-5. Visual pathways are crossed; thus, visual fields (and not eyes) are represented in each hemisphere. All of the field left of the fixation point (shaded region) is represented in the right visual cortex, and all of the field right of the fixation point is represented in the left visual cortex.

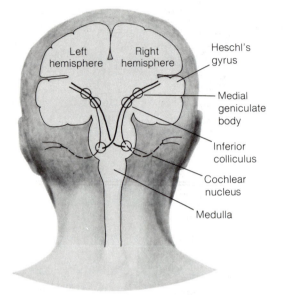

FIGURE 9-6. Auditory pathways from the ears to the cerebral auditory receiving areas in the right and left hemispheres are partially crossed. Although each hemisphere can receive input from both ears, the neural connections from one ear to the hemisphere on the opposite side are stronger than those to the hemisphere on the same side. When ipsilateral (same-side) and contralateral (opposite-side) inputs compete in the auditory neural system, it is thought that the stronger contralateral input inhibits or occludes the ipsilateral signals. (After Kimura, 1973.)

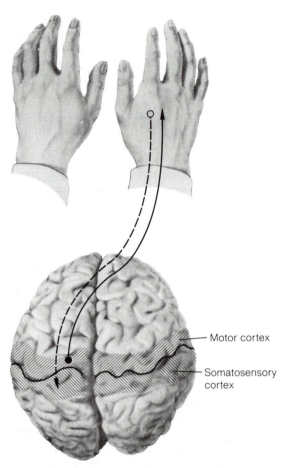

FIGURE 9-7. Somatosensory and motor pathways are almost wholly crossed; each hand is served primarily by the cerebral hemisphere on the opposite side.

such as reading Braille, with each hand separately. Differences in efficiency of performance by the two hands can be taken to imply functional asymmetry in the cerebral organization of the systems. For one type of experiment, Witelson devised a tactual version of the dichotic technique known as dichhaptic testing. She presented a different, unfamiliar, complex shape simultaneously to each hand out of sight. The subjects felt the objects and then visually identified the objects palpated from an array of objects. The results showed a left-hand—hence right-hemisphere—superiority in recognition of objects.

In a second line of studies tactile perception of Braille characters has been examined. Rudel et al. found that both blind and sighted subjects read Braille more rapidly with the left hand. Some children are actually fluent readers with the left hand but totally unable to read with the right. Since Braille patterns are spatial configurations of dots, this observation is congruent with the proposal that the right hemisphere has a role in processing spatial information not shared by the left hemisphere.

An interesting experiment by Kimura has confirmed Leipmann's early suggestion that the left hemisphere has a role in the control of complex movements that is not shared by the right hemisphere. It is a common observation that people often gesture when talking. By videotaping subjects while talking or humming Kimura was able to show that right-handed people tend to gesture with their right hands when talking but are equally likely to scratch, rub their nose, or touch their body with either hand. Left-handed subjects with speech represented in the right hemisphere gesticulated with their left hand, reflecting right-hemisphere involvement. The observed gesturing with the limb contralateral to the speaking hemisphere is interpreted to indicate a relationship between speech and certain manual activities. Further work has indicated that lesions of the left hemisphere result in apraxia (the inability to produce a series of skilled movements of either hand, such as copying a sequence of different hand or arm postures), whereas analogous right-hemisphere lesions do not have this effect.

A variety of laboratories have recently examined the well-known phenomenon that most people manifest: the difficulty in doing two complex tasks at the same time. If subjects are asked to balance a dowel on their left or right index fingers while talking, they are able to maintain the balance much longer with the left hand than with the right. Similar results are also reported for other complex tasks such as tapping a sequence of movements with the fingers. This result has been interpreted as support for the notion that there is an overlap of cerebral mechanisms of speaking and the sequencing of certain manual tasks in the left hemisphere.

Another fascinating observation of lateralization of movement control is that concentration on a difficult problem frequently causes the eyes, and often the head, to turn laterally to the left or right. Careful study indicates that right-handed people usually turn head and eyes to the right when solving verbal problems, but look up and to the left when solving numerical and spatial problems. This phenomenon, labeled lateral eye gaze, has been interpreted as resulting from predominant activation of the hemisphere most vigorously involved in processing the material of the task. In other words, people gaze right while doing a verbal problem because the activation of the left hemisphere "spills over," affecting motor activation toward the right side. The converse is true of spatial or numerical tasks. This phenomenon, while slow in gaining credibility among many neuropsychologists, is interesting and provocative.

Experiments demonstrating hemispheric asymmetry show that in normal subjects anatomical asymmetry is relative rather than absolute. For example, tachistoscopic work shows that the right visual field (left hemisphere) has a selective advantage for the perception of visually presented verbal material such as words (see Table 9-2). However, some words presented to the left visual field are perceived even though this field projects to the right, nonverbal, hemisphere. These data are not to be interpreted as showing evidence for right-hemisphere linguistic abilities. The corpus callosum, which joins the visual areas of the two hemispheres, is able to transfer the information from the right, nonverbal, hemisphere to the visual area in the left, verbal, hemisphere, as Figure 9-8 shows. The most likely reason for the observed asymmetry is that this route into the left hemisphere is inefficient, and information is lost. One would predict that if the corpus callosum, the connection between the hemispheres, were severed, the difference between the hemispheres would be absolute. This condition does indeed occur in the split-brain patient (see Chapter 20).

TABLE 9-2

Summary of relative asymmetry of function in studies of normal subjects

	Task	Left-hemisphere dominance[a]	Right-hemisphere dominance
Visual (tachistoscope)	Letters	1.2	1.0
	Words	1.5	1.0
	Two-dimensional point localization	1.0	1.2
	Dot and form enumeration	1.0	1.2
	Matching of slanted lines	1.0	1.1
	Stereoscopic depth perception	1.0	1.3
Auditory (dichotic listening)	Words	1.9	1.0
	Nonsense syllables	1.7	1.0
	Backward speech	1.7	1.0
	Melodic pattern	1.0	1.2
	Nonspeech sounds (cough, laugh, etc.)	1.0	1.1
Manual	Skilled movements	1.0	1.0
	Free movements during speech	3.1	1.0
	Tactual dot (Braille)		Significantly higher

[a] Numbers indicate the ratio of hemisphere dominance for each task.
Adapted from Kimura, 1973.

Electrical Recording. The electrical activity of the brain of normal subjects can be recorded (as noted in previous chapters) by both the EEG and the average evoked potential (AEP). Since the two hemispheres function differently, and since the EEG and AEP reflect the function of neurons, it follows logically that there ought to be asymmetry in the EEGs and AEPs recorded from the two hemispheres. Indeed, over the last 10 years numerous experiments have attempted to demonstrate this asymmetry, and there have been promising results, for on some behavioral tasks EEGs and AEPs do appear to be asymmetrical over the two hemispheres. The results are far from conclusive, however. In a recent review, Donchin et al. conclude that the literature is fraught with serious methodological inadequacies related to recording techniques, behavioral tasks, data analysis, and the like.

These problems are not insurmountable, however, and we concur with Donchin and his colleagues that although interhemispheric differences in EEG and AEP recordings are apt to be minute, the techniques are promising as a means of investigating hemispheric lateralization.

WHAT IS LATERALIZED?

It is tempting to conclude that the functional asymmetries described so far represent a larger fundamental difference in the basic cognitive processes of the left and right hemispheres. However, before considering this issue we will summarize the data, since any theoretical statements are best considered in light of the available information.

Table 9-3 summarizes the major data and

illustrates the range of functions lateralized principally in the left and right hemispheres respectively. In right-handed people the left hemisphere has a role in language and in controlling complex voluntary movement that is not shared by the right hemisphere, whereas the right hemisphere has a role in the control of visuospatial abilities not shared by the left hemisphere.

Theoretical Arguments

There have been three principal arguments regarding the fundamental difference between the hemispheres. The first clear proposal was made by Semmes in 1968. On the basis of her previous studies of World War II veterans suffering from penetrating brain injuries she concluded that the left hemisphere functioned as a collection of focalized regions, whereas the right hemisphere functioned more diffusely, in a manner consistent with Lashley's notions of mass action and equipotentiality. Her logic was as follows: she had noticed that small lesions of the left hemisphere produced a wide variety of specific deficits (e.g., impaired spelling, reading, etc.), the precise deficit depending upon the locus of the lesion; similar-sized lesions within the right hemisphere were frequently without obvious effect. In contrast, large lesions of *either* hemisphere produced a large number of deficits. To account for this differential effect Semmes argued that a person with a small lesion of the right hemisphere exhibits no deficits because specific functions are not localized in discrete regions in the right hemisphere, the functions being diffusely represented. A large lesion of the right hemisphere produces many more deficits than would be predicted from the total of smaller lesions because an entire functional field is removed—a proposition that is consistent with Lashley's idea of mass action. Large lesions of the left hemisphere produce many deficits

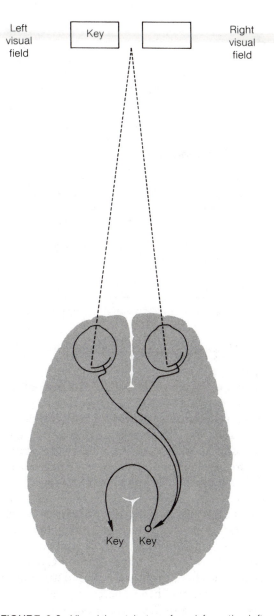

FIGURE 9-8. Visual input is transferred from the left visual field to the left visual cortex via the corpus callosum. Cutting the callosum would prevent such a transfer.

TABLE 9-3

Summary of data on cerebral lateralization[a]

Function	Left hemisphere	Right hemisphere
Visual system	Letters, words	Complex geometric patterns Faces
Auditory system	Language-related sounds	Nonlanguage environmental sounds Music
Somatosensory system	?	Tactual recognition of complex patterns Braille
Movement	Complex voluntary movement	?
Memory	Verbal memory	Visual memory
Language	Speech Reading Writing Arithmetic	
Spatial processes		Geometry Sense of direction Mental rotation of shapes

[a] Functions of the respective hemispheres that are predominantly mediated by one hemisphere in right-handed people.

simply because many small focal regions have been destroyed; the total is equal to the sum of the parts.

Semmes proposed that this differential organization of the two hemispheres is advantageous for efficient control of their respective functions. The diffuse organization of the right hemisphere is seen as advantageous for spatial abilities, since spatial analysis requires that different kinds of information (visual, auditory, tactual) be integrated into a single percept. Language functions are not integrated in the same manner, but remain as individual units.

From Semmes' basic idea subsequent writers such as Levy, Sperry, Bogen, Ornstein, and Jaynes have proposed a second argument: namely that the hemispheres represent two distinct modes of cognitive processing.

The left hemisphere operates in a more logical, analytical, computerlike fashion, analyzing stimulus information input sequentially, abstracting out the relevant details to which it attaches verbal labels; the right hemisphere is primarily a synthesizer, more concerned with the overall stimulus configuration, and organizes and processes information in terms of gestalts or wholes. (Harris, 1978, p. 463)

Although this second theory has recently stimulated interest among philosophers and the general public, it is important to remember that it is entirely an inference, one that has jumped a long way from the data summarized in Table 9-3. There is no direct support of the model, and there are good reasons to approach Semmes' results with caution. Her critical result—the absence of deficits from small right-hemisphere lesions—may reflect our ignorance about the functions of the right hemisphere rather than an absence of deficits. Recall that until the 1950s and 1960s right-hemisphere lesions had few known effects, and even today we understand the left, verbal, hemisphere far better than we do the right.

The third theoretical position, proposed by Kimura, is that although the left hemisphere mediates verbal function, it is specialized not for verbal function per se, but rather for certain kinds of motor function, both verbal and nonverbal. Kimura's argument is based on two premises. First, lesions of the left hemisphere disturb the production of voluntary movement, an impairment correlated with disturbance in speech. Second, Kimura proposes that verbal communication evolved from a stage that was primarily gestural, though with vocal concomitants, to one that is primarily vocal but that retains the capacity for manual communication. Since the neurological control of speech and language thus evolved out of a system of motor control of gesture, the left hemisphere is not specialized for language per se, but rather for motor control.

Kimura's theory is radically different from the previous ideas of Semmes and others, and unfortunately does not consider in the same detail the question of the right hemisphere. Nevertheless, we prefer Kimura's theory because: it is closely tied to the available data; the role of the left hemisphere in movement is testable; and it is possible to extend the theory to include the right hemisphere. For example, it could be argued that the two hemispheres became specialized for different aspects of motor control. The left hemisphere is specialized for fine motor control and the right hemisphere for gross motor movement in space.

Kimura discusses one aspect of cerebral asymmetry that other writers do not: the question of laterality in nonhuman species. Presumably any theory of what is lateralized in the human brain must eventually consider whether the nonhuman brain is asymmetrically organized, and if so, what is lateralized in those species. We consider this question later in the chapter.

Preferred Cognitive Mode

From the previous theoretical arguments it is possible to speculate that individual differences in the behavior of normal subjects result, at least in part, from individual differences in how the cerebral hemispheres are organized and how functions are lateralized. Thus, subjects who are very logical, analytical, and verbal could be assumed to be more efficient in using their left hemispheres to solve problems in everyday life, whereas subjects who are predominantly concerned with wholes or general concepts could be assumed to be more efficient in using their right hemispheres. For example (a tongue-in-cheek one), two professors, Alpha and Beta, are both excellent scholars, but are totally different in how they work and think.

Alpha is meticulous and leaves no detail to chance; when learning new material he masters every detail and has total command of the topic. Alpha is verbal and can easily win debates with his quick thinking and elegant arguments. His writing is clear and concise with flawless grammar and spelling. Alpha is athletic, being a nationally ranked tennis player. Curiously, he is only mediocre at other sports, but with prolonged practice he is able to master their details as well. Finally, Alpha's office is neat and tidy, with every item carefully placed in its correct location. On his desk is the project he is currently working on and nothing else.

Beta, on the other hand, only appears to learn the generalities of new material, and seldom recalls the minute details. He grasps ideas quickly, however, and is often able to tie very diverse concepts into a meaningful picture. His thinking often appears muddled to those around him, for he has difficulty expressing his ideas, but given enough time he often impresses his colleagues with his insight into problems. His writing is poor in comparison to Alpha's, for he expresses himself with tortuous constructions and is plagued by grammatical and spelling errors about which he appears totally unconcerned. Nevertheless, Beta has a remarkable knack for asking the correct questions and tying together seemingly diverse literature. Like Alpha, Beta is athletic, but unlike Alpha, Beta acquires the general motor skills of new sports rapidly, although he has never been able to become a top participant in any event. Beta's office is messy and his desk is a pile of papers and books, because he works on several projects concurrently.

Alpha and Beta represent extremes of what could be described as left-hemisphere and right-hemisphere individuals, respectively. The fundamental difference between them is that each attacks problems by using what has been described as a different **preferred cognitive mode.** Alpha is analytical, logical, verbal, and meticulous, whereas Beta is a synthesizer, more concerned with organizing concepts into meaningful wholes. Thus, in both the cognitive as well as motor skills of Alpha and Beta there is a basic difference that is assumed to reflect a fundamental difference in either brain organization or the "dominance" of one hemisphere over the other.

As intriguing as this analysis of Alpha and Beta appears to be, we caution that it is pure speculation, without empirical basis. It is probable that factors other than brain organization may contribute to preferred cognitive mode. For example, a recent study by Webster and Thurber demonstrates that cognitive set can affect some tests of lateralization. They repeated Witelson's dichhaptic test (described earlier), but added an additional variable. One group (the gestalt group) was encouraged to learn the shapes by imagining the overall appearance, or gestalt, whereas a second group (the analytic group) was encouraged to identify distinctive features and list them to themselves. This manipulation demonstrably influenced the degree of left-hand superiority, for the gestalt group had a significantly larger performance difference between the hands than did the analytic group. Although the basis for this effect is uncertain, it implies that strat-

egies used by subjects can significantly influence tests of lateralization. It thus seems reasonable to assume that differences in preferred cognitive mode may reflect socialization or environmental factors in addition to neuronal, biological, or constitutional factors. Nevertheless, that individual differences in behavior result in part from individual differences in brain organization seems a provocative assumption worthy of serious study.

SEX DIFFERENCES IN CEREBRAL ASYMMETRY

There is substantial anecdotal and experimental evidence of cognitive differences between males and females, and there have been several attempts to relate these to differences in brain organization. If any one principle can be abstracted to distinguish the sexes it is that males tend to be better than females at spatial analysis, whereas females tend to be more fluent than males in the use of language. These differences have been attributed to the possibility that the male brain has greater asymmetry of cerebral function, resulting in substantially less functional overlap between the verbal left and spatial right hemispheres of males than of females. The better performance of males on spatial tasks—such as recall and detection of shapes, mental rotation of two- or three-dimensional figures, geometry, maze learning, map reading, left-right discrimination, aiming at and tracking objects, and geographical knowledge—is explained by assuming that the overlap of verbal and spatial abilities in females hinders efficient spatial analysis. On the other hand, this overlap is presumed to account for the better verbal ability of females (as measured by tests of verbal fluency and articulation) because it conveys some advantage in verbal processing. Curiously, the apparent greater incidence of learning disorders in males suggests that cerebral specialization in males is associated with some hazard, whereas the lower incidence of language impairments in females after strokes suggests some advantage to a more symmetrical organization of brain function.

It should be noted, however, that both males and females vary substantially in performance of both verbal and spatial tasks. For example, although females are generally poorer than males at spatial skills, 20 to 25 percent of females exceed the average performance of males. In addition, and intriguingly, the variability of female performance on both verbal and spatial tests exceeds that of males, suggesting a greater variability in cerebral organization in females.

Evidence of Sex Differences

Evidence supporting the argument that there are significant sex differences in cerebral organization derive primarily from behavioral, anatomical, and neurological studies.

Behavioral Evidence. Sex differences are most dramatically demonstrated by an experiment called the *water level task,* used by Thomas (Figure 9-9). Subjects are shown a tilted flask and asked to indicate the water level. Thomas reports that among 62 randomly chosen college men the error in estimating the angle of the water was about 2° off the horizontal. Of 91 women, 28 (31 percent) showed the same performance as men whereas the remainder showed an error of 15 to 20°. In other words, although the men in his sample appreciated that the water level remained horizontal, 69 percent of the women did not. In developmental studies Thomas reports that by 12 years of age most males indicate that the water level is horizontal, but that females who perform in this way do so at a somewhat later age.

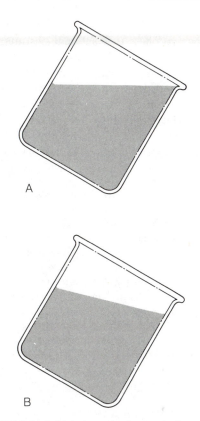

FIGURE 9-9. A. Line drawn to show waterline indicates comprehension of the concept of horizontality of fluid level. B. Line drawn incorrectly, indicating no comprehension of the concept. This response is typical of about two-thirds of females.

Several studies of male and female performance on tests of functional cerebral asymmetry—studies involving dichotic listening, dichhaptic testing, and tachistoscopic visual presentation—have generally indicated, respectively, greater ear, hand, and field effects for males than for females. (Details of the procedures and the expected lateralized effects were the same as in studies of asymmetry in normal subjects, described in the previous section.)

Some researchers have been impressed by anecdotal evidence that men appear to excel at chess and musical composition. In the Soviet Union, where chess is a national pastime, no women have achieved grand-master status, and women compete in separate tournaments. In music women appear to be as competent in performing as men, but fewer excel in composition. It has been suggested that men have an advantage in these fields because both involve heavy spatial loading. Harris described the spatial structure of music as follows:

> For instance, there is the sense in which certain kinds of sounds naturally seem to belong in certain parts of space relative to other sounds. Why are high notes and low notes *called* high notes and low notes? Why does the flute seem to float above the bassoon, and the violin above the cello? Pitch and resonance seem to impart "spatial" qualities to sound in more than a merely metaphorical sense....
>
> There are many other examples of spatial structure in music, including cross-relations (appearance in different voices of two tones of mutually contradictory character that normally are played as a melodic progression in one voice); cross-rhythms (simultaneous use of conflicting rhythmic patterns); bitonality; and polytonality.
>
> Perhaps the ability to recognize and to execute and, above all, to create, a melodic pattern is a spatial ability not unlike the visual detection of an embedded figure or the mental rotation of a geometrical form so as to anticipate how it will look from a different spatial perspective. The recognition of counterpoint or of variations on a theme may depend on similar abilities to [disassemble] a figure from a complex background, to remember it, and to follow it through a variety of transformations. (Harris, 1978, pp. 424–425)

There may be substance to the argument that sex differences in chess and musical composition can be attributed to spatial factors, but it is also easy to suggest cultural and environmental reasons why women have not exceeded in these areas. Similar arguments about the spatial aspects of literature could also be advanced, but it would be somewhat more difficult to demonstrate sex differences in creative writing ability.

Anatomical Evidence. Evidence for sex differences in anatomical asymmetry comes from two lines of work. First, one would expect to find anatomical differences in the brains of males and females if their behavioral differences result from differing cerebral function or organization. Specifically, in view of the greater functional asymmetry in males (described above) there ought to be greater structural asymmetry in the male than in the female brain. Wada and his colleagues reported just this finding in their analysis of the planum temporale and frontal operculum of human brains, although the data were rather variable and the sex effect rather small. Recall, however, that because females show large variability on spatial and verbal scores, large morphological variability might be expected. It would be instructive to correlate verbal and spatial skills with brain morphology, although this has not yet been done.

Second, the difference in functional organization of the male and female brain might result from differences in interhemispheric connections rather than in intrahemispheric organization per se. It could be speculated that cortical and subcortical fibers connecting the left and right halves of the brains of males and females differ in type, number, efficiency, or routing. Lansdell and Davie studied pneumoencephalograms of neurological patients for the presence of the massa intermedia (a band of tissue joining the thalami but absent in about one-third of males and one-quarter of females), and correlated performance on verbal and nonverbal sections of the Wechsler-Bellevue intelligence test. Whereas males with a massa intermedia had lower nonverbal scores than those without this structure, there was no comparable result in females. One interpretation of this result is that the presence of the massa intermedia in males produces competition and interference between the lateralized functions of the two hemispheres. This hypothesis remains to be proven, however.

Neurological Evidence. McGlone and her colleagues and Lansdell and his colleagues have provided substantial evidence that left- and right-hemisphere lesions have different effects in males and females. Their general finding is that cognitive deficits are less severe and less specific following unilateral lesion in females than in males. For example, McGlone reported three times more men than women with left-hemisphere lesions (strokes and tumors) were classified as aphasic. When aphasics were eliminated from her sample, males with left- but not right-hemisphere lesions exhibited a severer depression of verbal intelligence and memory. On the other hand, females with either left- or right-hemisphere lesions exhibited an overall depression of verbal intelligence. McGlone interpreted these results as indicating greater functional asymmetry in males than in females. Note, however, that this gender effect is relative, rather than absolute as McGlone's data might lead one to suppose. Milner and her colleagues, studying patients with more circumscribed cortical excisions, consistently found substantial functional asymmetry in males as well as in females, although there is a small sex difference. We are inclined to side with Milner: although gender may have a real effect on the outcome of brain damage, far and away the most significant factor is which side of the brain is damaged, not the subject's gender.

Environmental and Genetic Factors

Why, then, do spatial skills differ by gender? The most influential psychological view is that different environmental factors shape the be-

havior of males and females. In the case of spatial ability, it is presumed that male children are expected to exhibit greater independence than females, and thus engage in activities such as exploring and manipulating the environment—activities that improve spatial skills. In a recent review, Harris considered all of the research support for this argument and concluded that although a few studies can be found to support the view, the bulk of the evidence fails to support the idea. For example, in the Thomas et al. study on horizontality of liquid (Figure 9-9), women who had failed the task were repeatedly shown a bottle half-filled with red water that was tilted at various angles. They were asked to adjust the "pretend water level" by moving a disk half red, half white, in a second bottle. Even when the subjects simply had to adjust the pretend waterline to match the visible real waterline the women failed to show much improvement, and were likely to state that "water is level when the bottle is upright, but is inclined when the bottle is tilted." Males or females who perform correctly state that "water is always level." A priori, one would have expected females to have had as much experience as males with tilting vessels, and that even if they had not, special instruction would be helpful. This, however, does not seem to be the case.

A variety of authors have proposed that the major factor in differential spatial ability is genetic. It is postulated that a recessive gene on the X (female) chromosome is responsible. Every normal person has 46 chromosomes arranged in 23 pairs, one set from the male and one from the female. The twenty-third pair is composed of the sex chromosomes; if both are X, the child is female (XX), whereas if one is X and the other Y, the child is male (XY). If a gene is recessive, the trait will not be expressed unless the gene is present on both chromosomes—provided they are the same, as in females (XX). However, the gene need be present only on one chromosome if the other chromosome is different, as in males (XY). Thus, if a mother carried the gene on both chromosomes, all of her sons will present the trait, but whether her daughters will present it depends on whether the father also carries the recessive gene. Notice that for boys it is irrelevant whether or not the father carries the trait; males, then, have a greater chance of expressing the trait than girls, who require that both parents give them the gene. Figure 9-10 illustrates the principle. If this model were accurate, there would be a near-zero correlation between the spatial ability of a father and his son, since the father provided the Y chromosome; but there would be a significant correlation between mother and son as well as between father and daughter. These correlations are indeed demonstrated.

From the model in Figure 9-10 the number of males and females who would possess the trait can be predicted: 50 percent of males and 25 percent of females. From this we can predict that 25 percent of females will exceed the average male's score; as mentioned earlier, this percentage is consistently observed.

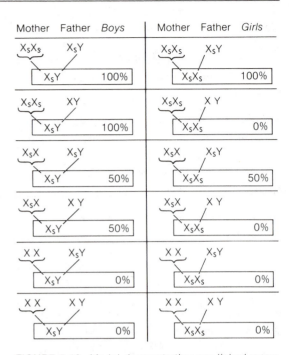

FIGURE 9-10. Model demonstrating sex-linked recessive trait for spatial ability. The percentages represent the number of offspring having the genotype for spatial ability. That genotype in males (X_sY) is more likely than in females (X_sX_s), since males have only a single X chromosome. Since the gene for spatial ability (s) is recessive, females require both X chromosomes to carry the gene before the trait is expressed. (After Harris, 1978.)

Neuropsychological Models

If a recessive gene carried by the X chromosome confers different spatial abilities, how does the gene alter brain function to produce the trait? Since a right-hemisphere function is affected by the gene, one might expect sex differences in tests of right-hemisphere function and cerebral laterality. Evidence confirming this expectation comes from three types of study.

First, tachistoscopic and dichotic studies of normal adults consistently demonstrate greater asymmetry of responses in males than in females. For example, Lake and Bryden found right-ear effects to be larger in males than in females on tests of dichotic listening to verbal material. About 75 percent of right-handed males showed a right-ear superiority, compared to only 62 percent of right-handed females.

The second source of evidence is analyses of clinical data indicating that cerebral lesions have different effects in males and in females. As noted earlier, McGlone, analyzing the effects of cerebral lesions on verbal and nonverbal abilities, found that adult males show a large decline in verbal intellectual ability following left-hemisphere lesions, and depressed nonverbal intelligence following right-hemisphere lesions. In contrast, women did not show selective verbal or nonverbal intellectual deficits after unilateral brain injury. It is disappointing that studies of patients with circumscribed cortical removals have generally failed to report patient gender, since McGlone's work would predict sex differences on a variety of specific tests of left- and right-hemisphere function. Similarly, one would expect significant sex differences in duration of aphasia following carotid sodium Amytal injection but analysis of these results with regard to sex has not been reported.

The third source of supporting evidence is electrophysiological data suggestive of sex differences in lateralization. Preliminary evidence reviewed by Harris indicates that the difference in shape of the auditory evoked potential is greater in the left hemisphere than in the right, and that this asymmetry is more pronounced in males than in females. Although analyses of sex effects in studies of regional blood flow have not yet been reported, analogous results could be expected from this measure as well.

So far we have implied that differences in neuropsychological profiles in males and females are a direct result of genetic factors. However, developmental studies indicate that a fundamental difference in male and female cerebral maturation may help account for sex differences observed in adulthood. It has long been known that girls begin to speak sooner than boys, develop larger vocabularies during childhood, and, as children, use more complex linguistic construction than do boys. Further, the speech of young girls may be better enunciated than boys' speech, and girls are generally better readers than boys. Although developmental studies of laterality in children have yielded conflicting results, dichotic and tachistoscopic studies frequently indicate an earlier evolution of asymmetry in girls than in boys. Since it is well known that females attain phys-

ical maturity at an earlier age than do males, it is reasonable to propose that the male brain matures more slowly than the female brain, and that maturation rate is a critical determinant of brain asymmetry. That is, the more slowly a child matures, the greater the observed cerebral asymmetry. A study by Waber demonstrates just this finding. She reported that, regardless of sex, early-maturing adolescents performed better on tests of verbal than of spatial abilities, whereas the late-maturing ones did the opposite. This study, then, implies that maturation rate may affect the organization of higher cortical function. Since, on average, females mature faster than males, superior spatial abilities in males may be directly related to their relatively slow development.

The relationship between maturation rate and cerebral asymmetry has an intriguing implication for the genetic model of spatial ability. It may be that what is transferred by the recessive gene is maturation rate, not spatial ability per se. Thus, superior spatial skills are an indirect effect of maturation rate, which is determined by the presence of the recessive gene. To test this prediction it would be necessary to show that females who develop slowly are the same ones who perform as well as the average male on spatial tests, and whose spatial ability correlates with their parents as predicted in Figure 9-10. This study has not been done.

Cognitive Mode in Males and Females

Although we have assumed that male and female differences in spatial abilities are directly related to neuropsychological factors, the relationship may in fact be more indirect. It may be that genetic, maturational, and environmental factors predispose males and females to prefer different modes of cognitive analysis. In other words, females develop in such a way that they prefer to solve problems primarily by using a verbal mode. Since this mode is less efficient at solving spatial problems, the female exhibits an apparent deficit. By the same logic, females should do better than males at primarily verbal tasks. This proposition has yet to be thoroughly investigated. It would be interesting to study the possibility that learning disabilities arise, in part, from an inability of some children, mostly males, to use the verbal mode in a highly verbal school system.

HANDEDNESS

There is little compelling evidence that nonhuman primates demonstrate consistent preference for one hand over the other, but there is strong evidence that early man was predominantly right-handed. Analysis of the cracked skulls of animals killed for food, of stone tools, and of cave drawings shows that the right hand was used more frequently than the left.

As the term sinister—usually used to mean wicked or evil, but originally meaning left-handed in Latin—implies, left-handedness has historically been viewed as somewhat strange or unusual. The most commonly cited figure for left-handedness is 10 percent, representing the number of people who write with the left hand, but when other criteria are used estimates range from 1 to 30 percent. The problem is that handedness is not absolute; some people are nearly totally right-handed, some are nearly totally left-handed, whereas others are ambidextrous (that is, they use either hand with equal facility). A rather useful distribution of handedness has been described by Annett (Table 9-4), who asked over 2000 adults to indicate the hand they used to perform each of 12 different tasks. It can be seen that the incidence of left-handedness on Annett's tasks varied from a low 5 percent when

TABLE 9-4

Percentages of "left," "right," or "either" responses to each question[a]

	Left	Either	Right
Dealing cards	17.02%	3.32%	79.66%
Unscrewing jar	16.50	17.49	66.01
Shoveling	13.53	11.89	74.58
Sweeping	13.49	16.89	69.62
Threading needle	13.10	9.74	77.16
Writing	10.60	0.34	89.06
Striking match	9.95	8.74	81.31
Throwing ball	9.44	1.29	89.47
Hammering	9.22	2.54	88.24
Using toothbrush	9.18	8.49	82.33
Using racket	8.10	2.59	89.31
Using scissors	6.20	6.81	86.99

[a] Percentages based on 2321 respondents
Adapted from Annett, 1970.

cutting with scissors to a high of 17 percent when dealing cards.

Family background allows left-handers to be subdivided into two populations: *familial left-handers,* who have a family history of left-handedness; *nonfamilial left-handers,* who have no family history of left-handedness. This distinction is important because neuropsychological tests have shown that the cerebral organization of nonfamilial left-handers is lateralized in a way identical to that of right-handed people, whereas familial left-handers have more bilaterally represented verbal and nonverbal functions. This distinction has been nicely demonstrated by Hécaen and Sauguet, who tested 50 different behaviors on left- and right-handed patients who had lesions in either the left or the right hemisphere. Depending upon whether they had a left- or right-hemisphere lesion, right-handed patients had different test results in 47 out of 50 tests. Nonfamilial left-handers had a similar test result pattern. Familial left-handers had different test results on only 4 of 50 tests. Thus, because lesions in either hemisphere could disrupt most behavior, it can be concluded that familial left-handers have less cerebral asymmetry than right-handers.

The anomalous cerebral organization of the familial left-hander has made it difficult to develop a simple theory of the functional utility of cerebral asymmetry. That is, why do most people have cerebral asymmetry unless it confers some adaptive advantage? Many studies have probed the cognitive capacities of left-handers in search of deficits or advantages that might account for their peculiar cerebral organization. Hardyck and Petrinovich, who reviewed and evaluated the studies, conclude that left-handed people do not differ from right-handed people in ability. Using a neuropsychological test battery administered to college students, Kolb and Whishaw have arrived at the same conclusion.

One caveat must be attached to the conclusion that there is no difference in ability between left- and right-handers: there is a larger incidence of left-handedness among mentally defective children and children with various neurological disorders than is found in the general population. This is not surprising, however, because if the dominant hemisphere is injured at an early age, handedness and dominance can move under the control of what would normally not be the dominant hemisphere. Since there are so many more right-handed children, by probability alone it would be expected that more right-handed children with left-hemisphere damage would switch to right-hemisphere dominance than would switch in the reverse direction. That this can occur, however, cannot be used as grounds for predicting cognitive deficits in the general population of left-handers.

Theories of Hand Preference

The many theories put forward to account for hand preference can be categorized according to their environmental, anatomical, or genetic emphases.

Environmental Theories. The three variations of environmental theories of handedness stress the utility of behavior, reinforcement, or accident as the major determining variable. The first variation, the behavioral, sometimes called the theory of the Peloponnesian Wars or the Sword and Shield hypothesis, is that a soldier who held his shield in his left hand better protected his heart and improved his chance of survival. Since the left hand was holding the shield, the right hand became more skilled in various movements and eventually was used for most tasks. According to a female variant to this theory, it is adaptive for a mother to hold an infant in her left hand so that it will be soothed by the rhythm of the mother's heart; the mother, like the soldier, then has the right hand free and so uses it for executing skilled movements. Such theories have difficulties, the most obvious being failure to consider the possibility that right-handedness preceded, and thus is responsible for, the behavior.

The second variant of environmental theories, that of reinforcement, has been elaborated by Collins. It is based on some ingenious experiments on "handedness" in mice: Collins raised mice in a world biased in such a way that the mice were forced to use either their left or right paws to obtain food located in a tube adjacent to the wall of their home cage. He found that the proportion of adult right- or left-pawed mice was directly related to the type of world in which they were raised. Thus, he suggested, their preference was established by the contingencies of reinforcement received in the environment in which they spent the first few weeks of life. This view can be adapted to humans. The child's world is also right-handed in many ways, which reinforces the use of that hand. In addition, children in the United States were once forced to write with their right hands. Although emphasizing the potential importance of environmental factors, Collins' theory does not account for the difference between familial and nonfamilial handedness or the relation of handedness to cerebral dominance. It also seems to be negated by what happened when children were given their choice of which hand to learn to write with in United States schools: the incidence of left-handed writing rose only to 10 percent, which is the norm in most societies that have been studied.

According to the third variant of environmental theories, there is a genetically determined bias toward being right-handed, but left-handedness occurs through some cerebral deficit caused by accident. To account for the familial aspect of left-handedness Bakan has argued that there is a high probability of stressful births among left-handers, which increases the risk of brain damage and so maintains the incidence of left-handedness. This theory would predict that some consistent deficit in cognitive functioning in adult left-handers should result from their brain damage, but, as we pointed out above, no such deficit has been shown. It could be argued that since the alleged damage occurs in infancy, the brain compensates in such a way that the only symptom that appears in adulthood is left-handedness; but this argument is hardly compelling support for the theory.

Anatomical Theories. Of the several anatomical theories of handedness, two, which are well documented, explain handedness by alluding to anatomical asymmetry. In the first theory right-handedness is attributed to enhanced maturation and ultimately greater development of the left hemisphere. Generalizing from this assumption, it is predicted that nonfamilial left-handers should show an asymmetry mirroring that of right-handers, whereas familial left-handers should show no anatomical asymmetry. These predictions are difficult to assess because no studies have specifically considered anatomical asymmetry with respect to handedness or with respect to familial history and handedness. A major problem with this theory is that it simply pushes the question one step backward, asking not "why handedness?" but instead "why anatomical asymmetry?"

The second theory, in part, addresses this problem. As Morgan has pointed out, many animals have a left-sided developmental advantage that is not genetically coded. For example, there is a left-sided bias for the location of the heart, the size of the ovaries in birds, the control of bird song, the size of left temporal cortex in humans, the size of the left side of the skull in the great apes, and so on. This predominance of left-favoring asymmetries puts the more celebrated left-hemisphere speech dominance in the more general perspective of all anatomical asymmetries. Since neither genetic evidence nor genetic theory accurately predicts these human asymmetries, Morgan assumes that they all result from some fundamental asymmetries in human body chemistry. The problem with Morgan's theory applied to handedness is that it fails to explain left-handedness in the presence of other "normal" asymmetries such as location of the heart.

Three studies have used ventriculograms or angiograms to visualize the outline of different structures in the brain, whereby to determine the relation between anatomical asymmetry and handedness. McRae et al. reported that in right-handed people the right **occipital horns** of the lateral ventricle were five times more likely to be longer than the left; in left-handed people there was an equal chance that the right might be longer than the left. LeMay and Culebras examined the arches formed by the arteries leaving the posterior ends of the Sylvian fissures and reported that there was an asymmetry in right-handed people that was not always present in left-handed people. Radcliffe repeated this study, and, knowing that about two-thirds of left-handers have speech in the left hemisphere, he correlated the angiography results with data on their hemispheric representation of speech. He found that left- and right-handers with speech in the left hemisphere had a mean right-left difference of 27° in the angle formed by the vessels leaving the posterior end of the Sylvian fissure. Left- and right-handers with speech in the right hemisphere or with bilaterally represented speech had a mean difference of 0°. The asymmetries, then, were related primarily to speech representation and not necessarily to handedness. This finding is extremely important because it means that handedness is not a reliable indicator of speech lateralization or anatomical asymmetry.

Genetic Theories. Of the many genetic models for handedness, most postulate a dominant gene or genes for right-handedness and a recessive gene or genes for left-handedness; but none of these models can accurately predict the probability of left-handedness.

The two best attempts to develop genetic models of handedness are those of Annett and of Levy and Nagylaki. Annett has proposed that there may be a gene for right-handedness but not for left-handedness. In the absence of the right-handed gene the displayed handedness will be random. The incidence of right-handedness would be slightly higher in this group because of environmental factors predisposing the choice of the right hand. The theory proposed by Levy and Nagylaki is somewhat more complex. This theory is a two-gene, four-allele model. That is, there is a gene for handedness and a gene for hemispheric representation of speech. The gene for left-handedness is recessive as is the gene for having speech in the right hemisphere. Ge-

netic theories have been criticized on a number of grounds (see Hardyck and Petrinovich), and none is totally satisfactory. For example, there is no attempt to differentiate between familial and nonfamilial left-handers.

From this brief review of theories of handedness it is clear that we do not know why there is handedness, and we may never know. (To the multiplicity of theories of handedness we add our own: a man named Noah was disliked by his fellow townspeople because he was right-handed and they were southpaws, and because he insisted on building an ark in the desert. A great flood came and everyone was drowned except Noah and his right-handed family. The rest is history.)

ASYMMETRY IN NONHUMANS

Anatomical and functional asymmetry of the cortex is not a uniquely human characteristic. Any theory that brain asymmetry is necessarily related to development of language in humans is jeopardized until the asymmetric laterality of nonhuman brains is clearly defined. It is not unreasonable to propose that the brain of different species evolved an anatomical and functional asymmetry in response to specialized ecological demands, and that the asymmetry therefore reflects fundamental differences among the brain–behavior relationships of different species; but this theory remains to be proven.

Our intent is not to thoroughly review all of the studies suggesting an asymmetry in the nonhuman brain, but rather to highlight the most stimulating and robust data gathered thus far on cerebral asymmetry, in birds, rats, cats, and monkeys. Each of these successive species has a brain more closely resembling the human's—although obviously not approximating its phylogenetic development.

Fernando Nottebohm made a startling discovery in 1971. In severing the canary left hypoglossal nerve, but not its right, he found severe disruption of bird song in the canary. Subsequently, he has found similar results from lesions all along the pathway from the hypoglossal nerve to the higher cerebral nuclei on the left but not on the right. If the left nerve is severed in young canaries, the right hypoglossal nerve assumes the control of bird song—a finding remarkably similar to that of human children with left-hemisphere damage in infancy who subsequently develop language centers in the right hemisphere. Although Nottebohm's results are provocative, he has also found that some highly vocal species such as parrots do not have lateralized control of song whereas some relatively inarticulate birds (e.g., domestic fowl) are lateralized.

Although the brain of the rat has been considered bilaterally symmetrical, recent findings imply that it is not. There appears to be a neuroanatomical asymmetry in its cerebral cortex, for Diamond et al. showed the right cortex to be thicker than the left. Dennenberg found a behavioral correlate of this difference, reporting that under certain conditions ablations of the right hemisphere produce extreme activity scores in open-field tests whereas analogous left-hemisphere lesions do not. Similarly, we have found that removal of the right frontal lobe but not of the left lobe produces increased activity in running wheels, although lesions do not asymmetrically affect a variety of other behavioral tasks. Further, Glick and his colleagues have found that rats given amphetamine tend to circle consistently to one side or the other. Since amphetamine increases dopamine levels in the brain, particularly in the caudate nucleus, they hypothesized that such circling could be induced by differential amounts of dopamine in the two caudate nuclei. Bioassays of rats confirmed this hypothesis, for normal rats have a 10 to 15 percent asymmetry in dopamine content in the

two caudate nuclei, a difference that is potentiated by amphetamine to 25 to 30 percent. Furthermore, the biochemistry and behavior are associated, because rats rotate toward the side with the lower level of dopamine. It becomes clear that the behavior–biochemistry relationship in rats is relevant to the understanding of human cerebral asymmetry when it is recalled that evidence of biochemical asymmetry in the human brain has recently been discovered—although there is not yet evidence that this asymmetry has any functional consequences. The data from the rat imply that it most likely does.

In an examination of cerebral asymmetry in cats, Webster used split-brain cats that had been trained to perform various problems prior to hemisphere disconnection. Following surgery, each hemisphere was tested separately on the problems by restricting visual input to that hemisphere. Webster found that some problems had been stored in both hemispheres, and other problems in only one hemisphere. Moreover, paw preference correlated significantly with the hemisphere that performed the various problems. Webster also found hemispheric asymmetry in the pattern of convolutions. About one-half of the cat brains he examined, including those of newborn kittens, evidenced fissural asymmetry, predominantly in the visual cortex. These results are suggestive, but really only imply a rough analogue to the asymmetry of the human brain. Studies addressed to finding functional asymmetry in the auditory system may hold more potential not only because the cat's auditory areas are very large but also because these may be more relevant than visual areas to studies of cerebral lateralization in humans.

Anatomical asymmetry in the brains of nonhuman primates was first noticed by Cunningham in 1892. As in human brains, there is a greater upward slope in the Sylvian fissure on the right in the chimpanzee, orangutan, and gorilla brains, and the right frontal pole is longer than the left in baboons. Such findings suggest that a functional asymmetry would be present in the great apes but not in other primate species.

The question of whether cerebral asymmetry or handedness occurs in primates has been most thoroughly studied by Warren and his associates. He concludes that handedness in rhesus monkeys is primarily the result of experience and not the expression of any basic asymmetry akin to that seen in humans. There is also little compelling evidence that chimpanzees, gorillas, and orangutans show handedness in the way that humans do.

Unequivocal evidence of functional asymmetry in monkeys has been elusive. Studies of the visual system have consistently yielded negative results, a surprising result considering the anatomical similarity of the visual systems in humans and other primates. Recent findings suggestive of functional asymmetry in the auditory system are somewhat more encouraging. Dewson removed Brodmann's area 22 in rhesus monkeys, producing a lasting deficit on an auditory-visual task if the lesion was in the left hemisphere, but not in the right. The monkeys were required to press a panel that activated one of two acoustic stimuli, either a 1 kHz tone or white noise. They were then presented with two panels, one green, one red. If the tone was heard, they pressed the red panel; if the white noise was heard, they pressed the green panel to receive the reward. Lesions to Brodmann's area 22 on the left impaired performance of this task, whereas lesions to the analogous area on the right did not.

An experiment appearing to confirm that there can be laterality in monkeys has been reported by Petersen and Beecher. They compared the ability of Japanese macaques to discriminate among communicatively relevant sounds and irrelevant sounds. The animals were able to discriminate communicatively relevant sounds presented to the right ear better than those presented to the left ear. The researchers suggest that the Japanese macaques engage in left-hemisphere processing in a way that is analogous to that of humans. These results are exciting, and may be an important step in demonstrating laterality in the nonhuman primate brain. The possible functional laterality of the human brain and the absence of consistent handedness implies that cerebral asymmetry and handedness in man may not be as closely related as had been assumed in the past.

CONCLUSIONS

No theory yet satisfactorily accounts for the asymmetric organization of the human brain. Most theories are based on the assumption that an asymmetrical brain must be of some advantage, but this assumption begs the question. For example, Levy has argued that an adaptive advantage results from restricting language to one hemisphere because it leaves one hemisphere free for visuospatial functions, which would otherwise be compromised. This idea has several pitfalls. Asymmetry is present in species that lack language. Further, Levy implies that people with bilateral speech areas should have impaired visuospatial functioning. The data are not compelling. According to a second theory, the left hemisphere is specialized primarily for control of complex movements. Language is located in the left hemisphere because originally it was primarily a motor function. Further, since the left hemisphere controls primarily the right hand, people are right-handed because of the privileged access to the hemisphere controlling skilled movements. This idea, too, has problems. What would be the advantage in specializing motor functions in one hemisphere? If there is an advantage, persons with bilateral speech areas should be at a disadvantage. Again, there is no compelling evidence that this is the case.

Asymmetry presumably offers some adaptive advantage, but left-handed people, especially those with bilateral speech and symmetrical brains, will continue to be a problem for any theory unless that theory can demonstrate some disadvantage in having a symmetrical brain.

REFERENCES

Annett, M. A classification of hand preference by association analysis. *British Journal of Psychology, 61* (1970), 303–321.

Bakan, P., G. Dibb, and P. Reed. Handedness and birth stress. *Neuropsychologia, 11* (1973), 363–366.

Cain, D. P., and J. A. Wada. An anatomical asymmetry in the baboon brain. *Brain, Behavior and Evolution, 16* (1979), 222–226.

Collins, R. L. Toward an admissible genetic model for the inheritance of the degree and direction of asymmetry. In S. Harnad, R. W. Doty, L. Goldstein, J. Jaynes, and G. Krauthamer, eds. *Lateralization in the Nervous System.* New York: Academic Press, 1977.

Cunningham, D. F. *Contribution to the Surface Anatomy of the Cerebral Hemispheres.* Dublin: Royal Irish Academy, 1892.

Dennenberg, V. H., J. Garbanati, G. Sherman, D. A. Yutzey, and R. Kaplan. Infantile stimulation induces brain lateralization in rats. *Science, 201* (1978), 1150.

Dewson, J. H. Preliminary evidence of hemispheric asymmetry of auditory function in monkeys. In S. Harnad, R. W. Doty, L. Goldstein, J. Jaynes, and G. Krauthamer, eds. *Lateralization in the Nervous System.* New York: Academic Press, 1977.

Diamond, M. C., R. E. Johnson, and C. A. Ingham. Morphological changes in the young, adult, and aging cerebral cortex, hippocampus, and diencephalon. *Behavioral Biology, 14* (1975), 163–174.

Donchin, E., M. Kutas, and G. McCarthy. Electrocortical indices of hemispheric utilization. In S. Harnad, R. W. Doty, L. Goldstein, J. Jaynes, and G. Krauthamer, eds. *Lateralization in the Nervous System.* New York: Academic Press, 1977.

Geschwind, N. Language and the brain. *Scientific American, 226* (1972), 340–348.

Geschwind, N., and W. Levitsky. Left-right asymmetries in temporal speech region. *Science, 161* (1968), 186–187.

Glick, S. D., T. P. Jerussi, and B. Zimmerberg. Behavioral and neuropharmacological correlates of nigrostriatal asymmetry in rats. In S. Harnad, R. W. Doty, L. Goldstein, J. Jaynes, and G. Krauthamer, eds. *Lateralization in the Nervous System.* New York: Academic Press, 1977.

Gordon, H. W., and J. E. Bogen. Hemispheric lateralization of singing after intracarotid sodium amylobarbitone. *Journal of Neurology, Neurosurgery, and Psychiatry, 37* (1974), 727–738.

Hardyck, C., and L. F. Petrinovich. Left-handedness. *Psychological Bulletin, 84* (1977), 385–404.

Harris, L. J. Sex differences in spatial ability: possible environmental, genetic, and neurological factors. In M. Kinsbourne, ed. *Asymmetrical Function of the Brain.* Cambridge: Cambridge University Press, 1978.

Hécaen, H., and J. Sauguet. Cerebral dominance in left-handed subjects. *Cortex, 7* (1971), 19–48.

Hicks, R. E. Intrahemispheric response competition between vocal and unimanual performance in normal adult human males. *Journal of Comparative and Physiological Psychology, 89,* (1975), 50–61.

Hughlings-Jackson, J. *Selected Writings of John Hughlings-Jackson.* J. Taylor, ed. New York: Basic Books, 1958.

Kimura, D. The asymmetry of the human brain. *Scientific American, 228* (1973), 70–78.

Kinsbourne, M. Eye and head turning indicates cerebral lateralization. *Science, 176* (1972), 539–541.

Kinsbourne, M., and J. Cook. Generalized and lateralized effects of concurrent verbalization on a unimanual skill. *Quarterly Journal of Experimental Psychology, 23* (1971), 341–345.

Kolb, B., and I. Q. Whishaw. A search for cerebral asymmetry in the frontal lobe of the rat. Unpublished manuscript.

Kolb, B., I. Q. Whishaw, and R. Barnsley. A comparison of neuropsychological test performance in left- and right-handed college students. In preparation.

Lake, D. A., and M. P. Bryden. Handedness and sex differences in hemispheric asymmetry. *Brain and Language, 3* (1976), 266–282.

Lansdell, H. A sex difference in effect of temporal-lobe neurosurgery on design preference. *Nature, 194* (1962), 852–854.

Lansdell, H., and J. Davie. Massa intermedia: possible relation to intelligence. *Neuropsychologia, 10* (1972), 207–210.

Lassen, N. A., D. H. Ingevar, and E. Skinhøj. Brain function and blood flow. *Scientific American, 239* (1978), 62–71.

LeMay, M., and A. Culebras. Human brain-morphologic differences in the hemispheres demonstrable by carotid arteriography. *New England Journal of Medicine, 287* (1972), 168–170.

Levy, J. The origins of lateral asymmetry. In S. Harnad, R. W. Doty, L. Goldstein, J. Jaynes, and G. Krauthamer, eds. *Lateralization in the Nervous System.* New York: Academic Press, 1977.

Levy, J. Possible basis for the evolution of lateral specialization of the human brain. *Nature, 224* (1969), 614–615.

Levy, J., and T. Nagylaki. A model for the genetics of handedness. *Genetics, 72* (1972), 117–128.

Levy, J., C. Trevarthen, and R. W. Sperry. Perception of bilateral chimeric figures following hemispheric deconnection. *Brain, 95* (1972), 61–78.

Maccoby, E., and C. Jacklin. *The Psychology of Sex Differences.* Stanford, Calif.: Stanford University Press, 1974.

McGlone, J. Sex differences in the cerebral organization of verbal function in patients with unilateral brain lesions. *Brain, 100* (1977), 775–793.

McGlone, J. Sex differences in human brain organization: a critical review. *Research Bulletin 399,* University of Western Ontario, 1979.

McGlone, J., and W. Davidson. The relation between cerebral speech laterality and spatial ability with special reference to sex and hand preference. *Neuropsychologia, 11* (1973), 105–113.

McGlone, J., and A. Kertesz. Sex differences in cerebral processing of visuospatial tasks. *Cortex, 9* (1973), 313–320.

McRae, D. L., C. L. Branch, and B. Milner. The occipital horns and cerebral dominance. *Neurology, 18* (1968), 95–98.

Milner, B. Hemispheric specialization: scope and limits. In F. O. Schmitt and F. G. Worden, eds. *The Neurosciences: Third Study Program.* Cambridge, Mass.: MIT Press, 1974.

Morgan, M. Embryology and inheritance of asymmetry. In S. Harnad, R. W. Doty, L. Goldstein, J. Jaynes, and G. Krauthamer, eds. *Lateralization in the Nervous System.* New York: Academic Press, 1977.

Morrell, L. K., and J. G. Salamy. Hemispheric asymmetry of electrocortical responses to speech stimuli. *Science, 174* (1971), 165–166.

Nottebohm, F. Asymmetries in neural control of vocalization in the canary. In S. Harnad, R. W. Doty, L. Goldstein, J. Jaynes, and G. Krauthamer, eds. *Lateralization in the Nervous System.* New York: Academic Press, 1977.

Oke, A., R. Keller, I. Mefford, and R. N. Adams. Lateralization of norepinephrine in human thalamus. *Science, 200* (1978), 1411–1413.

Petersen, M. R., M. D. Beecher, S. R. Zoloth, D. B. Moody, and W. C. Stebbins. Neural lateralization: evidence from studies of the perception of species-specific vocalizations by Japanese Macaques (*Macada puscata*). *Science, 202* (1978), 324–326.

Radcliffe, G. Arteriographic correlates of cerebral dominance for speech. Paper presented at International Neuropsychology Symposium, Oxford, 1978.

Robinson, R. G. Differential behavior and biochemical effects of right and left cerebral infarction in the rat. *Science, 205* (1979), 707–710.

Rubens, A. B. Anatomical asymmetries of human cerebral cortex. In S. Harnad, R. W. Doty, L. Goldstein, J. Jaynes, and G. Krauthamer, eds. *Lateralization in the Nervous System.* New York: Academic Press, 1977.

Rudel, R. G., M. B. Denckla, and E. Spalten. The functional asymmetry of Braille letter learning in normal sighted children. *Neurology, 24* (1974), 733–738.

Semmes, J. Hemispheric specialization: a possible clue to mechanism. *Neuropsychologia, 6* (1968), 11–26.

Sperry, R. W. Lateral specialization in the surgically separated hemispheres. In F. O. Schmitt and F. G. Worden, eds. *The Neurosciences: Third Study Program.* Cambridge, Mass.: MIT Press, 1974.

Taylor, J., ed. *Selected Writings of John Hughlings-Jackson.* London: Staples Press, 1958.

Teuber, H.-L. Physiological psychology. *Annual Review of Psychology, 6* (1955), 267–296.

Thomas, H., W. Jamison, and D. D. Hummel. Observation is insufficient for discovering that the surface of still water is invariantly horizontal. *Science, 181* (1973), 173–174.

Waber, D. P. Sex differences in cognition: a function of maturation rate? *Science, 192* (1976), 572–573.

Wada, J. A., R. Clarke, and A. Hamm. Cerebral hemispheric asymmetry in humans: cortical speech zones in 100 adult and 100 infant brains. *Archives of Neurology, 32* (1975), 239–246.

Wada, J., and T. Rasmussen. Intracarotid injection of sodium Amytal for the lateralization of cerebral speech dominance. *Journal of Neurosurgery, 17* (1960), 266–282.

Warren, J. M. Handedness and cerebral dominance in monkeys. In S. Harnad, R. W. Doty, L. Goldstein, J. Jaynes, and G. Krauthamer, eds. *Lateralization in the Nervous System.* New York: Academic Press, 1977.

Webster, W. G. Functional asymmetry between the cerebral hemispheres of the cat. *Neuropsychologia, 10* (1972), 75–87.

Webster, W. G., and A. D. Thurber. Problem solving strategies and manifest brain asymmetry. *Cortex, 14* (1978), 474–484.

Webster, W. G., and I. H. Webster. Anatomical asymmetry of the cerebral hemispheres of the cat brain. *Physiology and Behavior, 14* (1975), 867–868.

Witelson, S. F. Early hemisphere specialization and interhemispheric plasticity: an empirical and theoretical review. In S. J. Segalowitz and F. A. Gruber, eds. *Language Development and Neurological Theory.* New York: Academic Press, 1977.

Witelson, S. F. Sex and the single hemisphere: right hemisphere processing for spatial processing. *Science, 193* (1976) 425–427.

Witelson, S. F., and W. Pallie. Left hemisphere specialization for language in the newborn: neuroanatomical evidence of asymmetry. *Brain, 96* (1973), 641–646.

Yeni-Komshian, G., and D. Benson. Anatomical study of cerebral asymmetry in the temporal lobe of humans, chimpanzees and rhesus monkeys. *Science, 192* (1976), 387–389.

Zangwill, O. L. *Cerebral Dominance and Its Relation to Psychological Function.* Springfield, Ill.: Charles C Thomas, 1960.

PART FIVE

SENSORY AND MOTOR SYSTEMS

The *specificity of the morphological organization of the nervous system* is amazing. The more we know about the structure of the brain, the more we realize how this specificity can be traced to the minutest levels. It is the rule, rather than the exception, that even a small nucleus can be subdivided into parts or territories which differ with regard to cytoarchitecture, glial architecture, vasoarchitecture, fiber connections, synaptic arrangements and by its chemistry.... If one focuses attention on the fiber connections of the central nervous system one is struck by another feature of its organization: the *multiplicity of connections.* As a rule each small region receives fibers from a number of others and likewise emits fibers which pass to many other regions.... There may, of course, be great quantitative differences among the various contingents of afferent and efferent fibers of a nucleus. Nevertheless, a scrutiny of the fiber connections of the central nervous system as a whole leaves one with the conviction that there are morphological possibilities for an impulse from a certain part of the brain to be transmitted along circumvential routes of varying complexity to virtually every other part of the central nervous system! These multifarious interconnections between structures presumably provide possibilities for cooperation and integration of function between them and make it increasingly difficult and unjustified to describe a certain part of the brain as simply "motor," "visual," etc. (A. Brodal, Self-observations and neuro-anatomical considerations after a stroke. *Brain,* 96 [1973], 687–688.)

These comments by the anatomist Brodal were made with reference to symptoms of a stroke that he had suffered, which produced left hemiplegia (partial paralysis of the left side of the body). He concluded that he had had an occlusion of the right middle cerebral artery causing an infarction of part of the right internal capsule and its surroundings. This area contains the projection from the motor area of the right precentral gyrus. He also described himself as suffering changes in handwriting, concentration, and short-term memory; increased fatigue; and reduced initiative and reduced movements of emotional expression. Assuming that the diagnosis was correct, the symptoms associated with his right-hemisphere motor-system lesion were surprising to the author, and led him to acknowledge that the interaction of parts of the brain precludes its easy division into centers of function—or even into divisions as general as sensory and motor.

If it is difficult to divide the brain into sensory and motor areas on the basis of clinical evidence, it is even more difficult from a theoretical perspective. On the one hand, it is a simple matter to argue that the entire nervous system is motor, and that movements begin at the sensory receptor. Indeed, changes in receptor activity can potentially—and usually do—lead to changes in motor activity, be they as simple as knee-jerk reflexes or as complex as orienting responses. On the other hand, it can be as convincingly argued that the entire nervous system is sensory, for any change in muscle activity brings about changes in the stimulation of sensory receptors. This is true for all sensory systems, but particularly true for vision, where continuous shifts of the retina are mandatory for sustained perception. Although both sides of this argument could be thought to be extreme, both have merit and may be usefully applied in different situations. Both views are worth bearing in mind, for in this part we have divided the nervous system into sensory and motor components in the traditional way: Chapters 10 and 11 respectively. We have done so realizing that the division is in many ways arbitrary, and in some cases—particularly with respect to association areas of the cortex—unjustified on anatomical and functional grounds. We have made the division not to mislead, but to simplify description. In subsequent chapters the functions of many brain areas will be described from a perspective that acknowledges that they are in many ways both sensory and motor.

Two important principles underlie the discussion, in the next two chapters, of the sensory and motor systems: (1) Both systems are arranged in a hierarchy of levels of function. (2) Lateralization of function is greatest at the very highest levels of function and least at the lowest levels. In the sensory systems the lowest levels are composed of cells responsive to different forms of environmental stimulation. These receptor cells decode stimuli into a basic, simple form (for example, in the visual system, patterns of light and dark) and send it to the higher levels, where the input is synthesized into increasingly complex forms. At the highest levels there are cells receiving messages from several different sensory modalities, as well as from the memory systems; these cells allow us to experience a *percept* of the world around us. Konorski has termed these highest levels *gnostic areas* (from the Greek *gnosis,* meaning knowledge); thus, a disturbance of these regions is known as an **agnosia.** Within these gnostic areas cerebral asymmetry is found to be greatest; it is totally absent from the receptor levels. Within the motor system the lowest levels—housed in the spinal cord, lower brainstem, and cerebellum—function to control our movement patterns. Higher levels provide increasingly subtle and complex control of the movements produced by the lower levels. The highest levels allow long-range planning and programming of skillful movement. A skillful movement pattern is known as praxis (from the Greek, meaning action); thus, disturbances of a praxic movement are termed **apraxias**. As with gnostic areas in the sensory system, it is in the praxic areas of the motor system that there is asymmetry in the control of movement.

10

THE SENSORY SYSTEMS

Before the sensory systems are discussed the concepts sensation and perception must be distinguished: *sensation* is the result of activity of receptors and their associated afferent pathways to the corresponding primary sensory neocortical areas; *perception* is the result of activity of cells in the various sensory regions of the neocortex beyond the primary sensory cortex. Thus, in the neocortex sensory information is transformed into a percept by such factors as experience and context; the percept may differ in a number of ways from the sensory information sent to the neocortex. For example, if a motorist comes upon a road sign partially covered in mud and reading "ST" she would most likely stop her vehicle because her perception is of the word "STOP" although her sensation was only of "ST." From her previous experience with road signs the motorist's sensation is transformed by mediation processes to a perception with considerable meaning.

The clearest proof that perception is more than sensation is the transformation of the same sensory stimulation into totally different perceptions, and the fact that perceptions are affected by the context of the sensory input. The classical demonstration of the former effect is such ambiguous figures as Rubin's vases (see Figure 10-1). The figure may be seen either as a vase or as two faces, and if one fixates on the dot in the center the perceptions alternate even though the sensory stimulation has remained constant. Similarly, the Müller-Lyer illusion in Figure 10-1 demonstrates the influence of context. The top line is perceived as longer than the bottom although both are the same length. The contextual cues (the arrow heads) alter the perception of line length. Ambiguous figures and illusions involve complex perceptual phenomena that are mediated by the neocortex at a functional level beyond the primary sensory cortex. They also illustrate the complexity of perceptual phenomena produced by the secondary and tertiary sensory regions, and allow us some insight into the bases of cognitive processes.

The distinction between sensation and per-

A

B

FIGURE 10-1. Demonstration of the distinction between sensation and perception. A. An ambiguous or reversible figure first described by Rubin. The figure can be seen as a vase or as two faces. B. The Müller-Lyer illusion: the top line appears longer than the bottom line because of contextual cues (the arrowheads).

ception is particularly useful to neuropsychology because it allows different predictions to be made of the effects of lesions to lower (sensory) and upper (perceptual) components of the sensory systems. Specifically, damage to the sensory system, up to and including the primary sensory cortex, should produce distortions of the details of the world around us, whereas damage to the higher sensory regions of the neocortex, and in particular the gnostic regions, should result in deficits in understand-

ing or comprehending the meaning of the incoming sensory information. These predictions are indeed confirmed by the evidence.

Although in this chapter we discuss the workings of entire sensory systems, our primary focus is on the functioning of their perceptual components, which are largely found in the posterior portions of the hemispheres. After briefly reviewing the anatomy and physiology of the lowest levels of the sensory systems, we concentrate on disturbances of function (e.g., agnosias) resulting from damage at higher levels. Our discussion is limited to the visual, somesthetic, and auditory systems, because little is known about the neuropsychology of human olfaction and taste. Detailed discussions of sensory system anatomy and physiology being beyond the scope of this chapter, the reader is referred to discussions by Thompson and Uttal for more detailed reviews.

THE VISUAL SYSTEM

The visual system is composed of two distinct anatomical routes that converge on a final end point:

1. The **geniculostriate system** consists of the projections from the retina of the eye to the lateral geniculate nucleus of the thalamus, then to the neocortex in areas 17, 18, and 19, and finally 20 and 21.

2. The **tectopulvinar system** consists of projections from the retina to the superior colliculus, to the pulvinar and lateral posterior nucleus of the thalamus, and finally to areas 20 and 21 of the neocortex (see Figure 10-2).

Experimental evidence from monkeys suggests that these two anatomical systems have distinct functions: the geniculostriate system is involved in the perception of forms, colors, and patterns; the tectopulvinar pathway is in-

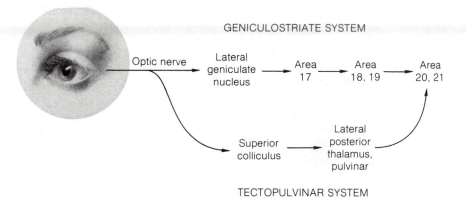

GENICULOSTRIATE SYSTEM

Optic nerve → Lateral geniculate nucleus → Area 17 → Area 18, 19 → Area 20, 21

Superior colliculus → Lateral posterior thalamus, pulvinar

TECTOPULVINAR SYSTEM

FIGURE 10-2. The connections of the visual system. One such subsystem, the geniculo-striate system, is specialized for pattern analysis; the other subsystem, the tectopulvinar system, is specialized for the detection of visual stimuli. Notice that the systems converge in the tertiary visual cortex.

volved primarily in locating visual stimuli in space. That is, the tectopulvinar system locates visual stimuli that are then analyzed for form and content by the geniculostriate system. These functions are, however, not mutually exclusive, for some degree of pattern vision is spared following lesions of the geniculostriate system, and vice versa.

Physiology

By the use of microelectrodes neurophysiologists have recorded the activity of cells in anesthetized cats and monkeys while visual stimuli are presented on a screen placed in the animals' visual field. It has been found that:

1. Cells at each level of the visual system are responsive to a specific region of the visual field, known as the cell's receptive field.

2. The entire visual field is re-represented at each level in the visual system.

3. Cells in different levels of the visual system respond to different properties of visual stimulation.

The higher the location of cells in the visual system, the more complex the visual stimulus must be to excite them. For example, cells in the retina are most responsive to spots of light falling in the center of their receptive fields. In some retinal cells this light produces a rapid increase in the firing rate of the cell, and in others produces an inhibition of all firing of the cell. In contrast, cells in area 17 of the visual cortex are most responsive to *bars* of light of a particular orientation. Some cells are most responsive to bars of light oriented at 90° from horizontal, whereas others are most responsive to bars oriented at other angles. Cells in areas 18 and 19 require more complex stimuli, being most responsive to bars of light oriented at a particular angle and moving in a particular direction. Still more complex cells are maximally responsive to more complex patterns of light, such as corners; in areas 21 and 22 cells may be responsive to particular shapes, such as that of a hand. In essence these microelectrode results confirm findings from more traditional techniques; that is, the successively higher levels of the visual system are more involved than lower levels in processing complex aspects of stimulation.

Effects of Lesions of the Visual System

The nature of a visual disturbance will depend upon the location of the damage (see Figure 10-3). Destruction of the retina or optic nerve of one eye produces **monocular blindness,** the loss of sight in that eye. A lesion of the medial region of the **optic chiasm** severs the crossing fibers, producing **bitemporal hemianopsia,** loss of vision of both temporal fields. A lesion of the lateral chiasm results in a loss of vision of one nasal field, or **nasal hemianopsia.** Complete cuts of the optic tract, lateral geniculate body, or area 17 will result in **homonymous hemianopsia,** blindness of one entire visual field. Should this lesion be partial, as is often the case, **quadrantic hemianopsia** occurs: destruction of only a portion of the visual field. Lesions of the occipital lobe frequently spare the central, or macular region, of the visual field, although the reason is uncertain. The most reasonable explanations of this **macular sparing** are: (1) The macular region receives a double vascular supply, from both the middle and posterior cerebral arteries, making it more resilient to large hemispheric lesions. Or, (2) the foveal region of the retina projects to both hemispheres, so that even if one occipital lobe is destroyed, the other receives projections from the fovea. Macular sparing helps to differentiate lesions of the tract or thalamus from cortical lesions, since macular sparing occurs only after lesions (usually large) of the visual cortex.

Small lesions of the occipital lobe often produce **scotomas,** small blind spots in the visual field. A curious aspect of these defects is that people are often totally unaware of them, because of **nystagmus,** constant tiny eye movements, and "spontaneous filling in." Because the eyes are in constant motion the scotoma moves about the visual field, allowing the brain to perceive all the information in the field. If the eyes are held still, the visual system actually completes objects, faces, etc., resulting in a normal percept of the stimulus. The visual system may cover up the scotoma so successfully that its presence can be demonstrated to the patient by "tricking" the visual system. This can be achieved by placing objects entirely within the scotoma, and, without allowing the patient to shift his or her gaze, asking what the object is. If no object is reported, the examiner moves the object out of the scotoma and it will suddenly appear in the intact region of the patient's visual field, thus demonstrating the existence of a blind region.

More complex effects on visual perception result from lesions in the visual system beyond the primary visual cortex. It is in these higher levels, especially in areas 20 and 21, that cerebral asymmetry becomes apparent, for lesions on the right produce larger deficits in perception of complex visual forms, such as faces and geometric patterns, whereas lesions on the left produce large deficits in perception of verbally related material. For example, lesions in the region of the Brodmann's area 39, particularly in the angular gyrus, produce **dyslexia,** deficits in reading, because letters no longer form meaningful words. We shall return to these perceptual deficits soon, in our discussion of agnosias.

Evidence for Two Visual Systems

Curiously, in neuropsychology, many ideas about brain function that were introduced around the turn of the century were extremely insightful although usually based on inference from only a few patients; most such ideas were ignored until the 1960s and 1970s. The idea that there are two parallel visual systems is a good case in point.

In 1918 Holmes reported a series of patients with unique visual deficits. These patients all had intact vision in the center of the visual field—that is, they could identify ob-

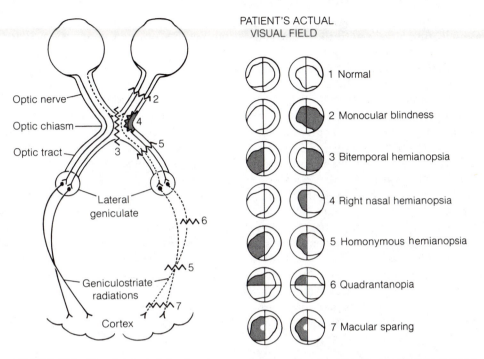

PATIENT'S ACTUAL
VISUAL FIELD

1 Normal

2 Monocular blindness

3 Bitemporal hemianopsia

4 Right nasal hemianopsia

5 Homonymous hemianopsia

6 Quadrantanopia

7 Macular sparing

FIGURE 10-3. Visual defects following damage at different levels of the visual system as denoted by numerals. A darkened region in the visual field denotes a blind area. (After Curtis, 1972.)

jects when asked to—but they often failed to notice objects that were within their range of vision. They had difficulty as well following moving objects with their eyes, judging depth, and orienting themselves visually in the space around them. These deficits implied to Holmes that there might be two components to the visual system: one to discriminate visual stimuli, and a second to locate and attend to stimuli in the visual field. This theory was supported by a phenomenon reported the previous year: Riddoch described patients who were apparently blind but were able to grasp objects in motion and could indicate the direction of motion, even if they reported not having seen the object! Weiskrantz recently dubbed this phenomenon blindsight, implying functional vision in cortically blind people.

Weiskrantz and others have extended Riddoch's observations. For example, we recently observed a man who suffered from nearly total cortical blindness, exhibiting only macular sparing. At one meter, this man could see a region about the size of a quarter. He was, however, capable of detecting objects outside this region. If an examiner moved his finger slowly into the area of vision and asked the patient to indicate when he first saw it, he failed to note its presence until it moved into the macular region. If the examiner moved his fingers rapidly in an oscillating motion and slowly moved toward the center of the visual field, no object was reported until it reached the macular region, but this report was accompanied by the statement "Oh, I saw that way out to the side!" Curiously, even with repeated practice the subject failed to acknowledge the oscillating fingers until they reached the macula, at which point he reported observing them earlier. Weiskrantz has labeled this phenomenon "hindsight in blindsight."

Riddoch and Holmes, and later others, have supplied evidence supporting the notion of two functional visual systems corresponding to the two anatomical pathways illustrated in Figure 10-2. The detection, location, and following of objects by the eyes are thought to be primarily functions of the tectopulvinar system, whereas form and color analysis are primarily functions of the geniculostriate system. Animal studies support this conclusion; several groups have developed convincing animal models of two anatomical and functional visual systems in species as diverse as hamsters and monkeys. Schneider, for example, demonstrated that ablation of the superior colliculus had little effect on pattern discrimination, but produced deficits in orientation to visual stimuli. Conversely, lesion of the striate cortex severely disrupted pattern vision, but did not impair orientation to visual stimuli.

Visual Agnosias

Visual agnosia is the term coined by Sigmund Freud for the inability to combine individual visual impressions into complete patterns—thus, the inability to recognize objects or their pictorial representations. Furthermore, patients with agnosias are unable not only to perceive objects but also to draw them or even to copy a representation of them. Agnosias cannot be explained as defects in sensation or as general disturbances of intellectual functioning. Rather, they are a defect in perception resulting from damage to a gnostic area. Luria has found that eye movements of agnosics are abnormal, adding further complexity to the syndrome. Normal subjects have a very complex but consistent manner of

looking at objects, pictures, etc. This pattern is completely disrupted in agnosic patients, who now produce random eye movements as illustrated in Figure 10-4. Luria also demonstrated perceptual defects similar to agnosias in patients without obvious perceptual difficulties by masking pictures of objects in ways similar to those diagrammed in Figure 10-5. There are several types of visual agnosias, summarized in Table 10-1 and described below.

Visual Object Agnosia. A patient with visual object agnosia when shown an object can see it but is unable to name it, demonstrate its use, or remember having seen it before. Hécaen and Albert describe one patient who identified a bicycle as "a pole with two wheels, one in front, one in back." Visual object agnosias are rare, leading to controversy over their existence and the precise location of a lesion leading to this condition. Hécaen and Angelergues found only 4 instances of object agnosia among 415 patients with cortical lesions. The general consensus is that a lesion of the left occipital lobe extending into subcortical white matter is necessary for the condition to occur. It is common for the damage to be bilateral, often including the corpus callosum and the inferior longitudinal fasciculus in the right hemisphere.

Visual Agnosia for Drawings. Visual agnosias affect recognition of a variety of drawn stimuli, including realistic representations of simple objects, complex scenes, schematic reproductions of objects, geometric figures, meaningless forms, incomplete figures, and abstract drawings. The lesion producing this condition is most likely located in secondary and tertiary visual cortex areas 18 through 21 in either hemisphere, although lesions in the right hemisphere may be more damaging.

Prosopagnosia: Agnosia for Faces. In 1947, Bodamer described the inability of three

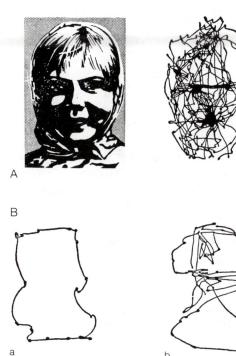

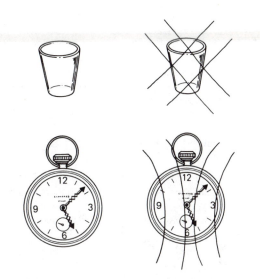

FIGURE 10-5. Luria's test of visual recognition of crossed-out figures found to be difficult for sufferers of visual agnosias. One response to the crossed-out watch was "chick hatching from an egg and some funny circles."

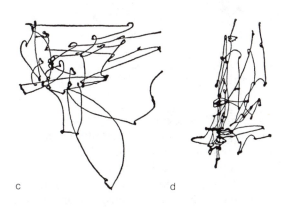

FIGURE 10-4. Eye movements during the examination of a visual stimulus. A. The concentration of normal eye movements (by a normal subject) to distinctive features of the face (eyes, nose, mouth); these movements are more directed at the left side of the photograph. B. The eye movements of a normal subject examining a sphere (a) and a bust (b); c and d represent the eye movements of an agnosic subject examining the same shapes. Note the random movements of the agnosic subject. (From A. R. Luria, *The Working Brain*. The Copyright Agency of the USSR. Reprinted by permission.)

patients to recognize faces although they were able to recognize objects, forms, and colors. This deficit, although rare, has since been confirmed by many others. According to Hécaen and Albert, sufferers from the disorder, although able to differentiate one face from another, cannot recognize previously known faces by relying only on the visual perception of them. Some patients may even be unable to recognize their own faces in a mirror! There is little agreement on the best explanation of **prosopagnosia.** Many studies have demonstrated that lesions of the right hemisphere alter the perception or memory of faces, implying that prosopagnosia results from damage to some critical area in the right hemisphere; but the necessary and sufficient damage is uncertain (see Meadows and Benson et al.). Less severe disturbances in the recognition and memory of faces are much more common than prosopagnosia. It appears that memory of faces is impaired by lesions of the

TABLE 10-1

Summary of the major agnosias

Type	Deficit	Most probable lesion site
Visual agnosias		
Object agnosia	Naming, using, or recognizing objects	Areas 18,19,20,21 on left + corpus callosum
Agnosia for drawings	Recognition of drawn stimuli	Areas 18,19,20,21 on right
Prosopagnosia	Recognition of faces	Areas 20,21 on right
Color agnosia	Association of colors with objects	Areas 18,19 on right
Color anomia	Naming colors	Speech zones or connections from areas 18,19,37
Achromatopsia	Distinguishing hues	Areas 18, 19, 37
Visual spatial agnosia	Stereoscopic vision, topographical concepts	Areas 18,19,37 on right
Auditory agnosias		
Amusia	Tone deafness; melody deafness; disorders of rhythm, measure, or tempo	Areas 42,22 on right
Agnosia for sounds	Identifying meaning of nonverbal sounds	Areas 42,22 bilaterally?
Somatosensory agnosias		
Astereognosia	Recognition of objects by touch	Areas 5,7
Anosognosia	Awareness of illness	Areas 7,40 on right
Anosodiaphoria	Response to illness	Areas 7,40 on right
Autotopognosia	Localization and naming of body parts	Areas 7,40? on left
Asymbolia for pain	Reaction to pain	Area 43?

right temporal lobe, and perception of faces by lesions of the right parietal lobe.

Color Agnosia. Impaired color recognition can take any of three different forms: achromatopsia, color anomia, and color agnosia. **Achromatopsia** is an inability to distinguish different hues in the presence of normally pigmented cells in the retina. It can be described as cortical color blindness, which differs from congenital color blindness in that achromatopsia affects all parts of the color spectrum. All colors appear less bright, and the environment is "drained of color" or, in severe cases, totally lacking color. Meadows concluded that achromatopsia results from *bilateral* lesions of areas 18, 19, and probably 37. **Color anomia,** or color aphasia, is an inability to name colors, and is generally associated with other aphasic symptoms. **Color agnosia** is an inability to associate particular colors with objects or particular objects with colors. Hécaen and Albert characterize color agnosia as: (1) preservation of color perception as determined by tests of color discrimination; and (2) inability to select all colors of the same hue from a group of colored objects, to pick out or point to colors on command, to name colors in the absence of aphasia, and to evoke the specific colors of color-specific objects such as tomato, grass, etc.

Anatomical studies have not conclusively indicated which lesions result in the various types of disturbances in color perception and recognition. Meadows presented a theoretical anatomical model, which we have altered somewhat: see Figure 10-6. It is assumed that lesions of areas 18, 19, and 37 produce achromatopsia because the cells responsible for color coding have been destroyed. Color aphasia or anomia results from a lesion of the speech zones or a disconnection of the speech zones from areas 18, 19, and 37, thus isolating the regions from one another. Color agnosia could result from a variety of lesions that disconnect the color cells from the memory functions. In this case, color could be seen but not recognized. Correlated defects in linguistic ability could result from damage to the connections with the language zones or to the language zones themselves.

Visual Spatial Agnosias. A variety of disorders of spatial perception and orientation have been described. These deficits, caused mainly by right posterior hemispheric lesions (particularly in the right parietal and occipital cortex), include defective stereoscopic vision, loss of topographical concepts, and neglect of one side of the world. We will return to spatial agnosias in our discussion of the parietal lobes.

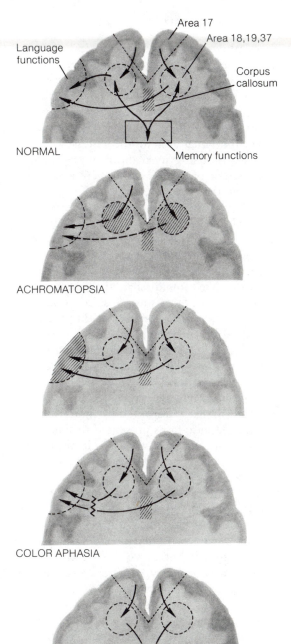

FIGURE 10-6. Cerebral function demonstrating possible mechanisms of various abnormalities of color vision. Each diagram represents a schematic section through the brain illustrating visual association cortex (areas 18, 19, 37), language functions, and a theoretical memory function. Memory functions are drawn as a single box, but it is understood that this is theoretical and may not actually represent a brain structure. (After Meadows, 1974.)

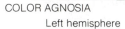

Are Faces Special?

Faces convey a wealth of social and affective information to humans. This importance of faces as visual stimuli led Teuber to postulate a special mode for the analysis of faces that is analogous to the left hemisphere's apparent innate predisposition for the analysis of words. When the visual system encounters words, a special processing mechanism in the tertiary visual region of the left hemisphere is invoked to allow their comprehension. Teuber suggested that when faces are encountered they are analyzed by a special processing mechanism in the right hemisphere so they are recognized in a manner analogous to words. An intriguing study by Yin supports Teuber's hypothesis. Yin found that the memory of photographs of faces was impaired in patients with right posterior lesions but this handicap was reduced when the photographs were presented upside down or when other complex visual stimuli, such as houses, were used instead. Yin concluded that photographs of faces presented upright are processed by a special mechanism that is disrupted by right posterior lesions. Because faces presented upside down do not stimulate the special mechanism, right posterior lesions do not affect the recognition of these stimuli.

The Teuber-Yin theory raises several questions. First, if there is a special processing mechanism for faces, where is it located? The tertiary cortex of the right parietal lobe is a likely candidate but, as we noted earlier, prosopagnosia is not very common, even in the presence of large right parietal lesions which produce many other deficits (see Chapter 12). Second, there is some doubt as to the nature of the special perceptual mechanism. Teuber appears to have assumed it to be a mechanism devoted to combining features of facial stimuli into a whole, or gestalt; but it is uncertain how this mechanism would be specific for faces. Fi-

nally, Yin's experiment confounds both perceptual and memory functions. If the Teuber-Yin view is correct, orientation would be expected to have an effect on a purely perceptual test as well. Kolb and his colleagues failed to confirm this prediction. They presented subjects with photographs of faces as illustrated in Figure 10-7. Each of the two lower photographs is a composite of the left or right side of the original face shown in the upper photograph. Asked to identify which of the composite photographs most resembled the original, normal subjects consistently matched the left side of the original photograph to its composite, whether or not the photographs were presented upright or inverted. This finding is not predicted by the Yin-Teuber theory. Furthermore, patients with either right temporal or right parietal removals failed to match consistently to either side of the face in either the upright or inverted presentation.

As intriguing an idea as the Teuber-Yin theory is, we believe that the data on facial perception and memory warrant a more parsimonious interpretation: the posterior part of the right hemisphere is specialized for the processing of complex visual patterns, whether they be faces, geometric patterns, or the like. Perception of faces is particularly sensitive to the effects of right posterior damage because faces are especially complex, and because there are so many different faces, many of which superficially appear highly similar. Indeed, the uniqueness of individual human faces is based on very small differences, and mastery of the differentiation of faces requires considerable practice, and possibly includes a genetic predisposition. In this regard, deficits in facial perception might result, in part, from deficits in the identificaton of the distinctive features used in differentiation, rather than in the flawed formation of an actual gestalt of a particular face. As we noted, if the normal pat-

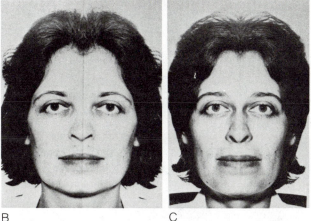

FIGURE 10-7. An example of the split faces test. Subjects were asked which of the two bottom pictures, B or C, most closely resembled the top picture, A. C was chosen by controls significantly more often than B. C corresponds to that part of A falling in the subjects' left visual field. (After Kolb, Milner, and Taylor, 1980.)

tern of visual scanning of faces is disrupted, recognition of faces might be impaired, in spite of a relatively intact percept of a given face. Indeed, the difficulty that normal adults initially have in differentiating individuals of an unfamiliar race may imply that one must learn to scan the faces of different racial groups in particular ways to identify the cues necessary for accurate identification.

THE AUDITORY SYSTEM

Anatomy

Auditory projections from both the left and right ears travel to both hemispheres (see Figure 9-6). Figure 10-8 illustrates the major connections of the auditory pathway crossing from the ear and cochlear nucleus to the in-

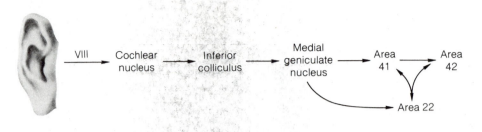

FIGURE 10-8. The major connections of the auditory system.

ferior colliculus, medial geniculate nucleus of the thalamus, and the cortex. The primary auditory region in the cortex is area 41, located in Heschl's gyrus, which is connected to the secondary auditory zones that include areas 42 and 22. Area 22 also receives direct connections from the medial geniculate, although it receives fewer than area 41. The crossed pathways to the hemisphere contralateral to each ear enjoy preferential access and input into the respective auditory cortical areas, as noted earlier in conjunction with the dichotic listening results.

Physiology

Microelectrode studies have shown that the neurons of the auditory system are arranged hierarchically: the auditory input travels from the auditory nerve to the cochlear nuclei, superior olivary nuclei, inferior colliculi, medial geniculate nuclei, and finally the auditory cortex. Single neurons in the auditory system code the frequency (or pitch) of sounds, different neurons being maximally sensitive to different sound frequencies. In general, cells low in the hierarchy are responsive to a broader band of frequencies than are cells higher in the hierarchy. Thus, a neuron in the cochlear nucleus may have a tuning curve with maximum sensitivity at 7000 Hz, with reduced sensitivity to frequencies between 1000 and 12,000 Hz, as compared to a neuron in

the auditory cortex whose tuning curve is also maximally sensitive to 7000 Hz but is partially responsive to frequencies between only 5000 and 9000 Hz. At the highest levels specificity of frequency is reduced slightly, because the cells are also responsive to particular spatial location as well as to certain special characteristics such as harmonics.

Effects of Lesions of the Auditory System

Whereas lesions in the primary visual pathways have devastating effects (i.e., blindness), brain lesions in the auditory system do not easily produce deafness. Lesions of the auditory nerve produce deafness in the connected ear as would be expected, but the only other way to induce deafness is by a bilateral lesion of the auditory system. For example, a bilateral lesion in Heschl's gyrus will produce deafness in both ears, but a unilateral lesion in either of Heschl's gyri will not produce deafness in either ear. The only consistent effect of lesions in the primary auditory projection cortex (area 41) described to date is an increase in the threshold for auditory sensation in the contralateral ear. In other words, a sound must be louder to be perceived.

Analysis of auditory perception in patients with lesions to secondary auditory cortex (areas 22 and 42) indicates clear asymmetry of function. For example, a deficit in the recall of dichotically presented digits is observed after left temporal lesions but not after right temporal removals. Rather than being specific to the right ear the deficit affects both ears, suggesting some sort of deficit in selectively attending to and differentiating simultaneous speech sounds. One might predict that patients so afflicted would have a very difficult time listening to a conversation in the midst of much background talking, such as at a party. A second deficit following left temporal lesions is found in phonemic hearing. According to Luria, patients asked to repeat pairs of oppositional phonemes, such as da-ta, ba-pa, or sa-za, have difficulty doing so correctly. Instead, the patients repeat da-da, pa-pa, and so on. This deficit is not seen in patients with anterior temporal lobectomies, implying that the damage involved is near Wernicke's area in the posterior part of area 22.

Lesions to the secondary zone of the right auditory cortex produce quite different results. First, analysis of music is impaired. For example, Milner gave patients the six subtests of the Seashore Measures of Musical Talents test: pitch discrimination, loudness, rhythm, time, timbre, and tonal memory. Patients with right temporal removals were impaired on the last two subtests, whereas analogous left temporal lesions failed to interfere with performance on any test. The timbre test measures the ability to distinguish between complex sounds that differ only in harmonic structure. It consists of 50 pairs of tones; for each pair the subject must judge whether the tone quality of the two is the same or different. On the tonal memory test a sequence of notes is played twice in rapid succession; the sequences are identical except that one note in the sequence is changed in the second playing. The subject must compare the two tonal patterns and identify, by its number in the sequence, the note that was changed at the second playing. Thus, the deficit in the analysis of

music observed after right temporal lobe damage is somewhat specific, because it affects only the more complex aspects of musical analysis, not the more basic aspects.

Shankweiler has reported one other auditory deficit following right temporal lesions. People with right temporal lobe damage were worse than people with left temporal lobe damage at locating the source of sounds in space. This result is consistent with the preferential assessment of visuospatial information by the right hemisphere.

Auditory Agnosias

An **auditory agnosia** is the impaired capacity to recognize the nature of *nonverbal* acoustic stimuli. The most common auditory agnosias are **amusia,** agnosia for music, and agnosia for other sounds (see Table 10-1).

Amusia. In 1926, Henschen reported 16 patients who had musical agnosia but had no language deficit. Since preservation of musical abilities in aphasic musicians had been documented many times since the 1830s, Henschen concluded that the two functions were in opposite sides of the brain. This argument was not unanimously accepted, and today it is difficult to find a convincing case of amusia in the absence of a language or perceptive disorder. Nevertheless, there is some evidence that Henschen's idea may be partly correct. For example, left-hemisphere lesions and left carotid injections of sodium Amytal can produce aphasia while leaving singing ability relatively intact. Thus, we are inclined to agree with Henschen: we think it reasonable to propose that some aspects of music and language are juxtaposed in the brain, and to expect right-hemisphere lesions to produce a condition of amusia analogous to the aphasia that results from left-hemisphere lesions. Further support for this idea comes from the common clinical observation that many severely aphasic patients can carry a tune and can even sing the words to previously learned songs. We saw a middle-aged woman with severe left hemisphere damage and dense aphasia who was able to sing with some coaxing and even managed a recognizable version of the national anthem—much to the surprise of herself, us, and the attending nurses.

Amusias can be subdivided into various forms, including tone deafness (the inability to discriminate various tones in a scale) and melody deafness (impaired recall or recognition of a melody), as well as disorders of rhythm, measure, or tempo. To date there are only scattered case reports of these various amusias, and there are no compelling quantitative studies demonstrating double dissociation to show they are independent. Lesions resulting in amusias usually have been located in the right middle temporal regions, roughly areas 22 and 42.

Agnosia for Sounds. Agnosia for sounds is characterized by an inability to identify the meaning of nonverbal sounds, such as a bell ringing. Sounds either may sound all alike to the patient, or, if they are distinguished, may be confused for one another. Thus, in the former case all sounds may be labeled as bird song, whereas in the latter case bird song and bell tinkling may be confused. Some patients remain able to recognize speech and music, but more usually amusia and word deafness are associated.

To date, the location of the lesions resulting in agnosia for sounds is uncertain, although the evidence favors bilateral temporal damage. We suspect that the syndrome of perceiving all sounds as similar may result from damage, perhaps bilateral, to secondary auditory areas (22 and 42). On the other hand, different sounds may be confused because the auditory percept is disconnected from the verbal or

memory components necessary to label the sound, much as is proposed as the cause of color agnosia (Figure 10-6).

THE SOMATOSENSORY SYSTEM

Anatomy

The somatosensory system includes the skin senses of touch, pressure, pain, temperature, itch, vibration, and tickle, as well as the body senses of joint position, muscle tension, and visceral state. Two neocortical regions are recognized as **somatosensory areas**: the primary somatosensory cortex (SI) corresponding to the postcentral gyrus (areas 1, 2, 3); and the secondary, or supplementary, somatosensory cortex (SII) located on the superior bank of the Sylvian fissure (area 43).

Penfield and others have demonstrated somatosensory maps for both SI and SII indicating a point-to-point representation of the skin on the neocortex. In general, the amount of cortex devoted to a particular body region is directly proportional to the sensitivity of that region. In humans, the hand and face areas are therefore proportionately much larger in both SI and SII. Skin sensation in these zones is consequently more likely to be affected by cortical damage than sensation elsewhere on the body, such as on the back, simply because the zones are so large. The SI and SII regions differ in that electrical brain stimulation of SI produces sensation primarily on the contralateral side of the body, whereas stimulation at some points in SII produces sensation simultaneously on both sides of the body. SI and SII are distinguished functionally by the input from the skin receptors. As in the visual system there are two pathways to the sensory association cortex. SI receives its input from the lemniscal system via the ventral basal complex of the thalamus, and SII receives its input

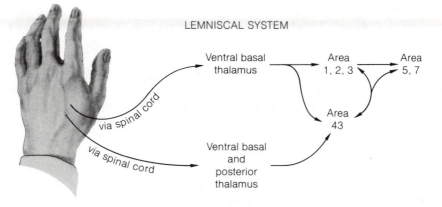

LEMNISCAL SYSTEM

EXTRALEMNISCAL SYSTEM

FIGURE 10-9. The major connections of the somatosensory system. Like the visual system it has two subsystems—the lemniscal system and the extralemniscal, or spinothalamic, system—which converge in the secondary somatosensory cortex. The lemniscal system may be specialized for touch information, the extralemniscal for pain and temperature information.

from the extralemniscal or spinothalamic system via the ventral basal complex and posterior thalamus (see Figure 10-9). The ventrobasal complex and posterior thalamus are amazingly different from one another in functional organization: the ventrobasal area has a topographical somatosensory map similar to the neocortical maps, whereas the posterior thalamus appears to be arranged haphazardly. These thalamic relays to the neocortex may account for the functional differences between SI and SII, but this possibility has not been clearly confirmed.

Physiology

Microelectrode studies have suggested that the somatosensory system is hierarchically arranged. Receptors in the skin transmit five basic sensations: light touch to the skin, deep pressure to the fascia below the skin, joint movement, pain, and temperature. Within the thalamus, cells are highly specific, any given cell being maximally responsive to only one mode of stimulation. Within the next higher level, in the cortex, the cells are just as specific to particular stimuli, but a given cell is responsive to a smaller region of skin. Thus, as one moves up the hierarchy in the somatosensory system there is increased discrimination of *spatial location,* not of the quality of the stimulation. This arrangement differs somewhat from that in the visual and auditory systems, where increased discrimination in the *quality* of the stimulation is found in the higher levels.

Effects of Lesions of the Somesthetic Cortex

Verger, in 1902, and Dejerine, in 1907, published the first descriptions of somatosensory loss resulting from cortical lesions. Symptoms of the Verger-Dejerine syndrome included loss of tactile localization, loss of sense of a limb's position in space, loss of tactile form discrimination, and impaired recognition of objects by touch (stereognosis). On the basis of thorough clinical studies Head elaborated the Verger-Dejerine syndrome, and concluded in 1920 that lesions of the somatosensory cortex produced three largely independent effects: (1) Spatial recognition is impaired, because information about the spatial position of a limb is lost. (2) The threshold for appreciation of the intensity of tactile, thermal, or painful stimuli is raised. (3) Stereognosis is impaired.

The effects of somatosensory cortical lesions were not quantified again until 1960, when Semmes et al. published a careful, large-scale study of patterns of somatosensory defects in patients with missile wounds of the brain. Their findings suggested asymmetry in the somatosensory system: missile wounds anywhere in the right hemisphere produced a sensory defect indicating that somatosensory function was diffuse throughout the right hemisphere. In the left hemisphere, by contrast, only lesions that invaded the region of the postcentral gyrus produced deficits. The implied asymmetry in somatosensory function is remarkable, and surprising, for two reasons: first, lesions to primary areas in the visual and auditory systems do not produce asymmetrical effects; second, many of the lesions studied must have been outside the primary sensory zone.

Other studies have been unable to confirm the Semmes et al. findings. Rather different conclusions came from the Corkin, Milner, and Rasmussen study assessing the effects of restricted cortical excisions on somatosensory function. The major findings of the Corkin et al. study were that lesions of SI produced abnormally high sensory thresholds, impaired position sense, and deficits in stereognosis. Further, these lesions produced difficulty on tests of pressure sensitivity, two-point threshold, and point localization on the skin of the hand contralateral to the lesion. If blindfolded,

the patients also had difficulty reporting whether the fingers of the contralateral hand were passively moved or not. Excisions sparing the postcentral gyrus—whether they be in the precentral gyrus or in the posterior parietal cortex—caused only transient deficits, if any. No evidence supported the asymmetrical representation of somatosensory function reported by Semmes et al. However, the Semmes et al. and Corkin et al. studies differed in a significant way: the subject population of the former study had suffered missile wounds; those of the latter study, surgical wounds. Because the cortical lesions in the Corkin et al. study would have greater specificity and delineation, their findings must be given more weight; but the issue is not yet resolved.

Lesions of the postcentral gyrus may produce a variety of other deficits not reported by the Semmes et al. and Corkin et al. studies. For example, Luria reported a symptom that he calls **afferent paresis:** movements of the fingers are clumsy because the patient has lost the necessary feedback about their exact position. If lesions of the postcentral gyrus cause loss of representation of the face area in the left hemisphere, another defect is often observed: **motor aphasia,** a transient aphasia in which the patient appears unable to figure out how to position the lips and tongue to pronounce the desired sounds. Although it is possibly analogous to Luria's afferent paresis, motor aphasia is not observed following lesions to the homologous region in the right hemisphere.

The effects of lesions localized to areas 5 and 7 and SII area 43 on somatosensory function in humans have not been quantified. Studies on nonhuman primates indicate that lesions of areas 5 and 7 produce defective form discrimination, reduced precision of grasping with the hands, and defective spatial analysis; but we are unaware of analogous studies on human subjects.

Somatosensory Agnosias

There are two major types of somatosensory agnosias: **astereognosia,** the inability to recognize the nature of an object by touch; and **asomatognosia,** the loss of knowledge or sense of one's own body and bodily condition.

Astereognosia. Astereognosias have been recognized since 1844. In 1895, Wernicke divided tactile agnosias into two categories: primary agnosia and secondary agnosia, or asymbolia. Primary agnosia is an inability to recognize tactile qualities of an object, allegedly because of an inability to evoke tactile images. In **asymbolia,** the tactile images are preserved but are disconnected or isolated from other sensory representations; thus, the full significance of the object cannot be appreciated. According to classic neurological doctrine, the principal locus for astereognosia is the posterior parietal cortex, roughly areas 5 and 7. The Corkin et al. study reviewed earlier failed to observe this effect, for tactile agnosias were consistently correlated with defects in sensation, implying that the lesion included primary sensory regions. Clinical cases of tactile agnosia in the absence of primary sensory defect have been reported, but they are admittedly rare. We suspect that they exist and that they represent a disconnection of tactile sensations and memory functions in a manner analogous to the model of color agnosia presented in Figure 10-6.

Asomatognosia. Asomatognosia, the loss of knowledge about one's own body and bodily condition, is one of the most curious of all agnosias. It is an almost unbelievable syndrome—until one has actually observed a person neglecting part of his or her body or denying an obvious illness. There are a variety of different asomatognosias, including **anosognosia,** the unawareness or denial of illness; **anosodiaphoria,** indifference to illness; **autotopognosia,** an inability to localize and name body parts; and asymbolia for pain, the absence of normal reactions to pain. A case study of a patient with asomatognosia is described in Chapter 12.

Asomatognosias may be for one or both sides of the body. Unilateral anosognosias and anosodiaphorias, resulting from lesions of the posterior parietal region in the right hemisphere, are most commonly of the left side of the body. Autotopognosias result from lesions of the left parietal cortex. The lesion location responsible for asymbolia for pain has not yet been established, although it most frequently results from left-hemisphere lesions, possibly because SII either has suffered a lesion or has been disconnected from affective regions of the brain.

HIGHER-LEVEL SENSORY-SYSTEMS INFLUENCES

As we have seen, the secondary and tertiary sensory zones produce a selective picture of the external world by a process known as perception. Normal perception may be disrupted either directly or indirectly. *Direct* disruption occurs either by an absence of sensory input, in which case there may be no perception at all as in blindness or deafness, or by a lesion of the secondary and tertiary sensory zones, in which cases there is an agnosia. *Indirect* disruption also can occur if higher-level control of the perceptual process is altered. As Figure 10-10 shows, sensory information is relayed to the frontal and anterior temporal lobes in the form of a perception; these higher levels, in turn, project back upon the sensory systems. Thus, a feedback loop is formed whereby perceptions can be influenced by previous experience, cognitive set, ongoing behavior, and so on—influences beyond the scope of the sen-

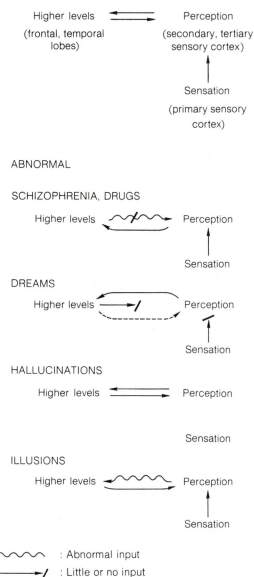

A   NORMAL

Higher levels ⟷ Perception

(frontal, temporal   (secondary, tertiary
lobes)   sensory cortex)

Sensation

(primary sensory
cortex)

B   ABNORMAL

SCHIZOPHRENIA, DRUGS

Higher levels ⟿ Perception

Sensation

DREAMS

Higher levels ⟶ Perception

Sensation

HALLUCINATIONS

Higher levels ⟷ Perception

Sensation

ILLUSIONS

Higher levels ⟿ Perception

Sensation

⟿   : Abnormal input
⟶/ : Little or no input

FIGURE 10-10. A. The role of higher levels in the activity of the sensory systems. Sensory input travels to the frontal and temporal (anterior and medial) lobes, which can in turn influence the perception via a feedback loop. B. Hypothetical disturbances in the higher-level control of sensory systems resulting in various perceptual phenomena.

sory representation of the external world. Consider the following possibilities.

If the sensory input is ambiguous, the perception may be influenced either by cognitive set or by a change in behavior. For example, imagine that you are walking through a park at dusk. Shapes become indistinct in the darkness because the sensory input is inadequate to provide a clear percept of your surroundings. If you are worried that a mugger might be hiding in the bushes (i.e., your set is for muggers), every noise and shape is perceived in that context. On the other hand, if you have no such set, the higher levels may produce behavior necessary to gather more information. Noises and vague shapes are explored to provide a clearer sensory representation and hence modify the perception.

The influence of the higher levels may also sometimes be inhibitory upon the sensory systems, preventing perceptions from dominating behavior. For example, one is unlikely to flee suddenly from the park because of one's perceptions concerning muggers. Fleeing is inhibited and frequently so-called displacement activities, behaviors such as whistling or humming, are produced instead.

The higher levels also allow sensory input to be interpreted in the context of behavior. If you move your eyes you do not perceive the world to move because there is **corollary discharge**: input from the frontal lobe informing the perceptual systems of the eye movement. If you gently push down upon your eyelid with your finger, the eye moves but there is no corollary discharge, so the world is perceived as moving when it did not. In the absence of higher-level input, the sensory stimulation is perceived literally and possibly erroneously. (The effects of frontal lobe lesions on corollary discharge are discussed in Chapter 14.)

Finally, the higher levels add the influence of experience to sensory input (recall our motorist who perceived "ST" as "STOP"). In the absence of higher-level input, sensory input is difficult to interpret, and perhaps can even be meaningless. Nakamura and Mishkin beautifully demonstrated this phenomenon in a recent experiment. They surgically removed the frontal cortex, parietal cortex, and portions of the temporal cortex of monkeys, leaving the visual and limbic systems intact. The remarkable result was that although the visual and limbic systems were intact the monkeys were behaviorally blind. Food could only be found by tactile and auditory cues; fearful objects were ignored; and unfamiliar environments were explored using only tactile cues. Two monkeys were kept alive for 200 days and they remained behaviorally blind. Although the visual system was intact it was unable to influence behavior because the sensory input was disconnected either from the motor output or from the descending influence of higher cortical areas.

Higher-Level Control Disorders and Perceptual Disorders

Seeing the sensory systems as hierarchical and as being influenced by higher-level input makes it possible to understand a number of complex perceptual phenomena such as illusions, hallucinations, and dreaming, in addition to complex perceptual disturbances found in drug intoxication or schizophrenia. We consider these phenomena below.

During the surgical treatment of epilepsy, Penfield, working with Jasper and with Perrot, discovered that stimulating the neocortex produced several remarkable phenomena: **illusions** (perceptual distortions), hallucinations (apparent perception of sights, sounds, etc. not actually present), and dreamlike states similar to what Hughlings-Jackson had described as dreamy states or psychical seizures in epileptic attacks. These phenomena reported by Penfield are of great interest, because they

provide a key to understanding illusions, hallucinations, and dreams under more normal circumstances.

Penfield reported illusions of four basic forms: (1) Auditory illusions (sounds seem louder, fainter, more distant, or nearer) occurred when the superior temporal gyrus (area 22) of either hemisphere was stimulated. (2) Visual illusions (objects are nearer, farther, larger, or smaller) occurred predominantly when the right temporal lobe was stimulated. (3) Illusions of recognition in which present experience seems either familiar (déjà vu) or strange, unreal, and dreamlike occurred predominantly when the right temporal lobe was stimulated. (4) Emotional illusions such as feelings of fear, loneliness, or sorrow occurred when either temporal lobe was stimulated.

Hallucinations took the form of dreamlike states in which familiar voices, music, scenes, etc. were experienced as being there, even when the patient knew that they could not be. Like illusions, the auditory hallucinations occurred when area 22 of either hemisphere was stimulated, whereas the visual hallucinations occurred primarily when the right temporal lobe was stimulated. An example of the responses of one of Penfield and Jasper's patients follows.

This French Canadian veteran, age 24, had had seizures for 6 years. His attacks were ushered in by a dizziness in which there was a sense of rotation. Then he might hear a voice calling "Sylvère, Sylvère, Sylvère." Sylvère was his own first name. As the years passed the warning changed to a feeling of nausea which he located behind his sternum. The warning gave him time to lie down so that he would not fall. There was a lapse of consciousness which might only last for 30 seconds. At times there was a major convulsive seizure.

Psychical precipitation. He volunteered the information that an attack was sometimes precipitated when he sought to recall the name of a person or to reflect whether or not he had seen a thing before. He illustrated this in a conversation with Dr. Robert Sears as follows, "Now, for example, if I thought I had seen you somewhere, perhaps in a crowd, and if I tried to make certain in my mind whether I had seen you or not, I might have an attack."

The precipitating factor seemed to be the intellectual process involved in comparing the present experience with the memory of past similar experiences. This is the same mechanism which must be interfered with during perceptual illusions. In an *illusion of familiarity* ("déjà vu") there is false activation of the mechanism. When this patient tried to make normal use of that mechanism he evidently precipitated an epileptogenic discharge in the temporal cortex.

The focus of the seizures was shown by preoperative electroencephalograms to be right temporal. Ventricular pneumography showed some enlargement of the right temporal horn of the ventricle.

Right osteoplastic craniotomy was carried out.

There was evidently an *arteriovenous anastomosis* within the temporal lobe. The substance of the temporal cortex was of normal consistency on its lateral aspect but the superior surface of the temporal lobe became quite abnormal where it lay in contact with the insula. Here it was yellow and tough. This toughness extended into the uncus and amygdaloid nucleus where it was grayish-yellow in color.

The Rahm stimulator was set at 50 cycles and 1 volt for points 1 to 5. After that it was changed to 2 volts for succeeding stimulations. The following were some of the responses to stimulation.

Numbers 1 to 13 mark the sites of origin of somatic sensory and motor responses. Curiously enough, at point 11 the patient opened his mouth. This was followed by a *sneeze* and chewing movements.

14. "Just like someone whispering, or something, in my left ear. It sounded something like a crowd." Warning was then given but no stimulation. He reported, "Nothing."

15. "Again someone trying to speak to me, a single person." When asked, he added, "Oh a man's voice, I could not understand what he said."

16. (While the electrode was held in place.) The patient said, "Something brings back a memory, I could see Seven-Up Bottling Company—Harrison Bakery."

Warning given again, but no stimulus applied. Again he was not fooled and replied, "Nothing."

17. (While the electrode was held in place.) "Again something I have heard of but I cannot remember it." On questioning he added that it was a word but he could not remember what word.

18. (Stimulus applied without warning the patient.) He said he was a little drowsy, then, "Someone was there in front of me right where the nurse is sitting."

19. (During stimulation.) "I am trying to find the name of a song. There was a piano there and someone was playing. I could hear the song, you know. It is a song I have sung before but I cannot find out quite what the title of the song is." The electrode was removed. After listening to the above dictation the patient added, "That was what I was trying to do when you finished stimulating!"

19. (Repeated without warning.) After withdrawal of the electrode, he said, "Someone speaking to another and he mentioned a name, but I could not understand it." When asked whether he saw the person, he replied, "It was just like a dream." When asked if the person was there he said, "Yes, sir, about where the nurse with the eyeglasses is sitting over there."

19. (Repeated again without warning the patient and without questioning him.) "Yes, 'Oh Marie, Oh Marie'—someone is singing it." He was then asked who it was and replied, "I don't know, Doctor, I cannot recognize the voice."

19. (Repeated again without warning.) He observed, while the electrode was being held in place, "Again, 'Oh Marie, Oh Marie.'" He explained that he had heard this before. "It is a theme song," he said, on a radio program. The program is called the 'Life of Luigi.'" The patient then discussed the identity of the song with Dr. Sears and he ended by singing the well

known refrain, "Oh Marie, Oh Marie." All in the operating room recognized the song.

21. "Someone telling me in my left [contralateral] ear 'Sylvère, Sylvère!' It could have been the voice of my brother."

23. "It is a woman calling something but I cannot make out the name."

24. (Deep stimulation with coated needle, the point being directed toward the buried transverse gyrus of Heschl.) "Buzzing sound."

25. (Stimulation without warning.) "There is someone near my left eye."

25. (Repeated without warning.) "Oh my left eye! I see someone." Then he explained that there were men and women. "They seemed to be sitting down and listening to someone. But I do not see who that someone might be."

22. Nausea.

19 was restimulated several times toward the close of exploration. Instead of causing him to hear the song, it produced nothing. The voltage was increased from 2 to 3 and the stimulation was repeated. This made him feel nauseated and he vomited, but it resulted in nothing else. (Penfield and Jasper, 1954, pp. 452–455)

The illusions and hallucinations described by Penfield and Jasper are remarkably similar to those observed in dreams or during epilepsy, sensory deprivation, drug intoxication, and other disorders. It is imperative to emphasize, however, that brain stimulation produces these states only in epileptic patients and not in patients with other neurological disorders, implying that epileptic brains are significantly different from other brains. Nonetheless, the similarity of spontaneous illusions and hallucinations to those observed by Penfield and Jasper is of great interest because it implies that these phenomena can be understood as disturbances in the normal functioning of the sensory systems.

Illusions. A variety of theoretical explanations have been proposed for illusions, but they are difficult to test empirically. Many such theories assume that illusions result from a failure of sensory and higher-level input to become synthesized, since normal perception is assumed to rely on the integration of input from these sources. The result is a distorted perception of the world.

Hallucinations. Hallucinations can be thought to result from stimulation of the sensory cortex without stimulation of the receptors. Normally the higher levels (presumably the frontal lobe) exert an influence to resolve this discrepancy. If this frontal influence is absent, a pathological state occurs. An example will illustrate: it is a common occurrence to "see" nonexistent things out of the corner of one's eye, "hear" nonexistent noises, or "feel" nonexistent irritations on the skin. Ordinarily this sensory input is confirmed or discarded by the higher levels, which direct orienting behavior to investigate the perceived stimulation. But what if this behavioral response were not produced? Consider what happens if you intentionally inhibit your response to reach for a possible insect on your skin: the stimulation becomes intolerable, both becoming more intense and increasing your uncertainty about the significance of the stimulation—even though there may be absolutely nothing here. Normally behavior is produced to resolve the ambiguity, but schizophrenics or people under the influence of psychogenic drugs may fail to produce this behavior normally, if at all. The result may be perception of stimuli not actually present. Support for this admittedly speculative proposal comes from indirect evidence of frontal-lobe dysfunction in both schizophrenia and drug intoxication. The neurochemistry of the tertiary zones of the frontal lobes is known to differ from that of other neocortical regions, because there are catecholaminergic synapses in the frontal lobe and apparently few, if any, elsewhere in the neocortex. Since schizophrenia and the effects of psychogenic drugs are generally thought to produce major changes in dopaminergic synapses in the neocortex and elsewhere, it is reasonable to suggest that the frontal lobe's higher-level influences on perception may be impaired. Although this interpretation is speculative, it is heuristic, providing a reasonable neuropsychological explanation of disordered perception in schizophrenia and drug intoxication.

Dreams. Penfield and Jasper, recall, produced "dreamy states" by electrically stimulating the higher-level sensory zones of the temporal lobes, especially of the right temporal lobe—suggesting that dreams may normally result from activation of the temporal lobes, possibly more so of the right than of the left. As electrophysiological work in cats has shown, sensory input from the receptors is blocked during dreaming, correlating with the common observation that people are difficult to arouse during dreaming. As Hughlings-Jackson originally proposed, it seems probable that during dreaming input from the frontal lobe and sensory systems is at least partially blocked from reaching the sensory zones. As a result the sensory zones are released from the influence of this source of higher control. These zones can still be influenced, however, by the medial temporal regions. Thus, the temporal-lobe memory system activates the sensory zones—which may account, in part, for the realism of many dreams. This admittedly speculative proposal obviously fails to explain *why* the temporal lobe (and hence dreaming) should be activated during certain periods of sleep, but it does explain the perceptual component of dream activity. Probably the sensory zones are activated by an ascending input from the brainstem, although the genesis of this input remains uncertain. One testable prediction of this model can be made: patients from whom a temporal lobe,

especially the right lobe, has been surgically removed should have significantly different dream activity, both in the content and nature of the sensory experience and, possibly, even in the frequency of dreaming. This remains to be studied.

SUMMARY AND QUESTIONS

Two fundamental principles describe the functional organization of the sensory systems:

1. The sensory systems are arranged hierarchically from the receptors at the bottom to the neocortex at the top, with complexity increasing at each higher level.

2. Function is lateralized at the highest levels.

Lesions in the primary visual, somatosensory, and auditory systems produce serious deficits in sensory discrimination by significantly reducing acuity. Often after lesions in the secondary zones acuity is preserved but, although intellectual functioning is not disturbed, there is an inability to recognize objects or patterns. Further, there is tentative evidence of specific neurological substrates of illusions, hallucinations, and dreaming.

A nagging question remains: How much of a sensory system must be spared to allow modality-specific processing? Why, for example, does unilateral removal of area 41, the primary auditory area, have negligible effects on resolution? A second question is: Do specific agnosias in fact consistently occur in the absence of other deficits? This issue has raised heated debate since the concept of agnosia was first proposed, and is far from settled. The disagreement has its historical roots in the debate over localization of function. If functions are truly localized, it is logical to presume that somewhere there are patients who have specific agnosias (e.g., for faces) and exhibit no other deficits. In principle, this would seem simple to determine. Skepticism develops, however, when there is consistent question about how thoroughly patients have been examined for other disorders. Given the considerable controversy over whether Broca's area is really necessary for language, the problem of convincingly demonstrating specific agnosias comes into perspective.

REFERENCES

Benson, D. F., J. Segarra, and M. L. Albert. Visual agnosia-prosopagnosia, a clinicopathological correlation. *Archives of Neurology, 30* (1974), 307–310.

Bodamer, J. (1947). Cited by H. Hécaen and M. L. Albert. *Human Neuropsychology.* New York: John Wiley and Sons, 1978.

Corkin, S., B. Milner, and T. Rasmussen. Somatosensory thresholds. *Archives of Neurology, 23* (1970), 41–58.

Curtis, B. Visual system. In B. A. Curtis, S. Jacobson, and E. M. Marcus, *An Introduction to the Neurosciences.* Philadelphia and Toronto: W. B. Saunders Co., 1972.

Dejerine, J. A propos de l'agnosie tactile. *Revue de Neurologie, 15* (1907), 781–784.

Hebb, D. O. *The Organization of Behavior.* New York: John Wiley and Sons, 1949.

Hécaen, H., and M. L. Albert. *Human Neuropsychology.* New York: John Wiley and Sons, 1978.

Henschen, S. E. On the function of the right hemisphere of the brain in relation to the left hemisphere in speech, music and calculation. *Brain, 49* (1926), 110–123.

Holmes, G. Disturbances of vision by cerebral lesions. *British Journal of Ophthalmology, 2* (1918), 353–384.

Holmes, G. Disturbances in visual orientation. *British Journal of Ophthalmology, 2* (1918), 385–407.

Kolb, B., B. Milner, and L. Taylor. Perception of faces by patients with localized cortical excisions. In preparation, 1980.

Konorski, J. *Integrative Activity of the Brain.* Chicago: The University of Chicago Press, 1967.

Ludel, J. *Introduction to Sensory Processes.* San Francisco: W. H. Freeman and Company, 1978.

Luria, A. R. *The Working Brain.* New York: Penguin Books, 1973.

Meadows, J. C. The anatomical basis of prosopagnosia. *Journal of Neurology, Neurosurgery and Psychiatry, 37* (1974), 489–501.

Meadows, J. C. Disturbed perception of colours associated with localized cerebral lesions. *Brain, 97* (1974), 615–632.

Milner, B. Laterality effects in audition. In V. B. Mountcastle, ed. *Interhemispheric Relations and Cerebral Dominance.* Baltimore: Johns Hopkins University Press, 1962.

Nakamura, K., and M. Mishkin. Blindness in monkeys after lesions of non-visual cortex. *Society for Neuroscience Abstracts, 3* (1977), 571.

Penfield, W., and H. H. Jasper. *Epilepsy and the Functional Anatomy of the Human Brain.* Boston: Little Brown, 1954.

Penfield, W., and P. Perrot. The brain's record of auditory and visual experience. *Brain, 86* (1963), 595–696.

Pompeiano, O. The neurophysiological mechanisms of the postural and motor events during desynchronized sleep. *Research Publications of the Association of Nervous and Mental Disorders, 45* (1967), 351–423.

Riddoch, G. Dissociation of visual perceptions due to occipital injuries, with special reference to appreciation of movement. *Brain, 40* (1917), 15–47.

Robinson, T. E., R. C. Kramis, and C. H. Vanderwolf. Two types of cerebral activation during sleep: relations to behavior. *Brain Research, 124* (1977), 544–549.

Schneider, G. E. Two visual systems. *Science, 163* (1969), 895–902.

Semmes, J., S. Weinstein, L. Ghent, and H.-L. Teuber. *Somatosensory Changes of Penetrating Head Wounds in Man.* Cambridge, Mass.: Harvard University Press, 1960.

Shankweiler, D. P. Effects of temporal lobe damage on perception of dichotically presented melodies. *Journal of Comparative and Physiological Psychology, 62* (1966), 115–122.

Teuber, H.-L., in personal communication, 1975.

Thompson, R. F. *Foundations of Physiological Psychology.* New York: Harper and Row, 1967.

Uttal, W. R. *The Psychobiology of Sensory Coding.* New York: Harper and Row, 1973.

Verger, H. Sur la valeur semeiologique de la stereo-agnosie. *Revue de Neurologia, 2* (1902), 1201–1205.

Weiskrantz, L., E. K. Warrington, and M. D. Saunders. Visual capacity in the hemianopic field following a restricted occipital ablation. *Brain, 97* (1974), 709–728.

Wernicke, C. (1895). Cited by H. Hécaen and M. L. Albert. *Human Neuropsychology.* New York: John Wiley and Sons, 1978.

Yin, R. K. Face recognition by brain-injured patients: a dissociable ability? *Neuropsychologia, 8* (1970), 395–402.

11

THE MOTOR SYSTEM

In the classical view the motor system was divided into two separate anatomical systems: the pyramidal and the extrapyramidal. The pyramidal system consisted of fibers that originated in the pericentral sulcus area (the precentral and postcentral gyrus) and descended directly to the spinal cord, decussating on the way through the pyramids (hence the name) of the brainstem. By definition all motor pathways that did not cross at the pyramids were called extrapyramidal. Although widely used, this classification is recognized to have inadequacies, the major one being that the systems are difficult to link to function in any coherent way. Rather than dwell on this two-systems theory and its inadequacies we present an alternate anatomical classification that has some demonstrated functional correlations and that simplifies and clarifies the way movement is produced. This classification derives largely from the work of Kuypers and Lawrence and their coworkers, but is based as well on electrophysiological and anatomical findings from many other people, whose work will not be given detailed review in our more general presentation.

The findings we present in this chapter suggest that the motor system can be subdivided into a number of subsystems so organized that they can differentially control independent movements of the fingers and of the limbs, and whole body movements. This organization can be seen in the development of movement, in the anatomical organization of the motor system, and to some extent, by reflection, in various disorders of movement. We review some of the supporting evidence in the following sections.

THE DEVELOPMENT OF MOVEMENT

The development of movement can be described from two general perspectives: phylogenetic and ontogenetic. From a phylogenetic perspective it is readily apparent that the movements we refer to as whole body movements evolved rather early. Primitive vertebrates and fish are restricted largely to whole body movements, which they use in swimming. Amphibians make whole body movements similar to those of fish, but have developed limbs as well, with which they can make patterned movements for locomotion. The ability to make relatively independent movements of the limbs developed only later, when mammals evolved; many mammals use one or two limbs independently of the others to engage in such behaviors as eating, nest-building, fighting, etc. Relatively independent movements of the fingers, however, are seen only in primates, and are most highly developed in humans. Thus, the phylogenetic story suggests the independent, sequential evolution of, first, whole body movements, then relatively independent limb movements, followed by relatively independent finger movements. This sequential evolution suggests that there should be a parallel evolution of brain structures to produce them. Subcortical motor systems are clearly involved in the production of whole body movements, such as those used in swimming and walking, whereas the motor systems of the neocortex evolved to produce relatively independent movements of the limbs. Of the cortical motor systems, the cells projecting directly to the spinal motor cells appear to have been the most recent evolutionary development, and are responsible for producing relatively independent finger movements.

Two developmental studies deserve mention in this brief section: those by Coghill and by Twitchell. In 1929 Coghill described the ontogeny of movement in the newt *Amblystoma*. Coghill observed how the first movements of turning developed into coiling, and how repeated coiling developed into a propulsion mechanism for moving the animal through the water. Since the development of swimming in *Amblystoma* recapitulated the evolution of swimming in vertebrates Coghill was moved to observe, "With the attainment of locomotion *Amblystoma* has passed one of the most significant landmarks in the evolution of animal behavior." The neural mechanisms that underlie coiling and swimming, also described by Coghill, seem to involve little more than a few spinal-cord circuits. The development of locomotion in *Amblystoma* does not stop with swimming, for the newt grows first front limbs and then hind limbs. At first its walking movements are secondary to swimming movements, its limbs being used only in conjunction with whole body coiling. As the animal matures the coiling diminishes in amplitude until the body is carried as a fixed trunk by the coordinated movements of the legs. This stage of motor development reached by *Amblystoma* is fairly representative of the movement controlled by the subcortical motor system.

The ontogeny of relatively independent arm movements and relatively independent finger movements is seen most clearly in the second of the two developmental studies mentioned above: Twitchell's 1965 description of the development of the grasping reaction in human infants. Before birth the infant's movements are essentially whole body movements, but after birth the infant gradually develops the grasping reaction, the ability to reach out with one limb and bring objects toward it. The grasping reaction develops in a number of stages. Shortly after birth the infant can flex all the joints of an arm in such a way that it could scoop something toward its body, but it is not at all clear that this movement is executed independent of other body movements. Between one and four months of age the infant can clasp objects that come in contact with its hands, but can do so only by clasping all of its fingers together. Between 3 and 11 months it orients its hand toward, and gropes for, objects which have contacted it. Between 8 and 11 months it develops the "pincher grasp," using the index finger and thumb in opposition to each other. The development of the pincher grasp is extremely significant, because it allows the infant to make a very precise grasping movement as well as to manipulate small objects or objects located in hard-to-reach places. In fact, in his baby book Dr. Benjamin Spock advises parents of babies of this age to observe them using the pincher grasp to pick up objects as small as pieces of dust. In summary, then, we see the sequential development of an independent limb movement quite clearly in the development of the infant's grasping reaction: first scooping, then reaching and grasping with all fingers, then independent movements of the fingers, as seen in the pincher grasp. Maturation of the motor cortex, as measured by its degree of **myelinization,** parallels the development of the grasping reaction: small motor fibers from the precentral gyrus become myelinated at about the time that reaching and grasping develop; the giant Betz cells of the precentral gyrus become myelinated at about the time the pincher grasp develops. As we shall point out, these different motor fibers are thought to control arm movements and finger movements respectively.

THE ANATOMICAL ORGANIZATION OF MOVEMENT

The Anatomy of the Motor System

The motor system can be subdivided into a number of general subsystems, which as they multiply can cause confusion. Much of the confusion can be avoided, however, if the motor system is described from the muscles inward and then classified into subsystems according to what part of the body each subsystem controls.

Few cells of the central motor system project to muscles. The special cells that do project, called **motor neurons,** are located in only a few places: in the nuclei of the cranial nerves and in the ventral portions of the spinal grey matter. (Sherrington called motor neurons **motoneurones,** including in this definition the cell body, its axon, and all of the muscle fiber to which the axon terminations connected.) As it turns out, no cells of the motor system of most nonprimates, and only a few cells in primates, connect directly with motor neurons. Rather, most connections are made via *interneurons* that lie in close proximity to the motor neurons. Figure 11-1 shows the location of the motor neurons in the *ventral zone* of the spinal grey matter, and the interneurons located more dorsally and medially in the *intermediate zone* of the spinal grey matter. Motor neurons and interneurons for the cranial nerves are similarly arranged, but for simplicity we will describe only the spinal-cord projections.

Motor Neurons and Interneurons. The motor neurons are organized systematically in the ventral zone of the spinal cord: motor neurons located dorsally and laterally innervate the distal musculature, including the fingers, hand, and arm; motor neurons located more ventrally and medially innervate the more proximal musculature of the trunk and shoulders.

The interneurons are similarly organized: interneurons located in the dorsolateral portion of the intermediate zone connect to dorsolateral motor neurons; interneurons located in the ventromedial portion of the intermediate zone connect to ventromedial motor neurons. As a result, the dorsolateral interneurons eventually control distal musculature, and the ventromedial motor neurons eventually control proximal musculature. Part C of Figure 11-1 shows this relation among body musculature, motor neurons, and interneurons.

LATERAL SYSTEM   VENTROMEDIAL SYSTEM

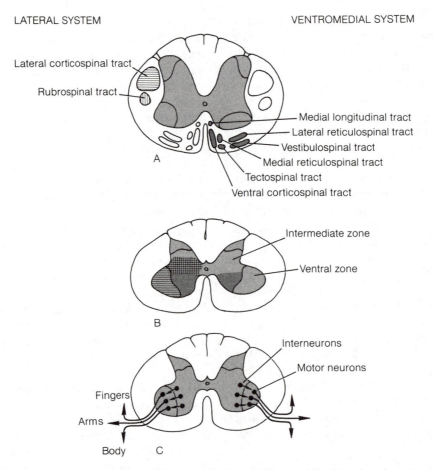

FIGURE 11-1. Spinal-cord motor organization. A. Tracts of the lateral and ventro-medial systems. B. Termination of tracts of the lateral and ventromedial systems in the ventral zone and motor neurons and intermediate-zone interneurons. C. Projection of interneurons of the intermediate zone onto motor neurons, and projection of motor neurons to body musculature. Note that the lateral system projects to distal musculature, and the ventromedial system projects to proximal musculature. (After Lawrence and Kuypers, 1968.)

The Motor Tracts. The motor tracts from the brain to the spinal cord are segregated into two groups as they descend through the spinal cord. This spatial separation has important implications for the differences in function between them. Part A of Figure 11-1 shows the location of these tracts. One group of tracts, located in the lateral columns of the spinal cord, makes up the *lateral system*. There are two major tracts in the lateral system: the *lateral corticospinal tract* and the *rubrospinal tract*. They originate in the cortex and *red nucleus* respectively. The second group of tracts, located in the ventromedial portion of the spinal cord, makes up the *ventromedial system*. There are six tracts in this system (see part A of Figure 11-1). The *ventral corticospinal tract* originates in the cortex; the other five tracts originate in several different nuclei of the brainstem.

Lawrence and Kuypers and others have described the relation between the descending motor tracts of the spinal cord and the interneurons and motor neurons of the spinal grey matter. If the axons of the descending tracts are lesioned and the spinal cord stained for degenerating end feet, each system develops a different pattern of degeneration (see Figure 11-1, part B). The lateral corticospinal tract connects primarily with motor neurons in the dorsolateral portion of the ventral zone, and with interneurons in the dorsolateral portion of the intermediate zone. The rubrospinal tract connects with interneurons in the dorsolateral portion of the intermediate zone; thus, the lateral system connects primarily with the distal musculature. The tracts of the ventromedial system synapse with interneurons in the ventromedial portion of the intermediate zone; thus, the ventromedial system connects primarily with the proximal musculature. In summary, then, the lateral system presumably controls movements of the fingers, hands, and arms; the ventromedial system presumably controls movements of the body and the proximal portion of the limbs.

Since some tracts in each lateral and ventromedial system have a cortical origin and some in each have a subcortical origin, the motor systems can be subdivided into a cortical motor system and a subcortical motor system and their organizations described.

The Cortical Motor System. Kuypers and Brinkman and others have described the projection of fibers from the primary motor cortex to the spinal cord. These fibers make up the lateral and ventral corticospinal tracts. Three statements can be made about the distribution of fibers in these tracts (see Figure 11-2).

1. Projections from the digit area of the motor cortex connect directly to motor neurons in the contralateral, dorsolateral portion of the ventral zone of the spinal grey matter. Many of the fibers in this projection are large and originate in large cells called the giant cells of Betz. This pathway decussates at the junction of the medulla and spinal cord, forming protuberances on the ventral aspect of the brainstem that are called the pyramids. Hence these fibers form a portion of what is known as the pyramidal tract. This direct corticomotor neuron projection is found only in primates and humans; since these are the only species capable of relatively independent finger movements, this projection is thought to produce these movements. (There may be exceptions to this generalization: hamsters and raccoons have some direct corticomotor neuron connections, and they also have better digit use than other animals such as cats, which have none.)

2. Cells in the digit, hand, and limb area of the motor cortex project to the interneurons in the dorsolateral portion of the intermediate zone in the contralateral spinal cord. They follow the course of the pyramidal tract. Because of their origin and termination, these fibers are thought to be responsible for producing relatively independent hand and arm movements.

3. Cells in the body area of the motor cortex project to the interneurons of the ventromedial portion of the intermediate zone both ipsilaterally and contralaterally. Part of this projection follows the pyramidal tract and part remains uncrossed to form the ventral corticospinal tract; thus, this projection, unlike the former two, is bilateral. Because of its origin and termination, this system is thought to control movements of the body and proximal limbs for such activities as walking.

Although this organization is not too surprising in itself, what is surprising is that the corticospinal tracts may show considerable

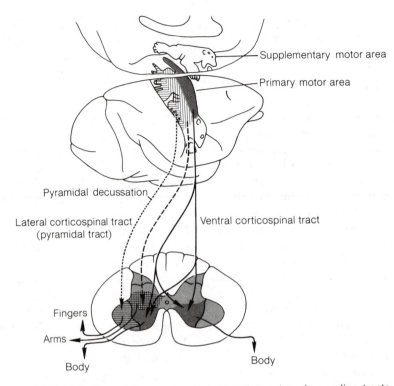

FIGURE 11-2. The relation among primary motor cortex, descending tracts, spinal-cord interneurons, motor neurons, and body musculature. (After Lawrence and Kuypers, 1968.)

variation among individuals. Nyberg-Hansen and Rinvik have described some of these variations; they include no uncrossed corticospinal tract, no crossed corticospinal tract, two crossed or two uncrossed corticospinal tracts. The functional significance of such variations is simply not known.

We should add that cells in the somatosensory area of the postcentral gyrus also project through the corticospinal tracts. However, they terminate in cells above the intermediate zone of the spinal grey matter, and at present their motor function is not understood.

The Subcortical Motor System. The subcortical motor system needs little further elaboration at this point. It is sufficient to note that the red nucleus in the midbrain sends

axons that cross in the midbrain and then descend as the rubrospinal tract to synapse with cells in the dorsolateral portion of the intermediate zone. Therefore, the red nucleus of one hemisphere controls distal musculature of the contralateral part of the body.

The projections from the other subcortical nuclei descend through the ventromedial system and connect bilaterally with interneurons in the ventromedial intermediate zone. Therefore, the ventromedial system controls body musculature and proximal limb musculature bilaterally.

Cortical Access to Motor Systems. In order that finger, arm, and body movements can be used under sensory and cognitive control, all regions of the cortex must have access to the different motor pathways. Kuypers and Lawrence and others have described a number of alternate routes through which movements can be controlled.

Figure 11-3 shows some of these alternatives. Figure 11-3 A shows the three corticospinal projections (already described) from area 4 that control finger, arm, and body movements respectively.

Figure 11-3 B shows indirect projections from area 4 into the lateral system through the red nucleus, and into the ventromedial system through the other brainstem nuclei. Additional projections may occur indirectly through the basal ganglia. The existence of these projections has been shown both anatomically and electrophysiologically. In the electrophysiological experiments the corticospinal tracts were cut in the lower brainstem, and the motor cortex was then stimulated electrically. Such stimulation no longer produced movements of the fingers, but still produced movements of the limbs and body, thus demonstrating that the motor cortex made connections with the subcortical motor systems.

Figure 11-3 C shows how other areas of the cortex obtain access to the motor pathways in area 4. Because only the postcentral gyrus projects into area 4, other posterior cortical regions must project into frontal cortex and from there into area 4. Brinkman and Kuypers and Haaxma and Kuypers have demonstrated such connections both anatomically and through behavioral studies.

Figure 11-3 D shows that there are alternate connections from frontal cortex and parietal cortex that bypass primary motor cortex and project into the brainstem motor systems either directly or indirectly, via the basal ganglia. Note that although these projections give these areas of the cortex access to control of arm movement via the lateral system, and of body movements via the ventromedial system, they have no access to the control of finger movements. Finger movements must be controlled through area 4 of the cortex. In general, these projections most probably control orientation of the head, body, and eyes, since stimulation of this cortex produces these types of movements.

Cerebellar Access to Motor Systems. The cerebellum is generally thought of as an important part of the motor system, but rather than sending projections directly to motor neurons or their interneurons, it projects to a number of nuclei that then join, either directly or indirectly, the lateral or ventromedial systems of the spinal cord. Figure 11-4 gives a simplified representation.

The archicerebellum composes the entire cerebellum in fishes, and is the first cerebellar structure to differentiate in the human fetus. In mammals it makes up the more medial and ventral portion of the cerebellum. Projections from the archicerebellum pass from its medial cerebellar nuclei to the reticular formation and the vestibular nuclei. Tracts from these areas form part of the ventromedial projection of the spinal cord, which, as we have seen, is instrumental in controlling more proximal movements of the body, such as posture and locomotion. Tumors or damage to this area disrupt upright posture and walking, but do not substantially disrupt other movements such as reaching, grasping, and finger movements. For example, a person with medial cerebellar damage may, when lying down, show few symptoms of such damage.

The paleocerebellum is the dominant cerebellar structure in quadrupeds from amphibians to mammals, and seems closely related to the development and use of the limbs in locomotion. Projections from the nuclei of this area go to the red nucleus, and possibly to the other brainstem nuclei as well. Thus, this system is probably involved in the control of limb movements through the lateral system, and body movements through the ventromedial system. The predominant effect of dam-

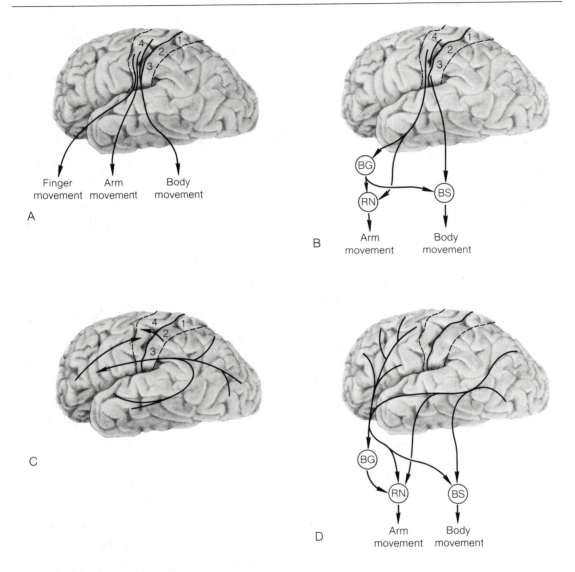

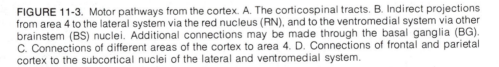

FIGURE 11-3. Motor pathways from the cortex. A. The corticospinal tracts. B. Indirect projections from area 4 to the lateral system via the red nucleus (RN), and to the ventromedial system via other brainstem (BS) nuclei. Additional connections may be made through the basal ganglia (BG). C. Connections of different areas of the cortex to area 4. D. Connections of frontal and parietal cortex to the subcortical nuclei of the lateral and ventromedial system.

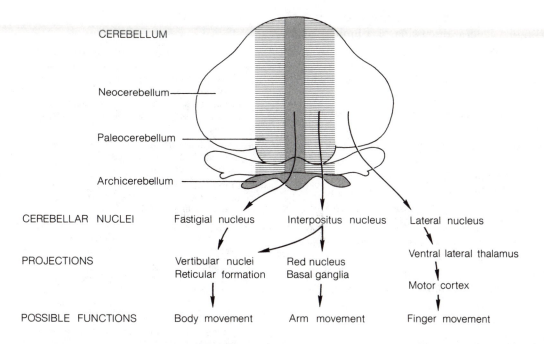

FIGURE 11-4. Projections from different cerebellar areas to spinal-cord motor pathways controlling different portions of body musculature.

age to this area, although such damage is rare, is an increase in rigidity of the limbs, which disrupts distal movement more than proximal movement.

The neocerebellum makes up the outermost lateral portion of the cerebellum. Although well developed in animals capable of non-symmetrical limb movements, it shows its greatest development in primates. Projections from the lateral nuclei that serve this area go to the ventral thalamus and from there to the precentral motor cortex. Thus, this area has access to the corticospinal tract that controls more distal movements of the arms and fingers as well as proximal movements of the body. Damage to the neocerebellum produces weakness and a tendency to fatigue, difficulty in localizing or pointing to body parts correctly, and a variety of deficits in the control of

the extremities such as overshooting the mark when pointing, flailing at the joints, staggering, and an inability to carry out repeated rhythmical movements.

In summary, therefore, the development and anatomy of these three cerebellar areas and their relations to other portions of the motor system suggest that they form an integral part of these systems and participate in differentially controlling whole body movements and relatively independent movements of the limbs and of the fingers.

DISORDERS OF MOVEMENT

Many more disorders of movement are attributable to malfunctions of various portions of the brain than can be discussed in this chapter. Therefore, the following section is limited to more general discussion of a limited number of disorders. Although we describe how brain lesions may affect movement, this discussion will have more of an idealized and experimental perspective than a strictly clinical perspective. Our purpose is to simplify the description of the effects of brain lesions, while permitting generalizations to clinical conditions. In addition, three types of motor disorders are sufficiently common or of sufficient theoretical importance to warrant special attention: Parkinson's disease; Huntington's chorea and related disorders; and apraxia, which is not a disease as such, but an inability to control movement. These motor disorders will be described in some detail. Table 11-1 gives some commonly used terms for movement disorders.

Brain Lesions

As can be seen from its anatomical organization, the motor system can be divided into cortical and subcortical systems. The cortical system controls all body movements, including arm and finger movements. The subcortical system controls distal movements through its lateral spinal cord projection, and proximal movements through its ventromedial spinal cord projection. To analyze the contributions made by these different systems Lawrence and Kuypers studied rhesus monkeys, which have a motor anatomy quite similar to that of humans. They made three types of lesions in the monkeys: (1) They cut the corticospinal tracts at the level of the pyramidal decussation in the medulla. (2) They then lesioned the rubrospinal tracts, either in the brain or in the cord by cutting its lateral columns. (3) They lesioned the tracts of the ventromedial column in the brain, or cut the ventromedial columns in the cord. The logic of this protocol was that first the functions of the corticospinal projections could be assessed, and then, since this system

TABLE 11-1

Some commonly used terms for movement disorders

Apraxia: Inability to carry out purposeful movements or movements on command in the absence of paralysis or other motor or sensory impairments. Usually follows damage to cortex tertiary areas.

Ataxia: Failure of muscular coordination or an irregularity of muscular action. Commonly follows cerebellar damage.

Hemiplegia: Complete or partial paralysis to one-half of the body. Usually follows damage to the motor cortex (area 4).

Paraplegia: Paralysis or paresis of the lower torso and legs, as can occur following spinal-cord damage.

Paralysis: Complete loss of movement or sensation in a part of the body. Usually permanent after damage to motor neurons; temporary after damage to the motor cortex (area 4).

Paresis: Slight or incomplete paralysis, or, often, a general loss of movement, such as follows syphilitic infection.

overlaps to some extent with the remaining lateral and ventromedial pathways, their function could be assessed independently in its absence.

The Function of the Corticospinal System. Within six to eight hours after surgery animals with corticospinal lesions were able to right themselves from a lateral posture, but their limbs tended to hang loosely or were poorly placed on the floor. Within 24 hours they could stand, grip the cage, and take a few climbing steps. They attempted to bite food, but for the first 10 to 15 days they could not swallow and so needed to be specially fed. Once they began to eat they would reach through their cage bars for food. However, they were hesitant to fully extend their arms and frequently caught their fingers on the opening. Once they reached the food their fingers closed in concert, but weakly, and grasping was associated with a hooking circumduction of the whole arm. Gradually, speed and strength of movements increased; yet the animals continued to display two striking deficits. First, they were not able to grasp food with the pincher grasp of the thumb and index finger opposed. Second, once they had grasped food with a whole-hand grip, they had difficulty releasing it; to do so they rooted for it with their snouts. During locomotion, however, they had no difficulty releasing the bars of the cage.

In summary, following corticospinal lesions, locomotion was minimally disturbed, whereas independent movements of the limbs in the absence of body movement were initially impaired, but recovered to near normal levels. In contrast, the animals never recovered the ability to fully use movements of the hand, as in releasing food, or to use relatively independent movements of the fingers to grasp food or manipulate objects. Beck and Chambers measured the functions of monkey limbs after lesions of the corticospinal tract. Their results comport with those given above. The monkeys showed slowed reaction times on two-choice tasks using the affected limb, showed greater loss of strength in flexion than in extension, and showed weaker flexion at the wrist than at the elbow or shoulder. From these and other observations it can be concluded that the corticospinal pathways provide speed, strength, and agility to limb movements, and provide the capacity to make discrete movements of the extremities—and in particular to make relatively independent movements of the fingers. The recovery from the initial difficulties in moving the limbs presumably can be attributed to actions of the rubrospinal projection of the lateral system.

The Function of the Rubrospinal System. Once the corticospinal system had been removed, lesions were made in the rubrospi-

nal system, either in the brain or by lateral cord section. After the lesions the animals were able to sit unsupported, stand, walk, run, and climb. The most striking changes in movement occurred in the limbs, particularly the forelimbs. When the animals were sitting the limbs hung loosely from the shoulder with the hand and fingers extended. The arm was not used for reaching for food, but if food was within reach the arm was moved from the shoulder to rake food in toward the mouth with the hand extended. If the hand fell on the food it was unable to grasp and hold it. In contrast to these deficits in using the limb for independent movements of reaching and grasping for food, it was used well, although somewhat weakly, in locomotor activities such as walking and climbing. Thus, interruption of the rubrospinal system severely disrupts the relatively independent use of the limbs in reaching and grasping, but spares their ability to participate in whole body movements.

The Function of the Ventromedial System. Once the corticospinal system was removed, lesions were made in the brainstem nuclei of the ventromedial system or by section of the ventromedial columns of the cord. Animals with such lesions showed striking abnormalities in posture, but were considerably less impaired in the use of their extremities. They showed a prolonged inability to achieve upright posture, severe difficulty in moving the body or in moving the limbs at the proximal joints. They also showed pronounced flexion of the head, limbs, and trunk, which lessened with recovery but did not disappear. They were not able to sit up for 10 to 40 days and required frequent repositioning and had to be fed by stomach tube. When they were able to sit they were unsteady and tended to slump forward with the shoulders elevated. Slight movements or sudden sounds made them fall, and when starting to fall they failed to make corrective movements to support themselves. The animals had great difficulty walking; they walked with a narrow-based gait, frequently veered off target, and bumped into things. In contrast to the severe impairments of body movement, the distal parts of the limbs and hands were less impaired. The animals could cling to cage bars, reach and grasp food, and bring it to their mouths. When reaching for food, they executed movements mainly at the elbows and hands while the rest of the body remained relatively immobile.

These experiments clarify to a great extent what has been a long-standing controversy about the functions of the corticospinal system in humans. People who suffer strokes, tumors, or lesions in the motor cortex initially show profound contralateral paralysis. Although such a patient may eventually recover sufficiently to use the affected leg as a support in walking, the arm may become flexed and rigid and unavailable for voluntary use. In some circles it had been thought that these symptoms were caused by damage to the corticospinal tracts. This seems not to be so.

Seldom are the corticospinal tracts interrupted without damage to other motor systems. Bucy, Keplinger, and Siqueira had the opportunity to study a man who had a section of one pyramidal tract as a therapy for a condition of repeated and disabling involuntary movements. They state:

> Following the operation he had complete left hemiplegia [inability to make voluntary movements]. Within a few days this began to recover and continued to do so for the next 7 or 8 months. When this condition became stationary the patient had no facial weakness and the movements of his left extremities were strong, useful and well-coordinated. These movements included fine movements of his hand and individual digits, and good movement of his foot and toes. (Bucy et al., 1964)

Autopsy on Bucy's patient revealed that only about 17 percent of his corticospinal fibers were spared. However, these remaining fibers may have been enough to ensure recovery. Lawrence and Kuypers found that if any corticospinal fibers were spared by their lesions there was recovery of independent finger movements. In fact, recovery was independent of the location of the spared fibers, presumably because the tract is not topographically organized. Thus, in the absence of more definitive evidence from humans, it seems possible to conclude that damage to the human corticospinal tract would most likely result in permanent loss of relatively independent finger movements, just as it does in monkeys, provided that all of the corticospinal tract is destroyed.

What, then, accounts for the lasting **paresis** (reduction in voluntary movement) following cortical damage? The severer effects of cortical damage result not only from damage to the corticospinal projections to the cord, but also from destruction of the major projections from the motor area into the red nucleus and into the other brainstem nuclei. Since together the corticospinal and rubrospinal projections provide all control of relatively independent limb movement, the removal of both together should produce a profound impairment in distal limb use. This is in fact what occurs, and parallels quite closely what occurs, as described above, following combined removal of these two systems in the monkey.

Parkinson's Disease

The isolated symptoms of **Parkinson's disease** had been described by physicians from the time of Galen. In 1817, James Parkinson, a London physician, published an essay in which he argued that several different motor symptoms could be considered together as a group forming a distinctive condition. His observations are interesting not only because his conclusion was correct, but also because he made his observations at a distance by watching the movements of parkinsonian victims in the streets of London. Parkinson's disease has been called at different times the shaking palsy or its Latin equivalent, *paralysis agitans,* but received its more common designation from Charcot, who suggested that the disease be renamed to honor James Parkinson's recognition of its essential nature.

Parkinson's disease is fairly common, estimates of its incidence varying from 0.1 to 1.0 percent of the population. It is also of considerable interest for a number of other reasons. First, the disease seems related to the degeneration of a small area of the brain called the **substantia nigra,** and to the loss of the neurotransmitter substance dopamine, which is produced by cells of the nucleus. The disease therefore provides an important insight into the role of this brainstem nucleus and its neurotransmitter in the control of movement. Second, because a variety of pharmacological treatments for Parkinson's disease relieve to some extent different features of its symptoms, the disease provides a model for understanding pharmacological treatments of motor disorders in their more general aspects. Third, although Parkinson's disease is described as a disease entity, the symptoms vary enormously among patients, thus making manifest the complexity with which the components of movement are organized to produce fluid motion. Fourth, because many of the symptoms of Parkinson's disease strikingly resemble changes in motor activity that occur as a consequence of aging, the disease provides indirect insight into the more general problems of neural changes in aging.

The symptoms of Parkinson's disease can be divided into two major categories: positive and negative. Positive symptoms are behaviors not seen in normal people or seen only so rarely and then in such special circumstances that they can be considered abnormal. Negative symptoms are marked, not by any particular behavior, but rather by and absence of a

behavior or by an inability to engage in an activity.

Positive Parkinsonian Symptoms. Since positive symptoms are common in Parkinson's disease they are thought to be held in check, or inhibited, in normal people but released from inhibition in the process of the disease. The most common positive symptoms are: (1) *Tremor at rest:* this consists of alternating movements of one or both of the distal limbs when they are at rest, but which stop during voluntary movements or during sleep. (2) *Muscular rigidity:* muscular rigidity consists of increased muscle tone simultaneously in both extensor and flexor muscles. It is particularly evident when the limbs are moved passively at a joint; they move in a series of interrupted jerks (sometimes called the cogwheel phenomenon) rather than as a smooth motion. The rigidity may be sufficiently severe to make all movements difficult. One man less severely afflicted by rigidity was moved to comment, "The slowness of movement is conscious but not willed. That is, I form a plan in my mind; for instance, I wish to uncork that bottle. Then I deliberately invoke the effort that sets the muscles in motion. I'm aware of the slowness of the process; I'm unable to increase ... [its speed], but I always get the bottle open." (3) *Involuntary movements:* these may consist of continual changes in posture, sometimes to relieve tremor and sometimes to relieve stiffness, but often for no apparent reason. These small movements or changes in posture, sometimes referred to as **akathisia** or "cruel restlessness," are not inconsistent with general inactivity. Other involuntary movements are distortions of posture, such as occur during oculogyric crisis (turns of the head and eyes to one side), which last for periods of minutes to hours. Since the positive symptoms are "actions," they are caused by the activity of some brain area. Before drug therapy became more common, one of the treatments used to stop them was to localize the source of the symptom and make a lesion there. For example, tremor was treated by lesions made in the ventral thalamus.

Negative Parkinsonian Symptoms. After detailed analysis of negative symptoms in severely parkinsonian patients Martin divided them into five groups. (1) *Disorders of posture:* these are disorders of fixation and equilibrium. A disorder of fixation consists of an inability to maintain, or difficulty maintaining, a part of the body (head, limbs, etc.) in its normal position in relation to other parts. Thus, a person's head may droop forward, or a standing person may gradually bend further forward until he or she ends up on the knees. Disorders of equilibrium consist of difficulties in standing or even sitting when unsupported. In less severe cases patients may have difficulty standing on one leg, or, if pushed lightly on the shoulders, they fall passively without taking corrective steps or attempting to catch themselves. (2) *Disorders of righting:* this consists of difficulty in achieving a standing position from a supine position. (3) *Disorders of locomotion:* normal locomotion requires support of the body against gravity, stepping, balancing while the weight of the body is transferred from one limb to another, and pushing forward. Parkinsonian patients have difficulty initiating stepping; and when they do, they shuffle with short footsteps on a fairly wide base of support because they have trouble maintaining equilibrium when shifting weight from one limb to the other. Often patients who have begun to walk demonstrate **festination:** they take faster and faster steps and end up running forward. (4) *Disturbances of speech:* these consist mainly of difficulties in the physical production of sound; rigidity may play a prominent role in these disturbances. (5) *Akinesia:* this refers to a poverty or slowness of movement, which may also manifest itself in a blankness of facial expression, and lack of blinking, swinging of the arms when walking, spontaneous speech, or normal movements of fidgeting. It is also reflected in difficulty making repetitive movements, such as tapping, even in the absence of rigidity. Patients who sit motionless for hours show **akinesia** in its most striking manifestation. Other negative symptoms include difficulty in chewing and swallowing, but these symptoms do not fit easily or clearly into any of the above five categories.

The symptoms of Parkinson's disease begin insidiously, often with a tremor in one hand and with slight stiffness in the distal portions of the limbs. Movements may next become slower, the face becoming masklike with loss of eyeblinking and poverty of emotional expression. Thereafter the body may become stooped, while the gate becomes shuffling with absence of arm swinging. Speech may become slow and monotonous, and difficulty swallowing saliva may make drooling a problem. Although the disease is progressive, the rate at which the symptoms worsen is variable, and only rarely is progression so rapid that a person becomes disabled within five years; usually 10 to 20 years elapse before symptoms cause incapacity. One of the most curious aspects of Parkinson's disease is its on-again/off-again quality: symptoms may suddenly appear and as suddenly disappear. Partial remission of Parkinson's disease may also occur in response to interesting and activating situations. Sacks recounts the famous incident in which a parkinsonion patient leaped from his wheelchair and rushed into the breakers to save a drowning man, only to fall back into his chair immediately afterward and become inactive again.

Causes of Parkinsonism. There are three major types of Parkinson's disease: postencephalitic, idiopathic, and drug-induced. Parkinson's disease may also have an arteriosclerotic cause, may follow poisoning by carbon monoxide or manganese intoxication, or may follow syphilis or the development of tumors. As is suggested by its name, the *idiopathic* cause of Parkinson's is not known. Its origin may be familial, or it may be part of the aging process, but it is also widely thought that it could have a virus origin. It most often occurs in people who are over 50 years of age. The *postencephalitic* form originated in the sleeping sickness (*encephalitis lethargica*) that first appeared in the winter of 1916–1917 and vanished by 1927. Although the array of symptoms was bewilderingly varied, such that hardly any two patients seemed alike, Constantin von Economo demonstrated a unique pattern of brain damage associated with a virus infection in the brains of patients who had died from the disease. A third of those affected died in the acute stages of the sleeping sickness, in states either of coma or of sleeplessness. Although many patients seemed to completely recover from the sickness, most subsequently developed neurological or psychiatric disorders and parkinsonism. The latency between the initial and subsequent occurrences of the disease has never been adequately explained. The third major cause of Parkinson's disease is more recent, and is associated with ingestion of various drugs, particularly major tranquilizers that include reserpine and several phenothiazine and butyrophenone derivatives. The symptoms are usually reversible, but difficult to distinguish from those of the genuine disorder.

Although parkinsonian patients can be separated into clinical groups on the basis of cause of the disease, it is nevertheless likely that the mechanisms producing the symptoms have a common origin. Either the substantia nigra is damaged, as occurs in idiopathic and postencephalitic cases, or the activity of its cells is blocked, as occurs in drug-induced parkinsonism. The cells of the substantia nigra contain a dark pigment (hence its name); in Par-

kinson's disease this area is depigmented by degeneration of the melatonin-containing neurons of the area. Why the relatively selective degeneration occurs is not known, but it is possible that in viral causes the virus disturbs the metabolic pathways related to the formation of the pigment. The cells of the substantia nigra are the point of origin of fibers that go to the basal ganglia in particular, but also, in the rat (and probably also in humans), project to the frontal cortex and to the spinal cord. The neurotransmitter at the synapses of these projections is dopamine. It has been demonstrated by bioassay of the brains of deceased parkinsonian patients, and by analysis of the major metabolite of dopamine, homovanallic acid, in living patients, that the amount of brain dopamine is reduced by over 90 percent, and is often reduced to undetectable amounts. Thus, the cause of Parkinson's disease has been identified with some certainty as a lack of dopamine, or, in drug-induced cases, with lack of dopamine action. However, dopamine depletion may not account for the whole problem in some people, since decreases of noradrenaline have been recorded, and there have been a number of reports that cells in some of the nuclei in the basal ganglia may degenerate as well.

The Nature of the Motor Defect. It is not known precisely how a reduction in brain dopamine produces Parkinson's disease, but Martin has performed the best analysis of the disease's negative symptoms. He compared the function of mechanisms controlling posture and locomotion in normal people with those controlling locomotion in parkinsonian patients.

In normal people postural reflexes are under the control of vision; the labyrinths, or balance receptors, of the middle ear; and proprioception, or sensation, from muscles and joints. Of these three senses proprioception appears to be the most important, because whereas adequate locomotion can still occur in the absence of vision and labyrinth function, locomotion is severely impaired if proprioception is absent. Martin described the difficulties of a man whose proprioceptive pathways of the spinal cord had been cut accidentally. His locomotor difficulties appear in some ways surprisingly like those of people with Parkinson's disease.

This patient, in spite of years of physiotherapy and training, has never regained the ability to walk in any normal manner. His greatest difficulty is in starting to walk and in propelling himself forward. When he first began to walk—about a year after his injury—he held his hands out in front of him, which, of course, had the effect of bringing his center of gravity forward. Now, after several years of practice, he advances his hands less and he bends his head and body forward. He walks on a wide base and rocks his body but he does not bend his legs and so shows no proper stepping. If he loses his balance, he shows no reaction to protect his equilibrium and he has learnt to fall with his body relaxed. When he falls he cannot rise without help. He is also unable to rise from a chair. He cannot crawl or place himself in the all-fours posture. When standing or walking he is entirely dependent on vision and falls down if he closes his eyes. At first he was unable to maintain his position on an ordinary chair when he closed his eyes but he had gradually acquired the ability to do this. (Martin, 1967, p. 32)

When Martin tested labyrinthine and proprioceptive function in Parkinson's disease patients he found the receptors and their afferent pathways intact, but still neither seemed to function to aid locomotion. Furthermore, the mechanisms for eliciting normal locomotion seemed intact, for if walking was brought more directly under visual control it appeared quite normal. Martin accomplished increased visual control by having the patients walk over a series of wooden blocks: as the patients walked over the blocks, walking suddenly and dramatically became normal, but ceased to be so when the last of the blocks was reached. Leaning the patients forward (or having them carry something before them, which accomplished the same effect), and rocking them from side to side, both of which are automatic reflexes of walking, also reinstated more normal walking. Thus, in Parkinson's disease, when the proprioceptive system is intact and the stepping mechanisms of the motor system are functional, normal walking nevertheless fails to occur. Thus, it can only be concluded that the connection between sensory input and motor output is not being made. Since dopamine is implicated in Parkinson's disease, and since a primary projection of the dopamine system is from the substantia nigra to the basal ganglia, it can be concluded that dopamine is required in the basal ganglia to maintain the connection between the proprioceptive sensory system and the movement system.

How is Parkinson's disease related to the three aspects of the motor system we outlined in the preceding discussion? There is, of course, no certain answer to this question; but the defects in such movements as righting, leaning forward, and rocking from side to side, and the absence of arm swinging when walking, etc., all suggest disturbed control of the ventromedial system that controls body movements and walking. The basal ganglia are known to make major connections with this system. The corticospinal system may function more normally, since patients can write, although their writing tends to become small, possibly because of reduced arm movements. In opposition to this viewpoint, however, Weaver and Brooks and others report that in patients with Parkinson's disease fine motor skills involving the digits are severely impaired.

Treatment of Parkinson's Disease. There is no known cure for Parkinson's disease, and none will be in sight until the factors that produce the progressive deterioration of the substantia nigra are known. As a result, treatment is symptomatic and directed toward support and comfort. The major symptoms of parkinsonism are influenced by psychological factors, a patient's outcome being affected by how well he or she can cope with the disability. As a result, patients should be counseled early regarding the meaning of symptoms, the nature of the disease, and the potential for most patients to lead long and productive lives. Physical therapy should consist of simple measures such as heat and massage to alleviate painful muscle cramps, and training and exercise to cope with the debilitating changes in movement. Several types of drugs have been used to treat symptoms, including: anticholinergics, l-dopa, amantadine, amphetamine, the monoamine oxidase inhibitors, and tricyclic mood elevators.

The drug treatments for Parkinson's disease are of considerable theoretical as well as practical interest. In recent years understanding of the structure and function of synapses has been greatly advanced. Parkinson's disease provides an excellent model for understanding brain function with respect to synaptic action, because a specific constellation of symptoms has been linked with changes in a known neurotransmitter. Pharmacological treatment has two main objectives: first, increase the activity in whatever dopamine synapses remain; second, suppress the activity in structures that show heightened activity in the absence of adequate dopamine action. Drugs such as l-dopa, which is converted into dopamine in the brain; amantadine; amphetamine;

monoamine oxydase inhibitors; and tricyclic mood elevators are used to potentiate effective dopamine transmission. Naturally occurring anticholinergic drugs, such as atropine and scopolamine, and synthetic anticholinergics, such as benztropine (Cogentin) and trihexyphenidyl (Artane), are used to block the cholinergic systems of the brain that seem to show heightened activity in the absence of adequate dopamine activity.

Effectiveness of Drug Therapy

The best description of the effects of drug therapy on the condition of Parkinson's disease is given in a series of case histories described by Sacks. Although drugs such as l-dopa have been called miracle drugs, they are not a cure for the disease. Generally it is necessary to treat each patient as an individual, experimenting with different available drugs and with different dosages. In some cases symptoms are dramatically relieved and patients are immensely helped; in other cases the drug treatments may prove to have side effects as unpleasant and as debilitating to the patient as the disease symptoms. An additional complexity in treatment is the progressive nature of the disease. Drug therapy must be continually reevaluated and it may become ineffectual in the latter stages of the disease. The following is an example of the "side effects" on a patient, Miss N., described by Sacks.

In September for the third time I gave her l-dopa and her responses were not quite different from either of the first two times. She complained of rapid breathing and difficulty in catching her breath, and she had the beginnings of respiratory crises. She developed very rapid "saluting" tics in both of her arms, her hand flying from her lap to her face three or four times every minute. She also developed palilalia, repeating her words innumerable times. Her reaction at this time was remarkably similar to that of her room-mate Miss D., so much so that I wondered if either was automatically "imitating" the other. By the middle of September, Miss N. was ... [producing tics] 60 times to the minute, 60 minutes to the hour, and saying an incessant palilalic repetition of the following verse she had learned years before:

I thought it said in every tic,

I am so sick, so sick, so sick.

Oh death, come quick, come quick,
come quick!

Come quick, come quick, come quick, come quick!

Since she was exhausting herself and maddening her fellow patients, I again found it necessary to stop l-dopa.

Following this excited state Miss N. showed a severe "rebound" when l-dopa was stopped, becoming so rigid, tremulous, akinetic and voiceless, and having so much difficulty in swallowing, that we had to tube-feed her. This "withdrawal reaction" continued for the remainder of September without any lessening in severity whatever. (From *Awakenings* by Oliver Sacks. Copyright © 1973 by Oliver Sacks. Reprinted by permission of Doubleday & Company, Inc., and Gerald Duckworth & Co., Ltd.)

It is unlikely that l-dopa would produce such side effects if given to normal people. It does so in parkinsonian patients because postsynaptic receptors proliferate as dopamine end feet degenerate; there being fewer and fewer synapses, there are concomitantly more and more receptors. Thus, as parkinsonian symptoms develop and as l-dopa becomes more necessary it also unfortunately produces more side effects.

Psychological Aspects of Parkinson's Disease

Although Parkinson's disease patients are often described as manifesting many features of depression, they are also widely thought to show no psychological changes that parallel their motor disabilities. This latter view may be incorrect. On the basis of clinical observations, Sacks suggests that there are cognitive changes parallel to those reflected in motor activity. Sacks emphasizes festination and resistance as positive symptoms of cognitive activity. As mentioned earlier, festination is manifest as an acceleration of walking, but it is also seen as a rushing of speech and even thought. Resistance, however, has the opposite effect: as soon as speech or thought is attempted, it may be blocked by resistance. Thus, the two positive effects are in a sense opposites, and patients might find themselves embattled, festination counteracted by resistance. Sacks has also emphasized that there are negative components of the disease in cognitive function. There is an impoverishment of feeling, libido, motive, and attention; patients may sit for hours apparently lacking the will to enter or continue on any course of activity.

Bowen has reported on the performance of parkinsonian patients on a number of more formal neurological and psychological tests. Although verbal IQ was normal, patients performed significantly less well on memory tests than their spouses, who were used as the control group. Parkinsonian patients also showed significant deficits on tests of extrapersonal orientation, personal orientation, the Wisconsin card-sorting test, and Aubert's test of setting an illuminated rod to the vertical. (These tests, which are sensitive to frontal-lobe damage are described in some detail in Chapter 14.) Thus, Parkinson's disease would seem to be associated with cognitive changes, particularly those changes normally found in patients with frontal-lobe or basal-ganglia lesions. In a sense this association is not so surprising, because there are intimate relations between the functions of the basal ganglia and of the frontal cortex, and because there are dopamine projections into the frontal cortex that might be expected to degenerate in the same way that those of the basal ganglia degenerate. Having also tested patients before and after l-dopa treatment Bowen reports that test performance is not noticeably improved by drug therapy.

Animal Models of Parkinson's Disease

In recent years considerable attention has been given to developing animal models of Parkinson's disease. Although no animal models reliably produce all of the symptoms of the human condition, many symptoms resembling those of parkinsonism appear in animals with experimentally reduced dopamine concentrations. Specifically, the injection of the **neurotoxin** 6-hydroxydopamine into the ventricles or into specific brain areas can greatly deplete dopamine. We have found that animals thus treated show many symptoms resembling those of Parkinson's disease, including akinesia, rigidity, abnormal postures, and compulsive fidgeting. Some of these symptoms can be relieved by administration of anticholinergic drugs or l-dopa, but the threshold for eliciting side effects is nearly the same as the threshold for relief of symptoms. The animal models provide insights into the neurological basis of the disease, and will be useful in the development of new pharmacological treatments and assessment of their therapeutic value. Also, in some relatively new developments, a number of people have reported that embryonic brain cells transplanted into adult rats will grow and seemingly make normal connections. This has been demonstrated for dopamine and noradrenaline cells: if the animals are previously depleted of these neurotransmitters, the brain grafts will begin to restore brain concentrations of the neurotransmitters, and to restore as well some features of more normal behavior. Theoretically, these results offer an unex-

pected new approach to the treatment of Parkinson's disease.

Huntington's Chorea

Huntington's chorea, or hereditary chorea, is a progressive degenerative disease of the basal ganglia and cerebral cortex that begins in adult life and is characterized by rapid, involuntary jerks of the limbs called choreiform movements, and by mental deterioration. The disease is caused by inheritance of a single dominant autosomal gene and may be transmitted by either sex, affecting about 50 percent of the offspring. It has been suggested that the disease may be caused by disturbances of an enzyme system, but to date such a defect has not been found. The disease usually appears in persons between the ages of 35 and 39 with the occurrence of abnormal movements. Involuntary jerky movements usually occur in the extremities; they are rapid and irregular, and become pronounced during voluntary movements. Some patients may attempt to mask the abnormal movements in purposeful movements. For example, a patient may sometimes walk with a peculiar gait resembling a dance. Patients with chorea are often unable to maintain protrusion of the tongue, and they show abnormal movements of the hands when the arms are placed above the head.

Although chorea can be associated with degeneration of the neocortex and basal ganglia, the symptoms are likely to be a result of dysfunction of several normally integrated neural systems, including the cortex, caudate nucleus, globus pallidus, and thalamus. Although there is no effective therapy for Huntington's chorea a number of drugs prove helpful. Curiously, they are drugs that can induce parkinsonism; they include reserpine, phenothiazines, and butyrophenones. On the other hand, drugs that potentiate dopamine action worsen chorea. In fact, about half of the people receiving l-dopa in therapy for Parkinson's develop choreatic disorders. This incidence has led to the suggestion that chorea is the opposite of parkinsonism: dopamine activity is excessive, either because of an abnormality in the dopaminergic system, or because some other system is malfunctioning that normally checks the activity of the dopamine system.

Two other conditions bear some similarity to Huntington's chorea. *Ballismus* consists of violent movements of the limbs resembling a forceful throwing movement, which exhaust and incapacitate a patient. The cause seems to be damage in the contralateral subthalamic nucleus, the result of vascular disease, tumor, or infection. The disease is usually self-limiting, and recovery occurs within two to six months. *Athetosis* is marked by abnormal movements and postures, usually involving one or both sides of the body. The movements usually involve the upper extremities as well as the face. Athetotic movements are distinguishable from choreatic movements by being slower, coarser, and more writhing. Most instances of athetosis occur in early infancy, before one year of age, and may involve congenital defects, anoxia, or trauma at birth. Athetosis occurring later in life may be part of other basal-ganglia disorders, or part of a heterogeneous group of conditions called cerebral palsy.

At present there is no adequate neural model to explain these symptoms, but Martin has examined chorea patients and found that some have disturbances of postural reflexes strongly resembling those of parkinsonian patients. Since only 5 out of 20 patients fell into this category, and since the symptoms of excessive limb movement differ in many ways from those seen in parkinsonian patients, disturbance of the motor system must be different in each disease. Involvement of the basal ganglia in both diseases suggests that they control movement in different ways. Since abnormal movements are most pronounced during normal locomotion it is possible that the basal ganglia have a role in integrating limb movements with locomotion.

Apraxia

Steinthal coined the term apraxia in 1871, but the symptoms had first been described some five years earlier by Hughlings-Jackson. He noted that some aphasic patients were totally unable to perform voluntary movements, such as protruding the tongue, even though there was no evidence of weakness in the muscles involved. Although this symptom was subsequently noted by several authors, it was Leipmann who began the first detailed analysis of apraxic symptoms. In 1900 he reported the case of an aphasic man who was unable to carry out hand movements when asked to do so. Curiously, he could follow directions if the required movement was a whole body movement, such as sitting down, and could make *spontaneous* hand movements. In the ensuing years Leipmann studied many patients with this unusual movement problem, and in 1920 he proposed his now classic theory of apraxia of which two important points were: (1) Apraxia results from lesions of the left hemisphere or of the corpus callosum. (2) There are several different types of apraxia, each most likely resulting from damage to a specific locus in the left hemisphere.

Strictly defined, *apraxia* means no action (the Greek *praxis* meaning action). The term apraxia, however, is hardly ever used in this strict sense; today it is used to describe all sorts of missing or inappropriate actions that cannot be clearly attributed to paralysis, paresis, or other more primary motor deficits on the one hand, or to lack of comprehension, motivation, etc., on the other.

Defining Apraxia. Until recently discussion of apraxia was invariably of specific case histories rather than of carefully designed scientific studies. The result was conflicting interpretations of the behaviors described. Consider the following case as an example.

> A woman with a biparietal lesion had worked for years as a fish-filleter. With the development of her symptoms, she began to experience difficulty in carrying on with her job. She did not seem to know what to do with her knife. She would stick the point in the head of a fish, start the first stroke and then come to a stop. In her own mind she knew how to fillet fish, but yet she could not execute the maneuver. The foreman accused her of being drunk and sent her home for mutilating fish.
>
> This same patient also showed another unusual phenomenon which might possibly be apraxic in nature. She could never finish an undertaking. She would begin a job, drop it, start another, abandon that one, and within a short while would have four or five uncompleted tasks on her hands. This would cause her to do such inappropriate actions as putting the sugar bowl in the refrigerator, and the coffee pot inside the oven. (Critchley, 1966, pp. 158–159)

Although we can agree with Critchley that the filleter had a motor problem that cannot be readily attributed to paralysis or paresis, we could argue that she had forgotten how to fillet fish, that she had an agnosia for fish, knives, etc., that she had attention problems, that she was absent-minded, and so on. A more systematic analysis of her behavior is obviously required if we are to understand her deficit.

The several standard clinical tests often used to assess apraxia have similar weaknesses. For example, a patient may be asked to demonstrate the use of a particular object in its absence, e.g., to comb the hair or to hammer a nail. An apraxic person's response may be to do nothing or else to use a part of the body as if it were the implement—to stroke a finger through the hair as if it were a comb, or to hit the table with a fist as though it were a hammer. A normal person would pretend to be holding the comb or hammer. Another test of apraxia might be to ask a patient to perform such symbolic movements as saluting or waving good-bye; the patient might remain still or respond by making an unrecognizable movement. Although these tests are useful for "on the spot" assessments of apraxia, they do not permit objective quantification or more penetrating analysis.

Clinical description presents a further difficulty, namely that classifications of apraxia tend to be somewhat arbitrary. Also, new types of apraxias tend to proliferate not because actual new symptoms are discovered, but because either new questions are put to the patients or new ways of assessing the responses are developed. As a result there are such terms as ideational apraxia, ideomotor apraxia, limb kinetic apraxia, etc., the definitions of which are often disputed. Finally, slight variations in lesion location might often be used as justification that one apraxia differs from another. Rather than pursue this type of analysis, let us turn to a different approach.

Recently a number of laboratories have begun to analyze apraxias under fairly rigorous experimental conditions. The objectives of these experiments are to: (1) use a standard test; (2) quantify the response; (3) define the range of motor responses that are impaired; and (4) categorize those responses that are unimpaired. The goal of this research is to eventually specify what function each area of the cortex has in generating particular movements.

In any study of apraxia it is necessary to distinguish between deficits that result from direct damage to the motor system and those that result from damage to other areas that

TABLE 11-2

Effects of right- or left-hemisphere lesions on various motor behaviors

A: Tests in which there is no bilateral impairment[a]	Basic reference
1. Hand strength	Kimura, 1977
2. Finger-tapping speed	Carmon, 1971
3. Steadiness in static position	Haaland et al., 1977
4. Undirectional moving steadiness	Haaland et al., 1977
5. Repetitive screw rotation	Kimura, 1980
6. Imitation of single hand posture	Kimura and Archibald, 1974
7. Imitation of single oral movements	Mateer and Kimura, 1977
8. Imitation of single facial movements	Kolb and Milner, 1980

B: Tests in which there is bilateral impairment	Basic reference
1. Demonstration of object use	de Renzi et al., 1968
2. Rapid directed arm movements	Wyke, 1967, 1968
3. Finger tapping—two keys	Wyke, 1967
4. Finger tapping—rhythms	Luria, 1973
5. Stylus maze	Haaland et al., 1977
6. Pegboard	Haaland et al., 1977
7. Pursuit rotor	Heilman et al., 1975
8. Manual sequence box	Kimura, 1977
9. Imitation of multiple oral movements	Mateer and Kimura, 1977
10. Imitation of multiple facial movements	Kolb and Milner, 1980
11. Oral movements upon request	Poeck and Kerschensteiner, 1975
12. Imitation of meaningful single oral movements (e.g., kiss, whistle)	de Renzi et al., 1966

[a] Note that in the absence of damage to the motor cortex there may be no impairment at all on these tests.

"command" it. With respect to finger, hand, and arm movements it can be noted whether the deficit is unilateral. (Remember, one hemisphere controls the contralateral limb; thus, a deficit in only the contralateral limb can be most parsimoniously attributed to motor-system damage.) Because other movements (face, head, body) are controlled bilaterally, a deficit in their control is most likely to be apraxic. Most studies of apraxia also include tests for paralysis and paresis; clearly, it is pointless to try to determine whether a paralyzed limb is under voluntary control.

Table 11-2 summarizes two groups of motor behaviors. Those listed in part A of the table—hand strength, finger-tapping speed, etc.—are ones on which people with brain damage usually show no impairment or only unilateral impairment. Therefore, these tests are not particularly useful for diagnosing apraxia, although they are good for assessing paralysis or paresis; that is, they are good control tests for assessing the ability to make movements.

Listed in part B of Table 11-2 are tests on which either no impairment or bilateral impairment has been demonstrated. These, then, are tests of apraxia; they are assumed to require higher-level control for their execution. Figures 11-5 and 11-6 show examples of two of these tests. In the Kimura box test (Figure 11-5) the patient is asked to either push the button, pull the lever, or depress the bar as a test of paresis, and then is asked to make the responses in sequence. The manipulanda are connected to timers and counters that record accuracy and speed. In the test in Figure 11-6, a test for paresis, the patient is asked to make any one of the individual movements. If able to make the individual movements, the patient is then asked to watch and repeat each of the sequences of movement. The patient's response is scored for the accuracy of each movement, for the number of correct movements, and for the sequence of response.

It is clear that these tests are very objective; the responses can be quantified; and different laboratories can use the tests with little difficulty. Furthermore, the tests can be designed to analyze different contributions to motor control, as a comparison of the tasks shown in Figures 11-5 and 11-6 illustrates. The box test primarily requires movement of the distal musculature of the hand and fingers in a fairly discrete spatial locus. The arm-movement test, on the other hand, requires movements of both the distal and proximal musculature over a large spatial area. In view of what is known about the differential input of the frontal and parietal cortex in the control of proximal and distal musculature, it is likely that tests of these kinds will be differentially affected by lesions to different regions of the cortex. This likelihood, however, remains to be studied.

Asymmetry of Movement Control. One of the most important proposals in Leipmann's theory of apraxia was that the left hemisphere plays a special role not shared by the right hemisphere in the control of movement. This feature of apraxia is reflected in all of the studies cited in part B of Table 11-2. In each study the bilateral impairment was produced by a left-hemisphere lesion.

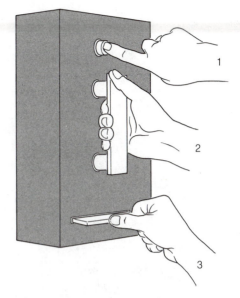

FIGURE 11-5. Kimura box test. Subjects are required to learn the movement series of (1) pushing the top button with the index finger, (2) pulling the handle as shown, and (3) pressing down on the bar with the thumb. Apraxic patients are impaired at this task, and may be unable to learn it at all, even with extended practice.

Another line of evidence supporting Leipmann's left-hemisphere proposal comes from a study by Milner and her colleagues. They taught patients a complex series of arm movements prior to intracarotid sodium Amytal injections. After the injections the patients were required to perform the movements. Only injections into the speaking hemisphere disrupted the movements, even though the movements were to be performed with the ipsilateral limb (controlled by the contralateral motor cortex that had not received an injection). Thus, the results of sodium Amytal injections support the results of lesion studies in confirming a special role for the left hemisphere in the control of movement.

Confronted with the left hemisphere's spe-

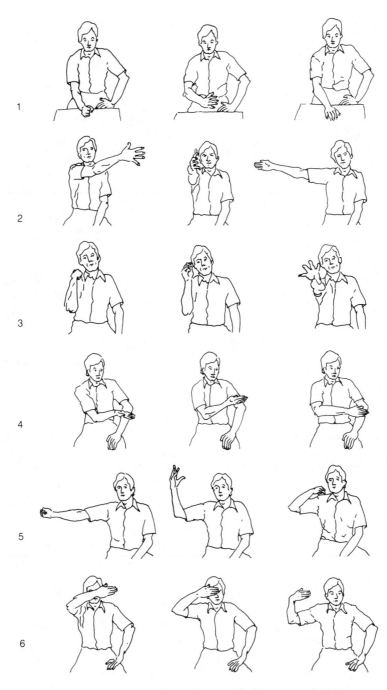

FIGURE 11-6. Serial arm movements and copying test. Patients are asked to copy each of the series (1–6) as accurately as they can. Patients with left-parietal or frontal lesions are impaired.

cial control of many types of movement the reader will immediately be moved to ask whether the right hemisphere might not also control certain types of movements. In fact, there is a group of movements that can be selectively disrupted by right-hemisphere lesions. These are used in tests in which a variety of components are to be assembled to form an object. Such tasks include: (1) assembling pieces of a jigsaw puzzle together to form a picture; (2) drawing a clock face, map, etc.; (3) copying a design with sticks of various lengths; (4) building bridges, towers, etc., with blocks; and (5) copying designs with different colored blocks. Deficits on such tests are sometimes called constructional apraxias.

What is special about these constructional tasks? All of them require that objects be ordered in extrapersonal space. Dealing with the spatial relations of objects is believed to be a function of the right hemisphere, especially of the right parietal cortex. Although left-parietal lesions can also produce some similar deficits, their occurrence can have a different cause: left-hemisphere deficits may result from the patient's inability to adjust the parts of his or her own body, rather than to adjusting the position of an external object. This theoretically interesting proposition has yet to be clearly tested experimentally.

Are Aphasia and Apraxia Correlated? Since many apraxias stem from left-hemisphere lesions, are they secondary to deficits in comprehension? Although aphasia frequently accompanies apraxia, three lines of evidence indicate that the symptoms can be dissociated. First, de Renzi gave patients tests of aphasia and apraxia; the test scores were poorly correlated. Second, patients with surgical incisions outside the speech zones may have no detectable dysphasias but may be apraxic. Third, nonhuman animals can be apraxic—and they of course do not speak. For example, Deuel reports that frontal lesions in monkeys, in the absence of primary sensory or motor deficits, can produce impairments in the completion of complex latch-box opening tasks. Similarly, Kolb and his colleagues have found that frontal-lobe lesions in rodents produce deficits in nest building, hoarding food, etc., behaviors that conceptually resemble those in tests of apraxia given to humans.

Neuroanatomical Basis of Apraxia. Classical neurological theory concerning the basis of apraxia is derived from a model originally proposed by Leipmann and subsequently popularized by Geschwind. Briefly, Leipmann proposed that the left parietal cortex (specifically around area 40) was the critical region for control of complex movement. This control was mediated via the left frontal lobe and area 4 in control of the right side of the body. Disruption anywhere along this route in the left hemisphere would produce apraxia of the right limbs. Control over the limbs of the left side was proposed to be mediated through a series of corticocortical connections running from the left parietal cortex to the left frontal cortex and finally to the right frontal cortex via the corpus callosum. There are three major problems with this model: (1) Section of the corpus callosum produces only a transient apraxia of the left limbs. (2) Impairment of motor control is much milder following surgical lesions of the parietal cortex than following natural lesions, which invade subcortical regions. (3) Even large lesions of the frontal cortex do not produce apraxia as severe as that resulting from parietal lesions. None of these data would be predicted from the Leipmann-Geschwind schema. In support of this theory, however, Brinkman and Kuypers, using the Leipmann-Geschwind design, have demonstrated apraxia-like deficits in the rhesus monkey. That is, isolating a "command" portion of the cortex from the motor component produces an apraxia. Alternately, Kimura suggests that there may be several complementary systems in movement control, and that some of these may not follow the classical corticocortical-area 4, or corticocallosal-area 4 pathways. They may instead use routes through the subcortical motor systems. Clearly, whatever theoretical approach one wishes to espouse, the work of Lawrence and Kuypers suggests that apraxias of the fingers and hand must involve some disconnection between "command" centers and area 4, whereas apraxias of other movements may involve alternate routes in addition to those through primary motor cortex.

REFERENCES

Beck, C. H., and W. W. Chambers. Speed, accuracy, and strength of forelimb movement after unilateral pyramidotomy in rhesus monkeys. *Journal of Comparative and Physiological Psychology, 70* (1970), 1–22.

Bowen, F. P. Behavioral alterations in patients with basal ganglia lesions. In M. D. Yahr, ed. *The Basal Ganglia.* New York: Raven Press, 1976.

Brinkman, J., and H. G. J. M. Kuypers. Cerebral control of contralateral and ipsilateral arm, hand and finger movements in the split-brain rhesus monkey. *Brain, 96* (1973), 653–674.

Bucy, P. C., J. E. Keplinger, and E. B. Siqueira. Destruction of the "pyramidal tract in man." *Journal of Neurosurgery, 21* (1964), 385–398.

Carmon, A. Sequenced motor performance in patients with unilateral cerebral lesions. *Neuropsychologia, 9* (1971), 445–449.

Coghill, G. E. *Anatomy and the Problem of Behavior.* New York and London: Hafner Publishing, 1964.

Critchley, M. *The Parietal Lobes.* New York: Hafner Publishing, 1965.

Denny-Brown, D. The nature of apraxia. *Journal of Nervous and Mental Diseases, 126* (1958), 9–33.

Economo, C. von. *Encephalitis Lethargica: Its Sequence and Treatment.* Oxford: Oxford University Press, 1931.

Elliott, H. C. *Textbook of Neuroanatomy.* Philadelphia and Toronto: J. P. Lippincott Co., 1969.

Geschwind, N. The apraxias: neural mechanisms of disorders of learned movement. *American Scientist, 63* (1975), 188–195.

Haaland, K. Y., C. S. Cleeland, and D. Carr. Motor performance after unilateral damage in patients with tumor. *Archives of Neurology, 34* (1977), 556–559.

Haaxma, R., and H. G. J. M. Kuypers. Intrahemispheric cortical connections and visual guidance of hand and finger movements in the rhesus monkey. *Brain, 98* (1975), 239–260.

Heilman, D. M., H. D. Schwartz, and N. Geschwind. Defective motor learning in ideomotor apraxia. *Neurology, 25* (1975), 1018–1020.

Kimura, D. The neural basis of language and gesture. In H. Avakina-Whitaker and H. A. Whitaker, eds. *Studies in Neurolinguistics,* New York: Academic Press, 1976.

Kimura, D. Acquisition of a motor skill after left-hemisphere damage. *Brain, 100* (1977), 527–542.

Kimura, D. Neuromotor mechanisms in the evolution of human communication. In H. D. Steklis and M. J. Raleigh, eds. *Neurobiology of Social Communication in Primates: An Evolutionary Perspective,* New York: Academic Press, 1980.

Kimura, D., and Y. Archibald. Motor functions of the left hemisphere. *Brain, 97* (1974), 337–350.

Kolb, B., and B. Milner. Performance of complex arm and facial movements after focal brain lesion. Unpublished manuscript, 1980.

Kolb, B., and I. Q. Whishaw. Double dissociation of prefrontal cortical subfields in the control of praxic behaviors in hamsters. Unpublished manuscript, 1980.

Kuypers, H. G. J. M. The descending pathways to the spinal cord, their anatomy and function. In J. C. Eccles and J. P. Schade, eds. *Organization of the Spinal Cord.* Vol. 11. Amsterdam: Elsevier, 1964.

Kuypers, H. G. J. M., and J. Brinkman. Precentral projections to different parts of the spinal intermediate zone in the rhesus monkey. *Brain Research, 24* (1970), 29–48.

Kuypers, H. G. J. M., and D. G. Lawrence. Cortical projections to the red nucleus and the brain stem in the rhesus monkey. *Brain Research, 4* (1967), 151–188.

Lawrence, D. G., and H. G. J. M. Kuypers. The functional organization of the motor system in the monkey. I. The effects of bilateral pyramidal lesions. *Brain, 91* (1968), 1–14.

Lawrence, D. G., and H. G. J. M. Kuypers. The functional organization of the motor system in the monkey. II. The effects of lesions of the descending brain-stem pathways. *Brain, 91* (1968), 15–36.

Leipmann, H. Die linke Hemisphäre und das Handeln. In *Drei Aufsätze aus dem Apraxiegebiet.* Berlin: Springer, 1908.

Luria, A. R. *The Working Brain.* New York: Penguin Books, 1973.

McLennan, J. E., K. Nakano, H. R. Tyler, and R. S. Schwab. Micrographia in Parkinson's disease. *Journal of Neurological Science, 15* (1972), 141–152.

Martin, J. P. *The Basal Ganglia and Posture.* London: Ritman Medical Publishing Co., Ltd., 1967.

Mateer, C., and D. Kimura. Impairment of nonverbal oral movements in apraxia. *Brain and Language, 4* (1977), 262–276.

Milner, B. Hemispheric asymmetry in the control of gesture sequences. *Proceedings of XXI International Congress of Psychology.* Paris, 1976, 149.

Nyberg-Hansen, R., and E. Rinvik. Some comments on the pyramidal tract, with special reference to its individual variations in man. *Acta Neurologica Scandinavia, 39* (1963), 1–30.

Parkinson, J. *Essay on the shaking palsy.* Reprinted in M. Critchley, ed. *James Parkinson.* London: Macmillan and Co., Ltd., 1955.

Poeck, K., and M. Kerschensteiner. Analysis of the sequential motor events in oral apraxia. In K. J. Zülch, O. Creutzfeldt, and B. C. Galbraith, eds. *Cerebral Localization.* Berlin: Springer-Verlag, 1975.

Renzi, E. de, A. Pieczuro, and L. A. Vignolo. Oral apraxia and aphasia. *Cortex, 2* (1966), 50–73.

Renzi, E. de, A. Pieczuro, and L. A. Vignolo. Ideational apraxia: a quantitative study. *Neuropsychologia, 6* (1968), 41–52.

Sacks, O. *Awakenings.* New York: Doubleday & Company, 1973.

Sherrington, C. *The Integrative Action of the Nervous System,* 2nd ed. New Haven: Yale University Press, 1961.

Twitchell, T. E. The restoration of motor function following hemiplegia in man. *Brain, 74* (1951), 443–480.

Twitchell, T. E. The automatic grasping response of infants. *Neuropsychologia, 3* (1965), 247–259.

Weaver, L. A., and G. W. Brooks. The effects of drug-induced parkinsonism on the psychomotor performance of chronic schizophrenics. *Journal of Nervous and Mental Diseases, 133* (1961), 148–154.

Wyke, M. Effect of brain lesions on the rapidity of arm movement. *Neurology, 17* (1967), 1113–1120.

Wyke, M. The effect of brain lesions in the performance of an arm-hand precision task. *Neuropsychologia, 6* (1968), 125–134.

PART SIX

FUNCTIONS OF ASSOCIATION AREAS

The regions of neocortex not specialized as primary sensory or motor regions are referred to as association cortex. This term derives from psychology theory prevalent in the early 1900s, when it was believed that messages from different senses met here and became associated with one another. Although Lashley's experiments of the 1940s disposed of this association idea, the term has endured. It is still useful to think of the secondary and tertiary zones of neocortex in the frontal, temporal, and parietal lobes as forming regions specialized for the mediation of complex cognitive processes, particularly since these areas have expanded tremendously as the mammals evolved. Chapters 12, 13, and 14 therefore discuss the association regions of the parietal, temporal, and frontal regions respectively. We provide a general overview of the functions of these zones, stressing the theoretical bases governing their operations. (The common functions of these zones—affect, memory, and language—are given detailed discussion in Part Seven.) Finally, we present strong evidence in each chapter suggesting that the association zones of nonhuman brains can provide excellent models of functioning in the association cortex of human brains. We demonstrate as well that much of our current understanding of human association cortex has evolved from a merging of studies of both humans and nonhumans.

12

THE PARIETAL LOBES

The patient with a gross lesion of the parietal lobe presents obvious and profound abnormalities of behavior. The interpretation of these abnormalities presents one of the most challenging puzzles in neuropsychology. A major source of the challenge is the absence of satisfactory nonhuman animal models of parietal-lobe function. Parietal-lobe function and organization are exceedingly complex. As a consequence of this complexity Luria has hypothesized that some portions of the parietal lobe constitute the specifically human portions of the brain. However, to date there is no clear evidence that such portions are exclusive to the human animal. In this chapter, we do not attempt to catalogue the myriad of behavioral abnormalities associated with parietal-lobe disease. We instead present a simple theoretical model of parietal-lobe function. The model is based on a similar one by Luria, and is supported with appropriate descriptions of the major symptoms of parietal-lobe disorder.

ANATOMY OF THE PARIETAL LOBES

The parietal lobe is the region of cerebral cortex underlying the parietal skull bone; this area is roughly demarcated anteriorly by the central fissure, ventrally by the Sylvian fissure, dorsally by the cingulate gyrus, and posteriorly by the parietal-occipital sulcus (see Figure 12-1). The principal regions of the parietal lobe include the postcentral gyrus (Brodmann's areas 1, 2, 3), the superior parietal lobule (areas 5, 7), the inferior parietal lobule (areas 40, 43), and the angular gyrus (area 39). These areas can be divided into two functional zones: an anterior zone including areas 1, 2, 3, and 43 as well as portions of areas 5 and 7; and a more posterior zone including the posterior portions of areas 5 and 7 as well as areas 39 and 40. The anterior zone is principally primary and secondary somatosensory cortex; the more posterior zone is true association cortex.

The principal afferents to the parietal cortex project from the lateral and posterior

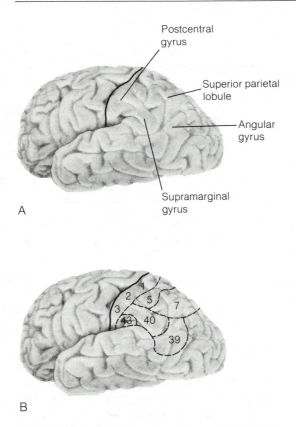

Postcentral
gyrus

Superior parietal
lobule

Angular
gyrus

Supramarginal
gyrus

A

B

FIGURE 12-1. Gross anatomy of the parietal lobe. A. The major gyri. B. Brodmann's cytoarchitectonic regions.

thalamus, hypothalamus, and primary and secondary sensory areas. The parietal lobe in turn sends its major projections to the frontal and temporal association cortex (Figure 12-2), as well as to subcortical structures including the lateral and posterior thalamus and the posterior region of the striatum, midbrain, and spinal cord. The corticocortical projections to the frontal lobe provide sensory input to the frontal lobe, because there are no direct sensory projections to this region. The descending projections to the striatum and spinal cord in particular likely function as a guidance control system in the control of movements in space (as described later in the chapter).

A THEORY OF PARIETAL-LOBE FUNCTION

No unitary theory of parietal-lobe function is possible because the parietal lobe is an artifact of gross anatomical definition rather than a reflection of cytoarchitectural or physiological unity. It is therefore not surprising that the parietal lobe does not have a unitary function. However, if the anterior (somatosensory) and posterior (association) zones are considered as functionally distinct regions, two independent functions of the parietal lobes can be identified. One is primarily concerned with somatic sensations and perceptions; the other is specialized for integrating sensory input from the somatic, visual, and auditory regions. This latter area extends beyond the formal boundary of the parietal lobe to include posterior portions of the temporal lobe, specifically area 37.

To discuss these two basic functions, we must first briefly review the hierarchical organization of the sensory systems (discussed in Chapter 8). Recall that the lowest cortical zone (Luria's primary zone), which receives projections from the thalamus, consists of highly specific neurons responsive to a single sensory modality. Lesions in the primary zones produce fundamental sensory losses, such as the scotoma that follows damage to area 17 in the visual system. The next cortical zone (Luria's secondary, or gnostic, zone) comprises the projection areas of the primary zones, which synthesize the sensory input into more complex forms. Again, the neurons, although more complex, are highly modality-specific; i.e., most are responsive to stimulation in just one modality. Lesions in this zone produce agnosias. Finally, in the highest zone (Luria's tertiary zone) sensory modalities overlap, enabling the sensory systems to integrate their input and to work in concert with one another and with information already stored in the nervous system.

The anterior portion of the parietal lobe

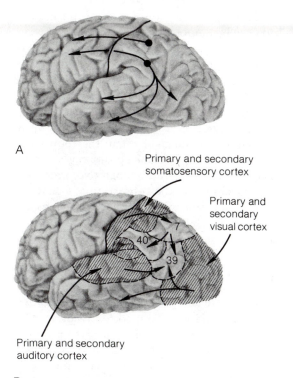

Primary and secondary
somatosensory cortex

Primary and
secondary
visual cortex

Primary and secondary
auditory cortex

FIGURE 12-2. A. Schematic of the long corticocortical projections of the parietal lobe to the frontal and temporal lobes. B. Schematic of the short corticocortical projections from the primary and secondary somatosensory, visual, and auditory cortex to the tertiary zone of the parietal lobe.

forms the primary and secondary zones of the somatic senses (see Figure 12-2), whereas the posterior region of the parietal lobe, in conjunction with the posterior temporal cortex, forms the tertiary zone. We are primarily concerned here with the function of the tertiary zone, the somatosensory functions having previously been discussed in Chapter 10.

Lesions of the tertiary zone do not produce deficits in vision, hearing, or somatic sensation or perception, but do produce severe disturbances in the integration and analysis of sensory information. An example of this type of

sensory integrating process is known as *cross-modal matching:* say an object is placed in a person's hand and palpitated but kept out of sight, and the person is then asked to choose the object visually from among a group of objects; the person must integrate the tactile and visual input to arrive at the solution—that is, to form a single percept of the object. Cross-modal matching can occur among any combination of visual, auditory, and somatic stimuli; in each case the matching is assumed to occur in the tertiary cortex where the inputs overlap. Lesions of this zone would be predicted to impair cross-modal matching, and indeed there is evidence that this is the case.

Another aspect of this integrative function of the tertiary cortex was seen in a patient of ours with a left posterior parietal astrocytoma. She was able to identify a clock as a clock, but was totally incapable of telling the time from the position of its hands. Thus, she did not have a visual agnosia, but rather a more complex deficit; she was unable to integrate the visual information necessary to decipher the meaning of the position of the hands.

We have greatly simplified the integrative function of the tertiary cortex of the parietal-temporal junction (we expand upon it in the next section). Nevertheless, this integrative function demonstrably represents the highest form of sensory analysis. This function is frequently also called cognition, a term in psychology essentially encompassing such mental abilities described by such English-language terms as reasoning, thought, perception, etc.

Asymmetry of Tertiary Sensory Function

One of the principles of hierarchical organization is that cerebral asymmetry is far more likely to be found at the highest functional levels. Thus, as would be expected, the greatest asymmetry is found in the cognitive functions of the tertiary zone. From our discussion of cerebral asymmetry in Chapter 9 we would expect the left parietal-temporal cortex to have a special role in language processes and the right parietal-temporal cortex to have a special role in spatial processes, and this is indeed the case. We shall describe each of these functions separately.

The left parietal-temporal region is specialized for processing symbolic-analytic information such as is found in language and arithmetic, in which the incoming sensory stimulation stands for, or abstractly symbolizes, something else. For example, the word "cat" describes a four-legged furry feline and assumes the characteristics of the animal (a form of cross-modal matching) even though the word itself in no way resembles a cat. Auditory, visual, and somatic input of a real object is therefore integrated and represented by an abstract stimulus that itself has auditory, visual, and somatic properties. One hears or reads the word "cat"—or, if the word is written in raised lettering, one can somatically "read" by touch the word "cat"—and in each case the object is understood. Geschwind, Luria, and others have proposed that this ability of cross-modally matching the various attributes of a real stimulus into an abstract, symbolic representation is the necessary foundation for the evolution of language. They hypothesize that the function is performed by the angular and supramarginal gyri, roughly areas 39 and 40. And, as previously mentioned, they question the existence of these regions in nonhuman primates on anatomical grounds, although their absence remains to be proven.

The right tertiary sensory zone is specialized for processing a different aspect of sensory input from that of the left. Analysis of visual, auditory, and somatic input requires that the information not only of *what* is incoming be integrated, but also of *where* it is coming from. In other words, only when the spatial characteristics of sensory inputs are integrated can a complete perception of the world around us

be developed. The complexity of this integration can be demonstrated in a number of ways. For instance, a student in a classroom is able to describe the room from the professor's point of view, even if the student has never stood where the professor stands. To do this, the student must construct an integrated spatial representation of the room, primarily visual and auditory, and then rotate the representation so that the professor's position is assumed. The complexity of this cognitive process is underscored by the observation, made by Piaget and others, that this ability does not develop in children until about 10 years of age.

Parietal-Lobe Motor Functions

Mountcastle and his colleagues have proposed that the tertiary parietal cortex receives afferent signals not only of the sensory representation of the world, but also of the position and movement of the body in space; the region uses this information to function as "a command apparatus for operation of the limbs, hands, and eyes within immediate extrapersonal space." Thus, not only does the parietal lobe integrate sensory and spatial information to allow accurate movements in space, but it also functions to direct or guide movements in the immediate vicinity of the body. Note, however, that the parietal lobe is not thought to control the details of muscular contraction during execution of movements—a function of the frontal lobe (principally area 4) and subcortical structures. Rather, it directs or aims movements toward behavioral goals. Note also that the parietal lobe is not considered to be the *only* motor command system, but rather one of several, each providing a different control function, as yet unspecified.

This view of parietal-lobe function accords with much anatomical and behavioral data. It is known that the parietal lobe has substantial efferents to subcortical motor structures, including the basal ganglia and spinal cord. These motor projections contribute to the control of proximal movements (e.g., gross limb movements), but not to distal movements (i.e., fine digit control), which are primarily controlled by area 4 of the frontal lobe. Thus, parietal-lobe lesions would be expected to disturb gross movements of the arms (in space) but to have little effect on distal movements of the fingers or face. Consistent with this prediction is the observation that parietal-lobe lesions produce severe bilateral apraxia when limb movements are required, but only mild apraxia when facial movements are required (see Chapter 11).

Like other functions of the parietal lobe, motor control of the left and right parietal cortex is asymmetrical. Because (as noted earlier) the left hemisphere has a special role in controlling movement, the theory would be expected to be more applicable to the left parietal lobe than to the right. Kimura has proposed that the left parietal control function provides a system for accurate internal representation of moving body parts and thus is important for controlling changes in their spatial positions. She argues that apraxia results from a disturbance in this function of controlling accurate positioning of limb and oral musculature. To move a limb from one position to another a person must have an accurate representation of where the limb is currently positioned. Without this information, changes of position are awkward and frequently in error. The right parietal lobe also has a motor function, as observed in constructional apraxia discussed in Chapter 11. We propose, however, that the two motor functions are totally unalike, for the right directs motor movements for reproducing the spatial properties of objects in the world. Right-parietal lesions disturb the motor control of drawing or constructional abilities, because the inadequate

sensory-spatial representation deprives the frontal motor system of sufficient information to carry out the appropriate movements. Thus, drawings are distorted; blocks are assembled in bizarre designs; maps lack spatial organization; etc.

Further Implications of the Theory

This relatively simple model of parietal-lobe function allows us to make inferences about the organization of other cognitive functions such as memory and personality.

Memory. For sensory input to be effectively integrated it must be held long enough to be used. It could therefore be predicted that parietal-lobe dysfunction would disturb short-term, or working, memory—that is, the memory for things that have just happened. For example, a person asked to repeat the digits 3292401 must hold them briefly in order to process and to repeat them; and indeed left parietal-temporal lesions seriously impair the ability to recall strings of digits. On the other hand, if there is no primary sensory defect, or agnosia, then a person with this lesion should be able to remember the digits with repeated practice, provided the mechanisms involved in long-term storage (located primarily in the medial temporal lobes) are intact. This prediction appears to be confirmed by observation. Furthermore, there is an asymmetry in this short-term memory function: the left parietal-temporal region is involved primarily in holding verbal material, and the right parietal-temporal region primarily in holding nonverbal material, such as the spatial location of particular sensory inputs.

Personality. We have seen that a person's behavior is influenced by the integration of sensory stimuli to produce a unified perception of the world. If a lesion in the left parietal lobe occurs, producing a disturbance of abstract symbolic integration, then behaviors such as talking, reading, writing, etc., are disturbed. Similarly, a disturbance of spatial integration resulting from lesion of the right parietal lobe produces a disturbance in behaviors requiring spatial orientation. Thus, since changes in sensory integration alter our behavior, it follows that how the affected person appears to others (that is, the person's personality) will be altered. And indeed, right parietal-temporal lesions commonly produce profound changes in personality. Luria describes a group of such patients with lesions (tumors and aneurysms) of the right parietal-temporal region who showed a severe loss of direct orientation in space and time.

> They firmly believed that at one and the same time they were in Moscow and also in another town. They suggested that they had left Moscow and gone to the other town, but having done so, they were still in Moscow where an operation had been performed on their brain. Yet they found nothing contradictory about these conclusions. Integrity of the verbal-logical processes in these patients, despite the profound disturbance of their direct self-perception and self-evaluation, led to a characteristic over-development of speech, to verbosity, which bore the character of empty reasoning and which masked their true defects. (Luria, 1973, p. 168)

EFFECTS OF PARIETAL-LOBE LESIONS

Although we have described a simple theory of how parietal-lobe function is organized, we have not discussed in any detail the bewildering array of symptoms characteristic of patients with parietal-lobe lesions. In this section we take a brief historical look at the interpretations of the symptoms of left and right parietal-lobe disease. We then describe some

of the typical symptoms observed in patients with parietal-lobe lesions.

Symptoms of Left Parietal-Lobe Lesions

In 1924, Josef Gerstmann described a patient with an unusual symptom following a left-parietal stroke—finger agnosia: the patient was unable to name or indicate recognition of the fingers on either hand. This discovery aroused considerable interest, and over the ensuing years other symptoms were reported to accompany finger agnosia, including: right-left confusion, **agraphia** (inability to write), and **acalculia** (inability to perform mathematical operations). These four symptoms collectively became known as the **Gerstmann syndrome.** Gerstmann and others argued that these symptoms accompanied a circumscribed lesion in the left parietal lobe, roughly corresponding to the **angular gyrus** (area 39). If these four symptoms occurred as a group the patient was said to demonstrate the Gerstmann syndrome, and the lesions could be localized in the angular gyrus. The storm of controversy that followed such claims continues to this day. The major issue is whether all of these symptoms occur together, and whether these are the only symptoms.

The important question from our point of view is whether these symptoms occur: they do. Do they ever occur as a pure syndrome? They probably do, but not often enough that the syndrome would be a useful diagnostic tetrad in routine investigations. Today various other symptoms of left-parietal lesions are known; many of these are illustrated in the following case history.

On 24 August 1975, Mr. S., an 11-year-old boy, suddenly had a seizure, which was characterized by twitching on the right side of the body, particularly the upper limb and face. He was given anticonvulsant medication, and was symptom-free until 16 September 1975, when he began to write upside down and backwards, at which time he was immediately referred to a neurologist, and diagnosed as having a left parietal malignant astrocytoma. Careful neuropsychological assessment revealed a number of symptoms characteristic of left parietal lesions. (1) Mr. S. had several symptoms of disturbed language function: he was unable to write even his name (agraphia); had serious difficulties in reading (dyslexia); and spoke slowly and deliberately, making many errors of grammar (**dysphasia**). (2) He was unable to combine blocks to form design, and had difficulties learning a sequence of novel movements of the limbs, suggestive of apraxia. (3) He was very poor at mental arithmetic (**dyscalculia**), and could not correctly solve even simple additions and subtractions. (4) He had an especially low digit span, being able to master the immediate recall of only three digits, whether they were presented orally or visually. (5) He was totally unable to distinguish left from right, responding at chance on all tests of this. (6) He had right hemianopia, probably because his tumor had damaged the geniculostriate connections. As Mr. S.'s tumor progressed, movement of the right side of his body became disturbed, because the tumor placed pressure on the frontal lobe. By the end of October 1975 Mr. S. died, neither surgery nor drug therapy being able to stop the growth of the tumor.

The symptoms that Mr. S. exhibited resemble those of other patients we have seen with left-parietal lesions. Curiously, he did not have finger agnosia, one of the Gerstmann symptoms, illustrating the point that even very large lesions do not produce the same effects in every patient. Thus, a parietal syndrome cannot be identified as Gerstmann had tried to do.

Symptoms of Right-Parietal Lobe Lesions

A perceptual disorder following right-parietal lesions was described by Hughlings-Jackson in 1874. However, not until the 1940s was the effect of right-parietal lesions clearly defined by Paterson and Zangwill. A classic paper by McFie and Zangwill, published in 1960, reviewed much of the previous work, and described several symptoms of right-parietal lesions, which are illustrated in the following patient.

Mr. P., a 67-year-old man, had suffered a right-parietal stroke. At the time of our first seeing him (24 hours after admission) he had no visual-field defect or paresis. He did, however, have a variety of other symptoms. (1) Mr. P. neglected the left side of his body and of the world. When asked to lift up his arms he failed to lift his left arm but could do so if one took his arm and asked him to lift it. When asked to draw a clock face he crowded all of the numbers onto the right side of the clock. When asked to read compound words such as ice cream or football he read "cream" and "ball." When he dressed he did not attempt to put on the left side of his clothing (a form of dressing apraxia); and when he shaved he shaved only the right side of his face. He ignored tactile sensation on the left side of his body. Finally, he appeared unaware that anything was wrong with him and was uncertain as to what all the fuss was about (anosagnosia). Collectively, these symptoms are referred to as **contralateral neglect**; we will return to them shortly. (2) He was impaired at combining blocks together to form designs (constructional apraxia), and was generally impaired at drawing freehand with either hand, copying drawings, or cutting out paper figures. When drawing, he often added extra strokes in an effort to make the pictures correct, but the drawings generally lacked accurate spatial relationships. Notice, in Figure 12-3, that the attempted drawing of a cube is spatially distorted and contains many superfluous lines. (3) He had a topographical disability, being unable to draw maps of well-known regions from memory. He attempted to draw a map of

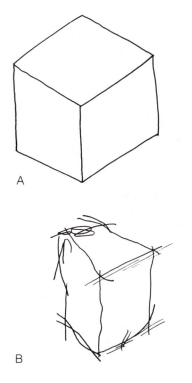

FIGURE 12-3. A. The model. B. The copy done by a patient with a right parietal stroke. Note the addition of lines to try to make the drawing correct.

his neighborhood, but it was badly distorted with respect to directions, the spatial arrangement of landmarks, and distances. In spite of all these disturbances Mr. P. knew where he was and what day it was, and could recognize his family's faces. He also had good language functions; he could talk, read, and write normally.

The contralateral neglect observed in Mr. P. is one of the most fascinating symptoms of brain dysfunction. Typically there is neglect of visual, auditory, and somesthetic stimulation on the side of the body and/or space opposite to the lesion and may be accompanied by denial of the deficit. Recovery passes through two stages: The first, **allesthesia**, is charac-terized by the patient's beginning to respond to stimuli on the neglected side, but doing so as if the stimuli were on the good side. The patient responds to and orients to visual, tactile, or auditory stimuli on the left side of the body as if they were on the right. The second stage is called **simultaneous extinction**: the patient responds to stimuli on the hitherto neglected side unless both sides are stimulated simultaneously in which case the patient notices only the stimulation on the side ipsilateral to the lesion.

Neglect presents several obstacles to understanding. For example, where is the lesion that can produce this effect? Figure 12-4 is a composite drawing of the region damaged (as inferred from brain scans) in 13 patients with neglect as described by Heilman and Watson. The area of most overlap among the lesions was the inferior parietal lobule. It should be noted, however, that neglect is occasionally observed following lesions to the frontal lobe and **cingulate cortex,** as well as to subcortical structures including the superior colliculus and lateral hypothalamus, among others. It is not clear, however, whether the same phenomenon results from these various lesions.

A second problem is why neglect occurs at all. There are two main theories: one, that it is caused by defective sensation or perception, and the other, that it is caused by defective "attention" or orientation. The strongest argument favoring the theory of defective sensation is that a lesion to the parietal lobes, which receive input from all of the sensory regions, could disturb the integration of sensation. Denny-Brown termed this function *morphosynthesis* and its disruption *amorphosynthesis*. In a current elaboration of this view it is hypothesized that neglect follows right-parietal lesion because the integration of the spatial properties of stimuli becomes disturbed; as a result, although stimuli are perceived, their location is uncertain to the nervous system and subse-

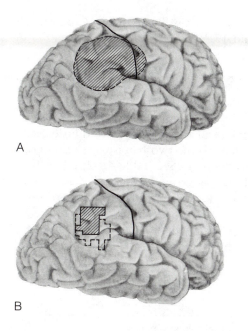

A

B

FIGURE 12-4. A. Composite drawing of the region damaged (as inferred from brain scans) in 13 patients with contralateral neglect as described by Heilman and Watson. The area of greatest overlap was the right inferior parietal lobule. B. Composite drawing of the region of overlap among lesions producing deficits in Warrington and Taylor's test of recognition of objects seen in unfamiliar views. The shaded region is the one of maximal overlap. Note the similarity between A and B.

quently they are ignored. The neglect is hypothesized to be unilateral because it is assumed that in the absence of right-hemisphere function, the left hemisphere is capable of some rudimentary spatial synthesis that prevents neglect of the right side of the world. This rudimentary spatial ability cannot compensate, however, for the many other behavioral deficits resulting from right-parietal lesion.

Critchley and later others, proponents of the other theory, have suggested that neglect results from an inability to attend to input that has in fact been registered. This view has most

recently been elaborated by Heilman and Watson. They propose that neglect is manifested by a defect in orienting to stimuli; the defect results from disruption of a system whose function is to "arouse" the individual when new sensory stimulation is present.

We are inclined to favor the former theory, the theory of defective perception, for two reasons. First, it is consistent with the general theory of parietal-lobe function; second, it does not require that an additional function be postulated for the parietal lobe.

Another common symptom of right-parietal-lobe lesion (which we did not look for in Mr. P.) has been described by Warrington and her colleagues: patients with right-parietal lesions, although capable of recognizing objects shown in familiar views, are badly impaired at recognizing objects shown in unfamiliar views. For example, a side-view photograph of a bucket is recognized easily; a top-view photograph of the same bucket is recognized with great difficulty (see Figure 12-5). Warrington concludes that the deficit is not in forming a gestalt, but rather in perceptual classification, the mechanism whereby two or more stimulus inputs are allocated to the same class. Such allocation can be seen as a type of spatial matching in which the common view of an object must be spatially rotated to match the novel view. Warrington and Taylor suggest that the focus for this deficit is roughly the inferior parietal lobule, the same region proposed as the locus of contralateral neglect (Figure 12-4).

Summary of the Major Symptoms

Our survey of the literature indicates 13 major reliable symptoms of parietal-lobe damage. Table 12-1 summarizes these symptoms, indicates the most probable lesion locus, and provides basic references in which these disorders have been quantified. Details of all of these

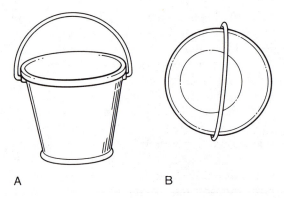

A   B

FIGURE 12-5. Drawing of a bucket in familiar (A) and unfamiliar (B) views. Patients with right-parietal lesions have difficulty recognizing objects in unfamiliar views such as this one.

symptoms can be found in Chapters 10, 11, and 12.

Left and Right Parietal Lobes Compared

Although we have discussed the left and right parietal lobes separately, and have described functional asymmetry, there is little doubt that lesions to the two hemispheres produce some overlapping. See Table 12-2, taken from the classic paper by McFie and Zangwill. Notice that lesions of either hemisphere are associated with behavioral deficits on four of their seven tests, although particular deficits were more likely to follow damage to one hemisphere.

TABLE 12-1

Summary of major symptoms of parietal-lobe damage

Symptoms	Most probable lesion site	Basic references
1. Disorders of tactile function	Areas 1, 2, 3	Semmes et al., 1960 Corkin et al., 1970
2. Visual or tactile agnosia	Areas 5, 7, 37?	Hécaen and Albert, 1978 Brown, 1972
3. Apraxia	Areas 7, 40 left	Brown, 1972 Geschwind, 1975 Kimura, 1980
4. Constructional apraxia	Areas 7, 40	Piercy et al., 1960
5. Disorders of language (alexia, aphasia)	Areas 39, 40 left	Hécaen and Albert, 1978
6. Acalculia	Areas 39, 40 left	Hécaen, 1969
7. Impaired cross-modal matching	Areas 37, 40	Butters and Brody, 1968
8. Contralateral neglect	Areas 7, 40 right	Heilman and Watson, 1977
9. Poor short-term memory	Areas 37, 40	Warrington and Weiskrantz, 1973
10. Disorders of body image	Area 7?	Hécaen and Albert, 1978
11. Right-left confusion	Areas 7, 40 left	Semmes et al., 1960 Benton, 1959
12. Disorders of spatial ability	Areas 7, 40 right	Semmes et al., 1963 Benton, 1969
13. Disorders of drawing	Area 40	Warrington et al., 1966

This partial overlap of symptoms is a common feature of lesions of association cortex, and implies functional overlap between the highest functions of the hemispheres. This partial overlap may be related to the concept of preferred mode of cognitive processing, introduced in Chapter 9. There we noted that many problems can be solved by using either a verbal cognitive mode or a spatial nonverbal cognitive mode, and that genetic, maturational, and environmental factors may predispose different people to use different modes. For example, a complex spatial problem, such as reading an upside-down map, can be solved either directly, by "spatial cognition" (the directions to travel are intuited spatially), or by "verbal cognition" (the spatial information is encoded into words and the problem is solved by being "talked" through step by step). There are people who are highly verbal and prefer the verbal mode even when it is less efficient; lesions of the left parietal lobe of these people would be expected to disturb functions that ordinarily are preferentially disrupted by right-parietal lesions, as can be seen in Table 12-2. Little direct evidence favors this explanation of functional overlap, but we believe it is a provocative idea that accounts in part for individual differences as well as for the apparent functional overlap revealed by lesion studies.

Clinical Neuropsychological Assessment

As we have seen, restricted lesions of the parietal cortex produce a wide variety of behavioral changes. It is logical to assume that behavioral tests used to evaluate brain damage in neurologically verified cases could be used to predict the locus and extent of brain damage or dysfunction in new cases. (See Chapter 21 for more detail on the rationale of neuropsychological assessment.) In this section we briefly summarize a number of tests that have

TABLE 12-2

Effects of left and right parietal-lobe lesions compared

	Percent of subjects with deficit[a]	
	Left	Right
Unilateral neglect	13%	67%
Dressing disability	13	67
Cube counting	0	86
Paper cutting	0	90
Topographical loss	13	50
Right-left discrimination	63	0
Weigl's sorting test	83	6

[a] Note the small but significant overlap in symptoms of left and right lesions respectively.
Based on data presented by McFie and Zangwill, 1960.

proven to be sensitive and valid predictors of brain injury (see Table 12-3). Although these tests do not assess all of the symptoms summarized in Table 12-1, they assess a broad range of parietal-lobe functions. It would be highly unusual for a person to perform normally on all of these tests but show other symptoms of parietal-lobe damage.

The two-point discrimination test assesses somatosensory thresholds. Recall that following lesions of the postcentral gyrus the somatosensory threshold increases in the contralateral side of the body. The test requires the blindfolded subject to report whether he or she felt one or two points touch the skin (usually on the palm of the hand or the face). The distance between the points is at first very large (e.g., 3 cm) and is gradually reduced until the subject can no longer perceive two points. In extreme cases the process is reversed: the distance must be increased to find that at which the subject first perceives two points.

The Seguin-Goddard formboard is a test of tactile form recognition; the blindfolded sub-

TABLE 12-3

Standardized clinical neuropsychological tests for parietal-lobe damage

Function	Test[a]	Basic reference
1. Somatosensory	Two-point discrimination	Corkin et al., 1970
2. Tactile form recognition	Seguin-Goddard formboard	Teuber and Weinstein, 1954
3. Visual perception	Gollin incomplete figures Mooney closure test	Warrington and Rabin, 1970 Milner, 1979
4. Spatial relations	Semmes locomotor map Right-left differentiation	Semmes et al., 1963
5. Language: speech comprehension reading comprehension	Token test Token test	de Renzi and Faglioni, 1978
6. Apraxia	Kimura box test	Kimura, 1977

[a] These are standardized tests validated on large samples of patients with known localized brain damage.

ject palpates 10 blocks of different shapes (e.g., star, triangle, etc.), and attempts to place them in similarly shaped holes on a formboard. When the test is completed the formboard and blocks are removed and the subject is asked to draw the board from memory. The precise locus of the lesion producing deficits on this test is controversial, and no claims have been proved. Nevertheless, research on tactile performance in monkeys with parietal lesions (see below) indicates that blindfolded tactual recognition is probably sensitive to lesions of areas 5 and 7, whereas in humans the drawing part—a test of both memory and cross-modal matching—is probably sensitive to lesions in the tertiary zone (areas 37, 40).

Visual perceptual capacity is easily assessed by either the Mooney closure test or the Gollin incomplete figure test. In both tasks a series of incomplete representations of faces or objects is presented, and the subject must combine the elements to form a gestalt to identify the picture. These tests are especially sensitive to right parietal-cortex damage.

The Semmes body placing and locomotor map tests are described in detail in Chapter 14 and will not be described here. In the right-left differentiation test a series of drawings of hands, feet, ears, and so on is presented in different orientations (upside down, rear view, etc.) and the subject's task is to indicate whether the drawing is of the left or right body part. The test is very sensitive to left parietal-lobe damage, but caution is advised, because patients with left frontal-lobe damage are also frequently impaired at this task.

The token test is an easily administered test of language comprehension. Twenty tokens—four shapes (large and small circles, large and small squares) in each of five colors (white, black, yellow, green, red)—are placed in front of the subject. The test begins with simple tasks (e.g., touching the white circle) and becomes progressively more difficult (e.g., touching the large yellow circle and the large green square). A reading-comprehension test can also be given by having the subject read the instructions out loud and then perform according to them.

It is unfortunate that there are no standardized tests of apraxia analogous to the token test for aphasia. However, the Kimura box test (see Figure 11-5) is probably the best test currently available, and may provide the desperately needed analogue. The subject is required to make three consecutive movements of pushing a button with the index finger, pulling a handle with four fingers, and pressing a bar with the thumb. This test is done very poorly by apraxics, and many patients appear unable to perform this very simple series of movements even with extensive practice.

Together, these nine tests provide a simple standardized and thorough collection of tests of parietal-lobe damage. We discuss the uses of these tests in Chapter 21.

NONHUMAN PARIETAL-LOBE FUNCTIONS

Certain claims have made studies of the organization of the parietal lobe of nonhumans especially important to our discussion of parietal-lobe function in humans. Luria, Geschwind, and others claim that the tertiary zone of the human parietal lobe either is not found in the nonhuman or functions differently there. This difference is taken to be significant in understanding the differences between humans and other primates. Unfortunately, the parietal cortex of nonhumans has drawn far less interest than the frontal and temporal cortex; current knowledge about nonhuman parietal-lobe function lags far behind knowledge about other association areas. To date, four types of experiments on the parietal lobes of nonhuman primates are relevant to this discussion: (1) those comparing neuroanatomical structure of the subregions of the parietal lobes; (2) those examining the behavioral capacities of different primates, especially on tests of cross-modal matching; (3) those examining the effects of parietal-lobe lesions on

behavior; (4) those examining the properties of cells in the parietal cortex.

Neuroanatomical Structure of Parietal Lobes

Luria, Geschwind, and Konorski have all argued that there are fundamental differences between the parietal lobes of humans and nonhuman primates. Luria and Geschwind have claimed that there is no homologue of the angular gyrus in nonhumans, and Konorski has questioned the existence of the **arcuate fasciculus,** which connects the posterior part of the parietal-temporal junction with the frontal cortex. In a thorough review of this issue Passingham and Ettlinger conclude that Konorski was in error, because there is clear evidence that the arcuate fasciculus exists in nonhuman primates, and to date there is no unequivocal evidence of major differences between the angular gyrus in humans and in other primates. Indeed, they point out that the only clear neuroanatomical difference between humans and other primates is the larger size of the human brain. Figure 12-6 provides a tentative summary of the extent and location of parietal cortex in the rat, cat, and monkey. The location of areas 39 and 40 in all three species is uncertain and somewhat controversial. Brodmann, for example, pointed out that his monkey area should be thought of as an undifferentiated area comparable to areas 7, 39, and 40 in humans. We have drawn these regions on the basis of available cytoarchitectonic, behavioral, and neuroanatomical degeneration studies.

Nonhuman Primate Cross-Modal Matching and Language Skills

Cross-modal matching ability has been widely implicated as a necessary correlate of language skills in humans; and it has been suggested

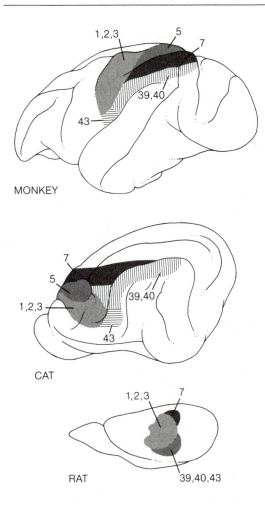

FIGURE 12-6. Gross anatomy of the parietal lobes of the monkey, cat, and rat. Tertiary zones (39, 40) are tentative pending further behavioral and anatomical work. The brains are not drawn to the same scale. Note that no evolutionary progression from one species to another is implied (see Chapter 6).

that nonhuman primates do not naturally have language because they lack this cognitive function. Because it is assumed that cross-modal matching is performed by the angular and supramarginal gyri, and because there are suggestions that nonhumans may not possess a homologue of this region, it is of particular interest to know whether nonhuman primates are capable of performing this behavior.

A variety of experimental situations have been devised to test this question. In the simplest of these tests an animal is presented three objects; one (the sample) he can see but not touch, and two others he can touch but not see. One of the hidden objects is identical to the sample. The subject's task is to select this one after palpating each of the hidden ones. If the chosen object matches the sample the animal is given a food reward. By using this procedure Davenport and his colleagues have unequivocally demonstrated cross-modal abilities in chimpanzees, for they not only can match a visually presented object with the tactile equivalent, but also can match photographs of an object with its tactile equivalent.

Until recently monkeys were reported to fail or give equivocal results in a matching task, but Jarvis and Ettlinger have recently shown that various species of monkeys are clearly capable of cross-modal matching and that early failures were an artifact of testing procedures. Furthermore, when they compared the performance of chimpanzees and rhesus monkeys on the same test problems, they found no clear superiority in the performance of the chimps. This result is surprising, for the chimpanzee has the larger parietal association cortex of the two.

The results of these studies imply one of two conditions: either cross-modal matching is not a correlate of language (although perhaps it is a prerequisite for language), or nonhuman primates are capable of some language abilities. Research on several species of apes has indicated that they are indeed capable of acquiring certain language abilities, such as the American Sign Language; thus, the neocortical organization of humans and other great apes may not differ qualitatively. We return to this issue in our discussion of language (Chapter 16); we conclude here that there is no compelling behavioral evidence for a significant difference between the parietal-lobe function in humans and their nearest primate relatives.

Behavior Following Parietal-Lobe Lesions in Nonhuman Mammals

If the parietal lobes of humans and nonhumans are similarly organized, then lesions of those of nonhumans should produce behavioral changes similar to those observed in humans. To date there have not been many studies of this type, but several authors have reported that unilateral parietal-cortex lesions in monkeys produce a phenomenon similar to the contralateral neglect described in humans. For example, Heilman and his associates observed that monkeys displayed extinction to simultaneous visual and somesthetic stimulation and decreased response to threat contralateral to the lesion, and occasionally even ignored food on the side contralateral to the lesion.

Bilateral lesions of areas 5 and 7 produce deficits in the capacity of monkeys to make tactile form discriminations in the dark. This deficit appears to resemble the impaired stereognosis of human patients with parietal lesions, particularly if they include the primary or secondary somatosensory cortex (see especially LaMotte and Mountcastle). In addition, monkeys with parietal lesions reach with poor accuracy, and the perception of the relationships among objects in space is impaired, although apparently not between the monkey's own body and objects in space (see Pohl and Moffet et al.). Recently, Petrides and Iverson studied the performance of monkeys on a behavioral analogue of the route-finding tests (e.g., mazes, maps, etc.) used to study spatial ability in humans. They chose a "bent-wire" problem, using metal rods bent to form various routes.

A ring-shaped sweet was threaded on the wire and the monkey's task was to remove the sweet so that it could be eaten. Monkeys with parietal lesions took significantly longer to remove the sweets; indeed they completely failed to solve about one-half the problems. These data demonstrate a visuospatial deficit analogous to those seen in humans with similar lesions.

We are unaware of any studies of lesions in areas 5, 7, 39, or 40 in cats, although McDaniel, Thomas, and their colleagues have made several reports on rats in recent years. They have found that large lesions of the entire parietal cortex produce deficits on a number of tasks (such as negotiating mazes) that require spatial processing but do not disrupt learning to discriminate visual patterns. It is uncertain if these spatial deficits are analogous to those observed in primates.

Monkey Parietal-Cortex Neurons

The study of the properties of single units in the parietal cortex yields findings consistent with the effects of lesions. Mountcastle and his colleagues studied the properties of single cortical cells in areas 5 and 7 and found that about 80 percent of the neurons in area 5 were activated by passive rotation of the limbs at their joints, passive stimulation of the skin, or stretching the muscle. Presumably, lesioning these neurons would reduce feedback about a movement, and could be responsible for afferent paresis. Another class of neurons that was found in both areas 5 and 7 was unexpected and fascinating. These cells were only responsive to projections of the arm or manipulations by the hand within the immediate space around the animal, to obtain an object such as food. These cells were not active during other movements in which the same muscles were used differently. Another type of cell in area 7 was active only when the animal fixated visually on an object he desired, such as food when hungry. The cell's activity continued during smooth visual following of the object if it moved. The activity of these cells depended on the object, its location, and the motivational state of the animals. Mountcastle and his colleagues concluded that area 7 contains large sets of neurons that function in a command fashion, directing visual attention to and exploration of the immediately surrounding extrapersonal space. Thus, the results of Mountcastle's studies confirm the importance of the parietal lobe of nonhumans in the integration of spatial information, and imply that this function may be more complex than previously believed.

Conclusions from Animal Studies

The results from all four lines of study of the nonhuman primate parietal lobe suggest that the monkey and chimpanzee may provide important models for understanding parietal-lobe function in humans. It would be particularly interesting to know whether lesions of the homologue of the angular and supramarginal gyri of monkeys and chimpanzees produce deficits in cross-modal matching or language. Further, since monkeys and apes are capable of cross-modal matching, are other intelligent species such as cats or dogs capable of this behavior? Finally, there is the as yet unanswered question of asymmetry of parietal association cortex function in nonhumans.

REFERENCES

Benton, A. L. *Right-Left Discrimination and Finger Localization.* New York: Hoeber Medical, Harper and Row, 1959.

Benton, A. L. Disorders of spatial orientation. In P. Vincken and G. Bruyn, eds. *Handbook of Clinical Neurology,* Vol. 3. Amsterdam: North Holland Publishing Co., 1969.

Brown, J. *Aphasia, Apraxia and Agnosia.* Springfield, Ill.: Charles C Thomas, 1972.

Butters, N., and B. A. Brody. The role of the left parietal lobe in the mediation of intra- and cross-modal associations. *Cortex, 4* (1968), 328–343.

Corkin, S., B. Milner, and T. Rasmussen. Somatosensory thresholds. *Archives of Neurology, 23* (1970), 41–58.

Critchley, M. *The Parietal Lobes.* London: Arnold, 1953.

Davenport, R. K., C. M. Rogers, and I. S. Russell. Cross-modal perception in apes. *Neuropsychologia, 11* (1973), 21–28.

Denny-Brown, D., and R. A. Chambers. The parietal lobes and behavior. *Research Publications of the Association for Research in Mental Disease, 36* (1958), 35–117.

Gerstmann, J. Some notes on the Gerstmann syndrome. *Neurology, 7* (1957), 866–869.

Geschwind, N. Disconnexion syndromes in animals and man. *Brain, 88* (1965), 237–294, 585–644.

Geschwind, N. The apraxias: neural mechanisms of disorders of learned movement. *American Scientist, 63* (1975), 188–195.

Graybiel, A. M. Studies on the anatomical organization of posterior association cortex. In F.

O. Schmitt and F. G. Worden, eds. *The Neurosciences: Third Study Program.* Cambridge, Mass.: MIT Press, 1974.

Hall, R. D., and E. P. Lindholm. Organization of motor and somatosensory neocortex in the albino rat. *Brain Research,* 66 (1974), 23–38.

Hécaen, H. Aphasic, apraxic and agnosic syndromes in right and left hemisphere lesions. In P. Vincken and G. Bruyn, eds. *Handbook of Clinical Neurology,* Vol. 4. Amsterdam: North Holland Publishing Co., 1969.

Hécaen, H., and M. L. Albert. *Human Neuropsychology.* New York: John Wiley and Sons, 1978.

Heilman, K. M., and R. T. Watson. The neglect syndrome—a unilateral defect of the orienting response. In S. Harnad, R. W. Doty, L. Goldstein, J. Jaynes, and G. Krauthamer, eds. *Lateralization in the Nervous System.* New York: Academic Press, 1977.

Jarvis, M. J., and G. Ettlinger. Cross-modal recognition in chimpanzees and monkeys. *Neuropsychologia, 15* (1977), 499–506.

Kimura, D. Acquisition of a motor skill after left hemisphere damage. *Brain, 100* (1977), 527–542.

Kimura, D. Neuromotor mechanisms in the evolution of human communication. In H. D. Steklis and M. J. Raleigh, eds. *Neurobiology of Social Communication in Primates: An Evolutionary Perspective.* New York: Academic Press, 1980.

Konorski, J. *Integrative Activity of the Brain.* Chicago: The University of Chicago Press, 1967.

LaMotte, R. H., and V. B. Mountcastle. Disorders of somesthesis following lesions of the parietal lobe. *Journal of Neurophysiology, 42* (1979), 400–419.

Luria, A. R. *The Working Brain.* New York: Penguin Books, 1973.

Lynch, J. C., V. B. Mountcastle, W. H. Talbot, and T. C. T. Yin. Parietal lobe mechanisms for directed visual attention. *Journal of Neurophysiology, 40* (1977), 362–389.

McDaniel, W. F., and R. K. Thomas. Temporal and parietal association cortex lesions and black-white reversal learning in the rat. *Physiological Psychology, 6* (1978), 300–305.

McFie, J., M. F. Piercy, and O. L. Zangwill. Visual spatial agnosia associated with lesions of the left cerebral hemisphere. *Brain, 73* (1950), 167–190.

McFie, J., and O. L. Zangwill. Visual-constructive disabilities associated with lesions of the left cerebral hemisphere. *Brain, 83* (1960), 243–260.

Milner, B. Complementary functional specialization of the human cerebral hemispheres. In press, 1980.

Moffet, A., G. Ettlinger, H. B. Morton, and M. F. Piercy. Tactile discrimination performance in the monkey: the effect of ablation of various subdivisions of posterior parietal cortex. *Cortex, 3* (1967), 59–96.

Mountcastle, V. B., J. C. Lynch, A. Georgopoulos, H. Sakata, and C. Acuna. Posterior parietal association cortex of the monkey: command functions for operation within extra-personal space. *Journal of Neurophysiology, 38* (1975), 871–908.

Passingham, R. F., and G. Ettlinger. A comparison of cortical functions in man and other primates. *International Review of Neurobiology, 16* (1974), 233–299.

Paterson, A., and O. L. Zangwill. Disorders of space perception associated with lesions of the right cerebral hemisphere. *Brain, 67* (1944), 331–358.

Petras, J. M. Connections of the parietal lobe. *Journal of Psychiatric Research, 8* (1971), 189–201.

Petrides, M., and S. D. Iverson. Restricted posterior parietal lesions in the rhesus monkey and performance on visuospatial tasks. *Brain Research, 161* (1979), 63–77.

Piercy, M., H. Hécaen, and J. de Ajuriaguerra. Constructional apraxia associated with unilateral cerebral lesions—left and right cases compared. *Brain, 83* (1960), 225–242.

Pohl, W. Dissociation of spatial discrimination deficits following frontal and parietal lesions in monkeys. *Journal of Comparative and Physiological Psychology, 82* (1973), 227–239.

Renzi, E. de, and P. Faglioni. Normative data and screening power of a shortened version of the token test. *Cortex, 14* (1978), 41–49.

Semmes, J., S. Weinstein, L. Ghent, and H.-L. Teuber. *Somatosensory Changes after Penetrating Brain Wounds in Man.* Cambridge, Mass.: Harvard University Press, 1960.

Semmes, J., S. Weinstein, L. Ghent, and H.-L. Teuber. Correlates of impaired orientation in personal and extra-personal space. *Brain, 86* (1963), 747–772.

Teuber, H.-L., and S. Weinstein. Performance on a formboard task after penetrating brain injury. *Journal of Psychology, 38* (1954), 177–190.

Thomas, R. K., and V. K. Weir. The effects of lesions in the frontal or posterior association cortex of rats on maze III. *Physiological Psychology, 3* (1975), 210–214.

Warrington, E. K., M. James, and M. Kinsbourne. Drawing disability in relation to laterality of cerebral lesion. *Brain, 89* (1966), 53–82.

Warrington, E. K., and P. Rabin. Perceptual matching in patients with cerebral lesions. *Neuropsychologia, 8* (1970), 475–487.

Warrington, E. K., and A. M. Taylor. The contribution of the right parietal lobe to object recognition. *Cortex, 9* (1973), 152–164.

Warrington, E. K., and L. Weiskrantz. An analysis of short-term and long-term memory defects in man. In J. A. Deutsch, ed. *The Physiological Basis of Memory.* New York: Academic Press, 1973.

13

THE TEMPORAL LOBES

In the late nineteenth century three major effects of temporal-lobe lesions on behavior were documented: in 1874 Wernicke described a language deficit; in 1899 Bekhterev reported memory impairment; and in 1888 Brown and Schaefer noted a disorder of affect and personality. Only in the last 30 years, however, have the functions of the temporal lobes—especially of the right—been elaborated. In this chapter (following the format of the previous chapter, on the parietal lobes) we review temporal-lobe anatomy, present a simple theoretical model of temporal-lobe function, describe the basic symptoms of temporal-lobe damage in humans, and briefly describe the effects of temporal-lobe lesions in non-humans.

ANATOMY OF
THE TEMPORAL LOBES

The temporal lobe comprises all of the tissue below the Sylvian fissure anterior to an imaginary line running roughly from the end of that fissure to the boundary of area 37 with area 19, and the boundary of areas 22 and 37 with the parietal association areas 39 and 40 (see Figure 13-1). The region enclosed by these boundaries includes not only neocortex (six layers) on the lateral surface, but also phylogenetically older cortex known as **archicortex** and **paleocortex** (three layers) on the medial surface. The neocortical regions include Brodmann's areas 20, 21, 22, 37, 38, 41, and 42. These areas are also sometimes described by the gyri that form them (illustrated in Figure 13-1): Heschl's gyrus (areas 41, 42), the superior temporal gyrus (roughly area 22), the middle temporal gyrus (roughly areas 21, 37, and 38), and the inferior temporal gyrus (roughly areas 20 and 37). The older cortex includes both the cortex on the medial surface of the temporal lobe, which forms the fusiform gyrus, parahippocampal gyrus, and uncus; as well as the hippocampus and amygdala (see Figures 13-1 and 13-2), which are subcortical. Thus, the temporal lobe includes

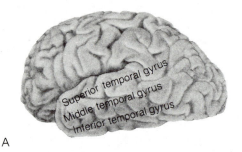

A

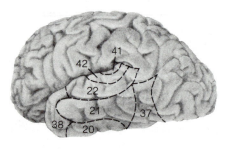

B

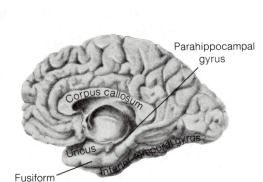

C

FIGURE 13-1. Gross anatomy of the temporal lobe.
A. The three major gyri visible on the lateral surface of
the temporal lobe. B. Brodmann's cytoarchitectonic
zones on the lateral surface. C. The gyri visible on a
medial view of the temporal lobe.

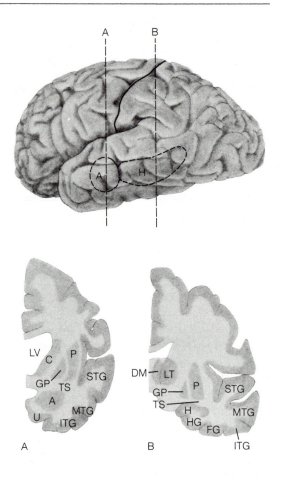

FIGURE 13-2. Top: Lateral view of the left hemisphere
illustrating the relative positions of the amygdala and
hippocampus buried deep in the temporal lobe. The
dashed lines A and B indicate the approximate location
of each section illustrated below. Bottom: Frontal sections through the left hemisphere illustrating the cortical and subcortical regions of the temporal lobe. A =
amygdala; C = caudate nucleus; DM = dorsomedial
nucleus of the thalamus; FG = fusiform gyrus; GP =
globus pallidus; H = hippocampus; ITG = inferior temporal gyrus; LT = lateral thalamus; MTG = middle temporal gyrus; P = putamen; STG = superior temporal
gyrus; TS = temporal stem; U = uncus. Shaded region
is the lateral ventricle.

auditory cortex, association cortex, and limbic cortex.

The temporal lobe is rich in internal connections, afferent projections from the sensory systems, and efferent projections to the parietal and frontal association regions, limbic system, and basal ganglia. The left and right temporal lobes are connected via the corpus callosum and anterior commissure, the neocortex through the former and the archicortex through the latter. As the complexity of its anatomy and connections suggests, the temporal lobe does not have a unitary function.

A THEORY OF TEMPORAL-LOBE FUNCTION

Being an arbitrarily defined anatomical region, the temporal lobe does not have a unitary function, since it houses primary and secondary auditory cortex, tertiary sensory cortex, as well as limbic cortex. However, if the primary and secondary auditory cortex are considered separately from the association and limbic cortex, three basic functions of the temporal lobes can be identified: one primarily concerned with auditory sensations and auditory and visual perception, one specialized for long-term storage of sensory input, and one functioning to add affective tone to sensory input.

The latter two functions are best understood by considering the analysis of sensory stimuli as they enter the nervous system. When a sensory stimulus is received, several processes must occur to allow the motor system to act upon the information. First, a percept must be formed, which requires that information about a given stimulus be integrated from different sense modalities, especially vision, audition, and somesthesis. This integration is the primary function of the associational area of the parietal lobe. Second, information may either

be stored for future use or compared to material stored previously. Higher animals characteristically are able to store large amounts of information that allows flexibility and adaptability to motor output. Storage requires two components. First, there must be a mechanism that functions to store and to retrieve information; this mechanism appears to be in the temporal lobes, especially the hippocampus. Second, there must be a mechanism for the actual storage of information; there are few clues about the location of this mechanism because brain lesions do not selectively destroy memories. We return to the problem of where memory is stored in Chapter 15.

The third function of sensory-input analysis is assigning connotative or affective properties to stimuli—that is, associating them with motivational or emotional significance. This function is crucial for learning because stimuli become associated with their positive, negative, or neutral consequences, and behavior is modified accordingly. In the absence of this system all stimuli would be treated as equivalent, and there would be a loss of affective response to them. Associating affective properties with particular stimuli is also a function of the temporal lobe, especially the medial temporal cortex and amygdala. Indeed, because of this function the medial temporal cortex has been called the association cortex of the limbic system. To date, most research on temporal-lobe function has been done on memory processes and very little on affective processes, partly because studying memory mechanisms is easier than studying affective mechanisms objectively. Indeed, both cognitive psychologists and neuropsychologists barely pay lip service to this latter function, although most would agree it plays an important role in the way we think and behave.

Although possible in principle at least, the anatomical separation of memory and affective functions in the temporal lobe has proven difficult to demonstrate. Visual or auditory input leaving the secondary sensory regions (see Figure 13-3) proceeds to the tertiary region of the temporal lobe, which includes areas 20, 21, 37, and 38. There are no strong empirical grounds for functionally differentiating these regions in humans, although work on nonhuman primates suggests that the anterior and posterior regions are likely to have different functions. The posterior region (area 37?) is primarily a sensory integrative region functionally associated with areas 39 and 40. The anterior region is primarily concerned with directing nervous-system "attention" to particular aspects of the sensory input, such as trying to remember a particular face from a large number (area 20?); the storage of visual and auditory memories (area 21?); and the association of affective properties with particular stimuli (area 38?). The sensory analysis performed in the tertiary zone then proceeds primarily to the medial regions of the temporal lobe, where, probably, the memory and affective systems are first clearly distinguished—although this has not been proved. The medial temporal cortex then projects primarily to the amygdala and hippocampus, which are relatively specialized for affective and memory functions respectively. Note, however, that the amygdala and hippocampus are probably not absolutely dissociated, because there is evidence in nonhuman primates that memory defects are more severe when the amygdala is also damaged, and affective changes have been associated with hippocampal lesions in cats (comparable data are not available from studies of primates).

Asymmetry of Temporal-Lobe Function

The sensitivity of the temporal lobes to epileptiform abnormalities, combined with the favorable outcome of treatment of epilepsy by surgical removal of the abnormal temporal lobe, has allowed neuropsychologists to care-

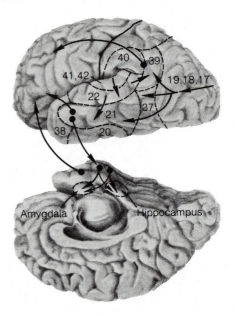

FIGURE 13-3. The flow of activity from the visual and auditory regions forward through the temporal lobes to the medial regions including the amygdala and hippocampus. Note that sensory input analyzed in either the temporal or the parietal lobe eventually arrives at the frontal lobe. Shaded area is tertiary temporal cortex, often called lateral temporal cortex.

fully study the complementary specialization of the temporal lobes. Comparison of the effects of left and right temporal lobectomy by Milner and her associates has revealed that specific memory defects vary according to which side the lesion is on: damage to the left temporal lobe is associated with deficits in verbal memory; damage to the right temporal lobe, with deficits in nonverbal memory. Little is known, however, about the relative role of the left and right temporal lobes in affective behavior; we are unaware of any studies specifically addressing the asymmetry of this function in the temporal lobes. The only hint of asymmetry comes from unquantified clinical observations that left and right temporal-lobe lesions appear to have different effects on personality.

In reviewing the literature on the effects of unilateral temporal lobectomy one is often struck by the relatively minor effects of removal of such a large zone of the cerebral hemispheres. However, it is incorrect to assume from these studies that removing both temporal lobes would have the effect merely of adding the symptoms of damage to each alone. Bilateral temporal-lobe removal produces dramatic effects on both memory and affect that are orders of magnitude greater than those observed following unilateral lesions. (See Chapters 15 and 17 for detailed discussion of the effects of bilateral lesions on memory and affect respectively.) Thus, although the temporal lobes are relatively specialized in their functions, there is substantial functional overlap: do not be overly impressed by the apparent functional asymmetry.

SYMPTOMS OF TEMPORAL-LOBE LESIONS

Six principal symptoms are associated with disease of the temporal lobes: (1) disturbance of auditory sensation and perception; (2) disturbance of selective attention of auditory and visual input; (3) disturbance of language; (4) impaired memory; (5) altered personality and affective behavior; (6) altered sexual behavior. Disorders of auditory sensation and perception were discussed in Chapter 10, and will not be repeated here. We discuss each of the remaining symptoms separately. Table 13-1 summarizes the major symptoms of temporal-lobe damage, lists the most probable lesion sites and cites basic references.

Disturbance of Selection of Visual and Auditory Input

Lesions of the temporal lobes outside the primary and secondary auditory and visual zones produce neither deficits of sensation nor ag-

nosias, producing instead disturbance in focusing attention on specific aspects of sensory input. This is best understood by first considering sensory selection in normal subjects.

People have a limited capacity to process the wealth of information in their environment, and hence must select which inputs to process. This selectivity is generally not conscious, for the nervous system automatically scans input and selectively perceives the environment. (Conscious control can be exerted, of course, as when one searches for a mailbox to post a letter.) Selectivity in auditory perception is best illustrated by the problem of listening to two conversations simultaneously. Because it is impossible to process the two competing inputs concurrently, the auditory system adopts one of two strategies: either one conversation is ignored, or attention shifts back and forth from one conversation to the other. In either case there is a selection of input. Selective perception in the visual system operates similarly. For example, because it is not possible to watch all events of a gymnastics meet simultaneously, attention either is focused entirely on one event or is shifted from one event to another.

Let us now consider the person with temporal-lobe damage. We shall see that there is an impairment of both auditory and visual selection of input, which is ordinarily demonstrated only by special testing procedures. Selective attention of auditory input can be tested by using a dichotic listening technique. As we noted in Chapter 9, if a series of pairs of words is presented dichotically, more of the words presented to the right ear will be reported; if tonal sequences are presented dichotically there will be a left-ear advantage. Exploiting this technique in patients with temporal-lobe lesions, Schulhoff and Goodglass have demonstrated that left temporal-lobe lesions result in an overall drop in the number of words reported, whereas right temporal lesions result in an overall drop

TABLE 13-1

Summary of major symptoms of temporal-lobe damage

Symptoms	Most probable lesion site	Basic reference
1. Disorders of auditory sensation and perception	Areas 41, 42, 22	Vignolo, 1969 Hécaen and Albert, 1978
2. Disturbance of selection of visual and auditory input	Areas 20, 21, 22, 37, 38	Sparks et al., 1970 Dorff et al., 1965 Milner, 1958
3. Disorder of language comprehension	Area 22 on left	Hécaen and Albert, 1978
4. Poor long-term memory	Areas 21, hippocampus (and possibly amygdala)	Milner, 1970
5. Changes in personality and affect	Areas 21, 38 plus amygdala	Blumer and Benson, 1975 Pincus and Tucker, 1974
6. Changes in sexual activity	?	Blumer and Walker, 1975

in the number of tonal sequences recognized, although the expected ear advantages are still present in both cases. One explanation for this effect is that the nervous system has difficulty focusing selectively on the input into one ear, and attempts to process all the input concurrently; as a result performance drops severely. Analogous findings are reported for visual input as well. Dorff et al. presented two different visual stimuli simultaneously, one to each visual field. Lesions of the left temporal lobe impaired recall of content of the right visual field, whereas lesion of the right temporal lobe impaired recall of content of both visual fields. Again, it may be that the nervous system is now unable to focus on distinctive features of the stimuli to allow efficient perception and storage of the input. In the case of visual input, however, it is noteworthy that right temporal lesions produce bilateral deficits, whereas left temporal lesions produce unilateral deficits. This difference implies that the right temporal lobe may have a greater role than the left temporal lobe in selective attention to visual input. Further evidence for this suggestion comes from a study by Milner. She presented

patients with items from the McGill picture anomaly test; the task is to recognize anomalous features of pictures. For example, in one item illustrating a monkey in a cage there is an oil painting on the wall of the cage—an obvious oddity or anomaly. But patients with right temporal lesions, although able to accurately describe the contents of the picture, are impaired at recognizing the anomalous characteristic of this and similar pictures. It could be argued that the picture is sufficiently complex that, to locate the anomalous characteristic, visual attention must be focused on different aspects of the picture rather than on the picture as a whole. In the absence of the right temporal lobe the visual system is unable to do this, and thus fails to locate the anomaly.

Language

Since the time of Wernicke, lesions of the left temporal association cortex (primarily area 22) have been associated with disturbed recognition of words, the extreme form being "word deafness": an inability to recognize words as such despite intact hearing of pure tones (a deficit given detailed discussion in Chapter 16).

In addition to producing deficits in language comprehension, lesions of temporal cortex beyond area 22 alter language processes in subtle ways. For example, Jaccarino-Hiatt has recently shown that nonaphasic patients with left temporal lobectomies have protracted latencies in producing word associations such as in "table-chair," "night-day," etc. Furthermore, patients with right temporal lobectomies are excessively talkative, suggesting a loss of inhibition of talking. (Excessive talkativeness is, however, a clinical impression not quantitatively documented.) In view of the temporal lobe's role in affect it would be interesting to know if the affective connotation of language is diminished by temporal lobectomy (we are unaware of any studies of this sort).

Memory

To many neuropsychologists the study of the temporal lobes is synonymous with the study of memory. In fact, in most physiological psychology and neuropsychology texts index references to the temporal lobes lead one to a discussion of amnesia. The interest in temporal lobes is synonymous with the study of memory which was stimulated in the early 1950s by the discovery that bilateral removal of the medial temporal lobes, including the hippocampus and amygdala, resulted in amnesia for all events after the surgery (anterograde amnesia). It is now clear that both the hippocampus and temporal neocortex are important for memory functions. Milner and her associates have demonstrated that disturbances of memory result from damage to area 21; the disturbance increases in direct proportion to the amount of hippocampus damaged. Studies by the same investigators have further indicated a strong asymmetry of temporal-lobe memory function

(both cortical and hippocampal): lesions of the left temporal lobe result in impaired recall of verbal material, such as short stories, word lists, and so on, whether presented visually or aurally; lesions of the right temporal lobe result in impaired recall of nonverbal material, such as geometric drawings, faces, tunes, and similar material. However, unlike parietal-lobe lesions, temporal-lobe lesions do not disturb the immediate recall of material such as strings of digits; thus, the temporal and parietal lobes have complementary rather than redundant roles in memory.

The following two patients demonstrate the role of the left and right temporal lobes in memory. Mr. B., a 38-year-old man, was suffering from an astrocytoma in the left temporal lobe. Prior to the onset he had been a successful executive in an oil company and was noted for efficiency. As his tumor developed he became forgetful, and at the time of hospital admission his efficiency had dropped drastically; he had begun to forget appointments and other important events. Forgetfulness had become such a problem that he had begun to write notes to himself to cover his memory problem, but often mislaid the notes, leading to even greater embarrassment. On formal tests of memory he had especial difficulty recalling short stories read to him a few minutes earlier. For example, in one test he was read the following story from the Wechsler memory scale and asked to repeat it as exactly as possible. "Anna Thompson of South Boston, employed as a scrub woman in an office building, was held up on State Street the night before and robbed of fifteen dollars. She had four little children, the rent was due and they had not eaten for two days. The officers, touched by the woman's story, made up a purse for her." Mr. B. recalled: "A woman was robbed and went to the police station where they made her a new purse. She had some children too." This is very poor performance for a person of Mr. B.'s intelligence and education. On the other hand, his immediate recall of digits was good; he could repeat strings of seven digits accurately, illustrating the integrity of his left parietal-lobe functions. Similarly, his recall of geometric designs was within normal limits, illustrating the asymmetry of memory functions, for his right temporal lobe was still intact.

Ms. C. illustrates the complement of Mr. B.'s syndrome. She was a bright 22-year-old college student who had an indolent tumor of the right temporal lobe. When we first saw her, following surgery, she complained of memory loss. She was within normal limits on formal tests of verbal memory, such as the story of Anna Thompson, but was seriously impaired on formal tests of visual memory, especially geometric drawings. For example, in one test she was shown geometric designs for 10 seconds and then asked to draw them from memory. Ten minutes later she was asked to draw them again. She had difficulty with immediate recall (see Figure 13-4), and after 10 minutes was unable to recall any of the drawings at all.

Affect and Personality

Although the temporal lobe has been known to be associated with disturbance of affect in humans for nearly 100 years, knowledge about the details of this role is still surprisingly fragmentary. Penfield and others reported that stimulation of the anterior and medial temporal cortex produces feelings of fear, an effect also occasionally obtained from the amygdala as well. Temporal-lobe epilepsy traditionally has been associated with personality characteristics in which there is an overemphasis on trivia and the petty details of daily life. Pincus and Tucker describe several symptoms of this personality, including pedantic speech, egocentricity, perseveration on discussion of personal problems (sometimes referred to as "sticky," because one is stuck talking to the person), paranoia, preoccupation with religion, and proneness to aggressive outbursts. This constellation of behavior produces what is described as a *temporal-lobe personality,* although very few patients combine all of these traits. Similar personality traits occur following temporal lobectomy. There appears to be a relative asymmetry in the symptoms as right temporal lobectomy appears more likely than left temporal lobectomy to be associated with paranoia, pedantic behavior, egocentricity, talkativeness, and stickiness. This observation has not been quantified, however, and warrants further study. Finally, although temporal-lobe epilepsy has long been linked anecdotally to psychosislike episodes, Slater and associates in 1963 first demonstrated a statistical relationship between the occurrence of temporal-lobe epilepsy and psychosis. Since no such relationship has been described between temporal lobectomy and epilepsy, it has been suggested that a chronic abnormally discharging temporal lobe may produce abnormalities in either biochemistry or electrophysiology of the brain, leading to psychotic behavior. We return to this issue in Chapter 17.

Sexual Behavior

The role of the temporal lobe in sexual behavior is poorly understood, but it has long been known that bilateral destruction of the entire temporal lobe results in a dramatic increase in sexual behavior that is indiscriminantly directed heterosexually and homosexually and toward inanimate objects. This condition is neither common nor well studied in humans, and does not occur following unilateral temporal-lobe removal. Indeed, although we are unaware that the sexual behavior of people with unilateral temporal lobectomies has been the subject of any formal studies, we have never heard any complaints of either increased

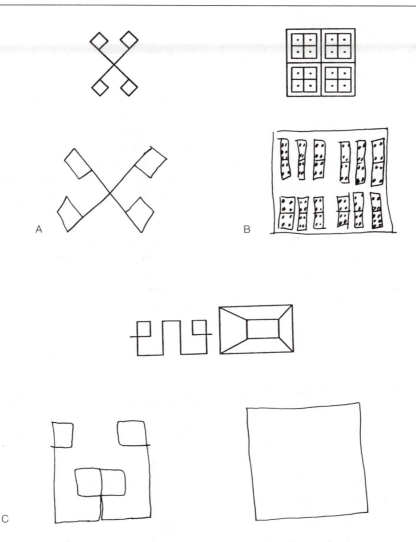

FIGURE 13-4. Illustration of impaired recall of geometric figures in the case of Ms. C. In each set shown (A, B, C) the top drawing is the original stimulus and the bottom drawing is Ms. C.'s sketch made immediately after viewing each figure for 10 seconds. Note that Ms. C.'s impairment is worse with the more complex figures. Ms. C. was unable to recall even the simplest figure 10 minutes after viewing it.

or decreased sexual activity in our experience with these patients. Temporal-lobe epilepsy is associated with altered sexual behavior, however: Blumer and Walker found 70 percent of their patient sample to have experienced a change in sexual activity, most commonly a decrease in sexual interest (see Table 13-2).

Among these patients it was not unusual for sexual arousal to occur as rarely as once a year. This result must be interpreted cautiously, however, for the data may not reflect the function of the temporal lobes so much as the effect of chronic abnormal electrical activity on temporal and limbic structures.

TABLE 13-2

Summary of the changes in sexual behavior
of 50 temporal-lobe epileptics

Symptoms	Number of patients showing symptom
Chronic global hyposexuality	29
Postoperative hypersexuality	2[a]
Hypersexuality induced by medication	1
Postictal sexual arousal	4[b]
Ictal sexual arousal	1
Homosexual behavior	2
	35 (70%)

[a] Both patients were preoperatively hyposexual.
[b] One patient also with homosexual behavior, another patient also with hypersexuality induced by medication (Mysoline).
From Blumer and Walker, 1975, p. 207.

Clinical Neuropsychological Assessment of Temporal-Lobe Damage

A number of standardized assessment tools have proven to be sensitive and valid predictors of temporal-lobe injury (see Table 13-3). Like clinical neuropsychological tests of parietal-lobe function, these tests do not assess all of the symptoms summarized in Table 13-1, but it would be highly unusual for a person to perform normally on all of these tests if there were damage to either temporal lobe.

Auditory and visual processing capacity can be assessed using dichotic listening and the McGill picture anomalies, as described earlier in the chapter. The picture-anomalies task is not as sensitive an indicator today as it was when first used in the 1950s, perhaps because television viewing has made the average person more sophisticated in visual perceptual abilities. Nevertheless, a poor score on this test almost invariably denotes right temporal abnormality.

The best test of general verbal memory ability is the Wechsler memory scale. However, because the Wechsler memory quotient is affected by nonspecific disorders of attention, two subtests—paired associates and logical stories—are often used as a purer measure of verbal memory capacity. Paired associates require a subject to learn a series of word pairs (e.g., north-south, cabbage-pen) such that when one word is read (e.g., north, cabbage) the paired associate word (south, pen) can be recalled. An example of the logical memory test was presented earlier in the chapter, in reference to Mr. B.'s verbal memory defect.

The Rey complex figure test has proven to be one of the best tests of the nonverbal memory function of the right temporal lobe. A printed copy of a complex geometric pattern is placed before the subject with the instructions, "Copy the drawing as accurately as you can." Forty-five minutes later the subject is asked to reproduce as much of the figure as he or she can remember. Although the scoring criteria provide an objective measure of nonverbal memory, the test has the drawback that depressed or poorly motivated subjects may perform poorly, not because there is right temporal-lobe damage, but because they refuse to seriously try to recall the figure. There is no easy solution to this problem, since all tests of nonverbal memory are subject to this complication.

Finally, a deficit in language comprehension could be the result of a lesion in any of the language zones of the left hemisphere (that is, in the parietal, temporal, or frontal lobe); there is currently no neuropsychological assessment tool that can localize the area of damage within the left hemisphere. For this reason we once again recommend the token test as the test of choice for language comprehension. Additional tests (described in Chapter 16) may prove useful after the initial screening with the token test.

TABLE 13-3

Standardized clinical neuropsychological tests for temporal-lobe damage

Function	Test	Basic reference
1. Auditory processing capacity	Dichotic words and melodies	Sparks et al., 1970
2. Visual processing capacity	McGill picture anomalies	Milner, 1958
3. Verbal memory	Wechsler memory scale: logical stories and paired associates	Milner, 1975
4. Nonverbal memory	Rey complex figure	Taylor, 1969
5. Language	Token test	de Renzi and Faglioni, 1978

ARE THE TEMPORAL LOBES SPECIAL IN HUMANS?

In the 1950s studies of memory defects in humans with temporal-lobe lesions led to the suggestion that the temporal lobes of humans might have functions unlike those of nonhumans, since severe memory defects could not be unequivocally demonstrated in nonhumans. An influential paper by Diamond and Hall in 1969 kindled interest in evolutionary questions regarding the temporal lobe. They proposed that the primate temporal lobe was special, and questioned whether or not carnivores even had a temporal lobe homologous to that of primates. Since Diamond and Hall's paper, research has indicated that this view is incorrect: both primates and carnivores appear to be good models of temporal-lobe function in humans. Without exhaustively surveying research on nonhuman temporal-lobe function, we will demonstrate that the symptoms of temporal-lobe lesions in nonhumans qualitatively resemble those observed in humans.

Anatomy of Nonhuman Temporal Lobes

The cortical extent of the temporal lobes of nonhumans is defined by cytoarchitecture, thalamic projections, and the electrophysiological properties of temporal-lobe cells. Figure 13-5 illustrates the general evolutionary increase in temporal-lobe neocortex in primates, especially in comparison to the rat. Indeed, it has been proposed that a major difference between primates and other mammals is in the increase in the size of both the temporal and the frontal lobes relative to the remaining cerebral cortex. Note the similarity, however, in the regions of the temporal lobes in cats and monkeys; both demonstrate the same cortical subareas, although the temporal neocortex may make up a larger percentage of the monkey brain. All mammalian species have the equivalent of medial temporal cortex, hippocampus, and amygdala.

Effects of Temporal-Lobe Lesions in Nonhumans

All of the major deficits associated with temporal-lobe lesions in humans (with the exception of language deficits) are observed in nonhumans, with no convincing qualitative differences. Moreover, many of the effects of temporal lesions are much easier to study in cats and monkeys than in humans. As a result, research on nonhuman animals has greatly

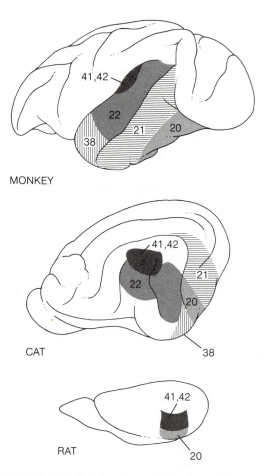

MONKEY

CAT

RAT

FIGURE 13-5. Relative sizes and locations of the temporal cortex of the monkey, cat, and rat. Depiction of area 22 in the cat may be an overestimate, because the zone's posterior region (the posterior ectosylvian gyrus) has both auditory and visual functions, and may actually be analogous to area 37 as well. The brains are not drawn to the same scale. No evolutionary progression from one species to another is implied.

clarified understanding of the human temporal lobe.

Auditory Processing

Dewson and his colleagues have demonstrated that unilateral lesion of the superior temporal gyrus (area 22) of the monkey produces deficits in performance of tasks requiring complex analysis of auditory input. For example, in one experiment monkeys with unilateral lesions confined to area 22 were trained to discriminate between paired sequences of auditory elements, combinations of pure tone (T) and white noise (N). Four sequences were presented: T-T, T-N, N-N, and N-T. The animals' task was to learn to press two bars in a unique sequence for each auditory pair. For example, for T-T the animals were trained to press the left bar twice; for T-N, to press the left bar, then the right. Monkeys with lesions of area 22 were severely impaired at this task. The auditory sensitivity of these animals proved to be normal, but there was a deficit in auditory memory. Lesions of the visual association cortex (areas 20, 21) had no effect on performance of this task.

Dewson has also demonstrated cerebral asymmetry in auditory processing in monkeys; lesions in area 22 on the left result in larger effects on auditory discrimination and association than similar lesions in the right. However, a crucial experiment remains to be done. Wollberg and Newman have shown that area 22 has cells differentially responsive to species-typical vocalizations such as hoots, howls, etc. The question is whether lesions of area 22 (especially on the left) would disturb perception of species-typical vocalizations. If so, a symptom analogous to "word deafness" in people might be demonstrated (although this may be pushing the analogy somewhat).

Visual Processing

The role of the temporal lobe in visual processing has drawn intense interest. A number of investigators have been able to functionally distinguish among the posterior temporal cortex (roughly area 20), an area anterior to it (roughly area 21), and the anterior and medial limbic cortex (roughly area 38 plus medial cortex) in monkeys and cats. Lesions of the posterior cortex produce an inability to discriminate and select the essential cues from a visual stimulus, and to maintain attention to them. Thus, the animal has difficulty distinguishing complex visual stimuli from one another, just as the human does with deficits in discriminating complex visual stimuli such as faces from one another. Lesions of area 21 produce a different type of deficit in which the animal has difficulty in forming visual memories. The monkeys are able to discriminate among complex visual stimuli, but are unable to remember the visual image for more than a few moments, and are thus impaired at problems requiring such visual memory. Finally, lesions of the anterior zone, including the amygdala, produce deficits in the process of associating visual stimuli with their reinforcement properties. To demonstrate this, a monkey is presented with two visual stimuli, such as a square and a cross. A food reward is associated with one of the stimuli; if the monkey chooses the correct stimulus it is reinforced with a peanut or raisin. Once this problem is mastered, the reward properties of the stimuli are reversed, the previously rewarded stimulus now being unrewarded and vice versa. This task therefore requires the animal to associate changing reward properties with the visual stimuli, a requirement that is difficult to meet in the absence of the anterior temporal cortex and/or amygdala.

The detailed studies of visual processing in monkeys with restricted temporal-lobe lesions beautifully illustrate how studies of nonhuman brain function can provide crucial clues to understanding human brain function. It is impossible to do parallel studies in humans, because neither surgical nor naturally occurring lesions conform to the anatomical subdivisions of the temporal lobe.

Memory

A clear demonstration of a severe memory defect in nonhuman animals analogous to that resulting from bilateral temporal-lobe removal in humans has been elusive. As a result, many propose that the functions of the medial temporal lobe in humans reflect an evolutionary shift. Until recently, studies meant to demonstrate analogous memory defects in nonhumans assumed that the critical structure for memory storage was the hippocampus, and it was repeatedly found that bilateral hippocampal lesions in rats, cats, and monkeys failed to produce the human syndrome of anterograde amnesia. A recent study by Mishkin sheds light on this apparent discrepancy: memory loss after removal of both the hippocampus and the amygdala in monkeys was much more severe than after removal of either structure alone. Mishkin suggested that both structures have an important role in memory.[1] This hypothesis remains to be studied further, especially in humans, where the amygdala is virtually always removed along with the hippocampus. It may be that the role of the amygdala has been underestimated in studies of humans. With respect to memory functions of area 21, we have already noted that these lesions in monkeys produce visual memory deficits, again consistent with the results of Milner's human studies.

Affect

Bilateral lesions of the amygdala, hippocampus, and lateral temporal cortex are known to produce alterations in affect in both monkeys and cats, but the precise role of each

---

[1] There is a further complication in understanding the locus of severe memory loss, as demonstrated in work by Horel. This issue is too complex to consider here and is discussed in detail in Chapter 15.

of these structures in affective control is not well understood. The amygdala and anterior temporal neocortex may have similar roles in affective control; Horel et al. reported that lesions of both regions reduced both attack and escape behavior, and made the animals less reluctant to approach novel stimuli. In addition, it is known that monkeys with lesions of either the anterior temporal cortex or the amygdala do not survive in the wild, because they no longer associate with other members of their species. By contrast, animals with more posterior lesions in the temporal lobe are still social creatures, behaving normally in the social group.

Sexual Behavior

Bilateral destruction of the temporal lobes is known to produce profound changes in sexual behavior—chiefly increasing sexual activity—in a variety of mammals. The crucial structure for this effect is the amygdala and its related archicortex and paleocortex. The hippocampus appears to play a minor role, and there is no clear indication of the role of the temporal neocortex in sexual behavior. It would be expected that damage to area 20 produces impaired discrimination of visual sexual objects, but this possibility has not been studied.

Summary

There is no convincing evidence that the temporal lobes of humans are qualitatively different from those of other mammals. Temporal-lobe lesions in monkeys and cats produce symptoms remarkably similar to those observed in humans. Studies of affect and sexual behavior of both human and nonhuman subjects with temporal-lobe lesions are sorely needed to complement the studies of the memory and sensory-processing functions of the temporal lobes.

REFERENCES

Blumer, D., and D. F. Benson. Personality changes with frontal and temporal lesions. In D. F. Benson and D. Blumer, eds. *Psychiatric Aspects of Neurologic Disease.* New York: Grune and Stratton, 1975.

Blumer, D., and E. A. Walker. The neural basis of sexual behavior. In D. F. Benson and D. Blumer, eds. *Psychiatric Aspects of Neurologic Disease.* New York: Grune and Stratton, 1975.

Campbell, A. Deficits in visual learning produced by posterior temporal lesions in cats. *Journal of Comparative and Physiological Psychology, 92* (1978), 45–57.

Cowey, A., and J. H. Dewson. Effects of unilateral ablation of superior temporal cortex on auditory sequence discrimination in *Macaca mulatta. Neuropsychologia, 10* (1972), 279–289.

Dewson, J. H. Preliminary evidence of hemispheric asymmetry of auditory function in monkeys. In S. Harnad, R. W. Doty, L. Goldstein, J. Jaynes, and G. Krauthamer, eds. *Lateralization in the Nervous System.* New York: Academic Press, 1977.

Diamond, I. T., and W. C. Hall. Evolution of neocortex. *Science, 164* (1969), 251–262.

Dorff, J. E., A. F. Mirsky, and M. Mishkin. Effects of unilateral temporal lobe removals on tachistoscopic recognition in the left and right visual fields. *Neuropsychologia, 3* (1965), 39–51.

Geschwind, N. Disconnexion syndromes in animals and man. *Brain, 88* (1965), 237–294, 585–644.

Hécaen, H., and M. L. Albert. *Human Neuropsychology.* New York: John Wiley and Sons, 1978.

Horel, J. A. The neuroanatomy of amnesia: a critique of the hippocampal memory hypothesis. *Brain, 101* (1978), 403–445.

Horel, J. A., E. G. Keating, and L. J. Misantone. Partial Klüver-Bucy syndrome produced by destroying temporal neocortex or amygdala. *Brain Research, 94* (1975), 349–359.

Iwai, E., and M. Mishkin. Two visual foci in the temporal lobe of monkeys. In N. Yoshii and N. A. Buchwald, eds. *Neurophysiological Basis of Learning and Behavior.* Osaka, Japan: Osaka University Press, 1968.

Jaccarino-Hiatt, G. Impairment of cognitive organization in patients with temporal-lobe lesions. Unpublished Ph.D. thesis, McGill University, 1978.

Jones, B., and M. Mishkin. Limbic lesions and the problem of stimulus-reinforcement associations. *Experimental Neurology, 36* (1972), 362–377.

Jones, E. G. The anatomy of extrageniculostriate visual mechanisms. In F. O. Schmitt and F. G. Worden, eds. *The Neurosciences: Third Study Program.* Cambridge, Mass.: MIT Press, 1974.

Milner, B. Psychological defects produced by temporal lobe excision. *Research Publications of the Association for Research in Nervous and Mental Disease, 38* (1958), 244–257.

Milner, B. Memory and the medial temporal regions of the brain. In K. H. Pribram and D. E. Broadbent, eds. *Biological Bases of Memory.* New York: Academic Press, 1970.

Milner, B. Psychological aspects of focal epilepsy and its neurosurgical management. *Advances in Neurology, 8* (1975), 299–321.

Mishkin, M. Memory in monkeys severely impaired by combined but not by separate removal of amygdala and hippocampus. *Nature, 273* (1978), 297–298.

Nonneman, A. J., and B. Kolb. Lesions of hippocampus or prefrontal cortex alter species typical behavior in the cat. *Behavioral Biology, 12* (1974), 41–54.

Penfield, W., and H. H. Jasper. *Epilepsy and the Functional Anatomy of the Human Brain.* Boston: Little, Brown, 1959.

Pincus, J. H., and G. J. Tucker. *Behavioral Neurology.* New York: Oxford University Press, 1974.

Renzi, E. de, and P. Faglioni. Normative data and screening power of a shortened version of the token test. *Cortex, 14* (1978), 41–49.

Schulhoff, C., and H. Goodglass. Dichotic listening: side of brain injury and cerebral dominance. *Neuropsychologia, 7* (1969), 149–160.

Slater, E., A. W. Beard, and E. Glithero. The schizophrenia-like psychosis of epilepsy. *British Journal of Psychiatry, 109* (1963), 95–150.

Sparks, R., H. Goodglass, and B. Nickel. Ipsilateral versus contralateral extinction in dichotic listening from hemispheric lesions. *Cortex, 6* (1970), 249–260.

Taylor, L. B. Localization of cerebral lesions by psychological testing. *Clinical Neurosurgery, 16* (1969), 269–287.

Vignolo, L. A. Auditory agnosia: a review and report of recent evidence. In A. L. Benton, ed. *Contributions to Clinical Neuropsychology.* Chicago: Aldine Publishing, 1969.

Weiskrantz, L. The interaction between occipital and temporal cortex in vision: an overview. In F. O. Schmitt and F. G. Worden, eds. *The Neurosciences: Third Study Program,* Cambridge, Mass.: MIT Press, 1974.

Wollberg, Z., and J. D. Newman. Auditory cortex of squirrel monkey: response patterns of single cells to species-specific vocalizations. *Science, 175* (1972), 212–214.

14

THE FRONTAL LOBES

There is no cerebral structure in which lesions can produce such a wide variety of symptoms, and thus a more bewildering range of interpretations, than the frontal lobes. Some authors have assigned the human frontal lobes the "highest" conceivable functions such as intellectual synthesis and the control of ethical behavior, whereas other authors demote them, failing to see any special importance in them. In this chapter we first describe the anatomy of the frontal lobes, then present a basic model of frontal-lobe function. The effects of frontal-lobe damage on human behavior are well documented. We attempt to summarize these effects in an effort to make sense of the extravagant claims as to the function of this vast area. We consider the question whether the frontal lobes are really special in humans, and discuss the idea that the frontal lobes are part of a functional system that includes a number of subcortical structures. First, however, it is necessary to review the anatomy of the frontal lobes.

ANATOMY OF THE FRONTAL LOBES

The frontal lobes of the human brain comprise all the tissue in front of the central sulcus. It is certainly not anatomically homogeneous, however; several areas are functionally and anatomically distinct. These include area 4, or primary motor cortex; area 6, or premotor cortex; Broca's area; medial cortex; and prefrontal cortex (see Figure 14-1). The functions of area 4 were described in Chapter 11.

In 1948, Rose and Woolsey noticed that the frontal lobes of all the mammalian species they examined had a region that received projections from the dorsomedial nucleus of the thalamus. They termed this region **prefrontal cortex.** The dorsomedial nucleus has three divisions, each of which projects to a distinct region of the prefrontal cortex, and each of which is functionally and anatomically distinct. In primates these regions are known as the dorsolateral cortex (roughly areas 9, 10, 44,

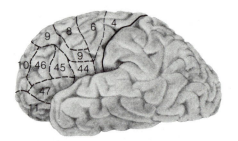

LATERAL VIEW

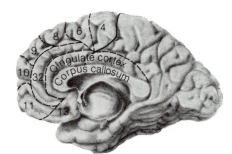

MEDIAL VIEW

A

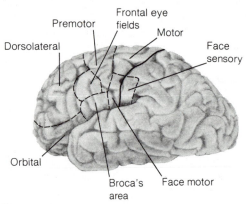

B

FIGURE 14-1. A. The lateral and medial views of Brodmann's cytoarchitectonic map of the frontal lobe. B. Approximate boundaries of functional zones of the frontal lobe.

45, and 46), **orbital frontal cortex** (so called because of its relation to the orbit of the eye, and roughly including areas 11, 12, and 47), and the frontal eye fields (including portions of areas 8 and 9). At one time the prefrontal cortex was called the frontal granular cortex, since the fourth layer of this region has large granular cells that clearly distinguish it from areas 4 and 6, which have no granular fourth layer but have instead a large fifth layer of giant pyramidal cells. This terminology is seldom used today because although all mammalian species have a prefrontal cortex, not all have granular cells, and hence a frontal granular cortex.

The transcortical and extracortical connections of the frontal lobe, and in particular of the prefrontal cortex, are exceedingly complex. Briefly, the prefrontal cortex receives afferents from the visual, auditory, and somatosensory areas, by way of the parietal cortex. It receives also fibers from many subcortical structures, most important being the caudate nucleus, the dorsomedial thalamus, the amygdala, and the hypothalamus. The prefrontal cortex sends heavy projections to the parietal and temporal association cortex and cingulate cortex, as well as to subcortical structures including the basal ganglia, dorsomedial thalamus, amygdala, hippocampus, hypothalamus, and other lower brainstem structures. As might be expected, each of the three subregions of the prefrontal cortex has its own separate connections, which are frequently connected to discrete regions of the structures mentioned above.

The complexity and breadth of the frontal-lobe connections no doubt contribute to the puzzling array of behavioral changes observed in people with lesions in this region. With respect to understanding the functions of the frontal lobes, the most important connections may well be those with the "motor" structures such as the basal ganglia, those with the limbic system, and those with the parietal and temporal association cortex.

A THEORY OF FRONTAL-LOBE FUNCTION

Background

Historically, claims about the functions of the frontal lobes have been extravagant and extreme. From the time of Gall until the 1930s the frontal lobes were thought by most to be the seat of highest intellect. Functions as varied as "abstract behavior," foresight, intellectual synthesis, ethical behavior, affect, and self-awareness were proposed by a variety of writers. Hebb's discovery in 1939 brought these prevailing views into question. Administering standard intelligence tests to patients with frontal-lobe removals for treatment of epilepsy, Hebb discovered that IQ was not reduced—an astonishing observation in light of the prevailing belief. This finding has been repeated by many others with the same results: IQ is not lowered by frontal-lobe lesions, and sometimes may actually be raised!

A major reason for the extremes of views regarding the frontal-lobe functions was that neurologists and neuropsychologists often based their conclusions on single cases. Many of these patients had tumors, and it is now well known that tumor patients frequently do not behave like patients with lesions resulting from other causes. Tumors may produce pressure on widespread parts of the brain, resulting in symptoms unrelated to the region where the tumor actually resides. Furthermore, tumors may include subcortical structures, or may result in the production of abnormal electrical discharges that themselves may alter the function of widespread areas of brain tissue. An additional problem is that

often frontal-lobe tumors are larger than tumors elsewhere in the brain. It may be that the large size of the frontal lobes allows a tumor to grow for longer periods without specific motor, sensory, or language problems arising as symptoms.

The advent of frontal lobotomies in psychosurgery provided large numbers of patients with frontal-lobe lesions, but studies on these patients did little to reduce extravagant claims of frontal-lobe function. Although IQs after frontal lobotomy were lower than those obtained much earlier, they were not, according to a study by Rosvold and Mishkin in 1950, lower than IQs obtained just prior to surgery. In other words, the lower IQ was caused not by the lobotomy per se, but by the psychiatric disease process necessitating the lobotomy. Hence the serious flaw in using psychosurgical patients in neuropsychological research. Because no groups of patients with similar psychiatric disease have lesions elsewhere in the brain, the effects of the disease cannot be separated from the effects of the lesion. Furthermore, we now know that severe psychotic disease of the type that might lead to psychosurgery produces serious deficits in neuropsychological test results without surgery.

Feuchtwanger, in 1923, did one of the first systematic studies of large numbers of patients with lesions other than tumors or lobotomies. His monograph should not have been ignored, as it was, by North American neuropsychology. Teuber has summarized the results of Feuchtwanger's study of 400 cases of gunshot wounds: 200 frontal and 200 nonfrontal. All of the wounds resulted from injuries during World War I.

A careful reading of Feuchtwanger's monograph would have prepared us for the surprises of the forties and fifties of this century: The increasing evidence is that frontal lesions, on the whole, have less effect on test intelligence, on categorizing, and on a variety of complex reaction-time tasks than lesions in other areas of the human brain. He concluded that specific changes were not to be sought, either in the intellectual sphere, or in that of "attention" or "memory," including recent memory. Instead, the more pervasive changes were those of mood and attitude, ranging from euphoria, or, less frequently, depression to a curious form of "other-directedness" on the patient's part—an incapacity for making plans. These changes were independent, in Feuchtwanger's view, from the occasional alterations in motor control: restlessness, hyperkinetic behavior, or, more rarely, slowing and torpor. (Teuber, 1964, p. 415)

During the 1950s, '60s, and '70s research on the frontal lobes has clarified many of the contradictions and inconsistencies of the earlier work. A theoretical model of frontal-lobe function is now possible that provides a unified explanation of the various symptoms of frontal-lobe damage.

Hierarchical Organization

Before the hierarchical organization of the frontal lobe is discussed, the organization of the cortical input to the motor system must first be reviewed briefly. The cortical motor system is thought to comprise three levels of function. The first level is composed of neurons whose cell bodies reside in area 4 and whose axons largely synapse directly on spinal motor neurons or cranial-nerve motor nuclei. This level is specialized for controlling fine hand, finger, and facial movements. Lesions in this level produce severe chronic deficits in fine motor control and also reduce speed and strength of limb movements.

The second level of cortical motor function is composed of neurons whose cell bodies lie primarily in areas 4, 6, and 8 of the frontal cortex and 5 and 7 of the parietal cortex.

These neurons contribute to two descending systems: one controlling limb movements; the other, body movements. All neurons of the limb-control system synapse in the red nucleus, although many synapse earlier as well, primarily in the basal ganglia. Similarly, all neurons of the axial system synapse in the brainstem reticular formation; but, again, many of these neurons synapse en route to the brainstem in the basal ganglia. Cortical lesions in this level of control do not abolish limb or axial movements, since subcortical structures (i.e., red nucleus, basal ganglia, thalamus, etc.) can still operate to produce basic limb and axial movements. Rather, the lesions alter more complex aspects of limb and axial movements, producing more subtle deficits. Lesions in areas 5 and 7 contribute to apraxias, probably because of damage in the visual and tactile guidance of limb and axial movements. The effects of lesions in areas 6 and 8, although still poorly understood, appear to impair the smooth transition of separate axial, limb, and hand movements into a fluid series of movements.

The third level of motor control is composed of the neurons forming the prefrontal cortex. These neurons receive input from the tertiary zones of the parietal and temporal cortex; they send efferents to cortical neurons in both the first and second levels as well as to the basal ganglia and brainstem nuclei of the motor system. The prefrontal cortex has a nonspecific role in movement control, and probably plays little role in actually controlling the components of movement. Rather, the prefrontal cortex controls the overall motor programs and adds flexibility to motor output by modifying behavior with respect to specific internal and external factors. Because of this flexibility, ongoing behavior requires continual monitoring, as do its consequences, such that behaviors are appropriate to particular circumstances. In the absence of this function, behavior becomes stereotyped, inflexible, and maladaptive. The prefrontal cortex also provides the highest control of affective behavior and is able to effect control of basic emotional behavior by virtue of its intimate connections with the limbic system. Lesions of the prefrontal cortex therefore usually produce alterations in basic aspects of personality and social behavior, and interfere as well with the planning and execution of complex behavioral programs. People with prefrontal lesions are therefore seldom able to hold jobs, and have difficulty looking after many daily activities. They are typically late for appointments and are often unable to maintain close relationships even with their immediate families.

The three levels of cortical motor control are hierarchical with respect to final motor output, the first level being closest to it and the third level being most removed. Whereas the first level synapses directly upon spinal motor neurons, the second level and, to a greater extent, the third level have multiple synapses en route to the spinal motor neurons. Thus, the effects of lesions in the first level are easily specified, since no other levels in the nervous system can assume the functions affected. But at the higher levels the effects of cortical lesions become progressively more difficult to define, because there are subcortical levels of control before the final motor output, in the spinal-cord and cranial-nerve nuclei.

Asymmetry of Frontal-Lobe Function

In view of the asymmetry in parietal and temporal association cortex function it could be expected that the frontal lobes are organized asymmetrically. This is indeed the case. Furthermore, as expected from the principles of hierarchical organization of the neocortex, this asymmetry is found principally in the prefrontal cortex, the highest level of the motor hierarchy. In keeping with the general asymmetrical organization of the cerebrum, the special role of the left frontal lobe is in control of movement primarily related to language, that of the right frontal lobe is in control of movement primarily related to nonverbal abilities. Like that of the parietal and temporal lobes, the asymmetry of frontal-lobe function is relative rather than absolute; studies of lesions indicate that both frontal lobes play a role in nearly all behavior. Milner has emphasized this point, noting that the laterality of frontal-lobe lesions is far less striking than that observed from more posterior lesions.

SYMPTOMS OF FRONTAL-LOBE LESIONS

The effects of lesions in the lower levels of the motor system were discussed in Chapter 11. Our primary concern here is with the effects of lesions to the prefrontal cortex. However, in our discussion two factors may produce discrepancies between our conclusions and others'. First, we deal primarily with the effects of *unilateral* frontal lesions. As with the temporal lobe there is reason to believe that the effects of bifrontal lesions cannot be duplicated by lesions of either hemisphere alone. Table 14-1 summarizes a study comparing the behavioral effects of unilateral and bilateral lesions. Patients with bifrontal lesions are severely impaired at reporting the time of day and in decoding proverbs, effects seldom seen following unilateral frontal lesions. Although its cause is uncertain, this effect is consistent with the results of much animal work—that is, unilateral frontal lesions have little or no effect on certain tasks whereas bifrontal lesions have severe effects.

The second factor in any discrepancy is that we have mainly drawn our conclusions from studies using patients with surgical removals

TABLE 14-1

Relative frequency of defective performance
on neuropsychological tests

Test	Percentage of group showing a deficit		
	Left	Right	Bilateral
Verbal fluency	70%	38%	71%
Verbal learning	30	13	86
Block construction	10	50	43
Design copying	10	38	43
Time orientation	0	0	57
Proverbs	20	25	71

Adapted from Benton, 1968.

for the relief of epilepsy or the excision of benign tumors, and patients with missile wounds of the brain. This choice of patients presents the difficulty that some phenomena may not be observed in these patients. For example, Denny-Brown and others described the release of hand and foot grasp reflexes, which appear to result only from very large frontal lesions, possibly bifrontal, such as result from slow-growing tumors or abcesses.

There appear to be about 10 reliable symptoms of prefrontal damage (Table 14-2); we discuss each of them separately and in some detail. We cannot describe patients with all of these symptoms, because few patients would have lesions so large as to include all of the functional subregions. Wherever possible, however, we illustrate the symptoms with examples.

Broca's Aphasia

The first symptom of prefrontal cortex damage to be described was the disturbance of language following lesion of the left frontal lobe, in 1861, by Broca. After studying additional patients Broca and others proposed that the

third frontal convolution of the left hemisphere, area 44, was specialized for producing motor programs for speech, a function Broca described as the "motor image of the word." In this type of aphasia the person has difficulty speaking, doing so only slowly and deliberately. Curiously, although this symptom of frontal-lobe damage was the first to be described, it remains the most controversial even to this day. Some question its existence; others, granting that it might really occur, question its nature. We shall return to this problem in our discussion of language in Chapter 16. To date there are no clear indications what area 44 in the right frontal lobe does. It is certain, however, that loss of this zone does not produce aphasia.

Impaired Response Inhibition and Inflexible Behavior

Perhaps the most commonly observed traits of frontal-lobe patients tested by clinical neuropsychologists are impaired response inhibition and inflexible behavior. Patients with frontal-lobe lesions consistently perseverate on responses in a variety of test situations, particularly those in which there are changing demands. The best example of this phenomenon is observed in the Wisconsin card-sorting test, which has been extensively studied by Brenda Milner. Figure 14-2 shows the test material as it appears to the patient. The patient is presented with four stimulus cards, bearing designs that differ in color, form, and number of elements. The patient's task is to sort the cards into piles in front of one or another of the stimulus cards. The only help the patient is given is being told whether the choice is correct or incorrect. The test works on this principle: the correct solution is first color; once the patient has figured out this solution, the correct solution then becomes, without warning, form. Thus, the patient must now inhibit

TABLE 14-2

Summary of major symptoms of frontal-lobe damage

Symptoms	Most probable lesion site	Basic references
1. Aphasia	Area 44 on left	Brown, 1972
2. Impaired response inhibition	Areas 9, 10	Milner, 1964 Perret, 1974
3. Poor voluntary eye gaze	Areas 8, 9	Teuber, 1964 Tyler, 1969
4. Poor recency memory	Dorsolateral	Milner, 1974
5. Reduced corollary discharge	Dorsolateral	Teuber, 1964
6. Poor movement programming	Dorsolateral	Kolb and Milner, 1980 Luria, 1973
7. Impaired spatial orientation	Dorsolateral	Semmes et al., 1963
8. Impaired social behavior	Orbital	Blumer and Benson, 1975
9. Altered sexual behavior	Orbital	Walker and Blumer, 1975
10. Reduced behavioral spontaneity	Orbital	Milner, 1964 Jones-Gotman and Milner, 1977
11. Impaired phonetic discrimination	Face	Taylor, 1979
12. Poor spelling	Face	Taylor, 1979

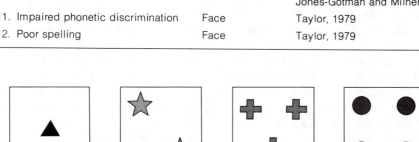

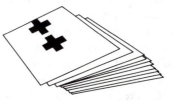

FIGURE 14-2. The Wisconsin card-sorting test, showing test material as presented to the subject. (From B. Milner, Some effects of frontal lobectomy in man. In J. M. Warren and K. Akert, eds., *The Frontal Granular Cortex and Behavior*, p. 315. Copyright © by McGraw-Hill, Inc. Used with the permission of McGraw-Hill Book Co.)

classifying the cards on the basis of color and shift to form. Once the patient has succeeded at selecting by form, the correct solution again changes unexpectedly, this time to number of elements. It will later become color again and so on. Shifting response strategies is particularly difficult for patients with frontal lesions, who may continue responding to the original stimulus (color) for as many as 100 cards until testing is terminated. Throughout this period they may comment that they know that color is no longer correct. They nevertheless continue to sort on the basis of color. For example, one patient stated (correctly): "Form is probably the correct solution now so this [sorting to color] will be wrong, and this will be wrong, and wrong again." Such perseveration is common on any task in which a frontal-lobe patient is required to shift response strategies, demonstrating that the frontal lobe is necessary for flexibility in behavior. It is important to note that on card-sorting tasks the subjects must not be given any hint that they are to expect a change in the correct solution, because many frontal-lobe patients improve dramatically when given this warning. The cue apparently allows enough flexibility in behavior to solve the problem.

It appears from Milner's work that the principal locus of this effect (on card sorting, at least) is roughly around Brodmann's area 9 in the left hemisphere. Lesions elsewhere in the left, and often the right, frontal lobe will also produce a deficit on this task, although a somewhat attenuated deficit.

Performance of the Stroop test further demonstrates loss of behavioral flexibility and response inhibition following frontal-lobe damage. Subjects are presented with a list of color words (blue, green, red, etc.), each word being printed in colored ink but never in the color denoted by the word (e.g., the word "yellow" is printed in blue, green, or red ink). The subject's task is to name the color in which each word is printed as quickly as possible. Correct response requires an inhibition of reading the color name, an inhibition that is difficult for many control subjects. Perret found that patients with left frontal lesions were unable to inhibit reading the words and thus were impaired at this task.

Deficits in Voluntary Gaze

A number of studies using quite different procedures have been reported in which frontal-lobe lesions produce alterations in voluntary eye gaze. For example, Teuber presented patients with an array of 48 patterns on a screen. The patterns could be distinguished by either shape or color or by both (see Figure 14-3). At a warning signal a duplicate of one of the 48 patterns appears in the center of the array, and the subject's task is to find the matching pattern and to identify it by pointing to it. Patients with frontal-lobe lesions are impaired at finding the duplicate pattern.

Luria recorded the patients' eye movements as they visually examined a picture of a complex scene. The eye-movement patterns of the patients with large frontal-lobe lesions were quite different from those of normal control subjects or of patients with more posterior lesions. For example, if a normal control was asked about the age of the people in a picture, his eyes fixed on their heads; if asked how they are dressed, the eyes fixed on the clothing, etc. Patients with large frontal-lobe lesions tended to glance over the picture more or less at random, and a change in the question about the picture failed to alter the direction or pattern of eye movements.

As mentioned earlier, the frontal eye fields are the region in the frontal lobe that is primarily concerned with eye movements. It is likely—although unproven—that these deficits in eye gaze and movements are most severe after lesions that include the eye fields.

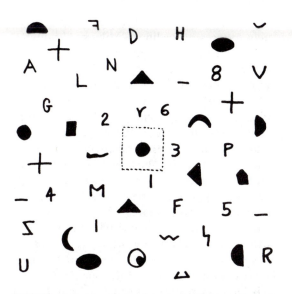

FIGURE 14-3. Visual search test adapted from Poppel-reuter (1917). The subject must locate a duplicate of the stimulus object placed inside the central base.

It would be interesting to know if the frontal lesions alter lateral eye gaze observed during different types of tests (see Chapter 9).

Memory

Many reports of the 1930s and '40s suggested that the frontal lobes played a role in some types of memory. Although consistent with research on nonhuman primates, this conclusion is, in a broad sense, not correct, because frontal-lobe lesions do not generally interfere with the long-term storage of material. However, one special function is mediated by the frontal lobes: namely, memory for recency. That is, patients with frontal-lobe lesions are impaired at remembering the order of events, although the memory of the events themselves does appear intact. Further, there is relative asymmetry in the frontal lobes in this regard: the right frontal lobe appears more important

for memory for nonverbal or pictorial recency; the left frontal lobe appears more important for verbal recency. For example, if a subject is read a series of words and then asked which of two words was read most recently, the frontal-lobe patient will have difficulty recalling, although he may clearly recall that both words were read. This latter storage function is performed by the temporal lobe. Nonverbal function can be tested by showing photographs instead of reading words; again, the order of presentation of the photographs is forgotten.

At first glance, the impaired memory for recency appears to be an exception to the theoretical role of the frontal lobe in motor control. However, it is essential to motor control that behaviors be distinguished from one another in time. In other words, the order in which behaviors are performed must be remembered, especially in the learning of complex skilled movements. Thus, it could be predicted that frontal-lobe patients with impaired recency memory for words or photographs would also be impaired at remembering the order of individual movements. This prediction remains to be tested.

Spontaneous Behavior

According to Zangwill, in a detailed study of the early literature, such authors as Feuchtwanger and Kliest observed that although patients with left frontal lesions anterior to Broca's area were not aphasic, they did have a type of verbal deficit. Zangwill described it as "a certain loss of spontaneity of speech" and a "difficulty in evoking appropriate words or phrases." Subsequent studies by a variety of authors—Milner and, later, Ramier and Hécaen among others—have been able to quantify this deficit. These researchers gave patients tests similar to Thurstone's word fluency test; patients were asked to write or to say, first, as many words starting with a given letter as they could think of in five minutes, then as many four-letter words starting with a given letter. Patients with frontal-lobe lesions have a low output of words in this test, producing an average of 35 words in total in Milner's sample. Although the principal locus of this defect appears to be in the left orbital frontal region, lesions in the right orbital frontal region may also produce a large reduction in verbal fluency. Again we see less asymmetry in the frontal lobes than one might expect. The following case is an example of low spontaneous verbal fluency from a lesion of the right frontal lobe.

Mrs. P., a 63-year-old woman with a BA degree, was suffering from a large astrocytoma of the right frontal lobe. Her word fluency is reproduced in Figure 14-4, where four features of frontal-lobe damage in this test performance are illustrated. First, her total output of words is remarkably low; only eight words beginning with "S" and six words beginning with "C." (Control subjects of similar age and education produce a total of about 60 words in the same time period.) Second, we see rule breaking, which is a common characteristic of frontal-lobe patients on this test. We told her several times that the words starting with "C" could have only four letters. She replied: "Yes, yes, I know, I keep using more each time." Even though she understood the instructions she could not organize her behavior to follow them successfully. Third, her writing is not fluid but rather jerky, much like that seen in a child learning to write, implying that her tumor had invaded area 4 or 6. Finally, Mrs. P. insisted on talking throughout the test—complaining that she simply could not think of any more words—and kept looking around the room for objects starting with the required letter.

Although one locus of low verbal fluency anterior to Broca's area appears to be in the orbital cortex, patients with lesions in the central face area actually have even lower verbal fluency scores, according to Milner. Although a peculiar result, it appears solid and reliable, and suggests that the face area has some special role in certain aspects of verbal abilities.

A recent study by Jones-Gotman and Milner raises the question whether this verbal fluency deficit might have a nonverbal analogue. The researchers devised an ingenious experiment in which they asked patients to draw as many different drawings, which were not supposed to be representational, as they could in five minutes. The patients were then asked to draw as many different drawings as they could, but this time using only four lines (a circle was counted as a single line). The results showed a beautiful analogue to the verbal fluency results. As can be seen in Figure 14-5, lesions in the right frontal lobe produced a very large drop in the production of *different* drawings. Normal controls drew about 35 drawings, left frontal-lobe patients about 24 drawings, and right frontal-lobe patients about 15 drawings. This deficit appears to be related to an impoverished output, high perseveration, and, in some cases, the drawing of nameable things. As with verbal fluency, lesions in the central face area actually appeared to produce a larger deficit than the more anterior lesions. There is not yet a clear indication whether orbital frontal lesions affect design fluency more than dorsolateral lesions do. More patients must be studied.

The question arises whether patients with frontal-lobe lesions might actually show a reduced spontaneity of behavior in general. Since frontal patients have been described as "pseudodepressed" (see below), this might indeed be the case; but we are aware of only two studies that have actually recorded the spontaneous behavior of patients. Kolb and his colleagues found that: (1) Patients with frontal-lobe removals displayed fewer spontaneous facial movements and expressions than did normal controls or patients with more poste-

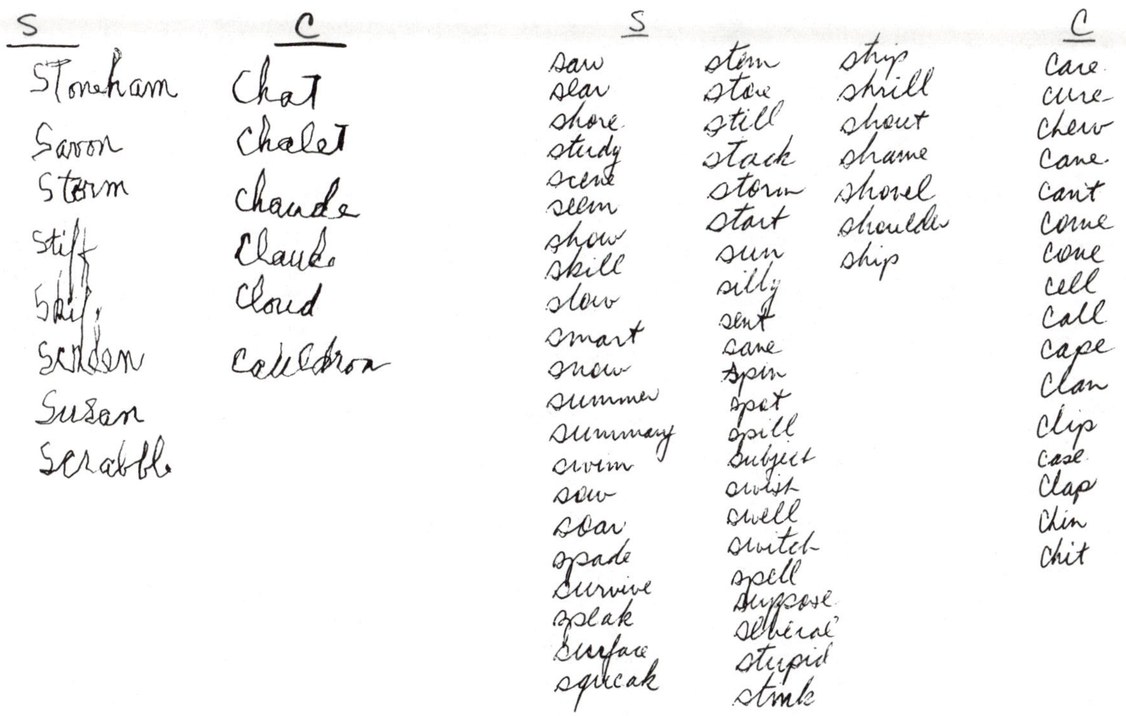

S	C	S		S	C
Stoneham	Chat	saw	stem	ship	care
Saxon	Chalet	sear	stow	shrill	cure
Storm	Chaude	shore	still	shout	chew
Stiff	Claude	sturdy	stack	shame	cane
Stiff	Cloud	scene	storm	shovel	can't
Seldon	Calledron	seem	start	shoulder	come
Susan		show	sun	ship	cone
Scrabble		skill	silly		cell
		slow	sent		call
		smart	sane		cape
		snow	spin		clan
		summer	spot		clip
		summary	spill		case
		swim	subject		clap
		sow	artist		chin
		soar	swell		chit
		spade	switch		
		survive	spell		
		speak	suppose		
		surface	several		
		squeak	stupid		
			strike		

FIGURE 14-4. Word fluency. Left: Mrs. P.'s lists. Right: A normal control subject's lists. Both subjects were given five minutes to write as many English-language words as possible starting with the letter "S," and four minutes to write as many four-letter words as possible starting with the letter "C." Note Mrs. P.'s low output and her rule breaking in the four-letter "C" words. (Mrs. P. was multilingual, although English was her first language.)

rior lesions. (2) There were dramatic differences in the number of words spoken by frontal-lobe patients during a neuropsychological interview: patients with left frontal removals rarely spoke, whereas patients with right frontal lesions were excessively talkative. Hence it would seem worthwhile to study in detail the spontaneous behavior of patients with frontal lesions, to determine whether altered spontaneity is a general feature of their behavior. The following quotation from Hécaen and Albert suggests that it might be.

Lack of initiative or spontaneity is a characteristic feature of frontal lobe pathology. These are linked to a general diminution of motor activity. The patient no longer voluntarily carries out the necessary daily activities of life, such as getting out of bed in the morning, washing or dressing himself, feeding himself, or even urinating or defecating in the toilet. These latter activities may be carried out at any time or place, without regard for the social consequences. The actual ability to carry out the various activities of daily living is not impaired—the patient is neither paralyzed, apraxic, nor confused. When he is vigorously urged to do something, he can do it. What is impaired is the ability to initiate spontaneously a desired or an automatic motor task.

It is this rupture between the patient and the external world, this diminution of activity in manipulating real objects, this reduction of interpersonal exchange that appear to be a loss of

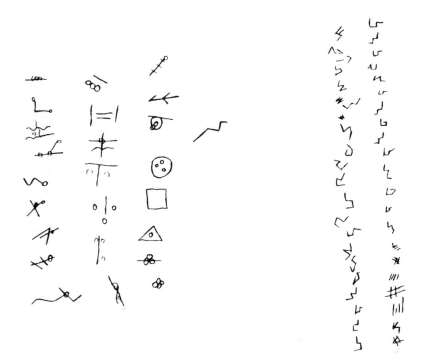

FIGURE 14-5. Design fluency. Left: A normal control subject's drawings. Middle: A frontal-lobe patient's drawings, showing perseveration. Right: A frontal-lobe patient's drawings, showing lack of spontaneity. (Adapted from Jones-Gotman and Milner, 1977.)

interest on the part of the patient. Whether there is a true loss of interest or an apparent loss of interest due to an impairment of spontaneous initiation of activity, the effect on the examiner remains the same. (Hécaen and Albert, 1975, p. 139)

Movement Programming

In a classic paper in 1950, Karl Lashley asked how movements are put together in a particular order. How is it, he asked, that a violinist can play an arpeggio so quickly and flawlessly? Clearly, each note is not "thought of" separately. Furthermore, how is it that during a game a tennis player can make very rapid movements, seemingly much too fast to have

considered each movement itself? Lashley presumed that this function—serially ordering complex chains of behavior in relation to varying stimuli—must somehow be a function of the neocortex. Although Lashley believed this to be a function of the entire neocortex, it appears more likely to involve only the frontal lobes.

To date, the major support for this role of the frontal lobe comes from animal work (see below) and inference from clinical observations. One experiment, however, does provide a direct test. Kolb and Milner asked patients with localized unilateral frontal removals to copy a series of arm or facial movements, as illustrated in Figure 14-6. The results, summarized in Figure 14-7, showed that patients

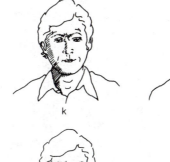

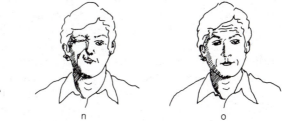

FIGURE 14-6. Patients with frontal lesions were impaired at copying the series of facial movements abc, def, ghi, jkl, and mno. Individual movements were performed correctly, but series were not combined properly. (From Kolb, 1977.)

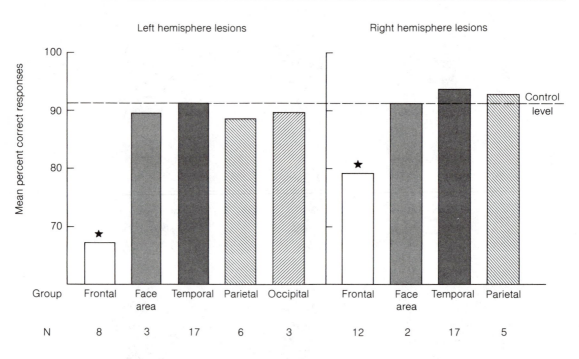

FIGURE 14-7. Summary of Kolb and Milner's study of facial series copying. Note that both left and right frontal lesions impaired the copying of the series of movements illustrated in Figure 14-6, whereas lesions of the face area or parietal cortex did not.

with left *or* right frontal removals were impaired at both the arm and facial-movement tasks. On analysis of the facial-movement task, the frontal-lobe groups made more errors of sequence than normal controls or other groups of patients. In other words, one deficit observed in the frontal-lobe groups was a difficulty in ordering the various components of the sequence into a chain of movements. The components were recalled correctly, but in the wrong order. To be sure, the frontal-lobe patients made other sorts of errors as well, including intrusions (making movements not belonging in the sequence) and omissions (leaving movements out). This study had one unexpected result: both right and left frontal lesions produced deficits on the tasks, although the left frontal group was more severely impaired. Perhaps this result is not so surprising,

because the effects of frontal-lobe lesions are consistently observed to be less asymmetrical than those of more posterior lesions.

Corollary Discharge

If one pushes on the eyeball the world appears to move. If one moves one's eyes the world remains stable. Why? Teuber proposed that for a movement to take place there must be a signal to produce the movement and also a signal that the movement is going to occur. Thus, when one moves the eyes there is a signal that it will happen and the world stays still. If the eyes are moved mechanically, there is no such signal and the world moves. This signal has been termed corollary discharge, or **reafference**.

In 1954 Teuber and Mishkin began to study

this process, using a task first designed by Aubert in 1861. If you tilt your head sideways in a lighted room, vertical lines between the ceiling and floor do not tilt; they remain upright. If you tilt your head or body in the dark while looking at a luminous line, the mechanism still works, but not as well. If the task is made more difficult so that you must try to orient a tilted luminous line to the vertical in the dark while your head is also tilted sideways, there will be errors of a few degrees. The task is very difficult. Teuber and Mishkin discovered that if the patients with frontal lesions were strapped into a chair that was then tilted, and the task was to set a luminous line to vertical, they were much more severely impaired than patients with more posterior lesions or than controls. This impairment disappeared if the chair was upright, indicating that the problem was not one of orienting the line but of doing so in an abnormal attitude.

On the basis of this study as well as others on cats, rats, and monkeys (see below), Teuber argued that the deficit in the tilted-chair experiment is one of corollary discharge. Stated simply, voluntary movements involve two sets of signals rather than one. There are simultaneously the movement command, through the motor system, to effect the movements, and a signal (corollary discharge) from the frontal lobe to the parietal and temporal association cortex that presets the sensory system to anticipate the motor act. Thus, a person's sensory system is able to interpret changes in the external world in light of information about the person's movement. For example, when one is running the external world remains stable, even though the sense organs are in motion, because there is corollary discharge from the frontal lobe to the parietal-temporal cortex signaling that the movements are occurring. A frontal lesion can therefore not only disturb the production of a movement but also interfere with the message to the rest of the brain that a movement is taking place. By this indi-rect means, perception of the world by the posterior association cortex is altered.

Spatial Orientation

Semmes and her colleagues were the first to demonstrate clearly that patients with frontal-lobe lesions have a deficit in spatial orientation. To do this, they devised parallel tests of personal orientation (egocentric spatial relations) and of extrapersonal orientation (allocentric spatial relations), both diagrammed in Figure 14-8. In the egocentric test the subject's task was to point to the location on his or her body represented by the various numbers shown on the figure. In the allocentric task the subjects carried a series of maps, one map at a time, in a room where nine dots were painted on the floor in an evenly spaced pattern. The subject's task was to pace out on the floor the route laid out on a given map.

Because the parietal cortex is known to be involved in spatial relations, Semmes expected the maximal deficits on both of these tasks to result from parietal lesions. But this was not the case. The results showed a double dissociation of egocentric and allocentric spatial relations; the frontal-lobe patients were impaired at the egocentric test and not the allocentric, whereas the parietal-lobe patients were badly impaired at the latter test, and only slightly at the former. Furthermore, performances on both tests were more severely affected by lesions of the left than of the right hemisphere. Semmes et al. interpreted the impairment following frontal-cortical damage as a difficulty with behaviors that depend on the accurate assessment of one's body orientation in space. In contrast, the impairment following parietal-cortex damage was interpreted as a difficulty with behaviors involving the spatial relationships among external stimuli.

Why personal orientation should be disrupted by frontal-lobe lesions, and, in view of the right hemisphere's importance in spatial

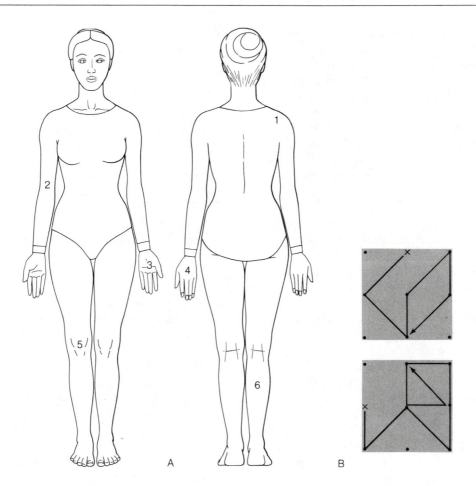

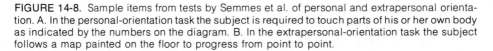

FIGURE 14-8. Sample items from tests by Semmes et al. of personal and extrapersonal orientation. A. In the personal-orientation task the subject is required to touch parts of his or her own body as indicated by the numbers on the diagram. B. In the extrapersonal-orientation task the subject follows a map painted on the floor to progress from point to point.

processing, why these deficits should result primarily from lesions in the left hemisphere cannot be easily explained. Teuber has proposed that maximum flexibility of behavior requires that the nervous system keep an ongoing record of where the individual is at any given instant—a kind of corollary discharge of all ongoing behavior. Thus, to Teuber, deficits in personal orientation result from an absence of corollary discharge. Further, it could be argued that since the left hemisphere is specialized for control of complex movement it may be the most efficient location for this behavioral recording system. Both of these conjectures remain to be proven.

Social Behavior and Personality

One of the most obvious and striking effects of frontal-lobe damage in humans is a marked change in social behavior and personality. Perhaps the most publicized example of personality change following frontal-lobe lesion is that of Phineas Gage, first reported by Harlow in 1868. Gage was a dynamite worker and survived an explosion that blasted an iron tamping bar (3 feet, 7 in. long, 1.25 in. wide at its widest point) through the front of his head (see Figure 14-9). After the accident his behavior changed completely. He had been of average intelligence and was "energetic and persistent in executing all his plans of operation." His posttrauma personality is described as follows:

> The equilibrium or balance, so to speak, between his intellectual faculties and animal propensities seems to have been destroyed. He is fitful, irreverent, indulging at times in the grossest profanity, manifesting but little deference for his fellows, impatient of restraint or advice when it conflicts with his desires, at times pertinaciously obstinate, yet capricious and vacillating, devising many plans of operation, which are no sooner arranged than they are abandoned in turn for others appearing more feasible. A child in his intellectual capacity and manifestations, he has the animal passions of a strong man. (Blumer and Benson, 1975, p. 153)

Gage's injury affected primarily the left frontal lobe from the medial orbital region upward to the precentral region.

Although Gage's skull has been examined carefully, the first patient with extensive frontal damage to actually undergo close scrutiny at autopsy was a furrier who fell 100 feet from a window. He suffered a compound fracture of the frontal bones and severe injury to the right frontal lobe, but, remarkably, was never unconscious and was confused only briefly. Before the fall the man had been good-natured and sociable, but afterwards became nasty and cantankerous. Autopsy, about a year after the accident, revealed deep scarring of the orbital part of both frontal lobes, although more extensively on the right.

From soon after the turn of the century until about 1950 there were many excellent psychi-

atric studies of the effect of brain lesions on personality. A consistent finding of this work (especially Kliest's) was that damage to the orbital regions of the frontal lobe was associated with more dramatic changes in personality than dorsolateral lesions, although these latter also have significant effects. Although there are abundant clinical descriptions of the effects of frontal-lobe lesions on personality, there are few systematic studies. At least two types of personality change have been clinically observed in such patients: Blumer and Benson have termed them as showing **pseudodepression** and as being **pseudopsychopathic.** Patients classified as showing pseudodepression exhibit such symptoms as outward apathy and indifference, loss of initiative, reduced sexual interest, little overt emotion, and little or no verbal output. Patients classified as pseudopsychopathic exhibit immature behavior, lack of tact and restraint, coarse language, promiscuous sexual behavior, increased motor activity, and a general lack of social graces. Incontinence is not uncommon with large traumatic lesions or tumors in the frontal lobes. The following two case histories illustrate the pseudodepressed and pseudopsychopathic frontal personalities respectively.

> At the age of 46, a successful salesman sustained a compound depressed fracture of the left frontal bone in a traffic accident. Treatment included debridement and amputation of the left frontal pole. Recovery was slow, and 9 months after the injury he was referred for long-term custodial management. By this time, he had recovered motor function with only a minimal limp and slight hyperreflexia on the right side, had normal sensation, no evidence of aphasia, and normal memory and cognitive ability (IQ 118). Nonetheless, he remained under hospital care because of marked changes in personal habits.
>
> Prior to the accident, the patient had been garrulous, enjoyed people, had many friends and talked freely. He was active in community affairs, including Little League, church activities, men's clubs, and so forth. It was stated by one

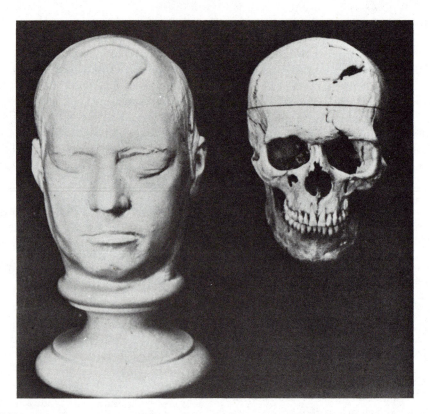

FIGURE 14-9. Bust and skull of Phineas Gage, showing the hole in the frontal bone made by the iron rod blown through his head. (From C. Blakemore, *Mechanics of the Mind.* Cambridge: Cambridge University Press, p. 3. Copyright © 1977. Reprinted by permission of Cambridge University Press.)

acquaintance that the patient had a true charisma, "whenever he entered a room there was a change in the atmosphere, everything became more animated, happy and friendly."

Following the head injury, he was quiet and remote. He would speak when spoken to and made sensible replies but would then lapse into silence. He made no friends on the ward, spent most of his time sitting alone smoking. He was frequently incontinent of urine, occasionally of stool. He remained unconcerned about either and was frequently found soaking wet, calmly sitting and smoking. If asked, he would matter-of-factly state that he had not been able to get to the bathroom in time but that this didn't bother him. Because of objectionable eating habits he always ate alone on the ward. His sleep pattern was reversed; he stayed up much of the night and slept during the day. He did not resent being awakened or questioned. He could discuss many subjects intelligently, but was never known to initiate either a conversation or a request. He could give detailed accounts of his life prior to the accident, of the hospitals he had been in, the doctors and treatment he had had but there was an unreality to his conversation. When asked, he would deny illness, state emphatically that he could return to work at any time, and that the only reason he was not work-ing was that he was being held in the hospital by the doctors. At no time did he request a dis-charge or weekend pass. He was totally uncon-cerned about his wife and children. Formerly a warm and loving father, he did not seem to care about his family. Eventually, the family ceased visiting because of his indifference and uncon-cern. (Blumer and Benson, 1975, pp. 156–157)

A 32-year-old white male was admitted for be-havioral evaluation. History revealed that he had sustained a gunshot wound in Vietnam 5 years previously. A high-velocity missile had entered the left temple and emerged through the right orbit. Infection necessitated surgical removal of most of the orbital surface of the right frontal lobe. On recovery, he was neither paralyzed nor aphasic but suffered a remarkable change in per-sonality.

Prior to injury he had been quiet, intelligent, proper, and compulsive. He was a West Point graduate and spent the ensuing years as a mili-tary officer attaining the rank of captain. Both as a cadet and later as an officer, he was known to be quiet, strict, and rigid. He was considered a good commander, trusted by his men, but never shared camaraderie with his troops or with his peers.

Subsequent to injury, he was outspoken, facetious, brash, and disrespectful. There was no evidence of self-pity, although he frequently made rather morbid jokes about his condition (for example, "dummy's head"). On admission to the hospital, he had just failed at an extremely simple job.

He was not aphasic but misused words in a manner that suggested inability to maintain specific meanings. For instance, when asked whether the injury had affected his thinking his response was, "Yeah—it's affected the way I think—it's affected my senses—the only things I can taste are sugar and salt—I can't detect a pun-gent odor—ha ha—to tell you the truth it's a blessing this way." When the examiner persisted, "How had it affected the way you think?" his response was "Yes—I'm not as spry on my feet as I was before." He was never incontinent, but did show a messiness in attire. His remarks to the nurses and other female personnel were open and frank but were never blatantly sexual. His premorbid IQ was reported at about 130. Present examination showed a full-scale IQ of 113. (Blumer and Benson, 1975, pp. 155–156)

Blumer and Benson are probably correct in their assertion that all elements of these syn-dromes are observable only after bilateral frontal-lobe damage. Nevertheless, some ele-ments of these two rather different syndromes can be observed in most, if not all, patients with frontal-lobe lesions. Pseudodepression appears most likely to follow lesions of the left frontal lobe; pseudopsychopathic behavior, le-sions of the right frontal lobe.

Sexual Behavior

Changes in sexual behavior are among the most difficult symptoms of frontal-lobe dam-age to properly document, largely because of social taboos against investigating people's sex lives. To date, there are no such empirical studies, but there is anecdotal evidence that frontal lesions do alter libido and related be-havior. Orbital frontal lesions may introduce abnormal sexual behavior (such as public mas-turbation) by reducing inhibitions, although the actual frequency of sexual behavior per se is not affected. On the other hand, dorsolateral lesions appear to reduce interest in sexual be-havior, although the patients are still capable of the necessary motor acts and can perform sexually if led through the activity "step by step."

Symptoms Associated with Damage to the Face Area

Over the years Taylor and his colleagues have accumulated some remarkable data from a small group of patients with localized surgical removals of the precentral and postcentral gyri containing, respectively, the motor and sensory representations of the face (see Figure 14-1 B). Unlike removal of the hand area (see Chapter 10), removal of the face area is seldom associated with long-lasting somatosensory deficits on the face, even if both the sensory and motor representations are removed completely. This finding is in keeping with the evidence that the face area is represented bilaterally in the cortex. There has been no systematic study of the facial motor abilities of patients with removal of both precentral and postcentral gyri, but Kolb and Milner found them able to perform normally the facial sequences illustrated in Figure 14-7. Furthermore, although they had difficulty making individual facial movements in the initial postoperative period, especially on the side of the face contralateral to the lesion, they appeared to have regained normal voluntary facial control a month after surgery, although closer examination might have revealed subtle defects. In addition, their faces were expressive, and they displayed normal spontaneous facial expressions at frequencies well within normal limits.

In the immediate postoperative period the patients with left-hemisphere face-area lesions are aphasic, being impaired at both language comprehension and production, as well as alexic. However, these symptoms subside rapidly, probably having resulted from swelling and trauma associated with the surgical procedure. Within about six months to a year of surgery only a slight residual expressive dysphasia remains. Yet these same patients are severely impaired at certain other language tests.

> They achieve an even lower score on the word fluency test than do our frontal lobe patients. They are also unable to make effective use of phonetic elements of language. When asked ...

to discriminate phonemes embedded in nonsense words, face area patients correctly identify less than one half of the 108 sounds they have heard, whereas other patient groups score significantly higher on the task. (Taylor, 1979, p. 171)

In addition, these same patients are very poor spellers, occasionally writing words that are unrecognizable. Their low verbal fluency is complemented by a very low design fluency; patients with right face-area lesions are worse at design fluency than frontal-lobe patients, even with very large anterior lesions. This lack of spontaneity in verbal and design fluency is remarkable, considering the normal spontaneity of facial expressions noted above.

In summary, unilateral removal of the face area results in no significant chronic loss in sensory or motor control of the face (presumably because of its bilateral representation in the cortex), but results surprisingly in chronic deficits in phonetic discrimination, spelling, verbal fluency, and design fluency. Taylor has preliminary data suggesting that these deficits may result primarily from damage to the precentral motor representation of the face, rather than to the postcentral sensory representation. The origin of these deficits is, however, unexplained to date.

Clinical Neuropsychological Assessment of Frontal-Lobe Damage

Considering the number and variety of symptoms associated with frontal-lobe damage, surprisingly few standardized neuropsychological tests are useful for assessing frontal-lobe function. The available tests (see Table 14-3) are very good, however. As with parietal- and temporal-lobe tests discussed in the previous two chapters, it would be highly unusual for a person to perform normally on all of these tests if there were damage to either frontal lobe.

TABLE 14-3

Standardized clinical neuropsychological tests for frontal-lobe damage

Function	Test	Basic reference
1. Response inhibition	Wisconsin card-sorting test	Milner, 1964
2. Personal spatial orientation	Semmes body placing	Semmes et al., 1963
3. Verbal fluency	Thurstone word fluency	Milner, 1964 Ramier and Hécaen, 1970
4. Motor	Hand dynamometer Finger tapping Sequencing	Taylor, 1979 Reitan and Davison, 1974 Kolb and Milner, 1980
5. Aphasia: language comprehension spelling phonetic discrimination	Token test	de Renzi and Faglioni, 1978 Taylor, 1979 Taylor, 1979

The Wisconsin card-sorting test (Figure 14-2), described earlier, is the best available test of dorsolateral frontal-cortex function. Briefly, the subject is told to sort the cards into piles in front of one or another of the stimulus cards bearing designs that differ in color, form, and number of elements. The correct solution shifts unbeknownst to the subject once he or she has figured out each solution.

The Semmes body-placing test (Figure 14-8), also described earlier, is a simple, easily administered test of personal spatial orientation. Left frontal-lobe patients do more poorly on this test than other patient groups, although left parietal-lobe patients often are impaired as well. For this reason the Semmes test should be given in conjunction with a left-right differentiation test (see Chapter 12), which often helps to differentiate between left-frontal and left-parietal patients. Although both groups are likely to be impaired at left-right discrimination and perform below control levels, the parietal-lobe patients are likely to be reduced to chance performance, whereas the frontal-lobe patients are more likely to perform above chance levels.

The Thurstone word fluency test, recall, re-quires patients to say or write as many words as possible beginning with a given letter in five minutes, and then as many four-letter words beginning with a given letter in four minutes. Although patients with lesions anywhere in the prefrontal cortex are apt to do poorly on this test, patients with face-area lesions perform the worst, patients with orbital lesions performing only slightly better. Performance is of course poorest when the lesion is in the left hemisphere.

Tests of motor function include tests of strength (hand dynamometer), finger tapping speed, and movement sequencing. Strength and finger-tapping speed are significantly reduced contralateral to a lesion that is in the vicinity of the precentral or postcentral gyri. Motor sequencing can be assessed by using the facial sequence test (Figure 14-6), although this test requires considerable practice in both administering and scoring. Simpler tests of movement programming such as the Kimura box test (Chapter 12) are not suitable because frontal-lobe patients are unlikely to perform very poorly unless the lesion extends into the basal ganglia.

As in previous chapters we recommend the

token test as a quick aphasia screening test, to be followed, if necessary, by more extensive aphasia testing (Chapter 16). Although it is widely believed that damage to Broca's area results in deficits in language production only and not in comprehension, we shall see in Chapter 16 that this is not strictly true. Left frontal lesions in the vicinity of Broca's area produce deficits in comprehension as well as in production. Spelling is seriously impaired by face-area lesions and can be assessed by any standardized spelling test. Phonetic differentiation, a test described by Stitt and Huntington and used for neurological patients by Taylor, is another means of assessing face-area function. A series of nonsense words, such as "agma," is presented and the subject's task is to identify the first consonant sound. This test proves difficult even for controls, but is most poorly performed by patients with face-area damage, especially on the left. However, frontal-lobe lesions outside the face area also may impair performance significantly on this test.

In the absence of language deficits it may prove difficult to localize frontal-lobe damage in either the left or the right hemisphere with neuropsychological tests, presumably because the two frontal lobes significantly overlap in function. Clinical evaluation of personality as pseudodepressed or pseudopsychopathic (as discussed earlier) may prove useful in localizing the dysfunction to the left or right hemisphere respectively, but caution is advised; unfortunately no standardized quantitative measures of these symptoms are available.

ARE THE FRONTAL LOBES SPECIAL IN HUMANS?

From the assumption, prevalent in the 1930s and '40s, that the frontal lobes house the highest human intellectual capacities, it was logical to conclude that they must be unique to humans. The fact that the frontal lobes markedly increase in size phylogenetically supported this view. The frontal lobes of humans are not, however, special. The frontal lobes have changed remarkably little functionally through phylogeny; thus, the nonhuman frontal lobes provide an excellent model for the study of human frontal lobes.

An exhaustive survey of the effects of frontal-lobe damage in nonhumans being beyond the scope of this book, we discuss only the major findings. We will consider mainly nonhuman primates and rats, largely because the most is known about these species, and because they represent extremes in the anatomical size of the frontal cortex and in diversity of behavior. Surely, if the effects of lesions to the frontal lobes of rats, monkeys, and humans are similar, the functions of the frontal lobes are likely to be similar across mammalian phylogeny.

Anatomy of the Frontal Lobes of Nonhumans

In 1948 Rose and Woolsey pointed out that all mammals appeared to have a frontal lobe composed of regions receiving projections from the dorsomedial nucleus of the thalamus (which they termed prefrontal cortex) as well as from the motor thalamus that projects to areas 4 and 6.

Figure 14-10 shows how the frontal lobes have generally increased as a proportion of the neocortex during mammalian evolution. In all mammals there is a region of prefrontal cortex, and in all but marsupials and monotremes this region appears to be anatomically dissociable into three regions, as is the human frontal lobe. In the rat, dog, and monkey there is clear evidence that these three regions are functionally dissociable as well.

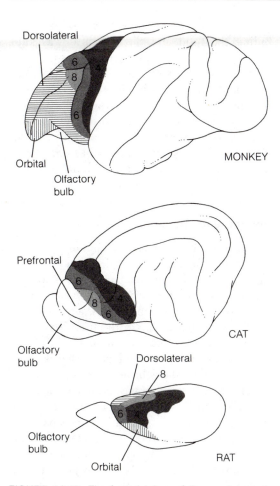

FIGURE 14-10. The frontal lobes of the monkey, cat, and rat. Notice the marked expansion of the frontal neocortex in primates. It is not currently possible to dissociate the prefrontal cortex of the cat into subzones that are analogous to those in the human, monkey, and rat. The brains are not drawn to the same scale. No evolutionary progression from one species to another is implied.

Effects of Frontal-Lobe Lesions in Nonhumans

The effects of frontal-lobe lesions in humans and other animals show a major difference: unilateral lesions in nonhumans seldom produce significant behavioral effects. What this differ-

ence implies is unknown, although it may be related to the apparent absence of laterality in nonhumans. Other than this one difference—and, of course, the lack of aphasia—there appear to be few qualitative differences. We now discuss the effects of frontal-lobe lesions, and the probable foci, as we did for humans.

Impaired Response Inhibition and Inflexible Behavior

Impaired response inhibition and inflexible behavior are behavioral deficits analogous to perseveration in card-sorting tasks by humans with frontal-lobe damage. Such behavior is a commonly observed effect of frontal-lobe lesions in rats, cats, dogs, and monkeys; it can be demonstrated on a wide variety of standard laboratory learning tasks. For example, if an animal is trained to find food under a foodwell located to its left, and the food reward is then shifted to a location under another foodwell to the animal's right, the animal with the frontal-lobe lesion persists in looking under the original foodwell. This perseverative responding may persist even with extended training, as we have observed rats to perseverate for up to a hundred incorrect choices in a row before adapting to the correct response. Normal control animals typically make fewer than 5 or 10 incorrect choices before altering response strategy. The primary focus for this perseverative response is the orbital frontal cortex, although this behavior also follows dorsolateral lesions.

Deficits in Voluntary Gaze

Lesions of the frontal eye fields (area 8) of monkeys impair performance on search tasks analogous to Poppelreuter's search task for humans. Eye movements are not a prominent feature of the behavior of cats, dogs, and rats, and we are unaware of any studies examining eye movements following area 8 lesions in these species. Nevertheless, there is evidence that all of these species have frontal eye fields, because stimulation there produces eye movements. We would be surprised if lesions to this region did not have some effect on eye movements.

Memory

In the 1930s Jacobsen gave impetus to a revolution in research on the frontal lobes when he observed that chimpanzees were impaired at a task called delayed response. In the delayed-response task, the animal is shown where food is located (e.g., under one of two cups), but is prevented from responding for some period of time, usually a few seconds. After this delay, the animal is allowed to respond, and its accuracy in choosing the correct hiding place for the food is measured. Monkeys, dogs, cats, and rats with frontal lesions are severely impaired at this task. This task was originally assumed to be a measure of short-term memory, but it later became clear that the spatial component of the task was essential to the deficit, since the animals are quite capable of forming object-discrimination learning sets that have no spatial component. Nevertheless, there is reason to believe that, like humans with frontal-lobe lesions, these species suffer a deficit in recent memory. From experiments by Harlow and later by Pribram and Tubbs it was observed that monkeys could not keep trials separate in memory. That is, what happened on the last trial as opposed to the previous one? Pribram and Tubbs found that if repeated trials on problems such as delayed response were separated by longer and longer periods of time, the performance of the monkeys improved. This could not be due simply to the spatial aspects of the task, because they remained constant; nor could it be a simple memory problem, because the period between hiding the food and the response was kept constant. The important variable was the time between trials. As the interval between trials lengthened, the trials became more distinct to the animals, and therefore easier to tell apart, suggesting a defect in recency memory analogous to that observed in humans with frontal-lobe lesions. This phenomenon has not, to our knowledge, been studied in rodents or carnivores.

Spontaneous Behavior

Behavioral spontaneity in humans was assessed by measuring verbal fluency, design fluency, and spontaneous facial expressions. It is difficult to find behavioral analogies of these behaviors in nonhuman species, although two studies are suggestive. In the first, Myers examined the frequency of spontaneous facial expressions and vocalizations in rhesus monkeys. These monkeys have a rich repertoire of vocalizations (hoots, howls, etc.) and facial expressions that are as important in social communication as facial expression and certain basic vocalizations (characteristic utterances such as "hmm," crying, laughing, etc.) are among humans. Myers reported that frontal-lobe removal resulted in drastically reduced frequencies of facial expressions and vocalizations. Indeed, it was this observation that led Kolb and Milner to study facial expressions in humans with frontal-lobe lesions. Unfortunately, because Myers failed to quantify this observation, it is difficult to assess the magnitude of the change in the number of expressions. In the second study, Kolb found that guinea pigs, who are normally very vocal, showed dramatic reductions (over 80 percent) in vocalizations following orbital frontal lesions. Although these observations do not conclusively establish reduced spontaneity of behavior as a frontal symptom in nonhumans, they suggest that further study may be fruitful. On the other hand, a large body of literature appears to contradict this conclusion. It has long been known that rats and monkeys with orbital frontal lesions increase locomotor activity. However, this paradoxical result may not be as inconsistent with the literature on humans as it appears. Although to date general locomotor activity levels of human frontal-lobe patients have not been systematically studied, numerous case studies (for example, see Ackerly) report increased locomotor activity in these people, especially if the lesion is on the right. It thus appears that frontal lesions may have differential effects on spontaneous levels of locomotor and other behaviors in both humans and nonhumans. This problem deserves additional study.

Habituation

Habituation is a gradual quantitative response decrement that results from repeated exposure to a stimulus. For example, when one first enters a bakery the odors are distinctive, but if one works in the same bakery there is rapid habituation to the odors and they are no longer noticed. A number of studies using monkeys, rats, and cats have suggested that frontal cortex, possibly the dorsolateral region, is involved in normal habituation. Animals with frontal cortex lesions fail to habituate normally, if at all, to novel stimuli or environments, whereas stimulation of the frontal cortex accelerates habituation to similar stimuli. Thus, in the absence of frontal cortex the animals' behavior appears stereotyped and repetitive, behavior that may contribute to the increased locomotor activity of animals with frontal-lobe lesions. We are unaware of any studies of habituation in humans with frontal-lobe lesions, but the reliability of this observa-

tion in a variety of nonhuman species suggests the worthiness of such studies.

Spatial Orientation

Monkeys, cats, dogs, rats, and hamsters with frontal lesions have all displayed deficits in learning problems and behaviors that require the use of spatial cues. In a classic study, Pohl was able to double dissociate the parietal and frontal lobes on two spatial tasks in a manner analogous to that done by Semmes and Teuber in humans. Pohl selected the two tasks of spatial reversal and landmark reversal. In the former task, after monkeys learned that food was placed under a cup to one side of them, the reward was shifted, without any cues or warning, to the cup on the opposite side. Once the animals had solved this reversal, the food was reversed again. Basically, the task requires the animal to learn egocentric orientation: the relationship of objects in space to the animal itself. Warren has suggested that this task is probably the best test of frontal-lobe damage in animals; the data support this view.

In the landmark-reversal task, a test of allocentric orientation, the animal must learn the spatial relationship between two objects: in this case, the food cup and some object located elsewhere. For example, the food will be found under the cup closest to a pop bottle located a few inches behind the cups. Once this relationship has been learned, the task is reversed—i.e., the reward is now to be found under the cup farthest from the pop bottle. The results of the landmark-reversal task have shown that frontal-lobe lesions (especially dorsolateral lesions) impair acquisition of the spatial-reversal task, whereas parietal-lobe lesions impair acquisition of the landmark-reversal task. This nice example of double dissociation is analogous to that observed in humans who have frontal- and parietal-lobe lesions.

Movement Programming

Serially ordering complex chains of behavior in relation to varying stimuli is as necessary a component of higher-level motor control in nonhumans as it is in humans. Many authors, most notably Pribram, have emphasized the role of the frontal cortex of the monkey in the highest levels of motor control (or, in Pribram's term, "executive" control) of behavior.

However, few studies have directly addressed the issue of the frontal lobe's role in apraxia in nonhumans. In a recent study, Deuel trained monkeys to open a complex latch box in which correct performance required a series of movements, including sliding a bolt along a track, lifting the bolt out, turning a crank 180°, and depressing a knob on the front of a box. To obtain a food reward, the monkeys had to perform these movements correctly and, more important, in the correct sequence. Deuel found that small dorsolateral lesions profoundly impaired performance, whereas parietal-lobe lesions did not. Gentile et al. found an analogous disruption of a latch-opening task in rats with frontal- but not parietal-cortex lesions. These motor tasks, similar to the Kimura box test used for studying human subjects, suggest that the frontal lobe of nonhuman primates is important in praxic functions. We have studied this function in a different way, by observing the chaining together of movement components of species-typical behavior.

Both rats and hamsters with frontal-lobe removals are impaired at such chaining to perform complex behaviors, such as nest building, grooming, food hoarding. Thus, when hamsters with frontal-lobe lesions attempt to build a nest the component behaviors of picking up nest material in the mouth, carrying it to the desired location, putting it down, and manipulating it into proper position are performed correctly, but not in the proper order—a deficit strikingly reminiscent of apraxia in primates.

To summarize, there is strong evidence that the frontal lobe of nonhumans also plays a significant role in serially ordering complex chains of behavior.

Corollary Discharge

There are two sources of evidence that the nonhuman primate frontal lobe plays a role in corollary discharge: studies of frontal eye-field cells and experimental use of prisms on the eyes. Bizzi and others have found that cells in the frontal eye fields fire simultaneously with movements of the eyes. These cells cannot be causing the eyes to move, for to do so they would have to fire prior to the eye movements (just as to accelerate an automobile you must first depress the gas pedal). Rather, these cells must be monitoring the ongoing movement—a process suspiciously similar to what would be expected from a region involved in corollary discharge.

Further evidence comes from a beautiful experiment by Bossom. In the early 1960s Held, Hein, and others performed experiments by fitting prisms to the eyes of animals and humans. As a result, whatever the subject saw was systematically displaced from its true location, all lines appearing subjectively curved and tilted, in keeping with the distortions imposed by the optics of the prism. After the prisms were worn for a few hours the distortions and displacements diminished, and acts such as reaching for objects were performed normally. Upon abrupt removal of the prisms the distortions were reinstated, requiring readaptation before perception was again normal. An important feature of these experiments was that passively sitting for a few hours did not produce the perceptual change; to induce the adaptation, the individual had to move about in the environment. This requirement implied that adaptation to the prism occurred in the motor system rather than in the sensory systems. With these experiments in mind, Bossom selectively removed frontal, temporal, parietal, or occipital cortex in monkeys to see which lesion, if any, would disrupt prism adaptation. As one would predict from the work of Held, only frontal lesions impaired adaptation to the distorting prisms; parietal, temporal, and occipital lesions did not. Teuber interprets this experiment as showing that corollary discharge is necessary for the adaptation to occur. In other words, the effects of movement must be monitored with respect to sensory input such that the brain can adjust the movements to make them accurate. To date, these studies have not been performed on other species (including humans), but they are suggestive and worthy of further study.

Social Behavior

Several studies show that frontal-lobe lesions in rats, cats, and monkeys significantly alter social behavior. In one interesting study, Butter and Snyder removed the dominant (so-called alpha) male from each of several groups of monkeys. They removed the frontal lobes from half the monkeys. When the animals were later returned to their groups they all resumed the position of dominant male, but within a couple of days all of the frontal monkeys were deposed and fell to the bottom of the group hierarchy.

Analogous studies of wild monkeys have shown similar results: frontal monkeys fall to the bottom of the group hierarchy and eventually die, because they are helpless alone. It is not known exactly how the social behavior of these animals has changed, but there is little doubt that it is as dramatic as the changes in social behavior of humans.

Sexual Behavior

As in humans, the role of the frontal lobes in the sexual behavior of nonhumans is very poorly understood. However, from the work of Larsson, Kolb, and others with rodents, it appears that lesions of the homologue of the human dorsolateral cortex reduces or abolishes sexual behavior in males. Lesions of the orbital cortex have little or no effect on the frequency of sexual behavior. If this result proves true for other species as well, it would add credence to similar anecdotal reports on the effects of frontal-lobe lesions in humans.

Summary

There is no evidence that the frontal lobes of humans are qualitatively special, for frontal-lobe lesions in species as diverse as rats and humans affect behavior in remarkably similar ways. It is probable that, in phylogeny, a significant specialization and elaboration of a basic movement control function has occurred, and that the complexity of movement control is highly correlated with the relative volume of the frontal lobe in mammals.

FRONTAL-LOBE SYSTEMS

We have noted several times that the prefrontal cortex is part of a system that has an important role in the control of movement. Rosvold and his colleagues have postulated that there are actually two frontal-lobe systems. One, a *dorsolateral system,* may involve the dorsolateral cortex, the anterodorsal sector of the caudate nucleus, the lateral portion of the dorsomedial thalamus, and the hippocampus. The other, an *orbital system,* may include the orbital cortex, the ventrolateral sector of the caudate nucleus, the medial portion of the globus pallidus, the medial region of the dorsomedial thalamus, the septal nuclei, and possibly the amyg-dala. Lesions of structures in either system would be expected to produce behavioral effects qualitatively similar to those observed from lesions of the dorsolateral or orbital regions respectively. Although there is anatomical and behavioral support for this type of frontal-lobe system in nonhumans, it remains mostly theoretical in humans. Nevertheless, two lines of evidence tend to support the idea in humans. First, movement disorders, especially Parkinson's disease, produce symptoms that are similar to those of frontal-lobe lesions—most particularly, reduced spontaneity of behavior, changed social behavior, and impaired corollary discharge. Second, Korsakoff's disease, which results from prolonged alcoholism (see Chapter 16), also produces several symptoms similar to frontal-lobe damage. For example, Korsakoff's patients are as impaired at the Wisconsin card-sorting test as are frontal-lobe patients. Although the idea that there are two frontal-lobe systems is intriguing, it is unlikely to derive much empirical support from human neuropsychology in the near future. The model must rely on research with nonhuman species.

REFERENCES

Ackerly, S. S. A case of bilateral frontal lobe defect observed for thirty years. In J. M. Warren and K. Akert, eds. *The Frontal Granular Cortex and Behavior.* New York: McGraw-Hill Book Co., 1964.

Benton, A. L. Differential effects of frontal lobe disease. *Neuropsychologia,* 6 (1968), 53–60.

Bizzi, E., and P. H. Schiller. Single unit activity in the frontal eye fields of unanesthetized monkeys during head and eye movement. *Experimental Brain Research, 10* (1970), 151–158.

Blakemore, C. *Mechanics of the Mind.* Cambridge: Cambridge University Press, 1977.

Blumer, D., and D. F. Benson. Personality changes with frontal and temporal lobe lesions. In D. F. Benson and D. Blumer, eds. *Psychiatric Aspects of Neurologic Disease.* New York: Grune and Stratton, 1975.

Bossom, J. The effect of brain lesions on adaptation in monkeys. *Psychonomic Science, 2* (1965), 45–46.

Brown, J. *Aphasia, Apraxia and Agnosia.* Springfield, Ill.: Charles C Thomas, 1972.

Butter, C. M., and D. R. Snyder. Alterations in aversive and aggressive behaviors following orbital frontal lesions in rhesus monkeys. *Acta Neurobiologiae Experimentalis, 32* (1972), 525–565.

Denny-Brown, D. The frontal lobes and their functions. In A. Feilnig, ed. *Modern Trends in Neurology,* New York: Paul B. Hoeber, 1951.

Deuel, K. K. Loss of motor habits after cortical lesions. *Neuropsychologia, 15* (1977), 205–215.

Divac, I. Neostriatum and functions of prefrontal cortex. *Acta Neurobiologiae Experimentalis, 32* (1972), 461–478.

Feuchtwanger, E. As cited in Teuber, 1964.

Fuster, J. M., and R. H. Bauer. Visual short-term memory deficit from hypothermia of frontal cortex. *Brain Research, 81* (1974), 393–400.

Gentile, A. M., S. Green, A. Nieburgs, W. Schmelzer, and D. G. Stein. Disruption and recovery of locomotor and manipulatory behavior following cortical lesions in rats. *Behavioral Biology, 22* (1978), 417–455.

Goldman, P. S., and H. E. Rosvold. Localization of function within the dorsolateral prefrontal cortex of the rhesus monkey. *Experimental Neurology, 27* (1970), 291–304.

Goldstein, K. Mental changes due to frontal lobe damage. *Journal of Psychology, 17* (1944), 187–208.

Griffin, J. O. Neurophysiological studies into habituation. In G. S. Horn and R. A. Hinde, eds. *Short Term Changes in Neural Activity and Behavior.* New York: Cambridge University Press, 1970.

Harlow, H. F., R. T. Davis, P. H. Seftlage, and D. R. Meyer. Analysis of frontal and posterior association syndromes in brain damaged monkeys. *Journal of Comparative and Physiological Psychology, 45* (1952), 419–429.

Hebb, D. O. Intelligence in man after large removals of cerebral tissue: report of four left frontal lobe cases. *Journal of General Psychology, 21* (1939), 73–87.

Hécaen, H., and M. L. Albert. Disorders of mental functioning related to frontal lobe pathology. In D. F. Benson and D. Blumer, eds. *Psychiatric Aspects of Neurologic Disease.* New York: Grune and Stratton, 1975.

Held, R. Dissociation of visual function by deprivation and rearrangement. *Psychology Forschung, 31* (1968), 338–348.

Jacobsen, C. F. Studies of cerebral function in primates. *Comparative Psychology Monographs, 13* (1936), 1–68.

Jones-Gotman, M., and B. Milner. Design fluency: the invention of nonsense drawings after focal cortical lesions. *Neuropsychologia, 15* (1977), 653–674.

Kliest, K. As cited in Zangwill, 1966.

Kolb, B. Dissociation of the effects of lesions of the orbital or medial aspect of the prefrontal cortex of the rat with respect to activity. *Behavioral Biology, 10* (1974), 329–343.

Kolb, B. Some tests of response habituation in rats with discrete lesions to the orbital or medial frontal cortex. *Canadian Journal of Psychology, 28* (1974), 260–267.

Kolb, B. Neural mechanisms in facial expression in man and higher primates. Paper presented at Canadian Psychological Association, Vancouver, 1977.

Kolb, B., and B. Milner. Performance of complex arm and facial movements after focal brain lesions. Unpublished manuscript, 1980.

Kolb, B., and B. Milner. The effects of focal cortical lesions and carotid sodium Amytal on spontaneous facial expressions. Unpublished manuscript, 1979.

Kolb, B., A. J. Nonneman, and R. K. Singh. Double dissociation of spatial impairments and perseveration following selective prefrontal lesions in rats. *Journal of Comparative and Physiological Psychology, 87* (1974), 772–780.

Kolb, B., L. Taylor, and B. Milner. Affective behavior in patients with localized cortical excisions: an analysis of lesion site and side. Unpublished manuscript, 1980.

Kolb, B., I. Q. Whishaw, and T. Schallert. Aphagia, behavior sequencing and body weight set point following orbital frontal lesions in rats. *Physiology and Behavior, 19* (1977), 93–103.

Larsson, L. Mating behavior of the male rat. In L. R. Aronson, E. Tobach, D. S. Lehrman, and J. S. Rosenblatt, eds. *Development and Evolution of Behavior.* San Francisco: W. H. Freeman and Company, 1970.

Lashley, K. S. The problem of serial order in behavior. In F. A. Beach, D. O. Hebb, C. T. Morgan, and H. W. Nissen, eds. *The Neuropsychology of Lashley.* New York: McGraw-Hill Book Co., 1960.

Latto, R. The effects of bilateral frontal eye-field, posterior parietal or superior collicular lesions on visual search in the rhesus monkey. *Brain Research, 146* (1978), 35–50.

Luria, A. R. *The Working Brain.* New York: Penguin Books, 1973.

Markowitsch, H. J., and M. Pritzel. Comparative analysis of prefrontal learning functions in rats, cats and monkeys. *Psychological Bulletin, 84* (1977), 817–837.

Milner, B. Some effects of frontal lobectomy in man. In J. M. Warren and K. Akert, eds. *The Frontal Granular Cortex and Behavior.* New York: McGraw-Hill Book Co., 1964.

Milner, B. Hemispheric specialization: scope and limits. In F. O. Schmitt and F. G. Worden, eds. *The Neurosciences: Third Study Program.* Cambridge, Mass.: MIT Press, 1974.

Mishkin, M., and F. J. Manning. Non-spatial memory after selective prefrontal lesions in monkeys. *Brain Research, 143* (1978), 313–323.

Myers, R. E. Role of the prefrontal and anterior temporal cortex in social behavior and affect in monkeys. *Acta Neurobiologiae Experimentalis, 32* (1972), 567–579.

Nauta, W. J. H. Neural associations of the frontal cortex. *Acta Neurobiologiae Experimentalis, 32* (1972), 125–140.

Pandya, D. N., and H. G. J. M. Kuypers. Cortico-cortical connections in the rhesus monkey. *Brain Research, 13* (1969), 13–36.

Passingham, R. Information about movements in monkeys (*Macaca mulatta*). *Brain Research, 152* (1978), 313–328.

Perret, E. The left frontal lobe of man and the suppression of habitual responses in verbal categorical behavior. *Neuropsychologia, 12* (1974), 323–330.

Pohl, W. Dissociation of spatial discrimination deficits following frontal and parietal lesions in monkeys. *Journal of Comparative and Physiological Psychology, 82* (1973), 227–239.

Poppelreuter, W. *Die psychischen Schädigungen durch Kopfschuss im Kriege 1914/16,* Vol. 1. Leipzig: Leopold Voss Verlag, 1917.

Pribram, K. H. The primate frontal cortex—executive of the brain. In K. H. Pribram and A. R. Luria, eds. *Psychophysiology of the Frontal Lobes.* New York: Academic Press, 1974.

Pribram, K. H., and W. E. Tubbs. Short-term memory, parsing and the primate frontal cortex. *Science, 156* (1967), 1765–1767.

Ramier, A.-M., and H. Hécaen. Role respectif des atteintes frontales et de la lateralisation lésionnelle dans les deficits de la "fluence verbale." *Revue de Neurologie, 123* (1970), 17–22.

Reitan, R. M., and L. A. Davison. *Clinical Neuropsychology.* New York: John Wiley and Sons, 1974.

Renzi, E. de, and P. Faglioni. Normative data and screening power of a shortened version of the token test. *Cortex, 14* (1978), 41–49.

Rose, J. E., and C. N. Woolsey. The orbitofrontal cortex and its connections with the mediodorsal nucleus in rabbit, sheep and cat. *Research Publications of the Association of Nervous and Mental Disease, 27* (1948), 210–232.

Rosvold, H. E. The frontal-lobe system: cortical-subcortical interrelationships. *Acta Neurobiologiae Experimentalis, 32* (1972), 439–460.

Rosvold, H. E., and M. Mishkin. Evaluation of the effects of prefrontal lobotomy on intelligence. *Canadian Journal of Psychology, 4* (1950), 122–126.

Semmes, J., S. Weinstein, L. Ghent, and H.-L. Teuber. Impaired orientation in personal and extrapersonal space. *Brain, 86* (1963), 747–772.

Shipley, J. E., and B. Kolb. Neural correlates of species-typical behavior in the Syrian Golden Hamster. *Journal of Comparative and Physiological Psychology, 19* (1977), 93–103.

Stitt, C., and D. Huntington. Some relationships among articulation, auditory abilities and certain other variables. *Journal of Speech and Hearing Research, 12* (1969), 576–593.

Taylor, L. Psychological assessment of neurosurgical patients. In T. Rasmussen and R. Marino, eds. *Functional Neurosurgery.* New York: Raven Press, 1979.

Teuber, H.-L. The riddle of frontal lobe function in man. In J. M. Warren and K. Akert, eds. *The Frontal Granular Cortex and Behavior.* New York: McGraw-Hill Book Co., 1964.

Teuber, H.-L. Unity and diversity of frontal lobe function. *Acta Neurobiologiae Experimentalis, 32* (1972), 615–656.

Teuber, H.-L., and M. Mishkin. Judgment of visual and postural vertical after brain injury. *Journal of Psychology, 38* (1954), 161–175.

Tyler, H. R. Disorders of visual scanning with frontal lobe lesions. In S. Locke, ed. *Modern Neurology.* London: J. and A. Churchill, 1969.

Walker, E. A., and D. Blumer. The localization of sex in the brain. In K. J. Zulch, O. Creutzfeldt, and G. C. Galbraith, eds. *Cerebral Localization.* Berlin and New York: Springer-Verlag, 1975.

Warren, J. M., H. B. Warren, and K. Akert. The behavior of chronic cats with lesions in the frontal association cortex. *Acta Neurobiologiae Experimentalis, 32* (1972), 345–392.

Zangwill, O. L. Psychological deficits associated with frontal lobe lesions. *International Journal of Neurology, 5* (1966), 395–402.

HIGHER FUNCTIONS

In Part Six we discussed the functions of each of the associational zones of the cortex separately, stressing the theoretical bases governing their operation. In Part Seven we take an overview of the highest functions of association cortex in order to discuss the integrated activity of these zones in affect, memory, and language. Some material from previous chapters is repeated, because ideas and concepts presented in Chapters 7 through 14 are extensively elaborated upon. Chapters 15, 16, and 17 can thus be considered as forming a bridge between neurology and the classical problems of cognitive psychology.

15

MEMORY

Psychologists began studying memory in the mid-nineteenth century, the first monograph, Ebbinghaus's, being published in 1885. Memory, however, has not been the sole province of psychologists. It has been a topic of interest to philosophers from the time of Plato and Aristotle, and more recently formed an important part of Freud's psychoanalytic theory. The neuropsychological study of memory dates back to about 1915, when Karl Lashley embarked on a lifetime project to identify the neural locations of learned habits. In most of his experiments he either removed portions of the neocortex or made cuts of fiber pathways in hopes of preventing transcortical communication between sensory and motor regions of the cortex. After hundreds of experiments Lashley was still unable to interfere with specific memories. In 1950 he concluded that "it is not possible to demonstrate the isolated localization of a memory trace anywhere in the nervous system. Limited regions may be essential for learning or retention of a particular

activity, but...the engram is represented throughout the region."

Ironically, only three years later, in 1953, a neurosurgeon, William Scoville, inadvertently made one of the most influential findings in neuropsychology, when he operated on the now famous patient H.M. Bilateral removal of the hippocampus in H.M. made him amnesic for virtually all events following the operation. From Lashley's extensive work no one could have predicted that removal of any structure, let alone a structure that was once believed to be primarily olfactory in function, would result in a person remembering things from the distant past but not from the recent past! The surgery had interfered with the process of storing or retrieving new memories, but had not touched stored memories themselves. The case of H.M. revolutionized the study of the memory process and shifted the emphasis from search for the location of memory to an analysis of the process of storing memories. Indeed, Scoville and Milner's description of

H.M. is probably the second most influential observation ever made in neuropsychology, with only Broca's surpassing it. Today, few areas in experimental psychology are as active as those relating to the processes involved in human memory.

In this chapter we describe the role of the temporal, frontal, and parietal lobes in memory. Specific attention is paid to the complementary specialization of the left and right hemispheres for the storage of verbal and nonverbal material respectively. We review the various disorders of memory, neuropsychological theories of memory, and studies of memory processes in nonhumans. But before we consider the facts regarding the pathology of memory let us examine several theoretical issues.

THE NATURE OF MEMORY

What Is Memory?

Memory is a process that results in a relatively permanent change in behavior. It is never observed and is always inferred. In other words, we cannot identify memories in the brain, but since behavior changes with experience, we logically infer that some process must occur to account for the behavioral change. The lesson to be learned from Lashley is that no region in the nervous system can be pointed to as the place where we remember. Lesions to a number of brain regions disturb memory, but these regions do not house memory or memories. They can be said only to be more involved in the process of remembering than other regions. It is likely that groups of neurons in different parts of the brain, especially in the cerebral hemispheres, are more or less important for the remembering of different types of information (e.g., verbal, pictorial), but even this specialization is relative rather than abso-

lute. It does not happen, for example, that a person is totally amnesic for verbal material but remembers nonverbal material.

If memories are not stored as discrete things in the brain, how might they be stored? This complex question has no clear answer as yet, but an analogy may help illustrate the kind of process that could be involved. Imagine a hill; water poured onto the soil at its top runs down the hill, eroding small channels in the earth. If more water is poured on the hill most of it follows the same route of the first water, further deepening the channels. Still more water continues the process. Since the water will always take the same route down the hill, we could say that there is a "memory" for that route. In neurological terms we could conceive the brain as the hill and the process of memory as the route. Sensory experience enters the brain (top of the hill), flows through the brain (the channels in the hill), and produces behavior (leaves the hill) at the bottom. We can see, therefore, that the memory was not stored in a place, but, rather, was a function of the activity of the entire brain. We do not wish to belabor this analogy, nor for it to be taken literally; but it does demonstrate a simple way in which to conceive of memory as a process of neuronal connectivity rather than as a thing to be found in the brain.

What Do We Remember from an Experience?

To consider the pathology of memory we must first examine what is normally remembered. In his classic book *Remembering* (1932) Bartlett made the point that remembering cannot be regarded as the mere revival of previous experience; rather, it is a process of active reconstruction. In Bartlett's words:

> Remembering is not the re-excitation of innumberable fixed, lifeless and fragmentary traces. It

is an imaginative reconstruction, or construction, built out of the relation of our attitude towards a whole active mass of organized past reactions or experience...and to a little outstanding detail which commonly appears in image or in language form. It is thus hardly ever really exact, even in the most rudimentary cases of rote recapitulation. . . . (Bartlett, 1932, pp. 213–214) It looks as if what is said to be reproduced is, far more generally than is commonly admitted, really a construction serving to justify whatever impression may have been left by the original. It is this "impression," rarely defined with much exactitude, which most readily persists. So long as the details which can be built up around are such that they would give a "reasonable" setting, most of us are fairly content, and are apt to think that what we build we have literally retained. (Bartlett, 1932, p. 176)

In other words, events are not stored *in toto;* only certain critical elements are stored from which the event can be reconstructed. The more cues or elements that are provided contextually, the more exactly the event can be reconstructed and "remembered."

Consider our hill analogy again: If only a trickle of water (minimal sensory input) is poured on the hill, the water will trace only part of the route to the bottom, bypassing many of the small side channels. As more water (i.e., more contextual information) is added, it travels faster down the hill, tracing more and more of the various channels originally followed (i.e., "remembers" the route more precisely).

After a long delay, remembering may identify correctly the essential elements of sensory experience yet incorporate additional elements that, although compatible with the essential sensory experience, are erroneous. It is widely believed that this incorrect embellishment of the critical experience may account for the fallibility of eyewitness evidence in which plausible but erroneous details are "remembered." To return to our hill analogy, if

water has not been poured on the hill recently, the channels become less distinct because of environmental processes such as wind erosion and so on. The major channels remain passable, but many of the smaller channels may be lost. When water is again poured on the hill, it retraces the major route but the details of the smaller side channels are lost and new ones, which may or may not coincide with the original, are formed.

Bartlett's proposition that remembering is reconstruction is particularly important in understanding the pathology of memory. An apparent defect in memory could result from a disorder not only in the storage of sensory experience, but also in the later reconstruction of sensory experience from the critical features. Indeed, in some disorders, such as the amnesia associated with Korsakoff's disease (see below), a deficit in reconstruction may well prove to be a significant component.

Two Types of Memory

In 1890 William James distinguished between what he called *primary* memory, one that endured for a very brief period of time, and *secondary* memory, "the knowledge of a former state of mind after it has already once dropped from consciousness" (James, 1890, p. 648). Not until 1958, however, were separate short-term and long-term memories specifically postulated, by Broadbent, although a number of authors (e.g., Miller) had hinted at this possibility. Since Scoville and Milner's description of H.M. the concept of two memory systems, short-term and long-term, has become central to neuropsychological theory. Neuropsychological evidence now supports the concept, since patients may suffer one kind of memory loss and not the other.

An experiment by Hebb nicely demonstrates the two kinds of memory behaviorally. College students were asked to repeat strings

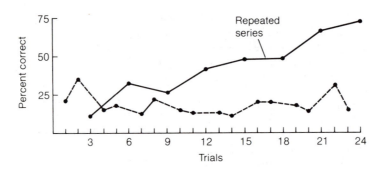

FIGURE 15-1. Performances on the Hebb recurring-digits test. Subjects were read sets of nine digits to recall immediately. Unbeknownst to the subjects every third set repeated the first set. The subjects gradually learned the repeating series, but continued to do poorly on the novel series. (After Hebb, 1961.)

of digits, such as 83759247. The number of digits that can be recalled is termed the memory span. The maximum memory span is about eight. There is little hope of repeating eight digits unless we listen very carefully and then repeat them at once. The memory is brief; and it is striking that even with sustained concentration items in short-term memory fade very quickly and are lost. In Hebb's experiment, nine digits were read aloud to the subjects. Since nine digits are beyond the memory span of most subjects, few correctly recalled the nine. The subjects were then read another set of digits, then a third, and so on, for a total of 24 sets of nine digits. However, unknown to the subjects, every third set repeated the first set. The results showed (see Figure 15-1) that although the short-term memory for nine digits is very brief, the subjects gradually learned the repeating series, as it was evidently stored in long-term memory. Hebb proposed that listening to a set of digits does more than set up a short-term memory. He suggested that some other long-term change must also be beginning, and is left behind in the nervous system. Although hearing another string of digits appears to completely wipe out the first

set of digits, only the short-term memory is wiped out completely, since permanent memory gradually develops as the repeating set is learned.

Hebb went a step further from the behavioral data and developed a theory of the neurological basis of short-term and long-term memory in his 1949 book. His genius was that using the associational learning theory of Hull and his contemporaries in the 1930s and '40s and using what was known of nervous-system activity, he described the basis of learning and memory. Hebb argued that short-term memory was an active process of limited duration, whereas long-term memory involved an actual structural change in the nervous system.

Hebb realized from the earlier anatomical work of Lorente de Nó that neurons in the brain are interconnected with many other neurons, and, in turn, each neuron receives input from many synapses upon its dendrites and cell body. The resulting neuronal loops (see Figure 15-2) contain neurons whose output signal may be either excitatory or inhibitory. Although the neuronal loops are usually drawn as though they were in the cortex, many of the loops probably run from the cortex to

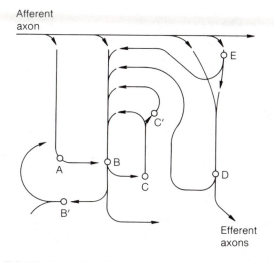

Afferent
axon

Efferent
axons

FIGURE 15-2. Simplified diagram of the interconnections of neurons to form neuronal loops. The entering axon excites four neurons, A, B, D, and E. Of these B and D send impulses out of the system (efferent axons) to excite other systems. A-B-B', B-C, and B-C-C' form closed loops. (After Hebb, 1972.)

the thalamus or other subcortical structures, such as the hippocampus, and back to the cortex. Because each neuron is believed to both send and receive thousands of outputs and inputs, the number of possible neuronal loops is truly immense.

In Hebb's theory each psychologically important event, be it a sensation, percept, memory, thought, emotion, etc., is conceived to be the flow of activity in a given neuronal loop. Hebb proposed that the synapses in a particular path become functionally connected to form a **cell assembly**. At this point Hebb made the assumption that if two neurons, A and B, are excited together, they become linked functionally. In Hebb's words: "When an axon of cell A is near enough to excite a cell B and repeatedly or persistently takes part in firing it, some growth process or metabolic change takes place in one or both cells such that A's efficiency, as one of the cells firing B,

is increased" (Hebb, 1949, p. 62). In Hebb's view the most probable way in which one cell could become more capable of firing another is that synaptic knobs grew or became more functional, increasing the area of contact between the afferent axon and efferent cell body and dendrites.

In Hebb's view the cell assembly is a system that is initially organized by a particular sensory event, but is capable of continuing its activity after the stimulation has ceased. Hebb proposed that to produce functional changes in synaptic transmission the cell assembly must be repeatedly activated. After the initial sensory input the assembly would therefore reverberate. Repeated reverberation could then produce the structural changes. Clearly this conception of information storage could explain the phenomena of short-term and long-term memory: short-term memory is reverberation of the closed loops of the cell assembly; long-term memory is more structural, a lasting change in synaptic connections.

In Hebb's theory there is yet another factor in long-term memory. For the structural synaptic changes to occur there must be a period in which the cell assembly is left relatively undisturbed. Hebb referred to this process of structural change as consolidation, a period believed to require 15 minutes to an hour. Its existence was supported by observations that retention failed when brain function was disrupted soon after learning, as, for example, in the amnesia for events just prior to a concussion. The description of H.M.'s case invited a logical extrapolation of Hebb's theory: the hippocampus was assumed to be especially important to the process of consolidation, although just how it was involved could not be specified. New material was not remembered because it was not consolidated; old material was remembered because it was consolidated before the hippocampal damage.

Finally, Hebb assumed that any cell assembly could be excited by others. This idea provided the basis for thought or ideation. The essence of an "idea" is that it occurs in the absence of the original environmental event that it corresponds to.

The beauty of Hebb's theory is that it attempted to explain psychological events by the physiological properties of the nervous system. Now, over 30 years since Hebb's landmark volume, his theory remains the best attempt to combine the principles of psychological reality and the facts of neuroscience. In a recent, thoughtful review Goddard revisited the cell assembly and found that, with a few modifications, it is still a sound metaphor for psychological activity. Goddard bases his argument largely on recent work providing physiological confirmation for Hebb's argument that there are separate neurological substrates for short-term and long-term memory. On the basis of earlier work by Eccles and others, Bliss and Gardner-Medwin demonstrated unequivocally in 1973 that electrical stimulation of a neuron can produce either brief or long-lasting changes in synaptic transmission, according to the characteristics of the brain stimulation. Brief pulses of current are delivered to an axon over a few seconds and the magnitude of the response is recorded from areas known to receive projections from the stimulated axon. After a stable baseline of response to the stimulation has been established the stimulation is changed to one of high frequency, driving the system very hard. This high-frequency stimulation is then discontinued and the brief test pulses are resumed. The magnitude of the postsynaptic response can thus be compared to the original baseline and the time course of the decay of changes in response magnitude can be measured as well. Two significant findings emerge from this study. First, response magnitude markedly increases immediately after the high-frequency stimulation (see Figure 15-3). This increase

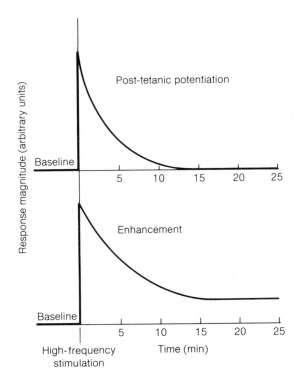

FIGURE 15-3. Time course of change in response magnitude following high-frequency stimulation. In the upper curve response magnitude returns to baseline, a phenomenon described as post-tetanic potentiation. In the lower curve response strength does not return to baseline, indicating enhancement. (After Goddard, 1979.)

declines over time and returns to baseline, the rate of decline depending upon the details of the stimulation. This short-term increase is called *post-tetanic potentiation*. Second, the change in response magnitude may not decline to baseline but instead remain elevated, possibly for days or as long as is technically practical to measure it. McNaughton has labeled this phenomenon *enhancement*. In some cases enhancement may be present after two months, and Barnes has shown that enhancement is prolonged by occasional repetition of the high-frequency stimulation. The original studies of post-tetanic potentiation and enhancement were done on the hippocampus, but there is no compelling reason at this time to believe that these phenomena cannot be demonstrated elsewhere in the brain.

Goddard emphasized the similarity between the phenomena of short-term memory and post-tetanic potentiation and between long-term memory and enhancement. He proposed that these physiological events provide a strong basis for Hebb's neuropsychological theory. As attractive as the physiological work is as a model of short-term and long-term memory, it is still a substantial theoretical leap to understanding the effects of lesions on memory, such as the differential effects of temporal-lobe and parietal-lobe lesions on short-term and long-term memory respectively. This apparent complication may be resolved in the future as more is learned about the mechanisms of enhancement and post-tetanic potentiation. The important point for us now is that there is tentative evidence to support Hebb's theory. As Goddard states:

> It is a tribute to Hebb that, even though some of his postulates concerning synaptic mechanisms were wrong, it is only by adopting his theoretical perspective that [we] have been able to see how the newly discovered details of synaptic plasticity have any importance at all. (Goddard, 1979, p. 22)

Terminology

The terminology in studies of disorders of memory can be confusing. **Amnesia** refers to the partial or total loss of memory. A difficulty in recalling events prior to the onset of the amnesia is known as **retrograde amnesia.** An inability to remember events subsequent to the onset of the amnesia is known as **anterograde amnesia.** These amnesias are usually not complete, but patchy instead, some events being remembered and others not.

TEMPORAL LOBES AND MEMORY

The first suggestion that the temporal lobes might play a critical role in human memory was provided by Bekhterev in 1899. He reported a patient who had shown a severe memory impairment, and demonstrated on autopsy a bilateral softening in the region of the uncus, hippocampus, and adjoining medial temporal cortex (see Figure 13-2).

In the 1950s the importance of the hippocampus in human memory was clearly demonstrated in reports describing several patients with bilateral hippocampal damage. Scoville and Milner's patient H.M. is the most thoroughly studied, having been followed for more than 20 years. He was a motor winder by trade and had experienced generalized epileptic seizures that had grown progressively worse in frequency and severity despite very high doses of medication. On 23 August 1953 William Scoville performed a bilateral medial temporal-lobe resection in an attempt to stop the seizures. Afterward H.M. experienced a severe anterograde memory impairment that has persisted with little improvement to this day.

The Case of H.M.

H.M.'s IQ is above average (118 on the Wechsler Adult Intelligence Scale), and he performed normally on several different types of perceptual tests such as the Mooney closure test (see Chapter 12). H.M.'s memory for events prior to the surgery is good, as is his capacity to recall remote events such as incidents from his school days or jobs he held in his late teens or early twenties, prior to his surgery. Socially, H.M. is quiet and well mannered. He dresses neatly but has to be reminded when to shave. He speaks in a monotone but articulates his words well and has a vocabulary in keeping with his above-average intelligence. His language comprehension is normal and he understands complex verbal material, including jokes.

H.M.'s recall of personal events is interesting and enlightening, as witnessed by the following description. Notice his severe handicap in everyday life and his ability to remember some events but only after prolonged repetition.

> H.M. has been cared for all this time by his mother, who usually accompanies him wherever he goes. It so happened, however, that in 1966 the mother was in Hartford Hospital, recovering from a minor operation, just when H.M. was about to leave for Boston. It was his father, therefore, who packed H.M.'s clothes for him and brought him to meet us at Dr. Scoville's office prior to the journey. The father had also taken the patient to visit his mother in hospital that very morning, the third such visit within a week. Yet when he questioned H.M., he seemed not to remember any of these visits, although he expressed a vague idea that something might have happened to his mother. On the journey to Boston, he kept saying that he felt a little uneasy and wondered if something might be wrong with one of his parents, though he could not be sure which one. On being asked who had packed his bag for the trip, he said "Seems like it was my mother. But then that's what I'm not sure about. If there is something wrong with my mother, then it could have been my father." Despite our explaining the situation to him repeatedly during the journey, H.M. was never able to give a clear account of what had happened, and was still feeling "uneasy" when he reached Boston, wondering if something was "wrong" with one of his parents. Gradually, this uneasiness wore off, and although he was told repeatedly that he could telephone home any time he wished, he no longer seemed to know why he should do so. Next day he appeared completely unaware that there had been any question of illness in his family. When asked again who had packed his suitcase, he said "It must have been my mother. She always does these things." It seemed to us instructive how the emotional tone (one of con-

cern and uneasiness), which was associated with the vague knowledge of his mother's illness, appeared to fade away nearly as rapidly as his knowledge of the events provoking it.

> During three of the nights at the Clinical Research Center, the patient rang for the night nurse, asking her, with many apologies, if she would tell him where he was and how he came to be there. He clearly realized that he was in a hospital but seemed unable to reconstruct any of the events of the previous day. On another occasion he remarked "Every day is alone in itself, whatever enjoyment I've had, and whatever sorrow I've had." Our own impression is that many events fade for him long before the day is over. He often volunteers stereotype descriptions of his own state, by saying that it is "like waking from a dream." His experience seems to be that of a person who is just becoming aware of his surroundings without fully comprehending the situation, because he does not remember what went before.

In December, 1967 (eighteen months after the visit to Boston), H.M.'s father died suddenly, and H.M. is said to have become temporarily quite irritable and intractable, rushing out of the house in anger one evening. The cause of the anger was finding that some of his guns were missing. These had been prize possessions of which he often spoke and which he had kept in his room for many years, but an uncle had claimed them as his legacy after the father's death. The patient was upset by what to him was an inexplicable loss, but became calm when they were replaced in his room. Since then, he has been his usual even-tempered self. When questioned about his parents two months later, he seemed to be dimly aware of his father's death. In these and similar respects, he demonstrates some capacity to set up traces of constant features of his immediate environment. In this instance, the continued absence of one of his parents may have served as an unusually effective clue. Until then, H.M.'s entire life had been spent at home with his father and mother.

After his father's death, H.M. was given protected employment in a state rehabilitation centre, where he spends week-days participating in rather monotonous work, programmed for severely retarded patients. A typical task is the mounting of cigarette lighters on the cardboard frames for display. It is characteristic that he cannot give us any description of his place of work, the nature of his job, or the route along which he is driven each day, to and from the centre.

In contrast to the inability to describe a job after six months of daily exposure (except for week-ends), H.M. is able to draw an accurate floor plan of the bungalow in which he has lived for the past eight years. He also seems to be familiar with the topography of the immediate neighbourhood, at least within two or three blocks of his home, but is lost beyond that. His limitations in this respect are illustrated by the manner in which he attempted to guide us to his house, in June, 1966, when we were driving him back from Boston. After leaving the main highway, we asked him for help in locating his house. He promptly and courteously indicated to us several turns, until we arrived at a street which he said was quite familiar to him. At the same time, he admitted that we were not at the right address. A phone call to his mother revealed that we were on the street where he used to live before his operation. With her directions we made our way to the residential area where H.M. now lives. He did not get his bearings until we were within two short blocks of the house, which he could just glimpse through the trees." (Milner, Corkin, and Teuber, 1968, pp. 216–217)

Formal Tests of H.M.'s Memory

H.M.'s memory has been the subject of literally dozens of papers. The following summarizes some of the major findings on the extent of his amnesia, the central feature of which is a failure in long-term retention for most events, in the absence of any general intellectual impairment or perceptual disorder.

1. *Learning and memory*. H.M. is impaired at virtually any kind of learning task in which there is a delay between presentation and recall, particularly if interfering material is pre-

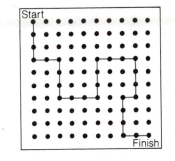

FIGURE 15-4. A visually guided stylus maze. The black circles represent metal bolt heads on a wooden base. The task is to discover and remember the correct route, indicated here by the line. Deficits on this task are correlated with the amount of right hippocampus damaged. (After Milner, 1970.)

sented between trials. For example, when shown photographs of people, he fails to recognize them two minutes later if asked to repeat digits in the interim. He is severely deficient on tests of verbal learning and recall, and cannot master sequences of digits beyond his immediate span. H.M. is also impaired at nonverbal tasks such as the delayed recall of a complex geometric design and the recognition of recurrent nonsense patterns.

2. *Maze-learning tests*. H.M. has been tested on both stylus and tactile maze tests. In the former test a wooden board has metal bolt heads sticking out as shown in Figure 15-4. The subject must discover and remember the correct route and is told only when he makes errors. H.M. failed to acquire the route even after extensive testing. He did, however, solve a radically shortened version of the maze, although it took him 155 trials. In the tactile maze test, the subject must learn a similar sort of problem, although in this case he is blindfolded and runs his fingers through alleys, again having to discover the correct route himself. Once again, H.M. failed to learn the complete maze, but eventually solved a shortened version of it.

3. *Classical conditioning.* The question whether H.M. can be classically conditioned has not been resolved. In 1962 Doreen Kimura attempted to condition galvanic skin responses, which were to be elicited by electric shock, to previously neutral stimuli. The experiment had to be abandoned as it turned out that H.M. showed no GSR response to the shock, even at levels of shock intensity that normal control subjects found disagreeably painful. H.M. apparently noticed the shocks but did not complain. The cause of this unexpected result has not been determined. Although classical conditioning has not been demonstrated in H.M., recent work by Warrington and Weiskrantz implies that H.M. probably can be classically conditioned. They classically conditioned an eyeblink response in two severe amnesics and demonstrated retention over an interval of 24 hours. This significant retention occurred in spite of the subjects' denial that they had ever seen the conditioning apparatus.

4. *Motor learning.* Although H.M. has a severe memory defect on tests of kinesthetic memory, memory for words, and visual location, he is surprisingly competent at motor learning. In one experiment Milner trained H.M. on a mirror-drawing task that required tracing a line between the double outline of a star while seeing the star and his pencil only in a mirror (Figure 15-5). This task is initially difficult even for normal subjects, but they improve with practice. H.M. had a normal learning curve and although he did not remember having performed the task previously, he retained the skill on following days! Subsequently, Corkin trained H.M. on a variety of manual-tracking and coordination tasks. Although his initial performances tended to be inferior to those of control subjects, he showed nearly normal improvement from session to session.

The dissociation between the motor-learn-

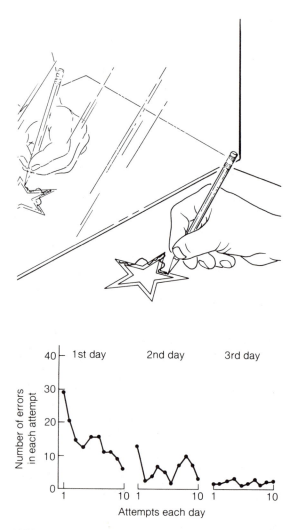

FIGURE 15-5. H.M. shows clear improvement in motor tasks. In this test the subject's task is to trace between the two outlines of the star while viewing his or her hand in a mirror. The reversing effect of the mirror makes this a difficult task initially. Crossing a line constitutes an error. (After Blakemore, 1977.)

ing and other types of tasks led Milner to speculate that motor skill is acquired independently of the hippocampal system. The question of *where* this might be has not been examined to date.

Additional Evidence for Hippocampal Role in Memory

Much has been written and theorized about H.M., but, as we have emphasized throughout the book, studies of single cases are not a legitimate basis for neuropsychological theory. If, for example, H.M. is in some way unusual, as he might very well be, conclusions about the hippocampus and memory drawn from this one subject may be grossly overstated. H.M. is not unusual, however, as we shall see in the evidence described in this section.

Other Examples of Bilateral Hippocampectomy

Milner has studied two other patients with severe memory defects who also are believed to have bilateral hippocampal damage. They showed many of the same phenomena seen in H.M. Once case, P.B., was a civil engineer whose left temporal lobe had been resectioned for relief of seizures. After surgery he had severe anterograde amnesia, which persisted and worsened until he died from unrelated causes 15 years later. At autopsy P.B. was found to have an atrophic right hippocampus opposite the surgically excised left hippocampus. Penfield and Milner proposed that P.B.'s right hippocampus was dead at the time of the operation, resulting in severe amnesia like H.M.'s.

Effect of Unilateral Hippocampal Lesions on Memory

Patients with unilateral lesions of the hippocampus do not suffer from H.M.'s severe amnesia, but they do have significant memory deficits. The role of the hippocampus in memory can be assessed by correlating the amount of hippocampus removed in the temporal lobectomy with the performance on memory tests. That is, since the surgeon removed only as much of the hippocampus as necessary to stop the abnormal epileptiform activity, different patients lose different amounts of hippocampus. Table 15-1 summarizes the results of such an analysis on the right hippocampus. Performance on maze-learning tasks is correlated with damage to the right hippocampus: the larger the removal, the larger the deficit. The same is true of a face-recognition task. On a test of spatial position (Figure 15-6) the patient marks the circle indicated on an exposed eight-inch line, then, after a short delay, attempts to reproduce this position on another eight-inch line. Again, performance is related to the extent of right hippocampus removed. In an ingenious experiment Corsi devised a spatial analogue to Hebb's recurring-digits test. A series of blocks is presented, and the subject learns to tap out a sequence on the block board illustrated in Figure 15-7. Just as there is a memory span for digits, normal subjects show a memory span for blocks: the maximum number that can be remembered. The subjects, patients and normal controls, are then tested on a series of block sequences that are one more than span. As on the Hebb repeating-digits experiment, one sequence repeats itself every third trial. Normal subjects learn the repeating sequence over several trials, although they are still poor at the novel sequences. Patients with damage to the right hippocampus do not learn the repeating sequence or do so very slowly (Figure 15-8), whereas patients with other cortical lesions perform as controls do. This test appears to be the best available noninvasive test of right hippocampal function.

The left-hand column of Table 15-1 summarizes a similar analysis of left hippocampus function. Recall of nonsense syllables (e.g., "PTB") is impaired in direct relation to the amount of hippocampus removed, as is performance on Hebb's repeating-digits test (see Figure 15-8).

TABLE 15-1

Summary of tests that correlate degree of memory defect
with amount of unilateral hippocampal removal[a]

	Site of lesion		
	Left hippocampus	Right hippocampus	Basic reference
Tactile maze learning	—	X	Milner, 1965
Visual maze learning	—	X	Corkin, 1965
Facial recognition	—	X	Milner, 1968
Spatial block span + 1	—	X	Corsi, 1972
Spatial position	—	X	Corsi, 1972
Recall of nonsense syllables	X	—	Corsi, 1972
Digit span +1	X	—	Corsi, 1972

[a] X = significant impairment; — = normal performance.

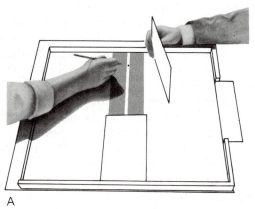

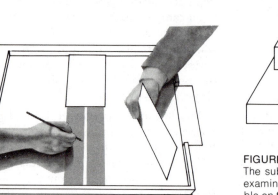

A

B

FIGURE 15-6. A procedure to test memory for spatial position. A. The subject marks the circle indicated on the exposed line to the left. B. After a short delay the subject attempts to reproduce this position as accurately as possible on the line on the right. (After Milner, 1972.)

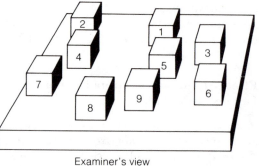

Examiner's view

FIGURE 15-7. Sketch of Corsi's block-tapping task. The subject must copy a sequence tapped out by the examiner on the blocks. The blocks' numbers are visible on the examiner side but not on the subject's. (After Milner, 1971.)

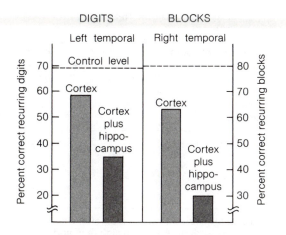

FIGURE 15-8. Summary of double dissociation of left and right hippocampal function. Left temporal lesions, including radical removal of the hippocampus, produced severe deficits on acquisition of the recurring digits, whereas right temporal lesions, including radical removal of the hippocampus, produced serious deficits on acquisition of recurring-block sequences. (Redrawn after Milner, 1970, 1971.)

These results illustrate that both hippocampi are essential for normal memory, and that the left and right hippocampi can be functionally dissociated. The left is more important in the memory of verbal material, and the right is more important in the memory of visual and spatial material.

Stimulation of the Hippocampus During Surgery

If it is assumed that stimulation of the hippocampus disrupts its functioning, then stimulation would be expected to impair memory functions. Chapman et al. stimulated the hippocampus bilaterally in 2 epileptic patients and unilaterally in 13 others, and found that bilateral stimulations produced retrograde amnesia that persisted for a few hours and reached back about two weeks. Immediate memory (digit span) and more remote memories were intact. Unilateral stimulation produced similar but lesser effects on memory.

Although these results appear to support the hypothesized role of the hippocampus in memory, there are problems with this interpretation. In their series at the Montreal Neurological Institute Rasmussen and his colleagues stimulated the hippocampus in well over 300 patients undergoing surgery for temporal-lobe epilepsy. Whenever the hippocampal stimulation produced hallucinatory or interpretational responses there were significant alterations of electrical activity on the temporal cortex. This implies that disturbances of memory from hippocampal stimulation may result from disruption of normal activity elsewhere in the brain. Furthermore, Doty and Overman found that electrical stimulation of the anterior commissure of monkeys prevented acquisition of a visual learning task, but stimulation elsewhere in the temporal lobe had no effect.

In conclusion, the results of stimulation of the hippocampus are somewhat ambiguous. Stimulation of the temporal lobe does disrupt memory, but the cause and principal locus of this effect have yet to be clearly demonstrated.

Carotid Sodium Amytal Memory Testing

Memory tests during sodium Amytal testing (see Chapter 9) have shown that if one hippocampus is damaged and the drug is injected into the contralateral hemisphere, there is amnesia for material presented during the action of the drug.

In memory testing during sodium Amytal, only very simple tests can be used, because the drug wears off within a few minutes. Before the drug injection the patient is presented with both verbal and nonverbal items and is told to remember them. For example, the patient is shown two pictures (e.g., hand and cup) and asked to name them and to remember them.

He is then distracted with mental arithmetic before being asked to recall the names of the pictures. A similar procedure is used for recall of a sentence (e.g., Peter is in the garden). After this baseline testing, injection is made into one hemisphere and testing is repeated, with the difference that the patient is shown two new pictures and given a new sentence to remember. After the drug has worn off, the patient is tested for recall and, failing this, recognition of all of the items.

Table 15-2, summarizing the incidence of amnesia following injections ipsilateral to a lesion, shows that although free recall is generally poor, recognition is very good. The table also shows that either hemisphere is capable of storing both verbal and nonverbal memories. In other words, the right hemisphere appears capable of storing the sentences, although not as efficiently as the left hemisphere.

Table 15-3 compares the effects of injection into the hemisphere ipsilateral and contralateral to a lesion. Injection into the contralateral (normal) hemisphere allows the efficiency of the impaired hemisphere's memory to be tested. Table 15-3 shows that if a patient suffers from temporal-lobe epilepsy with a unilateral focus, then, in the absence of the intact hemisphere during the period of anesthetization, the epileptic hemisphere is badly impaired at recognizing the pictures or sentences (47 percent failure). This compares to only 5 percent failure of recognition when the injection is made into the epileptic hemisphere. Comparison of the two failure rates indicates that normal memory function requires at least one temporal lobe to be functioning normally. Injection into the side contralateral to the lesion produces an unacceptable memory loss because neither hippocampus is operative. Table 15-3 also illustrates that patients with bilateral epileptic foci have significant memory defects when either hemisphere is injected, again implying that one normally functioning temporal

TABLE 15-2

Percent failure of recall and recognition after injection of sodium Amytal ipsilateral to lesion

	Free recall	Recognition
Pictures	60%	0%
Sentences	72%	6%

After Milner, 1975.

TABLE 15-3

Percent failure of recognition after injection of sodium Amytal ipsilaterally and contralaterally to lesion

	Side of injection	
	Ipsilateral to lesion	Contralateral to lesion
Unilateral epileptic focus	5%	47%
Bilateral epileptic focus	26%	35%

After Milner, 1975.

lobe is necessary for normal memory. Patients with bilateral epileptic foci are clearly poor risks for surgery, since injection of either hemisphere leaves the patient with unacceptable memory defects.

To summarize, there are three principal findings from the sodium Amytal studies. First, if the drug is injected ipsilaterally to the lesioned hemisphere, the patient retains 90 to 95 percent of both the verbal and nonverbal material. Thus, both temporal lobes are capable of storing both types of memories. This result does not impugn the previously described studies indicating an asymmetry in memory function, since the memory tests are very simple and do not nearly tax a person's mnemonic abilities. Second, injection of the drug contralateral to the damaged temporal lobe results in substan-

TABLE 15-4

Summary of the effects of left or right temporal lobectomy on various tests of memory[a]

	Site of lesion		
	Left temporal lobe	Right temporal lobe	Basic reference
Geometric recall (Rey)	—	X	Taylor, 1969
Paired-associate nonsense figures	—	X	Prisko, 1963
Recognition of nonsense figures	—	X	Kimura, 1963
Recurring nonsense figures	—	X	Kimura, 1963
Recognition of faces	—	X	Warrington and James, 1967 Milner, 1968
Recognition of tunes	—	X	Shankweiler, 1966
Recall of stories	X	—	Milner, 1967
Paired-associate words	X	—	Milner, 1967
Recognition of words, numbers	X	—	Milner, 1967
Recurring nonsense syllables	X	—	Corsi, 1972

[a] X = significant impairment; — = normal performance.

tial memory impairment, retention dropping to around 50 percent. In other words, if the injection is made into the intact hemisphere, the damaged hemisphere is impaired at storing the new material. Third, if injection ipsilateral to a known lesion results in impaired memory, there are strong grounds for predicting that the patient suffers from a bilateral lesion, as in the case of P.B. described above.

Role of the Temporal Neocortex in Memory

Although we have emphasized the role of the medial temporal lobes (hippocampus) in memory, the neocortex of the lateral temporal lobes is also important. Lesions of the anterior temporal lobe sparing the hippocampus result in a variety of memory impairments, although the global amnesia of H.M. is not observed. Milner and her colleagues have double dis-

sociated the effects of damage to the neocortex of the temporal lobe of each hemisphere on several memory tasks. They conclude that lesions of the right temporal lobe result in impaired memory of nonverbal material, whereas lesions of the left temporal lobe result in impaired memory of verbal material. These findings are summarized in Table 15-4, where it can be seen that removal of the right temporal lobe produces deficits on nonverbal tests, including recall of complex geometric figures, paired-associate learning of nonsense figures, and recognition of nonsense figures (see Figure 15-9), of tunes, and of previously seen photographs of faces. No deficits are seen, however, on tests of verbal memory. Removal of the left temporal lobe, on the other hand, produces deficits on verbal tests, such as recall of previously presented stories and of pairs of words, and recognition of words or numbers and of recurring nonsense syllables; such re-

FIGURE 15-9. Example from Kimura's recurring non-sense figures test. Subjects are shown a series of cards, on each of which is an unfamiliar design. Some designs recur, and it is the subject's task to say whether he or she has seen each design before. Right temporal lesions impair recognition on this task.

moval has little effect on the nonverbal tests. These studies indicate that although damage to the medial temporal lobe is associated with severe deficits of memory, so also is damage restricted to just the temporal neocortex associated with memory disturbance.

In a clever experiment, Jones-Gotman found that patients with left-hemisphere lesions could improve their verbal memory by encoding verbal information with the assistance of visual imagery. Thus, memory for a list of paired-associate words improved significantly if the person was told to remember pairs; for example, elephant-bouquet would be remembered by visualizing an elephant holding a bouquet in its trunk. Similarly, patients with right temporal lesions could benefit from the use of verbal encoding. Thus, for example, in the case of "elephant-bouquet" the patient was instructed to verbally encode the pair in a sentence such as "the elephant ate the bouquet." H.M. did not benefit from instructions to use these strategies, indicating that one intact hippocampus is necessary if this type of encoding scheme is to be of value.

Summary

Lesions to the temporal lobes produce significant and often tragically severe deficits in long-term memory. These deficits are not modality-specific, as they occur to both visual and auditory material no matter how the material is initially presented or memory is assessed. The deficits are material-specific, however, as left temporal lesions specifically impair memory for verbal material and right temporal lesions impair memory of nonverbal material. Although there is no question of memory defects following temporal-lobe lesions, there is substantial controversy over what the critical focus for the lesion is to produce the maximal deficit and why there are deficits at all. We address the first question in the next section and save discussion of the last question to our discussion of theories of amnesia.

PROBLEM: ROLE OF THE HIPPOCAMPUS IN MEMORY

Having emphasized the role of the temporal lobes, and especially of the hippocampus, in long-term memory a note of caution is desirable. Not even 25 years of study on amnesia and the temporal lobes have established with certainty that the hippocampus is the critical structure in the temporal-lobe amnesic syndrome. Certainly the extent of hippocampal involvement and the severity of memory impairment are correlated, but unresolved issues remain that must be confronted.

Functions of the Hippocampus in Nonhumans

The profound amnesia found in patients with bilateral medial temporal damage has not been observed in nonhumans with hippocampal damage, despite dozens of attempts to find it. In 1954 Mishkin established that bilateral removal of the temporal neocortex produced a severe and enduring impairment in learning visual material, but did not affect auditory and tactile modes—a pattern of effects unlike the modality-independent global amnesia observed in humans. Furthermore, these same studies found little or no impairment to follow bilateral hippocampectomy. The initial attempts at demonstrating hippocampal involvement in the memory processes of nonhuman species thus proved disappointing. But since 1954 at least four clear effects of bilateral hippocampal lesions in nonhumans, principally monkeys and rats, have emerged in the literature.

First, there is a tendency to perseverate on responses. That is, once an animal with a bilateral hippocampal lesion begins a response it will perseverate on that response. This deficit could be interpreted as a kind of memory deficit, since the animal may not "remember" what it has just done or what the consequences of that act were. But this behavior is more frequently interpreted as evidence of some type of response disinhibition. This interpretation is compatible with Warrington and Weiskrantz's idea that human amnesics have difficulty controlling and restraining the influence of prior learning on present performance.

The second effect is a deficit in the ability of animals with hippocampal lesions to order serially long chains of behavior. Thus, Sainsbury, Kolb, and others have shown that rats and hamsters with hippocampal lesions cannot build nests, hoard food, exhibit maternal behavior, and so on, largely because they appear to be unable to chain together the various motor acts necessary for the complex outcome. This deficit could explain some learning defects as well, since Winocur and Breckenridge have made a similar proposal to account for impaired maze performance. The idea that hippocampal animals cannot sequence motor acts is supported by the bulk of the recent hippocampal EEG literature, which has shown that rhythmical waves in the hippocampus are related to the moment-to-moment details of movement (see Chapter 8).

The third effect, demonstrated in experiments by a number of groups, is a memory defect in animals with hippocampal lesions, a defect that may be analogous to some aspects of the memory defect in amnesics. For example, several experiments have shown that learning and memory in hippocampal animals are disrupted by interfering stimuli. Correll and Scoville found that when monkeys with bilateral medial temporal lesions were required to learn six pattern discriminations concurrently they were severely impaired. The animals received only a single trial at a time on the individual problems, but trials on each of the six problems were interspersed with trials on the other five problems. Thus the presentation of one set of patterns interfered with the learning of other patterns. Interference need not come from concurrent learning, however: Jarrard found that if rats with hippocampal lesions were forced to run in a wheel after learning a spatial task their performance was impaired relative to controls or hippocampal rats that did not experience the interpolated activity.

Fourth, the most recent analysis of the hippocampus has been based on an ingenious set of experiments initiated by O'Keefe, Nadel, and Black. They have argued that the hippocampus functions to "construct spatial maps" by which animals locate themselves in space. This argument is supported by their own neurophysiological evidence that there are cells in the hippocampus that fire either when the animal finds itself in a particular spot in the environment, or when it encounters a strange object or the absence of an expected one. Hippocampal lesions are proposed to disturb maze learning, nest building, food hoarding, etc., because of the spatial requirement of the tasks.

In summary, lesions of the hippocampus of nonhuman species are known to produce perseverative responses, deficits in response sequencing, sensitivity to interfering stimuli, and spatial deficits. There is, however, no compelling evidence of a multimodal global amnesia. The failure to find the profound amnesia clinically observed in humans has been a serious obstacle to the understanding both of hippocampal function and of the amnesic syndrome.

Solutions

Failure to find global amnesia in nonhuman species has prompted a number of explanations. One argument is that there is an evolutionary break between humans and other species. Because humans and other animals are undeniably different, this absence of global amnesia could be another example of the differences in hippocampal anatomy, physiology, and apparent functions across all other mammalian species studied, as well as the general conservatism of development in nervous-system evolution (see Chapter 6).

A second possibility is that behavioral studies of hippocampectomized rats and monkeys have not used tests comparable to the ones used on people. Although more attractive than the first alternative, this also appears unlikely, since the memory deficits in nonhuman species generally appear to be minor compared with the global amnesia of H.M. and similar patients. Nevertheless, this possibility cannot be discounted yet in view of an intriguing series of experiments recently done by Gaffan, who attempted to devise behavioral tests more similar to those used to study human amnesics. In one experiment two monkeys were trained on a picture-recognition task somewhat similar to one used previously for amnesics by Warrington. The monkeys were shown a series of 25 pictures, each of which appeared twice per training session. The task was to make a response to a picture on its second appearance in a session, but to make no response on its first appearance. The difficulty of the test was varied by changing the average separation between the first and second presentation of pictures within a session. After the monkeys had learned the task with up to 18 intervening items, the fornix (a major output of the hippocampus) was surgically transected. After surgery neither monkey could reliably perform the task with more than three intervening items. The impairment was severe and was most plausibly ascribed to a memory defect similar to that observed in human amnesics. Gaffan's results are suggestive, but two problems must be considered experimentally before the memory impairments can be considered analogous to those in human amnesics. First, global amnesia is multimodal, and Gaffan has studied only visual problems to date. Second, Gaffan sectioned the fornix rather than directly damaging the hippocampus, thus making his experiment a somewhat indirect study of hippocampal function.

A final possibility is that the neuropathology responsible for the amnesia in humans has been inaccurately localized. The hippocampal damage is generally assumed to produce the amnesic syndrome, but a series of studies by Horel and Misantone and a more recent study by Mishkin bring this notion into serious question. Horel notes that major efferents of the temporal cortex pass through a narrow channel, known as the temporal stem (Figure 15-10), en route to the dorsomedial thalamus, frontal lobe, basal ganglia, and contralateral temporal lobe. After a careful examination of the literature Horel concludes that it is virtually impossible to surgically remove the hippocampus without damaging the temporal

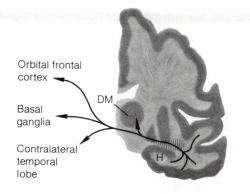

Orbital frontal
cortex

DM

Basal
ganglia

Contralateral
temporal
lobe

H

FIGURE 15-10. Major efferents of the temporal cortex pass through the temporal stem (shaded area) en route to the dorsomedial thalamus (DM), orbital frontal cortex, basal ganglia, and contralateral temporal lobe. Noting that removal of the hippocampus (H) invariably also damages the temporal stem, Horel posits that global amnesia may result from damage to the temporal stem rather than to the hippocampus.

stem; and the more hippocampus removed, the greater the damage to the temporal stem. Horel therefore concludes that damage to the temporal stem, and not to the hippocampus, may be critical in the amnesic syndrome. Some of the most convincing evidence favoring Horel's hypothesis comes from the autopsy data of Penfield and Milner's patient P.B., discussed earlier. Although autopsy confirmed Penfield and Milner's predictions that the hippocampus was damaged bilaterally, the posterior portion of one hippocampus was intact and appeared to be nearly normal, whereas the temporal stem appeared to be completely degenerated. Horel proposed that the bilateral damage to the temporal stem was responsible for P.B.'s amnesia, not the partial hippocampal damage. Horel supports his claim with studies showing that temporal-stem lesions in monkeys have severe consequences for visual discrimination learning. Although he has yet to examine auditory or tactile learning, Horel's proposal must be considered seri-

ously, especially in light of more recent work by Mishkin, who has emphasized a slightly different anatomical argument. Hippocampal lesions in humans usually are accompanied by damage to the amygdala as well. When Mishkin varied the extent of amygdala and hippocampal damage in monkeys he found that although bilateral hippocampal or amygdala lesions alone had little effect on a simple visual learning problem, simultaneous bilateral removal of the two areas produced a severe memory disorder. Unfortunately, like Gaffan and Horel, Mishkin has studied only visual learning to date. Be that as it may, both Horel's and Mishkin's experiments lead to the conclusion that the neuropathology of human amnesia cases requires reappraisal, with special attention to extrahippocampal damage.

Having sounded a note of caution regarding the interpretation of the temporal-lobe amnesic syndrome, we wish to emphasize that this in no way darkens the beautiful work of Milner and her colleagues as well as of others discussed earlier. Their descriptions of the cognitive behavior of amnesic patients are beyond question; only the anatomical basis for their observations remains controversial.

THE PARIETAL LOBES AND MEMORY

Warrington and her colleagues have presented evidence that the parietal lobes may be involved in short-term memory. They studied three patients with fairly restricted left parietal lesions who had severely impaired digit span but surprisingly intact memory of paired-associate words and short stories. Warrington has therefore argued that the left parietal lobe has an important role in the storage of short-term memory. Two objections can be raised to Warrington's conclusion. First, she does not convincingly demonstrate that the memory defect is not a secondary effect of aphasia, since all three of her patients were in fact dysphasic. Second, she does not demonstrate the effect to be specific to the left parietal lobe, for the lesions extend beyond this region. Despite these objections, there are indications that she is correct. For example, Table 15-5 summarizes the digit span and IQs from a series of nonaphasic patients with parietal removals (see Kolb and Milner for brain maps of the cortical excisions). Notice that the digit spans are significantly lower for those patients with left parietal lesions than with right parietal lesions. (Digit spans are also significantly reduced for groups with left frontal or left temporal lesions, although not as severely as the left parietal group.)

The left parietal lobe may be divisible into functional subregions, for Warrington and Weiskrantz report that patients with left parietal lesions have deficits on one type of short-term memory and not on another. They found that some patients apparently have defects in short-term recall of visually presented digits or letters but not for the same stimuli presented aurally. These patients have alexia but not aphasia. On the other hand, Luria reports patients with just the opposite difficulty: specific deficits for aurally presented but not visually presented verbal items. Luria's patients were aphasic but not alexic. Figure 15-11 shows Warrington and Weiskrantz's provisional anatomical location for these doubly dissociable deficits.

Note that the short-term memory deficits reported both by Luria and by Warrington and Weiskrantz occur in the absence of long-term memory defects. In other words, patients may exhibit surprisingly intact recall of verbal material over long delays in spite of markedly reduced short-term recall. This phenomenon implies that short-term and long-term memory are parallel processes and that material is stored separately in both. Neurologically, the parietal lobe appears to be involved in short-

TABLE 15-5

Summary of mean IQs and scaled digit-span scores on Wechsler Adult Intelligence Scale for patients reported in Kolb and Milner

		Full-scale IQ	Digit span[a]
Parietal	Left $n = 6$	98.2	6.8[b]
	Right $n = 5$	102.8	11.0
Frontal	Left $n = 9$	104.2	8.2[c]
	Right $n = 9$	107.2	9.7
Temporal	Left $n = 10$	105.1	9.1[c]
	Right $n = 10$	108.6	10.8
Normal controls	$n = 10$	114.3	10.1

[a] Refers to scaled score on Wechsler Adult Intelligence Scale. Controls from Kolb, Whishaw, and Barnsley, 1979.
[b] Differs significantly ($p < .05$) from homologous contralateral lesion.
[c] Differs significantly ($p < .05$) from all other groups.

term memory and the temporal lobe in long-term memory.

If the left parietal lobe is participating in the short-term storage of verbal material, is it possible that the right parietal lobe is participating in the short-term storage of nonverbal information? Although we are not aware of any published data on this point, the idea seems reasonable. One might expect, for example, that the span on the Corsi block-tapping test would be reduced in patients with right parietal lesions. This remains to be studied.

THE FRONTAL LOBES AND MEMORY

Historically there have been extravagant claims that the frontal lobes are responsible

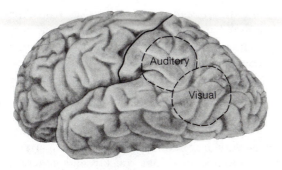

FIGURE 15-11. Provisional anatomical loci for most severe auditory and visual short-term memory defects. (After Warrington and Weiskrantz, 1973.)

for the highest intellectual functions, but until quite recently there was no evidence that the frontal lobes are involved in memory. In 1963, Prisko devised an experiment based on previous work on experimental animals. It was essentially a "compound-stimulus" task in which two stimuli in the same sensory modality were presented in succession, separated by a short interval. The subject's task was to report whether the second stimulus of the pair was identical with the first. On half the trials the stimuli were the same and on the other half they were different. Thus, the task required the subject to remember the first stimulus of a pair in order to compare it with the second, while suppressing the stimulus that occurred on previous trials. Prisko used pairs of clicks, light flashes, tones, colors, and irregular nonsense patterns as the stimuli. The same stimuli were used repeatedly in different combinations. Patients with unilateral frontal-lobe removals showed a marked impairment at matching the clicks, flashes, and colors.

The poor performance of the frontal-lobe patients is unlikely to have resulted from a defect of short-term or long-term memory, because the subjects performed normally on tests of these functions. Milner noted that in

the Prisko test the subject is required to suppress the memory of previous trials and concentrate only on the predelay stimulus. If this behavior is no longer possible after the frontal lesion, then, when a few stimuli constantly recur, the interfering effects of previous trials may seriously impair test performance. That is, because there is difficulty in discriminating the most recent stimulus from others that appeared earlier, the frontal-lobe patient's temporal discriminations become rather blurred. This possibility was tested more directly in an experiment by Corsi.

In Corsi's experiment there were two tasks, one verbal and one nonverbal, and two subjects were required to decide which of two stimuli were seen more recently. In the verbal task subjects were asked to read pairs of words presented on a series of cards (e.g., cowboy-railroad). From time to time a card appeared bearing two words with a question mark between them. The subject had to indicate which of the words he had read most recently. Sometimes both words had been seen before, but at other times only one had been. In the latter case the task became a simple test of recognition, whereas in the former case it was a test of recency memory. Patients with left temporal removals showed a mild deficit in recognition, as befits their difficulty with verbal memory; the frontal-lobe patients performed normally. However, on the recency test both frontal-lobe groups (left and right) were impaired, although the left-side group was significantly worse.

The nonverbal task was identical to the verbal, except that the stimuli were photographs of paintings rather than words. Patients with right temporal-lobe removals showed mild deficits on recognition, consistent with their visual-memory deficit, whereas those with right frontal-lobe lesions performed normally. On the recency test the frontal-lobe groups were impaired, but now the right-side group was significantly worse. Thus, Corsi's experiments confirm Prisko's results indicating a deficit in the memory of the temporal ordering of events; further, the results show an asymmetry in the function of the left and right frontal lobes.

Another memory deficit is observed in patients with frontal-lobe lesions. We have already noted that H.M. and patients with right hippocampal damage were impaired at tactile and visual mazes. When patients with frontal-lobe removals are tested on these tasks, patients with right frontal removals are impaired, patients with left frontal removals are not. Again we see an asymmetry in the memory functions of the frontal lobes. The major factor in this test is likely to be the spatial component, because frontal lesions appear to disturb various aspects of spatial ability.

OTHER AMNESIC SYNDROMES

Korsakoff's Syndrome and Wernicke's Disease

Korsakoff's syndrome and **Wernicke's disease** have historically been considered to be separate diseases, but it has recently become fashionable to consider them to be different components of the same disease.

Talland has described six major symptoms of Korsakoff-Wernicke disease:

1. *Anterograde amnesia:* The patients are unable to form new memories. On formal memory tests they are especially bad at learning paired-associate lists.

2. *Retrograde amnesia:* The patients show a loss of old memories.

3. *Confabulation:* Patients make up stories about past events rather than admit memory loss. These stories are often based on past experiences and are therefore often plausible.

4. *Meager content in conversation:* Korsakoff patients have little to say in spontaneous conversation, presumably in part because of their amnesia.

5. *Lack of insight:* Many patients are virtually completely unaware of their memory defect.

6. *Apathy:* Indifference and incapacity persevere in ongoing activities. The patients lose interest in things quickly and generally appear indifferent to change.

These symptoms are all observed in patients who otherwise appear quite normal. They have normal IQs, are alert and attentive, appear motivated, and generally lack other neurological signs of cerebral deficit such as abnormal EEG.

The symptoms of Korsakoff-Wernicke disease may appear suddenly within the space of a few days. The cause is a thiamine (vitamin B_1) deficiency resulting from prolonged intake of large quantities of alcohol. The syndrome, which is usually progressive, can be arrested by massive doses of vitamin B_1 but cannot be reversed. Prognosis is poor, only about 20 percent of patients showing much recovery over a year on a B_1-enriched diet. Many patients demonstrate no recovery even after 10 to 20 years.

Although there has been some controversy over the exact effect that the vitamin deficiency has on the brain, it is currently believed that there is damage in the medial thalamus, and possibly in the mammillary bodies of the hypothalamus, as well as generalized cerebral atrophy. It is widely believed that the severe memory defect results from hypothalamic damage because the mammillary bodies are a major recipient of hippocampal efferents through the fornix. There are three reasons to doubt this. First, in many cases only the medial thalamus is degenerated and not the mammillary bodies; the reverse is not observed. Second, the hippocampus appears not to project through the fornix to the mammillary bodies, but rather to the subiculum, which is the cortex lying near the hippocampus, and the subiculum appears in turn to project to the mammillary bodies. Third, there is considerable controversy over whether lesions to the fornix itself even produce amnesia. For example, Woolsey and Nelson report a case in which there was no apparent neuropsychological disturbance (that is, no obvious memory defect) from a malignant tumor that had destroyed the fornix bilaterally. Garcia-Bengochea et al. sectioned the fornix bilaterally as a treatment for epilepsy in 14 patients and reported that amnesia did not ensue. There have been two reports of memory loss after fornical section, but because these patients have not come to autopsy it is uncertain just where the lesion is. In sum, the bulk of the evidence suggests that damage to the dorsomedial thalamus, not damage to the hippocampal system, produces the memory loss. This conclusion supports Horel's argument, discussed above, that the role of the hippocampus in memory has been vastly overrated.

Electroconvulsive Shock

Convulsive therapy with metrazol-induced seizures was introduced by von Meduna in 1933, after the correlation between schizophrenia and epilepsy was observed to be extremely low; von Meduna proposed that they were mutually exclusive. In 1937, Cerletti and Bini replaced the previous agents with electricity: **electroconvulsive shock therapy** (**ECT** or **ECS**).

The method of ECT is to apply a 70–120-volt alternating current (AC) for about a half-second through temporal electrodes. Treatments are usually given one to three times a week, lasting for two to four weeks. To pro-

tect the body from the physical consequences of the convulsions, tranquilizers, muscle relaxants, and sometimes atropine are given just prior to the shock.

The clearest effect of ECT on psychological functioning is an adverse effect on memory, with three predominant features:

1. Total amnesia for the period of unconsciousness during treatment and for the period of confusion immediately following.

2. Retrograde amnesia for events just prior to treatment. The period of retrograde amnesia decreases over time, often shrinking to only about a 15–20-minute preshock period.

3. Anterograde amnesia for stimuli after the ECT, such as the names of people, the contents of books or articles read, etc. This amnesia may persist for as long as two to three weeks following the ECT, but by four weeks all subjects appear normal.

There have been claims that unilateral ECT has significantly less effect on memory than does bilateral ECT. The evidence for this is contradictory and not altogether convincing. In a recent review on ECT Robertson and Inglis conclude that manipulation of electrode placements is the most promising line of research to prevent or reduce memory impairments, but that much basic research remains to be done. It seems reasonable to expect that unilateral ECT on the left might preferentially disturb verbally mediated memory, whereas unilateral ECT on the right might preferentially disturb nonverbal memory. Indeed, there is preliminary evidence these expectations may be correct. Most of the claims made about the therapeutic powers of ECT remain unproven. In view of recent unpublished studies by Corkin showing that prolonged repetition of ECT has a very detrimental effect on general neuropsychological functioning, one wonders whether the risk is worth it.

Transient Global Amnesia

In 1958 Fisher and Adams described a previously unrecognized amnesic syndrome: transient global amnesia, a sudden and transient loss of memory. The onset is sudden and includes both retrograde and anterograde amnesia, without apparent precipitating cause. Although this syndrome has been subsequently confirmed by many others, little is known of the etiology. It has been linked to concussion, migraine, hypoglycemia, and epilepsy, but the most likely explanation appears to be vascular interruption in the territory of the posterior cerebral artery, from either a transient ischemic attack or an embolism.

Traumatic Amnesia

Head injuries commonly produce a form of amnesia, the severity of the injury determining the characteristics of the amnesia. There is typically a transient loss of consciousness followed by a short period of confusion. The period of retrograde amnesia generally shrinks over time, frequently leaving a residual retrograde amnesia of only a few seconds to a minute for events immediately preceding the injury. Further, there is usually an additional period of posttraumatic amnesia (i.e., anterograde amnesia) as well.

Duration of the posttraumatic amnesia varies. In one series of patients with severe head injuries Whitty and Zangwill found that 10 percent had durations of less than one week, 30 percent had durations of two to three weeks, and the remaining 60 percent had durations of over three weeks. Unfortunately, the authors fail to specify how long the amnesia might last in this latter group. Sometimes certain events, such as the visit of a relative or some unusual occurrence, may be retained as "islands of memory" during this amnesic period. According to Whitty and Zangwill the posttraumatic amnesia commonly ends quite sharply, often after a period of natural sleep.

Infantile Amnesia

One form of amnesia is experienced by everyone, and is therefore particularly intriguing: events or things experienced or learned in infancy are forgotten. (We refer readers to the excellent review by Campbell and Spear for more detail.)

The most paradoxical aspect of infantile amnesia is that the early years are generally regarded as being a time of critical importance in a child's development, yet these years are not remembered in adulthood. The evidence suggests that memory of early childhood begins in late preschool or early school years. Although there are some snatches of memory here and there from early childhood, it is difficult to know whether they are true memories, or have resulted from repetition of favorite stories by parents.

Infantile amnesia appears to have three plausible explanations. First, the information may still be there but be no longer retrievable. A fascinating experiment done by Yerkes in 1912 is germane to this theory. Yerkes trained worms in a Y-maze, one end of which had a shock grid; the other, moist earth. Once the worms had learned this problem Yerkes decapitated the creatures and retested the body on the maze over the ensuing days. The body appeared to retain the habit for a while, but appeared to lose the skill as a new head grew. To our knowledge this experiment has not been replicated, but the message of the data is intriguing: as the forebrain develops it either disrupts the memory or blocks its retrieval. Because in human ontogeny the brain clearly develops functionally in a caudorostral sequence, a similar explanation of infantile amnesia is plausible. In other words, as the new areas in the forebrain (i.e., cerebral hemispheres) mature and become functional, they preclude access to the memories laid down earlier.

A second, similar explanation of infantile amnesia suggests that one memory system is used by infants, and another develops for adults. Memories are lost because they are not stored in the new, adult system.

A third explanation is that the problem is cellular. As neurons mature, more and more dendritic processes grow. They interfere with the established memories, which are thus lost.

THEORIES OF AMNESIA

On the whole models of amnesia have been unsatisfactory for two reasons: either they have been restricted to very simple aspects of memory, or they have been based on communications theory or complex human cognitive theory, and are consequently difficult to reconcile with both neuropsychology and neurophysiology. Despite these shortcomings there is no shortage of theories. (Weiskrantz recently noted, tongue in cheek, that there are now more theories of the human amnesic syndrome than there are amnesic subjects.) For present purposes, however, theories of amnesia can be grouped into two broad categories: functional theories, which assume a defect in the sequential processing of information; and structural theories, which assume a blockage in a particular form of memory. Rather than attempt to review the multitudes of theories, we shall briefly discuss a few of the most popular versions of each of the two categories.

Defects in Sequential Processing

Most functional, or information-processing, models assume a functional defect in the process of memory storage or retrieval. Many theories also assume that memory traces are sequentially transferred from short-term to long-term memory—an assumption by no means universally accepted. Probably the oldest and most widely known sequential-processing model is the consolidation process, dating back to Müller and Pilzecker, in 1900. In the modern version of this theory it is assumed that for memory to become permanent, some structural change in the brain is required. The consolidation period is a brief period during which this structural change takes place. Thus, like gelatin, which takes time to set, the memory takes time to be "consolidated." Amnesia is presumed to result when the process of consolidation is disrupted and the memory trace fails to produce a structural change and is lost. More recent functional models of amnesia take a slightly different position; they propose that sensory experience produces a structural change in the normal manner, but that access to the memory trace is lost. The memory trace remains present in the brain but is inaccessible.

Multiple Memory System Theories

Structural theories assume that amnesia results from an impairment in one of several memory systems. Such theories assume that impairment of a psychological (or cognitive) structure leads to deficits in certain types of memory but not in others. In one theory of this type amnesics are thought to be incapable of forming certain types of associations, and thus practice faulty recognition. Stated in terms of Bartlett's constructional model of memory, discussed earlier, the amnesic is unable to reconstruct the memory on the background of available contextual cues. The most recent, and in many ways most novel, structural theory is the cognitive-map hypothesis of O'Keefe and Nadel. They propose that the hippocampus provides a spatial framework, or map, that provides spatial and temporal contexts for sensory experience. That is, the cognitive map provides a record of the associations among experiential events. Amnesia results from a disturbance in the cognitive map such that amnesics are unable to find order in their memorial worlds, just as tourists may fail to find order in a strange city in the absence of a map of the city.

The Problem of Knowing

As intriguing and appealing as some of these models of memory may be, none can satisfactorily explain all aspects of the amnesic syndrome. One interesting problem for current theories is that of "knowing when you know." Amnesics commonly appear unaware of their memories. For example, on tests of memory on which amnesics display long-term retention (such as H.M.'s motor-skill retention, illustrated in Figure 15-5), the subjects claim to have no recollection of ever having performed the test before, although they have obviously retained the task. Similarly, amnesics do not suffer from the "tip of the tongue phenomenon" of normal subjects, who "know they know," but are unable to demonstrate the retention. None of the current theories of the amnesic syndrome has been concerned with this striking dissociation between what subjects claim to remember and what they objectively remember. Weiskrantz has insightfully noted that this dissociation may be analogous to the "blindsight" of occipital patients (see Chapter 10); such patients are able to grasp objects in motion while reporting that they failed to see them. Phenomena such as "blindsight" and "knowing but not knowing" suggest that some neuropsychological deficits may occur because different levels or aspects of cognitive processing become dissociated rather than because a given level of processing

totally breaks down. This possibility of course has yet to be proven.

S.: A CASE OF TOTAL RECALL

We would be remiss if having presented H.M., the man who cannot form new memories, we were to close this chapter without mentioning S., the man who could not forget. So remarkable are the contrasts between the two that the neural capacity lost to H.M. through surgery seems to have been present in S. to excess. Of course, the notion is unlikely to ever be confirmed. Nevertheless, if H.M. has in any way shaped our notion of memory, so, too, should S.

S. was a newspaper reporter who never took notes at briefings as did other reporters, and so came to the attention of his employer. When questioned on the matter S. repeated verbatim the transcript of the briefing. S. had not considered himself unusual, although he had wondered why other people relied so much on written notes. Nonetheless, at his employer's urging he went to see a psychologist. In this way S. met Luria, with whom he began a 30-year study of his memory. Luria published an account of this investigation, and to this day *The Mind of the Mnemonist* is one of the most readable accounts of unusual memory.

We can document S.'s memory abilities by referring to Table 15-6. S. could look at this table for two or three minutes and then repeat the table from memory: by columns, by rows, by diagonals, in reverse, in sums, or as a single number. Tested unexpectedly as many as 16 or more years later, S. could repeat the performance without error.

For a good part of his life S. supported himself as a mnemonist, that is, a person who exhibits his memory in performances to audiences. During the course of his work he consigned hundreds of such lists, or lists of names,

TABLE 15-6

Example of tables memorized by S.

6	6	8	0
5	4	3	2
1	6	8	4
7	9	3	5
4	2	3	7
3	8	9	1
1	0	0	2
3	4	5	1
2	7	6	8
1	9	2	6
2	9	6	7
5	5	2	0
X	0	1	X

With only 2–3 minutes study of such a table, S. was able to reproduce it in reverse order, horizontally, vertically, or to reproduce the diagonals.

letters, nonsense syllables, etc., to memory and was able to recall any of these at some later date.

S.'s ability to commit things to memory hinged on three processes. He could visualize the stimuli mentally, recalling them simply by reading them from his internal image. He also made multisensory impressions of things. This ability, called synesthesia, involves processing any sensory event in all sensory modalities simultaneously. Thus, a word was recorded as a sound, a splash of color, an odor, a taste, as well as an object with texture and temperature. Finally, S. used the pegboard technique used by many other mnemonists; that is, he used a number of standard images with which he associated new material. In actuality, whereas most mnemonists used this technique as their primary memory device S. seemed to use it somewhat less, relying more on his internal visual images and his multisensory impressions. Here are some examples of how he saw numbers:

"Even numbers remind me of images. Take the number 1. This is a proud, well-built man; 2 is a

high-spirited woman; 3 a gloomy person (why, I don't know); 6 a man with a swollen foot; 7 a man with a mustache; 8 a very stout woman—a sack within a sack. As for the number 87, what I see is a fat woman and a man twirling his mustache." (Luria, 1968, p. 31)

"For me 2, 4, 6, 5 are not just numbers. They have forms. 1 is a pointed number—which has nothing to do with the way it's written. It's because it's somehow firm and complete. 2 is flatter, rectangular, whitish in color, sometimes almost a gray. 3 is a pointed segment which rotates. 4 is also square and dull; it looks like 2 but has more substance to it, it's thicker. 5 is absolutely complete and takes the form of a cone or a tower—something substantial. 6, the first number after 5, has a whitish hue; 8 somehow has a naive quality, it's milky blue like lime." (Luria, 1968, p. 25)

From Luria's description of S. it seems safe to conclude that there was absolutely no limit to his ability to remember. At least Luria, in the many tests that he gave S., was never able to reach such a limit. What was his ability with respect to short-term memory, long-term memory, and forgetting?

Luria never really tested S. to determine whether he had a short-term memory of the sort that most of us have. That is, once given an item of information did S. forget it a short while later? Luria's report seems to suggest that S. had no short-term memory—everything was put into long-term storage. In fact, S. worried about his inability to forget, and attempted to devise strategies for forgetting. He tried to write things down just as most of us do when we do not wish to carry them about as a memory, but the technique did not work.

"Writing something down means I'll know I won't have to remember it...so I started doing this with small matters like phone numbers, last names, errands of one sort or another. But I got nowhere, for in my mind I continued to see what I'd written....Then I tried writing all the notes on identical kinds of paper, using the same pencil each time. But it still doesn't work." (Luria, 1968, p. 70)

S. tried other strategies: burning the paper in his mind, or putting things on the blackboard and covering them up or erasing them in his mind. But none of these techniques worked either. These statements suggest that S. had no short-term memory; everything was stored as long-term memory.

Did S. forget? We have already said that his long-term memory was amazing, but from Luria's account he did not seem to forget in the same way as the rest of us. When he missed an item it was not because it was forgotten but because it was hidden from view or hard to see. He was always able to find it. Here is how he accounted for some of the items he had missed in a list:

> "I put the image of the *pencil* near a fence ... the one down the street, you know. But what happened was that the image fused with that of the fence and I walked right on past without noticing it. The same thing happened with the word *egg*. I had put it up against a white wall and it blended in with the background. How could I possibly spot a white egg up against a white wall?" (Luria, 1968, p. 36)

S.'s ability to use his imagination was not limited to memorizing things. He could raise his heart rate from 70–72 to 100 beats per minute by imagining that he was exercising, and could lower it to 64–66 by imagining that he was relaxing. He could also raise and lower the temperature of his hand by imagining that it was in warm or cold water. He could deal with pain by imagining that he was no longer in his body; and he could stop his sense of time passing by imagining that the hands of a clock no longer moved. He was even able to dark-

adapt himself in a lighted room by imagining that he was in a darkened room. This incredible control he had over his autonomic system contrasts with H.M., who was reported to show no changes of galvanic skin response even when receiving mild skin shock.

Did S. pay a price for his memory abilities? Luria clearly takes the position that he did. Luria characterizes S. as a person with little aim in life and seemingly dull and superficial. Luria suggests that S. was not able to reason, to categorize, and to see order in things seen by ordinary people. He also had little ability to deal with metaphors, and visualized and interpreted them literally (e.g., to weigh one's words) and so was puzzled by what was meant by them. He had difficulty understanding what was meant by simple statements, and had greater difficulty understanding the sense of poetry.

In summary we can agree with Luria that S. did have an apparently limitless memory. But whether he payed a penalty for it is another matter. Because Luria's assessments of this question were clinical, not experimental, it is impossible to assess in any objective way the nature and degree of S.'s supposed impairment. (In fact, we also had some difficulty with the meaning of poetry given to S. to interpret, and in many other situations we saw ourselves responding as S. did.) We conclude from the case of S., then, not that he paid a price, but that he is a person who has no short-term memory but a limitless long-term memory, and so is just the opposite of H.M., who had a short-term memory but no long-term memory. Whatever explanation of memory eventually evolves from the study of the nervous system it will have to account for each of these extremes.

REFERENCES

Barnes, C. A. Memory deficits associated with senescence: a neurophysiological and behavioral study in the rat. *Journal of Comparative and Physiological Psychology, 93* (1979), 74–104.

Bekhterev, V. M. Demonstration eines Gehirns mit Zerstorung der vorderen und inneren Theile der Hirnrinde beider Schlafenlappen. *Neurol. Zbl., 19* (1900), 990–991.

Bartlett, F. C. *Remembering.* Cambridge: Cambridge University Press, 1932.

Blakemore, C. *Mechanics of the Mind.* Cambridge: Cambridge University Press, 1977.

Bliss, T., and A. Gardner-Medwin. Long-lasting potentiation of synaptic transmission in the dentate area of unanesthetized rabbit following stimulation of the perforant path. *Journal of Physiology, 232* (1973), 357–374.

Broadbent, D. E. *Perception and Communication.* London: Pergamon Press, 1958.

Campbell, B. A., and N. E. Spear. Ontogeny of memory. *Psychological Review, 79* (1972), 215–236.

Chapman, L. F., R. D. Walter, C. H. Markham, R. W. Rand, and P. H. Crandall. Memory changes induced by stimulation of hippocampus or amygdala in epilepsy patients with implanted electrodes. *Transactions of the American Neurological Association, 92* (1967), 50–56.

Cofer, C. N. An historical perspective. In C. N. Cofer, ed. *The Structure of Human Memory.* San Francisco: W. H. Freeman and Company, 1975.

Corkin, S. Tactually-guided maze-learning in man: effects of unilateral cortical excisions and bilateral hippocampal lesions. *Neuropsychologia, 3* (1965), 339–351.

Corkin, S. Acquisition of motor skill after bilateral medial temporal-lobe excision. *Neuropsychologia, 6* (1968), 255–265.

Correll, R. E., and W. B. Scoville. Effects of medial temporal lesions on visual discrimination performance. *Journal of Comparative and Physiological Psychology, 60* (1965), 175–181.

Corsi, P. M. Human memory and the medial temporal region of the brain. Unpublished Ph.D. thesis, McGill University, 1972.

Doty, R. W., and W. H. Overman. Mnemonic role of forebrain commissures in *macaques.* In S. Harnad, R. W. Doty, L. Goldstein, J. Jaynes, and G. Krauthamer, eds. *Lateralization in the Nervous System.* New York: Academic Press, 1977.

Ebbinghaus, H. *Memory.* New York: Teachers College, 1913. (Originally published in 1885. Reprinted by Dover, New York, 1964.)

Fisher, C. M., and R. O. Adams. Transient global amnesia. *Transactions of the American Neurological Association, 83* (1958), 143.

Gaffan, D. Monkeys' recognition memory for complex pictures and the effect of fornix transection. *Quarterly Journal of Experimental Psychology, 29* (1977), 505–514.

Garcia-Bengochea, F., O. de La Torre, and O. Esquivel. The section of the fornix in the surgical treatment of certain epilepsies. *Transactions of the American Neurological Association, 79* (1954), 176–179.

Goddard, G. V. Component properties of the memory machine: Hebb revisited. In P. W. Jusczyk and R. M. Klein, eds. *The Nature of Thought: Essays in Honour of D. O. Hebb.* Hillsdale, N.J.: Lawrence Erlbaum Associates, in press, 1980.

Hebb, D. O. *Organization of Behavior.* New York: John Wiley and Sons, 1949.

Hebb, D. O. Distinctive features of learning in the higher animal. In J. F. Delafresnaye, ed. *Brain Mechanisms and Learning.* London: Blackwell, 1961.

Hebb, D. O. *Textbook of Psychology.* Toronto: W. B. Saunders Co., 1972.

Horel, J. A. The neuroanatomy of amnesia: a critique of the hippocampal memory hypothesis. *Brain, 101* (1978), 403–445.

Horel, J. A., and L. G. Misantone. Visual discrimination impaired by cutting temporal lobe connections. *Science, 193* (1976), 336–338.

Iversen, S. Do hippocampal lesions produce amnesia in animals? *International Review of Neurobiology, 19* (1976), 1–49.

James, W. *The Principles of Psychology.* New York: Henry Holt, 1890.

Jarrard, L. E. Role of interference in retention by rats with hippocampal lesions. *Journal of Comparative and Physiological Psychology, 89* (1975), 400–408.

Jones, M. K. Imagery as a mnemonic aid after left temporal lobectomy: contrast between material-specific and generalized memory disorders. *Neuropsychologia, 12* (1974), 21–30.

Kimura, D. Right temporal-lobe damage: perception of unfamiliar stimuli after damage. *Archives of Neurology, 8* (1963), 264–271.

Kolb, B., and B. Milner. Performance of complex arm and facial movements after focal brain lesions. Unpublished manuscript, 1980.

Kolb, B., I. Q. Whishaw, and R. Barnsley. Neuropsychological aspects of schizophrenia and depression. Progress report to Alberta Mental Health Advisory Council, 1979.

Lashley, K. D. In search of the engram. *Symposia of the Society for Experimental Biology, 4* (1950), 454–482.

Luria, A. R. *The Mind of a Mnemonist.* New York: Basic Books, 1968.

McNaughton, B. L. Dissociation of short- and long-lasting modification of synaptic efficacy at the terminals of the perforant path. Seventh Annual Meeting, *Society for Neuroscience Abstracts, 3* (1977), 517.

Milner, B. Visually-guided maze learning in man: effects of bilateral hippocampal, bilateral frontal, and unilateral cerebral lesions. *Neuropsychologia, 3* (1965), 317–338.

Milner, B. Brain mechanisms suggested by studies of temporal lobes. In F. L. Darley, ed. *Brain Mechanisms Underlying Speech and Language.* New York: Grune and Stratton, 1967.

Milner, B. Visual recognition and recall after right temporal-lobe excision in man. *Neuropsychologia, 6* (1968), 191–209.

Milner, B. Memory and the medial temporal regions of the brain. In K. H. Pribram and D. E. Broadbent, eds. *Biology of Memory.* New York: Academic Press, 1970.

Milner, B. Interhemispheric differences in the localization of psychological processes in man. *British Medical Bulletin, 27* (1971), 272–277.

Milner, B. Disorders of learning and memory after temporal lobe lesions in man. *Clinical Neurosurgery, 19* (1972), 421–446.

Milner, B. Memory. Unpublished neuroscience seminar. Montreal Neurological Institute, 1975.

Milner, B. Psychological aspects of focal epilepsy and its neurosurgical management. *Advances in Neurology, 8* (1975), 299–321.

Milner, B., S. Corkin, and H.-L. Teuber. Further analysis of the hippocampal amnesic syndrome: 14 year follow-up study of H.M. *Neuropsychologia, 6* (1968), 215–234.

Mishkin, M. Visual discrimination performance following partial ablations of the temporal lobe: II. Ventral surface vs. hippocampus. *Journal of Comparative and Physiological Psychology, 147* (1954), 187–193.

Mishkin, M. Memory in monkeys severely impaired by combined but not by separate removal of amygdala and hippocampus. *Nature, 273* (1978), 297–298.

Müller, G. E., and A. Pilzecker. Experimentelle Beitrage zur Lehre vom Gedachtnis. *Zeitschrift für Psychologie, 1* (1900), 1–288.

O'Keefe, J., and L. Nadel. *The Hippocampus as a Cognitive Map.* Oxford: Oxford University Press, 1978.

Olten, D. S., J. A. Walker, and F. Gage. Hippocampal connections and spatial discrimination. *Brain Research, 139* (1978), 255–308.

Penfield, W., and G. Mathieson. An autopsy and a discussion of the role of the hippocampus in experiential recall. *Archives of Neurology, 31* (1974), 145–154.

Penfield, W., and B. Milner. Memory deficit produced by bilateral lesions in the hippocampal zone. *Archives of Neurology and Psychiatry, 79* (1958), 475–497.

Posner, M. I. *Cognition: An Introduction.* Glenview, Ill.: Scott, Foresman, 1973.

Prisko, L. Short-term memory in focal cerebral damage. Unpublished Ph.D. thesis, McGill University, 1963.

Rasmussen, T., and B. Milner. Clinical and surgical studies of cerebral speech areas in man. In K. J. Zulch, O. Creutzfeldt, and G. C. Galbraith, eds. *Cerebral Localization.* Berlin and New York: Springer-Verlag, 1975.

Robertson, A. D., and J. Inglis. The effects of electroconvulsive therapy on human learning and memory. *Canadian Psychological Review, 18* (1977), 285–307.

Sainsbury, R. S., and G. W. Jason. Fimbria-fornix lesions and sexual-social behavior in the guinea pig. *Physiology and Behavior, 17* (1976), 963–967.

Scoville, W. B., and B. Milner. Loss of recent memory after bilateral hippocampal lesions. *Journal of Neurology, Neurosurgery and Psychiatry, 20* (1957), 11–21.

Serafetinides, E. A., R. D. Walter, and D. G. Cherlow. Amnestic confusional phenomena, hippocampal stimulation, and laterality factors. In K. H. Pribram and R. Isaacson, eds. *The Hippocampus.* Vol. II. New York: Plenum Press, 1975.

Shankweiler, D. Defects in recognition and reproduction of familiar tunes after unilateral temporal lobectomy. Paper presented at the 37th Annual Meeting of the Eastern Psychological Association, New York, 1966.

Shipley, J. E., and B. Kolb. Neuronal correlates of species-typical behavior in the Syrian Golden Hamster. *Journal of Comparative and Physiological Psychology, 91* (1977), 1056–1073.

Squire, L. R. A stable impairment in remote memory following electroconvulsive therapy. *Neuropsychologia, 13* (1975), 51–58.

Talland, G. A. *The Pathology of Memory.* New York: Academic Press, 1969.

Taylor, L. Localization of cerebral lesions by psychological testing. *Clinical Neurosurgery, 16* (1969), 269–287.

Warrington, E., and M. James. An experimental investigation of facial recognition in patients with unilateral cerebral lesions. *Cortex, 3* (1967), 317–326.

Warrington, E. K., and L. Weiskrantz. An analysis of short-term and long-term memory defects in man. In J. A. Deutsch, ed. *The Physiological Basis of Memory.* New York: Academic Press, 1973.

Warrington, E. K., and L. Weiskrantz. Further analysis of the prior learning effect in amnesic patients. *Neuropsychologia, 16* (1978), 169–177.

Weiskrantz, L. A comparison of hippocampal pathology in man and other animals. *Functions of the Septo-Hippocampal System,* Ciba Foundation Symposium. Amsterdam: Elsevier, 1978.

Weiskrantz, L., and E. K. Warrington. The problem of the amnesic syndrome in man and animals. In K. H. Pribram and R. Isaacson, eds. *The Hippocampus.* Vol. II. New York: Plenum Press, 1975.

Whitty, C. W. M., and O. L. Zangwill. Traumatic amnesia. In C. W. M. Whitty and O. L. Zangwill, eds. *Amnesia.* London: Butterworths, 1966.

Winocur, G., and C. B. Breckenridge. Cue-dependent behavior of hippocampally damaged rats in a complex maze. *Journal of Comparative and Physiological Psychology, 82* (1973), 512–522.

Woolsey, R. M., and J. S. Nelson. Asymptomatic destruction of the fornix in man. *Archives of Neurology, 32* (1975), 566–568.

Yerkes, R. M. The intelligence of earthworms. *Journal of Animal Behavior, 2* (1912), 332–352.

Zangwill, O. L. Remembering revisited. *Quarterly Journal of Experimental Psychology, 24* (1972), 123–138.

16

NEURAL MECHANISMS OF LANGUAGE

It is tempting to analyze the neurological correlates of language functions by considering the theoretical sensory-integrative, memory, and motor functions of the respective regions of association cortex discussed in the last three chapters. The activity of the association cortex of the left hemisphere integrates, however, to form a functional language system that is far more complex than an isolated analysis of the parietal, temporal, and frontal lobes would suggest. Thus, details of the neural mechanisms of language have been among the most difficult of the brain's functions to study. This difficulty has been compounded by the absence of language in other species, making models of the neural correlates of language difficult to test experimentally. In this chapter we briefly review the history of thought regarding the neurological basis of language, examine the cortical and subcortical speech zones as mapped by stimulation and lesion studies, consider disorders of language and theoretical models of language, and, finally, examine the phylogenetic origins of language.

HISTORICAL VIEWS

A brief review of the historical development of ideas about language function is the most effective approach to studying the organization of the neurological basis of language function. In the early 1800s, Gall, in his phrenology, was the first to propose a relationship between localized regions of the brain and specific behaviors. Bouillard agreed with Gall and attempted to provide clinical proof that the organ of language resided in the anterior lobes of the brain. Indeed, in 1825 Bouillard even proposed asymmetry of brain function, suggesting that the left hemisphere had a special role in complex movement such as fencing, writing, and speech. This proposal was supported a little later by Dax, in 1836, when he described a series of cases demonstrating that disorders of language were consistently associated with lesions of the left hemisphere. Although the hypothesis that speech is localized in the frontal lobe of the left hemisphere was revived in 1861 by Auburtin, it was Broca who provided the anatomical proof of the theory, and it is an irony of science that the anterior speech zone became known as Broca's area. The primary disturbance resulting from damage to Broca's area appeared to be a defect in the motor component of speech production. In 1875 Wernicke demonstrated that a lesion in the temporal-parietal cortex produced a form of language disturbance that differed from that described by Broca. This region became known as Wernicke's area. Wernicke proposed that Broca's area was the center of language production, whereas Wernicke's area was the center of language understanding. Wernicke's proposals led to a flurry of "brain diagrams" in the late 1800s, each purporting to describe how lesions to Broca's and Wernicke's areas, as well as associated regions and their interconnections, could produce specific disturbances in language functions.

Although the localizationists held the dominant view at the turn of the century, there were dissenting voices, most notably those of Hughlings-Jackson, Freud, Marie, and Head. Hughlings-Jackson contended that language was a dynamic process that derived from the integrated function of the whole brain, and although he conceded a special role for the left hemisphere in language, he believed that the right hemisphere and subcortical structures must also play a significant role in language function. He argued that the more complex a task was, the greater the number of regions and structures in the brain that were involved. For example, the ability to write one's name involved a much smaller, more localized brain region than the ability to write a book. Thus, a person might be unable to write a book after damage to virtually any region of the association cortex, but the ability to write one's name would be impaired only by a restricted lesion in the temporal-parietal cortex. By the 1920s the pendulum had swung in favor of a holistic view of language function, especially after the publication of Head's elegant and influential attack on localizationists in 1926. Not until the 1950s and '60s did the localizationist view of language function regain credibility, primarily through Geschwind's theoretical writings.

Today it is reasonable to say that the primary language functions of the brain are housed in broadly defined language zones in the left hemisphere, including Broca's and Wernicke's areas, as well as in other zones of association cortex within the left hemisphere, especially the tertiary zone of the left temporal cortex. Lesser, and poorly understood, roles are played by the association cortex of the right hemisphere and by subcortical structures, including especially the basal ganglia and posterior thalamus. This view of the neurology of language thus represents a compromise between the extremes of inflexible wiring diagrams of the late 1800s and the holistic views of the 1920s.

SPEECH ZONES AS MAPPED BY STIMULATION AND ABLATION

The zones of the neocortex involved in language, and particularly in speech, have been identified by careful investigations of the effects both of cortical stimulation during surgery and of the effects of surgery on behavior. Accumulating results from hundreds of patients has made it possible to construct statistically defined regions of the neocortex specifically concerned with language processes.

Electrical Stimulation

The investigations undertaken by Penfield and his associates on patients undergoing surgical treatment of epilepsy were the first to clearly identify the extent of the neocortical speech zones. Subsequent work by others has confirmed Penfield's findings, and has clarified and extended them by the use of more quantitative behavioral recording techniques. The major findings are as follows:

1. Stimulation of a number of cortical areas (Figure 16-1) with a low-voltage electric current interferes with speech. These areas include the classical areas of Broca and Wernicke in the left hemisphere, as well as the sensory and motor representations of the face in both hemispheres and in a region known as the supplementary motor area, or M II, of both hemispheres. (See Figure 6-3 for an illustration of the organization of M II.)

2. Penfield and Roberts conclude that stimulation produces two effects on speech:

a. Positive effects, meaning vocalization, which is not speech but rather a sustained or interrupted vowel cry, such as "Oh...." Vocalization can be elicited by stimulation of either the face area or the supplementary motor region of either hemisphere.

b. Negative effects, meaning the inability to vocalize or to use words properly. These include a variety of aphasia-like errors:

i. Total arrest of speech or an inability to vocalize spontaneously; this occurs from stimulation throughout the shaded zones in Figure 16-1.

ii. Hesitation and slurring of speech: hesitation occurs from stimulation throughout the zones of Figure 16-1; slurring occurs primarily from stimulation of the face area in either hemisphere.

iii. Distortion and repetition of words and syllables; distortion differs from slurring in that the distorted sound is an unintelligible noise rather than a word. These effects occur primarily from stimulation of the classical speech zones, although occasionally from the face area as well.

iv. Confusion of numbers while count-

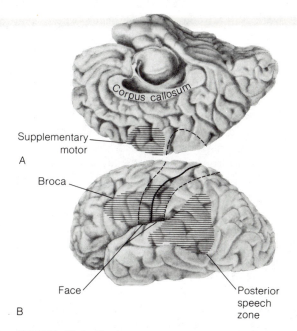

FIGURE 16-1. Shaded areas indicate the zones in which electrical stimulation may interfere with speech. Note that the posterior area is much larger than the classical Wernicke's area. Speech is also disrupted by stimulation in the face or supplementary motor area of the right hemisphere. A. The medial view of the left hemisphere. B. The lateral view of the left hemisphere.

ing; for example, a patient may jump from "six" to "nineteen" to "four" and so on. Confusion in counting results from stimulation of Broca's or Wernicke's area.

v. Inability to name despite retained ability to speak. "An example is 'That is a...I know. That is a...' When the current was removed, the patient named the picture correctly. Another example is, 'Oh, I know what it is. That is what you put in your shoes.' After withdrawal of the stimulating electrodes, the patient immediately said 'foot'" (Penfield and Roberts, 1959, p. 123). Naming difficulties arise from stimulation throughout the anterior (Broca's) and posterior (Wernicke's) speech zones.

vi. Misnaming; may occur when the patient uses words related in sound such as "camel" for "comb," uses synonyms such as "cutters" for "scissors," or perseverates by using the same name twice. For example, a picture of a bird may be named correctly but the next picture, a table, is also called a bird. Misnaming, like naming difficulties, occurs during stimulation of both the anterior and posterior speech zones.

3. Ojemann and Mateer report that during stimulation in the region of Broca's area, patients are unable to make voluntary facial movements similar to those illustrated in Figure 14-6. Curiously, stimulation of these same points may also disrupt phonemic discrimination as measured by the phonetic differentiation test described in Chapter 14. These authors also describe defects in short-term memory resulting from stimulation in roughly the zone identified from lesion studies and described in Figure 15-11.

4. Most reports agree that the extent of the cortical language zones as marked by stimulation varies considerably among subjects, although there is little indication of what this variation may reflect. In this regard, it would seem worthwhile to correlate the size of the speech zones with performance on a variety of verbal tests. Perhaps verbal ability is positively correlated with language ability, a suggestion that has intuitive appeal but which is obviously speculative and remains to be proven.

Several important conclusions can be drawn from these results. First, the data do not support strict localizationist models of language, since stimulation of the anterior and posterior speech zones has remarkably similar effects upon speech functions. Second, stimulation of the neocortex much beyond the classical areas of Broca and Wernicke disturbs speech functions. The area involved is remarkably similar to the speech zones defined more recently by the regional blood-flow studies (see Chapter 9). Compare, for example, Figures 9-4 and 16-1. Third, stimulation of the speech zones affects more than just talking, for there are deficits in voluntary motor control of facial musculature as well as of short-term memory. Fourth, removal of the cortex surrounding the posterior speech zone mapped in Figure 16-1 does not produce lasting aphasia, even though fibers connecting the visual areas to the speech regions may be disrupted. Thus, it seems clear that these connections are not essential in the coordination of these two areas. Fifth, it has proven difficult to classify the transient aphasia following surgery, because each patient appears to be unique. There is also little evidence for a distinctive type of aphasia associated specifically with damage to either the anterior or posterior speech zones. In other words, there is no evidence for pure motor or sensory aphasias as postulated by Wernicke. Sixth, chronic speech and language deficits occur only if lesions are made within the classical speech zones (see Figure 16-2). Although stimulation of the face areas and supplementary motor zones produces speech arrest, removal of these zones has no chronic effect on speech. Recall, however, that face-area lesions do chronically impair other language functions (see Chapter 14).

One issue arising from the study of lesion patients is the relative importance of the anterior and posterior speech zones. Recall that in 1906 Marie published his celebrated paper claiming that Broca's area played no special role in language. His conclusion was based on the study of cases in which there appeared to be destruction of Broca's area without aphasia, and of cases in which there was Broca's aphasia without damage to Broca's area. Marie undoubtedly overstated his case, but his point

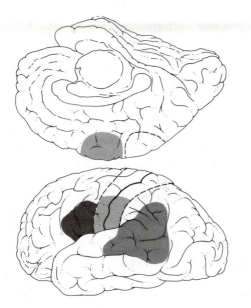

FIGURE 16-2. Summary of the effects of lesions on speech. Damage to the darker two areas produces chronic aphasia; damage to the lighter areas produces transient aphasia; and damage beyond these areas does not produce aphasia.

was well taken and led to a controversy that persists to this day. We are inclined to agree with Zangwill's suggestion that although Broca's area undoubtedly plays a significant role in the normal control of articulate speech, damage to the area does not have the severe consequences on language that lesions in the posterior speech zone have. Furthermore, the severity of aphasia is far more variable following lesions to Broca's area than to Wernicke's area. Some Broca's-area patients may have only mild articulatory disorders, whereas others have severe disturbances of both expression and comprehension. Jefferson was probably correct in his suggestion that this variability reflects the extent of subcortical damage in addition to the damage to Broca's area itself.

Subcortical Components in Language

At the same time that Broca was describing a cortical center for speech control, Hughlings-Jackson proposed that subcortical structures were critical to language. In 1866 he wrote: "I think it will be found that the nearer the disease is to the corpus striatum, the more likely is the defect of articulation to be the striking thing, and the farther off, the more likely it is to be one of mistakes of words." Although he was the first to propose that aphasias result from subcortical damage, this proposition was not seriously considered until 1959, when Penfield and Roberts proposed that the thalamus, especially the **pulvinar,** functions to coordinate the activity of the cortical speech zones. In recent years evidence from stimulation and lesion studies has supported Hughlings-Jackson's proposal, although the importance and the precise role of the thalamus is still under debate.

In the course of surgical treatment of **dyskinesia,** electrodes are placed in the thalamus and an electric current applied in order to precisely define the electrode's position. For example, movements evoked by stimulation would indicate placement in motor thalamus, whereas somatosensory changes such as tingling sensations in the skin would indicate placement in the somatosensory thalamus. When the electrode is properly placed, a stronger current is passed, producing a lesion intended to relieve the dyskinesia. Careful study of language functions during these procedures, especially by Ojemann and by Cooper and their respective colleagues, has indicated that the pulvinar and the lateral posterior-lateral central complex of the left thalamus have a role in language not shared by other subcortical structures (see Figure 1-14). Stimulation of the left ventrolateral and pulvinar nuclei of the thalamus produce speech arrest, difficulties in naming, **perseveration,** and a reduced speed of talking. Stimulation has also been reported to produce positive effects on memory, because it improves later retrieval of words heard during stimulation. As a result it has been proposed that the thalamus has some role in activating or arousing the cortex.

Lesions of the ventrolateral thalamus and/or pulvinar on the left have been associated with a variety of disturbances of speech and language processes. Symptoms include postoperative dysphasia, which is usually transitory; increased verbal response latency; decreases in voice volume; alterations in speaking rate and slurring or hesitation in speech; as well as impaired performance on tests of verbal IQ and memory.

To summarize, there is evidence that the left posterior thalamus, including the pulvinar, lateral posterior, and lateral ventral regions, has a significant role in language. The nature of this role is still uncertain.

DISORDERS OF LANGUAGE

Before the neurology of language is given a theoretical description, the disorders of language must first be considered, since theoretical formulations of language function must be able to account for the disorders observed. We first describe the types of deficits observed in language and then consider the classification of aphasias.

Language Deficits and Neurological Damage

Normal language depends upon a complex interaction among sensory integration and symbolic association, motor skills, learned syntactic patterns, and verbal memory. **Aphasia** refers to a disorder of language apparent in speech, writing (**agraphia**), or reading (**alexia**) produced by injury to brain areas specialized for these functions. Thus, disturbances of language due to severe intellectual impairment, loss of sensory input (especially vision and hearing), or paralysis or incoordination of the musculature of the mouth (**anarthria**) or hand (for writing) are not considered to be aphasic disturbances. These disorders may accompany aphasia, and complicate the study of it.

Goodglass and Kaplan have broken language disturbances down into nine basic types, which we have subgrouped into disturbances of comprehension and of production of language.

Disorders of Comprehension. Disorders of comprehension can be either auditory or visual, each related to the sensory modality of presentation of verbal material.

1. *Auditory comprehension.* Comprehension of auditory input may be disturbed even though the primary auditory cortex per se is not damaged. For example, a patient may act as though a word was not heard at all (so-called word deafness) or as though only fragments of the word were heard. The more common defect is not in failing to recognize that a word was spoken but rather in failing to attach meaning to the word (much as if the word were spoken in a foreign language unknown to the hearer). In some cases auditory comprehension is particularly impaired when words are presented in isolation rather than in the context of a sentence. In some aphasics comprehension of individual words is intact, but certain grammatical constructions are not discriminated properly. For example, the phrases "the lost man's wallet" and "the man's lost wallet" involve the same words but have totally different meanings.

2. *Visual comprehension.* Because compre-

hension of written material (i.e., reading) is based on prior mastery of auditory language, it is not surprising that deficits in reading (*alexia*) accompany deficits in auditory comprehension. A disturbance of reading is commonly associated with impaired comprehension of auditory material, but these two symptoms may occur independently of one another. As with auditory defects, defects in visual comprehension may involve a deficit in recognizing individual letters or words as being letters or words, or a deficit in attaching meaning to the symbols written on a page.

Disorders of Production. There are at least seven disorders of production, which range from an inability to form words to an inability to place words together to form a spoken or written sentence.

1. *Articulation.* Speaking requires the ability to make the sounds of vowels and consonants, which will then be placed in different combinations to form words and sentences. Patients with severe deficits in articulation are unable to produce simple sounds, even by imitation. Noises may actually be produced, but frequently each attempt to form a word produces the same nonsense syllable. In milder forms the patient may be able to articulate many sounds, especially vowel sounds, but usually will have extreme difficulty in making difficult sounds such as consonant blends. For example, one man that we saw would say "huah" for "ch" and "buh" for "bl." Deficits in articulation may result from any of three different causes. First, there may be a defect in the peripheral speech mechanisms of the larynx, pharynx, and tongue. This disorder is not an aphasia but is termed **dysarthria**. Second, there may be a defect in choosing the desired sound from all those available in a person's repertoire. Third, there may be a deficit in the motor system that prevents the desired sound from being properly pronounced.

2. *Word finding.* Words are formed by combining sounds; to do this correctly it is necessary to choose the appropriate words from the large available repertoire. Virtually all aphasics suffer from some restriction in the repertoire of words available, and even when words are produced it takes longer than normal to do so. If this difficulty in finding words occurs in the absence of other aphasic symptoms, the disorder is called **anomia**. Difficulty in word finding often results in the person's deliberately choosing a word that approximates the intended idea when the intended word cannot be found. For example, one woman we saw substituted words such as "cow" for "milk" and "cigar" for "pipe."

3. *Paraphasia.* Goodglass and Kaplan define **paraphasia** as the production of unintended syllables, words, or phrases during the effort to speak. Paraphasia differs from difficulties in articulation in that sounds are correctly articulated, but they are the wrong sounds, and either distort the intended word (e.g., "pike" instead of "pipe") or produce a completely unintended word (e.g., "my mother" instead of "my wife").

4. *Loss of grammar and syntax.* Words must be placed together to produce proper grammar and syntax. Some patients are totally unable to place words together into grammatically correct sequences, and so restrict their sentences to short utterances of two or three words. Choosing correct verb tenses may be especially difficult, in which case nearly all verbs are in the present tense, usually of a simple form such as "He go." It is curious that many of these aphasics are able to produce long strings of memorized sequences such as in counting numbers or reciting days of the week and months of the year; and some patients can even recite previously learned poetry or prayers. And some can even repeat sentences they have just heard. The preservation of these abilities, however, in the face of

inability to produce spontaneous sentences, demonstrates that some associative ability is missing or seriously impaired.

5. *Repetition.* Although many aphasics can repeat aurally presented material, others cannot, even though other language functions may appear fairly intact. Disorders of repetition may result either from deficits in comprehension or articulation—in which case there are associated aphasic symptoms—or from a selective dissociation between auditory-input and speech-output systems. In this latter case, of selective dissociation, the disorder of repetition may be the only significant language disturbance, and may go unnoticed except through special testing.

6. *Verbal fluency.* Verbal fluency is the ability to produce words in uninterrupted strings. Low verbal fluency may be associated with word-finding difficulty, or may occur in the absence of any other language disturbances. Recall that frontal lesions, even on the right, may reduce word output even though no other deficits in language use or production are known.

7. *Writing.* Writing, one of the most complex of language abilities, may be disturbed in a wide variety of ways. First, it may result from disturbance in movement of the limb to produce letters and words—although this disorder would not be a disturbance of language per se. At a more complex level, writing may be impossible (*agraphia*) because of inability to recall the form of letters or the correct movements necessary to produce them. Many of the deficits observed in oral language may also occur in written language, as in **paragraphia,** which is the writing of the incorrect word, or in perseveration, which would involve writing the same word repeatedly.

Classification of Aphasias

Since the time of Wernicke people have attempted to describe different types of aphasias by identifying clusters of symptoms associated with particular brain lesions. This has proven to be a difficult task, partially because so few cases are thoroughly studied, and partially because so few well-studied cases ever come to autopsy. Thus, there is constant debate over which lesions produce which cluster of aphasic symptoms. Although many authors have considered different types of aphasias to be totally independent of one another, there is no convincing empirical proof of this claim. As Brown puts it:

> ...all disorders of speech understanding, even those with the most limited pathology, are likely to have an expressive element, while some defect in speech comprehension should be a constant feature of the motor aphasias. The importance of this finding has certainly not received proper attention in the literature. One need only point to the fact that there is not one careful study of speech comprehension in restricted cases of Broca's aphasia, nor a comparable study, of the much rarer word-deafness, of the true state of expressive speech. (Brown, 1972, p. 14)

In spite of the considerable disagreement over the number of types of aphasias, there are at least five that most authors agree upon. These are summarized in Table 16-1, and we now discuss each.

Broca's Aphasia. In Broca's aphasia the patient has difficulty speaking, although he or she continues to understand speech. Broca's aphasia is also known as motor, expressive, or nonfluent aphasia. This aphasia features a pattern of speech in which a person speaks in a very slow, deliberate manner with very simple grammatical structure. Thus, all forms of a verb are likely to be reduced to the infinitive or a participle. Nouns are most apt to be expressed only in the singular, and conjunctions, adjectives, adverbs, and articles are very uncommon. Only the key words necessary for communication are used.

TABLE 16-1

Classification of aphasias[a]

Type of aphasia	Spontaneous speech	Comprehension	Repetition	Naming
1. Broca's aphasia Motor aphasia Nonfluent aphasia Expressive aphasia	Nonfluent	Intact	Limited	Limited
2. Wernicke's aphasia Sensory aphasia	Fluent	Impaired	Impaired	Impaired
3. Conduction aphasia	Fluent	Intact	Impaired	Impaired
4. Isolation syndrome Transcortical aphasia	Fluent	Impaired	Intact	Impaired
5. Anomic aphasic Amnesic aphasia	Fluent	Intact	Intact	Impaired

[a] Note that these aphasias are not totally independent of one another.
Based in part on Green, 1969.

There is still no adequate explanation for Broca's aphasia. Broca assumed that the problem was an impairment of the "motor image of the word," but it is uncertain what this supposition implies about brain function. Certainly, however, the deficit is not one of making sounds, but rather one of switching from one sound to another.

Wernicke's Aphasia. Classically, **Wernicke's,** or **sensory, aphasia** consists of an inability to comprehend words or to arrange sounds into coherent speech. Luria has proposed that this type of aphasia has three characteristics. First, to hear and make out the sounds of speech, one must be able to qualify sounds—that is, to include sounds in a system of phonemes that are the basic units of speech in a given language. An example will illustrate: in the Japanese language the sounds "l" and "r" are not distinguished; a Japanese hearing English cannot distinguish these sounds because the necessary template is not in the brain. Thus, although this distinction is perfectly clear to English-speaking persons, it is not to

native Japanese. This is precisely the problem that a person with Wernicke's aphasia has in his or her own language: the inability to isolate the significant phonematic characteristics and classification of sounds into known phonematic systems. The second characteristic of Wernicke's aphasia is that there is a defect in speech. The patient can speak, and may speak a lot, but confuses phonematic characteristics, producing a phenomenon often called word salad. The third characteristic is an impairment in writing. A patient who cannot discern phonematic characteristics cannot be expected to write, because he or she does not know the graphemes that combine to form a word.

Conduction Aphasia. Conduction aphasia is a paradoxical deficit: patients can speak easily, can name objects, and can understand speech, but cannot repeat words. The simplest explanation for this problem is that there is a disconnection of the "perceptual word image" in the parietal-temporal cortex and the "motor word image" of the frontal cortex. This explanation is not very convincing. There has never been any clear proof that cutting the connections actually causes this syndrome. And there is considerable debate over whether this symptom really occurs in the absence of other symptoms, especially impaired short-term memory.

Isolation Syndrome, or Transcortical Aphasia. Isolation syndrome, or **transcortical aphasia,** is a curious type of aphasia in which patients can repeat and understand words as well as name objects but cannot speak spontaneously. Or they are also unable to comprehend words although they can still repeat them. This type of aphasia is presumed to be caused by loss of the secondary sensory cortex (association cortex). Comprehension could be poor because words fail to arouse associations. Production of meaningful speech could be poor because even though the production of words is normal, words are not associated to other cognitive activity in the brain.

Anomic Aphasia. Patients with anomic aphasia comprehend speech, produce meaningful speech, and can repeat speech, but have great difficulty finding the names of objects. For example, we saw a patient who when shown the picture of a ship anchor simply could not think of the name and finally said, "I know what it does.... You use it to anchor a ship." Although he had actually used the word as a verb he was unable to use it as a noun. This symptom is most likely to result from a lesion in the angular gyrus, but nearly all aphasics have some naming difficulties. Luria and Hutton emphasize that this type of aphasia cannot be explained simply; it appears likely that the same symptom may result from any one of three causes. First, to name an object one must identify its distinguishing characteristics. A person having difficulties isolating these characteristics will not name it properly. Second, to name an object, having

isolated its characteristics, one must also develop the auditory form of the word. Thus, a person who does not retain the word's auditory structure will be unable to produce it. Finally, to produce the word, one must select the appropriate word from those expressing ideas closely associated with it. For example, when asked to name a butterfly, a person may have difficulty choosing the correct word from associated words such as moth, fly, insect, etc. In failing to do so the person may utter the word moth or even bird. Clearly this problem is quite different from the inability to identify distinguishing characteristics. It is possible that each of these three naming problems represents a separate neurological deficit, but this possibility is rather difficult to prove.

NEUROLOGICAL MODELS OF LANGUAGE

We noted earlier that there have been two major theoretical positions on the neurology of language: localizationism and non-localizationism. Although neither position is completely tenable today, in recent years Geschwind's reformulation and clarification of Wernicke's localization model has proven conceptually useful, forming a basis for more moderate positions on the neurology of language function.

The Wernicke-Geschwind Model

The Wernicke-Geschwind model is built on the assumption that the neural basis of speech and language involves the following structures: Broca's area, Wernicke's area, the arcuate fasciculus (which connects Broca's area with Wernicke's area), the precentral and postcentral face area, the angular gyrus, and the auditory and visual cortex (see Figure 16-3). Broca's area is assumed to house pro-

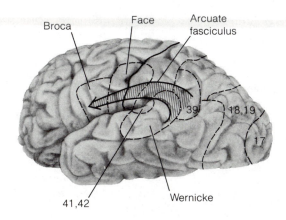

1 Spoken word ⟶ Area 41,42 ⟶ Wernicke (area 22) ⟶ Hear and comprehend word

2 Cognition ⟶ Wernicke ⟶ Broca ⟶ Face ⟶ Cranial Nerves ⟶ Speak

3 Written word ⟶ Area 17 ⟶ Area 18,19 ⟶ Area 39 (angular G) ⟶ Wernicke ⟶ Read

FIGURE 16-3. Geschwind's model of the neurology of language, showing the regions of the cortex involved. Items 1–3 show how the model explains different language functions.

grams for the complex coordination of muscles for speech; Wernicke's area, the mechanism for transforming auditory input into meaningful units, or words; the arcuate fasciculus joins the anterior and posterior speech zones; the face area directs the movements of the face, tongue, etc.; the angular gyrus combines sensory input to house "visual patterns" of letters, words, etc., and acts in some way to convert a visual stimulus into the appropriate auditory form. Geschwind has neatly summarized how these parts of the cortex function in the production of language.

When a word is heard, the output from the primary auditory area of the cortex is received by Wernicke's area. If the word is to be spoken, the pattern is transmitted from Wernicke's area to Broca's area, where the articulatory form is aroused and passed on to the motor area that controls the movement of the muscles of speech. If the spoken word is to be spelled, the auditory pattern is passed to the angular gyrus, where it elicits the visual pattern. When a word is read, the output from the primary visual areas passes to the angular gyrus, which in turn arouses the corresponding auditory form of the word in Wernicke's area. It should be noted that in most people comprehension of a written word involves arousal of the auditory form in Wernicke's area. Wernicke argued that this was the result of the way most people learn written language. He thought, however, that in people who were born deaf, but had learned to read, Wernicke's area would not be in the circuit.

According to this model, if Wernicke's area is damaged, the person would have difficulty comprehending both spoken and written language. He should be unable to speak, repeat, and write correctly. The fact that in such cases speech is fluent and well articulated suggests that Broca's area is intact but receiving inadequate information. If the damage were in Broca's area, the effect of the lesion would be to disrupt articulation. Speech would be slow and labored but comprehension should remain intact. (Geschwind, 1972, p. 344)

Further, damage to the arcuate fasciculus would not be expected to disturb either the comprehension or production of speech, but rather should make it difficult to repeat speech, because the auditory recognition and speech-production regions would be disconnected.

Two other abilities can be considered in this model: reading and writing. In theory, these abilities require the integrity of the angular gyrus to act as a way station between the visual and auditory regions (see Figure 16-3). To be meaningful, visual input must be translated into auditory form in this region. Similarly, before a word can be written, the auditory input must be translated into visual form. Thus, patients with lesions of the angular gyrus would be expected to be unable to either read or write. Although these patients can speak and can comprehend speech, they cannot recognize a word spelled aloud, nor can they spell a word aloud.

Problems with the Wernicke-Geschwind Model

However popular and useful the Wernicke-Geschwind model of language function has been, its rigid localizationist bias leaves it open to a number of criticisms. (1) As we described earlier, stimulation of speech zones does not always interrupt speech, and when speech is interrupted, the interruption is of the same type in both the anterior and posterior speech zones. Indeed, Ojemann has recently found that stimulation-induced naming errors are more likely to occur from stimulation of the anterior speech zone than of the posterior zone! Furthermore, Ojemann and Mateer report that stimulation of the same sites disrupted both the production of sequential oral-facial movements and the ability to discriminate phonemes such as "la" and "ba." The apparent functional homogeneity within widespread regions of the speech zones is difficult to reconcile with a strict localizationist view of language function. Different effects would have been expected from different portions of the speech circuitry. (2) Studies of lesion patients do not support a distinction between disorders of language production and understanding, since both expressive and receptive speech disorders are present in all aphasic patients with naturally occurring lesions, and surgical destruction of portions of the language zones seldom results in permanent aphasia. (3) The model does not include subcortical components of language, regions that play a significant, even if poorly understood, role in language. (4) The studies of Penfield and of Rasmussen and their colleagues indicate that the corticocortical connections from the visual and auditory regions to the speech zones, and the arcuate fasciculus joining the speech zones themselves, can apparently be surgically removed without incurring aphasia. This observation contradicts Geschwind's case studies, which show that accidental lesions of the cortex surrounding Wernicke's area produce aphasia. This discrepancy is explained by the considerable difference between the lesions in the patients studied by Geschwind and those done surgically. For example, the surgical lesions are shallower, bleed less, and are precise and restricted to the cortex; natural lesions almost certainly include subcortical damage, and remaining cortex may function abnormally.

In summary, although the Wernicke-Geschwind model of localization of language function is conceptually useful, it presents several serious difficulties. Other models have been proposed in recent years (e.g., those of Brown, of Caplan and Marshall, and of

Whitaker), but none is totally acceptable. A comprehensive model of language function must incorporate stimulation and lesion data, and include subcortical structures as well as mechanisms of affective control. Such a model will not be possible until more is known about each of these functions.

ASSESSMENT OF APHASIA

Since the Second World War there has been widespread interest in establishing a standard systematic procedure of aphasia assessment, for use both in providing standardized clinical descriptions of patients, and in facilitating comparison of patient populations in neuropsychological research. In the past 20 years a number of manuals on aphasia testing have appeared. Table 16-2 summarizes the most widely used. The first group of tests are considered to be test batteries, for they provide a large number of subtests designed to systematically explore the language capabilities of the subject. They typically include tests of: (1) auditory and visual comprehension; (2) oral and written expression including tests of repetition, reading, naming, and fluency; and (3) conversational speech. Because these test batteries have the disadvantage of being lengthy and they require special training to administer, some brief aphasia screening tests have been devised. The two most popular, the Halstead-Wepman and the token test, are frequently used as part of standard neuropsychological test batteries (Chapter 21), being short and easy to administer and to score. These tests do not replace detailed examination of the aphasia test batteries, but can be used to identify language disorders. If a fine description of the linguistic deficits is desired, the more comprehensive aphasia batteries must be given.

TABLE 16-2

Summary of the major tests of aphasia

Test	Basic reference
Aphasia test batteries	
Boston diagnostic aphasia test	Goodglass and Kaplan, 1972
Functional communicative profile	Sarno, 1969
Neurosensory center comprehensive examination for aphasia	Spreen and Benton, 1969
Porch index of communicative ability	Porch, 1967
Minnesota test for differential diagnosis of aphasia	Schuell, 1965
Wepman-Jones language modalities test for aphasia	Wepman and Jones, 1961
Aphasia screening tests	
Halstead-Wepman aphasia screening test	Halstead and Wepman, 1959
Token test	de Renzi and Vignolo, 1962

PHYLOGENETIC ORIGINS OF SPEECH AND LANGUAGE

Although no nonhuman primates have a verbal language analogous to the human's, one approach to the study of human language is to attempt to trace the phylogenetic origins of speech. Some recent demonstrations of languagelike processes in apes have generated interest in this approach, and the results have important implications for understanding human brain function—and may also have practical applications. For example, are there alternate forms of communication that can be substituted for the lost speech of the aphasic? In this section we will consider the evidence for languagelike processes in apes, the theories of the phylogenetic development of language, and the applications to humans of research on phylogenetic origins of language in nonhumans.

Evidence for Languagelike Processes in Apes

Several people have tried to teach chimpanzees to talk. The most persistent attempts were undertaken by Hayes and by the Kelloggs, who raised chimps in their homes with the idea that they might learn to talk if raised with humans from birth. They did not. Viki, Hayes's chimp, with extensive training, learned to make noises for about four words, none of them properly formed. For example, the word "cup" sounded like "krup" when Viki "said" it. These early studies were dismal failures in view of the obvious neurological similarity between apes and humans. Then in the 1960s two totally new approaches appeared virtually simultaneously. Both were based on the premise that auditory communication must be bypassed and something visual used. The Gardners pioneered the use of American Sign Language (Ameslan); Premack used plastic symbols. It is interesting that Yerkes, in 1925, first proposed the idea of teaching sign language to chimps. The notion was apparently not considered a worthwhile endeavor!

The Gardners began by bringing Washoe, a year-old chimp, into their home. The aim was to teach Washoe the hand movements, or signs, that refer to various objects or actions (known as exemplars) that are found in Ameslan. These signing gestures, analogous to words in spoken language, have specific movements that begin and end in a prescribed manner in relation to the signer's body (see Figure 16-4). The Gardners molded Washoe's hands to form the desired shapes in the presence of the exemplar of the sign, reinforcing her for correct movements. In addition, rather than using verbal language, the Gardners used Ameslan to communicate with one another in Washoe's presence. Thus, Washoe was raised in an environment filled with signs. Washoe learned, and learned well. She was able to correctly sign for objects and to ask for objects with high accuracy. Most of her errors were in the same class. For example, she might use the sign for cat when identifying a dog.

Washoe also picked up signs by observing the signing of others. One example was the sign for "smoke." Apparently several of the workers on the project smoked, and, using Ameslan, they would request, in front of Washoe, smokes (cigarettes) from fellow workers. Washoe was fascinated by smoking, and soon added the sign to her vocabulary. Another example was the sign for toothbrush. This sign is made by moving an extended forefinger back and forth in front of the teeth. Washoe learned this sign on her own as well. Washoe's signing did not include nouns only but also pronouns and action verbs. For example, she could sign statements such as "you go me," meaning "come with me."

Two questions are whether chimpanzees generalize the use of specific signs, and whether they can make up their own signs. In one experiment to test this question, a chimp had been taught five food-related signs including: food, fruit, drink, candy, and banana. The test was to show her new fruits and vegetables and to ask her what they were. The result was fascinating, as a couple of examples will illustrate: when a radish was shown, the chimp (who had previously eaten radishes) signed "cry-hurt-food"; for a watermelon she signed "candy-drink" or "drink-fruit." The sign "fruit" was used 85 percent of the time to label fruit, but only 15 percent of the time for vegetables, whereas "smell" was used 65 percent of the time to label citrus fruits, presumably because chimps eat the outer skin, which is rather aromatic when bitten into.

Another experiment addressed the question of abstraction. Could the chimps learn verbal

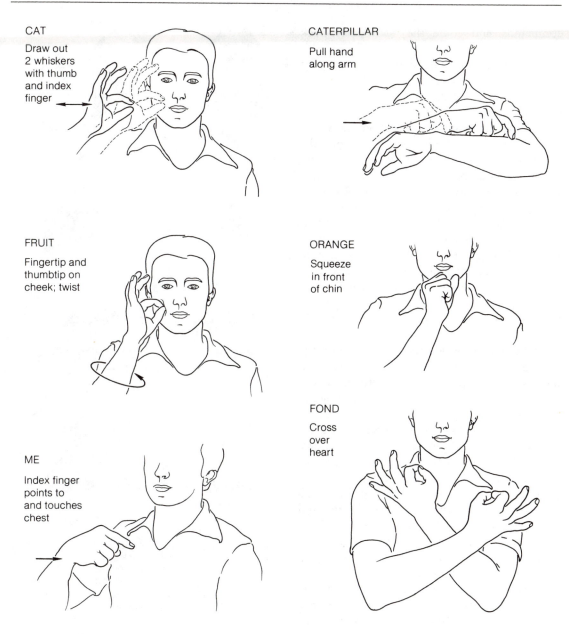

FIGURE 16-4. Examples from American Sign Language (Ameslan). The Gardners and others taught such symbols to the chimpanzees in their studies. (After Gustason et al., 1975).

commands, and could they generalize back and forth from signs to words? To test this idea, a chimp was trained on English words such as "spoon." Having learned that the verbal word spoon referred to an object, he was then taught the Ameslan sign for spoon, but not in the presence of the object, rather in relation to the auditory representation, the word "spoon." Would the chimp, if asked what the object was, be able to make the "jump" and sign for the object. The answer was yes.

A large number of chimps have now been studied, and although there are clear differences among the individual animals, all have mastered a large number of signs. Attempts to teach Ameslan to other species of great apes have proven very successful; Patterson has found gorillas to have an even better predisposition to acquire sign language than do chimpanzees.

Premack approached the study of language abilities of chimpanzees in a different way. He taught his chimpanzee, Sarah, to read and write with variously shaped and colored pieces of plastic, each representing a word (see Figure 16-5). Premack first taught Sarah that different symbols represented different nouns, just as Washoe had been taught in sign language. Thus, for example, Sarah learned that a pink square was the symbol for banana. Sarah was then taught verbs so she could write and read such combinations as "give apple" or "wash apple." Her comprehension could easily be tested by writing her messages (hanging up symbols) and then observing her response. This was followed by much more complicated tutoring in which Sarah successfully mastered the interrogative (Where is my banana?), the negative, and finally the conditional (if, then). It is readily apparent that Sarah had mastered a fairly complicated communication system analogous to simple human language.

A more recent project has demonstrated even more complex language learning in the

FIGURE 16-5. An example of a "conversation," using plastic symbols, with Premack's chimpanzee, Sarah. Note that the message is written from top to bottom. (After Ann James Premack and David Premack, Teaching language to an ape. Copyright © 1972 by Scientific American, Inc. All rights reserved.)

chimpanzee. After carefully studying the results of the Gardners' and Premacks' projects, Rumbaugh and his colleagues at the Yerkes Regional Primate Center launched Project Lana. This project involved teaching their chimp, Lana, to communicate by means of a keyboard programmed by a computer. The keyboard was composed of nine stimulus elements and nine primary colors, which could be combined together in nearly 1800 combinations (lexigrams), as illustrated in Figure 16-6, to form a language now known as Yerkish. This project differs from the previous ones in being a collaborative effort of a psychologist, linguists, and computer specialists.

Lana had to learn simply to type out her messages on the keyboard. She was first trained to press keys for various single incentives; the requirements then became increasingly complex as she mastered the various types of statements, such as the indicative (Tim move into room), the interrogative (Tim move into room?), the imperative (Please Tim move into room), and the negative (Don't Tim move into room). Lana is now capable of strings of six lexigrams and makes few errors, most being "typing errors" or errors caused by distraction.

One of the initial goals of Project Lana was to engage in conversation with a chimpanzee. This has been accomplished by having the experimenter type messages on the board and then allowing Lana to respond. She actually learned to initiate conversation on her own, and engaged in conversations such as that illustrated in Table 16-3.

Further studies by Rumbaugh's group have demonstrated that the chimpanzees are capable of symbolic communication with one another: two chimpanzees in adjoining rooms were able to use Yerkish to ask one another for specific foods. Further study showed they could even communicate reliably with regard to sharing tools for obtaining foods. When forced to rely on nonsymbolic means of communication, such as facial expression or body posture, their joint accuracy declined from 95 percent to 10 percent. This latter result implies that the chimpanzees comprehend the symbolic and communicative functions of the symbols that they use, and are not using subtle nonsymbolic cues to communicate.

Lenneberg and others have argued that human mathematical abilities are derived from the same foundation as language. Thus, whether chimpanzees possess the ability to acquire and use mathematical skills is an important question. Rumbaugh and his colleagues on Project Lana have begun to consider this problem. Lana has learned the concept of "more" and "less," and can accurately determine whether a group of four washers is more or less than a group of five washers, when surface area, mass, and spatial arrangement of the washers are varied randomly. The question now under study is whether Lana can learn names of precise numbers and the ordinal relationships involved among the numbers 1–10.

A Word of Caution

As provocative as the language studies in apes have proven, there have been criticisms. Terrace and his colleagues have raised an important issue that must be addressed before we know how relevant the ape language studies are to the study of human language. As Terrace notes, although apes can learn vocabularies of visual symbols, the important question is not whether the apes have a good memory for symbols but rather whether the apes can spontaneously combine such symbols by using a systematic grammar to create new meanings. After all, Terrace notes that whereas pigeons and other animals can learn complex chains of responses to obtain food reward, these responses are not related one to another as words in a sentence are. For example, a pigeon can be trained to peck on four keys of different colors in a particular sequence regardless of the physical position of the colors; nevertheless, colors do not combine to form a grammatical sentence. Likewise,

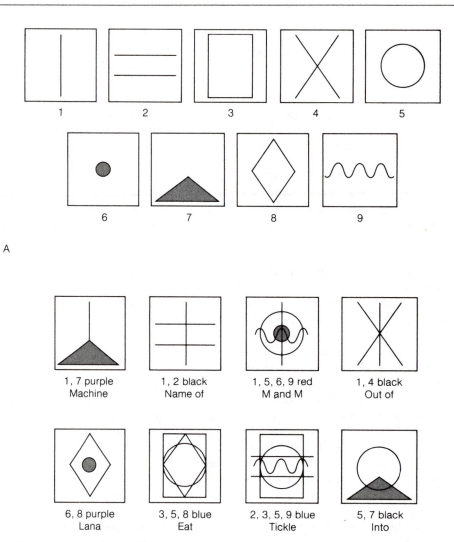

FIGURE 16-6. A. The nine basic design elements in Yerkish that are combined together to form lexigrams. B. Examples of lexigrams. (From E. von Glaserfeld, The Yerkish language and its automatic parser. In D. M. Rumbaugh, ed. *Language Learning by a Chimpanzee,* New York: Academic Press. Copyright © 1977. Reprinted by permission.)

TABLE 16-3

A conversation with Lana

Lana:	Milk name-of this.
Tim:	Yes
Lana:	Milk this ? Tim give Lana coffee
Tim:	No. (Although at times he has honored this request, this time he elected not to, for milk, not coffee, was the incentive appropriate to her state of heightened food motivation.)
Lana:	? Tim move milk coffee. (This was the first suggestion that she was going to ask Tim to move something from one point to another in space. She had not received specific training to ask that this be done.)
Tim:	(No response)
Lana:	? Tim move behind room
Tim:	Yes. (Thereupon Tim set down the pitcher of milk and moved behind the room to the general area of the vending devices where the milk would ordinarily be loaded into the machine. Lana's response was to hoot with apparent agitation; she also displayed piloerection and a furrowed brow. In a few seconds, Tim returned to the anteroom, picked up the milk, and stood once again in Lana's full view.)
Lana:	Milk of this coffee ? Tim give milk name-of. ? Tim move milk behind … (The sentence was not completed; however, Tim interpreted it to mean that Lana did not know how to finish what promised to be a novel question and one that was quite appropriate to the context.)
Tim:	? Behind what
Lana:	? Tim move milk behind room. (With this statement Lana had asked for the first time that a person move something other than his own body from one point to another in space.)
Tim:	Yes. (He then loaded the vending device with milk, and Lana began to work for it by requesting it repeatedly.)

From Rumbaugh and Gill, 1977, p. 175.

whereas an ape may produce sequences of symbols that a human observer sees as grammatically related, it does not follow that the ape was aware of the inferred relationships. If, for example, in response to the question "what that?" Washoe signed "water bird" in the presence of a swan, Washoe's response clearly appears creative and meaningful.

Nevertheless, there is no basis for concluding that Washoe was characterizing the swan as a "bird that inhabits water." Washoe had a long history of being asked "what that?" in the presence of objects such as birds and bodies of water. In this instance, Washoe may have simply been answering the question, "what that?" by identifying correctly a body of water and a bird,

in that order. Before concluding that Washoe was relating the sign "water" to the sign "bird," one must know whether she regularly placed an adjective (water) before, or after, a noun (bird). That cannot be decided on the basis of a single anecdote, no matter how compelling that anecdote may seem to an English-speaking observer. (Terrace et al., 1979, pp. 895–896)

To support their argument Terrace and his colleagues carefully analyzed more than 19,000 multisign utterances of an infant chimpanzee (Nim) as well as reanalyzing film of Washoe and other chimps. Although they found evidence for what appeared to be grammatical construction, that conclusion was invalidated by analyses of videotapes and films that showed that most of the apes' utterances were prompted by their teachers' prior utterances and could thus be adequately explained by simple nonlinguistic processes. Indeed, the authors were struck both by the absence of creativity in the apes' utterances and by the dependence of the apes' utterances upon the prior utterances of their teachers. This is quite unlike the advanced multiword sequences produced by young children.

We do not wish to belittle the remarkable achievements of the ape language projects, but for the moment it is best to proceed with caution and to resist overly rich interpretations of the language capabilities of apes. In view of the utility of Ameslan as a human language, it might initially appear that the machine language (e.g., Yerkish) studies were unnecessary and perhaps redundant. In view of Terrace's criticisms, however, it can easily be seen that the machine languages are more objective and easier to quantify and to analyze than Ameslan. Thus, the machine language approach is more likely to satisfy the criticisms of Terrace and his colleagues.

Applications of the Chimpanzee Studies

A major implication of the work with chimpanzees is that communication does not require talking or even the ability to talk. Thus, a person with severe aphasia could potentially be taught some other form of language. In view of the reports that strokes produce impairment in Ameslan signing in deaf patients, either the Premack symbols or the Project Lana Yerkish would seem more appropriate for this purpose. Glass, Gazzaniga, and Premack have used Premack symbols with encouraging results. Interestingly, noun symbols were learned readily, whereas verbs sometimes took weeks to learn. This difference is reminiscent of the observation that the right

hemisphere of the split-brain patient is unable to process natural-language verbs.

It is relevant in this context to note that a symbol language was devised and published by Bliss in 1942. This language, known as Bliss Symbols or semantographics, is essentially similar to a simplified Chinese, being the clear, pictorial representation of real things as we see them. Each symbol looks like the object it represents; abstractions and intangibles are represented by geometrical objects associated with them. The language is composed of 100 symbol elements that are recombined to form different words as illustrated in Figure 16-7.

The simplicity of this system is apparent. The language has now been tried with nonvocal children with very favorable results. For example, Harris-Vanderbeiden and her colleagues implemented a modified Bliss system for children with cerebral palsy. With about 20 hours of training these children had all mastered at least some symbols that could be used for communication. One child who had an IQ of about 56 learned about 75 symbols which she could use for both respondent and expressive communication.

To our knowledge this system has not yet been applied to aphasic patients, but appears very promising. It is considerably more complex than the chimpanzee symbol systems used to date, and its pictorial component might make it a better choice for aphasic patients than Yerkish.

Origin of Language

Although theorizing about human language ability is a centuries-old activity, until recently there had been virtually no speculation about its structure at the neurological level.[1] Hewes

---

[1] A beautiful little paper by Hewes summarizes the history of theories of the phylogenesis of speech. It is recommended reading for anyone interested in the problem.

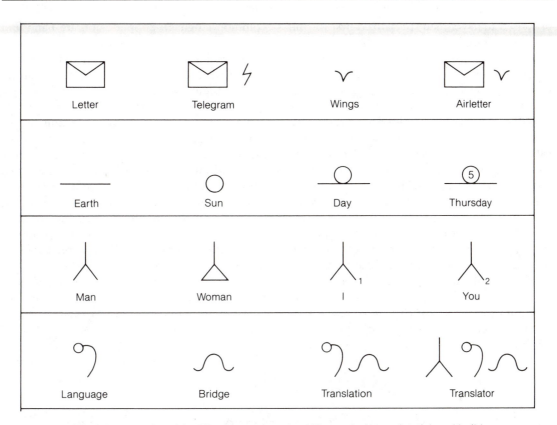

FIGURE 16-7. Examples of the Bliss language system. The symbols are pictorial, and build upon one another logically. This system has proven useful for teaching nonvocal children, and holds promise for use with aphasic adults.

notes that the first neurologically based theory appeared 10 years ago, and even today the theories are less than adequate. In our view, the most reasonable current theories emphasize the role of gesture in the evolution of language. We therefore review this type of theory, and recommend Hewes's article for those interested in others.

The gestural theories argue that language developed from gestures and other body movements. It is assumed that effective hunting and forming and maintaining social groups require some kind of communication system. Indeed, wild chimpanzees have a system of gestures and motions that communicate information. One example is begging, in which the hand is outstretched and the lower lips up-lifted, something like a pout. Menzel has provided evidence of more complex communication of the presence of food, of its location, of its quality, and so on. Studies like this and like the Gardners' make it clear that the chimpanzee nervous system is prepared for the learning and interpreting of others' gestures. Several authors (see especially Kimura) have proposed that lateralization in the brain precedes speech and is related to gesturing and tool making. Thus, the left hemisphere is proposed to have been specialized first for the control of complex movement. Since language requires the combination of complex movement of the mouth and vocal apparatus, language developed around a system already developed for complex movement.

A question that can be raised with respect to gestural theories is why there is a shift to vocalizing. Hewes proposes that this derives from facial expressions, grunts, etc., which themselves derive from gesturing. Two reasons are given for increased use of the face: (1) As the individual increases the use of tools the hands are full and cannot be used for gesturing. (2) As the language becomes more complicated there are clear upper limits on the number of possible facial and manual expressions.

A relevant observation that supports the gestural proposal is that hand gestures still accompany language. Indeed, in the absence of a common language people elaborate hand and facial gestures to communicate.

Myers has proposed a slightly different version of the gestural theory. He argues that the development of language is a logical consequence of the increasing development of the control of facial musculature. Prosimians are unable to produce facial expressions; rhesus monkeys and other monkeys are able to produce a limited range of facial expressions; chimpanzees have a complex repertoire of facial movements; but only humans have developed the movements for speech and the necessary changes in the vocal tracts. He proposes that the development of Broca's area creates a qualitatively different type of output. The need for increased facial control is assumed to result, at least in part, from the need for increasing communication to facilitate increasingly complex social interaction.

REFERENCES

Benson, D. F. Fluency in aphasia. *Cortex, 3* (1967) 373–394.

Bliss, C. W. *Semantography.* Sydney, Australia: Semantography Publications, 1942.

Brown, J. *Aphasia, Apraxia and Agnosia.* Springfield, Ill.: Charles C Thomas, 1972.

Brown, J. The neural organization of language: aphasia and lateralization. *Brain and Language, 3* (1976), 482–494.

Caplan, D., and J. C. Marshall. Generative grammar and aphasic disorders: a theory of language representation in the human brain. *Foundations of Language, 12* (1972), 583–596.

Chomsky, N. On the biological basis of language capabilities. In R. W. Rieber, ed. *Neuropsychology of Language.* New York: Plenum Press, 1976.

Cooper, I. S., I. Amin, R. Chandra, and J. M. Waltz. A surgical investigation of the clinical physiology of the LP-pulvinar complex in man. *Journal of Neurological Science, 18* (1973), 89–110.

Gardner, B. T., and R. A. Gardner. Two-way communication with an infant chimpanzee. In A. M. Schrier and F. Stolinitz, eds. *Behavior of Nonhuman Primates.* Vol. 4. New York: Academic Press, 1971.

Geschwind, N. Language and the brain. *Scientific American, 226* (1972), 76–83.

Glaserfeld, E. von. The Yerkish language and its automatic parser. In D. M. Rumbaugh, ed. *Language Learning by a Chimpanzee*. New York: Academic Press, 1977.

Glass, A. U., M. S. Gazzaniga, and D. Premack. Artificial language training in global aphasics. *Neuropsychologia, 11* (1973), 95–103.

Goodglass, H., and E. Kaplan. *The Assessment of Aphasia and Related Disorders*. Philadelphia: Lea and Febiger, 1972.

Green, E. Psycholinguistic approaches to aphasia. *Linguistics, 53* (1969), 30–50.

Gustason, G., D. Pfetzing, and E. Zawoklow. *Signing Exact English*. Silver Spring, Md.: Modern Signs Press, 1975.

Halstead, W. C., and J. M. Wepman. The Halstead-Wepman aphasia screening test. *Journal of Speech and Hearing Disorders, 14* (1959), 9–15.

Harris-Vanderbeiden, D., W. R. Brown, P. MacKenzie, S. Reinen, and C. Scheibel. Symbol communication for the mentally handicapped. *Mental Retardation,* (1975), 34–37.

Hayes, K. J., and C. H. Nissen. Higher mental functions of a home reared chimpanzee. In A. M. Schrier and F. Stolinitz, eds. *Behavior of Nonhuman Primates*. Vol. 4. New York: Academic Press, 1971.

Hewes, G. W. Language origin theories. In D. M. Rumbaugh, ed. *Language Learning by a Chimpanzee*. New York: Academic Press, 1977.

Hughlings-Jackson, J. Notes on the physiology and pathology of language. In J. Taylor, ed. *Selected Writings of John Hughlings-Jackson*. London: Hodder and Stoughton, Ltd., 1932.

Jefferson, G. Localization of function in the cerebral cortex. *British Medical Bulletin, 6* (1949), 333–340.

Kellogg, W., and L. Kellogg. *The Ape and the Child*. New York: McGraw-Hill Book Co., 1933.

Kimura, D. Neuromotor mechanisms in the evolution of human communication. In H. D. Steklis and M. J. Raleigh, eds. *Neurobiology of Social Communication in Primates: An Evolutionary Perspective*. New York: Academic Press, 1979.

Larsen, B., E. Skinhøj, and N. A. Lassen. Variations in regional cortical blood flow in the right and left hemispheres during automatic speech. *Brain, 101* (1978), 193–209.

Lenneberg, E. H. *Biological Foundations of Language*. New York: John Wiley and Sons, 1967.

Luria, A. R., and J. T. Hutton. A modern assessment of basic forms of aphasia. *Brain and Language, 4* (1977), 129–151.

Mateer, C. Asymmetric effects of thalamic stimulation on rate of speech. *Neuropsychologia, 16* (1978), 497–499.

Menzel, E. W. Communication about the environment in a group of young chimpanzees. *Folia Primatologia, 15* (1971), 220–232.

Myers, R. E. Comparative neurology of vocalization and speech: proof of a dichotomy. *Annals of the New York Academy of Sciences. 280* (1976), 745–760.

Ojemann, G. A., ed. The thalamus and language. *Brain and Language, 2* (1975), 1–120.

Ojemann, G. A., and C. Mateer. Cortical and subcortical organization of human communication: evidence from stimulation studies. In H. D. Steklis and M. J. Raleigh, eds. *Neurobiology of Social Communication in Primates: An Evolutionary Perspective*. New York: Academic Press, 1979.

Ojemann, G. A., and C. Mateer. Human language cortex: localization of memory, syntax, and sequential motor-phoneme identification systems. *Science, 205* (1979), 1401–1403.

Patterson, F. G. The gestures of a gorilla: language acquisition in another pongid. *Brain and Language, 5* (1978), 72–97.

Penfield, W., and L. Roberts. *Speech and Brain Mechanisms.* Princeton, N.J.: Princeton University Press, 1959.

Porch, B. E. *Porch Index of Communicative Ability.* Palo Alto, Calif.: Consulting Psychologists Press, 1967.

Premack, A. J., and D. Premack. Teaching language to an ape. *Scientific American, 227* (1972), 92–99.

Premack, D. *Intelligence in Ape and Man.* Toronto: John Wiley and Sons, 1976.

Rasmussen, T., and B. Milner. Clinical and surgical studies of the cerebral speech areas in man. In K. J. Zulch, O. Creutzfeldt, and G. C. Galbraith, eds. *Cerebral Localization.* Berlin and New York: Springer-Verlag, 1975.

Renzi, E. de, and L. A. Vignolo. The token test: a sensitive test to detect disturbances in aphasics. *Brain, 85* (1962), 665–678.

Ricklan, M., and I. S. Cooper. Psychometric studies of verbal functions following thalamic lesions in humans. *Brain and Language, 2* (1975), 45–64.

Rumbaugh, D. M., and T. V. Gill. Lana's acquisition of language skills. In D. M. Rumbaugh, ed. *Language Learning by a Chimpanzee.* New York: Academic Press, 1977.

Sarno, M. T. *The Functional Communication Profile: Manual of Directions.* New York: Institute of Rehabilitation Medicine, New York University Medical Center, 1969.

Savage-Rumbaugh, E. S., D. M. Rumbaugh, and S. Boysen. Symbolic communication between two chimpanzees. *Science, 201* (1978), 641–644.

Schuell, H. *Differential Diagnosis of Aphasia with the Minnesota Test.* Minneapolis: University of Minnesota Press, 1965.

Searleman, A. A review of right hemisphere linguistic capacities. *Psychological Bulletin, 84* (1977), 503–528.

Spreen, O., and A. L. Benton. *Neurosensory Center Comprehensive Examination for Aphasia.* Victoria, Canada: University of Victoria, 1969.

Steklis, H. D., and M. J. Raleigh. Requisites for language: interspecific and evolutionary aspects. In H. D. Steklis and M. J. Raleigh, eds. *Neurobiology of Social Communication in Primates: An Evolutionary Perspective.* New York: Academic Press, 1979.

Terrace, H. S., L. A. Petitto, R. J. Sanders, and T. G. Bever. Can an ape create a sentence? *Science, 206* (1979), 891–902.

Wepman, J. M., and L. V. Jones. *Studies in Aphasia: An Approach to Testing.* Chicago: University of Chicago Education-Industry Service, 1961.

Whitaker, H. A. *On the Representation of Language in the Human Brain,* Edmonton, Canada: Linguistic Research, Inc., 1971.

Zangwill, O. L. Excision of Broca's area without persistent aphasia. In K. J. Zulch, O. Creutzfeldt, and G. C. Galbraith, eds. *Cerebral Localization.* Berlin and New York: Springer-Verlag, 1975.

17

AFFECTIVE BEHAVIOR: AN OVERVIEW

In the past neuropsychologists studied primarily the easily quantifiable behaviors such as language and memory, and neglected some of the most salient changes in behavior following brain disease or injury. Virtually any alteration of central nervous system activity can change an individual's personality. This is especially true of cortical injuries, since impairments of language, perception, memory, or movement significantly affect how an individual behaves and is perceived by others. In the last decade interest in the neuropsychological analysis of social and affective behavior has been increasing, but to date research has concentrated on only a few aspects of social and affective behavior. Some research has been addressed specifically to examining the tone, or "emotion," of behavior; either the behavior of patients is observed, or perceptual changes are inferred from responses to visual or auditory stimuli. Other research has been addressed to searching for cerebral asymmetries in the perception, by normal subjects, of affective stimuli presented tachistoscopically or dichotically.

Other studies have been addressed to examining the appropriateness of social responses in neurological patients. Because patients with known neurological disorders (e.g., Parkinson's disease) behave very much like depressed or schizophrenic patients, it has been proposed that certain psychiatric disorders may have a neurological basis.

In this chapter we take a brief historical look at the study of the relationship between the brain and affective behavior. We then consider the neuropsychology of affective behavior, with emphasis on the localization and lateralization of functions within the neocortex. Finally, we examine the role of neurological disease in abnormal behavior, and look at abnormal behavior as neurological disease.

HISTORICAL VIEWS

In 1937, Papez proposed that the structures of the limbic lobe form the anatomical basis of emotions. Papez reasoned that the limbic structures acting on the hypothalamus produce emotional states. Although the neocortex plays no part in producing emotional behavior, it is necessary to the transforming of events produced by limbic structures into what we experience as "emotions." Papez based his theory on the observation of patients with rabies, since this disease affects the hippocampus and causes such emotional and behavioral changes as anxiety, rage, terror, and so on. The Papez theory had the appeal of combining behavioral phenomena with no known neurological substrates, with anatomical structures with no known function.

The idea of an emotional brain gained instant approval because of the predominance of Freudian thinking at the time. That an ancient, deep part of the central nervous system controls emotions and instincts unconsciously, with the neocortex producing consciousness, was a concept with natural appeal for a Freudian-based psychology. In 1939, Klüver and Bucy rediscovered an extraordinary behavioral syndrome that had first been noted by Brown and Schaefer in 1888. The observed behavior, resulting from bilateral anterior temporal lobectomy in monkeys, included: (1) tameness and a loss of fear; (2) indiscriminate dietary behavior, the monkeys being willing to eat many types of previously rejected foods; (3) greatly increased autoerotic, homosexual, and heterosexual activity, with inappropriate object choice; (4) **hypermetamorphosis,** or a tendency to attend to and react to every visual stimulus; (5) a tendency to examine all objects by mouth; and (6) visual agnosia.

The **Klüver-Bucy syndrome** has subsequently been observed in people with a variety of neurological diseases. For example, Marlowe et al. reported a patient with Klüver-Bucy symptoms resulting from meningoencephalitis.

As regards his visual functions, the patient seemed unable to recognize a wide variety of common objects. He examined each object placed before him as though seeing it for the first time, explored it repetitively and seemed unaware of its significance. As a result, he exhibited difficulty in the spontaneous employment of tools and other mechanical devices, but could initiate utilization of such objects by imitating the gestures of others, and could care for at least some daily needs in this way. Thus, when handed his razor, he would regard it in a bewildered fashion, but would accompany another patient to the bathroom and imitate all movements of his escort, even the most idiosyncratic, with precision; he could in this way succeed in shaving. Other ordinary tasks could be performed on the same imitative basis. Difficulties in recognition, it should be added, extended to people as well as to objects; he failed, for example, to recognize his parents during innumerable hospital visits. However, his ability to match simple pictures, geometric designs, letters of the alphabet and objects was demonstrably preserved when the tasks were taught non-verbally. Visual orientation was defective, the patient losing his way around the hospital when unattended, and visual distractibility was prominent; he seemed unable to distinguish between relevant and irrelevant objects and actions.

Behavioral patterns were distinctly abnormal. He exhibited a flat affect, and, although originally restless, ultimately became remarkably placid. He appeared indifferent to people or situations. He spent much time gazing at the television, but never learned to turn it on; when the set was off, he tended to watch reflections of others in the room on the glass screen. On occasion he became facetious, smiling inappropriately and mimicking the gestures and actions of others. Once initiating an imitative series, he would perseverate copying all movements made by another for extended periods of time. In addition, he commonly generated a series of idiosyncratic, stereotyped, gestures employing primarily his two little fingers which he would raise and touch end-to-end in repetitive fashion.

He engaged in oral exploration of all objects within his grasp, appearing unable to gain information via tactile or visual means alone. All objects that he could lift were placed in his mouth and sucked or chewed. He was commonly observed to place his fingers in his mouth and suck them. He did not attempt to pick up objects directly with his mouth, using his hands for that purpose, but was observed to engage in much olfactory behavior. When dining he would eat with his fingers until reprimanded and a fork placed in his hand; he was thereafter able to imitate use of a fork, but failed to remaster the task of eating with utensils spontaneously. He would eat one food item on his plate completely before turning to the next. Hyperbulimia was prominent; he ingested virtually everything within reach, including the plastic wrapper from bread, cleaning pastes, ink, dog food, and feces. Although his tastes were clearly indiscriminate, he seemed to prefer liquids or soft solids.

The patient's sexual behavior was a particular source of concern while in hospital. Although vigorously heterosexual prior to his illness, he was observed in hospital to make advances toward other male patients by stroking their legs and inviting fellatio by gesture; at times he attempted to kiss them. Although on a sexually mixed floor during a portion of his recovery, he never made advances toward women, and, in fact, his apparent reversal of sexual polarity prompted his fiancée to sever their relationship. (Marlow, Mancall, and Thomas, 1975, pp. 55–56)

The appearance of the Klüver-Bucy syndrome apparently requires that the amygdala and inferior temporal cortex be removed bilaterally. H. M., the patient described in Chapter 15, does not exhibit the syndrome in spite of bilateral removal of the medial temporal structures.

Around the time of Klüver and Bucy's discovery a less dramatic but in many ways more important discovery was made. Jacobson studied the behavior of chimpanzees on a variety of learning tasks following frontal-lobe removals. In 1935, he reported his findings on the effects of the lesions at the Second International Neurology Congress in London. He casually noted that one particularly neurotic chimp appeared more relaxed following the

surgery, leading a Portuguese neurologist, Egas Moniz, to propose that similar lesions in people might relieve various behavioral problems. Thus was born psychosurgery and the frontal lobotomy! Unbelievably, not until the late 1960s was any systematic research done on the effects of frontal-lobe lesions on the affective behavior of nonhuman animals. Frontal lobotomies in humans were thus performed without an empirical basis. Experiments by several laboratories have now clearly shown that frontal-lobe lesions in rats, cats, and monkeys all have severe effects on social and affective behavior. For example, frontal lesions in monkeys virtually eliminate social interaction, even when the surgical candidate is the dominant (or so-called alpha) monkey of the group. Social responses that remain following surgery are inappropriate and frequently lead to severe fights in which the frontal monkey is inevitably the loser. Removals of the neocortex other than the frontal lobes in monkeys has reduced or negligible effects on social behavior, implying that the frontal lobe is the primary neocortical zone involved in social behavior. Indeed, we noted earlier that one of the most characteristic results of frontal-lobe injury in humans is a marked, often dramatic alteration of personality.

Few would seriously argue today that the neocortex does not play a significant role in social behavior. In the four decades since Papez's model was first proposed the pendulum of thought regarding the neurological control of affective behavior has gradually swung from the extreme view placing this function in the limbic system to a view emphasizing the importance of the neocortex. Indeed, limbic structures such as the hippocampus would appear to have a minor role in the control of what Papez described as emotional behavior. Rather, the major forebrain structures involved in affective behavior now appear to be the orbital frontal cortex, amygdala, and portions of the anterior temporal cortex. These structures are intimately related anatomically, forming a system with important input to the hypothalamus.

NEUROPSYCHOLOGY OF AFFECTIVE BEHAVIOR

Current views on the role of the cerebral hemispheres in affective or social behavior have arisen from six major lines of work. Together these researches lead to the common conclusion that, as for nearly all behavior, there is complementary specialization of function of the cerebral hemispheres in respect to the control of affective behavior. The right hemisphere plays a major role in analyzing and producing emotionally toned stimuli and responses; the left hemisphere has a subordinate role, appearing to be more analytic or literal in its analysis of input. By way of loose analogy, the left hemisphere views or interprets socially relevant input irrespective of the tone, whereas the right hemisphere has the complementary role of analyzing the tone at the expense of the content. Thus, the statement "I hate you" can be interpreted literally as indicating disaffection, or it can be interpreted less than literally according to the tone of voice and circumstances. Lesions of either the left or the right hemisphere are therefore predicted to produce very different effects on affective behavior.

Perception of Relevant Stimuli

Normal Subjects. To date, in studies of perception of emotionally loaded stimuli, only visual and auditory modalities have been examined. For both modalities the stimulus usually is presented to one hemisphere selectively, either alone or in competition with information simultaneously presented to the opposite hemisphere. Two procedures have been used for the visual presentation. In one procedure,

faces with different expressions (e.g., sad, happy) are presented tachistoscopically to the left or right visual field, and the subject is asked to identify the facial expression. The results show the left visual field superior at correct identification. This superiority can be interpreted as demonstrating a right-hemisphere specialization for the perception of facial expression, an important aspect of nonverbal communication. The conclusion is consistent with the previous demonstrations of a right-hemisphere specialization for perception of faces (see Chapter 10). The second procedure involves an ingenious technique devised by Dimond. By the use of special contact lenses Dimond and his colleagues were able to selectively project several types of films to the left or right hemisphere. Subjects rated each film on a scale of 1 to 9 on the four emotional dimensions of humorous, pleasant, horrific, or unpleasant. Films presented to the right hemisphere were judged more unpleasant and horrific and produced greater autonomic nervous system activation (as measured by heart rate) than when presented to the left hemisphere of other subjects. Dimond and his colleagues concluded that the two hemispheres held an essentially different emotional view of the world. Curiously, if the films were shown to both hemispheres simultaneously, the ratings closely resembled those of the right visual field (the left hemisphere), suggesting that left-hemisphere perception is dominant. It could be predicted that a left-hemisphere lesion might result in a more negative view of the films, although this has not been studied.

We are aware of five studies of asymmetries in auditory perception of emotions (see Table 17-1 items 1 and 2 under Normal subjects). Three of these have employed a dichotic listening technique, and all have shown left-ear superiority for emotional material such as laughing, crying, etc. For example, dichotically presenting crying, shrieking, or laughing, Carmon and Nachshon found a left-ear super-

TABLE 17-1

Summary of experiments on perception of socially relevant stimuli

Test	Result	Basic references
Normal subjects		
1. Dichotic nonverbal sounds	Left-ear superiority	King and Kimura, 1972 Carmon and Nachshon, 1973 Haggard and Parkinson, 1971
2. Dichotic emotionally toned sentences	Left hemisphere comprehends content; right comprehends emotional tone	Safer and Leventhal, 1977
3. Tachistoscopic faces	Right-hemisphere superiority for recognition of facial expression	Ley and Bryden, 1979 Buchtel et al., 1978
4. Split-field movies	Elaboration of emotional tone by right hemisphere	Dimond et al., 1976; 1977
Neurological patients		
1. Judgment of mood in others	Right-hemisphere lesions impair comprehension	Heilman et al., 1975
2. Judgment of propositional affect	Left-hemisphere lesions impair comprehension	Kolb, 1977 Kolb et al., 1980
3. Comprehension of verbal humor	Left-hemisphere lesions impair comprehension	Gardner et al., 1975
4. Comprehension of non-verbal humor	Right-hemisphere lesions impair comprehension	Gardner et al., 1975
5. Matching pictures of emotional facial expressions	Right-hemisphere lesions impair performance	Kolb et al., 1980 Kolb, 1977

iority for the identification of both the stimulus and the subjects, which was either a male or a female, an adult or a child.

In a somewhat different type of experiment Safer and Leventhal presented the same material to both ears. The passages had three types of content (positive, negative, and neutral), each read in an appropriate tone of voice (positive, negative, or neutral). Thus, the positive tone passages were read in a "happy" fashion, the negative in an "angry" fashion, and the neutral in an objective manner. Subjects were instructed to listen with either the left ear or the right ear and then were asked to rate the emotion expressed in the passages. Slightly over 80 percent of the subjects who listened with the left ear rated the passages by the tone of voice and disregarded the content, whereas only about 60 percent of the subjects who lis-

tened with the right ear rated the passages by the content and disregarded the tone of voice. This result is somewhat analogous to that of Dimond et al., who found that the two hemispheres deal with *visual* material in a different way.

Neurological Patients. Three studies have examined the perception of emotionally loaded material in patients with unilateral lesions. Heilman and his colleagues asked patients to judge the mood of a speaker after listening to him read a sentence in which he successively feigned anger, joy, etc. Patients with right-hemisphere lesions, largely temporal-parietal, were more impaired at this task than patients with analogous left-hemisphere lesions. Similarly, Gardner and his colleagues examined the comprehension and

FIGURE 17-1. Examples from the study by Gardner et al. of sense of humor in neurological patients. Patients with right-hemisphere lesions had difficulty choosing the funny captionless cartoon (this page), whereas patients with left-hemisphere lesions had difficulty choosing the funny captioned cartoon (facing page). (After H. Gardner, P. K. Ling, L. Flamm, and J. Silverman, Comprehension and appreciation of humorous material following brain damage. *Brain, 98,* 399–412. Copyright © 1976. Reprinted by permission.)

appreciation of humorous material following left- or right-hemisphere lesions. They asked patients to choose the funniest of four cartoons, which were either with or without captions (Figure 17-1).[1] The results showed that all patients were impaired at the task, but there was an asymmetry in the pattern of errors. Patients with left-hemisphere lesions did well on the cartoons *without* captions, whereas patients with right-hemisphere lesions did well on the cartoons *with* captions. Further, the behavior of the two patient groups differed. Those with left-hemisphere lesions behaved "normally," whereas those with right-hemisphere lesions tended to exhibit one of two extreme reactions: either they laughed at nearly every item, even when their under-

---

[1] The appreciation of humor is of course idiosyncratic and difficult. For example, in the learning of a foreign language, humor is the most complex aspect of the language to grasp. The cartoons in Figure 17-1 may not strike everyone as being especially humorous, but most people will be able to identify which cartoon has an element of humor when compared to the other choices.

standing was doubtful, or, more commonly, they displayed little reaction to any item, even when their understanding seemed adequate.

Kolb et al. examined the comprehension of emotions in patients with unilateral removals of the left or right frontal, temporal, or parietal-occipital regions (Figure 17-2). Lesions anywhere in the right hemisphere produced impairments in a task requiring subjects to match photographs of different faces according to the emotion displayed. These data showed that lesions in the right hemisphere

had no focal effect—a surprising finding given that facial-recognition deficits are localized in the posterior regions of the hemisphere (see Chapter 10). Lesions anywhere in the left hemisphere produced an impairment in the perception of emotion in propositional speech. For example, the patients had difficulty pairing the correct emotion with a propositional statement such as "this man is at a funeral." This result is just the opposite of the deficit on the visual task.

It is instructive to compare the results of the

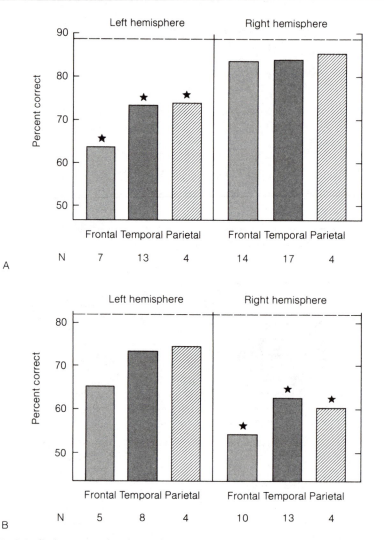

FIGURE 17-2. Performance of patients with surgical excisions on a test requiring descriptions of emotional situations to be matched with appropriate verbal description (A) and matching photographs of faces displaying the same emotional expression (B). Stars indicate significant differences with the group having excisions in the opposite hemisphere. The dotted lines indicate normal control. (After Kolb et al., 1980.)

studies by Heilman et al. and Kolb et al. In the former, one observes a *right*-hemisphere deficit in comprehension of the speaker's *tone*; in the latter, a *left*-hemisphere deficit in comprehension of the *content*. This asymmetry is reminiscent of Safer and Leventhal's study on normal subjects. Recall that they observed a left-hemisphere effect for analysis of content and a right-hemisphere effect for the analysis of tone.

To summarize, it appears that the right hemisphere tends to process faces and their expressions and the tone rather than content of auditory material, whereas the left hemisphere tends to process the content, not the tone of auditory material.

Production of Affective Behavior

Normal Subjects. Few studies have examined the neuropsychology by which affective behaviors are produced in normal subjects. All these studies have centered on the study of eye movements and facial expression. One study, by Schwartz et al., involved observing the direction of horizontal eye movements made during emotional and nonemotional tasks. Emotionally loaded statements, such as "Picture and describe the last situation in which you cried," produced significantly more gaze shifts to the left than to the right, whereas nonemotional questions such as "What is the primary difference between the meanings of the words 'recognize' and 'remember'?" produced more gaze shifts to the right than to the left. By use of the hypothesized relationship between gaze shift and lateralization, these results were interpreted as demonstrating a special role of the right hemisphere in regulating emotional processes. These data are provocative, but are not a very direct measure of affective behavior.

Recently, a series of studies (see Table 17-2) has demonstrated that facial expressions are not always symmetrical, but rather strongly tend to occur predominantly on the left side of the face. The asymmetries may range from the hardly noticeable, such as the flicker of a smile on the left side of Mona Lisa's face (on the right of the painting, of course), to the pronounced, such as a raised eyebrow, wink, or lopsided smile, on the left side of the face. In

one study Moscovitch and Olds surreptitiously recorded the laterality of facial expressions of people in restaurants, finding a left-sided preponderance of facial expression. They confirmed this observation by carefully analyzing video recordings of people recounting sad and humorous stories, again finding a left-sided bias in facial expressions. Asymmetrical production of facial expression can be interpreted as showing that the right hemisphere is specialized in that function, a conclusion consistent with its presumed specialization in the perception of facial expressions. It is tempting to speculate that right-hemisphere specialization in expressing and interpreting facial expression is analogous to the left-hemisphere specialization in expressing and interpreting language, but this has yet to be proven. In our discussion of the Teuber-Yin theory of facial perception (Chapter 10) we noted that the apparent specialization of the right hemisphere in the perception of faces could easily be interpreted as a specialization for the perception of complex visual stimuli, of which faces are an example.

Neurological Patients. Four groups of researchers have examined the production of emotional or social behavior in patients with unilateral brain lesions. Waxman and Geschwind reported hypergraphia (excessive writing behavior) in patients with temporal-lobe epilepsy, although no mention was made of the side of the epileptic focus. Tucker et al. asked patients to express particular affective states such as anger, happiness, etc., when they read emotionally neutral sentences. Patients with right-hemisphere lesions were more impaired than controls or patients with left-hemisphere lesions. This result parallels the Heilman et al. study showing that right-hemisphere lesions produce deficits in the perception of emotional tone in sentences read to the patients.

TABLE 17-2

Summary of experiments on production of socially relevant stimuli

Normal subjects		
1. Lateral eye gaze	Gaze shifts to left associated with emotion	Schwartz et al., 1975
2. Lateralization of facial expression	More facial expression on the left side of face	Chaurasia and Goswami, 1975 Campbell, 1978 Sackheim et al., 1978 Moscovitch and Olds, 1979
Neurological patients		
1. Hypergraphia	Temporal-lobe epileptics write excessively	Waxman and Geschwind, 1974
2. Expression of emotional states	Right-hemisphere lesions impair mimicry of emotional states	Tucker et al., 1977
3. Behavior of patients with natural lesions	Left-hemisphere patients show catastrophic reaction; right-hemisphere patients show indifference	Goldstein, 1939 Gainotti, 1972 Hécaen et al., 1951
4. Behavior of patients with surgical lesions	Frontal lesions reduce facial expressions Left frontal lesions reduce spontaneous talking; right frontal lesions increase talking	Kolb, 1977 Kolb et al., 1980
5. Sodium Amytal	A. Catastrophic reactions to left injection; indifference reactions to right injection B. No evidence of asymmetrical effects	Terzian, 1964 Rossi and Rosandini, 1967 Rovetta, 1960 Milner, 1967 Kolb and Milner, 1980

Gainotti categorized the behavior of patients according to the presence or absence of various emotional behaviors. Left-hemisphere lesions produced significant increases in the probability of what Gainotti calls "catastrophic or depressive behaviors" (e.g., tears, swearing), whereas right-hemisphere lesions produced significant increases in what he terms "indifference reactions" (e.g., joke telling, lack of interest). Although this intriguing experiment has been widely cited in both the neuropsychological and psychiatric literature, we believe that these results must be interpreted very cautiously. First, depressive-catastrophic reactions of the left-hemisphere patients are correlated with the presence of aphasia. This is important, because the behaviors usually appear after repeated failures in verbal communication. Second, the indifference reactions of the right-hemisphere pa-

tients are correlated with the presence of contralateral neglect. Third, in our experience, catastrophic or indifference reactions occur rarely following surgical excision of neocortex and more commonly in patients with naturally occurring lesions, which presumably include subcortical damage. Discussions of Gainotti's study have generally ignored these factors, but they are clearly important to any conclusions that may be drawn from this provocative work.

Kolb et al. recorded emotional behavior in patients with cortical excisions in quite a different way: they recorded not the content of the behaviors but rather the frequency of facial movements and spontaneous talking. An ethological recording technique was used to score the facial movements: brows raised, brows knitted, eyes closed, mouth open, slight smile, wide smile, open-mouth smile, lips tight, lips turned down at corners, lips pursed, lips pouting, tongue out, laughing, sighing, and miscellaneous. Excisions of either the left or right frontal lobe significantly reduced the occurrence of spontaneous facial expressions, whereas face-area, temporal, or posterior lesions had no differential effect (see Figure 17-3). On the other hand, during routine neuropsychological testing, left frontal lesions significantly reduced the incidence of spontaneous talking, whereas right frontal lesions significantly increased it. Lesions elsewhere in the cortex had no effect on this behavior. These patients were not aphasic, and did not exhibit contralateral neglect.

Taken together, the studies of neurological patients lead to four conclusions. First, lesions of the left and right hemispheres have differential effects on emotional behavior. Second, occurrences of aphasia and unilateral neglect are significant factors in predicting occurrences of depressive-catastrophic and indifference reactions respectively. Third, the frontal lobes appear to have a special role in producing facial expression; there is no evidence for asymmetry in this function. Fourth, the frontal lobes are clearly asymmetrical in relation to spontaneous talking: left-hemisphere lesions appear to inhibit spontaneous talking, whereas right frontal-lobe lesions appear to release it.

Affect under Sodium Amytal

From the above studies it is reasonable to expect that patients under the effects of carotid sodium Amytal would exhibit changes in personality related to the side of drug injection. For example, from Gainotti's results a depressive-catastrophic reaction could be predicted to follow injection of the speaking hemisphere, and an indifference reaction to follow injection of the nonspeaking hemisphere. Study results are, however, contradictory. The most widely cited results are those collected by Terzian and by Rossi and their

respective colleagues. They report that injections of the left hemisphere indeed provoke a catastrophic reaction as the drug wears off. The patient "despairs and expresses a sense of guilt, of nothingness, of indignity, and worries about his own future or that of his relatives, without referring to the language disturbances overcome and to the hemiplegia just resolved and ignored." As the drug wore off after injection of the right hemisphere a "euphorical" reaction was reported as the patient "appears without apprehension, smiles and laughs and both with mimicry and words expresses considerable liveliness and sense of well-being." These results have proven provocative. Unfortunately, a number of groups have been unable to confirm these observations. For example, in one report on 104 patients Milner noted only rare depression, and there was no systematic asymmetry in the euphoria. Furthermore, Kolb and Milner found no asymmetry in either the frequency or the quality (e.g., happy vs. sad) of facial expressions following injection of the left and right hemispheres respectively (see Figure 17-4).

The difference between the results of the Italian investigators and Milner's group is unlikely to be resolved in the near future. There is one relevant methodological difference: in the two Milner series each patient could be used as his own control, because both hemispheres were injected, although on different days. In the Terzian and Rossi studies most patients were injected in only one hemisphere. In any event, until such results are replicated by others they should be interpreted with caution.

Inferences from Commissurotomy

Lateralization of affective responses has not been studied intensively in split-brain patients. Preliminary indications imply that both hemispheres experience affect, although the patient is only able to talk about it if the stim-

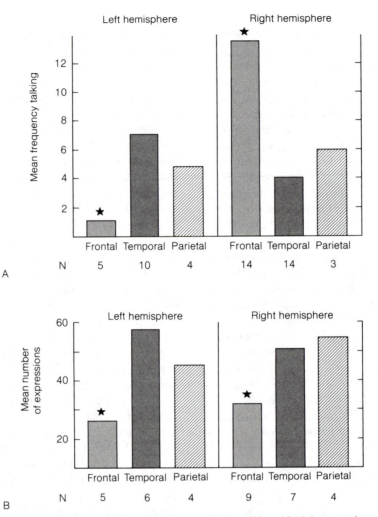

FIGURE 17-3. Relative frequencies of spontaneous talking (A) and facial expressions (B) during routine neuropsychological testing. Note that frontal-lobe lesions significantly reduce the number of facial expressions. The level of spontaneous talking is significantly reduced for left frontal lesions and increased for right frontal lesions. (After Kolb et al., 1980.)

uli are presented to the left hemisphere. For example, when a nude pin-up was flashed to the right hemisphere without warning within a series of rather mundane photographs, one split-brain patient broke into a "hearty grin and chuckle." When asked what was funny the patient replied that she didn't know. When the picture was unexpectedly presented to the left hemisphere she laughed again, but quickly reported the picture as being of a nude woman. Similarly, offensive odors presented to one nostril, and hence to one hemisphere, evoke

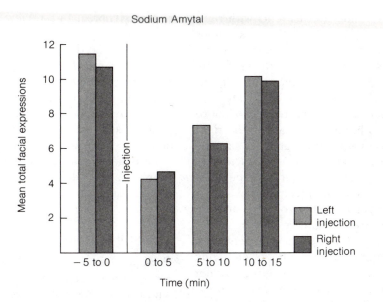

FIGURE 17-4. Changes in facial expression following injection into the left or right hemisphere. Note that injection into each hemisphere abolished expression briefly. Gradual recovery followed. There was no evidence of asymmetry. (After Kolb and Milner, 1980).

an emotional reaction no matter which hemisphere experiences it, but, as expected, only when the stimulus was presented to the left hemisphere could the patient talk about it.

Affect is difficult to lateralize in the split-brain patient for a number of reasons. First, emotional reactions to offensive odors or embarrassing photographs can presumably spread quickly through intact limbic-system connections to the opposite side. Second, various reactions such as blushing, giggling, frowning, and the like presumably help to bilateralize any emotion and make it very difficult to demonstrate concurrent conflicting emotional sets on the two sides.

ABNORMAL BEHAVIOR IN NEUROLOGICAL DISEASE

Psychiatry and neurology have traditionally been aloof from one another, clinicians in both

fields readily acknowledging a region of overlap but not clearly defining this borderland that until recently had remained a hinterland. In this section we briefly describe those neurological disorders consistently associated with behavior identified as abnormal in psychiatry.

Cortical Lesions Reviewed

In the chapters on the association cortex we noted that lesions to the frontal, parietal, and temporal regions all produce changes in personality and affect. In the previous section we described the experimental work on these changes. In general, right-hemisphere lesions appear to release talking, left-hemisphere lesions to reduce it. These effects are especially obvious following frontal-lobe lesions. The content of the talking released by right-hemisphere lesions has not been carefully studied, but it is our impression that it is significantly affected by the lesion site. Patients with right frontal lesions characteristically make poor jokes and puns and also tell pointless stories, often liberally embellished with profanity. Further, the right frontal patient is usually intensely amused by the stories he or she is telling, and will persist even if others are ambivalent to them. On the other hand, lesions of the right temporal and/or parietal lobe produce a totally different type of talking that is characterized by excessive concern for their own personal lives. They often go to great lengths to rationalize their personal shortcomings, and are generally unaware that others may be bored with their talking. Many of these patients also exhibit symptoms of paranoia, often being convinced that friends or family either are not supportive or are against them. They are excessively suspicious of neuropsychological assessments, insisting either that the assessments are unnecessary or that they would rather do them when they are "feeling better." We caution that this apparent qualitative difference between frontal and posterior lesions is a clinical impression and requires more systematic study.

Personality Changes Associated with Movement Disorders

Many movement disorders appear to have associated changes in personality. Pincus and Tucker estimate that as many as 90 percent of parkinsonian patients appear depressed. Because the caudate nucleus is anatomically closely related to the frontal lobe, the depression observed in such patients and in left frontal-lobe patients may be of a similar origin. Further, the biochemical changes in parkinsonism resemble those implicated in depression (see below).

In 1872, George Huntington defined "insanity with a tendency to suicide" as one of three distinguishing characteristics of Hun-

tington's chorea. In a review of the literature since Huntington's paper, McHugh and Folstein conclude that two psychiatric symptoms are consistently found in patients with Huntington's chorea: (1) a dementia syndrome that afflicts all the patients; and (2) an affective disorder that afflicts a considerable proportion of patients and can mimic in every way manic-depressive illness. Some patients manifest a delusionary-hallucinatory state but whether it should be considered a distinct syndrome of the disease is uncertain.

Presenile Dementias

Presenile dementia is defined as a general deterioration of behavior at a relatively young age, usually late middle age. It results from a variety of diseases, some known to result from viral infections. In most presenile dementias there is an atrophy of the neocortex, especially association cortex, although the principal region varies with the disease. Malamud reports that three presenile dementias—Alzheimer's, Pick's, and Jakob-Creutzfeldt's diseases—are often misdiagnosed as psychiatric disorders, and estimates that about 25 percent of patients with Pick's disease are initially misdiagnosed as having psychiatric disturbances. The following case history illustrates typical symptoms of presenile dementias. Notice how these symptoms resemble those of the frontal-lobe patients described in Chapter 14.

A 39-year-old white man had a history of normal prepsychotic personality, but at about the age of 34, while in the Army, he became withdrawn and slovenly in his personal appearance and was discharged from the service with a diagnosis of chronic schizophrenia. Three years later, he was admitted to a V.A. hospital because he had become increasingly mute and negativistic. Examination revealed negative neurological and laboratory studies, a clear sensorium, but emotional apathy, tendency to perseveration and incontinence. The diagnosis of schizophrenia was maintained and he received electroshock therapy without benefit. Prefrontal leucotomy was then recommended. When this was attempted, bilateral organized subdural hematomas were found compressing the brain. These were evacuated and the leucotomy was not performed. That patient's condition remained unchanged and he finally expired of bronchopneumonia.

The brain showed gross evidence of cerebral compression (by the old subdural hematomas) superimposed on the classic features of lobar atrophy, in which the involvement of the frontal, inferior temporal and posterior parietal regions was sharply demarcated from the well-preserved postcentral, superior temporal and occipital gyri. Microscopically, a diffuse loss of pyramidal cells especially in the third cortical layer was associated with scattered inflated neurons with argyrophilic inclusions, or so-called Pick cells. (Malamud, 1975, pp. 293–294)

Epilepsy

By nature of their interest and training, neurologists and neuropsychologists tend to pay little attention to the psychiatric symptoms of epilepsy. Historically, however, epilepsy was considered a form of insanity. Only in recent times has this stigma been removed. Among the various forms of epilepsy, temporal-lobe or psychomotor epilepsy has been identified as the form most likely to be associated with psychiatric disturbance. Blumer estimates that epileptics in general account for up to 10 percent of the total number of mental hospital admissions, and that as many as 50 percent of psychomotor epileptics may experience some form of psychiatric disorder.

Psychiatric changes rarely precede the onset of overt seizures, usually following them instead by about two years. The range of psychopathologic changes in temporal-lobe epilepsy is remarkable indeed. It may include decreased sexual arousal, which appears to re-

turn to normal when the seizures are controlled; impulsive, irritable behavior in the form of outbursts of anger or verbal or physical abuse; and good-naturedness and religiosity. A "temporal-lobe" personality is often described, being characterized by a deepening emotional response in which there is an overemphasis on trivia and the petty details of daily life. The probability of psychiatric, and particularly psychotic, disturbance in epileptics is related to two factors in epilepsy: there is typically a long history of anticonvulsant medication; and usually the medication only partially controls the seizures. That is, epileptics with psychotic symptoms usually have seizures, typically extending over more than a 10-year period, despite heavy medication.

NEUROLOGICAL FACTORS IN ABNORMAL BEHAVIOR

Accumulating evidence from the fields of neurochemistry, neurology, and neuropsychology indicates that diseases such as schizophrenia and depression are correlated with neurological abnormality.

Neurochemistry of Abnormal Behavior

From research on drug action, from autopsied brains, from the metabolites of psychotic patients, and from the observed side effects of movement-disorder treatments one conclusion is encouraged: there is strong evidence favoring the presence of neurobiochemical abnormalities in schizophrenia and depression. Although there is little agreement on the precise nature of these alleged abnormalities, the following neurotransmitters in particular have been implicated: noradrenaline, dopamine, serotonin, phenylethylamine, and endorphins.

During treatment of Parkinson's disease excessive medication with l-dopa has consistently been observed to result not only in relief of parkinsonian symptoms but also in the appearance of schizophrenic symptoms. Since l-dopa raises brain dopamine and noradrenaline levels it might be inferred that schizophrenia results from excessive levels of brain catecholamines. It is equally plausible, however, that the l-dopa medication increases the catecholamines, thus unbalancing a variety of neurochemical systems. Autopsy and brain metabolic studies also point to excessive levels of brain catecholamines, especially in the limbic system; but controversy surrounds many of these studies as well.

In a recent review article, Van Praag argued that certain types of depression are correlated with reduced levels of brain bioamines. In some depressions serotonin levels are alleged to be reduced; in others noradrenaline levels are low. But in still others both or neither may be reduced.

Biochemical studies have a primary shortcoming—they necessarily seek altered biochemistry within the known biochemical systems. In view of recent advances in knowledge about biochemical systems, it is not rash to presume that many systems, as yet uncharted, are potentially responsible for various psychotic disturbances.

Neurology and Abnormal Behavior

Trying to identify abnormalities in the brains of psychotic patients presents serious technical problems. By analogy, few would seriously doubt that something is seriously wrong with the brains of retarded individuals, even in the absence of supportive evidence. Thus, absence of evidence is certainly not evidence of absence. Nevertheless, there are preliminary indications that schizophrenics at least have neurological abnormalities. Haug did pneumoencephalograms (PEGs) on 278 mental patients diagnosed as either schizophrenic or having a nonorganic or an organic mental disorder. The schizophrenic group did not include patients with any indication of previous head trauma or alcoholism. Seventy-two percent of the "organics," 61 percent of the schizophrenics, and 48 percent of the "nonorganics" had abnormal PEGs. The mean size of the lateral ventricles in all groups was significantly greater than normal, thus indicating brain atrophy. Curiously, the "nonorganic" group showed a focal increase in ventricle size localized in the temporal horns. Few of the patients with abnormal PEGs were helped by *any* form of treatment, whereas most of the other patients were.

Rochford examined 65 hospitalized psychiatric patients before any psychotropic medications were administered, and assessed the presence or absence of the following minor neurological signs: (1) motor impersistence, (2) astereognosis, (3) agraphesthesia, (4) extinction during simultaneous bilateral stimulation, (5) bilateral marked hyper-reflexia, (6) coordination defects, (7) disturbance of balance and gait, (8) cortical sensory abnormalities, (9) mild movement disorders, (10) speech defects, (11) abnormal motor activity, (12) defective auditory-visual integration, (13) choreiform movements and adventitious motor overflow (tremor), (14) cranial-nerve abnormalities, and (15) unequivocally abnormal electroencephalograms. He reported that 36.8 percent of the patients had some neurologic abnormality, compared to an age-matched normal control population having only 5 percent abnormal signs. Patients diagnosed as schizophrenic showed the most symptoms, over 65 percent being abnormal. Somewhat surprisingly, patients diagnosed as having affective disorders showed no abnormalities. Similar results have been reported by Pollin and Stabenau.

Several groups have studied the neuropsychological test performance of schizophrenic patients. In general, schizophrenics are as severely impaired at a wide range of tests as are patients with known brain damage. In our experience, tests of frontal- and temporal-lobe function are performed especially poorly. A number of authors (e.g., Flor-Henry) have proposed that schizophrenics perform more poorly on tests of left- than of right-hemisphere function. We have been unable to replicate this finding using the tests described in Tables 12-3, 13-3, and 14-3. Rather, we found that schizophrenic patients were impaired at all tests of frontal- and temporal-lobe function but performed normally on tests of parietal-lobe function. This result is consistent with Hughlings-Jackson's proposals concerning the origin of schizophrenia (see Chapters 8 and 10): he believed schizophrenia to result from normally functioning sensory and perceptual systems that were released from inhibition by the frontal and temporal lobes. To date, however, neuropsychological hypotheses of schizophrenia remain intriguing but still unproven—hypotheses that are likely to generate considerable interest over the next decade.

CONCLUSIONS

The results of studies of neuropsychological aspects of affect demonstrate that although there is an asymmetry in the cerebral control of affective behavior, both hemispheres play a role in this type of behavior. Affect is not the sole domain of the right hemisphere, as has been previously proposed. Although the right hemisphere plays a special role not shared by the left hemisphere in analyzing affectively toned facial and auditory stimuli, both hemispheres play a role in producing affective behavior. The details of the respective roles of each hemisphere are the subject of considerable interest and controversy at present, and few firm conclusions are possible. Abnormalities of brain function and biochemistry are implicated in a variety of psychiatric disorders such as schizophrenia and depression. But, again, few conclusions can be made at this time.

The neuropsychology of affective behavior in patients with lateralized lesions is a relatively new field of study, and is likely to become more popular in the coming years, particularly because of the implications for the treatment and rehabilitation of both neurological and psychiatric patients. This research is likely to proceed cautiously, however, because it would be a tragedy to repeat past mistakes such as the widespread use of psychosurgery in the late 1940s and early 50s in a hurried attempt to improve the condition of patients with psychotic or affective disorders.

REFERENCES

Benson, D. F., and D. Blumer, eds. *Psychiatric Aspects of Neurological Disease.* New York: Grune and Stratton, 1975.

Blumer, D. Temporal lobe epilepsy and its psychiatric significance. In D. F. Blumer and D. Benson, eds. *Psychiatric Aspects of Neurological Disease.* New York: Grune and Stratton, 1975.

Brown, S., and E. A. Schaefer. An investigation into the functions of the occipital and temporal lobe of the monkey's brain. *Philosophical Transactions of the Royal Society,* Part B, *179* (1888), 303–327.

Buchtel, H., F. Campari, C. de Risio, and R. Rota. Hemispheric differences in discriminative reaction time to facial expressions. *Italian Journal of Psychology, 5* (1978), 159–169.

Campbell, R. Asymmetries in interpreting and expressing a posed facial expression. *Cortex, 14* (1978), 327–342.

Carlsson, A. Does dopamine have a role in schizophrenia? *Biological Psychiatry, 13* (1978), 3–21.

Carmon, A., and I. Nachshon. Ear asymmetry in perception of emotional nonverbal stimuli. *Acta Psychologia, 37* (1973), 351–357.

Chaurasia, B. D., and H. K. Goswami. Functional asymmetry in the face. *Acta Anatomica. 91* (1975), 154–160.

Davis, K. L., and P. Berger. Pharmacological investigations of the cholinergic imbalance hypotheses of movement disorders and psychosis. *Biological Psychiatry, 13* (1978), 23–49.

Dimond, S. J., and L. Farrington. Emotional response to films shown to the right or left hemisphere of the brain measured by heart rate. *Acta Psychologia, 41* (1977), 255–260.

Dimond, S. J., L. Farrington, and P. Johnson. Differing emotional response from right and left hemispheres. *Nature, 261* (1976), 690–692.

Farley, I. J., K. S. Price, E. McCullough, W. Deck, W. Hordynsku, and O. Hornykiewicz. Norepinephrine levels in chronic paranoid schizophrenia: above-normal levels in limbic forebrain. *Science, 200* (1978), 456–458.

Flor-Henry, P. On certain aspects of the localization of the cerebral systems regulating and determining emotion. *Biological Psychiatry, 14* (1979), 677–698.

Flor-Henry, P., L. T. Yeudall, W. Stefanyk, and B. Howarth. The neuropsychological correlates of the functional psychoses. *International Research Communications Systems; Medical Science, 3* (1975), 34.

Gainotti, G. Emotional behavior and hemispheric side of the lesion. *Cortex, 8* (1972), 41–55.

Gardner, H., P. K. Ling, L. Flamm, and J. Silverman. Comprehension and appreciation of humorous material following brain damage. *Brain, 98* (1975), 399–412.

Goldstein, K. *The Organism: A Holistic Approach to Biology, Derived from Pathological Data in Man.* New York: American Book, 1939.

Haggard, M. P., and A. M. Parkinson. Stimulus and task factors as determinants of ear advantages. *Quarterly Journal of Experimental Psychology, 23* (1971), 168–177.

Haug, J. O. Pneumoencephalographic studies in mental disease. *Acta Psychiatrica Neurologia Scandinavia,* Supplement 165, *38* (1962), 1–104.

Hécaen, H., J. de Ajuriaguerra, and J. Massonet. Les troubles visuo-constructifs par lesion parieto-occipitale droite. *Encephalé, 40* (1951), 122–179.

Heilman, K., M. R. Scholes, and R. T. Watson. Auditory affective agnosia. *Journal of Neurology, Neurosurgery and Psychiatry, 38* (1975), 69–72.

King, F. L., and D. Kimura. Left-ear superiority in dichotic perception of vocal nonverbal sounds. *Canadian Journal of Psychology, 26* (1972), 111–116.

Klüver, H., and P. C. Bucy. Preliminary analysis of the temporal lobes in monkeys. *Archives of Neurology and Psychiatry, 42* (1939), 979–1000.

Kolb, B. Neural mechanisms of emotional expression in man and higher primates. Paper at Canadian Psychological Association, Vancouver, Canada, 1977.

Kolb, B. and Milner, B. Observations on spontaneous facial expression in patients. Unpublished manuscript, 1980.

Kolb, B., L. Taylor, and B. Milner. Affective behavior in patients with localized cortical excisions: an analysis of lesion site and side. Unpublished manuscript, 1980.

Kolb, B., I. Q. Whishaw, and R. Barnsley. Neuropsychological aspects of schizophrenia and depression. Progress report to Alberta Mental Health Advisory Council, 1979.

Ley, R. G., and M. P. Bryden. Hemispheric differences in processing emotions and faces. *Brain and Language, 7* (1979), 127–138.

McHugh, P. R., and M. F. Folstein. Psychiatric syndromes of Huntington's chorea. In D. F. Benson and D. Blumer, eds. *Psychiatric Aspects of Neurological Disease.* New York: Grune and Stratton, 1975.

Malamud, N. Organic brain disease mistaken for psychiatric disorder. In D. F. Benson and D. Blumer, eds. *Psychiatric Aspects of Neurological Disease.* New York: Grune and Stratton, 1975.

Marlowe, W. B., E. L. Mancall, and J. J. Thomas. Complete Klüver-Bucy syndrome in man. *Cortex, 11* (1975), 53–59.

Milner, B. Brain mechanisms suggested by studies of the temporal lobes. In C. H. Millikan and F. L. Darley, eds. *Brain Mechanisms Underlying Speech and Language.* New York: Grune and Stratton, 1967.

Moscovitch, M., and J. Olds. Asymmetries in spontaneous facial expressions and their possible relation to hemispheric specialization. Unpublished manuscript, 1980.

Papez, J. W. A proposed mechanism of emotion. *Archives of Neurology and Psychiatry, 38* (1937), 725–744.

Pincus, J. H., and G. J. Tucker. *Behavioral Neurology.* New York: Oxford University Press, 1974.

Pollin, W., and J. Stabenau. Biological, psychological and historical differences in a series of monozygotic twins discordant for schizophrenia. In D. Rosenthal and S. Kety, eds. *Transmission of Schizophrenia.* London: Pergamon Press, 1968.

Reitan, R. M. Neurological and physiological bases of psychopathology. *Annual Review of Psychology, 27* (1976), 189–216.

Rochford, J. M., T. Detre, G. J. Tucker, and M. Harrow. Neuropsychological impairments in functional psychiatric diseases. *Archives of General Psychiatry, 22* (1970), 114–119.

Roemer, R. A., C. Shagass, J. J. Straumanis, and M. Amadea. Pattern evoked potential measurements suggesting lateralized hemispheric dysfunction in chronic schizophrenics. *Biological Psychiatry, 13* (1978), 185–202.

Rossi, G. F., and G. Rosandini. Experimental analysis of cerebral dominance in man. In C. H. Millikan and F. L. Darley, eds. *Brain Mechanisms Underlying Speech and Language.* New York: Grune and Stratton, 1967.

Rovetta, P. Discussion of paper "Amytal intracarotides per lo studio della dominanza emisferica." *Rivista di Neurologia, 30* (1960), 460–470.

Sackheim, H., R. S. Gur, and M. Saucy. Emotions are expressed more intensely on the left side of the face. *Science, 202* (1978), 434–436.

Safer, M., and H. Leventhal. Ear differences in evaluating emotional tones of voice and verbal content. *Journal of Experimental Psychology: Human Perception and Performance, 3* (1977), 75–82.

Schwartz, G. E., R. J. Davidson, and F. Maer. Right hemisphere lateralization for emotion in the human brain: interactions with cognition. *Science, 190* (1975), 286–288.

Terzian, H. Behavioral and EEG effects of intracarotid sodium Amytal injection. *Acta Neurochirurgica, 12* (1964), 230–239.

Tucker, D. M., R. T. Watson, and K. M. Heilman. Discrimination and evocation of affectively intoned speech in patients with right parietal disease. *Neurology, 27* (1977), 947–950.

Valenstein, E. *Brain Control.* New York: John Wiley and Sons, 1973.

Van Praag, H. M. Significance of biochemical parameters in the diagnosis, treatment and prevention of depressive disorders. *Biological Psychiatry, 12* (1977), 101–131.

Watson, S. J., P. A. Berger, H. Akil, M. J. Mills, and J. D. Barchas. Effects of naloxone on schizophrenia: reduction in hallucinations in a subpopulation of subjects. *Science, 201* (1978), 73–76.

Waxman, S. G., and N. Geschwind. Hypergraphia in temporal lobe epilepsy. *Neurology, 24* (1974), 629–636.

PART EIGHT

ISSUES

Three fundamental issues in neuropsychology have not yet been discussed: the problem of development of the brain and of cognitive processes, especially with regard to cerebral asymmetry; the study of recovery of function following brain injury in infancy or adulthood; and the idea that the functions of brain regions can be understood only in the context of the connections between them. Chapters 18, 19, and 20 address these issues respectively. Each chapter considers basic cortical functions discussed in previous sections from a different perspective, throwing light on vast developing areas of neuropsychological research.

18

DEVELOPMENTAL ISSUES

Developmental neuropsychology is becoming an area of increasing interest for many reasons. Some people are attracted to the area because they believe that children are neurologically simpler than adults and therefore easier to study. Others believe that analysis of the behavior and development of children will give important clues about the relative contributions of heredity and environment to the development of particular behaviors. Still others are compelled by practical necessity: they must develop programs for children with special problems in school. The growth of developmental neuropsychology as a field of inquiry has raised further questions. Why does the brain in early life appear to be so flexible in compensating for injury and for variations in the environment? Is there an optimal environment in which development should occur? Is there an optimal method of instruction that should be used in education? How can one brain be so much more efficient than another that appears so similar under superficial examination? Thus, the object of developmental

neuropsychology is to better understand nervous-system function in early life, and to see whether such an understanding can contribute answers to questions such as the above.

METHODOLOGY

Behavioral changes related to neural function can be examined in three ways. The first is to look at nervous-system maturation and correlate it with the development of specific behaviors. The second, the converse, is to look at behavior and then make inferences about neural maturation. The third is to relate brain malfunction or damage to behavioral disorders or cognitive deficits. Although each of these procedures is widely used, each is associated with methodological difficulties that deserve comment.

Initially, the first-named method, relating neural development to the emergence of specific behaviors, might seem ideal. The development of both the nervous system and behavior is orderly and similar in sequence from person to person, suggesting that correlations may be made easily. This approach has not been as useful as was expected, for a number of reasons. (1) The nervous system develops in a relatively unremitting way, whereas behavioral changes depend on education and learning. Thus, a behavior may emerge in one environment but not in another. (2) Because age-related changes in the human nervous system are observable only in extraordinary circumstances, it is impossible to observe relevant changes. Furthermore, the relevant neural substrate may be difficult to identify. For example, hundreds of studies on animals have attempted, with little success, to determine some anatomical or biochemical substrate of memory. This general failure bodes ill for such correlations in humans, because in theory it is easier to correlate a neural-behavioral change in animals. (3) Behaviors deemed important may also be irrelevant. For example, there is a tendency to emphasize school behaviors as most important for study; although these are certainly important, it must be remembered that the human brain did not evolve in a school-like environment. The basic functions and abilities of the brain may be revealed by the study of much more fundamental processes. Reading requires spatial skills and sequencing ability. How reading skills develop may be better understood by analyzing these more basic abilities than by studying reading per se. Because developmental research focused on nervous-system changes is difficult to conduct, most of it is done with animal models. Nevertheless, the principles obtained from this research should be applicable to humans.

The second approach, the analysis of nervous-system function by inference from sequential changes in behavior, is not widely used. This is partly because the psychologists most interested in human development have not been primarily interested in brain function. Also, hypotheses about brain function are hard to verify, because the human nervous system cannot be manipulated during development. Nevertheless, this approach is important because it is the only way models of the function of the normal human nervous system can be obtained.

The third approach, relating brain malfunction to behavioral disorders, is widely used in adult neuropsychology, but has drawbacks when applied to developmental problems. First, much evidence suggests that the function of an immature brain may not be comparable to that of an adult brain. Freud's work, and subsequently Piaget's, suggests, first, that the immature brain might be incapable of certain adult functions, and, second, that there is no *one* immature brain. That is, the brain may be changing such that principles applicable at one age are inappropriate for another age. This discontinuity may be one reason why estimates of intelligence obtained from very young children correlate poorly with their adult intelligence. Another obstacle to directly applying adult neuropsychology to developing brains is the plasticity or adaptability of the immature brain. Brain damage occurring in infancy may often go unnoticed because an undamaged portion of the brain adopts the function of the damaged zone. For example, if the speech zones of an infant's left hemisphere are damaged, speech may develop on the right. Such does not occur in an adult. Nevertheless, this approach remains important and provides major clues about the organization of the developing brain.

We point out these pitfalls in developmental neuropsychology not to deter study of developmental problems, but to caution that the neuropsychology of children may not be identical to that of adults. True, when adult standards are used, infants may look surprisingly like adults in a number of ways. But this similarity could be an artifact of researcher expectation: if the infant's brain is expected to be like the adult's, and if it is therefore studied only with tests initially designed for the study of adults, then phenomena peculiar to infants and children may be ignored.

The remainder of this chapter is divided into four sections. The first section looks at developmental problems from a neurological perspective; that is, what can be learned about behavior from studying the development of the nervous system. By its nature this area is largely experimental, leans heavily on animal research, and provides some good basic insights into developmental issues. The second section consists largely of work done on the development of cognitive functions from which inferences are made about nervous-system organization and development. As might be expected, it is informative, but its interpretation is speculative. The third section describes the effects of brain damage suffered in infancy, and compares these with the effects suffered by adults. The fourth section combines the different lines of research discussed in the chapter and presents a view of cognitive development that we believe may prove useful for understanding development.

A NEURAL PERSPECTIVE ON DEVELOPMENT

Cellular Basis of Brain Development

The process of brain growth and differentiation consists of a series of biological changes occurring at a particular age and in a relatively fixed sequence. These include: (1) the migration of cells; (2) the formation and growth of axons; (3) the formation of dendrites; (4) the formation of synaptic connections; and (5) myelinization. Because of either deficits in the genetic program, intrauterine trauma, the in-

fluence of toxic agents, or other factors, peculiarities or errors in development can occur that may contribute to obvious and severe deformities such as those listed in Table 18-1. Less pronounced deficits may become manifest in such things as learning disabilities, or may contribute only to subtle differences in individuality. In the following sections each of the above-named biological processes is briefly described, as are abnormalities that occur when the process is not properly completed.

Cell Migration. Nerve cells form by division in the inner, or ventricular, lining of the brain, and migrate from there to the surface of the brain. Once a group of cells has arrived at the surface, differentiation (formation of axons, dendrites, etc.) begins. Subsequently a new group of cells migrates from the inner lining through the layers already present to form a new outer layer. Thus, a structure such as the cortex matures from its inner to its outer surface. The mechanisms that guide migration are not known.

Migration can stop prematurely, leaving a group of cells that should normally appear as an outer layer instead scattered among inner layers of cells. Caviness and Sidman have made a major study of disturbed cell migration in the cortex of a genetic mutant mouse called the reeler mouse. In this animal the first-generated cells lie near the surface while the last-generated lie deepest, creating a cortex that is inverted from that of a normal mouse. Despite their aberrant position the cells receive and give off appropriate connections, but the mice have an abnormal, reeling, movement. Cases of failure or incomplete cell migration in humans have also been described.

Axonal Growth. Sprouting axons grow in a given direction either because the cell body is oriented in a particular way or because of other, unknown factors. The growing end of

TABLE 18-1

Types of abnormal development

Type	Symptom
Anencephaly	Absence of cerebral hemispheres, diencephalon, and midbrain
Holoprosencephaly	Cortex forms as a single undifferentiated hemisphere
Lissencephaly	The brain fails to form sulci and gyri and corresponds to a 12-week embryo
Micropolygyria	Gyri are more numerous, smaller, and more poorly developed than normal
Macrogyria	Gyri are broader and less numerous than normal
Microencephaly	Development of the brain is rudimentary and the person has low-grade intelligence
Porencephaly	Symmetrical cavities in the cortex, where cortex and white matter should be
Heterotopia	Displaced islands of grey matter appear in the ventricular walls or white matter, caused by aborted cell migration
Agenesis of the corpus callosum	Complete or partial absence of the corpus callosum
Cerebellar agenesis	Portions of the cerebellum, basal ganglia, or spinal cord are absent or malformed

the axon, called the growth cone, was first recognized and described by Ramón y Cajal in the 1890s. He wrote:

> I had the good fortune to behold for the first time that fantastic ending of the growing axon. In my sections of the three-day chick embryo, this ending appeared as a concentration of protoplasm of conical form, endowed with ameboid movements. It could be compared with a living battering ram, soft and flexible, which advances, pushing aside mechanically the obstacles which it finds in its way, until it reaches the area of its peripheral distribution. This curious terminal club, I christened the growth cone. (Ramón y Cajal, 1937)

In general, the axon grows at a rate of 7 to 170 microns (μ) per hour. Axon branching occurs at the growth cone. It is possible that the growth cone forms synapses, and retains the capacity to renew growth, which may thus underlie the formation of new synapses during the course of learning.

A major unanswered question in developmental neurobiology concerns the forces that initiate and guide axonal growth. Axons have specific targets that they must reach if the neuron is to survive and become functional. Some axons grow because they are towed from their cell bodies by a structure that is growing away from the region, such as when the muscles grow away from the spinal cord early in development. Other axons traverse enormous distances, and are able to overcome obstacles such as being moved to another location, having their cell bodies rotated, or having their targets moved. Although the forces that guide this homing are not understood, there are several possibilities: axons may follow an electrical or chemical gradient, or a particular physical substrate; or they may send out many branches, or shoots, and when one reaches an appropriate target the others follow. It is also possible that several such mechanisms may be operative simultaneously or sequentially.

The formation of appropriate neural pathways may be disrupted in any of a number of ways. Axons may be unable to reach their target if their way is blocked, as may happen following scarring from head trauma during the early months of life. Their development may be disrupted by anoxia, ingestion of toxic materials, malnutrition, etc. Several reports of anomalous fiber systems in mutant strains of mice also suggest that abnormalities could have a genetic basis. There have been cases in which the corpus callosum is of abnormal size or is absent, and cases in which the fiber pathways in the hippocampal system are abnormal. In a number of albino animal species, and possibly also in human albinos, the ipsilateral optic pathway is reduced in size and area of distribution. Since the brain processes information sequentially, similar disruption of transcortical or interhemispheric connections during development could be related to the cognitive difficulties that some humans have. In fact, it has been suggested that some learning disorders might originate in delayed, incomplete, or inappropriate formation of the cortical fiber system.

Axonal development might also be disrupted if the axons' target is damaged, in which case the axonal system may degenerate or may occupy an inappropriate target. Should the latter event occur the behavior supported by the invaded area may also be disrupted. In a well-documented study of abnormal fiber growth Schneider has shown that if the optic tectum in the hamster is removed on one side at birth, the fibers that should normally project to it project instead to the opposite side. This aberrant pathway is functional, but in a curious way. If a visual stimulus is presented to the eye contralateral to the damaged tectum, the hamster turns in the direction opposite that of the stimulus. The message has traveled from the eye to the wrong tectum, a tectum that would ordinarily receive input from the opposite side of the world. The abnormalities of posture and movement seen in some sorts of athetosis and dystonia in children may occur because fiber systems supporting posture and movement invade the wrong target, causing an intended movement to be disrupted by an inappropriate movement. Should this be the case, it is not surprising that lesions in the thalamus, which might sever such an abnormal connection, can result in improved posture and movement.

Dendritic Growth. The growth of dendrites parallels that of axons, growth and division also occurring at a growth cone. Generally, the growth of dendrites is timed to intercept the axons that are to innervate them. During development all dendrites go through a phase in which they have dendritic spines; later the dendrites of some cells lose their spines, whereas others reduce the number of their spines. The significance of dendritic spines is not well understood, but it is possible that they receive a particular class of synapse.

In studies of abnormalities of dendrites it is difficult to determine whether a disorder is specifically dendritic or is secondary to inappropriate cell location, abnormal innervation, ingestion of a neurotoxin, etc. Reduced afferent innervation is known to lead to a reduction in the number of dendritic spines. Studies of the cerebral cortex in various mental retardation conditions indicate a number of dendritic abnormalities. Dendrites may be thinner, with fewer than normal numbers of spines; the dendrites may be short stalks with small spines, or there may be simply a reduction in spine number. What causes these changes is not known, but the histology gives the general impression that the embryonic condition is retained.

Synaptic Formation. It is clear from many studies that a given brain region sends axons to only a limited number of other regions, and that synapses are made only in a specific part of certain cells in that region. The locations of synapses are determined in part by genetic instruction, in part by the orientation of the cell when the axons arrive, in part by the timing of axon arrival (axons apparently compete for available space), and in part by the use that they are given once a connection is made. In addition, the pharmacology of the synapse is flexible. For example, it has been found that individual neurons can become either noradrenergic or cholinergic depending upon their environment. Malfunctions in any of these features of synaptic formation may cause abnormal brain development.

Myelination. Myelination is the process by which the support cells of the nervous system begin to surround axons and provide them insulation. Although nerves can become functional before myelinization, it is assumed that they reach adult functional levels as myelination is completed. Thus, myelination provides an index of the maturity of structures from which axons project and to which they project.

If myelination is used as an index of maturation, then the anatomical developmental work of Flechsig indicates that the neocortex begins a sequential development at a relatively early age. The primary sensory areas and motor areas show some myelinization just before term. The secondary cortical areas become myelinated within the next four postnatal months, and by the fourth month the tertiary areas of the cortex are becoming myelinated. Although myelination begins during the early

postnatal period, it continues to increase beyond 15 years of age, and may increase in density as late as 60 years of age. Any disruption in this ongoing process can potentially cause neural and hence behavioral abnormalities.

ENVIRONMENTAL INFLUENCES ON DEVELOPMENT

The environment in which development occurs can profoundly influence behavior, as has been suggested by anecdotal reports about how deprivation has produced impoverished behavior in children. For example, Singh and Zingg report that children raised by wolves behave like wolves and are difficult to socialize; on the other hand, Skeels reports that children removed from substandard orphanages develop normal intelligence by adulthood whereas those that are not removed remain retarded. These reports have been fully confirmed by Harlow in formal studies on the effects of early deprivation on the maturation of monkeys. How do the conditions of early environment affect nervous-system development? There are several possibilities, each of which has received some support in recent experimental work: (1) The nervous system develops independently, but requires stimulation for maintained function. (2) The nervous system develops independently in part, but requires stimulation for continued maturation beyond some point. Inappropriate stimulation may change the system's properties. (3) The properties of the nervous system are not innate, but develop only with appropriate stimulation. Experimental work has been advanced most by studies using the visual system as a model, and provides support for each of these possibilities. In all cases the importance of stimulation is emphasized. The term **functional validation** is sometimes used to express the idea that to become fully functional a neural system requires stimulation at some point.

Environmental Influences on Brain Size

The simplest measure of the effects of environment on the nervous system is brain size. Environmental influences on animal brain size have been investigated; domestic animals have brains up to 10 to 20 percent smaller than those of animals of the same species and strain raised in the wild. These differences are apparently related to factors that occur early in life, since animals born in the wild and later domesticated have brains the same size as animals raised in the wild. The part of the brain that seems to be most affected by a domestic upbringing is the cortex, which is reduced in size by as much as 35 percent in some animals. This reduction may be related to smaller eye and retina size.

An extensive laboratory experimental literature now exists on the effects of environmental manipulation on brain size and anatomy. Exposure to an enriched environment increases brain size, most noticeably in the neocortex, with the greatest increase occurring in the occipital neocortex. Related to increased size are increases in the density of glial cells, in the number of higher-order dendritic spines on neurons, in the number of synaptic spines, and in the size of synapses. These changes are most pronounced if enriched experience is given in early life; similar but less pronounced effects can be obtained with more prolonged exposure given in later life. In addition to these anatomical changes, enriched animals can perform better than their impoverished counterparts on a number of tests of learning and memory. However, given that the enriched environment of the laboratory experiment may be less than or only equivalent to that of a wild habitat, these findings mean that exposure to an impoverished laboratory retards the development of the nervous system and reduces performance on a number of tests.

Environmental Influences on Function— Examples from the Visual System

Clinical studies have shown that disturbances of the optics of the eye, e.g., cataracts, astigmatism, etc., during early life cause long-lasting impairments of vision even after the optical defects are corrected. These impairments, called **amblyopia**—dimness of vision without obvious impairment of the eye—are presumed to be caused by changes in the central nervous system. Behavioral studies have shown that amblyopia can be produced in animals; its cause has been extensively analyzed in studies using cats and monkeys. This area of research now provides one of the most penetrating insights into factors affecting development and deserves careful study.

Hubel and Wiesel and others have described the response patterns of normal cells in area 17 of the visual cortex. They recorded the activity of cells in anesthetized animals while visual stimuli were presented on a screen placed in the animal's visual field. The cells respond to a number of properties of a visual stimulus, including its orientation and direction; they also respond according to which eye it is presented to, and are affected by binocular disparity (the different view each eye has of the stimulus). Using a profile of the activity of cells in a normal cat's area 17, Hubel and Wiesel addressed the question of the function of area 17 in kittens whose eyes had not yet opened. In eight-day-old kittens they found that although the cells are sluggish and become fatigued quickly, they show the properties of the adult cat's cells to the first presentation of visual stimulation. The results of this and similar studies suggest that the visual system has normal response capacity before being stimulated by light. What, then, of the environment's contribution?

To assess the contributions of the environment two conditions of visual deprivation have been used: **binocular deprivation** and **monocular deprivation**. In the first, animals are deprived by being reared in the dark or by their eyelids being sutured before they open. This deprivation produces no change in the retina, and only mild changes in the lateral geniculate nucleus, the major relay of the visual cortex. By contrast, cells in the visual cortex undergo disturbances of protein synthesis and have fewer and shorter dendrites, fewer spines, and 70 percent fewer synapses than normal. Analysis of the properties of these cells shows that after a number of months of early deprivation there are severe abnormalities, which disappear to some extent with normal visual experience. Deprivation in later life does not produce the same initial period of abnormality. Thus, visual stimulation in early life is important for continued development of visual cells, but the visual system retains some ability to compensate.

The second deprivation condition, monocular deprivation, surprisingly has a severer effect than binocular deprivation. If one eyelid is sutured during early life the eye appears to be essentially blind for a period of weeks after opening, although its function does improve somewhat with time. Cell-recording studies show either that stimulation in the deprived eye cannot activate cells in the cortex, or that in those few cases in which it can the cells are highly abnormal. The experiments also show that the earlier deprivation occurs, the shorter the deprivation period required and the severer the effects. These results confirm that deprivation can retard development, and that early deprivation is the most influential. The experiments also suggest that factors other than deprivation alone must be operative to produce the severe effects found.

Apparently competition also contributes to the severity of deficits in the deprived eye. Kratz et al. found that if the normal eye of an animal was removed after the other eye had been deprived for five months the deprived eye gave comparatively normal responses in 31 percent of the cells, compared with only 6 percent when the normal eye was present. This finding is confirmed by a number of more indirect experiments. These results imply that the deprived portion of the visual system has the capacity to function, but is inhibited from doing so by the good portion of the visual system. If inhibition of function is removed, the deprived portion of the visual system begins to function.

Can the visual system be changed by manipulation less drastic than complete sensory deprivation? Hirsch and Spinelli fitted kittens with lenses that brought a set of horizontal stripes into focus on one retina and a set of vertical stripes into focus on the other retina. After later removal of the lenses, they found that cells responded only if the stimulus was oriented close to the horizontal when viewed with the eye that had seen horizontal during the exposure period, and only to a stimulus oriented close to the vertical when viewed with the eye that had seen vertical stripes during the exposure period. These findings have been confirmed for kittens raised in an environment of stripes or of spots, or in an environment organized to be devoid of movement. In fact, work by Blakemore and Mitchell indicates that one hour of exposure on day 28 after birth is sufficient to bias a cortical unit to respond to a particular pattern.

In summary, this work suggests that the visual system is genetically programmed to make normal connections and normal responses, but can lose much of this capacity if it is not exercised during the early months of life. When part of the system is deprived, in addition to loss of capacity caused by the deprivation, the system is inhibited by the remaining functional areas, and the defect is potentiated. Removal of inhibition can permit some degree of recovery. Finally, if the environment is so arranged that the system is exposed to stimuli of one type, the cells in the system are biased to respond to stimuli of that type.

Although these conclusions come from experiments performed on a relatively low level of the visual system, the results can be generalized to other sensory systems and cortical areas. For example, our inability to perceive certain sounds in languages unfamiliar to us may result partly from disuse, inhibition, or the development of an incompatibility set within the auditory cortex. These experiments suggest speculative questions about the function of the brain. Under normal circumstances, how much do used portions of the brain tend to place inhibition upon unused portions of the brain? Does the development of language in one hemisphere inhibit its development in the other hemisphere? These questions will be asked in future experiments undertaken to analyze the secondary and tertiary areas of the cortex.

A BEHAVIORAL PERSPECTIVE ON DEVELOPMENT

Asymmetry

Just as the asymmetrical function of the adult's brain has been a focal point for neurological study, the development of asymmetry has been a focal point for developmental studies. Most studies with children have been designed to demonstrate lateralization of function, emphasizing the question of the age at which asymmetry first appears.

Asymmetry in the Auditory System

Asymmetry in the auditory system has been demonstrated in infants only a few weeks old. Entus combined the dichotic listening technique with a test known by the awesome name of the nonnutritive high-amplitude sucking paradigm. In the study the infant was given the opportunity to suck on a nipple and then to learn that if it increased its sucking rate it would receive an auditory stimulus through one or the other side of a pair of earphones. Entus presented phonemes such as /ma/ and /ba/, or the note A (440 Hz) played on different instruments, such as the piano or viola. Entus found that the infants changed their sucking rate in such a way that they received more phonemes through the right earphone than the left, and more musical notes through the left earphone than the right. This evidence suggested that there was a lateralized preference—left for phonemes, right for notes—as early as 22 days. In support of this conclusion a variety of evoked-potential and electroencephalographic studies suggest that very young infants have similarly lateralized preferences for phonemes and tones. In addition, many studies using the standard dichotic listening technique have found an adultlike asymmetry in children three years of age and older.

Asymmetry in the Visual System

There have been many attempts to use the tachistoscopic method of visual presentation to demonstrate perceptual asymmetries in the visual system of children. In a recent, thorough review, Witelson concluded that not one tachistoscopic study of left-hemisphere specialization in children is free of methodological difficulty, or provides unequivocal results. Tachistoscopic studies of right-hemisphere specialization have been more convincing, and have indicated right-hemisphere effects in children as young as six years of age. From their use of a strobe-light test Crowell et al. even suggest a right-hemisphere effect in newborns. Using findings that repetitive strobe-light flashes produce bilateral photic driving in adults—that is, particular EEG waves occurring in both hemispheres at the same frequency as the flash—he tested newborn babies for the same phenomenon. Newborns showed photic driving only in the right hemisphere (or in some cases not at all); Crowell interpreted this result as evidence of right-hemisphere specialization for the perception of rhythmic visual stimuli.

Asymmetry in Motor Control

The study of the development of hand preference is intriguing in view of the relationship between hand preference and cerebral control of language. Thus, the emergence of hand preference (presumably for the right hand) is commonly inferred to be indicative of left-hemisphere specialization. Although this inference is somewhat tenuous at best, it is nevertheless worthy of consideration. After hundreds of studies on this issue, considerable disagreement remains about results and their interpretation alike. The major problem is deciding how to measure hand preference. If frequency of reaching is taken as the measure there appears to be a *left* hand preference at about 4 to 5 months, followed by a switch to a *right* hand preference at about 6 to 9 months, which increases from then until 8 to 9 years. Measures of grasp duration, however, favor the right hand as early as one month of age. In general, although hand preference is evident in most tests by one year, the data at early ages are far from clear.

Observations favoring left-hemisphere specialization for motor control by age three or earlier include increased right-hand gesturing during speech (as seen also in adults), as well as reduced speed of finger tapping with the right hand, but not the left, when in competition with talking—a finding similar to those of analogous experiments in adults.

A study by Ingram is intriguing: she found both left- and right-hand effects in the same children, according to the task tested. At age three the right hand was stronger, the right fingers tapped faster, and the right hand showed increased gesturing during speech. Thus, the right hand showed an adult response pattern. The left hand copied hand postures of the deaf alphabet and finger spacing of a hand position significantly better. The left-hand tasks may be interpreted as measuring spatial control of hand and finger movements, thus indicating that the right hemisphere is specialized for certain aspects of spatial motor control as early as age three. Curiously, this result is not obtained with adults.

Does Asymmetry Develop?

According to many studies of the development of asymmetry, the differences become greater with age. Can this be taken as evidence that lateralization of function continues to develop? Apparently not, for the methodological and theoretical problems of such an inference have often been pointed out. Lateralization scores are usually used to indicate relative differences of function of the two hemispheres, and not degree of difference or specialization. Therefore, to use difference scores across different ages to indicate development of lateralization would be inappropriate. The emergence of such differences may indicate the development of cognitive ability, not of its lateralization.

What Determines the Development of Asymmetry?

According to an old doctrine called *Müller's law of specific nerve energy* an area of the brain performs its given function because it receives fibers from a given sensory system. For example, we see with the visual cortex because that region receives fibers from the eye. This doctrine's explanatory usefulness is open to dispute. And if the law is not an entirely adequate explanation of why we see with a particular area of the cortex (we could, for example, hear with color and see with sounds), what is the explanation for why we speak with one hemisphere? What is its special property that it can assume that function? What property allows the other hemisphere to support nonlanguage abilities? One explanation is that the anatomy of particular areas is well developed, making it easier for one hemisphere to adopt a given function than for the other. Thus, language becomes a left-hemisphere function because the left temporal cortex is genetically programmed to be well developed, and more easily subsumes language than the right; likewise, because the right hemisphere is well developed in other areas, for the same reasons it adopts other functions. We believe this the most likely explanation, although other theories have been proposed favoring either greater activity of the reticular activating system on one side than on the other, or environmental factors. Our explanation is at least consistent with the principles obtained from the cat's visual system. Lateralization is innate, but requires functional validation, as we shall see below.

Environmental Influences on Asymmetry

Although the evidence so far recounted suggests an inborn predisposition toward lateralization of cerebral function, there is convincing evidence that environmental factors play a significant role. Recall that although the cat's visual system appears functionally and anatomically mature when the eyes open, visual deprivation, especially of just one eye, seriously affects the system. Similarly, it is reasonable to suppose that environmental stimulation could enhance or retard the development of other cerebral functions such as language. Two lines of evidence support this proposition: (1) the absence of normal cerebral lateralization in illiterate or deaf adults; (2) anomalous hemispheric development following social isolation and experiential deprivation.

Asymmetry in Illiterate and Deaf People

Studies by Cameron et al. and by Wechsler have reported that aphasia is equally probable following either left- or right-hemisphere damage in illiterate persons. This is a provocative finding, for it implies that experience with language—particularly complex language skills such as reading and writing—somehow influences cerebral asymmetry.

An analogous finding is that literate, congenitally deaf persons have abnormal patterns of cerebral organization, as indicated by two different lines of work. First, according to Neville, two different laboratories have independently reported that congenitally deaf persons fail to show the usual right visual-field superiority in tasks of linguistic processing. This failure could be interpreted as evidence that if experience with auditory language is absent, lateralization of some aspect or aspects of nonauditory language functions is abolished. Second, Neville reported that, during perception of line drawings, visual evoked potentials were significantly larger on the *right* in children with normal hearing, and significantly larger on the *left* in deaf children who used American Sign Language to communicate. Curiously, there was no asymmetry at all in children who could not sign, but merely used pantomime to communicate. From the signers' left-hemisphere effect for line drawings Neville inferred that the deaf signers acquired their sign language much as normal children acquire verbal language: with their left-hemispheres. However, since sign language has a visuospatial component, certain visuospatial functions may have developed in the left hemisphere, producing an unexpected left-hemisphere effect. The lack of asymmetry in nonsigners could mean that the absence of language experience somehow abolished certain aspects of cerebral asymmetry, or, alternately, that the expression of cerebral asymmetry depends on language experience. If the nonsigners learn Ameslan, and do so before puberty (the reasons are discussed below), they might develop an asymmetrical evoked-potential pattern similar to those of children who already sign.

Although congenital deafness appears to alter certain aspects of cerebral organization, Kimura and her colleagues found a deaf aphasic patient with a left-hemisphere lesion to be impaired at sequential motor movements, just as hearing aphasics are. Thus, although experiential deprivation appears to alter the lateralization of verbal material in the left hemispheres of the deaf, it may not disturb the lateralization of control over praxic movements.

Genie: The Effect of Social Isolation and Experiential Deprivation on Language

It is well known that deprivation retards development. An important question is whether deprivation retards or prevents the development of cerebral lateralization, and, further, whether a child so deprived can "catch up," wholly or partly. Genie is a child whose isolation resulted from a deliberate attempt to keep her from normal social and experiential stimuli.

> Genie was found when she was 13 years, 9 months, at which time she was an unsocialized, primitive human being, emotionally disturbed, unlearned, and without language. She had been taken into protective custody by the police, and, on November 4, 1970, was admitted into the Children's Hospital of Los Angeles for evaluation with a tentative diagnosis of severe malnu-

trition. She remained in the Rehabilitation Center of the hospital until August 13, 1971. At that time she entered a foster home where she has been living ever since as a member of the family.

> When admitted to the hospital, Genie was painfully thin, had a distended abdomen, and appeared to be six or seven years younger than her age. She was 54.5 inches tall and weighed 62.25 pounds. She was unable to stand erect, could not chew solid or even semi-solid foods, had great difficulty in swallowing, was incontinent of feces and urine, and was mute.

> The tragic and bizarre story which was uncovered revealed that for most of her life Genie suffered physical and social restriction, nutritional neglect, and extreme experiential deprivation. There is evidence that from about the age of 20 months until shortly before admission to the hospital Genie had been isolated in a small closed room, tied into a potty chair where she remained most or all hours of the day, sometimes overnight. A cloth harness, constructed to keep her from handling her feces was her only apparel of wear. When not strapped into the chair she was kept in a covered infant crib, also confined from the waist down. The door to the room was kept closed, and the windows were curtained. She was hurriedly fed (only cereal and baby food) and minimally cared for by her mother, who was almost blind during most of the years of Genie's isolation. There was no radio or TV in the house and the father's intolerance of noise of any kind kept any acoustic stimuli, which she received behind the closed door, to a minimum. (The first child born to this family died from pneumonia when three months old after being put in the garage because of noisy crying.) Genie was physically punished by the father if she made any sounds. According to the mother, the father and older brother never spoke to Genie although they barked like dogs at her. The mother was forbidden to spend more than a few minutes with Genie during feeding. (Fromkin et al., 1974, pp. 84–85)

At Genie's birth (by Caesarean section) she was 7 pounds, 7.5 ounces and according to the pediatrician's records was within normal weight limits at 11 months. There is no suggestion of retardation, her only serious physical anomaly being a dislocated hip.

It is unknown whether Genie ever began to speak words prior to her isolation, but when she was discovered she did not speak at all. Her only sound was a "throaty whimper." Even when angry, although she would scratch at her face, blow her nose violently into her clothes, and urinate, she would not vocalize, possibly because she had been whipped by her father when she did. Genie's inability to talk may have been due to similar emotional factors, or may have had a physiological basis. Comprehensive tests of language comprehension were first administered about 11 months after Genie's discovery. By this time Genie was able to understand and produce individual words and names, although her comprehension was far beyond her ability to use words. One source of her problems in using words for talking was probably a physical difficulty in learning the necessary neuromuscular controls over her vocal organs. After all, while other children were learning this control she was learning to repress all sounds. As a result, Genie's speech is in a monotone and very low volume, although it has shown marked improvement with time.

In spite of her physical problems with speech Genie is clearly learning language. Hers is similar to development in normal children in that her speech is governed by rules: her basic sentence elements are in a fixed order, and syntactic and semantic relations are expressed systematically. Her speech does, however, differ from that of normal children. For example, although her vocabulary is much larger than that of children with equivalent syntactic abilities, she clearly has more difficulty than normal children learning rules of grammar. She uses no question words, no demonstratives, no particles, and no rejoinders. She produces negative sentences by the addition of the negative element to the beginning of the sentence rather than reorganizing the sentence as children at her stage in language development would do (e.g., "No can go").

Genie's cognitive development was quite rapid. In May 1973 her Stanford-Binet mental age was 5–8. Because this value far exceeds her linguistic abilities, Genie's right-hemisphere functions may be far superior to her left-hemisphere functions.

Results of her dichotic listening are provocatively unusual for a right-handed person: although both ears show normal hearing, there is a strong left-ear, hence right-hemisphere, effect for both verbal and nonverbal (environmental) sounds. In fact, the right ear is nearly totally suppressed, a phenomenon also characteristic of split-brain patients for the *left* ear. In short, the dichotic listening results imply that Genie's right hemisphere is processing both verbal and nonverbal acoustic stimuli, as would be the case in patients with a left hemispherectomy in childhood. The possibility that Genie is using her right hemisphere for language suggests that her capacity for language acquisition is limited, as it is in left hemispherectomy patients (see below). This conclusion is supported by her retarded development of syntactic skills despite possession of a large vocabulary.

To date, Genie has not been assessed for neuropsychological functions such as measured by visuospatial or praxic tests. In view of the Leipmann-Kimura theory that the left hemisphere controls movement, it would be interesting to determine whether Genie has difficulty performing sequential motor movements.

Genie's dichotic results suggest a curious puzzle: Why has deprivation of auditory and verbal experience caused a shift in speech lateralization? (Speculations of this type are risky at best, since there is no "average brain," and all inferences about brain function are based on group averages. Thus, any hypothesis about individual patients must be treated as pure conjecture and heavily spiced with skepticism. After all, it is possible that Genie's speech would have developed in the right hemisphere even if she were raised normally.) Given this caution, we will consider different hypotheses to explain why Genie's right hemisphere has speech along with nonspeech functions.

At least three explanations for Genie's abnormal lateralization are plausible. The first hypothesis is that disuse of the left hemisphere (functional validation) may simply have resulted in degeneration. Thus, it would be interesting to have a CT-scan on Genie's brain, to see if there are any gross morphological changes. The second hypothesis is that in the absence of auditory stimulation the left hemisphere is now actively inhibited by the right hemisphere or by some other structure. This possibility is congruent with the studies done on monocular deprivation in cats. Recall that after monocular deprivation in kittens, the experienced eye actively inhibited input from the deprived eye. This inhibition could only be released by inhibiting the active cells pharmacologically. By analogy, Genie's left hemisphere could be actively inhibited from assuming its function when the chance arose. Since Genie was not deprived of visuospatial experience, the right hemisphere would not be inhibited from assuming its normal functions. The third hypothesis is that Genie's left hemisphere is now performing some other functions. In the absence of a thorough neuropsychological assessment, it is difficult to theorize just what the new functions might be. One possibility is that the left hemisphere was able to assume its preferred role in motor control, and in the absence of competition from speech functions the left hemisphere has an even greater control of motor functions than normal. This idea actually suggests increased cerebral lateralization for at least one function

in Genie, but it remains to be tested. It is unfortunate that tests of praxic functions were not administered repeatedly throughout the period of language development.

BRAIN INJURY AND DEVELOPMENT

As a rule brain injury has milder and shorter-lived effects on behavior if sustained in childhood than in adulthood. We consider the possible mechanisms of this phenomenon in the next chapter. In this section we examine the effects of brain damage in infancy and childhood on adult behavior, considering especially the effects of hemispherectomy and damage in aphasia and hemiplegia.

Effects of Hemispherectomy

If a patient has life-threatening seizures resulting from severe infantile cerebral injury, the neocortex of an entire hemisphere may be surgically removed to control the seizures. Although most such surgery is performed during the patient's early adolescence, it is sometimes done in the first year of life, before speech has developed. These latter cases are particularly germane to the question of how cerebral lateralization develops. If the hemispheres were functionally different at birth, then left and right hemispherectomies would be expected to produce differential effects on cognitive abilities.

The general results of recent careful studies of linguistic and visuospatial abilities in patients with unilateral hemidecortications support the conclusion that *both* hemispheres are functionally specialized at birth, although both hemispheres appear rather plastic and capable of assuming some functions usually performed by the missing hemisphere. Table 18-2 summarizes these data. Notice that left hemidecortication produces no severe aphasia

TABLE 18-2

Summary of effects of hemidecortication on verbal
and visuospatial abilities

Intelligence	Left hemidecorticate	Right hemidecorticate
	Low normal	Low normal
Language tests		
simple	Normal	Normal
complex (e.g., syntax)	Poor	Normal
Visuospatial tests		
simple	Normal	Normal
complex	Normal	Poor

Based on data from Kohn and Dennis (1974) and Dennis and Whitaker (1976).

or obvious language deficits. Yet the right hemisphere cannot completely compensate for the left hemisphere, for the patients have deficits in using complex language. For example, Dennis and Whitaker found that, unlike right-hemisphere removals, left-hemisphere removals produced deficits in understanding auditory language when the meaning was conveyed by complex syntactic structure, particularly if the sentence contained an error (e.g., "Cash shouldn't send people through the mail since it might be stolen"); difficulty in repeating syntactically permutated sentences (e.g., "The tall guard wasn't shot by the armed robber"); as well as difficulty in determining sentence implication, integrating semantic and syntactic information to replace missing pronouns, and forming judgments of word interrelationships in sentences. Thus, although phonemic and semantic abilities are well developed in the absence of a left hemisphere, language development in an isolated right hemisphere is incomplete. An analogous pattern of results is observed on tests of visuospatial function. Kohn and Dennis found that although patients with right-hemisphere removals performed normally on simple tests of

visuospatial function, such as drawing, they were significantly impaired on complex tests such as maze problems or map-reading tests.

To summarize, each hemisphere can assume some of the opposite hemisphere's functions if that opposite hemisphere is removed during development; but neither hemisphere is totally capable of mediating all of the missing opposite's functions. Thus, although the developing brain gives evidence of considerable plasticity, there is convincing evidence against equipotentiality of the hemispheres: both appear functionally specialized at birth or shortly thereafter.

The results of hemispherectomy raise the question of whether one hemisphere can perform all of its own functions normally if it is partly preoccupied with the functions of the missing contralateral hemisphere following hemispherectomy. Milner, Teuber, and others have emphasized that there is clearly an intellectual price to pay when one hemisphere assumes functions of a damaged or absent hemisphere. With few exceptions, patients undergoing hemispherectomy are of below-average, or at best low-average, intelligence, and are frequently less than normally proficient at tests of

TABLE 18-3

Summary of studies of aphasia resulting from unilateral lesions

	Age range of subjects	Number of cases	Percent with right-hemisphere lesions
Childhood lesions			
Guttman, 1942	2–14	15	7%
Alajouanine and Lhermitte, 1965	6–15	32	0
McCarthy, 1963	After language acquisition	114	4
Basser, 1962	Before 5	20	35
Hécaen, 1976	3½–15	17	11
Total	2–15	198	8%
Adult lesions			
Russell and Espir, 1961	—	205	3%
Hécaen, 1976	—	232	0.43
Total	—	437	1.6%

Adapted from Krashen (1973) and Hécaen (1976).

the intact hemisphere's functions. These data suggest that one hemisphere cannot effectively assume the functions of both.

Effect of Brain Damage on Language

It has been known for nearly 100 years that language deficits resulting from cerebral injury in childhood are usually short-lived, and that recovery is nearly complete. Furthermore, transient language disorders following right-hemisphere damage are more common in children than in adults, the incidence running around 8 percent and 2 percent respectively (see Table 18-3).

Alajouanine and Lhermitte studied 32 cases of childhood aphasia, finding writing deficits in all and reading deficits in about half of the children, in addition to difficulty in speaking. Six months after the injury they observed total recovery of spontaneous language in about one-third, although significant improvement was noted in all of the others. When reexamined at one year or more postinjury, 24 of the 32 children had normal or almost normal language, although 14 still had some degree of dysgraphia; 22 of the children were eventually able to return to school.

Similarly, Hécaen followed postinjury recovery of aphasia and related symptoms in 15 children with left-hemisphere unilateral lesions, as summarized in Table 18-4. Besides disorders of speech, nearly all of the children had disorders of writing and calculation as well. Of these 15 children, 5 showed complete recovery within six weeks to two years. Most of the remaining children showed considerable improvement, the only remaining deficit often being a mild difficulty with writing, a finding similar to that of Alajouanine and Lhermitte. These studies confirm and quantify the clinical observation that early cerebral injury has a markedly milder effect on language than injury sustained in adulthood.

TABLE 18-4

Frequency of different symptoms in 15 cases caused by left-hemisphere lesions in childhood

	Number of cases	Percent	Evolution of symptoms
Mutism	9	60%	From 5 days to 30 months
Articulatory disorders	12	80	Persistent in 4 cases
Auditory verbal comprehension disorders	6	40	Persistent in 1 case
Naming disorders	7	46	Persistent in 3 cases
Paraphasia	1	7	Disappearance
Reading disorders	9	60	Persistent in 3 cases
Writing disorders	13	86	Persistent in 7 cases
Facial apraxia	2		Transient
Acalculia	11		(Not reported)

Adapted from Hécaen (1976).

Because of the striking, curious difference in how early and late lesions affect language, it has been proposed that the two hemispheres are equally able to mediate language at birth and in early childhood, becoming specialized or lateralized only during development. Lenneberg refined this idea by proposing that lateralization of function develops rapidly between the ages of two or three to five, and then proceeds more slowly until puberty, by which time it is complete. Lenneberg reasoned that if cerebral damage occurred before about age three, recovery would be complete and rapid, because language would be acquired by undamaged brain tissue. Damage to either cerebral hemisphere at this age could produce language disturbance, because the two hemispheres are equipotential for language, although the left one has a predisposition for development of language. Between the ages of 3 and 10, cerebral damage may produce aphasia, but recovery occurs over time because the cerebral hemispheres, particularly the right one, are still able to take over. Damage after age 10 would produce language disorders resembling those observed in adults, because the brain becomes decreasingly able to adapt and reorganize. By about age 14 the ability to reorganize is lost, and prognosis for recovery is poor. Lenneberg defined the time span from about age 2 to 14 as the critical period for the development of language and, more broadly, of cerebral lateralization.

Lenneberg's theory has not gone unnoticed, and has aroused considerable controversy. It appears that the critical period for hemispheric transfer of language may be much shorter than Lenneberg proposed. Krashen has noted that right-hemisphere aphasia nearly always occurs before age five. Furthermore, Milner has found that very few children who incur injuries to the left hemisphere after the age of five show a change in the pattern of speech representation as indicated by sodium Amytal testing. However, even if Lenneberg's theory is revised to incorporate these data, there are serious problems with it. First, he would predict that children with hemispherectomies prior to one year of age would develop normal language function in the right hemisphere. We noted above that this does not occur. Second, Lenneberg infers that recovery from childhood aphasia is being mediated by the right hemisphere. This precludes the possibility that the left hemisphere could mediate the recovery of language. Using the sodium Amytal test, Milner and her colleagues have shown that only direct damage to the left-hemisphere speech zones before age five results in a shift in language lateralization. Finally, the data on development in normal children discussed above clearly indicate functional specialization at birth or shortly thereafter.

Lenneberg's theory has generated much research and has proved a useful model, particularly insofar as it has encouraged the study of the ontogeny of cerebral function and lateralization. The fact remains that recovery is considerably greater following early damage than following later damage.

A THEORY OF COGNITIVE DEVELOPMENT

Three general theoretical positions can be postulated to account for the ontogeny of cerebral specialization. We have called these: (1) the equipotential theory, (2) the left-for-language theory, and (3) the parallel-development theory.

According to the *equipotential* theory, either hemisphere can be specialized for either language or nonlanguage functions, and the occurrence of specialization is entirely a matter of chance. According to the *left-for-language* theory the left hemisphere is special and is organized genetically to develop language skills; the right hemisphere is postulated to be a dumping ground for whatever is left over. According to the *parallel-development* theory, both hemispheres, by virtue of their construction, play special roles, one hemisphere being destined to specialize in language and the other in

nonlanguage functions. Although there are fairly good arguments for each theory, in our view a parallel-development theory that initially permits some flexibility or equipotentiality most usefully encompasses most of the available data. The cognitive functions of each hemisphere can be conceived hierarchically. Simple or lower-level functions are represented at the base of the hierarchy, corresponding to functions in primary, sensory, motor, language, or visuospatial areas. More complex or higher-level functions are represented further up the hierarchy, the most complex being at the top: these functions are the most lateralized. At birth the two hemispheres functionally overlap because each is processing low-level behaviors. By five years of age the newly developing higher-order cognitive processes have very little overlap, and each hemisphere thus becomes increasingly specialized. By puberty each hemisphere has developed its own unique functions (Figure 18-1).

Note that the cerebral hemispheres are not becoming more lateralized in development; rather, as Witelson has already pointed out, the developing cognitive functions are built upon the lower functions, which are innately located in one hemisphere or the other.

All models of cerebral development provoke the question of how functions become restricted to one hemisphere, rather than becoming bilateral. In a series of papers, Moscovitch has emphasized the possibility that one hemisphere actively inhibits the other (recall our earlier discussion of the effects of monocular deprivation in cats), thus preventing the contralateral hemisphere from developing similar functions. This active inhibition presumably develops around age five, as the corpus callosum becomes functional. Moscovitch proposes that this inhibitory process not only prevents the subsequent development of language processes in the right hemisphere, and

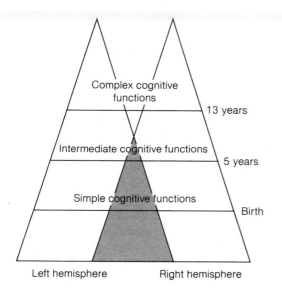

FIGURE 18-1. A model of the development of cognitive function in the left and right hemispheres of normal people. At the bottom of the pyramids cognitive functions are relatively simple (e.g., for language simple functions could include babbling and the use of simple nouns), and the functions of the two hemispheres overlap considerably. At the top of the pyramids, representing very complex functions, the functions of the two hemispheres do not overlap at all (e.g., for language complex functions could include the use of adult language structure). It is important to note that the hemispheres are not themselves becoming more lateralized with respect to a given function; rather they are developing new functions that are more specialized. Since both hemispheres show functional overlap in the early years of life, each can adopt the functions of the other if brain damage has occurred at an early age.

vice versa, but also inhibits expression of the language processes already in the right hemisphere. Support for this idea comes from the observation that the right hemisphere of commissurotomy patients would appear to have greater language abilities than expected from the study of normal patients, presumably because the right hemisphere is no longer subject to inhibition by the left. Furthermore, Netley reports that people born with no corpus callosum demonstrate little or no functional asymmetry as inferred from dichotic listening, suggesting that the absence of interhemispheric connection results in attenuated hemisphere differentiation. This phenomenon follows directly from the Moscovitch proposal.

REFERENCES

Alajouanine, T., and F. Lhermitte. Acquired aphasia in children. *Brain, 88* (1965), 653–662.

Basser, L. Hemiplegia of early onset and the faculty of speech with special reference to the effects of hemispherectomy. *Brain, 85* (1962), 427–460.

Blakemore, C., and D. E. Mitchell. Environmental modification of the visual cortex and the neural basis of learning and memory. *Nature, 241* (1973), 467–468.

Cameron, R. F., R. D. Currier, and A. F. Haerer. Aphasia and literacy. *British Journal of Disorders of Communication, 6* (1971), 161–163.

Caviness, V. S., Jr., and R. L. Sidman. Time of origin of corresponding cell classes in the cerebral cortex of normal and reeler mutant mice: an autoradiographic analysis. *Journal of Comparative Neurology, 148* (1973), 141–152.

Crowell, D. H., R. H. Jones, L. E. Kapuniai, and J. K. Nakagawa. Unilateral cortical activity in newborn humans: an early index of cerebral dominance? *Science, 180* (1973), 205–208.

Curtiss, S. *Genie: A Psycholinguistic Study of a Modern-Day "Wild Child."* New York: Academic Press, 1978.

Dennis, M., and H. A. Whitaker. Language acquisition following hemidecortication: linguistic superiority of the left over the right hemisphere. *Brain and Language, 3* (1976), 404–433.

Entus, A. K. Hemispheric asymmetry in processing of dichotically presented speech and nonspeech stimuli by infants. In S. J. Segalowitz and F. A. Gruber, eds. *Language Development and Neurological Theory.* New York: Academic Press, 1977.

Flechsig, P. *Anatomie des menschlichen Gehirns und Rückenmarks.* Leipzig: Georg Thieme, 1920.

Freud, S. *The Standard Edition of the Complete Psychological Works of Sigmund Freud.* J. Strachey, trans. and ed., in collaboration with A. Freud. London: Hogarth Press, 1954.

Fromkin, V. A., S. Krashen, S. Curtiss, D. Rigler, and M. Rigler. The development of language in Genie: a case of language acquisition beyond the "critical period." *Brain and Language, 1* (1974), 81–107.

Guttman, E. Aphasia in children. *Brain, 65* (1942), 205–219.

Harlow, H. F. *Learning to Love.* San Francisco: The Albion Publishing Co., 1971.

Hécaen, H. Acquired aphasia in children and the ontogenesis of hemispheric functional specialization. *Brain and Language, 3* (1976), 114–134.

Hirsch, H. V. B., and D. N. Spinelli. Modification of the distribution of receptive field orientation in cats by selective visual exposure during development. *Experimental Brain Research, 13* (1971), 509–527.

Hubel, D. H., and T. N. Wiesel. Receptive fields of cells in striate cortex of very young, visually inexperienced kittens. *Journal of Neurophysiology, 26* (1963), 994–1002.

Ingram, D. Motor asymmetries in young children. *Neuropsychologia, 13* (1975), 95–102.

Kimura, D., R. Battison, and B. Lubert. Impairment of nonlinguistic hand movements in a deaf aphasic. *Brain and Language, 3* (1976), 566–571.

Kohn, B., and M. Dennis. Selective impairments of visuo-spatial abilities in infantile hemiplegics after right hemidecortication. *Neuropsychologia, 12* (1974), 505–512.

Krashen, S. D. Lateralization, language learning and the critical period: some new evidence. *Language Learning, 23* (1973), 63–74.

Kratz, K. E., P. D. Spear, and D. C. Smith. Postcritical-period reversal of effects of monocular deprivation on striate cortex cells in the cat. *Journal of Neurophysiology, 39* (1976), 501–511.

Lenneberg, E. *Biological Foundations of Language.* New York: John Wiley and Sons, 1967.

McCarthy, G., 1963. Quoted in Krashen, 1973.

Milner, B. Psychological aspects of focal epilepsy and its neurological management. *Advances in Neurology, 8* (1975), 299–321.

Moscovitch, M. The development of lateralization of language functions and its relation to cognitive and linguistic development: a review and some theoretical speculations. In S. J. Segalowitz and F. A. Gruber, eds. *Language Development and Neurological Theory.* New York: Academic Press, 1977.

Netley, C. Dichotic listening of callosal agenesis and Turner's syndrome patients. In S. J. Segalowitz and F. A. Gruber, eds. *Language Development and Neurological Theory.* New York: Academic Press, 1977.

Neville, H. Electroencephalographic testing of cerebral specialization in normal and congenitally deaf children: a preliminary report. In S. J. Segalowitz and F. A. Gruber, eds. *Language Development and Neurological Theory.* New York: Academic Press, 1977.

Piaget, J. *Biology and Knowledge.* Chicago: The University of Chicago Press, 1971.

Ramón y Cajal, S. *Recollections of My Life.* Memoirs of the American Philosophical Society, 8 (1937).

Russell, R., and M. Espir. *Traumatic Aphasia.* Oxford: Oxford University Press, 1961.

Schneider, G. E. Early lesions of superior colliculus: factors affecting the formation of abnormal retinal projections. *Brain Behavior and Evolution,* 8 (1973), 73–109.

Segalowitz, S. J., and F. A. Gruber, eds. *Language Development and Neurological Theory.* New York: Academic Press, 1977.

Sidman, R. L. Development of interneuronal connections in brains of mutant mice. In F. P. Carlson, ed. *Physiological and Biochemical Aspects of Nervous Integration.* Englewood Cliffs, N.J.: Prentice-Hall, 1968.

Singh, J. A. L., and R. M. Zingg. *Wolf Children and Feral Man.* New York: Harper, 1940.

Skeels, H. M. Adult status of children with contrasting early life experiences. *Monographs of the Society for Research in Child Development,* 31 (1966), 1–65.

Teuber, H.-L. Recovery of function after brain injury in man. In *Outcome of Severe Damage to the Nervous System.* Ciba Foundation Symposium 34. Amsterdam: Elsevier-North Holland Publishing Co., 1975.

Wechsler, A. F. Crossed aphasia in an illiterate dextral. *Brain and Language,* 3 (1976), 164–172.

Witelson, S. F. Early hemisphere specialization and interhemispheric plasticity: an empirical and theoretical review. In S. J. Segalowitz and F. A. Gruber, eds. *Language Development and Neurological Theory.* New York: Academic Press, 1977.

19

RECOVERY OF FUNCTION

On the afternoon of June 16, 1783, Dr. Samuel Johnson, the famed English lexicographer, sat for his portrait in the studio of Miss Frances Reynolds, the sadly untalented sister of Sir Joshua Reynolds. Despite his 73 years and marked obesity, Johnson afterwards walked the considerable distance from the studio to his home. He went to sleep at his usual hour in the evening and awoke according to his account around 3 a.m. on June 17. To his surprise and horror, he found that he could not speak. He immediately tested his mental faculties by successfully composing a prayer in Latin verse. Next he tried to loosen his powers of speech by drinking some wine, violating his recently acquired habits of temperance. The wine only put him back to sleep. Upon reawakening after sunrise, Johnson still could not speak. He found, however, that he could understand others and that he could write. His penmanship and composition were somewhat defective. . . . Johnson proceeded to summon his physicians, Drs. Brocklesby and Heberden, who came and examined him. They prescribed blisters on each side of the throat up to the ear, one on the head, and one on the back, along with salts of

hartshorn (ammonium carbonate). Heberden, who was one of London's leading doctors, predicted a speedy recovery. His confidence proved quite justified: the therapeutic regimen was so efficacious that Johnson's speech began returning within a day or two. Recovery proceeded smoothly over the next month, and even the mild disorders in writing lessened. Johnson finally was left with a slight but stable dysarthria until he succumbed to other causes later in the next year. (Rosner, 1974, p. 1)

After what was presumably a left-hemisphere stroke or arterial occlusion Dr. Johnson exhibited the phenomenon of recovery of function. Dr. Johnson's recovery was surprisingly rapid and complete. Luria described a more typical case in his book, *The Man with a Shattered World*. This book describes the condition of a former soldier, Lyova Saletsky, who received a fractured skull and accompanying brain damage from a bullet wound in the battle of Smolensk. The damage was centered in the posterior left hemisphere in the intersections of the occipital, temporal, and parietal cortex. Luria first saw Saletsky three months after the injury and then at three-week intervals for the next 26 years. During this time Saletsky painfully and slowly "relearned" the art of reading and writing. (It may have been a matter of relearning to use his remaining skill rather than relearning the skill per se.) In doing so he compiled a diary in which he gives a moving account of his initial deficits, recovery, and residual problem. The following is an example of what Saletsky had to say about his condition.

> I remember nothing, absolutely nothing! Just separate bits of information that I sense have to do with one field or another. But that's all! I have no real knowledge of any subject. My past has just been wiped out!
>
> Before my injury I understood everything people said and had no trouble learning any of the sciences. Afterwards I forgot everything I learned about science. All my education was gone.
>
> I know that I went to elementary school, graduated with honors from the middle school, completed three years of courses at the Tula Polytechnic Institute, did advanced work in chemistry, and, before the war, finished all these requirements ahead of time. I remember that I was on the western front, was wounded in the head in 1943 when we tried to break through the Germans' defense in Smolensk, and that I've never been able to put my life together again. But I can't remember what I did or studied, the sciences I learned, subjects I took. I've forgotten everything. Although I studied German for six years, I can't remember a word of it, can't even recognize a single letter. I also remember that I studied English for three straight years at the institute. But I don't know a word of that either now. I've forgotten these languages so completely I might just as well never have learned them. Words like *trigonometry, solid geometry, chemistry, algebra,* etc., come to mind, but I have no idea what they mean.
>
> All I remember from my years in the secondary school are some words (like signboards, names of subjects): *physics, chemistry, astronomy, trigonometry, German, English, agriculture, music,* etc., which don't mean anything to me now. I just sense that somehow they're familiar.
>
> When I hear words like *verb, pronoun, adverb,* they also seem familiar, though I can't understand them. Naturally, I knew these words before I was wounded, even though I can't understand them now. For example, I'll hear a word like *stop!* I know this word has to do with grammar—that it's a verb. But that's all I know. A minute later, I'm likely even to forget the word *verb*—it just disappears. I still can't remember or understand grammar or geometry because my memory's gone, part of my brain removed.
>
> Sometimes I'll pick up a textbook on geometry, physics, or grammar but get disgusted and toss it aside, since I can't make any sense out of textbooks, even those from the middle school. What's more, my head aches so badly from trying to understand them, that one look is enough to make me nervous and irritable. An unbearable kind of fatigue and loathing for it all comes over me. (Luria, 1972, 140–142)

One factor that certainly influences recovery is the type of lesion sustained. A person who has a stroke, as Dr. Johnson did, or penetrating injuries, as Lyova Saletsky suffered, will clearly be worse off than before the trauma. But if a person is suffering from a tumor or from epilepsy, surgery may improve his or her condition. This remedy perhaps deserves further comment.

Because focal cortical lesions are most often performed to relieve epilepsy, interpreting recovery from these lesions is complicated by ambiguity: Does the postsurgical recovery represent recovery from surgery or from epilepsy? To answer this question Milner has tested the intelligence of epileptics before and shortly after surgery, a year later, and 5 to 20 years later. Before surgery IQ is found to be fairly stable from one test to the next; it declines by 10 to 15 points in the early postoperative period, returns to normal by one year, and may actually increase by 5 to 10 points thereafter. These findings have been interpreted to indicate that the epileptic's intelligence has been suppressed by the disease, and begins to approximate its true value only after epilepsy has been controlled. This situation, then, is one in which malfunctioning brain tissue is worse than no tissue. Of course, removal of the tissue still leaves an impairment, but that impairment was likely to have already been present to some extent because of the malfunctioning and epileptogenic tissue.

RECOVERY FROM BRAIN DAMAGE

Brain damage is widely recognized to be followed by a succession of three events: (1) a period of shock or diaschisis; (2) a period of recovery; (3) a chronic impairment that reflects the locus and extent of the tissue destroyed. (Brain damage may of course be followed by secondary complications, but these are not relevant to the present discussion.)

Diaschisis

One of the earliest theories of recovery of function was formulated by Munk, in 1881. He suggested that regions of the brain that were not otherwise occupied could assume functions previously mediated by the injured area. The area substituting for the damaged one would ordinarily not have become involved in mediating the function in question. However, there is little evidence that any portions of the brain are standing by unused until required. Subsequent proposals variously suggested that recovery occurs through regrowth, compensation by surrounding areas, removal of inhibition from surrounding areas, etc. Munk's and some subsequent proposals failed to recognize that the initial deficits may not have been entirely due to focal damage.

Von Monakow recognized another factor. In 1911 he formulated the concept that he called **diaschisis** (from the Greek, meaning to split in two or to split apart): after a brain injury not only is neural tissue and its function lost, but several neural areas related to the damaged area are also depressed and their function is consequently absent for a period of time. In von Monakow's words:

> What characterizes all kinds of shock is a temporary cessation of function which affects a wide expanse of physiologically built up functions, and a restitution which goes on in well defined phases, sometimes shorter, sometimes longer, sometimes even retrospectively in the shape of fragments of functions in retrograde amnesias. The diaschisis proper has its point of attack beyond the limits of anatomically disturbed tissue in those parts of the grey substance which are connected with the focus by fibers. (von Monakow, 1911, p. 241)

The term diaschisis has been described by some as peculiar at best and horrible at worst, because what neural changes were to be encompassed within its meaning have never been precisely specified. Von Monakow meant that some aspects of recovery could be attributed to reemergence of function of the depressed zones rather than to **plasticity**, rewiring, **sprouting** of remaining fibers, or other neural changes that might be occurring at the same time. Certainly, something like general depression or shock is common after brain damage: for example, after spinal-cord section there is a period of spinal shock; after damage to the motor cortex there is a period of contralateral paralysis; and after many head injuries there is often a period of coma, loss of orientation, loss of memory, etc. Furthermore, it is well known that removal of brain tissue in several small operations produces substantially milder shocklike effects than what follows one large removal.

One aspect of neural change might be encompassed within the framework of diaschisis:

edema, or swelling, occurs in the area surrounding a lesion, but may, through pressure and other mechanisms, affect distant areas. Some early deficits may be in part secondary to edema, such as, for example, the drop in IQ immediately after cortical surgery for the treatment of epilepsy, as reported by Milner. A year later IQ had returned to preoperative levels. These changes are shown in Figure 19-1. The initial drop in IQ appears to be due partially to postsurgical edema, for treatment with cortisone lessens the transient decrease in IQ.

Probably many other neural changes should also be encompassed by diaschisis, such as arrested production of neurotransmitter substance, sudden changes in the function of neurotransmitter receptors, changes in axon transmembrane potentials. Sherrington, for example, showed fairly conclusively that tissue damage was not solely responsible for spinal shock. He sectioned the spinal cord and observed shock as manifest by a depression of all reflexes. When reflexes recovered he sectioned the cord again, but failed to reestablish shock. Work by Grillner suggests that neurotransmitters may be involved in shock; he found that stimulating noradrenaline receptors with various pharmacological agents could arrest spinal shock in the cat. Grillner's demonstration indicates that if the mechanisms of shock can be understood, recovery might be accelerated by preventing the initial period of diaschisis.

Recovery

There is not one process of recovery but two (and probably more). The first known process is the emergence from diaschisis; the second known process is recovery or reorganization in the remaining portions of the area that received the initial insult. Since these two processes are likely to be very different we describe them separately.

Recovery from Diaschisis. Recovery from diaschisis does not appear to be a sudden restitution of function, but rather, often, a slow change that follows a relatively predictable sequence. Examination of the stages of the sequence and their associated behaviors reveals an apparent reemergence of lower-level functions in succession. More normal behavior is manifest only in the last stage of the sequence. In Hughlings-Jackson's terms the lesion or trauma produces a complete devolution of the behavior followed by re-evolution. (As Teitelbaum and his coworkers have pointed out tellingly, recovery often parallels the sequential development of the behavior in infants.) Several examples of such events are worth considering.

1. *Recovery from spinal-cord section.* In Chapter 8 we described the effects of complete spinal-cord section in humans. Briefly, there is an initial period of shock lasting from 1 to 6 weeks, after which first flexor and then extensor reflexes emerge. Reports of the development of reflexes in preterm infants indicate that flexor reflexes develop before extensor reflexes. Thus, recovery from shock parallels the sequence of original reflex development.

Nathan and Smith report that patients who had one-half of the spinal cord cut to relieve pain from cancer recovered from paralysis within a few days and were walking well enough to go up and down stairs. Here there was not a sudden recovery in the sectioned portion of the cord; rather, the connections already present from the contralateral portion of the cord were able to support the reemerging behaviors. Furthermore, the recovered behaviors consisted of whole body movements, which develop early in infants, and not relatively independent arm and finger movements, which develop later.

2. *Recovery from hypothalamic lesions.* In 1951, Anand and Brobeck observed that lesions of the lateral hypothalamus of rats and

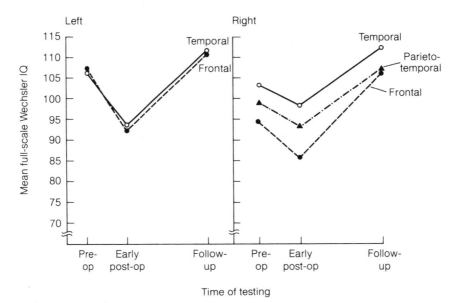

FIGURE 19-1. Mean preoperative, early postoperative, and long-term follow-up Wechsler IQ ratings for 51 patients (38 male, 13 female), classed according to side and site of the cortical excision carried out to relieve epilepsy. Number of cases: left temporal, 19; left frontal, 6; right temporal, 13; right frontal, 6; right parieto-temporal, 7. (From B. Milner, Psychological aspects of focal epilepsy and its neurosurgical management. In D. P. Purpura, J. K. Penry, and R. D. Walker, eds. *Advances in Neurology*. Vol. 8. New York: Raven Press. Copyright © 1975. Reprinted by permission.)

cats produced **aphagia** (inability to eat or chew), which ultimately led to death. Teitelbaum and Stellar reported three years later that if the animals are artificially fed for a period of time they recover the ability to eat. Analyzing this recovery process Teitelbaum and Epstein found feeding behavior recovered in an orderly sequence: first the animals ate only small amounts of wet food, and maintained themselves on this diet; later they began to eat dry food, and eventually maintained themselves on dry food and water. Many workers have observed this sequence of recovery in many species of animals that have received hypothalamic and other types of brain lesions that affect feeding. Interestingly, this sequence of recovery bears close resemblance to the development of eating in young

animals. Teitelbaum and others have thus argued that the process of recovery is analogous to the process of **encephalization**: ontogenetic development of behavior in the individual as successively higher levels of function mature.

The same analytical technique has been extended to behaviors other than feeding. Numerous studies with many species of animals had suggested that large lesions of the posterior portions of the hypothalamus produce **somnolence** that leads eventually to death. In 1969, McGinty found that with care rats would recover from somnolence and eventually sleep less than normal rats. Analyzing the processes of recovery Robinson and Whishaw argued that the somnolence was due more to a loss of voluntary movement than to disruption of a sleep center. Sleep abated as movement recovered, and the residual impairment was an inability to initiate and maintain voluntary movement. More recently Golani, Wolgin, and Teitelbaum have supported this suggestion. To analyze the details of the recovery of movement, they used a version of the Eshkol-Wachmann system of movement notation—originally developed for ballet choreography and analysis.

Figure 19-2 gives examples of sequential recovery of movement. During recovery the animal first develops antigravity support, which allows it to stand and support its weight. Then the animal develops scans of the head in a forward and lateral direction, which progressively increase in amplitude over days until the animal can turn completely around as well as walk forward. Interestingly, each time the animal initiates walking it does so with the sequence of movements illustrated during recovery. The development of movement in infant rats follows a similar sequence, and many of its components can be observed each time a normal animal begins to move.

In the two examples given above the diaschisis is manifest as a complete absence of eating or of movement. Both abilities recover, but do so in stages that appear to parallel behavioral development in infant animals. This parallelism suggests that recovery represents a sequential emergence of higher levels of function. Finally, if hypothalamic damage is not excessive the animals recover a level of function that approximates normal. Many studies on animals with lesions indicate that if the initial lesions are small, the animals begin to recover at more advanced stages; but they nevertheless follow the same sequence. If the lesions are particularly large, recovery may be arrested short of completion.

3. *Recovery from motor-cortex damage.* Twitchell has given a very detailed description of recovery from hemiplegia produced by thrombosis, embolism, or stroke of the middle cerebral artery. Immediately following arterial occlusion there was onset of hemiplegia marked by complete flaccidity of the muscles and loss of all reflexes and voluntary movements. Recovery occurred over a period of days or weeks, and followed a relatively orderly sequence in each patient. Some patients recovered relatively normal use of their limbs; for others recovery was arrested at one or another stage. Complete recovery of use of the arms, when it occurred, appeared between 23 and 40 days after the lesion. Recovery occurred in the following sequence: (1) return of tendon and stretch reflexes, (2) development of rigidity, (3) grasping that was facilitated by, or occurred as a part of, proprioception (that is, as part of postural reflexes of turning, righting, etc.), (4) development of voluntary grasping (this involved recovery of movement in the sequence of shoulder, elbow, wrist, and hand, first in the flexor musculature, then in the extensor musculature), (5) facilitation of grasping by tactual stimulation of the hand, and, finally, (6) grasping that occurred predominantly under voluntary control. Voluntary grasping continued to improve until independent movements of the fingers were well developed. About 30 percent of patients reached the last stage of recovery; the others showed arrested recovery at one of the preceding stages.

In these patients diaschisis was initially profound and many cases it resulted in complete suppression of all reflexes, including spinal reflexes, so that the muscles were left completely flaccid. The sequential recovery involved first the return of spinal-tendon and stretch reflexes, then rigidity and proprioceptive facilitation from the midbrain, then tactile facilitation from the forebrain, and finally the return of voluntary control. The actual degree of recovery was no doubt determined by the extent of cortical damage. Some patients who never went through the latter stages probably had the most severe cortical damage. Subse-

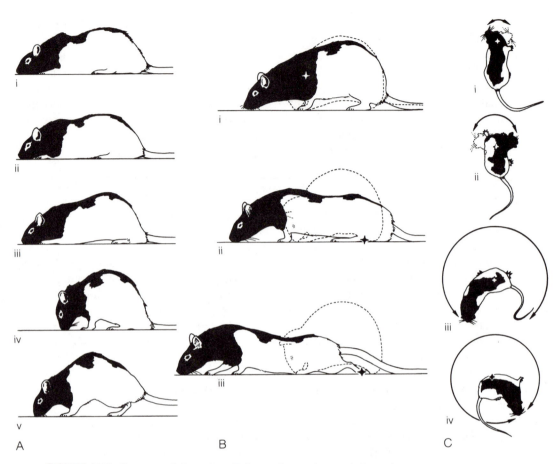

FIGURE 19-2. Recovery of, A, posture; B, forward scanning; and, C, turning in a rat that had been given large posterior lateral hypothalamic lesions. Broken-line and solid-line drawings indicate the extreme positions that the rat assumes during each phase. Recovery occurs over time, in the sequence indicated by the Roman numerals. In each sequence recovery begins with the head and proceeds caudally. (After I. Golani, D. L. Wolgin, and P. Teitelbaum, A proposed natural geometry of recovery from akinesia in the lateral hypothalamic rat. *Brain Research, 164* [1979], 237–267. Reprinted by permission.)

quently, Twitchell analyzed the development of the grasp response in infants. It develops in stages that parallel those seen in the recovery from hemiplegia: grasping develops from a proprioceptive response to a tactually activated response, and finally comes under voluntary control to be executed independently of direct sensory stimulation.

4. *Recovery from aphasia.* To date no studies have clarified the details of sequential recovery from aphasia. As the following case history illustrates, however, there is gradual recovery, which may well follow a logical course and which would be well worth investigation.

Mr. H., a professor of architecture, began to experience tingling sensations in the right side of his face, which rapidly developed into motor seizures of that side of the face. He sought neurological treatment. CT-scan showed a small tumor in the Rolandic region, which was removed surgically by Dr. W. Feindel at the Montreal Neurological Institute. The excision removed the sensory and motor representation of the face up to Broca's area, as determined by electrical stimulation during surgery. The hand region of area 4 was spared.

On the day following surgery Mr. H. could not make any sounds but could open his mouth and move his tongue. His right arm was paralyzed, and his face had a pronounced right-sided weakness. In addition, he was apraxic; he could not imitate simple movements of the left hand or imitate individual facial movements. Mr. H. was unable to read and could not follow simple verbal commands or answer questions by nodding, implying a severe comprehension deficit. Within a week of surgery Mr. H. regained gross arm movements and began to make noises but still could not make any intelligible words. He was still apraxic and alexic. He attempted to write messages with his left hand but the messages were totally meaningless. For example, he wrote "DRICHTRD-HHOL, DRIEH, T, H, GTUTU."

By the end of the second postoperative week he was making intelligible sounds and had regained partial use of his fingers, but still wrote with his left hand. He was now able to make individual facial movements, but still had a right facial weakness. His written messages improved, but he was unable to spell even the simplest words correctly. He was able to read simple nouns but could not understand short sentences.

Clear progress was evident in the third and fourth postoperative weeks. Mr. H. was no longer apraxic: he easily performed the arm-sequence test (Figure 11-6) and facial-sequence test (Figure 14-6) as well as control subjects do. His right hand was nearly totally recovered, although it was still weaker than the left hand. His language functions were markedly improved, for he could speak, although slowly and with great difficulty in pronunciation. His comprehension was still somewhat impaired; he performed below normal on the token test in either oral or written form. He could read simple sentences, and his writing had improved, although spelling was still atrocious. For example, he wrote "NECESSY OPERPEPTION" meaning "necessary operation."

Mr. H.'s language skills improved slowly over the following months, and a year after surgery his comprehension was normal, his verbal IQ had returned to near its preoperative level of 129, and he had returned successfully to his job as a professor. He still spoke slowly, however, and was impaired at tests such as spelling and phonemic discrimination, tests we previously noted to be sensitive to face-area lesions.

5. *Recovery from amnesia.* There are many reports of the loss of memory and its subsequent recovery following brain lesions or concussions. There is some difference in opinion on the sequence of events during recovery. Barbizet reports a case that illustrates one point of view, or possibly one type of syndrome of recovery. A 40-year-old man suffered a head trauma and was in a coma for seven weeks. Five months after the trauma he was completely amnesic for the two preceding years and had gross memory disturbances for events back to early childhood. Eight months after trauma the period of complete amnesia had shrunk to one year, and the period of partial amnesia extended back to the age of four. Sixteen months after trauma his amnesia was limited to the two-week period before trauma. Thus, his recovery represented a progressive shrinkage of the amnesia, from past to present.

Whitty and Zangwill report a somewhat different pattern of recovery following less severe head injury. They report that as a rule retrograde amnesias are very short, usually of a few seconds' duration. If they are longer the shrinkage of amnesia may not be strictly chronological. Sometimes more recent events are recalled first and then serve as a magnet for piecing together a continuous memory.

Despite the difference of opinion (a not uncommon event in areas of memory research, and one that may be attributable to differences in type of damage, location, etc.), both the above reports present a period of complete amnesia, a period of recovery either of time or events, and a period of residual deficit. The nature of the deficit and the processes of recovery seem reminiscent of those we have just described for other types of deficits: that is, a sequential recovery from diaschisis with some residual deficit. The parallel between the recovery of memory and the recovery from aphagia, paralysis, etc., suggests that recovery from all types of brain trauma involves a common process.

Descriptions of recovery as a sequential development have obvious practical and theoretical utility. From a practical perspective good sequential descriptions allow any patient to be monitored for rate and degree of recovery. If recovery is arrested before completion, residual abilities can be understood within the context of the recovery stage reached. Theoretically, stages of recovery provide insights into the brain's organization, and provide background information for enhancing recovery or for overcoming residual deficits.

Recovery through Reorganization. So far we have dealt with recovery from diaschisis, but a substantial portion of overall recovery is thought to involve reorganization of remaining undamaged tissue, or else reorganization of tissue around the area of lesion. Flourens

first propounded this latter idea, but Lashley brought it to prominence in the first half of this century.

Lashley believed that recovery of function was not only expected but was relatively easy to explain, since the brain worked on the principles of *mass action* (the entire cortex participates in each function) and *equipotentiality* (each area of the cortex is equally able to assume control of any given behavior). Although Lashley's original position was extreme he moderated it, applying the notions of mass action and equipotentiality only to functional areas. The following experiment illustrates the type of evidence that Lashley brought forth in support of his position. Lashley electrically stimulated the area of the precentral gyrus of rhesus monkeys on 4 separate occasions over a period of 18 days. On each test he obtained relatively constant responses from each site stimulated, and on different tests he found that arm and leg areas, etc., remained relatively fixed. However, within any one area stimulation of the same point on different tests resulted in widely different movements, and at different times the same movement was obtained from separate and shifting areas. These results suggested to Lashley that "within the segmental areas the various parts of the cortex may be equipotential for the production of all of the movements within that area" (Lashley, 1929, p. 154).

Subsequent work has given Lashley's conclusion little support, because use of more refined techniques to perform the same experiments did not confirm his results. Doty and his coworkers repeatedly stimulated the motor cortex of dogs, and found that the movements obtained from a given site are amazingly constant over long periods of time. Craggs and Rushton implanted an array of electrodes into the cortex of a baboon, and found remarkable stability of response with repeated stimulation. In Lashley's experiments the surgical procedures were repeated on each test, whereas in Doty's and in Craggs and Rushton's the animals were chronically implanted so that after initial surgery the electrodes were fixed and no further surgical trauma occurred. It seems likely that Lashley's results can be attributed in part to trauma (tissue edema, etc.), and in part to slight differences in the placement of his electrodes. Certainly it is now accepted that Doty's findings on what is called the stability of points negate the belief that recovery occurs because of equipotentiality alone.

Strictly speaking, equipotentiality means that every subarea of a region is involved in mediating a given function. Although, as shown above, there is little evidence to support such a strict view, there is evidence that under certain circumstances equipotentiality, if more flexibly defined, is realized. In this view an area may play no role in the control of a particular behavior until a lesion occurs, at which point reorganization takes place, giving other areas, particularly adjacent areas, some part of the damaged area's function. The experiments of Glees and Cole support just such a hypothesis. They identified the thumb area of the monkey neocortex with electrical stimulation, removed the area, and then remapped the surrounding tissue after a period of recovery. During recovery the animals began to use the thumb, and when the cortex was remapped, the areas surrounding the lesion were found to produce thumb movements.

A modified equipotentiality interpretation may explain the recovery in the following case reported by Bucy, Keplinger, and Siqueira. They studied a man with a pyramidal tract sectioned in the lower brainstem as a treatment for involuntary movements. During the first 24 hours after surgery he had complete flaccid hemiplegia, followed by slight return of voluntary movement in his extremities. By the tenth day he was able to stand alone and walk with assistance. By the twenty-fourth day he could walk with a walker, and by the twenty-ninth day he could walk unaided. Within seven months maximum recovery seemed to have been reached, and he could move his feet, hands, fingers, and toes with only slight impairment. At autopsy, two and a half years later about 17 percent of his pyramidal-tract fibers were found to be intact. The recovery in his ability to move his toes and fingers seems attributable to that remaining 17 percent, doing the job previously done by the entire tract. This suggests that the system displays substantial equipotentiality. Lawrence and Kuyper's experiments with pyramidal-tract lesions in rhesus monkeys might be interpreted as supporting this conclusion. They found that a few remaining pyramidal-tract fibers could support relatively independent finger movements, apparently irrespective of the location of the fibers. If all of the fibers were removed there was no recovery of finger movement.

If it is accepted that functional areas have the ability to compensate for damage, how does this occur? Several neural mechanisms have been suggested as important in mediating such recovery, including: (1) regeneration, (2) sprouting, (3) denervation supersensitivity, and (4) release of potential compensatory zones from inhibition. Associated with these mechanisms are several possible ways of facilitating the processes of recovery.

1. *Regeneration.* **Regeneration** is a process by which neurons damaged by trauma regrow connections to the area that they previously innervated. Regeneration is a well-known and common occurrence in the peripheral nervous system, where both sensory and motor neurons send forth new fibers to reinnervate their previous targets. It is believed that Schwann cells, the cells that provide myelin on peripheral fibers, multiply and provide a tube or tunnel that guides the regenerating fibers to their appropriate destination. Although con-

nections are regenerated in the amphibian central nervous system, it is either an uncommon or an ineffective process in the mammalian central nervous system, because regenerating fibers cannot reach their appropriate targets; glial cells provide no guidance for growing sprouts, which thus either fail to grow or become entangled or kept from their target by scar tissue.

There have been a number of attempts to devise ways of facilitating regeneration. One is the use of a substance called **nerve-growth factor** (NGF), a high-molecular-weight protein that is either produced or taken up from glia by nerve terminals and then transported to the cell body to play some role in maintaining normal growth or the health of a cell. There have been a number of attempts to determine whether injection of NGF into lesioned areas will promote functional regeneration, but as yet there has been no conclusive evidence that it does so.

Two approaches have been formulated for developing ways of helping regeneration fibers to bridge areas of scarring. One is to build artificial tubes or bridges across the area of scarring; the second is to place relatively undifferentiated neural tissue in the lesion to provide a medium through which regenerating fibers can grow. Kromer, Björklund, and Stenevi have reported some success with this technique. They sectioned the cholinergic pathway, which innervates the septum from the hippocampus, transplanted embryonic brain tissue into the gap, and found that regenerating cholinergic fibers grew through the bridge to reinnervate the hippocampus in what appeared to be a normal fashion. A particularly interesting feature of these results is that the embryonic tissue, in addition to providing a bridge, stimulates the damaged system to regenerate. These experiments appear to provide one of the most promising avenues for developing ways of stimulating functional

regeneration. A similar experiment by Björklund, Segal, and Stenevi is particularly exciting. They removed the noradrenaline system in the brain with a neurotoxin and then transplanted embryonic noradrenaline cells into pockets of the neocortex and found that the cells grew and sent functional connections to many brain areas. The practical results of such research will clearly have applications for many biochemical diseases of the brain.

2. *Sprouting.* Some early studies on the effect of sectioning some of the afferent fibers to muscles suggested that the remaining fibers sprouted branches that occupied the sites left vacant by the lesioned axons. Convincing evidence now shows that similar sprouting takes place in the brain after lesions. Lynch and his coworkers and others have examined the rate at which sprouting occurs and have examined the question of whether the newly formed connections are functional. Using the rat's hippocampus as their model they cut one of the inputs to the granule cells of the hippocampus. They then addressed the question of function by recording evoked potential from the denervated area. In addition, they examined the anatomical basis of regrowth by staining the hippocampus with chemicals that highlight the synaptic terminals of interest so that synaptic distribution could be assessed with the electron microscope. Their results show that: (1) Remaining fibers send sprouts to reinnervate vacated portions of the granule cells. (2) Other fiber systems from adjacent portions of the cell sprout and reinnervate the unoccupied area. (3) Even fibers not connected with the cells grow and occupy a deserted space. The process of sprouting appears to be quite rapid and may be complete in 7 to 10 days. Evoked potentials indicate that the new connections are electrophysiologically functional. Whether they are behaviorally functional is open to inquiry.

3. *Denervation supersensitivity.* The idea of

denervation supersensitivity arose from the work of Cannon and Rosenblueth in 1949. They found that when the afferent fibers to a muscle were cut, the muscle became hyper-responsive to the application of its neuro-transmitter. Hypersensitivity is presumed to occur because receptors proliferate on the muscle cell in areas where they were not pre-viously located. As a result a given amount of drug produces a greater effect because there are more receptors available to be stimulated. Similar receptor proliferation is thought to occur in the brain.

Denervation supersensitivity appears to be a particularly pronounced occurrence after cer-tain biochemical lesions of the nervous system. For example, it has been found that when the dopamine terminals of the brain are destroyed with a neurotoxin, animals previously unaf-fected by injections of l-dopa (which, recall, is converted to dopamine in the brain) become profoundly activated by the drug. It is sug-gested that this effect occurs because the re-moval of dopamine synapses produces a pro-liferation of dopamine receptors.

A question remains about denervation supersensitivity: Is it a mechanism with some adaptive or compensatory value? There is a certain appeal in the idea that supersensitivity may compensate for reductions in neuro-transmitter supply (caused by lesions, poisons, or aging), but as yet there is no evidence to suggest that this happens.

4. *Disinhibition of potential compensatory zones.* In 1971, Wall and Egger mapped the thalamic and neocortical regions in which stimulation of a rat's forelimb or hindlimb re-sulted in an evoked potential. After then cut-ting the pathway from the lower spinal cord to the brain to sever the connections with the hindlimb they again stimulated the forelimb or hindlimb. As expected, there was no response in the hindlimb regions, but the forelimb re-gion was normal. After three days, however,

there was a remarkable change. The region that previously exhibited evoked potentials to stimulation of the hindlimb now showed these potentials to stimulation of the forelimb. The response looked normal, as if it had always been wired up to the forelimb. Why?

Most available evidence indicates that sprouting could not account for the effect: evoked potentials elicited over pathways formed by sprouting generally take between 7 and 10 days to occur. It seems likely, therefore, that fibers from the forelimb were always con-nected to the hindlimb area, but were kept under some form of inhibition and thus were not functional. Once fibers from the hindlimb area were severed the competing input was lost and the area became functionally a forelimb area. These findings seem to suggest that an area that could *potentially* become in-volved in a response is larger than mapping studies usually suggest. The results also sug-gest that the areas may not become involved in a response unless competing or inhibitory sys-tems are abolished; that is, unless **disinhibition** occurs. A good example of the applicability of this idea has been previously mentioned. If one eye of a kitten is occluded, the cells that it should normally drive are taken over by the nonoccluded eye. In fact, the animal appears completely blind to stimulation of the previ-ously occluded eye. However, Kratz et al. have found that if the good eye is removed the previously blind eye becomes functional to a rather surprising extent. The blindness of the previously occluded eye seems to be due to in-hibition from the good eye. Duffy et al. found that drugs which block inhibiting synapses (bicuculline) were also able to restore vision to the blind eye. In fact, in a rather ingenious experiment Guillery and Sherman et al. de-stroyed a small part of one retina and occluded the other eye. When the occluder was re-moved the animal was blind in all parts of the occluded eye except that part corresponding to the damaged portion of the retina of the nonoccluded eye. Apparently areas of the cortex that would normally receive input from the damaged part of the retina require input to inhibit the function of the corresponding area of the other eye.

These findings suggest that in various parts of the brain there is considerable overlap in innervation, but that specificity is maintained through inhibition. Removal of inhibition allows some takeover by the previously inhibited area. How general is this effect? The answer is not known, but Geschwind has raised the question of whether the recovery of language is mediated by such a mechanism. He suggests that language may be learned in both hemispheres, but its use in the subordinate hemisphere is inhibited in some way. Damage in the dominant hemisphere disinhibits the subordinate hemisphere, and recovery can be attributed to this release. Although there is not much firm evidence to support this suggestion, it illustrates an imaginative use of the concept of disinhibition.

THE CHRONIC EFFECTS OF BRAIN DAMAGE IN ADULTS

The use of such words as "plasticity" and the emphasis placed on recovery of function in a great deal of basic research give the impression that the brain has an unlimited potential for recovery and reorganization after injury. Although there is a paucity of information on long-term recovery, the available evidence indicates that there are always residual and permanent deficits, and that extensive recovery is the exception, not the rule.

Teuber and Dresser and their respective coworkers have conducted long-term follow-up studies on wounded veterans of World War II, the Korean War, and the Vietnam War. These are excellent groups for study because they received standard tests after induction into the Army and were relatively young at the time of injury; the immediate aftermath of the injury is documented; and the kind and extent of recovery can be documented through prolonged follow-up by veterans' services.

In Teuber's analysis the deficits of veterans on tests given one week after injury were compared with those given 20 years later. They found that 44 percent showed some recovery from motor defects, 36 percent showed some recovery from somatosensory defects, 43 percent showed some recovery from visual defects, and only 24 percent showed some recovery from initial dysphasia. These findings are probably quite reliable if we can generalize from the visual-field tests; according to Teuber, the Harms procedure of determining field defects allows for an extremely accurate assessment, and is highly reliable in the hands of different testers at different times. The failure of more than 75 percent of patients to show recovery from dysphasia is not encouraging. This figure is supported by Luria's report that 66 percent of dysphasic patients show no recovery. In fact, many people have concluded that recovery of speech is minimal even when speech therapy is given.

These results testify to a central point throughout much of this book: the effects of brain damage are usually permanent. We can conclude, therefore, that much of the recovery seen in patients is recovery from diaschisis, and that, at least in adults, the brain's ability to reorganize is limited. However, despite the permanent effects of lesions, Teuber, Milner, and others report that performance on intelligence tests is not permanently affected by the lesion unless the damage is in the left temporal-parietal region (posterior tertiary zones). Furthermore, the studies by Dresser and others on injured veterans from the Korean War showed that approximately 80 percent were employed.

RELATIONS BETWEEN AGE
AT INJURY AND RECOVERY

There is considerable evidence that the age at which brain injury is incurred significantly affects the likelihood of recovery, or **sparing,** of function. However, there are really two questions here: First, is the effect of an early lesion less than one sustained later in life? Second, does the child pay a price for enhanced recovery? In other words, does a reduced deficit in language following a left-hemisphere lesion result in unexpected deficits on other types of behaviors?

Woods and Teuber have studied about 50 patients with prenatal or early postnatal brain damage to either the left or right hemisphere. Using normal siblings as controls they came to the following conclusions: (1) Language survives after early left-sided injury. (2) Much of this survival seems attributable to a kind of de-repression of a potential language zone in the right hemisphere. (3) This release of language is not without a price, because some kinds of visuospatial orientation are impaired. (4) Early lesions of the right hemisphere produce deficits similar to those produced by lesions in adulthood. In other words, if a child sustains a lesion of the left hemisphere that produces right hemiplegia, language functions are remarkably more intact than after a comparable lesion in an adult, presumably because some, or all, of the language abilities have moved to the right hemisphere. However, language crowds into the right hemisphere at the expense of visuospatial functions. On the other hand, a lesion of the right hemisphere, which produces left hemiplegia, results in deficits on visuospatial tasks; apparently they do not crowd into the left hemisphere. These results are summarized in Figure 19-3. In this regard it is interesting to note that we are unaware of any reports of visual neglect following early lesions to the right hemisphere, and

that Teuber's failure to observe sparing of function following right-hemisphere damage may be due, in part, to the choice of behavioral tests.

Milner and her colleagues have reported data similar to Teuber's. Lesions of the left hemisphere early in life often result in speech moving to the right hemisphere, as can be seen in Table 19-1. This table compares the location of speech (as determined in sodium Amytal testing) in patients with and without early brain damage. Notice particularly that left-handed patients with early lesions were more likely to have speech in the right hemisphere than in the left. Of particular interest is the age at which this shift in hemispheric locus of speech occurs. Milner reports that very few children with injuries to the left hemisphere occurring after the age of five years show a change in the pattern of speech representation. She notes, however, that older children may still show more recovery of language after left-hemisphere damage than would be seen after comparable brain lesions in the adult, but her evidence from both carotid sodium Amytal tests and cortical ablations for epilepsy suggests that this recovery is usually achieved by an *intra*hemispheric reorganization, rather than by the development of speech functions in the right hemisphere. This view accords with the recent work of Krashen and Hécaen (see Chapter 18).

Why does damage to the left hemisphere not always result in language functions moving to the right hemisphere? Rasmussen and Milner have found that the locus of the original damage is a critical factor. It appears that damage to the speech regions results in speech shifting, whereas damage to the regions outside speech does not. They also report that damage to only one of the speech regions in the left hemisphere in early childhood is likely to shift only that speech region to the opposite hemisphere. For example, damage to Broca's

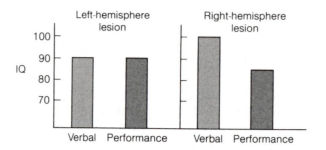

FIGURE 19-3. IQs on subtests of the Wechsler Intelligence Test for adults who while infants had suffered a lesion of the left or right hemisphere, as determined by the occurrence of hemiparesis. Note that both verbal and performance scores are depressed by left-hemisphere lesions, whereas only performance scores are depressed by right-hemisphere lesions. The results suggest that if language moves to the right hemisphere, that hemisphere's functions are sacrificed to accommodate this shift. The results also suggest that right-hemisphere functions do not shift sufficiently to interfere with language. (After Teuber, 1975.)

TABLE 19-1

Changes in hemispheric speech representation
following early brain damage

| | | Percent with speech representation | | |
	Handedness	Left	Bilat-eral	Right
No early damage	Right	96%	0%	4%
	Left or mixed	70	15	15
Early damage	Right	81	7	12
	Left or mixed	28	19	53

Adapted from Rasmussen and Milner, 1975, pp. 248–249.

area may result in Broca's area moving to the right, whereas Wernicke's area remains on the left. These patients would thus appear to have bilateral speech, as can be shown in sodium Amytal testing.

Functions lying outside the primary speech areas of the left hemisphere show very little sparing of function even after early injury. Left-temporal damage thus still produces specific impairments in memory, and left frontal lesions are still associated with enduring defects on tests such as the Wisconsin card-sorting test. Thus, the brain places an emphasis on preserving speech, and it will shift speech functions even at the cost of somewhat reducing the functions of the invaded hemisphere.

Another source of data about sparing and recovery of function has been the results of studies of patients with an entire hemisphere surgically removed for the relief of epilepsy in early childhood. Kohn and Dennis have extensively studied such patients, and their results concur with Teuber's and Milner's. Early damage to the left hemisphere in the speech regions results in speech moving to the right hemisphere (see Table 18-2).

The results of early lesions raise a final question: Until what age does the brain retain enough plasticity to compensate in some way, even partially, for recovery? To a limited extent plasticity may be retained to a quite late age. Hurt and Teuber have found that on a number of tests, recovery by soldiers from natural lesions in the 17–20 age group is greater than in the 21–25 age group, which in turn is greater than for age groups 26 and over (Figure 19-4). Perhaps 40 years is the upper limit, for Milner reports that patients over 40 who have removals near the posterior temporal speech zone of the left hemisphere show little recovery in IQ.

Experimental Approaches to Early Recovery

It is becoming increasingly clear that mechanisms mediating recovery of function from injury sustained in infancy are behaviorally and anatomically quite different from mechanisms that mediate recovery after lesions inflicted in adults. The best illustration of the role of age comes from a series of studies on the function of the dorsolateral and orbitofrontal areas of the prefrontal cortex.

The dorsolateral cortex receives projections from the parvocellular subdivision of the dorsomedial nucleus of the thalamus. In fact, the distribution of this projection defines this cortical zone. Many studies of the function of this area show that if it is damaged in adult monkeys, rats, or other animals they show profound impairments on spatial delayed responses or spatial delayed alternations. The features of these tasks are that the animal must make a choice between two spatially located

objects, and each trial is separated by a delay. For example, a monkey must remember that a peanut is located in one of two cups, but each trial is separated by a short delay during which it cannot see the cup. Generally, lesioned animals do not perform above chance on this task, and the deficit is not attributable to interference with performance by sensory or motor difficulties, surgical shock, or lack of opportunity to learn. That is, even though they seemingly "know" what to do they make errors. On a host of other tasks, visual discriminations, etc., these monkeys show no deficits. In addition to showing this behavioral deficit, histological analysis shows that the projecting fibers from the dorsomedial nucleus die after lesioning, and the cell bodies of these fibers degenerate.

Akert et al. and subsequently others have removed the dorsolateral cortex within the first two months of life and studied the monkeys on spatial reversals over the next year of life. During this time the monkeys show no impairment when compared with age-matched control animals. Nevertheless, degeneration of cells in the thalamus are found. These early studies seemed to suggest that other brain structures, most likely the basal ganglia, could assume this function. However, this simple interpretation was complicated by Goldman's 1971 finding that if the monkeys were tested for as long as two years they gradually developed the adult deficit, or as it has been phrased "they grew into the deficit." These results are instructive, first because they show that a subcortical structure can control the behavior in a seemingly normal way for a period of time, and second, because they show that the function is "given up" with maturation.

More recently, Goldman and Galkin studied the behavior and anatomy of monkeys that had been removed from the womb before term, subjected to surgery, and then replaced. These animals show no deficits as infants or

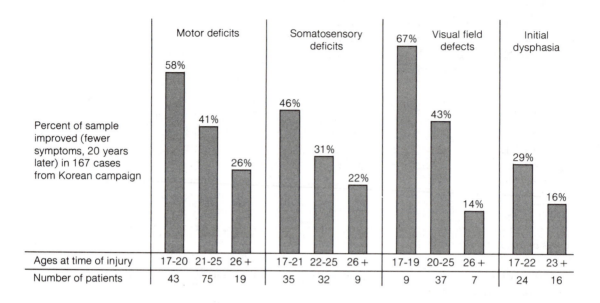

FIGURE 19-4. Estimated improvement from initial examination (within no more than one week of injury) and follow-up examination (20 years later) for some body regions (extremities, sides of face) for which symptoms were recorded (reflex changes, paralysis, weakness) for the motor system; noted sensory losses for somatosensory system; estimated improvement in visual field (diminution in number of quadrants known to be affected) and in symptoms interpreted as dysphasia. Note the advantage of groups of lower age at the time of wounding. (After Teuber, 1975.)

when mature, and also show no cellular degeneration in the dorsomedial thalamus. Kolb and Nonneman have obtained identical results with the rat, which does not require preterm surgery because it is more immature at birth than the monkey. The studies of Goldman and Galkin and of Kolb and Nonneman imply that if cortical damage occurs sufficiently early in life the brain is able to reorganize in some way to achieve complete compensation. One type of evidence for reorganization is that the monkeys have gyri and sulci not observed in normal monkeys. Other evidence is that cells of the dorsomedial nucleus remain intact, permitting the hypothesis that the new connections that they make most likely sustain behaviors of delayed alternation. Goldman and Galkin have suggested a number of types

of reorganization that might account for the survival of these cells (Figure 19-5): (1) *Transient collaterals.* The fibers that enter the dorsolateral cortex from the dorsomedial thalamus may initially have collaterals going elsewhere, which under normal conditions degenerate, but which in instances of dorsolateral cortex damage survive. (2) *Oversupply.* There is an oversupply of neurons in the dorsomedial nucleus, but normally only those that innervate the dorsolateral cortex survive. (3) *Collateral sprouting.* The immature neurons do not die, because in early life they can sprout collaterals to new cortical areas and so replace their severed axons. (4) *Lesion-induced neurogenesis.* Although the original neurons are killed by the lesion, new cell bodies form and replace them. (5) *Autonomy of undifferentiated*

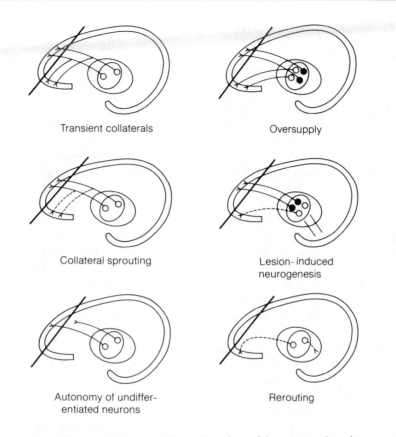

Transient collaterals

Oversupply

Collateral sprouting

Lesion- induced
neurogenesis

Autonomy of undiffer-
entiated neurons

Rerouting

FIGURE 19-5. Diagram of possible alternative explanations of the preservation of neurons in the dorsomedial nucleus of the thalamus after surgical resection of the dorsolateral frontal cortex in the monkey prior to birth. Black circles indicate degenerated neurons; open circles, preserved neurons. (From P. S. Goldman and T. W. Galkin, Prenatal removal of frontal association cortex in the fetal rhesus monkey: anatomical and functional consequences in postnatal life. *Brain Research, 152* [1978], 451–485. Reprinted by permission.)

neurons. Although normal neurons die if their target is destroyed, undifferentiated neurons can survive to make new connections. (6) *Rerouting.* The last possibility is that if axons from the thalamus have not yet entered the neocortex they are able to seek out and innervate alternate targets.

These studies of frontal-lobe function in developing animals provide a number of novel hypotheses for why behaviors may survive early lesions. There is, however, one other

mechanism of interest. Almli et al. have found that if large lesions are made in the lateral hypothalamus of adult or seven-day-old infant rats they are aphagic and adipsic and require tube feeding to live. The same lesions in day-old infants produce no behavioral deficits. The explanation for this finding is that feeding and drinking are supported by dopamine fibers that course from the brainstem, through the lateral hypothalamus, to the forebrain. Because these fibers pass through the lateral hypothalamus between day one and three, the earlier lesions spare them and the later lesions section them. Presumably, after the early lesion they simply grow around the lesion site. Since many behavioral deficits in adults may be due to disconnection, absence of deficits in infants that have received similar lesions may be attributable to events such as those described by Almli.

Although there is striking recovery from infant injury, as demonstrated in the experiments we have just described, equally careful studies have failed to obtain either recovery or compensation after infant lesions. Lawrence and Hopkins cut the corticospinal tract in infant monkeys, and studied the monkeys as they matured. This tract controls speed, agility, and strength of distal movements, and more specifically it produces relatively independent finger movements in adult monkeys. When the monkeys lesioned in infancy matured they showed deficits identical to monkeys lesioned when adult. Their speed, agility, and strength were reduced, and they were unable to make relatively independent finger movements, such as those requiring opposition of thumb and forefinger to grasp small objects located in holes in wooden boards.

What accounts for the differences in results obtained by experiments that show compensation and those that do not? There are a number of differences in the experimental procedures. In the studies of the Goldman type, damage is inflicted on the terminals of the projection of interest, possibly allowing the projection to make other connections. In the Lawrence and Hopkins study, the actual projection itself is cut. A second difference is that the Goldman studies are dealing with tertiary cortex, and Lawrence and Hopkins are dealing with projections from primary cortex. A third difference is that Goldman is dealing with a cognitive ability, whereas Lawrence and Hopkins are studying a motor task. The last difference may be particularly important. Kolb and Whishaw found that after neonatal prefrontal neocortex lesions in the rat, species-typical behaviors, such as food hoarding or nest building, are lost whereas cognitive behaviors, such as spatial-reversal learning, are spared. This finding suggests that although the neural basis of certain behaviors is fixed, for others there is sufficient plasticity to support recovery. Probably all of these variables account in some part for the differences in results between the two types of studies. The important lesson of these differences is that recovery from infant lesions is not invariable, but depends very much on the type of damage, the system damaged, and the type of function subserved by that system. This principle seems consistent with reports (described above) that language abilities are more likely to survive early lesions than are some other abilities.

REFERENCES

Akert, K., O. S. Orth, H. F. Harlow, and K. A. Schultz. Learned behavior of rhesus monkeys following neonatal bilateral prefrontal lobotomy. *Science, 132* (1960), 1944–1945.

Almli, R. C., D. L. Hill, N. T. McMullen, and R. S. Fisher. Newborn rats: lateral hypothalamic damage and consummatory-sensorimotor ontogeny. *Physiology and Behavior, 22* (1979), 767–773.

Anand, B. K., and J. R. Brobeck. Hypothalamic control of food intake. *Yale Journal of Biology and Medicine, 24* (1951), 123–140.

Barbizet, J. *Human Memory and Its Pathology.* San Francisco: W. H. Freeman and Company, 1970.

Björklund, A., M. Segal, and U. Stenevi. Functional reinnervation of rat hippocampus by locus coeruleus implants. *Brain Research, 170* (1979), 409–426.

Bucy, P. C., J. E. Keplinger, and E. B. Siqueira. Destruction of the "pyramidal tract" in man. *Journal of Neurosurgery, 21* (1964), 385–398.

Cannon, W. B., and A. Rosenblueth. *The Supersensitivity of Denervated Structures.* New York: Macmillan, 1949.

Craggs, M. D., and D. N. Rushton. The stability of the electrical stimulation map of the motor cortex of the anesthetized baboon. *Brain, 99* (1976), 575–600.

Doty, R. W. Conditioned reflexes formed and evoked by brain stimulation. In D. E. Sheer, ed. *Electrical Stimulation of the Brain.* Austin: University of Texas Press, 1961.

Dresser, A. C., A. M. Meirowsky, G. H. Weiss, M. L. McNeel, A. G. Simon, and W. F. Caveness. Gainful employment following head injury. *Archives of Neurology, 29* (1973), 111–116.

Duffy, F. H., S. R. Snodgrass, J. L. Burchfield, and J. L. Conway. Bicuculline reversal of deprivation amblyopia in the cat. *Nature, 260* (1976), 256–257.

Eshkol, N., and A. Wachmann. *Movement Notation.* London: Weidenfeld and Nicolson, 1958.

Geschwind, N. Late changes in the nervous system: an overview. In D. G. Stein, J. J. Rosen, and N. Butters, eds. *Plasticity and Recovery of Function in the Central Nervous System.* New York: Academic Press, 1974.

Glees, P., and J. Cole. Recovery of skilled motor function after small repeated lesions of motor cortex in macaque. *Journal of Neurophysiology, 13* (1950), 137–148.

Golani, I., D. L. Wolgin, and P. Teitelbaum. A proposed natural geometry of recovery from akinesia in the lateral hypothalamic rat. *Brain Research, 164,* (1979), 237–267.

Goldman, P. S. Functional development of the prefrontal cortex in early life and the problem of neuronal plasticity. *Experimental Neurology, 32* (1971), 366–387.

Goldman, P. S., and T. W. Galkin. Prenatal removal of frontal association cortex in the fetal rhesus monkey: anatomical and functional consequences in postnatal life. *Brain Research, 152* (1978), 451–485.

Grillner, S. Locomotion in the spinal cat. In R. B. Stein, K. G. Pearson, R. S. Smith, and J. B. Redford, eds. *Control of Posture and Locomotion.* New York: Plenum Press, 1973.

Guillery, R. W. Binocular competition in the control of geniculate cell growth. *Journal of Comparative Neurology, 144* (1972), 177–130.

Hécaen, H. Acquired aphasia in children and the ontogenesis of hemispheric functional specialization. *Brain and Language, 3* (1976), 114–134.

Kohn, B., and M. Dennis. Selective impairments of visuo-spatial abilities in infantile hemiplegics after right hemidecortication. *Neuropsychologia, 12* (1974), 505–512.

Kolb, B., and A. J. Nonneman. Sparing of function in rats with early prefrontal cortex lesions. *Brain Research, 151* (1978), 135–148.

Kolb, B., and I. Q. Whishaw. Failure to find sparing of species-typical behaviors following prefrontal cortex lesions. *Society for Neuroscience Abstracts, Atlanta, 9* (1979), 629.

Krashen, S. D. Lateralization, language learning and the critical period: some new evidence. *Language Learning, 23* (1973), 63–74.

Kratz, K. E., P. D. Spear, and D. C. Smith. Postcritical-period reversal of effects of monocular deprivation on striate cortex cells in the cat. *Journal of Neurophysiology, 39* (1976), 501–511.

Kromer, L. F., A. Björklund, and U. Stenevi. Utilization of embryonic hippocampal implants to promote regeneration of the cholinergic input to the hippocampus in the adult rat. *Neuroscience Abstracts, 8* (1978), 532.

Lashley, K. S. Temporal variation in the function of the gyrus precentralis in primates. *American Journal of Physiology, 65* (1923), 585–602.

Lashley, K. S. *Brain Mechanisms and Intelligence.* Chicago: The University of Chicago Press, 1929.

Lawrence, D. G., and D. A. Hopkins. The development of motor control in the rhesus monkey: evidence concerning the role of corticomotorneuronal connections. *Brain, 99* (1976), 235–254.

Lawrence, D. G., and H. G. J. M. Kuypers. The functional organization of the motor system in the monkey: I. The effects of bilateral pyramidal lesions. *Brain, 81* (1968), 1–14.

Lomas, J., and A. Kertesz. Patterns of spontaneous recovery in aphasic groups: a study of adult stroke patients. *Brain and Language, 5* (1978), 388–401.

Luria, A. R. *The Man with a Shattered World.* Lynn Solotoroff, trans. New York: Basic Books; London: Jonathan Cape, Ltd., 1972.

Lynch, G. S., R. L. Smith, and C. W. Cotman. Recovery of function following brain damage: a consideration of some neuronal mechanisms. In *Recovery of Function Following Brain Damage,* in press.

McGinty, D. J. Somnolence, recovery and hypersomnia following ventromedial diencephalic lesions in the rat. *Electroencephalography and Clinical Neurophysiology, 26* (1969), 70–79.

Milner, B. Psychological aspects of focal epilepsy and its neurosurgical management. *Advances in Neurology, 8* (1975), 299–321.

Monakow, C. V. von. Lokalization der Hirnfunktionen. *Journal für Psychologie und Neurologie, 17* (1911), 185–200. Reprinted in G. von Bonin, trans. *The Cerebral Cortex,* Springfield, Ill.: Charles C Thomas, 1960.

Munk, H. *Ueber die funktionen der Grosshirnrinde. Gesammelte Milleilunger aus den Jahren.* Berlin: August Hershwald, 1877–1880.

Nathan, P., and M. Smith. Effects of two unilateral cordotomies on the mobility of the lower limbs. *Brain, 96* (1973), 471–494.

Rasmussen, T., and B. Milner. The role of early left-brain injury in determining lateralization of cerebral speech functions. *Annals of the New York Academy of Sciences, 299* (1977), 355–369.

Rasmussen, T., and B. Milner. Clinical and surgical studies of the cerebral speech areas in man. In K. J. Zulch, O. Creutzfeldt, and G. C. Galbraith, eds. *Cerebral Localization.* Berlin and New York: Springer-Verlag, 1975.

Robinson, T. E., and I. Q. Whishaw. Effects of posterior hypothalamic lesions on voluntary behavior and hippocampal electroencephalograms in the rat. *Journal of Comparative and Physiological Psychology, 86* (1974), 768–786.

Rosner, B. B. Recovery of function and localization of function in historical perspective. In D. G. Stein, J. J. Rosen, and N. Butters, eds. *Plasticity and Recovery of Function in the Central Nervous System.* New York: Academic Press, 1974.

Sherman, S. M., R. W. Guillery, J. H. Gaas, and K. J. Sanderson. Behavioral electrophysiological and morphological studies of binocular competition in development of geniculocortical pathways of cats. *Journal of Comparative Neurology, 158* (1974), 1–18.

Sherrington, C. S. *The Integrative Action of the Nervous System.* 2nd ed. New Haven: Yale University Press, 1947.

Teitelbaum, P., and A. N. Epstein. The lateral hypothalamic syndrome: recovery of feeding and drinking after lateral hypothalamic lesions. *Psychological Review, 69* (1962), 74–90.

Teitelbaum, P., and E. Stellar. Recovery from the failure to eat produced by hypothalamic lesions. *Science, 120* (1954), 893–895.

Teuber, H.-L. Recovery of function after brain injury in man. In *Outcome of Severe Damage to the Nervous System.* Ciba Foundation Symposium 34. Amsterdam: Elsevier-North Holland Publishing Co., 1975.

Twitchell, T. E. The restoration of motor functions following hemiplegia in man. *Brain, 74* (1951), 443–480.

Twitchell, T. E. The automatic grasping response of infants. *Neuropsychologia, 3* (1965), 247–259.

Wall, P. D., and M. D. Egger. Formation of new connections in adult rat brains after partial deafferentation. *Nature, 232* (1971), 542–545.

Whitty, C. W. M., and O. L. Zangwill. Traumatic amnesia. In C. W. M. Whitty and O. L. Zangwill, eds. *Amnesia.* London: Butterworths, 1966.

Woods, B. T., and H.-L. Teuber. Early onset of complementary specialization of cerebral hemispheres in man. *Transactions of the American Neurological Association, 98* (1973), 113–117.

20

DISCONNECTION SYNDROMES

So far we have emphasized the importance of neocortical and subcortical regions in controlling various aspects of behavior. We have associated particular behavioral deficits with different brain lesions and from these deficits have tried to infer the function of the missing region. In looking at brain function in this way we have postponed discussion of the function of the connections between various regions. In this chapter we consider the function of various cerebral connections and the effects of cutting them. The process of cutting connections is called *disconnection,* and the ensuing behavioral effects are therefore called *disconnection syndromes.* We begin by reviewing the major connections of the cerebral hemispheres.

ANATOMY OF CEREBRAL CONNECTIONS

There are three major types of connections of the neocortex: projection fibers, commissural fibers, and association fibers.

Projection Fibers

Projection fibers include ascending fibers from lower centers to the neocortex, such as projections from the thalamus, as well as descending fibers from the neocortex to the brainstem and spinal cord.

Commissural Fibers

Commissural fibers primarily function to join the two hemispheres, and include principally the corpus callosum, anterior commissure, and hippocampal commissure. The **corpus callosum** provides the major connection of neocortical areas. Most homologous regions of the hemispheres are interconnected by this route, although there are exceptions. For example, area 6 has heavy connections not only with the contralateral area 6 but also with areas 4, 5, 7, and 39. Area 4, on the other hand, directly connects only with the contralateral area 4. Furthermore, the prefrontal cortex and inferior parietal lobule are only partially interconnected, because portions of these regions are not connected with the contralateral hemisphere.

The *anterior commissure* is much smaller than the corpus callosum, and functions to interconnect portions of the anterior temporal lobe, the amygdala, and the paleocortex of the temporal lobe surrounding the amygdala. In humans reported to have been born with no corpus callosum (a condition called agenesis of the corpus callosum), the anterior commissure is greatly enlarged to connect far greater regions of the neocortex.

The hippocampal commissure interconnects the hippocampal formations of the two hemispheres. Little is known about the significance of these connections.

Association Fibers

Two types of association fibers can be distinguished: (1) long fiber bundles that interconnect distant neocortical areas, and (2) short subcortical U-fibers that interconnect adjacent neocortical areas. The long fiber bundles include the uncinate fasciculus, the superior longitudinal fasciculus, the cingulum, the inferior longitudinal fasciculus, and the inferior frontal occipital fasciculus. These pathways were illustrated in Figure 1-11.

THE BEHAVIORAL EFFECTS OF DISCONNECTION

The clinical effects of disconnection were first seriously considered by Wernicke, in 1874. He predicted the existence of an aphasic syndrome (conduction aphasia) that would result from severing fiber connections of the anterior and posterior speech zones. Later, in 1892, Dejerine was the first to demonstrate a distinctive behavioral deficit resulting from pathology of the corpus callosum. However, in a series of papers published around 1900 Leipmann most clearly demonstrated the importance of severing connections as an underlying causal factor in the effects of cerebral damage. Having carefully analyzed the behavior of a particular patient Leipmann predicted a series of disconnections of the neocortex that could account for the behaviors. In 1906, after the patient died, Leipmann published the postmortem findings, which supported his hypothesis. Leipmann wrote extensively on the principle of disconnection, particularly with respect to the idea that some apraxias might result from disconnection. Leipmann reasoned that if a patient were given a verbal command to use the left hand in a particular way, only the verbal left hemisphere would understand the command. To move the left hand a signal would then have to travel from the left hemisphere through the corpus callosum to the right hemispheric region that controls movements of the left hand, as illustrated in Figure 20-1. Interrupting the portion of the corpus callosum that carried the command from the left hemisphere to the right would disconnect the right hemisphere's motor region from the command. Thus, although the subject comprehended the command the left hand would be unable to follow it (see Figure 20-1). This apraxia would occur in the absence of weakness or incoordination of the left hand, as would occur if there were a lesion in the motor cortex of the right hemisphere, which controls the actual movement of the left hand.

Leipmann's deduction, although brilliant, was ignored for a number of reasons. First, it was published in German and so was not widely read by English-speaking neurologists; to this day Leipmann's papers have not been translated into English. Second, except in the extremely unusual case of a patient with a natural lesion of only the corpus callosum, any observed behavioral deficits could be attributed to damage of grey matter itself without

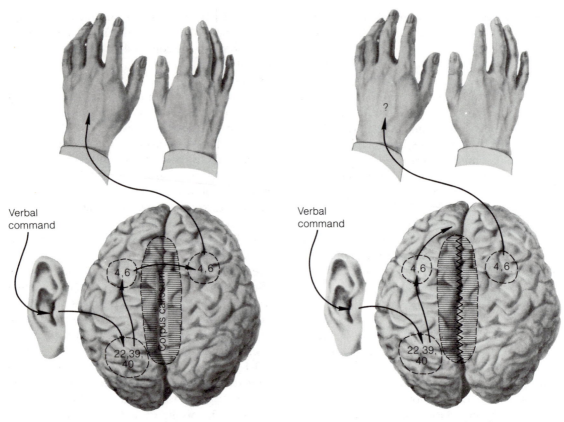

FIGURE 20-1. Leipmann's theory of apraxia resulting from lesion of the corpus callosum. (The jagged line indicates section of the callosum.) The verbal command has no way of reaching the motor cortex (area 4) of the right hemisphere to move the left hand. Geschwind proposed that bilateral apraxia could result from a lesion disconnecting the posterior speech zone (areas 22, 39, 40) from the motor cortex of the left hemisphere. In this case the verbal command cannot gain access to either the left or the right motor cortex.

reference to connections. Third, a large number of animal studies consistently purported to demonstrate that no significant behavioral effects followed the cutting of the corpus callosum. Not until the late 1950s and '60s did it become clear that the results from the animal studies could be largely attributed to crude behavioral testing.

An important series of papers by Myers and by Sperry in the early 1950s revived interest in the effects of disconnecting neocortical re-

gions. They examined the behavioral effects of severing the corpus callosum of cats. Their work confirmed others' earlier observations that the animals were virtually indistinguishable from their unoperated counterparts, and indeed appeared normal under most tests and training conditions. Unlike the previous studies, however, their studies revealed that under special training procedures the animals could be shown to have severe deficits. Thus, if the sensory information were allowed separate access to each hemisphere, each could be shown to have its own independent perceptual, learning, and memory processes. Myers's and Sperry's remarkable results were quickly duplicated by dozens of laboratories around the world. The corpus callosum did indeed have an important function. This conclusion has been clearly demonstrated in the subsequent studies by Sperry and his colleagues on the effects of surgical disconnection of the cerebral hemispheres of humans for the treatment of intractable epilepsy.

The success of the Myers and Sperry experiments stimulated interest in other connections of the brain. Geschwind and his colleagues began to reassess the clinical effects of naturally occurring neocortical lesions as possibly indicating disconnection of various regions of the cerebral hemispheres. In parallel work, Mishkin and his colleagues began to construct animal models of human disconnection syndromes; by disconnecting related neocortical regions from one another, they have demonstrated their critical interdependence. In the remainder of this chapter we first discuss the work of Sperry on the "split-brain" patient, this patient providing an excellent model of disconnection syndromes. Next we reconsider Geschwind's reinterpretation of three classic symptoms of cortical damage (aphasia, apraxia, and agnosia) as disconnection syndromes. Finally, we briefly study Mishkin's animal models of disconnection in the visual and somesthetic systems, the only systems that have been studied in this way to date.

A HUMAN MODEL OF DISCONNECTION

Epileptic seizures may begin in a restricted region of one hemisphere (most frequently the temporal lobes) and then spread via the fibers of the corpus callosum or anterior commissure to the homologous location in the opposite hemisphere. These seizures can usually be controlled by anticonvulsant medication, but in some cases the medication is of little value and the seizures may actually become life-threatening because they may recur often, sometimes several times in an hour. To relieve this seizure condition, the corpus callosum and anterior commissure can be surgically sectioned to prevent the spread of abnormal electrical activity from one hemisphere to the other.

From Leipmann's early theorizing it should be possible to demonstrate conditions such as apraxias in patients with this sort of surgery. Sperry and his colleagues have extensively studied the effects of hemispheric disconnection on behaviors related to both sensory and motor systems.

Olfaction

Unlike all of the other senses the olfactory system is not crossed. The input from the left nostril goes straight back to the left hemisphere, and the input from the right nostril goes to the right hemisphere. Fibers traveling through the anterior commissure join the olfactory regions in each hemisphere, just as fibers traveling through the corpus callosum join the motor cortex of each hemisphere.

If the anterior commissure is severed odors presented to the right nostril cannot be named, because the left hemisphere, where speech is centered, is disconnected from the information. Similarly, the right hemisphere has the information, but has no control of speech. The olfactory function is still intact, however, because the patient can use the *left* hand to pick out an object, such as an orange, that corresponds to the odor smelled. In this case, no connection with speech is necessary, the right hemisphere both containing the olfactory information and controlling the left hand.

If requested to use the right hand the patient would be unable to pick out the object because the left hemisphere, which controls the right hand, is disconnected from the sensory information. Thus, the patient appears normal with one hand and anosmic with the other (see Figure 20-2).

Vision

As described previously (see Figure 9-5), the visual system is crossed. Information flashed tachistoscopically to one visual field travels selectively to the corresponding region of the visual cortex. Recall that by using this procedure Kimura and her associates demonstrated left and right visual-field superiorities for different types of input. For example, verbal material (such as words) is more accurately perceived when presented to the right visual field, presumably because the input travels to the left, speech, hemisphere. On the other hand, various types of visuospatial input produce a left visual-field superiority, since the right hemisphere appears to have a more important role in analyzing this information. Note, however, that the visual-field superiority observed in normal subjects is *relative.* That is, words presented to the left visual field, and hence right hemisphere, are sometimes perceived, although not as accurately or consistently as when they are presented to the right visual field. The relative effects of course occur because either hemisphere potentially has access to input to the opposite hemisphere via the corpus callosum, which joins the visual areas (see Figure 9-8). In the commissurotomy patient there is no longer such access because the connection is severed. Since speech is housed in the left hemisphere of right-handed patients, visual information presented to the left visual field will be disconnected from verbal associations because the input goes to the right, nonlinguistic, hemisphere. Similarly,

complex visual material presented to the right visual field would be inadequately processed, because it would not have access to the visuospatial abilities of the right hemisphere. It follows that if material is appropriately presented it should be possible to demonstrate aphasia, agnosia, alexia, and acopia in a patient who ordinarily exhibits none of these symptoms. This is indeed the case, as we now demonstrate.

Consider the language-related deficits aphasia, alexia, and agnosia. If verbal material were presented to the left visual field the commissurotomy patient would be unable to read it or to verbally answer questions about it, since the input is disconnected from the speech zones of the left hemisphere. Presentation of the same verbal material to the right visual field presents no difficulties, since the visual input projects to the verbal left hemisphere (see Figure 9-8). Similarly, if an object is presented to the left visual field the patient would be unable to name it and thus would appear to be either agnosic or aphasic. If presented to the right visual field this same object would be correctly named, because the left visual cortex "perceives" the object and has access to the speech zones. Thus, we can see that the split-brain patient is aphasic, alexic, and agnosic if verbal material or an object requiring a verbal response is visually presented to the right hemisphere, but appears normal if material is presented to the left hemisphere.

A further deficit can be seen if the patient is asked to copy a complex visual figure. As discussed earlier, the right hemisphere is specialized for the perception of complex visual material. Since the right hemisphere controls the left hand we might predict that the left hand would be able to copy the figure but that the right hand, deprived of the expertise of the right hemisphere, would be severely impaired. The left hand draws the figure well, whereas the right hand cannot and is thus acopic.

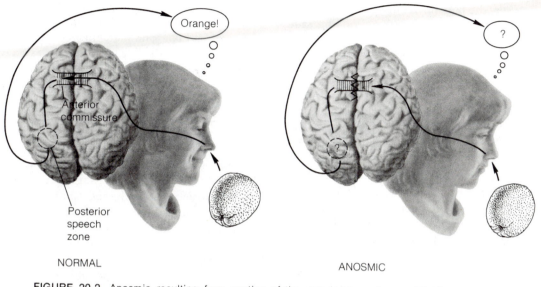

NORMAL ANOSMIC

FIGURE 20-2. Anosmia resulting from section of the anterior commissure. (The jagged line indicates the lesion of the anterior commissure.) Olfactory input to the right nostril travels directly back into the right hemisphere, crosses the anterior commissure, and thus gains access to the left (speech) hemisphere. When the pathway is severed, the left hemisphere has no way of knowing what odor the right hemisphere perceived.

Somesthesis

Like the visual system, the somatosensory system is completely crossed. Sensations of touch in the left hand travel to the right hemisphere, whereas those in the right hand travel to the left hemisphere. An object placed in the left hand can be named because the tactile information projects to the right hemisphere, crosses to the left, and subsequently has access to the speech zones. Similarly, if a subject is blindfolded and the right hand molded to form a particular shape, the left hand is able to copy it because the tactile information goes from the right hand to the left hemisphere, then across the corpus callosum to the right hemisphere, and the left hand forms the same shape.

If the two hemispheres are disconnected from one another, the somatosensory func-

tions of the left and right parts of the body become independent. For example, if some object is placed in the left hand of a blindfolded patient, who is then asked to choose the presented object from an array of objects, the left hand can pick out the object whereas the right hand cannot. If an object is placed in a blindfolded patient's right hand the patient can name it, but not if it is placed in the left hand, because the sensory input is disconnected from the left, speech, hemisphere.

The disconnection effects can also be demonstrated without the use of objects. For example, if the patient is blindfolded and one hand is shaped in a particular way, the opposite hand is unable to mimic the posture. One hand has no way of "knowing" what the other hand is doing in the absence of input coming from the opposite hemisphere via the corpus callosum. If the patient is not blindfolded, however, the patient can find out what the opposite hand is doing simply by looking at it.

Audition

The auditory system is somewhat more complex than the other systems because it has both crossed and uncrossed connections (Figure 9-6). Although the left hemisphere appears to receive most of its input from the right ear, it also receives input from the left ear. Words played into the left ear can therefore travel directly to the left hemisphere, or can go to the right hemisphere and then to the left via the corpus callosum. In normal subjects dichotic listening tasks clearly show that the contralateral input is preferred because words presented to the right ear are selectively perceived over words presented to the left ear. Remember, however, that this difference is relative, some words presented to the left ear also being reported.

The bilateral anatomical arrangement just described appears to reduce the effects of disconnection, but nevertheless one effect has been demonstrated. In the dichotic listening task input from the left ear is totally suppressed; the patient reports only those words played to the right ear. That is, digits or words played to the right ear are reported, but no input to the left ear is reported. This is a little surprising, since words played to the left ear, even under these conditions, would have been expected to attain some direct access to the left hemisphere. This direct access does not appear to occur.

Movement

Because the motor system is largely crossed, disconnection of the hemispheres could be predicted to induce several kinds of motor difficulties. First, on any task involving either a verbal command for the left hand to follow or verbal material for the left hand to write, a form of apraxia and agraphia could be expected, because the left hand does not receive instruction from the left hemisphere. That is, the left hand would be unable to follow the command (apraxia) or write (agraphia). These disabilities would not be seen in the right hand, which has access to the speech hemisphere. Similarly, if the right hand were asked to copy a geometric design it might be impaired (acopia) because it is disconnected from the right hemisphere, which ordinarily has a preferred role in the drawing of this type of material. These symptoms of disconnection are in fact observed in commissurotomy patients, although the severity of the deficit declines significantly over time after surgery, possibly because the left hemisphere's ipsilateral control is being used.

A second situation that might be expected to produce severe motor deficits in commissurotomy patients is one in which the two arms must be used in cooperation. Ordinarily, one hand is informed of what the other is doing via the connection of the corpus callosum. Preilowski and later Zaidel and Sperry carefully examined the effect of disconnection on this type of bimanual cooperative movement. Patients required to make alternating tapping movements of the index fingers were severely impaired at the task. Similarly, in a task similar to an Etch-a-Sketch, one requiring that a line inclined at an angle be traced, callosal patients did very poorly. This task requires the use of two cranks, one operated by each hand; one makes the tracing pen move vertically, whereas the other makes the tracing pen move horizontally. A high degree of manual cooperation is required to trace the line smoothly. If the hemispheres have undergone disconnection, this cooperation is severely retarded since the left and right motor systems are unable to gain information as to what the opposite side is doing, except indirectly, by the patient's watching them.

Dramatic illustrations of conflict between hands can be seen in the following descriptions.

> In one case the patient (W.J.) would repeatedly pick up a newspaper with his right hand and lay it down with his left hand. This would be performed several times until finally the left hand threw the newspaper on the floor. Another patient (R.Y.) was described by a physiotherapist: "He was buttoning his shirt with his right hand and the left hand was coming along just behind it undoing the buttons just as quickly as he could fasten them." However, as in the praxic impairments described earlier, instances of intermanual conflict were generally confined to the first post-operative months and again seemed related to the age of the patient and extent of extra-callosal damage. It is of interest to note that the same patients while inhibiting these episodes of intermanual conflict were able to use their left hand in a purposeful and cooperative manner when "not thinking of what they were doing." For example, they could pour coffee out of a pot held in the right hand into a cup held by its handle with the left hand. The above-mentioned peculiarities in motor functions were observed only in the complete split-brain patients. (Preilowski, 1975, p. 119)

The Problem of Partial Disconnection

Results from tests of callosal patients raise the question whether a partial section of the corpus callosum would have as severe effects as a complete disconnection. Recently, surgeons have experimented with partial surgical disconnection of the hemispheres, hoping to attain the same clinical relief from seizures but with fewer neuropsychological side effects. Although the results are still preliminary, partial disconnection, in which the posterior part of the corpus callosum is left intact, appears to combine markedly milder effects than the complete commissurotomy with the same therapeutic benefits for epilepsy. For example, Sperry and colleagues have found that patients with partial disconnection are significantly better at motor tasks such as the Etch-a-Sketch. Research on monkeys with partial commissurotomies suggests that the posterior portion of the corpus callosum (splenium) subserves visual transfer (as does the anterior commissure), whereas the region just in front of the splenium affects somatosensory transfer. The functions of the more anterior portions of the corpus callosum are largely unknown, but presumably transfer of the motor information may be one function.

Conclusions

The results of studies on surgical disconnection of the hemispheres indicate that many symptoms, including aphasia, alexia, agnosia, agraphia, acopia, and apraxia, can be demonstrated *in the absence of any direct damage to particular cytoarchitectural or functional neocortical regions.* They can also occur for one side of the body and not the other. Symptoms such as aphasia, agnosia, etc., can be thought of as resulting from disconnection of cortical regions rather than as necessarily resulting from damage to cortical regions. We will return to this idea below.

LESION EFFECTS REINTERPRETED AS DISCONNECTION SYNDROMES

In 1965, Geschwind published a theoretically significant monograph, "Disconnexion Syndromes in Animals and Man," that tied together a vast amount of literature and anticipated many of the effects of callosal surgery. Although Geschwind's arguments are extremely complex his thesis is that certain types of behavioral deficits can be seen as resulting from disconnections between hemispheres, within a hemisphere, or a combination of both. The value of this monograph is not the review of data, but rather that it forcefully reintroduces the concept first proposed by Dejerine and Leipmann nearly 70 years earlier, that disconnecting neocortical regions can cause a variety of neurological symptoms. To demonstrate the utility of the model we discuss only the three classic symptoms of left-hemisphere damage: apraxia, agnosia, and alexia.

Apraxia

Earlier in this chapter we noted that if a lesion of the corpus callosum disconnected the left hand from the left hemisphere, that hand would be unable to respond to verbal commands and would be considered apraxic (see Figure 20-1). Suppose, however, that the right hand is unable to respond to verbal commands. Geschwind speculated that this deficit results from a lesion in the left hemisphere that disconnects its motor cortex, which controls the right hand from the speech zone; thus, the right hand could not respond to verbal commands and would be considered apraxic.

Although Geschwind's model can explain bilateral apraxia in some patients, it must be emphasized that disconnection is not the only cause of apraxia. Because the posterior cortex has direct access to the subcortical neural mechanisms of arm and body movements (as described in Chapter 11), parietal input need not go through the motor cortex except for control of finger movements. Furthermore, as we noted earlier, patients with sections of the corpus callosum are initially apraxic, but show substantial recovery despite a disconnection of the motor cortex of the left and right hemispheres.

Agnosia and Alexia

Geschwind theorized that agnosia and alexia can be produced by disconnections of the posterior speech area from the visual association cortex. They can be produced by a lesion that disconnects the visual association region on the left from the speech zone in addition to a lesion which disconnects the right visual association cortex from the speech zone by damaging the corpus callosum as illustrated in Figure 20-3. Thus, the patient, although able to talk, is unable to identify words or objects because the visual information is disconnected from the posterior speech zone in the left hemisphere.

Conclusions

In this section lesions that disconnect regions within or between hemispheres were demonstrated to at least theoretically be able to produce many neuropsychological symptoms. It is likely that the effects of naturally occurring lesions result from a combination of direct damage to a region and disconnection of different regions. If so, localization of brain damage on the basis of behavior becomes more complicated.

EXPERIMENTAL VERIFICATION OF DISCONNECTION EFFECTS

Disconnection of different neocortical regions to produce a variety of behavioral symptoms can be used experimentally to demonstrate the function of various brain regions. Downer, for example, devised an ingenious experiment to demonstrate the effects of temporal lobectomy. He removed one temporal lobe in a monkey that had previously undergone a split-brain operation. He then showed that if

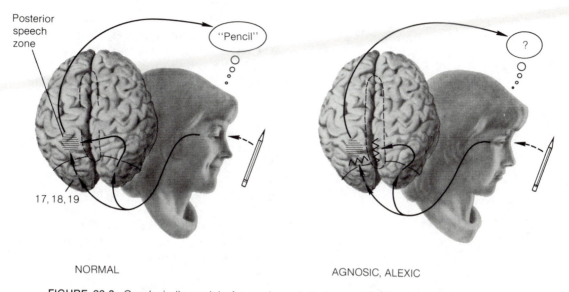

Posterior
speech
zone

"Pencil"

17, 18, 19

?

NORMAL

AGNOSIC, ALEXIC

FIGURE 20-3. Geschwind's model of agnosia and alexia resulting from disconnection of the visual cortex from the posterior speech zone. (The jagged lines indicate the lesion of the pathways.) Normally, the visual input of both hemispheres travels to the posterior speech zone and tertiary sensory cortex, where it is processed to allow speech describing the written word or object. In the absence of the connection this is no longer possible, and agnosia and alexia result.

only the hemisphere with the temporal lobectomy receives visual information, the monkey acts like Klüver and Bucy's monkeys, being completely tame and placid. On the other hand, when the visual input is restricted to the intact hemisphere the monkey is normal and far from tame. So astounding was this phenomenon that it was at first widely doubted, but having been replicated by other investigators it is now generally accepted. The experiment clearly demonstrates that the two hemispheres can act independently of one another.

Mishkin and others have exploited the disconnections of different brain areas in animals to demonstrate the functional connections in the hierarchical organization of the visual system and, more recently, the somatosensory system. This research clearly demonstrates the

usefulness in the disconnection approach and has led to significant progress in our understanding of the sensory systems.

The Visual System

Previous discussion of the visual system's hierarchical nature did not consider the connections between the system's various regions. These are summarized in Figure 20-4 A. In each hemisphere connections run from area 17 to area 18 and 19 in the same hemisphere. Connections from 18 and 19 cross the corpus callosum to the analogous area on the opposite side, as well as connecting with area 20 on the same side. Area 20 connects to area 21 and the amygdala on the same side, and on the opposite side via the anterior commissure. What would happen to vision if the connections were

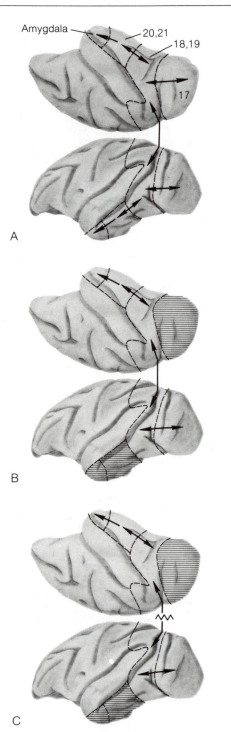

A

B

C

cut? This question has been addressed in experiments using monkeys as subjects.

Consideration of this question requires that monkeys first be tested to determine their visual capabilities? The easiest method is to teach the animal a visual discrimination such as a "+" vs. an "0." Food reinforcement is associated with one stimulus and not with the other. The monkey's task is to identify the correct stimulus and respond to it. Control monkeys learn this problem in 100 to 150 trials or fewer, so if a monkey that has been operated on fails to learn this problem in 1000 trials, it is assumed that it will not learn it at all; the lesion can thus be inferred to have some important effect on the monkey's ability to discriminate visual stimuli.

By using tasks of this sort, Mishkin and others have demonstrated that bilateral lesions in areas 17, 18, and 19, or in 20 and 21, result in impaired, or abolished, acquisition of visual-discrimination problems. Because unilateral lesions do not have such an effect, what seems to be necessary is one intact area each of 17, 18, and 19, and one intact area 20 and 21. There is, however, one constraint: the remaining regions must be connected. Thus, in Figure 20-4 B a lesion in area 17 on the right and 20 and 21 on the left does not disturb performance, since there is still an intact system that can be used. If the connection between the hemispheres were now severed the neocortical areas would still be intact but not connected, and the result is failure on the visual-discrimination problem (Figure 20-4 C). Clearly the neocortical regions do not function

FIGURE 20-4. Disconnection effects in the visual system of monkeys. A. The visual system is intact. B. The left visual cortex still has access to the visual association cortex of the right hemisphere, so vision is still possible. C. The intact components of the visual system are disconnected, producing major visual deficits. (After Mishkin, 1979.)

properly if they are not connected to one another.

Mishkin first studied the region of area 20, 21, thinking them to be the final step in the neocortical visual system. More recently he has studied the problem of how visual stimuli might gain what he calls "motivational" or "emotional" significance. Recall that the Klüver-Bucy monkeys with bilateral temporal lobectomies attached no significance to visual stimuli. Thus, they would repeatedly taste nasty-tasting objects, or place inedible objects in their mouths. In his 1965 paper Geschwind proposed that this symptom represented a disconnection of the amygdala from the visual system. That is, theoretically at least, although an animal's visual sensory system might be intact the animal would behave as if it were not because it is disconnected from another system that attaches meaning to visual information. Figure 20-5 A illustrates the additional connections when the amygdala is included in an extended visual system. Area 20, 21 connects with the amygdala on the same side and on the opposite side via the anterior commissure.

To test Geschwind's proposal, Mishkin devised the experiment illustrated in Figure 20-5 parts B and C. The amygdala was lesioned on the left and the inferior temporal cortex on the right. This arrangement left one complete system of areas 17, 18, 19, 20, 21, amygdala, and using it the monkey's performance on visual problems was normal, as would be expected. The anterior commissure was then cut, leaving all of the necessary pieces of the system intact,

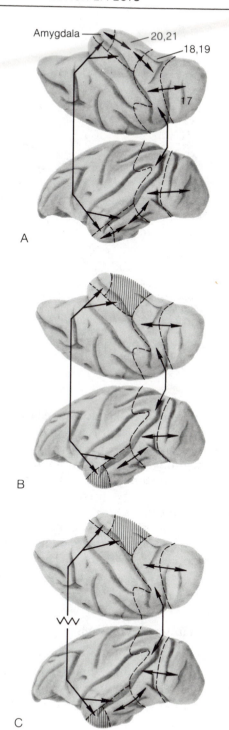

FIGURE 20-5. Disconnection of affect from visual input. A. The connections of the normal visual system, including both the callosal and anterior commissural connections. B. Even if parts of the system are damaged it can still function. C. If the anterior commissure is severed, visual input is separated from affect, resulting in visual deficits. (After Mishkin, 1979.)

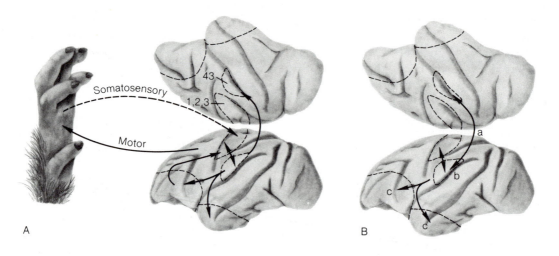

FIGURE 20-6. Mishkin's somatosensory model. A. The major intracortical connections of the
somatosensory system involved in performing a tactile discrimination. Input travels from the hand
to areas 1, 2, 3, to area 43, and then to the medial temporal and orbital frontal areas. This input
then travels to the motor cortex to produce a response. B. A lesion at a would render the left hand
unable to perform a task learned by the right because the memory is in the left hemisphere. Also,
b and c show that lesions at these points would render the trained right hand unable to perform the
task because the primary area is disconnected from the remainder of the system. (After Mishkin,
1979.)

but disconnecting the intact amygdala from
the neocortical portion of the system. Performance on visual problems instantly deterio-
rated, indicating that there was some interruption of the normal processing of visual
material, as would be predicted from Geschwind's model. Other experiments by
Mishkin and his colleagues have demonstrated
that the orbital frontal cortex may also play an
important role in the system, possibly to guide
behavioral responses to biologically relevant
visual information.

The Somatosensory System

The logic used in studying the connection of
the visual system can be applied to the study
of the somatosensory system. Consider the following type of experiment: a monkey is

trained to make a discrimination of two objects by touch alone, using just one hand.
Once this problem is learned, the opposite
hand, when tested, performs well on the task,
either because the information stored in the
trained hemisphere is accessible to that hand
(see Figure 20-6), or because the information
is stored in both hemispheres. The next step is
to cut the corpus callosum. Failure of the
left hand to solve the problem would indicate that memory of the task is stored in
the trained hemisphere. The hand indeed
fails, indicating that the memory of the task is
stored in the trained hemisphere. Notice,
however, that the trained hand will still be
able to solve the problem. The next question
to ask is: Which connections within the trained
hemisphere are necessary to continue to perform normally on this task? Mishkin proposes

that the connections are something like those diagrammed in Figure 20-6. That is, the primary somatosensory cortex is connected to the secondary somatosensory cortex of both hemispheres. This region, in turn, is connected to the medial temporal region and/or the orbital frontal region. If this is true then the following predictions can be made. First, a lesion at point *a* in Figure 20-6 B would render the left hand unable to do a task learned by the right hand because the memory is in the trained hemisphere as noted above. Second, a lesion of *b* or *c* would render the right, trained, hand unable to do the problem because the primary area is disconnected from the remainder of the system. These predictions remain to be tested directly. Notice that if there were lesions to *b* or *c* the callosum would not have to be cut, because the memory is not stored in the opposite hemisphere.

CONCLUSIONS

We have demonstrated that the connections of various cortical and subcortical regions are as important as the regions themselves in understanding the effects of brain damage. Conditions such as apraxia, agnosia, and alexia may be produced by disconnections of neocortical regions that normally function as part of an interconnected system. In humans it is extremely difficult to know whether behavioral symptoms are a result of disconnection or of regional damage, but in experimental work with nonhumans the data are much clearer. Mishkin and his colleagues have clearly shown that the visual and possibly the somatosensory systems are composed of a series of sequential steps beginning with the primary sensory cortex and terminating in the medial temporal lobe and/or orbital frontal cortex.

REFERENCES

Akelaitis, A. J. A study of gnosis, praxis and language following section of the corpus callosum and anterior commissure. *Journal of Neurosurgery, 1* (1944), 94–102.

Downer, J. L. de C. Changes in visual gnostic functions and emotional behavior following unilateral temporal pole damage in the "split-brain" monkey. *Nature, 191* (1961), 50–51.

Gazzaniga, M. S. *The Bisected Brain.* New York: Appleton-Century-Crofts, 1970.

Geschwind, N. Disconnexion syndromes in animals and man. *Brain, 88* (1965), 237–294, 585–644.

Klüver, H., and P. C. Bucy. Preliminary analysis of functions of the temporal lobes in monkeys. *Archives of Neurology and Psychiatry, 42* (1939), 979–1000.

Mishkin, M. Analogous neural models for tactile and visual learning. *Neuropsychologia, 17* (1979), 139–152.

Myers, R. E. Functions of the corpus callosum in interocular transfer. *Brain, 57* (1956), 358–363.

Nebes, R. D. Hemispheric specialization in commissurotomized man. *Psychological Bulletin, 81* (1974), 1–14.

Preilowski, B. Bilateral motor interaction: perceptual-motor performance of partial and complete "split-brain" patients. In K. J. Zulch, O. Creutzfeldt, and G. C. Galbraith, eds. *Cerebral Localization.* Berlin and New York: Springer-Verlag, 1975.

Sperry, R. W. Lateral specialization in the surgically separated hemispheres. In F. O. Schmitt and F. G. Worden, eds. *Neurosciences: Third Study Program.* Cambridge, Mass.: MIT Press, 1974.

Zaidel, D., and R. W. Sperry. Some long term motor effects of cerebral commissurotomy in man. *Neuropsychologia, 15* (1977), 193–204.

PART NINE

APPLIED HUMAN NEUROPSYCHOLOGY

This final part of the book describes the application of the fundamental principles of human neuropsychology to both neuropsychological assessment and the understanding of a variety of socioeducational problems. Chapter 21 discusses the assessment of cerebral damage and dysfunction in neurological and psychiatric settings. Chapter 22 discusses the direct application of neuropsychological principles to the design of programs ranging from the rehabilitation of neurological patients to the schooling of children with learning disabilities.

The true potential of neuropsychology lies not only in its contribution to the understanding of brain function but also—and this will be its real test—in the applicability of the basic knowledge to human problems. There are moral and ethical responsibilities to apply the basic knowledge wisely, with the utmost care and caution. Neuroscientists in other areas will be watching with a very critical eye. Perhaps the major difficulty in successful application of neuropsychological principles is the problem of individual differences. Up to this point in the book we have emphasized the consistent relationship between brain function and behavior. In practice, however, brain–behavior relationships vary considerably from person to person. Such variability can be attributed to a number of factors. For example, individuals in the general population vary widely in their ability at any particular skill, and this variance influences the effects of brain injury or dysfunction. An architect with injury to the right hemisphere may suffer deficits in visuospatial analysis that make it impossible for him to return to work as an architect—even though he is still better at visuospatial ability than the average person! Further, personality variables influence a person's response to brain injury and affect the degree of recovery following it. In other disciplines in applied neurology, variation, although it must also be contended with, is less of a burden because those disciplines deal largely with physical signs and symptoms that are much less variant than the differences in cognitive processes measured by neuropsychologists. It is for this reason that neuropsychological principles must be applied carefully and conservatively to avoid serious errors harmful both to individual patients and (less importantly) to the reputation of a field with so much potential. Thus, those who would be called neuropsychologists *must* have a solid grounding in the fundamentals of neuroscience, and in neuropsychology in particular. Throughout this book we have emphasized the importance of a basic understanding of how the nervous system operates, to its minute particulars, whether it be a neuron or a synapse. Failure to learn basic lessons before applying neuropsychological principles will only ensure, at best, mediocrity or, worse, incompetence. At the same time, competent neuropsychologists must not be *overly* cautious, because if the competent fail to apply the basic knowledge, the incompetent will surely fill the field.

21

NEUROPSYCHOLOGICAL ASSESSMENT

After World War II many neuropsychological laboratories were established in Europe and North America. These have been principally responsible for the development of neuropsychological assessment as a tool in clinical neurology. We make no attempt to thoroughly review all the tests used in neurological assessment (we recommend Lezak's recent book for further discussion of the range of available tests). Rather, we review: (1) the rationale and goals of neuropsychological assessment; (2) the types of disorders for which it is most useful; (3) the characteristics of useful neuropsychological tests; (4) several currently used test batteries; and (5) examples of the use of test results in the diagnosis of individual patients' problems.

RATIONALE OF ASSESSMENT

Throughout Chapters 10 to 20 we have seen that circumscribed lesions in different cortical regions may produce discrete behavioral changes. In Chapters 12, 13, and 14 we argued that it would thus seem reasonable to assume that one could work backward from this knowledge to localize unknown brain damage. That is, given a particular behavioral change, one should be able to predict the site or sites of the disturbance most likely causing the behavioral change. There are, however, several problems in working backward in such a manner. First, research patients are often chosen for specific reasons. For example, whereas patients with rapidly expanding tumors would not be chosen for research, because the results are so difficult to interpret, neurosurgical patients, on the other hand, are ideal research subjects because the extent of damage is known. This difference in etiology of the neurological disorder might thus be expected to make assessment difficult if the tests are based on data collected from patients with totally different etiologies.

The second problem is related to the size of the lesion and the sensitivity of the tests. If a large region of the brain is dysfunctioning, then the assessment test need not be particularly sensitive to demonstrate the dysfunction. On the other hand, if the lesion is small, the behavioral effect may be rather specific (as we have seen). For example, a lesion in the right somatosensory representation of the face may produce very subtle sensory changes, and unless specific tests of nonverbal fluency are used (see Chapter 14), the cognitive changes may go unnoticed, even with dozens of tests.

The third problem, a related one, is assessment time. Since neuropsychological tests must be sensitive to changes in a vast number of behaviors and skills, many different tests must be administered for a diagnosis to be made. Thus, existing one-shot tests of organic impairment, organicity, or brain dysfunction are invalid when used alone. Although it is true that many patients with brain damage do poorly on some of these tests, it is also true that many patients with known brain damage do well on them. And even among those patients who are impaired at them, there is no localization of the neurological problem. In addition, there is the continual problem of false positives. Patients may be impaired at *particular* tests for many reasons, only one of which may be brain damage or dysfunction. An adequate assessment requires time, often six or more hours, which clearly requires more than one sitting with the patient.

The fourth problem is that various factors may interact with the brain pathology to make interpretation of test results difficult. Tests are seldom developed for subjects who are 80 years old or who are culturally disadvantaged. Test scores therefore cannot be interpreted with strict cutoff criteria—that is, performance below a particular level cannot always be taken as indicating brain damage. Further, intelligence alters the investigators' expectations of performance on different tests: someone with an IQ of 130 may be relatively impaired on a test of verbal memory but, compared to someone with an IQ of 90, may appear normal. Thus, unlike standard psychometric assessment, neuropsychological assessment must be flexible. This clearly makes interpretation difficult and requires extensive training in fundamental neuropsychology and neurology as well as in neuropsychological assessment.

A final problem is that current neuropsychological assessment procedures cannot easily discriminate between patients with extensive brain damage and patients with gross cerebral *dysfunction* such as occurs in schizophrenia. Although schizophrenic patients would not appear to have focalized lesions, they do certainly appear to have grossly dysfunctioning brains.

Goals of Neuropsychological Assessment

The goal of assessment in general clinical psychology is the diagnosis of the disorder for the purpose of effecting behavioral change. For example, intelligence and achievement tests may be given to schoolchildren as a means of trying to identify particular problem areas, as an aid in teaching. Similarly, personality tests are used with an eye toward defining and curing a behavioral disorder.

The goals in clinical neuropsychology are different in some respects. First, the assessment aims to diagnose the presence of cortical damage or dysfunction and to localize it where possible. Second, assessment is used to facilitate patient care as well as rehabilitation. A related goal is to identify unusual brain organization that may occur in left-handers or in people with childhood brain injury. This information is particularly valuable to the surgeon, who would not wish to inadvertently remove primary speech zones during surgery. In such disorders as focal epilepsy the primary evidence corroborating abnormal EEG may be behavioral, because radiological procedures often fail to demonstrate the abnormal brain tissue giving rise to the seizures. In addition, because some recovery of function may be expected following brain injury, this recovery must be documented not only with rehabilitation in mind but also to determine the effectiveness of any medical treatment, particularly for neoplasms or vascular abnormalities. Further, the patient and the family must understand the patient's possible residual deficits, so that realistic life goals and rehabilitation programs can be planned.

Application of Neuropsychological Assessment to Specific Disorders

Neuropsychological assessment is most useful on patients with cerebral vascular disorders, acute traumatic lesions, neoplasms, and epilepsy; it is of limited value on patients with infections of the brain, progressive brain disease such as multiple sclerosis, or dementias, all of which are not localized. Once a patient behaves as if demented, test results have little validity.

The importance of comprehensive neuropsychological assessments in patients with cerebral vascular disorders or traumatic lesions cannot be overemphasized: in such patients a partial assessment is often worse than none at all. For example, standardized intelligence tests may produce results that misleadingly suggest dementia, because IQ tests emphasize verbal skills and ignore other skills necessary for day-to-day living. On the other hand, just the opposite may also be true: patients with normal or near normal IQs may fail to perform normally on other tests of specific mental functions critically important in normal daily activities. An inadequate assessment may fail to diagnose these deficits, leading to invalid conclusions about an individual's neuropsychological functioning.

In the case of cerebral tumors, neuro-

psychological studies may provide baselines for assessing initial and later effects of surgery, irradiation, or chemotherapy. In the absence of radiological evidence such studies may also promote proper clinical neurological assessment by providing evidence of brain dysfunction resulting from disease processes.

Neuropsychological assessment has a most important diagnostic role in the preoperative localization of lesions in focal epilepsy. It is not uncommon for focal epileptics to demonstrate no positive signs in radiological or other neurological tests while demonstrating clearly localized behavioral deficits. Further, particularly in the case of temporal-lobe epilepsy, where there may be risk to memory, neuropsychological assessment may be invaluable in identifying hippocampal damage in the hemisphere contralateral to the major focus.

Finally, neuropsychological assessment is beginning to be used to evaluate undesirable side effects of various pharmacological treatments, particularly in the treatment of movement disorders such as Parkinson's disease. Because the effects of various pharmacological treatments for both psychiatric and neurological disorders are as yet poorly understood, side effects of high or chronic doses of various drugs are common. Neuropsychological assessment can provide an objective measure of unwanted deficits in cognitive functioning.

Although neuropsychological assessment has many roles and goals in the diagnosis and treatment of neurological disease, we must emphasize a serious concern. Hebb once wrote, "a half-baked psychologist is worse than none at all." It is also true that "a half-baked neuropsychologist is worse than none at all." Neuropsychological assessment is complex and requires extensive training to properly evaluate the results. Experience in interpreting personality or intelligence tests is not sufficient background to begin neuropsychological assessment.

Characteristics of Useful Neuropsychological Tests

At least five important criteria characterize useful neuropsychological tests.

1. *Thoroughness.* To be useful a group of tests must test a wide variety of functions. They must identify the hemisphere containing speech; measure general intelligence and memory; measure sensory, perceptual, and motor functions; assess language functions; and, finally, examine the performance on tests sensitive to frontal-lobe damage.

Laterality of speech is most easily determined by a verbal dichotic listening test, and general intelligence is most frequently measured by one of the Wechsler scales (Wechsler-Bellevue or Wechsler Adult Intelligence Scale). Memory testing requires consideration of both verbal and nonverbal aspects as well as short-term and long-term memory. The Wechsler memory scale, widely used as a general test of memory, is primarily verbal and must be supplemented with visual tests.

Visual and auditory sensory functions are usually thoroughly examined by neurologists, but somatosensory function is not—largely because it is tedious and time consuming. If there is any evidence of a lesion to the central regions, somatosensory tests are invaluable. Motor functions such as reflexes, balance, gait, and the like are usually thoroughly examined by neurologists, but praxic functions frequently are not, again because of time limitations. These tests of apraxia are, however, easy to administer and score and should be included if practical.

Language functions can be assessed by tests of the patient's speech and also by the many tests of aphasia, reading, writing, and arithmetic abilities. Tests of language functions should not be limited to a simple conversation, for subtle defects may often be overlooked.

Finally, a thorough assessment protocol will include tests of left and right frontal-lobe function.

2. *Ease and cost.* Tests should be easy to administer and score. Much of the testing often must be done by psychometrists, and the results interpreted by the neuropsychologist. Thus, it is essential that tests be given in a standard format and scored objectively, so that the neuropsychologist can be assured of consistent results from tests being administered by more than one psychometrist. The tests should also be inexpensive. Cost constraints are not a good reason to administer a partial assessment protocol.

3. *Time.* Tests should not take excessively long to administer. Because patients are often weak and easily tired, it is desirable to complete testing as quickly as possible without compromising thoroughness.

4. *Adaptability.* Often patients are not very mobile, possibly being restricted to wheelchairs or even bedridden. It is therefore essential that the tests be portable and adaptable to varying constraints determined by the health of the patient.

5. *Flexibility.* Research is continually improving tests and devising newer, better tests. It is important that tests be substituted or improved in the light of new data. Test batteries that employ complex formulae or cutoff scores are thus less desirable because they necessarily lose their flexibility.

TEST BATTERIES: DESCRIPTIONS AND CRITICISMS

It is evident that to be thorough a useful neuropsychological assessment requires a series of different tests. Hence the development of neuropsychological batteries that are given routinely as a group—although most batteries are flexible enough that certain tests may be added or deleted depending upon the nature of the assessment. In this section we discuss the types of test batteries and the uses of intelligence testing in neuropsychological batteries; finally we describe an example of each type of battery.

There are three basic types of neuropsychological test batteries: (1) clinically based batteries; (2) theoretical psychometric batteries; and (3) theoretical nonpsychometric batteries. Clinically based batteries include those in which the tests used were originally chosen because they successfully discriminated between persons with brain damage and persons without such damage. In these tests there is frequently no intuitive reason *why* the tests should work because they may not be theoretically based. The tests themselves, however, are generally psychometrically sound, being standardized, having reasonable norms for comparison, and being reliable. An example of this type of battery is the Halstead-Reitan battery.

In theoretically based batteries the tests included are based directly on research findings. The psychometric and nonpsychometric types differ in how deficits are inferred. On tests of the psychometric type, performance on each test is compared to a set of norms, often adjusted for IQ, and a neuropsychological deficit is identified *quantitatively*. Most neuropsychological batteries are of the psychometric type, an example being the Montreal Neurological Institute test battery. On nonpsychometric batteries, performance on each test is compared *qualitatively* to the performance of normal controls. By this method, deficits are thus inferred, not from numbers, but from deviations in subjectively assessed behavior on highly standardized tests. The nonpsychometric type of test battery closely resembles the format of the neurological exam, the best example being Luria's Neuropsychological Investigation.

Intelligence Testing in Neuropsychological Batteries

Most neuropsychological test batteries begin with either the Wechsler Adult Intelligence Scale (WAIS) or one of the Wechsler-Bellevue scales. Although the Wechsler-Bellevue forms are rather dated, they do provide alternate forms of the WAIS, which are necessary for repeated testing, and they correlate highly with the scores obtained on the WAIS. The Wechsler scales have proven invaluable in providing a base level of cognitive functioning. McFie has also found them to be extremely useful diagnostic tools in themselves. These scales present a distinct advantage: they provide separate scores for verbal and for performance subtests, as well as an overall IQ.

The verbal scale consists of six subtests: (1) Information: questions such as "Where is Egypt?" "Who wrote *Hamlet?*" (2) Comprehension: questions requiring some reflection before answering, e.g., "Why are child labor laws needed?" (3) Arithmetic: e.g., "How many hours will it take a man to walk 24 miles at the rate of three miles an hour?" (4) Similarities: the subject is asked in what way two items are alike, e.g., an orange and a banana, an egg and a seed. (5) Digit span: tests the number of digits that can be repeated in correct sequence, forward and backward. (6) Vocabulary: asks for the meaning of words ranging from easy (e.g., winter) to difficult (e.g., travesty).

The performance scale consists of five subtests: (1) Digit symbol: nine symbols (e.g., ⊥) are paired with digits 1–9 in a key above the response sheet. The task is to pencil in as many of the symbols corresponding to each of 90 digits as possible in 90 seconds. This requires rapid eye movement and short-term visual store. (2) Picture completion: the subject indicates what is missing in each of a series of pictures. (3) Block design: red and white blocks must be used to form a design presented on a card. (4) Picture arrangement: several cards with cartoonlike drawings are presented in mixed-up order, and the subject is required to order them so that they tell a coherent story. (5) Object assembly: pieces of simple jigsaw puzzles are given to the subject who must assemble them as quickly as possible.

Although the verbal versus performance distinction between these subtests is serendipitous the subtests have proven extremely useful as a rough measure of left- and right-hemisphere function, respectively. The IQs obtained on the verbal and performance sections both have a mean of 100 and a standard deviation of 16, and the standard error of the difference at a 95 percent confidence level is around 10. In other words, a difference of more than 10 points between the verbal and performance scores is abnormal. A number of studies have shown that well-defined left-hemisphere lesions produce a relatively low verbal IQ, whereas well-defined right-hemisphere lesions produce a relatively low performance IQ. Diffuse damage, on the other hand, tends to produce a low performance IQ, leading to the erroneous belief that the verbal–performance IQ difference is not diagnostically useful. Although a reduced performance IQ is not definitive, it is rare to obtain a relatively low verbal IQ, and its appearance should not be ignored.

Halstead-Reitan Battery

The most widely known battery is the Halstead-Reitan battery, presumably because it is the most readily available. Essentially it is based on a series of tests originally devised by Halstead in the late 1940s. It began as a battery of seven tests selected for their power to discriminate between patients with frontal-lobe lesions and other patient groups or normal controls. The current version of the battery consists of about 10 basic tests, 8 of which are listed below and several others of which are given mention.

1. *Wechsler intelligence scale.* Either the Wechsler Adult Intelligence Scale (WAIS) or the Wechsler-Bellevue intelligence scale, Form I, is administered.

2. *Category test.* A category test is primarily a test of abstracting ability. A variety of stimulus figures varying in size, shape, number, intensity, color, and location are projected on a screen for the patient's viewing. These figures can be grouped by abstract principles, and it is the patient's task to determine the principle. This test is sensitive to left or right frontal-lobe damage.

3. *Critical flicker fusion test.* The rate at which flashing lights appear steady or fused into a constant light is assessed by using a light-flashing stroboscope. This test is often not included in the battery.

4. *Tactual-performance test.* The Seguin-Goddard formboard test described in our discussion of parietal-lobe tests in Chapter 12 is a tactual-performance test. Blindfolded patients are asked to place blocks of wood of various shapes (square, star, half-moon, etc.) into holes of similar shape in the formboard; later they are asked, without having seen the board, to draw it from memory. Although Halstead and Reitan believed this was a frontal-lobe test, many authors, including ourselves, have found that frontal-lobe patients are not impaired at this task whereas right-parietal patients are. Indeed, it is difficult to understand why this test would have been considered a test of frontal-lobe pathology.

5. *Rhythm test.* The rhythm test, a subtest of the Seashore test of musical talent, requires the patient to discriminate between like and unlike pairs of musical beats. Patients with right temporal-lobe removals are impaired at this task.

6. *Speech-sounds perception test.* The speech-sounds perception test is an auditory acuity test in which the subject listens to a tape recording of 60 spoken nonsense words, all of which have an "ee" vowel sound in the middle with different beginning and ending consonant sounds. The subject selects the word heard from a series of alternatives. This is a test of left-hemisphere function, presumably taxing mainly either the left posterior temporal-parietal cortex around Wernicke's area or possibly the left face area.

7. *Finger-oscillation test.* On the finger-oscillation test the subject's finger-tapping speed is measured on a key resembling a Morse code key. Halstead found a slight slowing of tapping speed in patients with cortical lesions, and Reitan has claimed this test to be one of the most sensitive in the battery. This conclusion is not universally accepted and we have found the test to be unreliable in lateralizing pathology, especially if the lesion is in the temporal or occipital cortex.

8. *Time-sense test.* A time-sense test measures the subject's visual-motor reaction time and ability to estimate elapsed time. The task is to watch a clock hand rotate around a clock face and then to estimate sweep time from memory. The memory component of this test has not proven useful and is not generally used.

9. *Auxiliary tests.* Other tests included in the original battery but not always administered include the trail-making test, aphasia screening test, and Minnesota Multiphasic Personality Inventory (MMPI). The trail-making test requires subjects to draw lines to connect either consecutive numbers or letters scattered randomly on a page and in a second part to alternate between the two sequences (i.e., A-1-B-2-C-3...); the aphasia screening test is an altered version of the Wepman aphasia test; and the MMPI is a widely used self-report questionnaire alleged to diagnose psychiatric abnormalities.

To ascertain the presence of brain damage, a summary value is obtained, known as the *Halstead Impairment Index.* This index is determined by counting the number of tests on which the results fall in the range characteristic of the performance of brain-damaged subjects.

Although the Halstead-Reitan battery is widely used and has been an important pioneer effort in neuropsychological assessment, it is subject to a number of serious criticisms. The tests are not theoretically based, but rather are largely derived from 27 tests that Halstead originally chose in hopes of finding tests to identify patients with frontal lesions. Thus, the 10 tests that are used are really clinically based and are difficult to interpret theoretically. Furthermore, the battery has not been substantially altered in the last 20 years despite marked advances in the understanding of human brain function during that period. Memory functions are poorly and naively assessed, even though more probably is known about memory and its assessment than about any other cerebral function. In addition, the tests are not sensitive enough, because many patients with small focalized lesions would have no significant abnormalities on the battery. The test is also not sensitive to the effects of aging on behavior and cannot reliably discriminate between subjects 45 years of age or older and brain-damaged subjects. An additional problem is that the battery, and particularly the category test, is not really portable and is thus difficult to administer to bedridden patients. The most serious problem, however, is that the battery, although containing a large number of tests, does not meet our criteria of thoroughness (as discussed above). There is no measure of somatosensory function, praxic function, or gnostic function. Furthermore, there is evidence that the tests used are highly correlated, and therefore redundant, and that some of the individual tests (e.g., the trail-making test) may actually be better predictors of brain damage than the impairment index. A final problem, by no means unique to the Halstead-Reitan battery, is its inability to distinguish between psychotic and brain-damaged patients. For example, Watson et al. found that Reitan-trained examiners were unable to differentiate, at better than a chance level, patients with known brain damage from patients diagnosed as schizophrenic. This inability is a chronic problem of all neuropsychological batteries, no doubt reflecting the gross frontal and temporal-lobe dysfunction in schizophrenia discussed in previous chapters.

Montreal Neurological Institute Battery

The tests comprising this battery are based on about 30 years of research at the Montreal Neurological Institute by Milner, Taylor, and their colleagues. The battery is based primarily on research with patients with surgical excisions for indolent tumors or epilepsy. Although not all of the tests were developed in Montreal, all have been extensively researched on neurosurgical patients before and after surgery, as well as later in follow-up, sometimes pursued over periods of 20 years after surgery.

Table 21-1 summarizes the tests in the battery, most of which have been discussed in other contexts earlier in the book (see Chapters 12, 13, and 14); each test will thus be discussed only briefly. First, general intelligence and speech lateralization are assessed using standard techniques, namely Wechsler scales and dichotic digits. Visuoperceptual abilities are assessed by a series of pictures making up the McGill picture-anomalies test: looking at a series of pictures, each containing something strange or unusual, the subject must point to the oddity in the picture. The Mooney faces test requires the subject, examining an incomplete sketch of a face, to per-

TABLE 21-1

Summary of Montreal Neurological
Institute battery

1. Determination of speech lateralization
   a. Handedness questionnaire
   b. Dichotic digits

2. General intelligence: WAIS or Wechsler-Bellevue scales

3. Visuoperceptual
   a. McGill picture anomalies
   b. Mooney faces
   c. Rey complex figures—copy

4. Memory
   a. Wechsler memory scale
   b. Rey complex figures—delayed recall
   c. Delayed recall of stories, paired associates, and drawings

5. Spatial
   a. Right-left differentiation
   b. Semmes body-placing test

6. Somatosensory
   a. Passive movement
   b. Point localization
   c. Two-point discrimination
   d. Simultaneous extinction

7. Language
   a. Object naming
   b. Chapman-Cook speed of reading
   c. Spelling
   d. Phonetic discrimination
   e. Token test

8. Hippocampal function
   a. Corsi recurring blocks
   b. Hebb recurring digits

9. Frontal lobe
   a. Wisconsin card-sorting test
   b. Chicago word-fluency test

10. Motor function
    a. Dynamometer
    b. Kimura box test
    c. Complex arm and facial movement copying

ceive the face, and then indicate the sex and age of the person. Finally, the Rey complex figure is copied as accurately as possible. The Mooney faces and Rey figure are particularly sensitive to right parietal-lobe damage, whereas the McGill picture anomalies is most sensitive to right temporal-lobe damage.

Memory is assessed by a number of tests. The widely used Wechsler memory scale complements the Wechsler intelligence scales and includes subtests of general information (names of heads of state) and orientation (date, etc.), as well as recall of simple logical stories, forward and backward recall of strings of digits, a paired-associates list, and simple drawings. In addition to immediate recall of the stories, drawings, and paired associates, these items must be recalled after a delay of about 30 minutes. Finally, there is a delayed recall of a complex figure previously copied. The verbal-memory tests are sensitive to left temporal-lobe damage, the nonverbal tests to right temporal-lobe damage.

Among the spatial tests are a right-left differentiation test and the Semmes body-placing test. Somatosensory tests include tests of sensitivity of the hands, face, and feet to light touch and passive movement. Language functions are assessed by standard tests of naming, reading, spelling, and language comprehension, the only unusual test being that of phonetic discrimination, described in the frontal-lobe chapter. Tests of hippocampal, frontal-lobe, and motor function have all been discussed previously, in Chapters 12, 13, and 14.

The principal advantage of the Montreal battery is that the hundreds of research cases upon which it is based have surgically induced lesions that are carefully photographed and sketched by the surgeons so that test performance can be accurately correlated with lesion location and extent. Since the patients are tested both preoperatively and postoperatively, as well as in follow-up, those tests that are not reliable indicators of localized brain injury have been eliminated. There are, however, several criticisms of the battery. First, being based on patients with focal lesions, the battery has not been adequately researched on patients with diffuse brain dysfunction. Thus, like other batteries, it is uncertain that it can reliably differentiate schizophrenia from diffuse

brain dysfunction of other etiologies. A related, but invalid, criticism is that because many of the research patients had epilepsy and/or early brain injuries the tests are not valid for patients with disorders such as tumors and strokes. This, however, is not the case, the tests having proven to be even more sensitive to the latter disorders. A third criticism is that the battery is not published as a battery and is therefore not as widely known or accessible to clinical neuropsychologists as one might hope.

Luria's Neuropsychological Investigation

Luria's test battery is not widely known in the Western world, having been first published in English as a battery by Christensen in 1975. Based on about 30 years of research by Luria and his colleagues in Russia it is probably the most thorough battery available, as the summary of the tests in Table 21-2 shows. Because the nonpsychometric nature of Luria's battery makes it difficult to describe all of the tests briefly, we have presented an example of one test and its interpretation in Tables 21-3 and 21-4.

The principal advantages of Luria's battery are: (1) It is based on theoretical principles of neuropsychological functioning, making the interpretation a logical conclusion of the theory. (2) It is thorough, inexpensive, easy to administer, flexible, and brief, taking only about one hour to administer. (3) It measures the actual behavior of the subject rather than inferred cognitive processes, thus making interpretation more straightforward. There are, however, also disadvantages of the Luria procedure: (1) The scoring is subjective and is based on clinical experience. It is unlikely that a novice to neuropsychology or neurology could easily master the interpretation without extensive training. On the other hand, experienced neuropsychologists or neurologists ought to find the battery easy to learn. (2) Because the manual that accompanies the battery

TABLE 21-2

Summary of Luria's Neuropsychological Investigation

1. Determination of cerebral dominance

2. Investigation of motor functions
   a. Motor functions of the hands
   b. Oral praxis
   c. Speech regulation of the motor act

3. Investigation of acousticomotor organization
   a. Perception and reproduction of pitch relationships
   b. Perception and reproduction of rhythmic structures

4. Investigation of the higher cutaneous and kinesthetic functions
   a. Cutaneous sensation
   b. Muscle and joint sensation
   c. Stereognosis

5. Investigation of the higher visual functions
   a. Visual perception of objects and pictures
   b. Spatial orientation
   c. Intellectual operations in space

6. Investigation of impressive speech
   a. Phonemic hearing
   b. Word comprehension
   c. Understanding of simple sentences
   d. Understanding of logical grammatical structures

7. Investigation of expressive speech
   a. Articulation of speech sounds
   b. Reflected (repetitive) speech
   c. The nominative function of speech
   d. Narrative speech

8. Investigation of writing and reading
   a. Phonetic analysis and synthesis of words
   b. Writing
   c. Reading

9. Investigation of arithmetical skill
   a. Comprehension of number structure
   b. Arithmetical operations

10. Investigation of memory processes
    a. The learning process
    b. Retention and retrieval
    c. Logical memorizing

11. Investigation of intellectual processes
    a. Understanding of thematic pictures and texts
    b. Concept formation
    c. Discursive intellectual activity

Adapted from Christensen (1975).

offers no validation studies, it must be taken on faith that the tests really measure what Luria claims they do. This criticism is the most serious, because most Western neuropsychologists are likely to continue to use psychometric assessment tools reporting validation studies. Recently, Golden and his colleagues have begun validation and standardization studies of the Luria battery, but insufficient data have been published to date to make this battery very useful.

EXAMPLES OF ASSESSMENT

The use of neuropsychological tests in the assessment of brain damage or dysfunction is most clearly illustrated by case histories. In this section we describe the test results that we obtained from four different patients tested on an abbreviated form of the Montreal battery. Table 21-5 shows the scores of the four patients, tabulated and compared to a normal control. Abnormally poor scores are indicated by an asterisk.

Case 1

A 28-year-old right-handed woman had undergone emergency surgery following the bursting of a large aneurysm in the right temporal lobe. Surgical reports indicated that portions of the right temporal and parietal cortex were damaged, and she had a left quadrantic hemianopsia, indicating that the lesion extended posteriorly into the visual cortex. Testing was performed two years after the surgery, at which time the woman was in good health and was attending a university. She was referred to us for assessment because she was having social problems as well as difficulty with mathematics. Her test results suggested that speech was in the left hemisphere and that

TABLE 21-3

Example of Luria's assessment tests.
Test 1, Investigation of higher visual functions

Procedure	Materials

1. Investigation of objects and pictures
   a. The patient is asked to examine carefully objects or clearly drawn pictures of objects (with no time limit) and to name them.
 	
      If speech is disturbed, nonverbal communication can be used.
 	
   b. The patient is asked to examine and name complicated or indistinct pictures of objects.
 	
   c. The patient is asked to examine and name pictures of objects that are scribbled over or superimposed one on another (Poppelreuter's test).
 	
   d. The patient is asked to identify a figure in a complex design (Gottschaldt).
 	
   e. The patient is asked to complete a structure from which a portion is missing by choosing from a series of offered insets the one that matches the particular structure (example from Raven's test). No time limit is imposed.
	Objects and pictures

The presentation of these tests may be varied. The figure may be presented for only a short period of time, or the pictures may be presented in the wrong position.

In simplified forms the patient is asked to trace the outline of the figure with his finger, or he may be given leading questions, or the examiner may point to any one of the essential signs.

From Christensen (1975), p. 69.

her intelligence was high average, as was her verbal memory. The only deficits that she presented were on tests of visuoperceptual function and nonverbal memory, both of which were severely impaired. These results are consistent with her known right-hemisphere lesion.

Case 2

A 22-year-old woman was referred to us by a clinical psychologist to assess the possibility of "organic" dysfunction. She had on several occasions engaged in bizarre behaviors such as undressing in public and urinating on other people, and on one occasion had attacked her roommate. Following these episodes she was confused and amnesic for her behavior during the "attack" as well as for the period just prior to the outburst. Her neuropsychological test results indicated that her left temporal lobe was abnormal, because her verbal memory as well as reading and object naming were impaired (see Table 21-5). Our diagnosis of temporal-lobe epilepsy with a left-sided focus was partially confirmed by a neurologist when EEG studies showed left-hemisphere abnormality. As frequently occurs in epilepsy a CT-scan failed to reveal any unusual features, and there is nothing in the woman's history to account for the epilepsy. The seizures are com-

TABLE 21-4

Interpretative guideline for Luria's test of objects and pictures

Behavior	Lesion
1. Perception of objects and pictures	
Objects and pictures The patient perceives only one sign—the most conspicuous or prominent—but fails to correlate it with the other signs or to integrate the necessary group of signs; he draws premature conclusions regarding the meaning of the pictures, guessing at it from a single fragment that he has perceived. E.g., he may identify the pair of spectacles ... as "a bicycle" because he cannot synthesize two circles and a series of lines into the required image. In less marked cases these difficulties are only brought to light during the examination of the most complex visual structures. The patient hardly ever expresses confident opinions regarding the meaning of pictures; he is constantly in doubt or he complains of his poor eyesight.	Lesions in the occipito-parietal divisions of the cortex. *Optic agnosia*
The patient can perceive a picture and evaluate it properly, but he can only perceive one picture or one element at a time.	*Simultaneous agnosia*
The patient loses sight of the whole picture if he examines its details. His examination of the objects is accompanied by ataxia of gaze.	
The patient looks at the picture passively; he does not change the direction of his gaze and he does not seem to attempt to "seek out" the identifying signs; usually he reaches a confident conclusion about what the picture represents; he shows no doubt and there is no attempt at correction.	Lesion of the frontal lobes
The patient evaluates the picture in the position it is shown to him; he does not turn it over and he makes no attempt to invert it mentally. Complex visual stimuli give him the impression of chaos. ... He may also persevere in the same perception, i.e., the different pictures begin to be interpreted in the same way.	
The patient neglects the left side.	Lesion of the right hemisphere

From Christensen (1975), pp. 72–73.

pletely controlled with dilantin, but her neuropsychological deficits remain.

Case 3

A 48-year-old left-handed man began to have generalized seizures and was found to have a large malignant tumor of the left dorsolateral frontal lobe. Neuropsychological testing revealed serious impairment on tests sensitive to both left frontal- and left temporal-lobe damage. Thus, his performance on tests of memory, language, praxic function, and frontal-lobe function was significantly disturbed.

TABLE 21-5

Examples of patient assessments on a modified version of the Montreal Neurological Institute battery

Test	Normal control	Case 1: right temporal	Case 2: left temporal	Case 3: left frontal	Case 4: schizophrenia
1. Speech lateralization					
dichotic words: left ear	25	18	2*	25	29
right ear	46	50	15	38	37
handedness	R	R	R	R	R
2. General intelligence					
full-scale IQ	107	113	104	114	98
verbal IQ	109	117	95*	106*	100
performance IQ	105	107*	111	117	95
3. Visuoperceptual					
Mooney faces (abbreviated)	18/19	12/19*	16/19	18/19	15/19
Rey complex figures—copy	32/36	24/36*	31/36	29/36	35/36
4. Memory					
Wechsler memory quotient	107	115	87*	92*	90*
Rey complex figures—recall	22/36	11/36*	18/36	24/36	1/36*
delayed recall of stories and paired associates	13	17	7*	9	8*
delayed recall of drawings	12	6*	10	12	9
5. Spatial					
right-left differentiation	52/60	48/60	43/60	48/60	44/60
Semmes body placing	32/35	30/35	30/35	18/35*	16/35*
6. Language					
reading	12	12	7*	8*	6*
object naming	23/26	20/26	14/26*	19/26	20/26
7. Frontal lobe					
Wisconsin card-sorting test	6.0 cat	5.8 cat	4.0 cat	2.0 cat*	2.5 cat*
Chicago word fluency	62	50	38	25*	30*
8. Motor function					
complex arm	92%	94%	89%	83%*	70%*
face	88%	90%	89%	72%*	68%*

* Abnormally poor score.

Dichotic listening suggested that his speech was in the left hemisphere, as would be expected from his impaired verbal functions.

Case 4

This case, of a 31-year-old man, is included to demonstrate the difficulty in differentiating patients with psychotic disturbances from patients with widespread brain damage. This man was diagnosed independently by two psychiatrists as being schizophrenic, but when tested by us he had been on a small dose of chlorpromazine for two days and appeared rather lucid, having no delusions or hallucinations during the testing. His test results, however, showed serious neuropsychological abnormalities, especially in tests of left-hemisphere function. In particular, this man showed symptoms similar to those seen in case 3. We have found this pattern of abnormality in other diagnosed schizophrenics, confirming the suggestion that some schizophrenics suffer from severe neuropsychological deficits.

Summary

The most important lesson from these case histories is that neuropsychological assessment batteries can differentiate patients with different localized cortical lesions, irrespective of the cause of the lesions. We emphasize, however, that the picture is less clear for patients with more diffuse brain injury, especially when it results from head trauma or drug abuse, or for patients with dementias or cerebral infections such as encephalitis. Finally, identifying the existence or location of brain damage with any certainty clearly requires an extensive battery of tests.

REFERENCES

Christensen, A.-L. *Luria's Neuropsychological Investigation.* New York: Spectrum Publications, 1975.

Golden, C. J., T. A. Hammeke, and A. D. Purisch. Diagnostic validity of a standardized neuropsychological battery derived from Luria's neuropsychological tests. *Journal of Consulting and Clinical Psychology,* 46 (1978), 1258–1265.

Kimura, D., and J. McGlone. *Neuropsychology Test Procedures.* Manual used at the University Hospital, London, Ontario, Canada, 1979.

Lezak, M. D. *Neuropsychological Assessment.* New York: Oxford University Press, 1976.

McFie, J. *Assessment of Organic Intellectual Impairment.* New York: John Wiley and Sons, 1975.

Milner, B. Psychological aspects of focal epilepsy and its neurosurgical management. *Advances in Neurology,* 8 (1975), 299–321.

Reitan, R. M. Psychological deficits resulting from cerebral lesions in man. In J. M. Warren and K. Akert, eds. *The Frontal Granular Cortex and Behavior.* New York: McGraw-Hill Book Co., 1964.

Reitan, R. M., and L. A. Davison. *Clinical Neuropsychology: Current Status and Application.* New York: John Wiley and Sons, 1974.

Smith, A. Neuropsychological testing in neurological disorders. *Advances in Neurology,* 7 (1975), 49–109.

Taylor, L. B. Localization of cerebral lesions by psychological testing. *Clinical Neurology,* 16 (1969), 269–287.

Taylor, L. B. Psychological assessment of neurosurgical patients. In T. Rasmussen and R. Marino, eds. *Functional Neurosurgery.* New York: Raven Press, 1979.

Watson, C. G., R. W. Thomas, D. Anderson, and J. Felling. Differentiation of organics from schizophrenics by use of the Reitan-Halstead organic test battery. *Journal of Consulting and Clinical Psychology,* 32 (1968), 679–684.

22

APPLICATIONS OF
NEUROPSYCHOLOGY

Having surveyed the basic principles of neuropsychological theory and assessment, we must now try to answer the difficult but essential question: How can this technology be applied to the world we live in? To date, neuropsychology has been applied to at least three major areas (neurology, psychiatry, and education), and is increasingly being used, and fruitfully so, as an assessment tool by psychologists dealing with a wide variety of clinical problems ranging from retardation to delinquency, as well as in their general counseling.

APPLICATION TO SPECIFIC TARGET POPULATIONS

Neurological Patients

The application of neuropsychology to diagnosis and assessment of neurological problems has been discussed throughout the book and need not be considered in detail again here. Neuropsychology has an important additional application with neurological patients, however, long after the patient has stopped visiting the neurologist. Witness the following case history.

Mr. J. was a 37-year-old man who had been in a traffic accident some 15 years earlier. He was in a coma for six weeks and suffered secondary injury from brain infection. At the time of his accident Mr. J. was a student in a graduate program in journalism, having previously obtained a BA with honors in English literature. When we first met Mr. J. he had severe motor problems, needing canes to walk, and was both apraxic and ataxic. He had great difficulty pronouncing words, especially when hurried or stressed, but careful language testing revealed no aphasic symptoms; his language problems were actually anarthric. Since the time of his accident Mr. J. had lived at home with his parents and had not learned the social skills necessary to cope with his handicap. In short, Mr. J. was being treated as though he was retarded and was being completely looked after by his family. Indeed, Mr.

J. himself believed he was retarded and he was very reluctant to attempt rehabilitation programs. At the suggestion of his family we gave Mr. J. a thorough assessment (using the Montreal Neurological Institute battery) to evaluate his potential. His results were surprising, even to us. His IQ was superior (WAIS verbal IQ of 127) and most of his other tests, except those involving motor skills, were average or above average. Mr. J., despite his obvious motor deficits and obvious word-pronunciation difficulties, clearly was not retarded. Armed with our test results we were able to show Mr. J., and his family, that he was capable of much more than he was doing. We convinced him that he could look after himself and should seek occupational therapy through a government agency for the handicapped.

Mr. J. is not an isolated case. Literally thousands of people who have suffered neurological disorders have never been evaluated by a neuropsychologist and are totally unaware of their potential, or, in many cases, of their deficits. We do not suggest that these people should all now be evaluated simply because the assessment tools are available. But we do stress that there is a need for the application of neuropsychological technology in helping a significant number of these people adjust to their handicaps.

Psychiatry

In our discussion of affective behavior we noted that psychotic behavior is associated with a variety of neurological, neurochemical, and neuropsychological abnormalities. Although it is unlikely that neuropsychological assessment will be useful in the near future for differentially diagnosing various types of psychotic disorders, the following case history illustrates a major application of neuropsychological technology.

Ms. T., a 23-year-old woman, was admitted to the psychiatric ward of a general hospital.

She was exhibiting schizophrenic symptoms, including delusions, hallucinations, and inappropriate affect. Assessment by the Montreal Neurological Institute battery showed an average IQ along with significant impairments on all tests of frontal- and temporal-lobe functioning, similar to those observed in case 4 in Chapter 21. The patient was placed on phenothiazine therapy by her psychiatrist and a month later was discharged as an outpatient. When she was reassessed by us two months later her schizophrenic symptoms had disappeared and she was unsuccessfully attempting to return to her job as a secretary. Her neuropsychological test results showed a marked improvement, but her verbal-memory and verbal-fluency scores were still significantly impaired. We recommended extending her leave of absence from her job for a couple of months. In view of her memory deficit it appeared unlikely to us that she would be able to cope with the job requirements. Follow-up assessment three months later found all of her test results to be within the normal range and she returned to her job. She has been able to cope successfully and her medication is gradually being reduced.

The case of Ms. T. demonstrates the usefulness of neuropsychological assessment in the monitoring of treatment outcomes in psychotic patients. Patients often show remission of obvious psychotic symptoms while their cognitive abilities remain far from normal, and a hasty return to society—and the job setting in particular—can frequently have disastrous consequences for effective rehabilitation.

Educational System

The educational system is perhaps the most challenging field for the application of neuropsychological technology, not only because of the sheer numbers of students entering the system but also because of the practical difficulty of teaching the same core curriculum to students with such varied innate cognitive abilities and environmental experience. This latter problem is most clearly seen in dealing with the 10 to 15 percent of children with so-called learning disabilities. The following case is representative.

Ross, an 11-year-old sixth-grade boy, was referred to us by the school psychologist. When we saw him he was reading at below third-grade level but was keeping up in other school subjects. On formal testing Ross presented a picture that is characteristic of many children with reading problems. His intelligence was strictly average, with a Wechsler IQ of 99. There was no significant difference between verbal and performance scales. Ross performed normally on frontal-lobe tests such as the Wisconsin card-sorting test and the Semmes body-placing test, and his verbal and nonverbal memory scores were low average. His real problems were readily apparent, however, on tests of parietal-lobe function. Ross had a severe left-right confusion and a very low digit span, and copied drawings of geometric figures very poorly. In view of his performance on these tests it was hardly surprising that Ross could not read, since dyslexia is commonly associated with left-right confusion and poor digit span in adult parietal-lobe patients. Ross had no evidence of parietal-lobe damage, however. Why did he show these symptoms, and what could we as neuropsychologists do to help him? To answer these questions we must take a broader look at the neuropsychology of learning disabilities.

The idea that neurological abnormalities are a primary causal factor in learning disorders has received growing attention over recent years, but few areas in neuroscience have occasioned such discord. In a light vein, Fry published a "Do-It-Yourself Terminology Generator," shown in Table 22-1, to emphasize the proliferation of terms in the field and the inaccuracies in description. From this

list about 2000 terms can be fabricated that have been or could be used to describe the syndromes observed. This explosion of terms has led to misunderstanding and confusion. We use the term learning disability to encompass all of Fry's terms. There is little doubt that there are many different forms of learning disability, but so little is known about the causes that we will make no attempt to distinguish them here. A commonly used criterion for establishing learning disability is that the child is at least two years behind in a particular subject, such as reading or arithmetic, but not in others. Thus, the child is performing unevenly, achieving normal or near normal performance in some subjects but retarded performance in others. This definition has been criticized by many because it fails to consider either the child's age, the tests used, or the fact that the children usually also have other symptoms, as in the case of Ross's left-right confusion and low digit span.

Disagreement over the definition of learning disabilities makes it difficult to estimate the incidence. Gaddes tried to determine the proportion of children with learning disabilities as reported in various prevalence studies from both North America and Europe. He reported that most estimates of the need for special training for learning disabilities range between 10 and 15 percent of the school-age population, although only about 2 percent actually receive special education.

It has proven extraordinarily difficult to clearly define the symptoms of learning disabilities, largely because of the wide range of symptoms observed. The U.S. Department of Health, Education, and Welfare identifies 10 characteristics as most often cited by various authors: (1) hyperactivity; (2) perceptual-motor impairments; (3) emotional lability; (4) general coordination deficits; (5) disorders of attention (short attention span, distractibility, perseveration); (6) impulsivity; (7) disorders of memory and thinking; (8) specific learning

TABLE 22-1

"Do-It-Yourself Terminology Generator"[a]

Qualifier	Area of involvement	Problem
Secondary	Nervous	Deficit
Minimal	Brain	Dysfunction
Mild	Cerebral	Damage
Minor	Neurological	Disorder
Chronic	Neurologic	Desynchronization
Diffuse	CNS	Handicap
Specific	Language	Disability
Primary	Reading	Retardation
Developmental	Perceptual	Deficiency
Disorganized	Impulsive	Impairment
Organic	Visual-motor	Pathology
Clumsy	Behavior	Syndrome
Functional	Psychoneurologic	Complex

[a] Directions: Select any word from first column, add any word from second and third columns. If you don't like the result, try again. It will mean about the same thing. (From Fry, 1968. Reprinted with permission of Edward Fry and the International Reading Association.)

disabilities including especially reading (dyslexia), arithmetic, writing, and spelling; (9) disorders of speech and hearing; (10) equivocal neurological signs and irregular EEG.

A serious difficulty with identifying learning disability with any certainty is that not all disabled children exhibit all of the symptoms. Critchley points out that for every learning-disabled child with coordination problems, there is a child with better than normal coordination. This variability underscores the points that not all learning disabilities are the same and that there are presumably multiple causes.

Five major neurological factors are most frequently cited as possible causes of learning disabilities: (1) structural damage; (2) physiological dysfunction; (3) abnormal cerebral lateralization; (4) maturational lag; and (5) environmental deprivation. Although no data unequivocally and totally support any one of these theories, there is reason to believe that all of these factors may contribute to disabilities.

Structural Damage. Since the symptoms of brain damage in adulthood resemble childhood learning disabilities (e.g., dyslexia), the cause of learning disabilities may be structural damage, perhaps resulting from birth trauma, encephalitis, anoxia, etc. Although no doubt a cause for a small minority of children, structural damage is not likely to be the cause in most children, since many neurological symptoms associated with brain damage in adults are not typically observed in children. For example, children with developmental dyslexia do not have hemianopsias or scotomas, which are symptoms that would certainly occur in a large percentage of dyslexic adults. Further, to date, EEG studies have not demonstrated structural damage: abnormal EEGs similar to those correlated with known brain damage are not consistently correlated with learning disabilities.

Brain Dysfunction. It is not necessary to have direct brain damage to have neurological deficits. As we noted earlier, for example, there is little doubt that schizophrenia results from abnormal brain function; but brain lesions do not produce schizophrenia. Rather, some abnormal physiological or biochemical process is most likely responsible. A similar logic has been applied to the study of learning disabilities: such disabilities may result, not from direct damage, but from malfunction of some portion of the cerebral cortex. Tentative support for this view comes from electrophysiological recording studies associating specific high-frequency EEG abnormalities with various types of learning disabilities. These studies are controversial, however. In a recent review Hughes concludes that EEG and AEP studies of children with learning disabilities are encouraging enough to justify further investigation of these techniques as diagnostic tools, but to date no firm conclusions have been reached.

One view of the brain dysfunction hypothesis holds that the dysfunction results from defective "arousal mechanisms." Since the neocortex is normally activated by subcortical structures, it is argued that if the subcortical input were missing or abnormal, then a particular cortical region would dysfunction. This conclusion has been inferred from two principal sources. First, Douglas and her colleagues have found that learning-disabled children have difficulty on continuous-performance tests requiring them to react to particular stimuli while ignoring others. Similarly, reaction-time studies show the children to have slower mean reaction times to signals. On tests of visual searching—in which the child is asked to search among several alternatives to find a picture identical to a standard picture—the learning-disabled children choose impulsively and quickly, making many more errors than normal children, who per-

form more slowly. Douglas concludes that the deficits on these types of tasks result from some form of inadequate cerebral activation. It could be predicted that learning disabilities—or some types, at least—should improve with drugs that increase cerebral activation. This is indeed the case: both amphetamine and caffeine, cerebral stimulants, improve performance on the Douglas et al. tests, and are frequently used effectively in the treatment of hyperactive children.

An alternative dysfunction theory proposes that brain malfunction results from abnormal metabolism, due either to diet or to abnormal metabolic processes. Recent work has shown that if diet is modified—especially if foods containing sugar are reduced—learning disabilities are significantly mitigated. This finding supports the idea that inadequate diet may contribute to learning disabilities by causing abnormal brain function. One difficulty in treating learning disabilities with proper nutrition is that people's needs for various minerals, vitamins, etc., vary widely. It may be that some children require certain nutrients in amounts far exceeding the usual. For example, vitamin D resistant rickets is a disorder requiring amounts of vitamin D that would be lethal to most people. Although it is conceivable that extremely large amounts of some vitamin or mineral are required in children with learning disorders, the missing factor would be extremely difficult to identify. A recent study is intriguing in this respect. Analyzing specimens of hair from normal and learning-disabled children, Pihl and Parkes found significant differences between the groups in the levels of sodium, cadmium, cobalt, lead, manganese, chromium, and lithium. When levels of these elements were measured in the hair it was possible to accurately pick 98 percent of all of the children diagnosed as learning-disabled from a second sample of children. Although Pihl and Parkes could not identify the cause of abnormal levels of trace elements, their success in diagnosing additional children leads us to seriously consider biochemical factors as causal factors in learning disabilities.

Abnormal Cerebral Lateralization. Around 1900 there were several reports of children with normal intelligence who appeared unable to learn to read, exhibiting so-called developmental dyslexia. In 1925, Orton began to study such children, and proposed that some anomaly in cerebral dominance was responsible for the difficulties; he termed such dyslexia *strephosymbolia.* Orton's concept (and term) was largely ignored until its revival in the 1960s, with the growing interest in human neuropsychology. Today a variety of theories rest on the premise that learning disabilities result from reduced or abnormal cerebral lateralization. This premise is based on the assumption that, since language is lateralized in the left hemisphere of most adults, such lateralization must be advantageous, and its absence would be deleterious to the acquisition of language skills. Normal lateralization could be absent for a number of reasons. For example, we noted earlier that some inhibitory process may normally act to prevent left-hemisphere functions from developing in the right hemisphere, and vice versa. If this inhibitory process were inactive, the brain would be less asymmetrical. Inhibition could be absent because of a number of factors, retarded myelinization of the corpus callosum being one.

Orton's explanation of learning disabilities would seem to be easy to evaluate experimentally. For example, if children were divided into two groups (normal and learning-disabled) and then tested for dichotic and visual-field asymmetries, the disabled group should not show asymmetries. In the last 15 years dozens of studies have examined dichotic and visual-field asymmetries in this way, but the data are far from unequivocal. In a recent review Satz concludes:

> One might ask what light the preceding review of laterality studies sheds, if any, on the problem of cerebral dominance and reading disability. The answer should be—not much. The reason for this somewhat discouraging view lies in the numerous methodological and conceptual problems that continue to plague research efforts in this area. (Satz, 1976, p. 288)

Proposing a somewhat different theory of abnormal cerebral lateralization, Witelson argues that there may be an association between developmental dyslexia and two neurological abnormalities: a lack of right-hemisphere specialization for spatial processing, and a dysfunction in left-hemisphere processing of linguistic functions. That is, being located in both hemispheres, spatial functions result in an interference with the left hemisphere's processing of linguistic functions. The person approaches linguistic functions in a visual-holistic manner rather than a phonetic-analytic manner, which would be expected to produce deficits in language but superiority in spatial skills. Witelson's position is intriguing and warrants further study.

Because of current popular interest in hemispheric asymmetry, the belief that impaired cerebral lateralization is the source of problems in learning-disabled children has become attractive. Kinsbourne and Hiscock have been outspoken critics of this theory. Their principal criticism centers on the assumption that reduced lateralization of language should be detrimental to language development and school performance. As discussed in Chapter 9, anomalous language lateralization in left-handers is not consistently correlated with cognitive deficit; nor is left handedness consistently correlated with learning disability. We concur with Kinsbourne and Hiscock's criticisms and endorse the view of Spreen and others that unless we have proof about the state of the brain, it is wise to pursue only description. Performing neurological diagnosis in the absence of data can only be harmful in the long run.

Maturational Lag. Maturational lag postulates that cognitive functions involved in language, reading, and other complex behaviors are organized hierarchically, and the levels in the hierarchy develop sequentially during ontogeny. Should one level of the hierarchy be slow to develop, the entire hierarchy is retarded in development, since higher functions depend on the integrity of lower ones. The delayed maturation of cortical functions could result from a variety of factors; two examples are delayed myelinization of a particular region, and slow development of the connections of association regions, which delays the hook-up of sensory and motor regions with associative cortex. Although some studies suggest that various functions in learning-disabled children are slow in maturing, the type of study needed here is a careful longitudinal analysis of children tested on a large number of perceptual, motor, and cognitive skills for a period of 10 to 15 years. This remains to be done.

Environmental Deprivation. The work of Krech, Rosensweig, Bennett, Diamond, and their colleagues has shown that environmental factors can alter the neocortical development of rats. Rats raised in enriched environments have a thicker cortex with increased numbers of dendritic spines than rats raised in impoverished environments. This work implies, then, that the environment in which children are raised may affect behavior indirectly by altering brain development. This notion has considerable appeal, and has led to the development of programs such as Operation Headstart. To date there is no unequivocal experimental evidence that environmental factors, short of impoverishment like that suffered by Genie (Chapter 18), can produce

learning diabilities, but the possibility continues to receive serious investigation.

Having briefly surveyed the proposed causes of learning disabilities we are left with the problem of what neuropsychology can offer the educational system. First, as we have seen in the example of Ross, neuropsychology offers a means, not offered by classical academic achievement tests, of accurately identifying the cognitive deficits of children with learning disabilities. Usually, children are not dyslexic or dyscalculic alone, but have a number of associated symptoms of brain dysfunction. Teachers and parents are usually unaware of the associated deficits, and once the deficits are explained, it is often easier for both teachers and parents to understand the nature of the child's handicap. It is worth noting that if the *only* symptom were dyslexia or dyscalculia one might entertain the possibility of emotional or other environmental factors as primary causes of the learning problems. Second, once specific problem areas of individual children have been identified, specialized teaching programs can be devised to circumvent the neuropsychological handicaps. For example, children of junior high school age who are reading at an early elementary level can be taught alternate language systems such as Bliss Symbols or Braille, systems that use other brain areas that are functioning normally. Third, neuropsychology can offer a way of thinking about learning problems. Children do not all have equal cognitive abilities. Many children will simply never be able to read beyond the first- or second-grade level despite a normal IQ (see case history below), because the neurological requisites are either not present or not functioning properly. We know, for example, that patients with left face-area lesions will never be able to spell adequately, so there is little use in recommending practice. Similarly, many children will never learn to spell, to read, etc.; there is little point in forcing the children to fail repeatedly, especially once they have reached junior high school and are still performing at an early elementary level. Rather, the children can be taught alternative skills to deal with their handicap. This view does not accord well with many educators, who believe that one should never give up trying to teach children to read, write, etc. The message from neuropsychology is clear, however: if the requisite neurological structures are not present the skill cannot be mastered, no matter how hard both pupil and teacher try. To be beneficial, however, the tests of neuropsychological functioning must be valid and must be interpreted cautiously and intelligently to avoid serious errors. We stress again that it is thus extremely important that people using the technology of neuropsychology thoroughly understand the basics of neuropsychology.

GENERAL APPLICATIONS

The technology of neuropsychology can be applied to virtually any problem in which psychologists use traditional assessment techniques. This range includes general counseling, vocational guidance, assessment of juvenile delinquents for the courts, assessment related to legal matters such as suits arising from injuries in traffic accidents, and placement of retarded people in occupational training programs. Neuropsychology does not offer a panacea for any of these problems, but can add an important tool to the arsenal used in general psychological assessment. The following case is a representative example.

Ms. P., a 19-year-old woman, was referred to us by a friend of hers. She was working as a nurse's aide and had found her work so enjoyable that she was considering entering a nursing program. However, she had not completed high school and generally had a poor academic record. She came to us for guidance as to whether or not she could handle the nurs-

ing program. In discussing her academic record we learned that Ms. P. had particular difficulty with language skills, and her reading was so poor that she was unable to pass the written exam for a driver's license. In view of Ms. P's real interest in further education in nursing we decided to administer a complete neuropsychological battery to see if the requisite cognitive abilities were present. The results showed an overall IQ on the WAIS of 85, but there was a 32-point spread between her verbal IQ of 74 and her performance IQ of 106—a difference so large as to suggest that her left hemisphere was functioning very poorly at best. Her performance on specific tests of left-hemisphere function confirmed this hypothesis, because her verbal memory, verbal fluency, spelling, reading, and arithmetic skills were extremely poor. On the other hand, her spatial skills were good, as were her nonverbal memory and her performance on tests such as the Wisconsin card-sorting and Semmes body-placing tests. In short, her language skills were those of a 6-year-old although she had attended school for 11 years. This verbal ability contrasted with her other abilities, which were normal for a person of her age.

In view of the test results we explained to Ms. P. our belief that it was unlikely that she could handle a nursing program because of her deficient language skills. We believed also that she was unlikely to develop these skills, especially since—as we inadvertently discovered—none of her five brothers and sisters could read either! We explained to Ms. P. that she was by no means retarded, but that just as some people had no musical ability whatsoever, she had no verbal ability. (Further, we were able to arrange an aural administration of the driver's test, which she passed.) Finally, we explained Ms. P.'s problem to her husband, a well-educated man with a master's degree. In the short time they had been married he had become totally frustrated with her inability to balance the bank account, read recipes, etc., and was beginning to believe his wife was either "crazy or retarded." Whatever the marital outcome will be we do not know, but at least Mr. P. now has an understanding of his wife's problem, and they are able to work out domestic routines to circumvent her handicap.

The case of Ms. P. illustrates how neuropsychological technology can be used as a tool in counseling. It certainly cannot cure Ms. P.'s problem, nor is it a substitute for other clinical tools and skills, but it provides additional useful information in general counseling situations.

A Word of Caution

We have emphasized the usefulness of neuropsychological information for a variety of applied settings, but we would be remiss if we failed to caution against overuse or abuse of this information. As useful as neuropsychological data can be for general counseling, we are not proposing that neuropsychological technology be applied to every person who sees a neurologist, psychologist, psychiatrist, counselor, etc. First, it would be a waste of resources, since the vast majority of clinical problems presented to mental health and counseling services are related to problems in coping with everyday life and are largely unrelated to neurological functioning, at least at our current state of knowledge.

Second, there is a real risk of labeling people as brain-damaged or organic because of failure to perform normally on particular tests. As we saw in our discussion of learning disabilities, there are numerous reasons for poor performance on psychological tests, only one of which is actual brain damage. In the absence of physical symptoms or a sudden change in behavior it would be an error to assume the cause of poor performance to be brain damage. Furthermore, there is a tendency to assume that identifying a person as brain-damaged solves the clinical problem, and to stop there. This is of course a false assumption, since the goal of the clinician is treatment as well as assessment. Labeling a person as brain-damaged does little in the way of treatment, and may actually deter treatment if the label is interpreted as meaning that nothing can be done. Indeed, we have found that the decision to administer and to use neuropsychological information requires a healthy dose of common sense in addition to technical savvy.

Conclusion

The usefulness of any scientific endeavor is eventually measured by its technological applicability to the betterment of mankind. We believe that in the decades to come neuropsychology will indeed be applied to a plethora of human problems. It is up to those in the field to apply it wisely.

REFERENCES

Critchley, M. *Developmental Dyslexia*. Springfield, Ill.: Charles C Thomas, 1964.

Douglas, V. I. Perceptual and cognitive factors as determinants of learning disabilities: a review chapter with special emphasis on attentional factors. In R. M. Knights and D. J. Bakker, eds. *The Neuropsychology of Learning Disorders*. Baltimore: University Park Press, 1976.

Fry, E. A do-it-yourself terminology generator. *Journal of Reading, 11* (1968), 428–430.

Gaddes, W. H. Prevalence estimates and the need for definition of learning disabilities. In R. M. Knights and D. J. Bakker, eds. *The Neuropsychology of Learning Disorders.* Baltimore: University Park Press, 1976.

Hughes, J. R. Electroencephalographic and neurophysiological studies in dyslexia. In A. L. Benton and D. Pearl, eds. *Dyslexia: An Appraisal of Current Knowledge.* New York: Oxford University Press, 1978.

Kinsbourne, M., and M. Hiscock. Does cerebral dominance develop? In S. J. Segalowitz and F. A. Gruber, eds. *Language Development and Neurological Theory.* New York: Academic Press, 1977.

Orton, S. T. Word-blindness in school children. *Archives of Neurology and Psychiatry, 14* (1925), 581–615.

Pihl, R. O., and M. Parkes. Hair element content in learning disabled children. *Science, 198* (1977), 204–206.

Rosensweig, M. R., D. Krech, E. L. Bennett, and M. C. Diamond. Effects of environmental complexity and training on brain chemistry and anatomy: a replication and extension. *Journal of Comparative and Physiological Psychology, 55* (1962), 427–429.

Satz, P. Cerebral dominance and reading disability: an old problem revisited. In R. M. Knights and D. J. Bakker, eds. *The Neuropsychology of Learning Disorders.* Baltimore: University Park Press, 1976.

Spreen, O. Neuropsychology of learning disorders: post-conference review. In R. M. Knights and D. J. Bakker, eds. *The Neuropsychology of Learning Disorders.* Baltimore: University Park Press, 1976.

United States Department of Health, Education and Welfare. Minimal brain dysfunction in children. *National Institute of Neurological Diseases Monograph, 3* (1966), 1–18.

Witelson, S. F. Early hemisphere specialization and interhemispheric plasticity. an empirical and theoretical review. In S. J. Segalowitz and F. A. Gruber, eds. *Language Development and Neurological Theory.* New York: Academic Press, 1977.

GLOSSARY

Ablation. Intentional destruction or removal of portions of the brain or spinal cord; brain lesion.

Absence attack. Temporary loss of consciousness in some forms of epilepsy.

Acalculia. Inability to perform arithmetical operations.

Accessory cells. Cells that, originating from germinal cells (spongioblasts), contribute to the support, nourishment, conduction, and repair of neurons; occasionally the origins of tumors. The accessory cells are the astrocytes; oligodendrocytes; and ependymal, microglial, and Schwann cells.

Achromatopsia. Inability to distinguish different hues despite normally pigmented cells in the retina. Sometimes called cortical color blindness.

Acopia. Inability to copy a geometric design.

Action potential. The brief electrical impulse by which information is conducted along an axon. It results from brief changes in the membrane's permeability to potassium and sodium ions.

Afferent. Conducting toward the central nervous system or toward its higher centers.

Afferent paresis. Loss of kinesthetic feedback resulting from lesions to postcentral gyrus (areas 1, 2, 3), producing clumsy movements.

Agnosia. Partial or complete inability—unexplainable by a defect in elementary sensation or by a reduced level of alertness—to recognize sensory stimuli.

Agraphia. Decline or loss of the ability to write.

Akathisia. A condition of motor restlessness, ranging from a feeling of inner disquiet to an inability to sit or lie quietly.

Akinesia. Absence or poverty of movement.

Akinetic seizures. Seizures producing temporary paralysis of muscles. Characterized by a sudden collapse without warning. Most common in children.

Alexia. Inability to read.

Allesthesia. The sensation of touch experienced at a point remote from the place touched.

Alpha rhythm. A regular (approximately 10 Hz) wave pattern in the EEG, found in most subjects when they are relaxed with eyes closed.

Amativeness. Inclination to love. Localized by the phrenologists in the nape of the neck.

Amblyopia. Dimness of vision without obvious impairment of the eye itself.

Ammon's horn. Part of the hippocampus.

Amnesia. Partial or total loss of memory.

Amusia. Inability to produce (motor) or to comprehend (sensory) musical sounds.

Amygdala. A set of nuclei in the base of the temporal lobe; part of the limbic system.

Anarthria. Incoordination of the musculature of the mouth, resulting in speechlessness.

Anastomosis. The connection between parallel blood vessels such that they can communicate their blood flows.

Aneurysm. Vascular dilations resulting from localized defects in vascular elasticity; a sac is formed by the dilation of the walls of an artery or of a vein and is filled with blood.

Angiography. Radiographic imaging of blood vessels filled with a contrast medium.

Angioma. Collections of abnormal blood vessels, including capillary, venous, and arteriovenous malformations, resulting in abnormal blood flow.

Angular gyrus. Gyrus in the parietal lobe corresponding roughly to Brodmann's area 39. Important in language functions.

Anomia. Difficulty in finding words, especially those naming objects.

Anopia. Loss of vision.

Anosmia. Absence of the sense of smell.

Anosodiaphoria. Indifference to illness.

Anosognosia. Loss of ability to recognize or to acknowledge bodily defect; usually associated with right parietal lesions.

Anterior commissure. Fiber tract that joins the temporal lobes.

Anterograde amnesia. Inability to remember events subsequent to some disturbance of the brain such as head injury, electroconvulsive shock, or certain degenerative diseases.

Aphagia. Inability to eat.

Aphasia. Defect or loss of power of expression by speech, writing, or signs or of comprehending spoken or written language due to injury or disease of the brain.

Apraxia. Inability to carry out purposeful movements in the absence of paralysis or paresis.

Arachnoid. A thin sheet of delicate collagenous connective tissue that follows the contours of the brain.

Archicortex. Portion of cerebral cortex that develops in association with olfactory cortex and is phylogenetically older than the neopallium and lacks its layered structure. Also called archipallium, allocortex, and olfactory cortex. Corresponds to the dendate gyrus and hippocampal gyrus in mature mammals.

Arcuate fasciculus. A long bundle of fibers joining Wernicke's and Broca's areas.

Argyll-Robertson pupil. Constriction of the pupil to accommodation, but not to light. Used to diagnose damage to the midbrain relays of the third nerve (oculomotor).

Asomatognosia. Loss of knowledge or sensory awareness of one's own body and bodily condition. May occur on one or both sides of the body. Most commonly results from damage to the right parietal lobe.

Association cortex. All cortex that is not specialized motor or sensory cortex. (The term survives from earlier belief that inputs from the different senses meet and become associated.)

Astereognosis. Inability, with no defect of elementary tactile sensation, to recognize familiar objects by touch.

Astrocytes. A type of glial cell. *See also* accessory cells.

Astrocytoma. A slow-growing brain tumor resulting from the growth of astrocytes.

Asymbolia. Inability to employ a conventional sign to stand for another object or event.

Ataxia. Failure of muscular coordination; any of various irregularities of muscular action.

Auditory agnosia. Impaired capacity to identify nonverbal acoustic stimuli.

Automatic behaviors. Stereotyped units of behavior linked in a fixed sequence, e.g., grooming and chewing. Also called reflexive, consummatory, and respondent behaviors.

Autotopagnosia. Inability to localize and name the parts of one's own body; e.g., finger agnosia (*see* agnosia).

Average evoked potential (AEP). The computerized average of a number of evoked potentials from sensory input.

Axon. A thin neuronal process that transmits action potentials away from the cell body to other neurons (or to muscles or glands).

Axon hillock. The site of origin of a nerve impulse.

Basal ganglia. A group of large nuclei in the forebrain, including the caudate nucleus, putamen, globus pallidus, claustrum, and amygdala.

Beta rhythm. Irregular EEG activity of 13–30 Hz generally associated with alert state.

Bilateral. Occurring on or applying to both sides of the body.

Binocular deprivation. Removal of visual stimulation from both eyes by raising an animal in the dark, bandaging the eyes, etc.

Bitemporal hemianopsia. Loss of vision in both temporal fields due to damage to the medial region of the optic chiasm.

Brain abcess. A localized collection of pus in the brain formed from tissues that have disintegrated as a result of infection.

Brain scan. *See* radioisotope scan.

Brainstem. Defined in this book to include the hypothalamus, midbrain, and hindbrain. Some authorities also include the thalamus and basal ganglia.

Broca's aphasia. An expressive or nonfluent aphasia; chiefly a defect of speech; results from a lesion to Broca's area.

Broca's area. A region of the left frontal lobe (frontal operculum) believed to be involved in the production of language. Damage results in Broca's aphasia.

Brodmann's map. A map of the cerebral cortex devised by Brodmann; it is based on cytoarchitectonic structure and labels anatomical areas by number. (Conforms remarkably closely to functional areas based on lesion and recording studies.)

Caudate nucleus. A nucleus of the basal ganglia.

Cell assembly. A hypothetical collection of neurons that become functionally connected; proposed by Hebb to be the basis of ideation, perception, and memory.

Central sulcus. A fissure running from the dorsal border of the hemisphere near its midpoint, obliquely downward and forward until it nearly meets the lateral fissure, dividing the frontal and parietal lobes. Also called fissure of Rolando.

Cerebellum. A major structure of the hindbrain specialized for motor coordination.

Cerebral arteriosclerosis. Condition marked by loss of elasticity and by thickening and hardening of the arteries. Eventually results in dementia.

Cerebral compression. A contraction of the brain substance due to an injury that has caused hemorrhage and the development of a hematoma.

Cerebral contusion. A vascular injury resulting in bruising and edema and hemorrhage of capillaries.

Cerebral cortex. The layer of grey matter on the surface of the cerebral hemispheres composed of neurons and their synaptic connections that form 4–6 sublayers.

Cerebral laceration. A contusion severe enough to physically breach the brain substance.

Cerebral vascular accident. *See* stroke.

Cerebrospinal fluid (CSF). A clear, colorless solution of sodium chloride and other salts that fills the ventricles inside the brain and circulates around the brain beneath the arachnoid layer in the subarachnoid space.

Cingulate gyrus. A strip of limbic cortex lying just above the corpus callosum along the medial walls of the cerebral hemispheres.

Class-common behaviors. Those behaviors and behavioral capacities common to all members of a phylogenetic class.

Color agnosia. Inability to associate particular colors with objects or objects with colors.

Color anomia. Inability to name colors; generally associated with other aphasic symptoms. Also called color aphasia.

Commissure. A bundle of fibers connecting corresponding points on the two sides of the central nervous system.

Commissurotomy. Surgical disconnection of the two hemispheres by cutting the corpus callosum.

Concussion. A condition of widespread paralysis of the functions of the brain that occurs immediately after a blow on the head.

Conduction aphasia. A type of fluent aphasia in which, despite alleged normal comprehension of spoken language, words are repeated incorrectly.

Contralateral. Residing in the side of the body opposite the reference point.

Contralateral neglect. Neglect of part of the body and/or space contralateral to the lesion.

Contrast x-ray. Radiographic procedure using the injection of radio-opaque dye or air into the ventricles, or of dye into the arteries, for purposes of diagnosis.

Corollary discharge. Transmission by one area of the brain to another, informing the latter area of the former's actions. Commonly used more specifically for a signal from the motor system to the sensory systems that a particular movement is being produced.

Corpus callosum. Fiber system connecting the homotopic areas of the two hemispheres. Split-brain patients are those whose corpus callosum has been severed.

Cortex. An external layer. In this text, synonymous with neocortex.

Cranial nerves. A set of 12 pairs of nerves containing sensory and motor signals to and from the head.

CT-scan. Computerized tomography. An x-ray procedure in which a computer draws a map from the measured densities of the brain; superior to a conventional x-ray since it provides a three-dimensional representation of the brain. Also called by the trade name EMI-Scan.

Cytoarchitectonic map. A map of the cortex based on the organization, structure, and distribution of the cells.

Decerebrate rigidity. Excessive tone in all muscles, producing extension of the limbs and dorsoflexion of the head because antigravity musculature overpowers other muscles; caused by brainstem or cerebellar lesions.

Decortication. Removal of the cortex of the brain.

Decussation. Crossing of pathways from one side of the brain to the other.

Delusions. Beliefs opposed to reality but firmly held despite evidence of their falsity; characteristic of some types of psychotic disorders.

Dendrites. Treelike processes at the receiving end of the neuron.

Denervation supersensitivity. A condition of increased susceptibility to drugs, resulting from proliferation of receptors after denervation (removal of terminations) of an area.

Depolarization. Inward transfer of positive ions erasing a difference of potential between the inside and the outside of the neuron.

Dermatome. The area of skin supplied with afferent nerve fibers by a single spinal dorsal root.

Diaschisis. A special kind of shock following brain damage in which areas connected to the damaged area show a transitory arrest of function.

Dichotic listening. A procedure of simultaneously presenting a different auditory input to each ear through stereophonic earphones.

Diencephalon. A region of the brain that includes the hypothalamus, thalamus, and epithalamus.

Diplopia. Perception of two images of a single object; double vision.

Disconnection. Severing, by damage or by surgery, of the fibers that connect two areas of the brain such that the two areas can no longer communicate; also, the condition that results.

Disinhibition. Removal of inhibition from a system.

Dissolution. According to an unproven theory, the condition whereby disease or damage in the highest levels of the brain would produce, not loss of function, but rather a repertoire of simpler behaviors as seen in animals who have not evolved that particular brain structure.

Distal. Being far apart; remote.

Dorsomedial thalamus. A thalamic nucleus providing a major afferent input to the prefrontal cortex; degenerates in Korsakoff's disease, leading to a severe amnesic syndrome.

Double dissociation. An experimental technique whereby two areas of neocortex are functionally dissociated by two behavioral tests, each test being affected by a lesion to one zone and not the other.

Dura mater. A tough, double layer of collagenous fiber enclosing the brain in a kind of loose sack.

Dysarthria. Difficulty in speech production caused by incoordination of speech apparatus.

Dyscalculia. Difficulty in performing arithmetical operations.

Dyskinesia. Any disturbance of movement.

Dyslexia. A difficulty in reading.

Dysphasia. Impairment of speech caused by damage to the central nervous system.

Efferent. Conducting away from higher centers in the central nervous system and toward muscle or gland.

Electroconvulsive shock therapy (ECT or ECS). The application of a massive electric shock across the brain, as a treatment for affective disorders.

Electroencephalogram (EEG). Electrical potentials recorded by placing electrodes on the scalp or in the brain.

Electromyography (EMG). Recording of electrical activity of the muscles as well as the electrical response of the peripheral nerves.

Embolism. The sudden blocking of an artery or vein by a blood clot, bubble of air, deposit of oil or fat, or small mass of cells deposited by the blood current.

Encephalitis. Inflammation of the central nervous system as a result of infection.

Encephalization. The process by which

higher structures such as the cerebral cortex have taken over the functions of the lower centers; may imply either a phylogenetic or an ontogenetic shift of function.

Encephalization quotient (EQ). The ratio of the actual brain size to the expected brain size for a typical mammal of that body size.

Encephalomalacia. Softening of the brain, resulting from vascular disorders caused by inadequate blood flow.

Encephalopathy. Chemical, physical, allergic, or toxic inflammation of the central nervous system.

Encorticalization. The process by which the cerebral cortex has taken over the functions of the lower centers; may imply either a phylogenetic or an ontogenetic shift of function.

Ependymal cells. Glial cells forming the lining of the ventricles; some produce cerebrospinal fluid.

Epilepsy. A condition characterized by recurrent seizures of various types associated with a disturbance of consciousness.

Epithalamus. A collection of nuclei forming the phylogenetically most primitive region of the thalamus; includes the habenulae, pineal body, and stria medullaris.

Equipotentiality hypothesis. The hypothesis that each part of a given area of brain is able to encode or produce the behavior normally controlled by the entire area.

Ergotamine. A drug used in the treatment of migraine and tension headaches and that acts by constricting cerebral arteries.

Evoked potential (EP). A short train of large, slow waves recorded from the scalp, reflecting dendritic activity.

Fasciculation. A small local contraction of muscles, visible through the skin, representing a spontaneous discharge of a number of fibers innervated by a single motor-nerve filament.

Festination. Tendency to engage in behavior at faster and faster speeds; usually refers to walking, but can include other behaviors such as talking and thinking.

Fissure. A cleft, produced by folds of the neocortex, that extends to the ventricles.

Focal seizures. Seizures that begin locally and then spread; e.g., from one finger to the whole body.

Forebrain. Term used in this book for the cerebral hemispheres, basal ganglia, thalamus, amygdala, hippocampus, and septum.

Frontal lobes. All of the neocortex forward of the central sulcus.

Frontal operculum. The upper region of the inferior frontal gyrus.

Functional maps. Maps of the cortex constructed by stimulating areas of brain electrically and noting elicited behavior, or by recording electrical activity during certain behaviors. Such maps relate specific behaviors to brain areas.

Functional validation. According to theory, the need of a neural system for sensory stimulation if it is to become fully functional.

Generalized seizures. Bilaterally symmetrical seizures without a local onset.

Geniculostriate system. A system consisting of projections from the retina of the eye to the lateral geniculate nucleus of the thalamus, then to areas 17, 18, 19, and then to 20, 21; involved in perception of form, color, and pattern.

Gerstmann syndrome. A collection of symptoms due to left parietal lesion, alleged to include finger agnosia, right-left confusion, acalculia, and agraphia. A source of some controversy.

Glial cells. Supportive cells of the central nervous system.

Glioblastoma. A highly malignant, rapidly growing brain tumor; most common in adults over 35 years of age; results from the sudden growth of spongioblasts.

Glioma. Any brain tumor that arises from glial cells.

Gnosis. Knowledge.

Graded potential. An electrical potential in a neuron or receptor cell that changes with the intensity of the stimulus. Also known as a generator potential.

Grand mal. Seizure characterized by loss of consciousness and stereotyped, generalized convulsions.

Graphesthesia. The ability to identify numbers or letters traced on the skin with a blunt object.

Grey matter. Any brain area composed predominantly of cell bodies.

Gyrus. A convolution of the cortex of the cerebral hemispheres.

Habituation. Gradual quantitative decrease of a response after repeated exposure to a stimulus.

Hallucinations. Perceptions for which there are no appropriate external stimuli; characteristic of some types of psychotic disorders.

Hematoma. A local swelling or tumor filled with effused blood.

Hemiparesis. Muscular weakness affecting one side of the body.

Hemiplegia. Paralysis of one side of the body.

Hemispherectomy. Removal of a cerebral hemisphere.

Hindbrain. A region of the brain that consists primarily of the cerebellum, medulla, pons, and fourth ventricle.

Hippocampus. Primitive cortical structure lying in the anterior medial region of the temporal lobe.

Homeostasis. The maintenance of a chemically and physically constant internal environment.

Homonymous hemianopsia. Total loss of vision due to complete cuts of the optic tract, lateral geniculate body, or area 17.

6-Hydroxydopamine. A chemical that is selectively taken up by axons and terminals of noradrenergic or dopaminergic neurons and acts as a poison, damaging or killing them.

Hypermetamorphosis. A tendency to attend and react to every visual stimulus, leading to mental distraction and confusion.

Hypothalamus. Collection of nuclei located below the thalamus; involved in nearly all behavior including movement, feeding, sexual activity, sleeping, emotional expression, temperature regulation, and endocrine regulation.

Idiopathic seizures. Seizure disorders that appear to arise spontaneously and in the absence of other diseases of the central nervous system.

Illusions. False or misinterpreted sensory impressions of real sensory images.

Infarct. An area of dead or dying tissue resulting from an obstruction of the blood vessels normally supplying the region.

Infection. Invasion of the body by disease-producing microorganisms and the reaction of the tissues to their presence.

Inferior colliculus. The nucleus of the tectum of the midbrain that receives auditory projections and is involved in whole body orientation to auditory stimuli.

Interneuron. Any neuron lying between a sensory neuron and a motor neuron.

Ipsilateral. Located on the same side of the body as the point of reference.

Isolation syndrome. *See* transcortical aphasia.

Kindling. Production of epilepsy by repeated stimulation.

Klüver-Bucy syndrome. A group of symptoms resulting from bilateral damage to the temporal lobes. Characterized especially by hypersexuality, excessive oral behavior, and visual agnosia.

Korsakoff's syndrome. An amnesic syndrome resulting from degeneration of the dorsomedial thalamic nucleus; produced by chronic alcoholism.

Korsakoff-Wernicke disease. A metabolic disorder of the central nervous system due to a lack of vitamin B_1 (thiamin); often associated with chronic alcoholism.

Lateral fissure. A deep cleft on the basal surface of the brain that extends laterally, posteriorly, and upward, thus separating the temporal and parietal lobes. Also called Sylvian fissure.

Lesion. Any damage to the nervous system.

Limbic system. An elaboration of the structures of the limbic lobe to form a hypothetical functional system originally believed to be important in controlling affective behavior.

Localization of function. Hypothetically, the control of each kind of behavior by a different specific brain area.

Macular sparing. A condition in which the central region of the visual field is not lost even though temporal and/or nasal fields are.

Mass-action hypothesis. The hypothesis that the entire neocortex participates in every behavior.

Massa intermedia. Mass of grey matter that connects the left and right thalami across the midline.

Medulla oblongata. The portion of the hindbrain immediately rostral to the spinal cord.

Medulloblastoma. Highly malignant brain tumor found almost exclusively in the cerebella of children; results from the growth of germinal cells, which infiltrate the cerebellum.

Meninges. The three layers of protective tissue—the dura mater, arachnoid, and pia mater—that encase the brain and spinal cord.

Meningioma. An encapsulated brain tumor growing from the meninges.

Meningitis. Inflammation of the meninges.

Mesencephalon. Middle brain; term for the middle one of the three primary embryonic vesicles, which subsequently comprises the tectum and tegmentum.

Metastatic tumor. A tumor that occurs through the transfer of tumor cells from elsewhere in the body.

Midbrain. The short segment between the forebrain and hindbrain including the tectum and tegmentum.

Migraine. A type of headache characterized by an aching, throbbing pain, frequently unilateral. It may be preceded by a visual aura presumed to result from ischemia of the occipital cortex induced by vasoconstriction of cerebral arteries.

Monocular blindness. Blindness in one eye caused by destruction of its retina or optic nerve.

Monocular deprivation. Deprivation of visual experience to one eye by closure, bandaging, etc.

Motoneurone. Sherrington's term for the unit formed by motor neurons and the muscle fiber to which their axon terminations are connected.

Motor neuron. A neuron that has its cell body in the spinal cord and that projects to muscles.

Mycotic infection. Invasion of the nervous system by a fungus.

Myelin. The lipid substance forming an insulating sheath around certain nerve fibers; formed by oligodendroglia in the central nervous system and by Schwann cells in the peripheral nervous system.

Myelinization. Formation of myelin on axons. Used by some people as an index of maturation.

Myoclonic spasms. Massive seizures consisting of sudden flexions or extensions of the body and often beginning with a cry.

Narcolepsy. Condition in which a person is overcome by uncontrollable, recurrent, brief episodes of sleep.

Nasal hemianopsia. Loss of vision of one nasal field due to damage to the lateral region of the optic chiasm.

Neocortex. Newest layer of the brain, forming the outer layer or "new bark"; has 4–6 layers of cells. In this text, synonymous with cortex.

Nerve growth factor (NGF). A protein that plays some role in maintaining the growth of a cell.

Nerve impulse. Movement or propagation of an action potential along the length of an axon; begins at a point close to the cell body and travels away from it.

Neuroblast. Any embryonic cell that develops into a neuron.

Neurofibril. Any of numerous fibrils making up part of the internal structure of a neuron; may be active in transporting precursor chemicals for the synthesis of neurotransmitters.

Neurologist. A physician specializing in the treatment of disorders of the nervous system.

Neuron. The basic unit of the nervous system; the nerve cell; its function is to transmit and store information; includes the cell body (soma), many processes called dendrites, and an axon.

Neuropsychology. The study of the relation between brain function and behavior.

Neurotoxin. Any substance that is poisonous or destructive to nerve tissue; e.g., 6-hydroxydopamine, placed in the ventricles of the brain, will selectively destroy the noradrenaline and dopamine systems.

Neurotransmitter. A chemical released from a synapse in response to an action potential and acting on postsynaptic receptors to change the resting potential of the receiving cell; chemically transmits information from one neuron to another.

Neurotropic viruses. Those viruses having a strong affinity for cells of the central nervous system; as opposed to pantropic viruses, which attack any body tissue.

Node of Ranvier. A space separating the Schwann cells that form the covering or myelin on a nerve axon; because the nerve impulse jumps from one node to the next its propagation is accelerated.

Noradrenergic neurons. Neurons that contain noradrenaline in their synapses or use noradrenaline as their neurotransmitter.

Nucleolus. An organelle within the nucleus of a cell that produces ribosomes.

Nucleus. A spherical structure in the soma of cells; contains DNA; also, a group of cells forming a cluster that can be identified histologically.

Nystagmus. Constant, tiny eye movements that occur involuntarily and have a variety of causes.

Occipital horns. Most posterior projections of the lateral ventricles that protrude into the occipital lobe.

Occipital lobes. A general area of the cortex lying in the back part of the head.

Olfaction. The sense of smell or the act of smelling.

Oligodendrocytes. Specialized support or glial cells in the brain that form a covering or myelin on nerve cells to speed the nerve impulse. Also called oligodendroglia.

Optic chiasm. The point at which the optic nerve from one eye partially crosses to join the other, forming a junction at the base of the brain.

Orbital frontal cortex. Cortex that lies adjacent to the cavity containing the eye but that, anatomically defined, receives projections from the dorsomedial nucleus of the thalamus.

Organic brain syndrome. A general term for behavioral disorders that result from brain malfunction attributable to known or unknown causes.

Paleocortex. That portion of the cerebral cortex forming the pyriform cortex and parahippocampal gyrus. Also called the paleopallium.

Pantropic viruses. Those viruses that attack any body tissue. *See also* neurotropic viruses.

Papilledema. Swelling of the optic disc; caused by increased pressure from cerebrospinal fluid. Used as a diagnostic indicator of tumors or other swellings in the brain.

Paragraphia. The writing of incorrect words or perseveration in writing the same word.

Paraphasia. The production of unintended syllables, words, or phrases during speaking.

Parasite. An organism living upon or within another living organism (the host) at the expense of the host.

Paresis. A general term for loss of physical and mental ability due to brain disease, particularly from syphilitic infection; a term for slight or incomplete paralysis.

Parietal lobes. A general region of the brain lying beneath the parietal bone.

Parkinson's disease. A disease of the motor system that is correlated with a loss of dopamine in the brain and is characterized by tremors, rigidity, and reduction in voluntary movement.

Peripheral nerves. Those nerves that lie outside the spinal cord and the brain.

Perseveration. Tendency to repeatedly emit the same verbal or motor response to varied stimuli.

Petit mal. Seizure characterized by a loss of awareness during which there is no motor activity except blinking and/or turning of the head, rolling of the eyes, etc.; of brief duration (10 seconds typically).

Phagocytes. Cells that engulf microorganisms, other cells, and foreign particles.

Phrenology. The study of the relation between the skull's surface features and mental faculties. Long discredited.

Pia mater. A moderately tough connective tissue that clings to the surface of the brain.

Pineal body. An unsymmetrical structure in the epithalamus, thought by René Descartes to be the seat of the soul, but now thought to be involved in circadian rhythms.

Planum temporale. The cortical area just posterior to the auditory cortex; Heschl's gyrus within the Sylvian fissure.

Plasticity. According to theory, the ability of the brain to change in various ways to compensate for loss of function due to damage.

Pneumoencephalography. An x-ray technique in which the cerebrospinal fluid is replaced by air introduced by a lumbar puncture.

Pons. A portion of the hindbrain; composed mostly of motor fiber tracts going to such areas as the cerebellum and spinal tract.

Postsynaptic membrane. The membrane lying adjacent to a synaptic connection across the synaptic space from the end foot.

Praxis. An action, movement, or series of movements.

Precentral gyrus. The gyrus lying in front of the central sulcus.

Preferred cognitive mode. Use of one type of thought process in preference to another, e.g., visuospatial instead of verbal; sometimes attributed to the assumed superior function of one hemisphere over the other.

Prefrontal cortex. Cortex lying in front of primary and secondary motor cortex; thus, tertiary or association cortex in the frontal lobe.

Presynaptic membrane. The end-foot membrane adjacent to the subsynaptic space.

Primary projection area. An area of the brain that first receives a connection from another system.

Primary sensory area. An area of the cortex that first receives projections from a sensory system.

Primary zones. Areas of the cortex that first receive projections from sensory systems or that project most directly to muscles.

Projection maps. Maps of the cortex made by tracing axons from the sensory systems into the brain, and by tracing axons from the neocortex to the motor systems of the brainstem and spinal cord.

Prosencephalon. Front brain; term for the most anterior part of the embryonic brain, which subsequently evolves into the telencephalon and diencephalon.

Prosopagnosia. Inability, not explained by defective visual acuity or reduced consciousness or alertness, to recognize familiar faces. Very rare in pure form, and thought to be secondary to right parietal lesions.

Proximal. Being close to something.

Pseudodepression. A condition of personality following frontal-lobe lesion in which apathy, indifference, and loss of initiative are apparent symptoms but are not accompanied by a sense of depression in the patient.

Pseudopsychopathic. Describing a condition of personality following frontal-lobe lesion in which immature behavior, lack of tact and restraint, and other behaviors symptomatic of psychopathology are apparent but are not accompanied by the equivalent mental or emotional components of psychopathology.

Psychoactive drug. Any chemical substance that alters mood or behavior by altering the functions of the brain.

Psychometrics. The science of measuring human abilities.

Psychosis. A major mental disorder of organic or emotional origin in which the individual's ability to think, respond emotionally, remember, communicate, interpret reality, and behave appropriately is sufficiently impaired so that the ordinary demands of life cannot be met. The term is applicable to conditions having a wide range of severity and duration (e.g., schizophrenia, depression).

Psychosurgery. Surgical intervention to sever fibers connecting one part of the brain with another or to remove or destroy brain tissue with the intent of modifying or altering disturbances of behavior, thought content, or mood for which no organic pathological cause can be demonstrated by established tests and techniques (e.g., lobotomy).

Ptosis. Drooping of the upper eyelid from paralysis of the third nerve (oculomotor).

Pulvinar. Thalamic nucleus that receives projections from the visual cortex and superior colliculus and sends connections to secondary and tertiary temporal and parietal cortex.

Putamen. A nucleus of the basal ganglia complex.

Putative transmitters. Chemicals strongly suspected of being neurotransmitters but not conclusively proven to be so.

Pyramidalis area. Area 4.

Quadrantic hemianopsia. Blindness in one quadrant of the visual field due to some damage to the optic tract, lateral geniculate body, or area 17.

Radioisotope scan. Scanning of the cranial surface with a Geiger counter after an intravenous injection of a radioisotope has been given, to detect tumors, vascular disturbances, atrophy, etc.

Reafference. Confirmation by one part of the nervous system of the activity in another. *See also* corollary discharge.

Reciprocal inhibition. Activation of one muscle group with inhibition of its antagonists.

Red nucleus. A nucleus in the anterior portion of the tegmentum that is the source of a major motor projection.

Regeneration. A process by which neurons damaged by trauma regrow connections to the area that they previously innervated.

Resting potential. Normal voltage across a nerve cell membrane; varies between 60 and 90 millivolts in the cells of different animals.

Reticular formation. A mixture of nerve cells and fibers in the lower and ventral portion of the brainstem, extending from the spinal cord to the thalamus and giving rise to important ascending and descending systems.

Reticular matter. An area of the nervous system composed of intermixed cell bodies and axons; has a mottled grey and white or netlike appearance.

Retrograde amnesia. Inability to remember events that occurred prior to the onset of amnesia.

Rhinencephalon. Alternative term for the limbic system.

Rhombencephalon. The hindmost posterior embryonic part of the brain, which divides into the metencephalon and myelencephalon.

Righting reflex. A reflex whereby an animal placed in an inverted posture returns to upright; survives low decerebration, hence a reflex.

Roentgenography. Photography using x-rays.

Saccule. One of two vestibular receptors of the middle ear; stimulated when the head is oriented normally; maintains head and body in an upright position.

Saltatory conduction. Propagation of a nerve impulse on a myelinated axon; characterized by its leaping from one node of Ranvier to another.

Schizophrenia. A type of psychosis characterized by disordered cognitive functioning and poor social adjustment (literally splitting of thought and emotive processes); probably due to brain malfunction.

Schwann cells. Glial cells that form myelin in the peripheral nervous system.

Scotoma. Small blind spot in the visual field caused by small lesions or epileptic focus or migraines of the occipital lobe.

Secondary projection area. An area of the cortex that receives projections from or sends projections to a primary projection area.

Sensory aphasia. See Wernicke's aphasia.

Septum. A nucleus in the limbic system that when lesioned in rats produces sham rage and abolishes the theta EEG wave form.

Simultaneous extinction. Second stage of recovery from contralateral neglect; characterized by response to stimuli on the neglected side as if there were a simultaneous stimulation on the contralateral side.

Somatosensory zone. Any region of the brain responsible for analyzing sensations of fine touch and pressure and possibly of pain and temperature.

Somnolence. Sleepiness; excessive drowsiness.

Sparing. The saving (sparing) of some brain functions from disruption after the occurrence of a lesion early in life (usually before that function has developed).

Spatial summation. Tendency of two adjacent events to summate; hence two adjacent postsynaptic potentials add or subtract.

Spinal cord. The part of the nervous system enclosed in the vertebral column.

Spinal reflex. Response obtained when only the spinal cord is functioning.

Spongioblasts. Immature cells that develop into glial cells.

Sprouting. The phenomenon, following partial damage, whereby remaining portions of a neuron or other neurons sprout terminations to connect to the previously innervated area.

Stereognosis. The recognition of objects through the sense of touch.

Stimulation. The act of applying a stimulus or an irritant to something; the occurrence of such a stimulus or an irritant.

Stimulus. An irritant or event that causes a change in action of some brain area.

Storage granules. Vesicles in the end foot that are presumed to store neurotransmitters.

Stretch reflex. The contraction of a muscle to cause stretching; mediated through a muscle spindle, a special sensory receptor system in the muscle.

Stroke. The sudden appearance of neurological symptoms as a result of severe interruption of blood flow.

Substantia nigra. A nucleus area in the midbrain containing the cell bodies of axons containing dopamine. In freshly prepared human tissue the region appears black, hence the name (Latin, meaning black substance).

Sulcus. A small cleft produced by folding of the cortex.

Superior colliculus. Nucleus of the tectum in the midbrain that receives visual projections and is involved in whole body reflexes to visual stimuli.

Sylvian fissure. *See* lateral fissure.

Synapse. The junction between an axonal end foot and another cell.

Synaptic knob. Another term for end foot; also called synapsis, synapse, bouton termineau, terminal knob.

Synaptic vesicles. Small vesicles visible in electron-microscope pictures of end feet; believed to contain neurotransmitter.

Tachistoscope. A mechanical apparatus consisting of a projector, viewer, and screen by which visual stimuli can be presented to selective portions of the visual field.

Tactile; tactual. Pertaining to the sense of touch.

Tectopulvinar system. Portion of the visual system that functions to locate visual stimuli. Includes superior colliculus, posterior thalamus, and areas 20 and 21.

Tectum. The area of the midbrain above the cerebral aqueduct (the roof); consists of the superior and inferior colliculi, which mediate whole body response to visual and auditory stimuli, respectively.

Tegmentum. The area of the midbrain below the cerebral aqueduct (the floor); contains sensory and motor tracts and a number of nuclei.

Telencephalon. Term for the endbrain; includes the cortex, basal ganglia, limbic system, and olfactory bulbs.

Temporal lobes. Lobes found laterally on the head, below the lateral sulci adjacent to the temporal bones.

Temporal summation. Tendency of two events related in time to summate; hence two temporally related postsynaptic potentials add or subtract.

Tertiary projection area. An area of the cortex that receives projections from or sends projections to a secondary projection area. Also known as association cortex.

Thalamus. A group of nuclei of the diencephalon.

Thermoregulation. The ability to regulate body temperature.

Theta rhythm. A brain rhythm with a frequency of 4–7 Hz.

Threshold. The point at which a stimulus produces a response.

Thrombosis. A plug or clot in a blood vessel, formed by the coagulation of blood.

Topographic maps. Maps of the neocortex showing various features, projections, cell distributions, etc.

Tract. A large collection of axons coursing together within the central nervous system.

Transcortical aphasia. Aphasia in which patients can repeat and understand words and name objects but cannot speak spontaneously, or can repeat words but cannot comprehend them.

Transient ischemia. A short-lived condition of inadequate supply of blood to a brain area.

Tumor. A mass of new tissue that persists and grows independently; a neoplasm; it surrounds tissue and has no physiologic use.

Uncinate fasciculus. A fiber tract connecting temporal and frontal cortex; a hooked or curved tract.

Unit activity. The electrical potential of a single cell.

Ventral root. The tract of fibers leaving the spinal cord, hence motor, on the ventral portion of the spinal cord of animals or on the anterior portion of humans.

Ventricles. The cavities of the brain that contain cerebrospinal fluid.

Ventriculography. An x-ray technique whereby, to highlight the contours of the ventricles, an opaque medium is introduced into the ventricle through a cannula inserted through the skull.

Vestibular system. A sensory system with receptors in the middle ear that respond to body position and movement.

Viruses. Encapsulated aggregates of nucleic acid causing infections and nonspecific lesions.

Visual agnosia. Inability to combine visual impressions into complete patterns—therefore an inability to recognize objects; Inability to perceive objects and to draw or copy them.

Voluntary movement. Any movement that takes an animal from one place to another; can be elicited by lower-level sensory input and/or executed through lower and postural support and reflex systems. Also called appetitive, instrumental, purposive, and operant movement.

Wernicke's aphasia. Inability to comprehend speech or to produce meaningful speech; follows lesions to posterior cortex.

Wernicke's area. The posterior portion of the superior temporal gyrus, roughly equivalent to area 22.

White matter. Those areas of the nervous system rich in axons covered with glial cells.

INDEX OF NAMES

INDEX OF TOPICS